The Grand Scribe's Records

VOLUME II

The Basic Annals of Han China

The Grand Scribe's Records

VOLUME II

The Basic Annals of Han China

by Ssu-ma Ch'ien

William H. Nienhauser, Jr.

Editor

Weiguo Cao, Scott W. Galer,

William H. Nienhauser, Jr., and

David W. Pankenier

Translators

INDIANA UNIVERSITY PRESS

Bloomington & Indianapolis

This book is a publication of

Indiana University Press
601 North Morton Street
Bloomington, Indiana 47404-3797 USA

http://iupress.indiana.edu

Telephone orders 800-842-6796
Fax orders 812-855-7931
Orders by e-mail iuporder@indiana.edu

The paper used in this publication meets the minimum
requirements of American National Standard for Information
Sciences—Permanence of Paper for Printed Library
Materials, ANSI Z39.48-1984.

Manufactured in the United States of America

Library of Congress Cataloging-in-Publication Data

Ssu-ma, Ch'ien, ca. 145–ca. 86 B.C.
The grand scribe's records.

Includes bibliographical references and index.
Contents: v. 1. The basic annals of pre-Han China — v. 2. The basic annals of
Han China — v. 7. The memoirs of pre-Han China.
1. China—History—To 221 B.C. 2. China—History—Ch'in dynasty, 221–207 B.C.
3. China—History—Han dynasty, 202 B.C.–220 A.D.
1. Nienhauser, William H. II. Cheng, Tsai Fa. III. Title.
DS741.3.S6813 1994
931—dc20   94-18408
ISBN 0-253-34021-7 (v. 1)
ISBN 0-253-34022-5 (v. 2)
ISBN 0-253-34027-6 (v. 7)

1 2 3 4 5 07 06 05 04 03 02

CONTENTS

THIS VOLUME IS DEDICATED TO

Burton Watson

for conveying much of the music

ACKNOWLEDGEMENTS

Seven years have passed since the last volume of *The Grand Scribe's Records* appeared. Throughout this period we have been working regularly on the translation and revision of these chapters and drafts for the following volumes. Whether the increased time and care has improved the quality of the translations and supporting material will be for the reader to determine.

On thing is certain, however. Over this lengthy period more people have been involved in the production of this volume. First and foremost I would like to thank my students in the Department of East Asian Languages and Literature at the University of Wisconsin-Madison. They have been patient enough to read and comment on these chapters several times. Special thanks go to the Group of Nine who have been meeting every other Saturday in my dining room for the last two years: Cao Weiguo, Chen Zhi, David Herrmann, Huang Hongyu, Bruce Knickerbocker, Hans-Georg Möller, Shang Cheng, Su Zhi, and Sun Jingtao.

This group came together gradually after the publication of volumes 1 and 7 of *The Grand Scribe's Records* in 1994 and the departure of my four cotranslators for that volume from the project (although Lu Zongli has remained an active correspondent and advisor). The translations for this volume actually began in 1994-5 when I was in Taipei supported by Fulbright-Hays and ACLS fellowships. They continued through classes taught at the University of Wisconsin in 1995-6 when the team of new translators began to take shape, Cao Weiguo and Scott Galer being the first to join.

In the summer of 1996 Tu Cheng-sheng 杜正勝 made it possible for me to visit Academia Sinica and to work in the library there (again supported by Fulbright-Hays and the Graduate School of the University of Wisconsin). I am also grateful to Wang Shu-min 王叔岷 who during this Nankang sojourn answered a number of my questions concerning his own *Shih chi* research. At the end of the summer I was fortunate to attend the large conference celebrating the 2140th anniversary of Ssu-ma Ch'ien's birth in Xian and to meet many of the scholars who are now working on the *Shih chi* in China. My thanks to the conference organizer, Xu Xinghai 徐興海 of Shaanxi Normal University for his hospitality. I also owe Imataka Makoto 今鷹真 a debt of thanks for introducing me to the series of early Japanese manuscripts of various Han *pen-chi* 本紀 during this conference.

During the next academic year (1996-7), David W. Pankenier, who had proofread many of the chapters in the first volume for us, agreed to join our team for this third volume of translations. By June 1997 the draft renditions of these five chapters were finished. From 17-23 August 1997 the first Workshop on Early Chinese History and Historiography was held here in Madison hosted by my colleague, Robert Joe Cutter, and myself. The week-long gathering brought Chen Zhi (National Singapore University), Scott Cook (Grinnell University), David Honey (Brigham Young University), Lu Zongli (Hong Kong University of Science and Technology), and David W. Pankenier (Lehigh University) to campus. Each visiting scholar presented a paper and then led the discussion of a chapter of our translations ("Kao-tsu pen-chi" was discussed by Zongli Lu, "Lü T'ai-hou pen-chi" 呂太后本紀 by David Honey, "Hsiao Wen pen-chi" 孝文本紀 by Scott Cook, "Hsiao Ching pen-chi" 孝景本紀 by Chen Zhi, and "Hsiao Wu pen-chi" 孝武本紀 by the entire group). Our debt to the participants of this Workshop is enormous. (Chen Zhi, Scott Cook, and Zongli Lu have remained involved in the translation and revision of chapters for future volumes.) Gratitude is also owed Dean Philip Certain of the College of Letters and Science, University of Wisconsin-Madison, for his support of this gathering.

After the five chapters in this volume were revised in light of comments offered during the Workshop, we were privileged to have several scholars read chapters for us in the last several years: Rafe de Crespigny (Chapters 8-10), Michael Loewe (Chapter 8), John Page (Chapters 8-10), and Michael Puett (Chapter 8).

I made several other trips abroad that had significance for the current volume. I spent the summer of 1997 in Staatsbibliothek (Berlin) working parttime on the draft translations left by Erich Haenisch and parttime revising my chapters. My thanks to the Dr. Hartmut Walravens and the Alexander von Humboldt Foundation for their support. In October 1997 I visited the Museé Guimet and was allowed to view all of the manuscripts of Chavannes' unpublished translations.[1] My thanks to Jacques Gernet for his help in arranging this visit and for showing me Chavannes' personal library which has been kept virtually intact in the library of the Societé Asiatique. The following year, in November 1998, I was invited by Wang Yundu 王雲度 to visit Xuzhou Normal University. Through his auspices I was also able to visit P'ei and Feng Counties, to see sites related in popular lore to Liu Pang's birth and childhood, and to acquire a complete set of a local journal, *Liu Pan yen-chiu* 劉邦研究 (1990-93). The kindness of the Alexander von Humboldt Foundation allowed me to visit the University of Bonn during the summer of 1999 and to exchange ideas on our project with Wolfgang Kubin and Rolf Trauzettl. I am grateful to Kawai Kôzô 川合康三 for inviting me to spend a semester at Kyoto University in late 1999 as a Research Professor in the Faculty of Letters. During these months Professor Kawai made it possible for me to view and xerox sections of a number of editions not available to us in Madison as well as to meet and exchange ideas with several Japanese scholars who work on the *Shih chi,* most notably Fujita Katsuhisa 藤田勝久. Professor Fujita was a gracious host for a visit to his Ehime University and also provided me with a number of bibliographic materials on Japanese *Shih chi* Studies. Ozawa Kenji 小沢賢二 gave invaluable advice on editions. Isobe Akira 磯部彰 was kind enough to guide me through the library and archives at Tohoku University in order to review their collection of materials and photos relating to Takigawa Kametarô 瀧川龜太郎 (1865-1946)–this during a two-month extension in early 2000 financed by a Japan Foundation Grant. Yamaguchi Yogi 山口謠司 and Kamitaka Tokuharu 神鷹徳治 made it possible for us to obtain a copy of the Higaku 祕閣 mss. of "Kao-tsu pen-chi" 高祖本紀 and also discussed with me Ho Tz'u-chün's 賀次君 work on this and related Japanese *Shih chi* manuscripts.

Others who should be mentioned here include Jens Petersen, who provided unique assistance in accessing electronic versions of the *Shih chi,* Teresa Nealon, who oversaw the finances of our project, Wu Shuping 吳樹平 and Zhang Lie 張烈 for providing

[1]This trip also resulted in a paper, "A Note on Édouard Chavannes' Unpublished Translations of the *Shih chi* 史記," which is slated to appear in a volume of essays on the *Shih chi* edited by Michael Puett.

me with copies of their books, the Research Committee of the Graduate School, which has regularly given support to this project, the Alexander von Humboldt Foundation for two recent grants of support and for the intial award in 1975-6, which spurred my interest in early Chinese narrative, Cao Weiguo and Bruce Knickerbocker, who as my Project Assistants have spent several semesters going over these translations, and, of course, my wife Judith, who provided her usual good humor even in the face of proofreading with me several hundred pages of these stimulating chapters. Despite the assistance of so many, errors and omissions no doubt remain. The responsibility for all such problems remains with the editor.

Indiana University Press has been extremely supportive in preparing this volume. It is hard to imagine more help than I received from the former head, John Gallman, but the new director, Mr. Peter-John Leone, and his staff, have proved every bit as competant and knowledgeable. I am especially grateful to Robert J. Sloan for his encouragement and Pamela S. Rude for her careful guidance in technical matters.

Finally, our debt of gratitude to Burton Watson has been clear from the first months we worked on this text nearly thirteen years ago. What is amazing about Burton Watson's translation work with the *Shih chi* is not that he did so much, but that he did so much so quickly. Like Chavannes, Watson's *Shih chi* work was his first major sinological project; yet within a period of a little over three years (a period not unlike that which Chavannes devoted to the text) he had produced a masterpiece not only for Sinology, but for those general readers interested in China's most important history.[2] This volume is dedicated to Professor Watson and his accomplishments in making the *Shih chi,* which he calls *The Records of the Historian,* a part of world history.

William H. Nienhauser, Jr.
13 January 2002

---

[2]See Watson's comments on pp. 202-3 in his "The *Shih Chi* and I," *CLEAR* 17 (December 1995): 199-206.

Introduction

I tell parts of a story
that once occurred
and I laugh with surprise at what disappeared
though I remember it well.
     from "Talking" by W. S. Merwin (*Flowers & Hand,* [Townsend,
     Washington: Copper Canyon Press, 1997], p. 121)

I. The *Shih chi* and *Han shu* Texts

There are two points that should be made at the outset. First, that the basic text of the *Shih chi* 史記 differs little in the various early manuscripts and editions from the text that we have today. Most of the variants are relatively minor, scarcely effecting the understanding of the overall text.[1] Second, for better or worse, the Chung-hua text of the *Shih chi* is considered the *textus receptus* and our goal in this project is to render that text into English.[2] Thus we need not overly concern ourselves with the recent studies by a handful of Western scholars who have attempted to show that portions of the *Shih chi* have been lost and then recopied from the *Han shu.*

However, since we have read a good portion of the *Shih chi* and the *Han shu* 漢書 parallels now, and since this is the first volume of *The Grand Scribe's Records* to treat Han dynasty chapters, some comments on the relationship between these two early histories seem in order. Let me start with a generalization. The chapters we have read with some care and translated suggest uniformly that the *Shih chi* is a patchwork text, put together from earlier sources for the most part with temporal transitions added by its compiler. Such transitions are needed because it would seem Ssu-ma Ch'ien was often not certain of the dates of various events. Liang Yü-sheng's 梁玉繩 (1745-1819) *Shih chi chih-yi* 史記 志疑 (Records of Doubtful Points in the *Grand Scribe's Records*) contains nearly 7,500 entries which criticize portions of the *Shih chi* text; a great number of these entries—perhaps half—involve problems in chronology or dating. Liang often uses the parallel texts in the *Han shu* to resolve a question of dates. The *Han shu* (again in the portions we have read) is a much more tightly organized history, with relatively few problems in dating. This

---

[1]There are over one hundred passages ascribed to the *Shih chi* in *lei-shu* and other texts which have been collected by Wang Shu-min 王叔岷 in an appendix to his *Shih chi chiao-cheng* 史記斠證 (Taipei: Chung-yang Yen-chiu Yüan, Li-shih Yü-yen Yen-chiu So, 1982) titled "*Shih chi* yi-wen" 史記逸文 (10:3501-9), but they await further study.

[2]There are some problems with this text and its predecessor the Chin-ling Shu-chü 金陵書局 edition as I have tried to show in my "Chang Wen-hu and His Text of the *Shih chi,*" Wang Ch'eng-mien 王成勉, ed., *Ming Ch'ing wen-hua hsin-lun* 明清文化新論 (Taipei: Wen-chin, 2000), pp. 275-309, but again these problems are relatively minor.

situation suggests that the accepted opinion–that Pan Ku and his predecessors who worked on the *Han shu* took the portions of the *Shih chi* text which treated Han-dynasty events and characters and then corrected and revised these accounts–is valid. In contrast, it is difficult for me to imagine how a group of copyists attempting to fill out missing portions of the *Shih chi* could possibly have taken the well organized *Han shu* accounts and put them into the chronological and stylistic disparity of sections of the current *Shih chi.*

Generalizations aside, a word-by-word comparison of the respective parallel chapters or portions thereof in the *Shih chi* and *Han shu* would no doubt be the best manner to illustrate the relationship between these two texts. Before turning to such a comparison, however, it seems imperative to offer a few comments on textual criticism in general and the composition of the *Shih chi* and *Han shu* texts in particular.

Although in recent comparisons of these two histories much has been made of the concept of *brevior lectio praeferenda est* (the simpler reading is to be preferred), it would seem that in fields with a lengthier history of textual comparisons a more balanced view of variants reigns. Bruce M. Metzger, for example, summarizes this view as held by New Testament scholars in his "Recent Trends in the Textual Criticism of the Iliad and the Mahâbhârata" (in Metzger, *Chapters in the History of New Testament Textual Criticism* [Leiden: Brill; Grand Rapids: Eerdmans, 1963], pp. 153):

> New Testament scholars have been well acquainted for more than two centuries with the canon of criticism, *brevior lectio praeferenda est.* It goes without saying that responsible textual critics have never applied this canon in a mechanical way. The merits and demerits of the Alexandrian, Western, and Koine texts of the New Testament must be evaluated by weighing the evidence for each variant reading and forming from these separate judgments an opinion regarding the text as a whole.

Indeed, we shall attempt to apply the approach suggested by Metzger to differences between the *Shih chi* and *Han shu* examined below.

More recently, J. Harold Greenlee has argued that the "first and most basic principle of textual criticism" is that "the reading from which the other readings could most easily have developed is most likely the original."[3] This, too, has offered insights into these two early histories as will be demonstrated in the pages that follow.

As for the composition of the *Shih chi* and *Han shu,* it should be reemphasized that the autographs of these early histories were most likely not the product of a single brush. In addition to the two families, the Ssu-mas and the Pans, there were no doubt a number of other scribes and scholars involved. In a recent study[4] I have tried to argue that the *T'ai-shih Chang-ku* 太史掌故 (Authority on Ancient Matters of the Grand Scribe)

---

[3]J. Harold Greenlee, *Scribes, Scrolls, and Scripture: A Student's Guide to New Testament Textual Criticism* (Grand Rapids, Michigan: W.B. Eerdmans Publishing Co., 1985), p. 56.

[4]"Sentence Fragments and the Methods of Composition of the *Shih chi* 史記," a draft paper under consideration for publication.

assigned to the office of the *T'ai-shih ling* 太史令 (Prefect of the Grand Scribes) during the Former Han dynasty (there were thirty of these "Authorities") could well have been in charge of copying and organizing texts of the "dependent chapters" (those based on earlier sources–this term was coined by Bernhard Karlgren in his "Sidelights on Si-ma Ts'ien's Language," *Bulletin of the Museum of Far Eastern Antiquities* 42 [1970]:297). They may also have been involved in the writing (or carving) of the two autographs Ssu-ma Ch'ien left[5]–it is not likely the Grand Scribe himself would have copied the 526,000-graph text twice! As Grant Hardy (p. xi) points out, the *Shih chi* in its original form (bamboo slips tied together by silken cords) "would have taken a cart to contain it." Thus to move the work around would have required a small team of assistants as well. It seems equally possible that the Pans had similar help.

II. A Comparison of "Kao-tsu pen-chi" 高祖本紀 and "Kao-ti chi" 高帝紀

What follows is a study and comparison of selections from a single chapter of the *Shih chi* that is translated below, "Kao-tsu pen-chi" 高祖本紀 (The Basic Annals of the Exalted Ancestor), and the corresponding chapter in the *Han shu,* "Kao-ti chi" 高帝紀 (The Annals of the Exalted Emperor). All conclusions will have to limit themselves to these chapters.[6] I have not found it possible, as A.F.P Hulsewé and David Honey did,[7] to extrapolate conclusions from this comparison to the other Han-dynasty chapters of the *Shih chi.* Indeed, the problem of the relationship of the texts of these two great histories is complex and comparing different sections of these two works may lead to different conclusions.

In the comparisons below, every attempt has been made to consider various editions of the *Shih chi,* including the text referred to as the "Higaku text" 祕閣 by Japanese scholars (i.e, the early, manuscript preserved in the Kunaichô 宮内庁 in the form

[5] Cf. *Shih chi,* 130.3320.

[6] There are also comments on related specific textual comparisons by the translators of *Shih chi* Chapters 9-12, William H. Nienhauser, Jr., Cao Weiguo, Scott W. Galer, and David W. Pankenier, in their footnotes and translators' notes.

[7] See, for example, Hulsewé's comments on p. 89 of his "The Problem of the Authenticity of the *Shih-chi* Ch. 123," *TP* 61 (1975), and Honey's assertion on p. 95 of his "The *Han-shu,* Manuscript Evidence, and the Textual Criticism of the *Shih-chi:* The Case of the 'Hsiung-nu *lieh-chuan,*'" *CLEAR* 21 (1999): 67-97. Hulsewé –he has tempered these claims considerably in his accounts of the *Han shu* and *Shih chi* in Michael Loewe's *Early Chinese Texts, A Bibliographic Guide* (Berkeley: The Society for the Study of Early China and The Institute of East Asian Studies, University of California, Berkeley, 1993), pp. 130 and 406 respectively and in his final comments to the note he published in *T'oung Pao* 76 (1993), "A Striking Discrepancy between the *Shih chi* and the *Han shu,*" p. 322: "[My re-discovery] is perhaps important from the historiographical standpoint, because it teaches us to be circumspect when dealign with textual contradictions or irregulaties. The *Shih chi* and the *Han shu,* each with an independent textual tradition, should be constantly consulted as a check on each other, regardless of the question as to which of these two texts is primary."

of an unpaginated scroll).[8] The following additional sources also provided material for the discussion: the *Han chi* 漢紀 (Annals of the Han) by Hsün Yüeh 荀悅 (148-209), Mizusawa Toshitada's 水澤利忠 textual notes (found as *Shiki kaichû koshô fu kôhô* 史記會注考證附校補, reprinted in two volumes by Shanghai: Shang-hai Ku-chi, 1986), and parallel passages in other works such as the *Lun heng* 論衡 by Wang Ch'ung 王充 (127-ca. 200).[9] David Honey has recently pointed out that in Ho Tz'u-chün's 賀次君 sample "of fourteen variants" from these chapters "seven verify the reading of either the *Han-shu* or the *Han-chi*" and the "remaining seven are demonstrated to be wrong without reference to these parallel readings." Honey also argues that "Liang Yü-sheng's treatment of the same chapter, without benefit of the MS preserved in Japan, does follow the *Han-shu* reading about seventy percent of the time."[10] However, there is a problem in using such studies in relationship to the question of which of these chapters on Liu Pang is primacy. Although both Ho and Liang pointed out errors in the *Shih chi* and then tried to correct them based on other texts including the *Han shu*, neither Ho nor Liang questioned the primacy of the *Shih chi* text.[11] Ho worked through the mid-1950s as Ku Chieh-kang's 顧頡剛 (1893-1981) project assistant in constructing the Chung-hua *Shih chi* text,[12] and Liang Yü-sheng spent nineteen years working on his *Shih chi chih-yi*. Obviously neither of them felt the *Shih chi* text was basically flawed. Both Ho and Liang point out the errors in the Grand Scribe's writings; Liang especially often corrects Ssu-ma Ch'ien's chronology–many times with the help of the *Han shu*. But in comparing the two texts these scholars argue only that the *Han shu* has corrected errors in the *Shih chi,* not that it was the primary text.

    Discussing and interpreting such secondary texts, however, is not the best method of addressing this question of primacy. Let us therefore turn to the *Shih chi* and *Han shu*

---

[8]On this text see Ho Tz'u-chün 賀次君, *Shih chi shu-lu* 史記書錄 (Shanghai: Shang-wu Yin-shu-kuan, 1958; rpt. Taipei: Ti-p'ing-hsien Ch'u-pan-she 地平線出版社, 1972), pp. 26-7.

[9]The relationship between parallel texts in the *Lun heng* merits a more detailed study than is possible here. In the chapter titled "Wen K'ung p'ien" 問孔篇, for example, Wang Ch'ung discusses contents of the "Hsiao Wen pen-chi" 孝文本紀 ([Emperor Wen the Filial, Basic Annals], a text sometimes considered to have been lost early in the transmission of the *Shih chi* (*Lun heng,* 2:526).

[10]Honey, "The *Han-shu*," p. 91. Honey implies in his n. 18 on p. 91 that Ikeda Shirojiro's 池田四郎次郎 comments in his (and Ikeda Eiyû's 池田英雄)*Shiki kenkyû shomoku kaidai (kôhon)* 史記研究書目解題(稿本) [Tokyo: Meitoku Shuppansha, 1978], pp. 41-2 are also related to textual problems in the *Shih chi* mss., but Ikeda's remarks are clearly limited to a physical description of the mss.

[11]Moreover, Ho's assumption that the Higaku text is of T'ang provenance has been disputed by many Japanese scholars who believe the mss. is an Edo era copy of a Song-dynasty original. Cf. Kanda Kiichirô's 神田喜一郎 review of Ho's *Shih chi shu-lu* in *Chûgoku bungaku hô* 中国文学報 10 (April 1959): 146-51.

[12]See William H. Nienhauser, Jr., "Historians of China," *CLEAR* 17 (1995): 212 [207-16].

themselves. In our comparison below, although we shall not compare every single line of these two chapters, we begin with an uninterrupted, line-by-line analysis of the first sections, and then move to a sampling of later parallel passages.

The opening lines of "Kao-tsu pen-chi" and "Kao-ti chi" already reveal minor differences:

> *Shih chi*, 8.341[13]: 高祖，沛豐邑中陽里人，姓劉氏，字季。父日
> 太公，母日劉媼。
> *Han shu*, 1A.1: 高祖，沛豐邑中陽里人也，姓劉氏。

The Higaku text (no pagination) of the *Shih chi* here is completely identical to that of the Chung-hua edition. The *Han shu* version has a *yeh* 也 after identifying Kao-tsu as a man of Chung-yang Hamlet in Feng Township in P'ei. The *Han shu* does not contain the passage giving Kao-tsu's *agnomen* (*tzu* 字) or the names of his father and mother. No conclusion can be drawn from these differences, since it is as possible that someone added the names of Kao-tsu's parents to the text as it is that Pan Ku decided to omit this information.[14]

If the opening lines above may be considered the exposition of our main character, the next passage introduces the exciting force which induces great changes in the Liu Family:

> *Shih chi*, 8.341: 其先劉媼嘗息大澤之陂，夢與神遇。是時雷電晦冥，太
> 公往視，則見蛟龍於其上。
> *Han shu*, 1A.1: 母媼嘗息大澤之陂，夢與神遇。是時雷電晦冥，父太公往
> 視，則見交龍於上。

Whereas previous scholars might have been tempted to discuss the variants *chiao* 蛟 and *chiao* 交,[15] the more significant changes here should garner our attention: the expression *ch'i hsien* 其先 (found also in the Higaku text) which begins the *Shih chi* line and the *ch'i* 其 which modifies *shang* 上 at the end of the line (there is also the difference between Liu Ao 劉媼 in the *Shih chi* and mu Ao 母媼 in the *Han shu*). Both expressions are problematic. *Ch'i hsien* can mean either "his ancestor" or "formerly." Chavannes (2:325) translates it as "auparavant." Chang Wen-hu 張文虎 (1808-1885; *Chiao-k'an Shih chi*

[13]References to chapter and page numbers are for the Chung-hua editions of these texts. A translation of the *Shih chi* passages can be found in the rendition of "Kao-tsu pen-chi" below. Discrepencies in the *Han shu* account are translated in the discussion which follows each example.

[14]Hsün Yüeh's 荀悅 (148-209) *Han chi* 漢紀 (Annals of the Han, 1.2b, *SPTK*) gives both Kao-tsu's *ming*, Pang 邦, and his *tzu*, Chi 季.

[15]Rather than a question of *brevio lector*, this is simply a matter of usage; in the *Shih chi* we find the expression *chiao lung* 蛟龍 four times in addition to this passage–*Shih chi*, 6.263, 29.1413, 47.1926, and 117.3017-3018–whereas in *Han shu* only *chiao lung* 交龍 occurs (twice).

"Chi-chieh," "So-yin," "Cheng-yi," cha-chi 校刊史記集解索引正義札記. 2v. [Rpt. Peking: Chung-hua, 1977], 1:87) believes it is an interpolation, Mizusawa, 8.254 notes a Northern Sung edition which has the phrase. Moreover, the *Lun heng* (completed before the *Han shu* in 70-80 A.D.) contains a similar passage which reads "Kao-tsu's ancestor, Liu Ao, once rested on the banks of a great marsh" 高祖之先,劉媼曾息大澤之陂 (*Lun heng chu-shih* 論衡注釋, ed. by Pei-ching Ta-hsüeh Li-shih-hsi *Lun heng* Chu-shih Hsiao-tsu , 4v. [Peking: Chung-hua, 1979], 1:386, "Lei-hsü p'ien 雷虛篇"). Thus it seems likely that *ch'i hsien* was an early textual tradition. The term is quite common in the *Shih chi,* occurring four times in the annals preceeding this chapter.[16] On the other hand, this expression occurs not a single time in the *Han shu* basic annals. Moreover, with Greenlee's principle that "the reading from which the other readings could most easily have developed is most likely the original" in mind, it seems that the *Shih chi* text must be the original here. It is likely that the two possible understandings of *ch'i hsien* here perturbed Pan Ku and he then streamlined the passage. I have argued below (see n. 5 to the translation of *Shih chi* Chapter 8) that the meaning of "his ancestor" here, although resulting in the strange reading of "His ancestor Mother Liu," would be in line with Ssu-ma Ch'ien's general tone in this chapter. Ssu-ma Ch'ien may intend a resonance with the usage of *ch'i hsien* in his own comments to "Ch'in pen-chi" 秦本紀 (The Basic Annals of Ch'in) which read:

> The *cognomen* of the Ch'in's ancestors was Ying. Ch'in's descendants were enfeoffed with parceled out [lands] and adopted the names of their states as their *cognomens.* There were *nomens* such as Hsü, T'an, Chü, . . . and Ch'in. Nevertheless, the Ch'in, because their ancestor [*ch'i hsien*] Tsao-fu was enfeoffed with Chao-ch'eng 趙城, made their *nomen* Chao 趙" (*Grand Scribe's Records,* 1:123 and *Shih chi,* 5.122).

This passage was a tribute to the long royal line of the Ch'in. In contrast, Ssu-ma Ch'ien realized Liu Pang, as a commoner, had no ancestry, royal or otherwise, that could be identified beyond his parents. He therefore may have incorporated the format he used to depict the Ch'in royal house and their *nomen* here in a sardonic description of the Lius.

The second difference between the *Shih chi and Han shu* here is the *ch'i* 其 towards the end of the passage (also found in the Higaku edition). While the *Han shu* version could be translated "T'ai-kung went to look for her and saw a kraken above," the *Shih chi* text is more graphic and perhaps insulting to Mother Liu and the subsequent line of Han emperors: "T'ai-kung went to look for her and saw a kraken atop her."[17] Once again, it is difficult to see how the *Shih chi* text could have developed from the *Han shu* and the *Shih chi* seems to be the primary, if slightly salacious, version.

[16]Cf. *Shih chi,* 4.170, 5.178, 5.192 and 5.221. It also appears as *ch'i hsien-tsu* 其先祖 on *Shih chi,* 4.122.

[17]The *Lun heng* here offers two variant readings which do not match either the *Shih chi* or *Han shu* current texts: 交龍在上 ("Chi-yen p'ien" 吉驗篇, 1:132) and 交龍居上 ("Ch'i-kuai p'ien" 其怪篇, 1:226).

The texts continue:

> *Shih chi,* 8.341: 已而有身，遂產高祖。
> *Han shu,* 1A.1: 已而有娠，遂產高祖。

The variants here, *shen* 身 in the *Shih chi,* and *chen* 娠 in the *Han shu,* are not that significant. Y*u shen*有身 occurs fourteen times in the *Shih chi* and the same number of times in the *Han shu. Yu chen*有娠 occurs only in this passage in *Han shu.*[18] The Higaku manuscript reads *shen.*

> *Shih chi,* 8.342: 高祖為人，隆準而龍顏，美須髯，左股有七十二黑子。
> *Han shu,* 1A.2: 高祖為人，隆準而龍顏，美須髯，左股有七十二黑子。

This passage depicting Kao-tsu's character and appearance is identical in both texts.

> *Shih chi,* 8.342: 仁而愛人，喜施，意豁如也。
> *Han shu,* 1A.2: 寬仁愛人，意豁如也。

Here the texts differ again. The Higaku manuscript is identical with the Chung-hua *Shih chi* version. Both the *T'ai-p'ing yü-lan* (87.1b) citation of this *Shih chi* passage and the *Han chi* (1.2b) have identical readings to that of the *Han shu–k'uan jen ai ren,* "was indulgent, humane, loved people."[19] However, this chapter later depicts Hsiang Yü, in the words of Wang Ling, as one who "was humane and loved people" (*jen erh ai jen; Shih chi,* 8.381), and it seems that Ssu-ma Ch'ien may have enjoyed the irony of describing these two enemies with the same phrase. With the Greenlee Principle in mind, the *Han shu* omisson of *hsi shih* 喜施, which we read as "fond of charitable acts, largesse" following Wu and Lu (8.281), makes it difficult to see how the *Han shu* text here could be the original.

> *Shih chi,* 8.342-3: 常有大度，不事家人生產作業。及壯，試為吏，為泗水亭長，廷中吏無所不狎侮。
> *Han shu,* 1A2: 常有大度，不事家人生產作業。及壯，試吏，為泗上亭長，廷中吏無所不狎侮。

[18]*Yu shen* occurs on *Shih chi,* 9.402-3, 37.1597-8, 49.1978-9, 59.2100, 78.2396-7-8 (2x), 78.2398, 85.2508, 85.2508, 85.2511, 111.2922, 116.2995-6, 118.3075 (2x); since some of these passages are in pre-Han chapters, it is impossible that the expression was borrowed from the *Han shu; yu chen* 有娠 occurs not a single time in *Shih chi.*

[19]*K'uan-jen* echoes the *Shang shu* description of T'ang 湯 (*Shang shu chu-shu* 尚書注疏, 8.4b, *SPPY*) and is applied to Kao-tsu elsewhere by General Ch'ai Wu 柴武 in the *Han shu* (33.1854). The *Shih chi* parallel passage (93.2635) also has Ch'ai Wu depict Kao-tsu as *k'uan-jen.*

These passages are nearly identical in both texts. There are only two differences: first, the omission of *wei* 為 from the *Han shu* phrase *shih li* 試吏 (the *Shih chi* reads *shih wei li* 試為吏). From Ying Shao's 應劭 (ca. 140-203/204) comment (cited in "Chi-chieh") on *shih wei li*–"*shih pu li*" 試補吏 "he tested to be appointed as an official"–it is likely that the *Shih chi* expression puzzled Latter Han writers. Second, the *Han shu* reads "Chief of the Precinct on the Ssu" (*Ssu-shang T'ing-chang* 泗上亭長) for "Chief of the Ssu River Precinct (*Ssu-shang T'ing-chang* 泗水亭長). Although there are differing opinions on the best reading here,[20] overall is seems once again that the *Han shu* text could be derived from the *Shih chi* here, but not the other way around.

> *Shih chi,* 8.343: 好酒及色。
> *Han shu,* 1A.2: 好酒及色。

These passages are identical in both texts.

> *Shih chi,* 8.343: 常從王媼、武負貰酒，醉臥，武負、王媼見其上常有龍，怪之。高祖每酤留飲，酒讎數倍。
> *Han shu,* 1A.2: 常從王媼、武負貰酒，時飲醉臥，武負、王媼見其上常有怪。高祖每酤留飲，酒讎數倍。

Here again there are minor differences between the two texts. The *Han shu* has an additional *shih yin* 時飲, "often he drank," before *tsui wo* 醉臥, which resembles that *Han chi* (1.2b) language, *mei yin tsui* 每飲(醉), "whenever he drank (he became drunk)." The *Lun heng* ("Chi-yen p'ien" 吉驗篇, 1:132) reads *yin tsui chih wo* 飲醉止臥 "he drank until he was drunk, stopped and lay down." The Higaku mss. reads simply *yin* before *tsui wo.* This is one of the fourteen questions raised by Ho Tz'u-chün (p. 26). Ho here notes that the Higaku text is identical to a passage cited in the *Yi-wen lei-chü* 藝文類聚.[21] Despite Honey's claims, Ho makes no suggestion that the *Han shu* version is primary (although both Takigawa [8.6] and Wang Shu-min [8.299] cite passages from *T'ai-p'ing yü-lan* that have *shih* 時 here). Moreover, in textual matters citations in *lei-shu* should be employed with great care. The same *Yi-wen lei-chü* passage that provides the *yin* for Ho's argument begins with the line: 高祖諱邦自季，沛豐邑中陽里人, an opening that matches neither the *Han shu* nor the *Shih chi.* Even without the *yin* here, the *Shih chi* text makes good sense, and its formulation seems to fit the idea of a habitual action, "when he got drunk and lay down." Applying the Greenlee Principle, the more elaborate *Han shu* text might seem to be the more likely original. But given that Pan Ku can be seen in many other passages clarifying obscure passages in Ssu-ma Ch'ien's writing, this could also be an addition which makes clearer, in Pan Ku's eyes, Kao-tsu's drinking habits. It seems that Hsün Yüeh's version is also an attempt to add a temporal context to Kao-tsu's binges.

The second variance here involves what Mother Wang saw hovering above the besotted future emperor. In the *Shih chi* it is a dragon (or dragons–all important *Shih chi*

[20]See *Han-shu pu-chu* (1.3a), Wang Nien-sun (1.20a-b), and Wang Shu-min (8.299).

[21]See *Yi-wen lei-chü.* 2v. (Rpt. Shanghai: Shang-hai Ku-chi, 1982 [1965]), 1:12.226.

printed editions, as well as the citation on *T'ai-p'ing yü-lan,* 87.1b, read *lung* 龍 "dragon");
in the *Han shu* it is "strange things" (*yu kuai* 有怪–見其上常有怪). The Higaku mss.
adds a third possibility; it reads: 武負、王媼見其上常有龍怪之屬 "Old Woman Wu and
Mother Wang saw that there were regularly things like dragons and anomalies above
him."[22] Ho Tz'u-chün believes that this version is close to the original (p. 26). Once again,
however, he does not argue that the *Han shu* text is primary here. Two further considerations
also support the *Shih chi* version. The most compelling is the use of *lung* 龍 "dragon" as a
sort of leitmotif which Ssu-ma Ch'ien uses to lend royal authority to Liu Pang: we see the
dragon first, of course, in Liu Pang's conception, next in his visage (*lung yen* 龍顏), and
finally here. Wang Ch'ung's discussion of these dragons in *Lun heng* ("Ch'i-kuai p'ien"
奇怪篇, 1:226) makes it evident they were perceived by Han readers as well. Secondly, it
is easy to see how, if the appearance of a dragon above Kao-tsu troubled Pan Ku, he could
have simplified the *Shih chi* lines that read 王媼見其上常有龍，怪之 to his own 王媼見
其上常有怪 merely by deleting the *lung* and the final particle *chih* 之.[23] The *Han chi*
(1.2b) varies a bit here, but supports the *Shih chi* text by having Old Woman Wu marvel
at what she saw: "Above their house they saw radiant anomalies and [Old Woman] Wu and
the rest considered him different" 上嘗見光怪，負等異之. Finally, the same *Yi-wen
lei-chü* passage that Ho Tz'u-chün cited above is here identical to the Chung-hua *Shih chi*
text.

> *Shih chi,* 8.343: 及見怪，歲竟，此兩家常折券棄責。
> *Han shu,* 1A.2: 及見怪，歲竟，此兩家常折券棄責。

These passages are identical in both texts.

> *Shih chi,* 8.344: 高祖常繇咸陽，縱觀，觀秦皇帝，喟然太息曰：「嗟乎，
> 大丈夫當如此也！」
> *Han shu,* 1A.3: 高祖常繇咸陽，縱觀秦皇帝，喟然大息，曰：「嗟乎，大
> 丈夫當如此矣！」

These passages are nearly identical. The only difference is the awkward repetition of *kuan*
觀 (縱觀，觀秦皇帝 "[the common people] were permitted to look [at the emperor], and
when he looked at The August Emperor of Ch'in . . .) in the *Shih chi.* There would be no
reason for someone who was copying a text to make the language more awkward, as would
have to be the case if the *Han shu* version was primary here. On the other hand, it is quite
logical that Pan Ku would want to polish Ssu-ma Ch'ien's rather shaky syntax.

> *Shih chi,* 8.344: 單父人呂公善沛令，避仇從之客，因家沛焉。沛中豪桀
> 吏聞令有重客，皆往賀。

[22] A number of *Shih chi* manuscripts held in Japan also read *shu* 屬 after *kuai chih* 怪
之 (see Mizusawa, 8.255 and Wang Shu-min, 8.299).

[23] There is also the possibility, of course, that the *lung* was omitted by a scribe.

Han shu, 1A.3: 單父人呂公善沛令，辟仇，從之客，因家焉。沛中豪傑吏聞令有重客，皆往賀。

These passages are virtually identical (the Higaku mss. is the same as the Chung-hua *Shih chi* text). The *Han shu* omits the place-name P'ci at the end of the first sentence. The difference in terms of content is whether Master Lü moved into P'ei (*Shih chi*) or into the prefect's house (*Han shu*). But once again it would be difficult for the *Shih chi* text to be based on the simpler *Han shu* version–there would be no way for some later 'author' of the *Shih chi* passage to add the idea of moving into P'ei from the *Han shu*'s version.

Shih chi, 8.344: 蕭何為主吏，主進，令諸大夫曰：「進不滿千錢，坐之堂下。」高祖為亭長，素易諸吏，乃紿為謁曰「賀錢萬」，實不持一錢。謁入，呂公大驚，起，迎之門。
Han shu, 1A.3: 蕭何為主吏，主進，令諸大夫曰：「進不滿千錢，坐之堂下。」高祖為亭長，素易諸吏，乃紿為謁曰「賀錢萬」，實不持一錢。謁入，呂公大驚，起，迎之門。

These passages are identical in both texts. The Higaku text omits *chin* 進 in 進不滿千錢 and *chih* 之 in 坐之堂下.

Shih chi, 8.344: 呂公者，好相人，見高祖狀貌，因重敬之，引入坐。
Han shu, 1A.3-4: 呂公者，好相人，見高祖狀貌，因重敬之，引入坐上坐。

Here, again, we find a small variance between the two texts, namely the *shang tso* 上坐 which concludes the line. The Higaku mss. is identical to the *Han shu*. But even here Ho Tz'u-chün (p. 26) states that he believes the two texts "are identical in meaning" (*t'ung yi* 義同) and that the two graphs *shang tso* were omitted during the printing of the *Shih chi* in early Sung times. Despite the evidence of the Higaku mss., there is some internal logic to the *Shih chi* text without *shang tso*. There Master Lü leads Liu Pang in "to be seated." This is before Liu Pang himself dares "to take the seat of honor without a second thought" 遂坐上坐，無所詘. In the *Han shu* account it is Master Lü who leads him to the seat of honor. This deflates the bravado the *Shih chi* text lends to Liu Pang here. It also undermines the force of the following lines–"Taking advantage [of Master Lü's high opinion of him], Kao-tsu, to slight the other guests, proceeded to take the place of honor without a second thought." If Master Lü allows him the seat of honor, then it is he, not Liu Pang, who slights the other guests.

Shih chi, 8.344: 蕭何曰：「劉季固多大言，少成事。」高祖因狎侮諸客，遂坐上坐，無所詘。
Han shu, 1A.4: 蕭何曰：「劉季固多大言，少成事。」高祖因狎侮諸客，遂坐上坐，無所詘。

These passages are identical in both texts.

Shih chi, 8.344: 酒闌，呂公因目固留高祖。高祖竟酒，後。
Han shu, 1A.4: 酒闌，呂公因目固留高祖。竟酒，後。

Here the minor difference is the "Kao-tsu" in the *Shih chi* account (the Higaku version is the same as the Chung-hua again). In it, it is Kao-tsu who finishes his wine and stayed behind. In the *Han shu* account Kao-tsu stays behind after "the wine is finished." It seems unlikely that the *Shih chi* text could be derived from the *Han shu* version; on the other hand, it would not be unlikely that Pan Ku might want to suggest that it was only after *all* the guests had finished their wine that the following conversation could take place.

> *Shih chi*, 8.345: 呂公曰：「臣少好相人，相人多矣，無如季相，願季自愛。臣有息女，願為季箕帚妾。」酒罷，呂媼怒呂公曰：「公始常欲奇此女，與貴人。
> *Han shu*, 1A4: 呂公曰：「臣少好相人，相人多矣，無如季相，願季自愛。臣有息女，願為箕帚妾。」酒罷，呂媼怒呂公曰：「公始常欲奇此女，與貴人。

The Higaku text is identical to the Chung-hua *Shih chi* version here. And, except for the omission of "Chi" 季 (Liu Pang's *agnomen*) in the *Han shu* account, the passages in both histories are identical. As above, it seems unlikely that the *Shih chi* version could be derived from that of the simpler *Han shu* text.

> *Shih chi*, 8.344-5: 沛令善公，求之不與，何自妄許與劉季？」呂公曰：「此非兒女子所知也。」卒與劉季。呂公女乃呂后也，生孝惠帝、魯元公主。
> *Han shu*, 1A.4: 沛令善公，求之不與，何自妄許與劉季？」呂公曰：「此非兒女子所知。」卒與高祖。呂公女即呂后也，生孝惠帝、魯元公主。

The only difference in these parallels is the lack of the particle *yeh* after Master Lü's comment and the discrepancy between the *Shih chi* calling Liu Pang "Liu Chi" 劉季 while the *Han shu* has "Kao-tsu" 高祖 (the Higaku text is identical to the Chung-hua *Shih chi* in these two points, but it omits *ti* 帝 after Hsiao Hui 孝惠 and *kung-chu* 公主 following Lu Yüan 魯元). *Yeh* seems a stylistic difference; we shall deal with the varying references to Liu Pang when they recur below. Once again it seems improbable that someone copying the *Han shu* text into a *Shih chi* lacuna would vary from a standard, making the spuriousness of his text more apparent.

> *Shih chi*, 8.346: 高祖為亭長時，常告歸之田。
> *Han shu*, 1A.5: 高祖嘗告歸之田。

Here the *Shih chi* text (the Higaku mss. is identical) offers another example of what can be seen as a corpus of anecdotes organized around the opening phrase, "When Kao-tsu was precinct chief . . . ." 高祖為亭長時 . . . . It is likely that these stories were collected together by storytellers and told as a sequence or that Ssu-ma Ch'ien had access to a written version of these tales.[24] The *Han shu* text omits reference to 'precinct chief' here

---

[24]On such clusters of oral tales, see Robert W. Funk and the Jesus Seminar, *The Acts of Jesus, The Search for the Authentic Deeds of Jesus* (San Francisco: Harper Collins, 1998), p. 2: "The followers of Jesus no doubt began to repeat his witticisms and parables during his lifetime.

(although it does contain one of these tales in its text immediately below). The *Lun heng* parallel text ("Ku-hsiang p'ien" 骨相篇, 1:161) reads "When Kao-tsu was precinct chief of Ssu-shang" 高祖為泗上亭長, approximating the *Shih chi*. The *Han chi* (1.3a) does not mention either Kao-tsu's position or his asking for leave and reads simply: "Once an stopped and begged a drink of something" 嘗有老父過乞漿. Thus based both on the larger sense of a series of 'precinct chief tales' and the smaller textual support from the *Lun heng* there seems little possibility that the *Shih chi* text could have been derived from the more simpler *Han shu* version.

> *Shih chi*, 8.346: 呂后與兩子居田中耨，有一老父過請飲，呂后因餔之。
> *Han shu*, 1A.5: 呂后與兩子居田中，有一老父過請飲，呂后因餔之。

These passages reveal only one difference: the *Shih chi* text specifies that Lü Hou and the children were "weeding" in the fields. The Higaku version is identical to the Chung-hua *Shih chi* text. The single graph *nou* 耨 (to weed, hoe) could more easily have been omitted from the *Han shu* than added (based on what?) to the *Shih chi*.[25] The *Lun heng* parallel text (*ibid.*) omits *nou* and reads *lao kung* 老公 "elderly gentleman" for *lao fu* 老父 "old father." The *Han chi* (1.3a), as noted just above, reads *ch'i chiang* 乞漿 here for the *Shih chi*'s *ch'ing yin* 請飲 "asked for something to drink."

> *Shih chi*, 8.346: 老父相呂后曰：「夫人天下貴人。」令相兩子，兒孝惠，曰：「夫人所以貴者，乃此男也。」相魯元，亦皆貴。老父已去，高祖適從旁舍來，呂后具言客有過，相我子母皆大貴。高祖問，曰：「未遠。」乃追及，問老父。老父曰：「鄉者夫人嬰兒皆似君，君相貴不可言。」高祖乃謝曰：「誠如父言，不敢忘德。」及高祖貴，遂不知老父處。
> *Han shu*, 1A.5: 老父相后曰：「夫人天下貴人也。」令相兩子，兒孝惠帝，曰：「夫人所以貴者，乃此男也。」相魯元公主，亦皆貴。老父已去，高祖適從旁舍來，呂后具言客有過，相我子母皆大貴。高祖問，曰：「未遠。」乃追及，問老父。老父曰：「鄉者夫人兒子皆以君，君相貴不可言。」高祖乃謝曰：「誠如父言，不敢忘德。」及高祖貴，遂不知老父處。

The conclusions to this story reveal several minor differences in the *Shih chi* and *Han shu* accounts. First, the *Shih chi* refers to Lü Hou as "Empress Lü" 呂后 throughout, whereas in the first reference to her the *Han shu* calls her simply *hou* 后, "the empress." Second, the *Han shu* adds the particle *yeh* 也 following the old man's statement that "Your ladyship will become an honored person throughout the world" (the *Lun heng* text [*ibid.*]

They soon began to recount stories about him, perhaps about his encounters with critics or about his amazing way with the sick and demon-possessed. As time went by, the words were gathered into compounds and clusters suggested by common themes or by catchwords to make them easier to remember and quote."

There are two other stories in these annals which begin "As Kao-tsu was serving as precinct chief." The first (*Shih chi*, 8.346) follows this narrative about reading faces and tells how Kao-tsu "made a hat out of the outer skin of the bamboo" which he later wore and which became "none other than the so-called Liu Family Hats." The second (*Shih chi*, 8.347) follows that narrative in turn and depicts how Kao-tsu, while escorting a group of convict-laborers to also has *yeh*; the Higaku manuscript does not). Third, although both the *Shih chi* and the *Han shu* also have *yeh* following the elderly father's second pronouncement ("The means by which your ladyship will become honored is none other than this boy" 夫人所以貴者，乃此男也。), the Higaku text omits it. Fourth, the *Han shu* adds *ti* 帝 "emperor" follow the first mention of Hsiao Hui 孝惠. Neither the *Lun heng* nor the Higaku manuscript have this *ti* (the *Han chi* text abbreviates this section so much that it does not seem relevant to the discussion). Sixth, the *Han shu* adds *kung chu* 公主 "princess" after the first mention of Princess Yüan (neither the Higaku text nor the *Lun heng* parallel add *kung chu*). Seventh, the *Han shu* reads *erh tzu* 兒子 "children" for the *Shih chi*'s *ying erh* 嬰兒 "infants." Each of these readings has a parallel: the *Lun heng* reads *ying erh*, but the Higaku manuscript echoes the *Han shu* reading of *erh tzu*. Finally, and perhaps most significantly, the *Han shu* has *yi chün* 以君 "through you, sir" for the *Shih chi*'s *ssu chün* 似君 "resemble you, sir" in the line 鄉者夫人嬰兒[or 兒子]皆似君，君相貴不可言. Thus for the *Shih chi*'s "though the lady and infants I examined just now all resemble you, sir, your appearance in so honorable that I cannot put it into words," the *Han shu* has "though the lady and infants I examined just now all [appear honored] through you, sir, your appearance in so honorable that I cannot put it into words." Homer Dubs after considering all the commentaries on this passage adopts the *Shih chi* reading in his *Han shu* translation. The *Lun heng* and Higaku texts both read *ssu chün*. The *Han chi* (1.3a) is distinct, but supports the *Han shu* reading: 夫人兒子蒙君之力也 "the lady and children have received your power, sir."

Here we may begin to see some patterns in the closer relationship between the *Han shu* and the *Han chi*, whereas the *Lun heng* text seems often to be allied to that of the *Shih chi*. The *Han shu* prefers more explicit titles, but the abbreviated *Shih chi* titles have the support of the Higaku manuscript and the *Lun heng* in this regard.

Let us move now to the final example from the anecdotes which form the front frame of this chapter:

> *Shih chi,* 8.348: 秦始皇帝常曰「東南有天子氣」，於是因東游以厭之。高祖即自疑，亡匿，隱於芒、碭山澤巖石之閒。呂后與人俱求，常得之。高祖怪問之。呂后曰：「季所居上常有雲氣，故從往常得季。」高祖心喜。沛中子弟或聞之，多欲附者矣。

> *Han shu,* 1A.8: 秦始皇帝嘗曰「東南有天子氣」，於是東游以猒當之。高祖隱於芒、碭山澤間，呂后與人俱求，常得之。高祖怪問之。呂后曰：「季所居上常有雲氣，故從往常得季。」高祖又喜。沛中子弟或聞之，多欲附者矣。

These passages differ in more significant fashion and will require a more detailed examination.[26] The first difference in the texts can be found in the second clauses of these passages, which in the *Shih chi* version reads "At this, he took advantage of a tour of

[25]The detail about Lü Hou and the children weeding is not found in the *Han chi*.

[26]The *Han chi* version (1.3a) is quite distinct here, rearranging the order of the passage. It further describes the emanations of the Son of Heaven as "red in color" (*ch'ih-se yün-ch'i* 赤

inspection to the East to repress it" 於是因東游以厭之。The *Han shu* omits *yin* 因 "took advantage of," and adds *tang* 當 following *yen* 猒, changing the meaning to "At this he took a tour of inspection to the East to repress and block him" ("him," *chih* 之, referring to the source of this emanation of a Son of Heaven).[27] The Higaku text here is identical to the current *Han shu* version.[28] The *Han chi* (1.3a) has a similar line: 秦始皇帝乃東游欲以猒之, "Only then did the August First Emperor of Ch'in take his tour of inspection to the East, intending by this means to repress him." In a parallel passage in the *Lun heng* ("Chi-yen p'ien" 吉驗篇, 1:132) this sentence is exactly the same as the *Han shu* version.

A second variance can be found in the line which follows: "Kao-tsu, immediately suspecting that he himself [was the source of the emanation], fled and hid, retreating to the area of mountains and marshes, cliffs and rocks between Mang and Tang" 高祖即自疑，亡匿，隱於芒、碭山澤巖石之閒. The *Han shu* omits 即自疑，亡匿 "immediately suspecting that he himself [was the source of the emanation], fled and hid." The *Han shu* also omits *yen shih* 巖石, "cliffs and rocks." The *Lun heng,* in what seems to be a synoptic version of this passage, reads: 高祖之起也，與呂后隱於芒、碭山澤間 "Kao-tsu having risen up [in rebellion], he hid together with Lü Hou among the marshes and mountains of Mang and Tang."[29] The *Han chi* (which presents these events in a different order) reads: 高祖亡，避吏於山澤中, "Kao-tsu fled, avoiding the officials amidst the mountains and marshes." But the Higaku text, which paralleled the *Han shu* version in the first discrepancy, here follows the Chung-hua *Shih chi* edition word for word.

The final variance between these two passages occurs in the penultimate sentence. The *Shih chi* reads: "Kao-tsu was pleased" 高祖心喜. The *Han shu* reads: 高祖又喜, "Kao-tsu was again pleased." The Higaku manuscript is identical to the *Shih chi.* Neither the *Han chi* nor the *Lun heng* describe Kao-tsu's feelings here.

All of the major *Shih chi* editions are identical to the Chung-hua edition here. Mizusawa (8.256d-7a) notes no variants in other versions of the text. *Yin* makes sense in the historical context since the First Emperor did make an excursion to the East in 210 B.C. (*Shih chi,* 6.260). As for w*ang ni* 亡匿 "fled and hid," the expression is quite common in the *Shih chi,* occurring ten times, most of the passages relating to situations during the first few years of the Han dynasty; it is also used, for example, to describe how Chang Liang, later one of Kao-tsu's fellow men, hid from the First Emperor after attempting to assassinate him (*Shih chi,* 55.2034). If we return to the basic principle of Greenlee's that "the reading from which the other readings could most easily have developed

色雲氣). On such emanations, see also n. 3 on Dubs, 1:36-7.

[27]Cf. Shih Ting 施丁, *Han shu hsin-chu* 漢書新注, 4v. (Sian: San Ch'in, 1994), 8.4n.

[28]The Higaku text also omits the *shih* 始 in the First Emperor's title (unlike either the current Chung-hua *Shih chi* or *Han shu* texts).

[29]The text has actually been emended by the members of the History Department at Beijing University who prepared the *Lun heng chu-shih*: they read *ch'i* 起 for *ch'i* 氣, a change which they claim is based on the contextual meaning (p. 134, n. 14), but could also be based on a variant in a Sung-dynasty manuscript (see *Lun heng chiao-shih* 論衡校釋, ed. by Huang Hui 黃暉. 4v. [Peking: Chung-hua, 1990], 1:6.297n.). The Sung variant may stem from the same

is most likely the original," it would seem that the *Shih chi* once again should be the primary text. At the same time, the repetition of one *Han shu* line in the Higaku text, and the approximate parallels between the *Han shu* version and that of the *Lun heng,* once again suggest that some of the questions of textual relations between these two great histories may remain, pending further discoveries, a mystery.

That having been said, we have seen that in all cases but one, the early stories of the respective chapters in the *Shih chi* and *Han shu*–which form the first section of the chapters–point to the *Shih chi* text as primary. Let us now move to the second section, that which is structured chronologically by year in a more normal "annals" style.

> *Shih   chi,   8.349:* 秦二世元年秋，陳勝等起蘄，至陳而王，號為「張楚」。
>
> *Han shu,* 1A.9: 秦二世元年秋七月，陳涉起蘄，至陳，自立為楚王，遣武臣、張耳、陳餘略趙地。八月，武臣自立為趙王。

Here at first glance the *Han shu* text seems the fuller. But this is because the last portion of its text is added here. "The Basic Annals of Kao-tsu" in the *Shih chi* does not mention that Ch'en She sent Wu Ch'en, Chang Erh, and Ch'en Yü to overrun territory in Chao or that Wu Ch'en set himself up as King of Chao,[30] events Pan Ku may well have taken from Ch'en Yü's biography (*Shih chi,* 89.2573-6). Actually, the more precise dating ("in the seventh month of autumn . . .") in the *Han shu* is likely taken from "Hsiang Yü pen-chi," *Shih chi,* 7.297. But that text similarly makes no mention of Wu Ch'en and the others. The *Han shu* omits reference to "others" (*teng* 等) who rose at the same time as Ch'en She, probably because these other rebels cannot be precisely identified. The *Han shu* then fails to refer to the problematic title "Chang Ch'u" 張楚 "The One Who Claims to [Restore] Ch'u to Greatness" (which occurs only in this passage in the *Shih chi*[31]), opting to merely state that "Ch'en She. . . reached Ch'en and enthroned himself as King of Ch'u." The Higaku text is identical to the Chung-hua *Shih chi* version except for the substitution of *yüeh* 越 "crossed over" for *ch'i* 起 "rose up." There is no mention of Wu Ch'en *et al.* in the *Han chi* or the *Lun heng.* The *Han chi* (1.3a-b) gives a more detailed account of how Ch'en She and Wu Kuang 吳廣 were sent as officials of Ch'in to Ch'i 蘄

problem: the text with *ch'i* reads awkwardly here.

[30]The *Shih chi* (8.351) does note that after Ch'en She had moved west to Hsi the following year: "Yen, Chao, Ch'i and Wei all enthroned themselves as kings" 秦二世二年，陳涉之將周章軍西至戲而還。燕、趙、齊、魏皆自立為王.

[31]See also the discussion of the title Chang Ch'u in its earliest known occurrence in the *Wu hsing chan* 五星占 text found with the Ma-wang-tui materials in Liu Nai-ho 劉乃和, "Po-shu so chi 'Chang Ch'u' kuo-hao yü Hsi Han fa-chia cheng-chih" 帛書所記 '張楚' 國號與西漢法家政治, *Wen-wu,* 1975.5: 35-7.

This title may be related to Ch'en Sheng having Wu Kuang call out and say, "Great Ch'u will rise up and Ch'en Sheng will be king" 狐鳴呼曰「大楚興，陳勝王」 (cf. *Shih chi,*

and then, because a storm caused them to be delayed–a 'crime' punishable by death–decided to rebel.

This passage then continues:

Shih chi, 8.349: 諸郡縣皆多殺其長吏以應陳涉。沛令恐，欲以沛應涉。掾、主吏蕭何、曹參乃曰：「君為秦吏，今欲背之，率沛子弟，恐不聽。願君召諸亡在外者，可得數百人，因劫眾，眾不敢不聽。」乃令樊噲召劉季。劉季之眾已數十百人矣。

Han shu, 1A.9: 郡縣多殺長吏以應涉。九月，沛令欲以沛應之。掾、主吏蕭何、曹參曰：「君為秦吏，今欲背之，帥沛子弟，恐不聽。願君召諸亡在外者，可得數百人，因以劫眾，眾不敢不聽。」乃令樊噲召高祖。高祖之眾已數百人矣。

By omitting *chu . . . chieh* (諸 . . . 皆) the *Han shu* passage weakens the *Shih chi* argument that "In *every* commandery and county many killed the high-ranking officers in response to Ch'en She." The Higaku text is identical to the Chung-hua *Shih chi* for this line. The *Han shu* continues to provide a chronological frame ("in the ninth month") for the following actions, but omits reference to any specific motive behind the Magistrate of P'ei's decision to align P'ei with Ch'en She (the *Shih chi* says he did so because "he was afraid" [*k'ung* 恐]). The Higaku text also has *k'ung* and Mizusawa lists no other *Shih chi* variants here. The *Han shu* text then omits *nai* 乃 from the *Shih chi* line "Hsiao Ho and Ts'ao Ts'an then said" 蕭何、曹參乃曰, reads *shuai* 帥 for the *Shih chi's shuai* 率, and replaces "Liu Chi" in the final two lines with "Kao-tsu," making its text consistent in referring to Liu Pang throughout the first sections as "Kao-tsu."[32] Finally, the *Han shu* says that Liu Pang's following at this time was "several hundred men" (*shu pai jen* 數百人) as we have it in the text a line or two above, whereas the *Shih chi* claims he had gathered "several tens to a hundred men" 數十百人. The Higaku text is virtually identical to the Chung-hua *Shih chi,* although it adds "Ch'en" to the line 欲以沛應陳涉, "[the Prefect of P'ei] wanted to use P'ei to respond to Ch'en She's call," reads *pei* 倍 (a homophone which could be substituted for *pei* 背 with the meaning "to turn the back on") for *pei* 背 repeats *tzu ti* 子弟 in the line "率沛子弟，「子弟」恐不聽," and reverses *chao chu* 召諸 to read *chu chao* 諸召, all changes which do not alter the basic meaning of the lines. The *Han shu* text is more precise in the chronology of these events and omits

48.1950).

[32]In the preceding pages of the *Shih chi* concerning Kao-tsu's life before the rebellion against Ch'in, Liu Pang is referred to by his posthumous title as "Kao-tsu," the Exalted Ancestor. This suggests these passages were put into their final form some time after Kao-tsu had died. Here he is called simply by his name, Liu Chi, as the style switches to an annalistic account of current affairs. In the subsequent sections of *Shih chi* Chapter 8 Liu Pang is referred to by each of his official titles as he attains them and exercises duties related to them–from the Magistrate of P'ei, to the King of Han, and finally to the Exalted Ancestor, Kao-tsu, again. Thus the use of Liu Chi here makes good sense. The *Han shu,* which follows no such practice, has simply standardized all references to Liu Pang as "Kao-tsu." Once again, it is difficult to imagine how the varied *Shih chi* practice of referring to Liu Pang could have derived from the consistency of

details which may seem questionable: the unknown associates in Ch'en She's rebellion are not mentioned, nor is the magistrate's fear, and the number of Liu Pang's followers, which is presented in the awkward, but standard, expression "several tens to a hundred" in the *Shih chi* version,[33] is kept simpler and consistent with Hsiao and Ts'ao's prediction in the Pans' account. While this may make the *Han shu* passage here more historically reliable, it also—as a seeming 'reduction' of the *Shih chi* text—makes it clearly derivative (there is no logical way to assume that this *Shih chi* passage could have been rewritten from what the *Han shu* provides here).

> *Shih chi*, 8.355-6: 「秦二世二年」呂臣軍彭城東，項羽軍彭城西，沛公軍碭。章邯已破項梁軍，則以為楚地兵不足憂，乃渡河，北擊趙，大破之。當是之時，趙歇為王，秦將王離圍之鉅鹿城，此所謂河北之軍也....秦二世三年，楚懷王見項梁軍破，恐，徙盱台都彭城，并呂臣、項羽軍自將之。以沛公為碭郡長，封為武安侯，將碭郡兵。封項羽為長安侯，號為魯公。呂臣為司徒，其父呂青為令尹。
> *Han shu*, 1A.15-6: 「秦二世二年九月」呂臣軍彭城東，項羽軍彭城西，沛公軍碭。魏咎弟豹自立為魏王。後九月，懷王并呂臣、項羽軍自將之。以沛公為碭郡長，封武安侯，將碭郡兵。以羽為魯公，封長安侯，呂臣為司徒，其父呂青為令尹。
> 章邯已破項梁，以為楚地兵不足憂，乃渡河北擊趙王歇，大破之。歇保鉅鹿城，秦將王離圍之。

The narrative here picks up the activities of Hsiang Yü and Liu Pang shortly after the Ch'in general Chang Han 章邯 has defeated an arrogant Hsiang Liang and killed him. The initial difference in these two passages is, of course, the more specific dating of the initial events in the *Han shu* (". . . in the ninth month"). The second major discrepancy is the *Han shu* presentation of Chang Han's actions following Hsiang Liang's death, after the description of Lü Ch'ing's appointment as Premier. Third, only the *Shih chi* mentions the 'Army North of the Ho' (*Ho pei chih chün* 河北之軍). This title does not appear at all in the *Han shu*. Fourth, in the *Han shu* it is not King Huai of Ch'u who decides himself to move to P'eng-ch'eng, but Hsiang Yü and Liu Pang who cause him to be moved there; this is thus ostensibly the reason that Lü Ch'en, Hsiang Yü and Liu Pang position themselves about the city (*Han shu*, 1A.15: 沛公、項羽方攻陳留，聞梁死，士卒恐，乃與將軍呂臣引兵而東，徙懷王自盱台都彭城); "Only when the Magistrate of P'ei and Hsiang Yü, having just attacked Ch'en-liu, heard that [Hsiang Liang] had died and his officers and men were afraid, did they lead their troops together with General Lü Ch'en and head east, moving King Huai from Hsü-yi and causing him to make his capital at the *Han shu*.

[33]This expression, *shu shih pai jen* 數十百人, explained in "So-yin" (*Shih chi*, 8.349), is common in the *Shih chi*, occurring eight times and especially in accounts of the founding of the Han. It is employed, for example, to depict how many men Hsiang Chi 項籍 killed at the start of the rebellion, as well as to describe the total Hsiang Yü slew as he was surrounded by Liu Pang's troops at the end of it (cf. *Shih chi*, 7.297 with *Grand Scribe's Records*, 1:183, and *Shih*

P'eng-ch'eng"). Moreover, this move is set in 207 B.C. in the *Shih chi* account, but occurs late in 208 B.C. in the *Han shu* version. Finally, there is no mention of Wei Pao becoming King of Wei in the *Shih chi* account. The Higaku text is identical with the Chung-hua *Shih chi* for this passage. Other differences in the *Shih chi* and *Han shu* here are stylistic rather than substantive.

The *Han chi* (1.8a) places Hsiang Liang's death in the ninth month of 208 B.C. and also records Wei Pao's ascension to the throne in that same month. The chronological tables of the *Shih chi* (16.768-9) note Wei Pao's actions in addition to several of the appointments by King Huai, the former in the ninth month and the latter in the intercalary month after the ninth. Thus rather than a case of one of these texts providing more information and the other less, these parallel passages reveal the *Han shu* providing more accurate chronology and a better sequence (based on all available sources) to the events depicted. This is in keeping with what has been traditionally considered a general tendency of Pan Ku to realign the chronology of the *Shih chi,* as can be realized by reading Liang Yü-sheng's comments on any parallel chapter or section of the *Shih chi.*

Finally, let us look at a brief passage from the seventh year of Kao-tsu's reign:

> *Shih chi,* 8.384: 七年，匈奴攻韓王信馬邑，信因與謀反太原。
> *Han shu,* 1B.63: 秋九月，匈奴圍韓王信於馬邑，信降匈奴。

The Higaku text is indentical to the Chung-hua *Shih chi* here and there are no variants noted by Mizusawa. The major difference between these passages is clearly the date. Aside from some minor variants in the first clause (the *Shih chi's kung* 攻 "to attack" is *wei* 圍 "to surround, to invest" in *Han shu,* which also adds the locative particle *yü* 於 before Ma-yi), there is also the rather distinct second clause in which the *Shih chi* text may suggest Hann Hsin's motivation for turning his back on the Han. Translations of both texts might read:

> *The Grand Scribe's Records:* In the seventh year (200 B.C.), the Hsiung-nu attacked [Hann] Hsin, the King of Hann, at Ma-yi, and Hsin took advantage of this to join them and plot rebellion in T'ai-yüan.
> *The History of the Han:* In the ninth month of the autumn [of the sixth year, 201 B.C.], the Hsiung-nu surrounded [Hann] Hsin, the King of Hann, at Ma-yi; Hsin surrendered to the Hsiung-nu.

The *Han chi* (3.13a) account of these events confirms the *Han shu* dating, but argues that the Hsiung-nu attacked T'ai-yüan, not Ma-yi: 秋九月匈奴圍太原、韓王信於馬邑。信降匈奴; "In the ninth month of the autumn the Hsiung-nu surrounded T'ai-yüan and [Hann] Hsin, the King of Hann, at Ma-yi. Hsin surrendered to the Hsiung-nu." While Hsün Yüeh echoes Pan Ku's dating, he differs from both the *Shih chi* and the *Han shu* by placing the Hsiung-nu attack at T'ai-yüan. In other words, the Hsiung-nu were attacking a point between Hann Hsin and the Han capital, effectively cutting him off (Ma-yi was located about one hundred miles north of Chin-yang, which is just to the southwest of modern T'ai-yüan, near modern Shuo 朔 County in Shansi–T'an Ch'i-hsiang, 2:9).

Before turning to the rebellion, let us address the question of dating. Liang Yü-sheng (6.232) notes that both the "seventh year" given in the *Shih chi* text here and "the fifth year" given in its chronological tables (*Shih chi,* 17.807) are incorrect. The correct date is given in Hann Hsin's biography (see discussion below) as well as in the *Han shu* and *Han chi* versions. Once again, however, Liang says nothing about the *primacy* of either text. He is simply noting that the information given by Pan Ku is correct, while that provided by Ssu-ma Ch'ien is erroneous.

The account of Hann Hsin's rebellion also occurs in his biography (*Shih chi,* 93.2632-3). It occurs after we have been told that Kao-tsu believes he may have made a mistake by making a capable general like Hann Hsin king of an area that was noted for its crack troops (he had been made King of Hann 韓, ruling the Ying-ch'uan 潁川 region, with his capital at Yang-ti 陽翟,[34] during the previous year):

Shih chi, 93.2632: 迺詔徙韓王信王太原以北，備禦胡，都晉陽。信上書日：「國被邊，匈奴數入，晉陽去塞遠，請治馬邑。」上許之，信乃徙治馬邑。秋，匈奴冒頓大圍信，信數使使胡求和解。漢發兵救之，疑信數閒使，有二心，使人責讓信。信恐誅，因與匈奴約共攻漢，反，以馬邑降胡，擊太原。

Then he issued a decree moving [Hann] Hsin, the King of Hann, to be king of [the territory] north of T'ai-yüan, to defend against the Tartars, with his capital at Chin-yang. Hsin submitted a letter saying: 'My state covers the frontier area and the Hsiung-nu have made several incursions. Chin-yang is distant from the fortifications [i.e., the wall built to hold out the Hsiung-nu]; I request to administer from Ma-yi. The sovereign agreed to this and Hsin thus moved his administration to Ma-yi. In the autumn, Mo-tu,[35] the Hsiung-nu [Shan-yü], surrounded Hsin with a great [force]. Hsin sent envoys several times to the Tartars seeking that they make a pact to relieve [the siege]. The Han [court] sent out troops to rescue him, [but] being suspicious of Hsin having a duplicitous mind for having several times sent envoys in secret [to the Hsiung-nu], they sent someone to reproach him. Hsin feared being executed and took advantage of this to come to an agreement with the Hsiung-nu to join together and attack Han. When he rebelled, he surrendered to the Tartars with Ma-yi and attacked T'ai-yüan.

Thus it can be seen that in Ssu-ma Ch'ien's eyes Hann Hsin was well aware of the danger he was in. He knew that in the year since Kao-tsu had become emperor, Tsang T'u 臧荼, Li Chi 利幾, and Han Hsin 韓信 had all rebelled (cf. *Shih chi,* 8.382-4), in part because of Kao-tsu's growing mistrust of his former confederates. This mistrust can be seen clearly in Hann Hsin's request to be sent closer to the fortifications, something that would place him further from Ch'ang-an and Han power. The *yin* 因 (or take advantage of) in the *Shih chi* account (因與謀反太原) is therefore significant, reminding the reader of Hann Hsin's fears

---

[34]Near modern Yü 禹 County in Honan about sixty miles southeast of Lo-yang (T'an Ch'i-hsiang, 2:19).

[35]On the pronunciation of this name and some basic biographical information, see Wu and Lu, 93.2571n.

further from Ch'ang-an and Han power. The *yin* 因 (or take advantage of) in the *Shih chi* account (因與謀反太原) is therefore significant, reminding the reader of Hann Hsin's fears and Kao-tsu's mercurial frame of mind, something that Pan Ku preferred to understate in his version.

These comparisons, even of parallel versions for a single chapter, could go on to form the basis of a lengthy monograph. We have not, for example, considered larger changes made by Pan Ku, such as the incorporation of imperial edicts into his annals (none are found in the *Shih chi* account of Kao-tsu). Such a study is, however, beyond the scope of this introduction. What in general can be assumed from the texts compared (and from the other passages that have been read carefully in preparation for the translations which follow) is that in most cases it is impossible to view the often shorter, less detailed *Han shu* texts as primary here. In cases where more information is provided in the *Han shu* parallel, it is usually because Pan Ku is correcting an error or omission in the *Shih chi*. Although admittedly it is difficult to *prove* that even this chapter of the *Shih chi* is the primary text, the conclusions that can be drawn from the comparisons above are overwhelmingly in support of that assumption. It may well be that, in the study of the *Shih chi*, the relationships between *The Grand Scribe's Records* and the *Han shu* will have to remain an open question, much like in the study of Biblical manuscripts. Paul Johnson's recent conclusion that "analyzing this mass of evidence [Biblical manuscripts, quotations in other texts, etc.] in the search for the perfect text is probably self-defeating. Beyond a certain point, scholarship tends to raise as many problems as it solves."[36] Nevertheless, it is to be hoped that the analysis provided above will at the very least call upon all scholars to use both of these texts with care and discretion.[37] And for all of us to keep in mind Daniel B. Wallace's caveat: "In historical investigation, one looks for a *probable* reconstruction on the basis of available evidence–both external and internal. There is always a degree of doubt, an element of subjectivity. But this factor does not give one the right to replace the probable with the merely possible. Any approach that does so is operating within the constraints of an a priori."[38]

[36]Paul Johnson, *History of Christianity* (Rpt. Harmondsworth: Penguin, 1990 [1976]), p. 26.

[37]On comparisons between the *Shih chi* and *Han shu* texts, see also Wu Fu-chu 吳福助, *Shih, Han kuan-hsi* 史漢關係 (Taipei: Wen-shih-che, 1987 [1975]), Park Jae-Woo 朴宰雨, *Shih chi, Han shu pi-chiao yen-chiu* 史記漢書比較研究 (Peking: Chung-kuo Wen-hsüeh, 1994), Shih Ting 施丁, "Ma Pan yi-t'ung san-lun" 馬班異同三論, in *Ssu-ma Ch'ien yen-chiu hsin-lun* 司馬遷研究新論, edited by Shih Ting and Ch'en K'o-ch'ing 陳可青 (Chengchow: Ho-nan Jen-min, 1982), and the bibliography on pp. 223-4 in *The Grand Scribe's Records*, v. 1.

[38]Daniel B. Wallace, "The Majority Text Theory: History, Methods and Critique," in *The Text of the New Testament in Contemporary Research*, edited by Bart D. Ehrman and Michael W. Holmes (Grand Rapids, Michigan: Eerdmans, 1995), p. 315.

III. The *Textus Receptus* and Chang Wen-hu

Despite the comparison to critical studies and translations of Western classical literature above, there is little doubt that textual work on the *Shih chi,* like that on most traditional Chinese texts, has lagged.[39] When the current translation project was begun, several colleagues suggested that we concern ourselves with establishing a better text of the *Shih chi* than the received version, rather than attempting a translation. This idea was rejected in part because we realized such a task would very likely be beyond the capabilities of our small team. We did consider this possibility for a time, rejecting it only after determining that the variations discovered in comparing passages of the *Shih chi* were negligible in the impact that they would have upon our translation and could be dealt with in the scholarly apparatus. Translation of over thirty pre-Ch'in chapters over the early years of the 1990s and most of the *shih-chia* 世家 chapters in the last four-five years have not altered this initial impression.

We were confident that our base text, the Chung-hua Shu-chü edition published in 1959 (6v. hardback, 10v. softbound) was the best available modern edition.[40] It has been based on the Chin-ling Shu-chü 金陵書局 edition, a text we believed to have been carefully prepared by Chang Wen-hu after he had perused a number of important early editions. Our conclusions were based on the two "Ch'u-pan shuo-ming" 出版説明 (Publishing Notes) penned by the Chung-hua editors for their edition of the *Shih chi* and for the punctuated edition of Chang's *Chiao-k'an Shih chi "Chi-chieh," "So-yin," "Cheng-yi," cha-chi* 校刊史記集解索引正義札記 they published in two volumes in 1977. The "Publishing Note" in the latter, followed by a list of seventeen editions, appeared to suggest that Chang had seen and collated all these texts. At least that is what we believed until I purchased a copy of the original 1873 edition of the Chin-ling Shu-chü *Shih chi* in Peking in October 1998. When I examined this original edition, I was surprised to find that Chang Wen-hu had written a colophon that for some reason had not been punctuated and published in the 1977 edition of his *Chiao-k'an.* As a result, a more detailed examination of Chang Wen-hu's editorial efforts on the Chin-ling edition seemed in order.

I began by re-reading the section on Chang Wen-hu and the Chin-ling Shu-chü in the "Publishing Note" (p. 5) to the Chung-hua edition,[41] where I found a troubling sentence to which I had not paid close attention previously:

---

[39]Textual criticism of most Chinese texts has remained primarily at the word level, not the narrative level. The major exception is David Hawkes' remarkable analysis of the textual strata in the biography of Ch'ü Yüan in the *Shih chi* (see Hawkes, "Qu Yuan," in his *The Songs of the South, An Anthology of Ancient Chinese Poems by Qu Yuan and Other Poets* [Harmondsworth: Penguin, 1985], pp. 51-60).

[40]On the compilation of the Chung-hua edition see also William H. Nienhauser, Jr., "Historians of China."

[41]*Shih chi* (Peking: Chung-hua, 1959), v. 1.

This edition had been examined and corrected by Chang Wen-hu based on a collated edition of Ch'ien T'ai-chi and various ancient and modern editions which Chang himself had seen; [Chang] selected the best [emendations] and followed them. This is a comparatively fine edition from the later period of the Ch'ing dynasty.

這個本子經張文虎根據錢泰吉的校本和他自己所見到的各種舊刻古本，時本加以考訂，擇善而從，是清朝後期較好的本子.

Thus, the scholar Ch'ien T'ai-chi 錢泰吉 (1791-1863)[42] was also an important figure in the transmission of the *Shih chi* text. Although information is readily available on Ch'ien himself, little is known of his collated edition of the *Shih chi*. In order to reassess Chang Wen-hu's debt to Ch'ien, I decided to explore Chang Wen-hu's life in more detail. The following sections (IIIA-D) are based on the author's recently published article, "Chang Wen-hu and His Text of the *Shih chi*."[43]

III.A. Chang Wen-hu's Life

There are several sources for a brief biography of Chang Wen-hu–his voluminous writings and a memorial inscription, for example.[44] For our purposes, however, excerpts from the already succinct account in the *Ch'ing shih kao* 清史稿 (Draft History of the Ch'ing)[45] will suffice:

. . . there was Chang Wen-hu 張文虎 of Nan-hui 南匯.[46] Wen-hu's cognomen was Hsiao-shan 嘯山 (Roaring in the Mountains).[47] He was a first-degree graduate. He read the books of various schools [such as] Mr. Hui 惠 of Yüan-ho 元和,[48] Mr.

[42]On Ch'ien T'ai-chi, see the notice in Arthur W. Hummel, *Eminent Chinese of the Ch'ing Period* (Rpt. Taipei: Ch'eng-wen, 1967, pp. 155-6–hereafter cited as *ECCP*).

[43]Published in Wang Ch'eng-mien 王成勉, ed., *Ming Ch'ing wen-hua hsin-lun* 明清文化新論 (Taipei: Wen-chin, 2000), pp. 275-309.

[44]A punctuated version of this inscription has been reprinted from Miao Ch'üan-sun's 繆荃孫 (1844-1919) *Yi-feng T'ang wen-chi* 藝風堂文集 in the front-matter to Chang Wen-hu's *Shu-yi Shih shih-ts'un* 舒藝室詩存 (Taipei: Ta-hua 大華, 1968), pp. 1-5.

[45]*Ch'ing shih kao chiao-chu* 清史稿校注. Chu Huai-sen 朱淮森, ed. Taipei: Kuo-shih Kuan 國史館, 1990), 489.11123.

[46]About twenty-five miles southeast of modern Shanghai city near the seacoast in the modern Shanghai district (T'an Ch'i-hsiang, 8.17).

[47]Which matches his given name, Wen-hu or "Literary Tiger." He also had another *tzu*, Meng-piao 夢彪 "Dreaming of the Tiger Cub" (see *Ch'ing shih kao*, 489.11123, n. 135).

[48]Hui Tung 惠棟 (1697–1758), a textual critic and scholar from Soochow (see *ECCP*, pp. 357-8). He was the founder of what became known as the Wu 吳 or Soochow School. This school was a part of Han-hsüeh 漢學, "The School of Han Studies," which emphasized textual criticism and evidential research.

Chiang 江 of Hsi 歙,[49] Mr. Tai 戴 of Hsiu-ning 休寧,[50] and Mssrs. Ch'ien 錢 of Chia-ting 嘉定,[51] and sighed with deep feeling [realizing] that in doing scholarship there was naturally a basis [in textual study and evidential research]; taking the commentaries and the explanations of the Classics from the Han, T'ang and Sung dynasties, through their form and sound he was able to master their graphs, through glosses and explanations he was able to understand their meaning, through calculations and terminology he was able to determine [the date and circumstances of] their composition, through the language and historical references he was able to glance at the profound and subtle meaning of the sages and worthies of antiquity. In addition, as regards the philosophical and historical works, he was able to investigate all their textual histories and variants. He was skilled in astronomy and mathematics and especially strong in the collation of texts. In the fifth year of the T'ung-chih 同治 reign period [1866], when the Liangkiang Book Company[52] was opened, by collating the *Shih chi* and its "Three Commentaries" [Chang] Wen-hu was able to complete a *Reading Notes* [*Cha-chi* 札記] in five *chüan;* it is said to be sublimely excellent. When he passed away, he was seventy one.[53] Among his writings there is the *Shu-yi Shih yi-shu* 舒藝室遺書 (Textual Legacy from the Study Where One Expands the Legacy of Books from the Past).

... 有南匯張文虎。文虎，字嘯山。諸生。嘗讀元和惠氏、歙江氏、休寧戴氏、嘉定錢氏諸家書，慨然歎為學自有本，則取漢、唐、宋注疏、經説，由形聲以通其字，由訓詁以會其義，由度數名物以辨其制作，由語言事蹟以窺古聖賢精

[49]Chiang Yu-kao 江有誥 (1790 or earlier–1851) was a philologist whose work was lauded by Tuan Yü-ts'ai 段玉裁 (1735-1815) and Wang Nien-sun 王念孫 (1744-1832)—see his biography in *Ch'ing shih kao,* 481:13220-1. Among more than a dozen books which Chiang wrote his *Ch'ün ching yün-tu* 群經韻讀 and *Shih ching yün-tu* 詩經韻讀 may have especially appealed to Chang Wen-hu.

[50]Tai Chen 戴震 (1727–1777), a native of Hsiu-ning (modern Anhwei), was a great scholar associated with a number of famous contemporaries including the historian Wang Ming-sheng 王鳴盛 (1722-1798); he also taught the noted scholar Wang Nien-sun (see note immediately above). Tai worked on the compilation of the *Ssu-k'u ch'üan-shu* 四庫全書 and edited over fifty works during his lifetime (*ECCP,* pp. 696-9).

[51]This refers to the brothers Ch'ien Ta-hsin 錢大昕 (1728-1804) and Ch'ien Ta-chao 錢大昭 (1744–1813), from Chia-ting in the modern Shanghai district. Ch'ien Ta-chao was a specialist in the Han era, as his *Han shu pien-yi* 漢書辨疑 and *Hou Han shu pien-yi* 後漢書辨疑 testify (*ECCP,* p. 152). Ch'ien Ta-hsin (*ECCP,* 152-4) was a noted historian and the author of the *Nien-erh shih k'ao-yi* 廿二史考異 (1780), a text that Chang Wen-hu often used in his collation of the *Shih chi.*

[52]Apparently an alternate name for the Chin-ling Shu-chü. Chin-ling was the seat of the Liangkiang (i.e., Kiangsu and Chekiang) government, and was perhaps used interchangeably with Liangkiang.

[53]According to the *Hsü pei chuan chi* 續碑傳集, ch. 75, he died at age 78. This dating, 1808-1885, is more widely accepted by scholars and conforms better to the events of Chang Wen-hu's life.

義，旁及子史，莫不考其源流同異。精天算，尤長校勘。同治五年，兩江書局
開，文虎為校史記三注，成札記五卷，最稱精善。卒，年七十有一。著有舒藝
室遺書。

This brief account of Chang's life provides us several important facts to guide subsequent
inquiries. First, by emphasizing the books he read, rather than the teachers he studied
with, the text suggests what can be discovered in Chang's own writings. He was self
taught. Orphaned at the age of fifteen,[54] Chang was forced to continue his studies on his
own, making his living by moving from job to job.[55] Second, the circle of masters he
came to prefer in his reading left him clearly within the confines of the School of Han
Learning 漢學, thereby devoted to textual criticism (*chiao-k'an hsüeh* 校勘學) and evidential
research (*k'ao-cheng* 考證). It was the methodology Chang learned through his readings–the
third fact of interest from the biography–that which led him to win patronage from the
Ch'ien 錢 family in Chin-shan 金山 (about forty-five miles southeast of modern Soochow
and thirty miles southwest of Shanghai, not far from the Kiangsu–Chekiang border and
only thirty miles west of his hometown of Nan-hui).[56] Just ten years after his father had
died, and still only in his mid-twenties, Chang Wen–hu was invited by the bibliophile
Ch'ien Hsi-tso 錢熙祚 (1800–1844)[57] to work in his huge library housed in the Shou-shan
Ko 守山閣 (Pavilion Close to the Mountains).[58] Chang stayed with the Ch'ien family for
most of his adult life, with the exception of the eight years he spent working on the *Shih
chi* for Tseng Kuo-fan 曾國藩 (1811-1872) and several brief sojourns at the Wen-lan Ko
文瀾閣 library in Hangchow where he collated over eighty works and copied nearly five
hundred.[59] In 1835 he married a Ms. Yao 姚 from Chin-shan and moved in with her
family. In 1839 they had a son, almost nothing is known about him.[60] During the 1830s
Chang edited the *Shou-shan Ko ts'ung-shu* 守山閣叢書 (Collectanea of the Pavilion
Close to the Mountains) among numerous other works. Ch'ien Hsi-tso had also invited
several other scholars to help with the editing of books including Li Shan-lan 李善蘭

[54]See Chang's "Hsing-chai Yao-shih chia chuan" 惺齋姚師家傳 in *Shu-yi Shih tsa-chu*
舒藝室雜著 (Miscellaneous Writings from the Studio Where One Expands the Legacy of Books
from the Past; rpt. Taipei: Ta-hua 大華 Yin-shu-kuan, 1968 [1874]), p. 381.

[55]See his second letter to Juan Yüan 阮元 (1764-1849), "Shang Juan Hsiao-kuo" 上阮
相國, dated 1844, *Shu-yi Shih ch'ih-tu* 舒藝室尺牘, 17b.

[56]T'an Ch'i-hsiang, 8:17.

[57]*ECCP*, p. 36.

[58]This and much of the following information comes from a grave inscription written
for Chang by Miao Ch'üan-sun 繆荃孫, *Hsü pei chuan chi*, 75:1a.

[59]See Chang's biography in the *Ch'ing shih lieh-chuan* 清史列傳 (Peking: Chung-hua,
1987), 73.6067-8.

[60]His daughter married a third–degree graduate named Wang Pao-ju 王保如 and they
had a son named Wang Hsiao-tseng 王孝曾.

(1810-1882),[61] who became a close friend and colleague to Chang.[62] In 1843 Chang Wen-hu accompanied Ch'ien Hsi-tso on a trip to Peking (possibly to present copies of the newly published collectanea to scholars and officials in the capital). While in Peking, Ch'ien passed away (early in 1844). Chang accompanied the coffin back to Chin-shan, but he seems to have detoured to Yangchow to visit the noted scholar and official Juan Yüan 阮元 (1764-1849), then in his eighties and living in retirement.[63] Chang gave him a copy of the collectanea he had edited and initiated a correspondence that may have been intended to seek a patron to replace Ch'ien Hsi-tso.[64] Once back in Chin-shan, however, Ch'ien's nephew, Ch'ien P'ei-sun 錢培蓀, soon filled that role, insisting that Chang stay in Chin-shan and complete the projects begun under his uncle.

In the early 1850s Li Shan-lan left Chin-shan to work with the English scholars Joseph Edkins (1823-1905) and Alexander Wylie (1815-1887) at the London Missionary Society in Shanghai. Li was a noted mathematician and in Shanghai he assisted in translating mathematical treatises and other works into Chinese. Chang continued his editing in Chin-shan. In 1856 he moved his family out of his wife's family home to Chang-ching Yen 張涇堰 (= 張堰鎮??, which is about ten miles southeast of Chin–shan, see T'an Ch'i-hsiang, 8:17). For the next few years, however, Chang was forced to move with his family to avoid the disruptions caused by military movements of the Taipings.

In 1863, after Tseng Kuo-fan[65] had secured An-ch'ing 安慶 for the Ch'ing, he set up an official press called the Chin-ling Shu-chü 金陵書局 (Chin-ling Press), to edit and produce new editions of various classical and historical texts, ostensibly because many of these texts had not survived the turmoil of the warfare that had engulfed the Lower Yangtze Region for nearly a decade. In reality, it seems that most of the major *Shih chi* texts were unaffected by the Taiping destruction and that Tseng's motives may have been more self-aggrandizing. Late in 1863,[66] Tseng invited Chang Wen-hu to join his staff as a

[61]*ECCP*, pp. 479-80.

[62]See Cheng Wei-chang 鄭偉章. "Chin-shan Ch'ien-shih k'o-shu k'ao" 金山錢氏刻書考, *Shu-lin ts'ung-k'ao* 書林叢考 (Canton: Kuang-tung Jen-min, 1995), pp. 115–25. Chang claims that in the late 1830s there were forty people collating books in this library.

[63]*ECCP*, pp. 399-402.

[64]Juan wrote a preface for the collectanea and the two exchanged poems for a time (letters to Juan Yüan titled "Fu Juan Hsiao–kuo" 復阮相國 and "Shang Juan Hsiang–kuo" 上阮相國, *Shu–yi Shih ch'ih-tu*, 15a and 17a).

[65]*ECCP*, pp. 751-6.

[66]We can date his arrival in An-ch'ing in part through a poem celebrating Su Shih's 蘇軾 (1036–1101) birthday held in Chou Hsüeh-chün's home (*Shu-yi Shih shih-ts'un*, pp. 268-9). It had long been Chang Wen-hu's practice to celebrate Su Shih and other ancient literati's birthdays with parties (see, for example, his poem written on a similar occasion while Chang was still in his hometown of Nan-hui, *Shu-yi Shih shih-ts'un*, pp. 39-41). Li Shan-lan was also in attendance at Chou's party and was probably summoned to join Tseng's staff at about this

scholar.[67] In the summer of the following year most of the operations of the press moved from An-ch'ing to Nanking when the latter city was taken by Tseng's troops. In 1865 Tseng was ordered north to face the Nien insurgency in northwestern Anhwei, but he had seen to it that Chang was given a position at a school in Nanking.[68] Moreover, Li Hung-chang 李鴻章 (1823-1901)[69] became the Acting Governor General of Liangkiang and immediately emphasized the importance of producing new editions of the classics and histories destroyed during the fighting. At this time the Chin-ling Press was headed by Chou Hsüeh-chün 周學濬.[70] It was probably Chou who involved Chang with the collation and editing work. Regardless of whom it was that brought Chang to the Press, during his eight-year employment there he was asked to edit new editions for a number of histories, classics and related texts, including the *Ssu shu* 四書, several of the other classics, the *Han shu* 漢書, the *San-kuo chih* 三國志, the *Wen hsüan* 文選, Wang Nien-sun's *Tu-shu tsa-chih* 讀書雜志, and, of course, the *Shih chi*.[71]

Work on the classics took precedence and new editions were printed in spring of 1867.[72] The editing of the *Shih chi* was begun by T'ang Jen-shou 唐仁壽 (1829–1876),[73] a student of Ch'ien T'ai-chi,[74] who, as will be seen below, also played a major, if indirect, role in the editing of the Chin-ling *Shih chi*. Ch'ien had joined Tseng Kuo-fan at An-ch'ing to support the fight against the Taipings, but died shortly after reaching Tseng's base. His son, Ch'ien Ying-p'u 錢應溥, remained with Tseng's troops, moved on to Nanking when they did, and sometime in late 1865 or 1866 recommended T'ang Jen-shou to Li Hung-chang. For a time T'ang and Chang worked on the *Shih chi* together; then the work was entrusted to Chang Wen-hu.[75] Details on how it was completed follow in the time.

Confirmation for the date of Chang joining Tseng's staff can be found in the prose piece Chang wrote for Tseng's sixtieth birthday, *Shu-yi Shih tsa-chu*, p. 201.

[67]On Tseng's use of the *mu-fu* 幕府 system of advisors, see Kenneth E. Folsom, "The *Mu-fu* System under Tseng Kuo-fan," in Folsom, *Friends, Guests, and Colleagues; the Mu-fu System in the Late Ch'ing Period* (Berkeley: University of California Press, 1968), pp. 58-77.

[68]See the grave inscription by Miao Ch'üan-sun, *Hsü pei chuan chi,* 75.1b.

[69]*ECCP*, pp. 464-71.

[70]Liu Shang-heng 劉尚恆, "Chin-ling Shu-chü hsiao-k'ao" 金陵書局小考, *T'u-shu-kuan tsa-chih* 圖書館雜誌, 1987.5: 54-5.

[71]*Ibid.*

[72]See Chang's letter to Tseng Kuo-fan's younger brother, Tseng Kuo-ch'üan 曾國荃 (1824-1890), "Shang Tseng Yüan-p'u Kung-pao" 上曾沅浦宮保, written in the eighth month of 1867, *Shu-yi Shih ch'ih-tu*, 33b-35a. On Tseng Kuo-ch'üan, see also *ECCP*, pp. 749-51.

[73]The following account is based on an unofficial biography of T'ang Jen-shou, "T'ang Tuan-fu pieh-chuan" 唐端甫別傳, written by Chang Wen-hu (*Shu-yi Shih tsa-chu*, pp. 165-9).

[74]Ch'ien was a grandson of Ch'ien Ch'en-ch'ün 錢陳群 (1686-1874); he was also a lifelong student of the *Shih chi* (see *ECCP*, pp. 155-6 and n. 42 above).

[75]T'ang was associated with this work long after he had ceased to be involved, it

colophon. The *Shih chi* edition has been called the best edition produced by the Chin-ling Press, validating the fourth claim–that his work on the *Shih chi* was "sublimely excellent"–of Chang's biography in the *Ch'ing shih kao*. Chang's final years after leaving the press in 1873 were spent in the Fu Yüan 復園 (Restoration Garden) of the Ch'ien family (outside the east gate of Sung-chiang 松江). At the request of his hometown magistrate, Nan-hui, he was asked to compile a local history. He seems to have finished this work in the late 1870s.[76] Although he was appointed chief lecturer in the Nan-ching Shu-yüan 南菁書院 in Chiang-yin 江陰 in 1883, a severe foot problem (gout?) prevented him from taking the position. His illness worsened and he died in 1885.

III.B. The Colophon and Chang's Work on a New *Shih chi* Edition

Having taken over the project in late 1867, Chang worked the next few years to complete a new edition of the *Shih chi*. Although in a letter to Tseng Kuo-fan written in 1869 he observes that he had first been intent to take a good edition and reprint it with some notes on variants, he was eventually convinced by Chou Hsüeh-chün to take this opportunity to compile a new, critical edition.[77]

But let us not anticipate Chang's own colophon for his edition of the *Shih chi*. This text is provided here both in translation and in the original text, since it was ignored by the Chung-hua editors in their critical edition of Chang's *Chiao-k'an Shih chi Chi-chieh, So-yin, Cheng-yi cha-chi* 校刊史記 集解索隱正義札記 (2v. Peking, 1977).[78] To my

seems. Thus Chang Wen-hu found it necessary to explain to Tseng Kuo-fan in a letter written in 1869 that T'ang was working on other texts such as the *Chin shu* 晉書, whereas he himself was in charge of the *Shih chi* project; *Shu-yi Shih ch'ih-tu*, 35b-37a.

[76]The *Nan-hui hsien chih* 南匯縣志 in 22 *chüan* is listed in the "Yi-wen chih" 藝文志 of the *Ch'ing shih kao*. 清史稿 by Chao Erh-hsün 趙爾巽 (1844-1927; see *Ch'ing shih kao chiao-chu* 清史稿校註 [Taipei: Kuo-shih Kuan, 1986], v. 5, p. 4080).

[77]*Shu-yi Shih ch'ih-tu*, 35b-37a.

[78]The publisher's preface mentions no reason for omitting the colophon.

This preface, moreover, notes that (p. 2) "In the process of putting the text in shape, we benefitted from the kindness of Comrade Wu Tse-yü 吳則虞 who loaned us the copy of Chang Wen-hu's Chin-ling Shu-chü *Shih chi* containing Chang's collation notes which Wu had in his library; we used it to correct a few printing errors in the [printed version of] the *Reading Notes*." [I assume that *p'i-chiao* 批校 here indicates "marginal collation notes."]

As was the norm in the late 1970s in Peking, we are not told who edited the *Reading Notes* to make this critical edition. It is perhaps noteworthy that Hsü Wen-shan 徐文珊, Ku Chieh-kang's student who co-edited the *Shih chi, Pai-wen chih pu* 史記白文之部 (Peiping: Kuo-li Pei-p'ing Yen-chiu Yüan, Li-shih Yen-chiu Hui, 1936), mentions in his preface (pp. 1-2) to that work that he had punctuated Chang Wen-hu's text and planned to publish it. It would seem that this edited version was to appear with the "San-chia chu" and other back-matter in a separate second volume ("Chu-shih chih pu" 注釋之部) which never appeared. Although it seems impossible to verify, it is possible that Chung-hua may have used Hsü's version in their knowledge this is the first attempt to provide not only a translation, but also punctuation for this text.

Colophon to the *Reading Notes* on the Collation and Printing of the *Grand Scribe's Records* and the *Collected Explanations [of the Grand Scribe's Records], Probing the Obscure [in the Grand Scribe's Records]*, and *Correcting the Meaning [of the Grand Scribe's Records]*[79]

The *Grand Scribe's Records* has had lacuna and interpolations since the Han dynasty. Down to modern times it has been another one-thousand and several hundred years in which the text was repeatedly transmitted by handwritten copies so that the accumulated errors [were accepted] in the correct version. There have been some places where we clearly understand there are errors, but we are unable to revise them. Mr. P'ei [Yin 裴駰] in his preface to his *Collected Explanations* claims, "I took from the Classics, the commentaries, and the Hundred Schools, together with the sayings of the Former Confucians. All those related things that were beneficial to this [commentary] have all been copied and included."[80] Today, beneath the text of the history, [P'ei's] comments are few and far between and in large part cannot represent the complete book. Only the *Probing the Obscure* has been printed in a unique edition by the Chi-ku Ko 汲古閣 (Pavilion Which Draws from Antiquity),[81] and the main text which appears there often surpasses those editions in common circulation. However, in changing the large characters of the Sung editions to the smaller characters [of later editions], a number [of characters] have been confused. And, furthermore, some have been revised according to the popular forms [of characters]; contrary to [their intention] [the Chi-ku Ko editors] lost the truth of Little Ssu-ma [Ssu-ma Chen 司馬貞]. Mr. Chang's *Correcting the Meaning* only survives in the editions which have printed all [the commentaries] together since the Southern Sung dynasty, its deletions already numerous, its errors extremely severe. In the "Three Commentaries" there are also instances of duplications of one text in the other causing errors and confusion.

editing.

[79]In *Shu-yi Shih tsa-chu*, p. 104.

[80]"*Shih chi Chi-chieh* hsü" 史記集解序, *Shih chi* (Peking: Chung-hua, 1959), v. 10, [Back-matter], p. 4.

[81]The Chi-ku Ko indicates the library (and studio-name) of Mao Chin 毛晉 (1599-1659) who reprinted the Northern Sung Secretariat Large Character 秘省大字 edition of the *Shih chi So-yin* 史記索隱 as part of Mao's *Shih-ch'i shih* 十七史 begun in 1628 and reprinted in 1660 (*ECCP*, pp. 565-66); the *Shih chi So-yin* itself was published in 1641, see Ho Tz'u-chün's 賀次君 entry on this edition in his *Shih chi shu-lu* 史記書錄 (Rpt. in *Shih chi fu-pien* 史記附編 [Taipei: Ting-wen, 1990]), pp. 34-49.

Before this [collation], the educational official, [Ch'ien] T'ai-chi 錢泰吉, [i.e.] Ch'ien [*hao*] Ching-shih 錢警石[82] of Chia-hsing 嘉興,[83] once assembled and collated various editions (of the *Shih chi*) over a period of more than thirty years. He invariably recorded in detail even the minor differences of a dot or a line [written incorrectly in a graph]. The Censor, [Chou] Hsüeh-chün [周]學濬, [i.e.] Chou [*hao*] Man-yün 周縵雲 of Wu-ch'eng 烏程,[84] borrowed [Ch'ien's] edition, examined it and recorded [notes], selecting the best [from Ch'ien's edition] and following them.

In the fifth year of the T'ung-chih reign period (1866), [Chou] asked the honorable Li [Hung-chang] 李[鴻章, 1823-1901] of Ho-fei 合肥,[85] Acting Governor General of the Kiangs [Kiangsu and Kiangsi, i.e., Liangkiang], Earl Su-yi 肅毅 and the present Chancellor of State, to entrust T'ang [style-name] Tuan-fu 唐端甫 of Hai-ning 海甯, [i.e.] the literary scholar [T'ang] Jen-shou 仁壽,[86] an eminent disciple of the educational official [Ch'ien T'ai-chi], to further collate [the manuscript] and hand it over to be printed. In the spring of the next year (1867), His Honor Tseng Wen-cheng 曾文正 [Tseng Kuo-fan], chancellor and Marquis of Hsiang-hsiang 湘鄉,[87] returned to Chin-ling 金陵 from Huai-pei 淮北 and ordered me, Wen-hu, to collate [the text] with him [T'ang]. I discussed [the work] with the Censor and His Honor Mr. T'ang. As the newly printed historical text and commentaries were not all based on a single edition, I feared this would give rise to doubt in the readers, and asked to append notes on the variants in each edition at the end of the completed printed version, together with the reasons for which something was accepted or rejected. [Tseng] Wen-cheng assented to this.

In the winter of the seventh year (1868), when His Honor [Tseng] was about to be transferred to take up a post in the capital area,[88] he ordered that if there were those things which should be changed in those fascicles for which

---

[82]See n. 42 above.

[83]Near the modern city of the same name about forty-five miles south of Soochow in Chekiang (T'an Ch'i-hsiang, 8:31).

[84]As noted above, Chou became the head of the Chin-ling Press in 1866; see also T'ao Hsiang 陶湘, ed., *Chao-tai ming-jen ch'ih-tu* 昭代名仁尺牘 (Taipei: Wen-hai, 1980), p. 277.

Wu-ch'eng is located near modern Hu-chou 湖州 City just southwest of Lake T'ai 太湖 in Chekiang (T'an Ch'i-hsiang, 8:31).

[85]See n. 69 above.

[86]Biographical materials in Min Erh-ch'ang 閔爾昌, ed., *Pei chuan chi pu* 碑傳集補 and *Pei chuan chi, san pien* 碑傳集，三編 by Wang Chao–yung 汪兆鏞 (in *Chin-tai Chung-kuo shih-liao ts'ung-k'an hsü-pien* 近代中國史料叢刊續編 [Taipei: Wen-hai, 1980], pp. 1733-7).

[87]About forty miles southwest of modern Changsha in Hunan (T'an Ch'i-hsiang, 8:37).

[88]To help stave off the approach of the Nien cavalry towards Peking (see *Cambridge History of China*, v. 10, *Late Ch'ing, 1800-1911, Part I* [Cambridge: Cambridge University Press, 1978], pp. 456ff).

the blocks had already been cut, as the occasion demanded [the errors] should be cut away and [the corrections] patched in [on the blocks]. Because of this it was not until the summer of the ninth year (1870) that the text could be printed and circulated. Then I wrote a draft and made it into my *Reading Notes* 札記.[89]

In the winter of that year (1870), His Honor again took on the position of Governor General of Liangkiang. I, Wen-hu, took the two fascicles which were completed first and respectfully offered them (to him). His Honor considered them excellent. Last winter (1871), the work was completed. I asked His Honor to write a preface at the head of the book. His Honor ordered that the *Reading Notes* should first be given to the [woodblock] carver, and that I should append a narrative giving the origins of the work at the end. Alas, who would have thought that before he had finished writing, His Honor would have passed away without time to make a preface for it.[90]

Of those variants which were recorded, the great majority of the material was taken from the collated edition by Ch'ien [T'ai-chi]. The rest was taken equally from the systematic discussions [of the *Shih chi*] by various scholars, those of Mr. Liang [Yü-sheng]'s (1745-1819) *Chih-yi* 志疑 (Records of Doubtful Points) and Mr. Wang [Nien-sun]'s (1744-1832) *Tu-shu tsa-chih* 讀書雜志 (Miscellaneous Records Made While Reading Books) being most numerous. We did not identify [entries on] those small points which I, Wen-hu, or His Honor Mr. T'ang saw [in the text]. Credit for those points which unconsciously duplicated what previous worthies [had written] was all returned to the previous worthies, in order to avoid the derision of taking credit due to others. As for other collational principles, they can be seen here and there in our notes. Limited by what we heard and saw, it would have been difficult to have avoided leaving out [something of importance]. [It is to be hoped] that those who are determined to collate [further] this history, using this text as a basis, would further refine our study, in order to achieve an excellent edition. [If such an edition is actually to appear,] it would be in accord with the fine encouragement [offered] later scholars by the two noble ministers.

校刊史記集解索隱正義札記跋

史記自漢已殘缺竄亂。迄今又千數百年，展轉傳寫，積非成是。蓋有明知其誤而不能改者矣。裴氏【集解】序稱，"采經傳百家，并先儒之說，豫是有益，悉皆鈔納。"今史文之下，箸注寥寥，大非完帙。

---

[89]*Cha* 札 were wooden slips on which notes were written in ancient times; by the Ch'ing dynasty, however, *cha-chi* had become a generic title for notes taken while reading (see, for example, Lu Wen-ch'ao's 盧文弨 [1717-1796] *Chung-shan cha-chi* 鍾山札記 [1790] and *Lung-ch'eng cha-chi* 龍城札記 [1796]).

[90]Li Hung-chang also seems to have been requested to write a preface, which he completed; but it is not included in the Chin-ling edition I own nor have I located it in Li's writings.

惟索隱有汲古閣單刻，所出正文，每勝通行之本。然其注改宋本大字為
小字，頗有混淆。又或依俗改竄，反失小司馬之真。張氏正義僅存於南
宋以來之合刻本，刪削既多，舛誤彌甚。三家注又有互相重複錯亂者。
　　先是，嘉興錢警石學博泰吉，嘗彙校各本，歷三十餘年。點畫小
殊，必詳記之。烏程周縵雲侍御學濬，借其本過錄，擇善而從。
　　同治五年，請於署江督肅毅伯，今相國合肥李公，以屬學博高弟
海寧唐端甫，文學仁壽，覆校付刊。及明年春，相侯湘鄉曾文正公自淮
北回金陵，命文虎同校。文虎與侍御及唐君議，以新刊史文及注皆不主
一本，恐滋讀者疑，請於刊竣之後附記各本異同及所以去取意。文正頷
之。
　　七年冬，公將移任畿輔，命凡已刻之卷，有宜改者，隨時剜補。
以是，至九年夏始克印行。乃屬稿為札記。
　　是年冬，公復任江督。文虎以先成稿二卷呈公，公以為善。去冬，
既蕆事，請公序其簡端。公命先以札記授梓氏，并附述緣起於末。烏乎，
孰意寫未竟而公薨，不及為之序乎。

　　　　所記異同，大半取資於錢校本。其外兼采諸家緒論，則梁氏【志
疑】，王氏【讀書雜志】為多。文虎與唐君管見所及，不復識別。其有
偶與前賢闇合者，悉歸之前賢，以避攘善之譏。餘例散見記中，限於聞
見，不免挂漏。有志於校史者，以此為質而益精攷之，以成善本。庶有
當於兩爵相嘉惠來學之意云。

The most important new facts to emerge from this colophon are the role of Ch'ien T'ai-chi in the composition of the Chin–ling Shu-chü *Shih chi* and Chang Wen-hu's reliance on works like Liang Yü–sheng's *Shih chi chih yi* and Wang Nien-sun's *Tu shu tsa-chih*. Since Ch'ien was a supporter of Tseng Kuo-fan and since his own disciple, T'ang Jen-shou, was working on the *Shih chi* project, it would have been logical for Ch'ien to have spoken to Chou Hsüeh-chün about his *Shih chi* collation. This may have been the means for introducing Ch'ien's *Shih chi* collation into the work at the Chin-ling Shu-chü.

This also means, however, that there was much less "collation" of rare editions and more dependence on previous collations (sometimes of texts Chang Wen-hu probably was unable to consult) and other evidential scholarship. With no access to Ch'ien T'ai-chi's manuscript, we are forced to reexamine Chang's *Reading Notes* item by item in an attempt to see what kind of changes he suggested and the reasons for those changes. Towards this goal, I have selected a few of Chang Wen-hu's notations from the "Cheng shih-chia" 鄭世家 (Hereditary House of Cheng), chapter forty-two of the *Shih chi,* for further examination.

III.C. Chang's Suggested Changes in Chapter 42

The *Reading Notes* (2:42.419-22) for the "Hereditary House of Cheng, Number 12" 鄭世家，第十二 contain forty-four entries by Chang Wen-hu. Many deal with potential problems in the "San-chia chu" and will not concern us. Since Chang is claiming to revise editions in circulation during the mid-nineteenth century, we shall use the Wu-ying Tien 武英殿–the so-called "Palace Edition" (Rpt. Taipei: Wen-hsing 文馨 Ch'u-pan-she, 1978)–as a basis for comparison.

The first change in our text suggested by Chang involves a proper name. The Palace Edition (p. 700, 42.4a) reads: 祝瞻射中王臂; "Chu Chan shot an arrow which struck the king's arm." Chang Wen-hu (p. 419) notes 各本訛瞻。依〔考異〕改; "Each edition erroneously has Chan 瞻. I changed it based on the *Investigations of Differences.*" The *K'ao-yi* or *Investigation of Differences* refers to Ch'ien Ta-hsin's 錢大昕 (1728-1804) *Nien-erh shih k'ao-yi* 廿二十考異 (Investigation of Differences in the Twenty-two Histories; 1782) which has about one-hundred pages of notes or entries on the *Shih chi.* The *Ch'ing shih kao* biography of Chang Wen-hu translated above, it should be recalled, tells us that Ch'ien Ta-hsin and his brother Ch'ien Ta-chao 錢大昭 (1744–1813) were among the scholars Chang studied (see also n. 50 above). There is indeed a note on the name Chu Chan in the *K'ao-yi*[91] and it was sufficient evidence to allow Chang to alter the Chin-ling *Shih chi* text to read "Chu Tan 祝耽." It should also be noted that the *So-yin* commentary in the Palace Edition (p. 700, 42.4a) reads: 左氏作祝耽; "Mr. Tso's [book] has Chu Tan 祝耽," and this, as much as the *K'ao-yi,* may have swayed Chang.

Another entry by Chang is of a completely different nature. The Palace Edition (p. 700, 42.4a) reads: 夜令祭仲問王疾, "At nightfall [the duke] ordered Chai Chung to inquire of the king's injury." Chang comments (p. 419): 舊刻無〔王〕字, "An old woodblock [edition] does not have the graph *wang* 王 (king)." Although such a reading might be possible, since there is neither textual support nor comments from earlier scholars on this, and since Chang does not identify the 'old woodblock edition,'[92] his comment seems of questionable value.

A third error Chang notes (p. 419) in this chapter refers to a date given. The original reads (Palace Edition, p. 700, 42.4b): 九月辛亥，忽出奔衛。己亥，突至鄭，立。是為厲公; "On the *hsin-hai* day of the ninth month [of 701 B.C., the forty-third year of Duke Chuang 莊 of Cheng], Hu went out [of the city] and fled to Wey. On the *chi-hai* day, T'u reached Cheng and was established. This was Duke Li." Chang's comment reads: 〔志疑〕云傳是〔丁亥〕。下文有己亥，則此文〔辛〕字誤可知; "The *Record of Doubtful Points* [by Liang Yü-sheng] reads: 'In the *[Tso] chuan* [the date] is *ting-hai.*' In my opinion, since the text reads *chi-hai* below, it is obvious that the *hsin* graph in this text is an error." Yet even with this amount of evidence, Chang did not alter the text of the Chin-ling *Shih chi* (42.4a), which still reads "*hsin-hai* 辛亥." The Chung-hua editors who used the Chin-ling *Shih chi* and Chang's *Reading Notes* to create their text, however, changed *hsin-hai* 辛亥 to *ting-hai* 丁亥 (*Shih chi*, 42.1762).

A fourth example involves a proper name again. In the Palace Edition we are introduced to a Grand Master of Cheng named Fu Hsia 甫瑕 (p. 701, 42.6a). Chang notes (p. 420): 索隱本作〔假〕。故引〔左傳〕異文以證之。各本作〔瑕〕，蓋後人依〔左〕改; "The *So-yin* edition has Hsia 假. For this reason, [Ssu-ma Chen 司馬貞] has cited the different text in the *Tso chuan* as evidence [for reading Hsia 瑕]. Each edition that has *hsia* 瑕 was presumably revised by some later person according to the *Tso.*" Here

[91]Rpt. Kyoto: Chûbun 中文 Shuppansha, 1980, p. 58.

[92]The Chung-hua editors believe this was the edition held by a Mr. Yü 郁 of Shanghai (probably Yü T'ai-feng 郁泰峰), but are uncertain as to its date (see *Cha-chi,* 1.1:1).

we find the unusual case where a text commonly available in the mid-nineteenth century–the Palace Edition–offered a reading Chang Wen-hu believed to be correct (Fu Hsia 甫瑕), but based on the *Shih chi So-yin* (i.e., the Chi-ku Ko edition, see also n. 45 above), Chang felt more comfortable maintaining a reading he felt was traditional. Since Chang believed the Palace edition was in error and also argued that the Hsia 瑕 in all other texts must all be interpolations, he suggests that the erroneous Hsia 假 was in the original text that Ssu-ma Ch'ien left us. This is especially questionable in light of the two occurrences of the name Fu Hsia, each written with the graph 瑕, in Ssu-ma Ch'ien's comments at the end of chapter 42.

As we shall see in this fifth example, sometimes Chang simply suggests a correction based on textual evidence within the *Shih chi* itself. The Palace Edition reads (p. 705, 42.14a): 十三年，定公卒; "In the thirteenth year [517 B.C.], Duke Ting expired." Chang notes (p. 421): 案表云〔十六年〕，此〔三〕字誤; "In my opinion, since the tables read 'the sixteenth year,' this 'three' [in thirteen] is a mistake." The error was already noted by the *K'ao-cheng* 考證 notes in the Palace Edition (p. 707) and it is difficult to see what Chang's note adds. Although Chang realizes "thirteen" is an error, the Chin-ling *Shih chi* still reads "In the thirteenth year."

As a sixth and final example of Chang Wen-hu's comments, let us look at a more complex case. The Palace Edition (p. 705, 42.14a-14b) reads: 孔子嘗過鄭。與子產如兄弟云。及聞子產死，孔子為泣曰: 〔古之遺愛也〕。兄事子產; "Confucius once passed through Cheng. He and Tzu Ch'an were like older and younger brothers. When he heard Tzu Ch'an had died, Confucius wept and said, 'He [exemplified] the love handed down from antiquity!' He [Confucius] served Tzu Ch'an like an elder brother." Chang comments (p. 421): 各本此下有〔兄事子產〕四字。與上文〔與子產如兄弟云〕複，且不當雜出於此 . . . 志疑 . . . 説同。此蓋後人旁注誤混。今刪; "Every edition has the four graphs ' he served Tzu Ch'an like an elder brother' below this. They are a reduplication of the text above–'He and Tzu Ch'an were like older and younger brothers' and, moreover, should not randomly appear here . . . the explanation in the *Record of Doubts* is the same. This was probably a marginal note by some later person which was erroneously mixed in [with the text] . . . Now I delete it." This is certainly the most radical change Chang proposes in chapter 42. The Po-na 百衲 Huang Shan-fu 黃善夫 edition of the *Shih chi* (2nd printing of a reprint, Taipei: T'ai-wan Shang-wu Yin-shu-kuan, 1995, p. 579, 42.15a) has these four graphs; modern scholars like Ku Chieh-kang and Hsü Wen-shan (in their *Shih chi, Pai-wen chih pu* 史記，白文之部 [Peiping: Kuo-li Pei-p'ing Yen-chiu Yüan, Shih-hsüeh Yen-chiu Hui, 1936]) also retained them–although both Ku and Hsü had read Chang's *Reading Notes* and Hsü had punctuated Chang's text in preparation to append it to a second volume of their work! Chang's deletion, moreover, has had a significant impact on modern Chinese studies of the *Shih chi* through its influence on the Chung-hua edition of the *Shih chi*. Thus the two major modern vernacular-language translations, Wang Li-ch'i's 王利器 *Shih chi chu yi* 史記注譯 (4v.; Sian: San Ch'in, 1988) and Wu Shu-p'ing 吳樹平 *et al., Ch'üan-chu ch'üan-yi Shih chi* 全注全譯史記 (Tientsin: T'ien-chin Ku-chi and

Kuo-chi Wen-hua Ch'u-pan Kung-ssu, 1995) seem to have used the Chung-hua *Shih chi* as a base text; although they don't include these four characters, they seem unaware of the problem and offer no notes (see Wang Li-ch'i, 42.1298 and Wu Shu-p'ing, 42.1625).

III.D. Remaining Problems with the Chung-hua Edition

There is no question that Chang Wen-hu contributed much to our understanding of the *Shih chi* text and its problems. However, as Chang himself argued in his colophon, the principles behind his work on the *Shih chi* only become apparent when one applies his *Chiao-k'an* to the text of the Chin-ling Shu-chü *Shih chi*. As we have seen in the examination of six examples above, it then becomes clear that decisions on revising the *Shih chi* text or deleting passages from it were based on a number of criteria, some of which were not textual in nature. In light of this, Chang's text of the *Shih chi* remains significant. But it, as well as the Chung-hua Shu-chü edition which it engendered, must both be used in concert with Chang's reading notes and those texts to which he had no access, primarily the Po-na and Ching-yu 璟祐 editions (the latter also known as the Academy Edition 監本, i.e., Pei Sung Ching-yu [Kuo-tzu] Chien pen 北宋璟祐〔國子〕監本, printed in the Ching-yu era [1034-1037] and reprinted in Taipei by the *Erh-shih-wu shih* Pien-k'an Kuan 二十五史編刊館 in 1955).

It should also be reasserted, however, that all of this is something of a tempest in a teapot, since textual variants between the major editions are generally as insignificant as they are infrequent. In comparing the Po-na edition of chapter 42 to the Chung-hua version, for example, besides the variants, *hsia* 假 / *hsia* 瑕, and Chang Wen-hu's deletion of the four characters 兄事子產–all discussed above–I found only the following differences between the Po-na and Chung-hua (i.e., Chin-ling) editions:

1a. Chung-hua 42.1766.13:   而卒立子蘭為太子。
1b. Po-na, p. 576, 42.9a: 卒而立子蘭為太子。
2a. Chung-hua 42.1769.1:   或欲還
2b. Po-na, p. 576, 42.10b: 或從還
3a. Chung-hua 42.1769.5,6,9 and 10:   揚
3b. Po-na, pp. 576-77, 42.11a–11b: 楊
       The name Chieh Yang 解揚 occurs five times in this passage. The Po-na edition has the correct graph once and the incorrect Yang 楊 four times.
4a. Chung-hua 42.1769.10:   為人臣無忘盡忠得死者!
4b. Po-na, p. 577, 42.11b: 為人臣毋忘盡忠得死者!
5a. Chung-hua 42.1775.14:   三十六年人
5b. Po-na, p. 579, 42.15b: 二十六年人
6a. Chung-hua 42.1776.2:   共公三年，三晉滅知伯。
6b. Po-na, p. 579, 42.16a: 共公三年，晉滅知伯。
7a. Chung-hua 42.1776.2:   三十一年，共公卒。
7b. Po-na, p. 579, 42.16a: 三十年，共公卒。

In all, ten relatively minor discrepancies which suggest, if anything, that the Po-na edition should be used with care!

Finally, in preparing this study a shadowy figure related to the *Shih chi* text has emerged (again). In re-reading the preface to the modern critical edition of the *Reading Notes* (Peking: Chung-hua, 1977), I found reference to a text of the *Notes*–possibly the original draft that Chang Wen-hu used–now in the possession of "Comrade Wu Tse-yü 吳則虞同志" in Peking. This text and its marginalia (*p'i chiao* 批校) by Chang Wen-hu were employed in the editing of the Chung-hua critical edition of *Reading Notes*. But the preface tells us little of this text. It is a pity that even in modern times the *Shih chi* continues to foster mystery.

IV. A Recapitulation

As we have seen, several major *Shih chi* scholars in the West advocated the primacy of the *Han shu* versions of events in the chapters they worked on. There may well be solid basis to their claims–this is something we shall address when we come to the chapters they translated and/or studied. But based on our reading of the five annals translated in this volume, there seems little reason to accept the more general argument that most or many of the Han-dynasty chapters in the *Shih chi* were in any fashion based on *Han shu* counterparts.

Moreover, although Burton Watson seems to have used Takigawa Kametarô 瀧川龜太郎 for his translation and David Honey has recently argued in favor of the Po-na edition,[93] for the great majority of scholars today, be it in Beijing or Berlin or Bloomington, the Chin-ling Shu-chü edition published in 1959 by Chung-hua Shu-chü is clearly the received text of the *Shih chi* today. From what we have examined above, this seems proper. Yet it is well to repeat the caveat offered the first volume of *The Grand Scribe's Records* (1:xv) that readers should employ the Chung-hua edition in tandem with the Po-na and Chien-pen editions. Despite some reservations over Chang Wen-hu's methods in preparing the Chin-ling edition (also demonstrated above), the Chung-hua text remains the only modern critical edition of the *Shih chi* and should continue to function as the *textus receptus*.

Finally, in assessing textual problems in the *Shih chi,* it should be kept in mind that Ssu-ma Ch'ien probably worked with a group of scribes or underlings who may have played an important role in copying texts for him, perhaps even in light editing. Since he left two copies of the text, there was no single "autograph" of the *Shih chi* and variants undoubtedly existed from the beginning. When we add to this the problem of whether Ssu-ma Ch'ien ever finished a final editing of the text,[94] errors in the text should not

[93]Watson did his work in Japan where Takigawa was the obvious choice. The Po-na edition is clearly a useful edition, but it was not available in mainland China for a good part of the last century and has not been used in the establishment of a modern critical text or by any major translator as the base text. Further problems with the Po-na text have been discussed in section III.D above.

[94]Aside from the problems of finding the time to work on the text (Ssu-ma Ch'ien held increasingly important official positions during the last years of his life), we ought to

surprise us. That the *Han shu* is better organized and better edited has long been accepted. This should not, however, lead us to believe that its texts are primary. Every chapter, every passage requires careful collation and comparison with all available parallels. The burden of proof should always be on those who want to change or exchange the *Shih chi* accounts.

William H. Nienhauser, Jr.
3 January 2002

recall that the "manuscript" was an enormous physical object, one that could scarcely be spread out in a single room. As Grant Hardy has pointed out, the *Shih chi* "was written with brush and ink on thousands of bamboo slips, packaged into about 130 bundles (*pian*), each held together by three or four silken cords and rolled up like so many window shades. It would have been impossible to hold the original *Shiji* in one's hands; in fact, it would have taken a cart to contain it" (Hardy, *Worlds of Bronze and Bamboo* [New York: Columbia University Press, 1999], p. xi). Not something to be easily edited and/or collated.

ON USING THIS BOOK

Most **Texts** are cited by chapter and page in a particular edition–*Shih chi* 62.2185 indicates *chüan* 卷 62, page 2135 of the Chung-hua edition (see **List of Abbreviations**)–but references to the *Lun yü* 論語 (Analects of Confucius) and *Meng Tzu* 孟子 (Mencius) are according to chapter and verse (學而時習之 is thus *Lun yü* 1/1) and to *Lao Tzu* 老子 (Lao Tzu) by section. When comments in a modern critical edition are relevant, however, we cite it. All dynastic history references are to the modern punctuated editions from Chung-hua Shu-chü 中華書局. For many other citations we have referred to the ***Ssu-pu pei-yao*** 四部備要 or ***Ssu-pu ts'ung-kan*** 四部叢刊 **Editions** to allow the reader to more easily locate the passage. Other abbreviated titles can be found in the **List of Abbreviations.**

In one important aspect we have deviated from accepted practice–**Names**. In the pre-Ch'in period there were four basic types of name–*hsing* 姓, *shih* 氏, *ming* 名 and *tzu* 字–one more than in later eras. The *ming,* given at birth, and the *tzu,* given at maturity in a male and marriage in a female, posed no new problems. The *hsing* has also remained the name given to those related by blood throughout Chinese history. But the *shih* is unique to pre-Ch'in times. Originally it was used to designate separate clans within the same *hsing.* The *shih* were usually created by using the official position (Ssu-ma 司馬), location (Chao 趙), noble title (Kung-tzu 公子), or profession (Shih 史) of the clan leader. In earliest times *shih* were only held by nobles, but during the Warring States era they were more widely held until *shih* and *hsing* became virtually indistinguishable (thus causing confusion for later scholars, including Ssu-ma Ch'ien). Given this extra name, and because we were not satisfied that any translation norms were universally followed for these terms, we have adopted a new scheme based primarily on Roman practice: "The Romans generally bore three names, the *praenomen,* corresponding to our Christian name; the *nomen,* the name of the *gens* or clan; the *cognomen,* the name of the family . . . a fourth name was sometimes added, the *agnomen*" (cf. Sir Paul Harvey, "Names of Persons," in Harvey's *The Oxford Companion to Classical Literature* [Rpt. Oxford: Oxford University Press, 1980], pp. 284-5). Well aware that there is not a perfect correspondence between these four name-types and those of pre-Ch'in China, we have adopted these terms: thus *hsing* is *cognomen, shih* is *nomen, ming* is *praenomen,* and *tzu* is *agnomen* (alternative renderings can be found in Endymion Wilkinson, *Chinese History, A Manual* [Cambridge, Massachusetts: Harvard University Asia Center, 1998], p. 98).

In earlier volumes we had mentioned that we hoped to publish a glossary. That hope has been realized in the appended **Glossary** intended primarily to clarify translations of specific terms in this volume and volume 1 (pre-Han basic annals).

For **Personal Names** in the early chapters we have hyphenated those two-syllable names we cannot analyze (e.g., Ch'a-fu 差弗), but separated those with titles or honorifics (e.g. Kung Liu 公劉). We have followed Ssu-ma Ch'ien's penchant for using several types of names to refer to the same character in a single chapter, but tried to alert the reader to this practice in our notes.

Locations of **Place Names** are based on T'an Ch'i-hsiang 譚其驤, ed. *Chung-kuo li-shih ti-t'u chi* 中國歷史地圖集, *Vol. I: Yüan-shih she-hui–Hsia, Shang, Hsi Chou, Ch'un-ch'iu, Chan-kuo shih-ch'i* 原始社會一夏，商，西周，春秋，戰國時期, *Vol. II: Ch'in, Hsi Han, Tung Han shih-ch'i* 秦，西漢，東漢時期 (Shanghai: Ti-t'u Ch'u-pan-she, 1982). T'an's identifications are not without problems, but they have been adopted by a number of large projects in China (such as the *Chung-kuo ta pai-k'o ch'üan-shu* 中國大百科全書) and provide the only practical means to attempt to identify the great number of place names in the *Shih chi*. On occasion we have added information from Ch'ien Mu's 錢穆 *Shih chi ti-ming k'ao* 史記地名考 (Rpt. Taipei: San-min Shu-chü, 1984), or Wang Hui's 王恢 *Shih chi pen-chi ti-li t'u-k'ao* 史記本紀地理圖考 (Taipei: Kuo-li Pien-i Kuan, 1990). Chinese characters for the major states of pre-Ch'in China (Chao 趙, Cheng 鄭, Ch'i 齊, Chin 晉, Ch'in 秦, Ch'u 楚, Han 韓, Lu 魯, Shu 蜀, Sung 宋, Wu 吳, Yen 燕, Yüeh 越, etc.) are generally not given. Wei 魏 is distinguished from Wey 衛 by romanization. We have found it difficult to decide when to translate a place name. Our basic principle has been to translate names which seem to still have meaning in the *Records* and to leave untranslated those which were understood by Ssu-ma Ch'ien primarily as toponyms. Where we were unsure, we gave a translation at the first occurrence only. Words like *yi* 邑, *ch'eng* 城 or *chün* 郡 (in two-syllable compounds) are treated as suffixes and transliterated rather than translated. For example, place names like An-yi 安邑, Tung-ch'eng 東城, and Nan-chün 南郡, in which *yi, ch'eng* and *chün* are similar to the "-ton" in Washington or "-ville" in Nashville, are transliterated as An-yi, Tung-ch'eng, and Nan-chün, rather than translated as An Town, East City or Southern Commandery. For modern cities and provinces we have used the postal-system romanization (Peking, Szechwan, etc.).

Another difficulty is, of course, that the location of many of these places is tentative at best. Although we have not been able to resolve such problems, we have given attention to the logic of locations within a given passage. In other words, if an army fought first at Point A and then took Point B, we have attempted to follow modern identifications which would accord with these events. Where the narrative lends support to identifying locations or campaigns (as in Chapter 8), we have provided outline **Maps** (at the end of the backmatter).

Official Titles in the Han chapters follow Hans Bielenstein, *The Bureaucracy of Han Times* (Cambridge: Cambridge University Press, 1980) except where otherwise noted. This is a departure from the pre-Han volumes. We have again often made reference to *Chung-kuo ku-tai chih-kuan ta tz'u-tien* 中國古代職官大辭典, Lu Zongli [Lü Zongli] 呂宗立, ed. (Chengchow: Ho-nan Jen-min Ch'u-pan-she, 1990), to Hsü Lien-ta 許連達, ed., *Chung-kuo li-tai kuan-chih tz'u-tien* 中國歷代官制詞典 (Hofei: An-huei Chiao-yü Ch'u-pan-she, 1991), and to the traditional commentators. Official titles are cross-listed (by translated title and romanized title) in the **Index.**

Weights and Measures are generally given in romanization only. More information is often provided in the notes and especially in the "Weights and Measures" section below.

Dates given according to the sexagenary cycle have been romanized: *chia-tzu jih* 甲子日 becomes "the *chia-tzu* 甲子 day."

We have used a slightly modified version of Wade-Giles' **Romanization**: *i* is written throughout as *yi* to avoid the confusion between the English first-person pronoun and Chinese proper names. For Chinese passages over four characters in length, romanization is usually not provided.

Our **Base Edition** has been that edited by Ku Chieh-kang 顧頡剛 (1893-1980) *et al.* and entitled *Shih chi* 史記. It was based on the Chin-ling Shu-chü 金陵書局 edition and published in ten volumes by Chung-hua Shu-chü in 1959. References to this edition are given by chapter and page (69.2250) in the notes and by page numbers in emboldened brackets in the translation itself **[2250]**.

In citing the standard three **Commentaries**–"Chi-chieh" 集解, "Cheng-yi" 正義, and "So-yin" 索隱–page numbers are given only if the reference is to a chapter other than that being translated. In other words, in the translation of 61.2124 no page number is provided for a citation from the "Cheng-yi" if that citation occurs on 61.2124 or 61.2125, since the reader should easily be able to locate it. If a "Cheng-yi" comment is provided from another section or chapter of the *Shih chi,* the reader is referred to the appropriate chapter and page. A brief introduction to these commentaries can be found in the Introduction to Volume 1. This volume also appends a list of **Frequently Mentioned Commentators** (those cited often in footnotes) and two more detailed **Biographical Sketches of *Shih chi* Commentators,** a feature we hope to continue in future volumes.

Our **Annotation** has attempted to identify major textual problems, place names, book titles, rituals, unusual customs, individuals and groups of people. We generally provide, however, only one base note for those items which occur repeatedly in the text (such as Jung and Ti–n. 10 to Chapter 4) and the reader is expected to use the index for help in locating the base note.

Chinese Characters are normally given at their first occurrence and repeated only in personal names in that person's "biography." In other words, the characters 張儀 are given at their first occurrence (69.2250) and again in Chang Yi's memoir (Chapter 70).

The translation of each chapter is followed by a **Translators' Note** and a short **Bibliography**. The former may provide a summary of analyses from traditional commentators, point out problems in the text, or discuss its relations to other chapters. The latter includes the major studies and translations.

A **General Bibliography** of works was published in volume one of *The Grand Scribe's Records.* A list of **Selected Recent Studies of the *Shih chi and Related Works*** is appended.

WEIGHTS AND MEASURES

Throughout the text we have given words indicating weights and measures in their romanized form followed (at the first occurrence) by the Chinese character (e.g., *jen* 仞). This is in part because there are no standards for each era or each region dealt with in the "basic annals." Yet most of the values given in the following charts were fairly stable from the Warring States era into the early Han in most states.

Generally speaking, the basic unit of length, the *ch'ih* 尺, was the most stable. It varied from 23.1 cm in Warring States to about 23.2 cm in the Western Han. In terms of volume, one *sheng* 升 was roughly equal to 200 cc throughout the period. The greatest variance can be seen in weights, but even there we can assume that one *chin* 斤 remained equal to approximately 250 g through the era.

However, in order to avoid confusion between *chin* 金 (which when preceded by a number indicated so many *yi* 鎰 of bronze or copper [1 *yi* = 20 *liang* 兩]) and *chin* 斤 (the standard measure for gold or *huang-chin* 黃金 which consisted of 16 *liang*), we refer to the former as *chin* and the latter as "catties."

The following list is arranged by category (Length, Capacity, etc.) and under each category by the importance of the term. Variances are listed with the most ancient value first. A selected list of sources (along with a key to the abbreviated sources cited in the list) is appended.

Length

Unit Name	Western Equivalent (Era)	Source (see appended Bibliography)
ch'ih 尺	23-23.7 cm (Western Han)	*K'ao-ku hsüeh*
ts'un 寸	1/10th *ch'ih*	
pu 步	6 *ch'ih* = 138.6 cm (Ch'in-Han) 138 cm	*Tz'u-hai* "Han Weights and Measures"
jen 仞	7 *ch'ih* (Western Han)	*Ku-tai wen-hua*
hsün 尋	8 *ch'ih*	*Ku-tai wen-hua*
chang 丈	10 *ch'ih*	
ch'ang 常	16 *ch'ih*	*Ku-tai wen-hua*

Unit Name	Western Equivalent (Era)	Source (see appended Bibliography)
Length (continued)		
ch'un 純	4 *tuan* 端 (cloth; 1 *tuan* = 2 *chang*)	"Chi-chieh" (*Shih chi,* 69.2250)
yin 引	10 *chang*	
li 里	415 m 416 m = 300 *pu* or 180 *chang*)	"Han Weights and Measures" *Ku-tai wen-hua*
she 舍	30 *li*	
Area		
mu 畝	240 *pu*^{2} (Warring States, Ch'in, Han; 457.056 m.^{2}) 0.1139 English acre	*Ku-tai wen-hua* "Han Weights and Measures"
li 里	often stands for x-*li on a side* (i.e., x by x *li*)	
Capacity		
sheng 升	from 194-216 cc (Ch'in)	*K'ao-ku hsüeh*
yü*eh* 龠	1/2 *ho* = about 10 cc	
ho 合	1/10 *sheng* = about 20 cc 19.968 cc.	"Han Weights and Measures"
tou 斗	10 *sheng* = 1900 cc (Ch'in dynasty)	Ch'en Meng-chia
hu 斛	10 *tou* = 19,968 cc.	"Han Weights and Measures"
fu 釜 chia	20,460-20,580 cc	*K'ao-ku hsüeh,* Ch'en Meng-
Weight		
chin 斤	244-268 g (Western Han) 245 g (Western Han)	Ch'en Meng-chia "Han Weights and Measures"
liang 兩	1/16 *chin*--about 15.625 g-15.36 g	"Han Weights and Measures"

Unit Name	Western Equivalent (Era)	Source (see appended Bibliography)

Weight (continued)

chu 銖	1/24 *liang*--about 0.651 g-0.64 g	"Han Weights and Measures"
tzu 錙	6 *chu* 1/4 *liang* = about 3.906 g	
yi 溢	20 *liang*	See introduction to "Weights and Measures" above
chün 鈞	30 *chin* = about 7,500 g-7,350 g	"Han Weights and Measures"
tan 石	120 *chin* = about 30 kg 29.5 kg	"Han Weights and Measures"
chin 金 = *yi* (of copper or bronze, in pre-Ch'in times) 1 *chin* = 1 $ts'un^3$ of gold = 238-251 g (Ch'in-Han)		See introduction to "Weights and Measures" above

Key to Abbreviated Sources

Ch'en Meng-chia — Ch'en Meng-chia 陳夢家. "Chan-kuo tu-liang heng shih-lüeh shuo" 戰國度量衡史略説, *K'ao-ku,* 6.6(1964): 312-4.

"Han Weights and Measures" — "Han Weights and Measures," in *The Cambridge History of China, Volume 1, The Ch'in and Han Empires.* Denis Twitchett and Michael Loewe, eds. Cambridge: Cambridge University Press, 1986, p. xxxviii.

K'ao-ku hsüeh — *Chung-kuo ta pai-k'o ch'üan shu, K'ao-ku hsüeh* 中國大百科全書, 考古學. Peking and Shanghai: Chung-kuo Ta Pai-k'o Ch'üan Shu Chu-pan-she, 1986.

Ku-tai wen-hua — *Ku-tai wen-hua ch'ang-chih* 古代文化常識. Yang Tien-k'uei ·楊殿奎 *et al.,* eds. Tsinan: Shan-tung Chiao-yü Ch'u-pan-she, 1984, pp. 271-92.

Shih chi tz'u-tien — *Shih chi tz'u-tien* 史記辭典. Ts'ang Hsiu-liang 倉修良, ed. Tsinan: Shan-tung Chiao-yü Ch'u-pan-she, 1984

Tz'u-hai — *Tz'u-hai* 辭海. 3v. Shanghai: Shang-hai Tz'u-shu Ch'u-pan-she, 1979.

Selected Bibliography

Ho Ch'ang-ch'ün 賀昌群. "Sheng tou pien" 升斗辨, *Li-shih yen-chiu*, 1958.6: 79-86.

Hulsewé, A. F. P. "Ch'in-Han Weights and Measures," in Hulsewé, *Remnants of Ch'in Law*. Leiden: E. J. Brill, 1985, p. 19.

___. "Weights and Measures in Ch'in Law," in *State and Law in East Asian: Festschrift Karl Bünger*. Dieter Eikemeier and Herbert Franke, eds. Wiesbaden: Harrassowitz, 1981, pp. 25-39.

Kuo-chia Chi-liang Tsung-chü 國家計量總局. *Chung-kuo ku-tai tu-liang-heng t'u-chi* 中國古代度量衡圖集. Peking: Wen-wu 文物, 1981.

Loewe, Michael. "The Measurement of Grain during the Han Period," *TP*, 49(1961): 64-95.

Tseng Wu-hsiu 曾武秀. "Chung-kuo li-tai chih-tu kai-shu" 中國歷代尺度概述, *Li-shih yen-chiu*, March 1964, esp. pp. 164-6 and 182.

Wang Chung-ch'üan 王忠全. "Ch'in-Han shih-tai chung, hu, tan hsin-k'ao" 秦漢時代鐘, 斛, 石新考, *Chung-kuo-shih yen-chiu*, 1988.1, 11-23.

Wu Ch'eng-lo 吳承洛. *Chung-kuo tu-liang-heng shih* 中國度量衡史. Shanghai: Shang-wu, 1937.

Yang K'uan 楊寬. *Chung-kuo li-tai ch'ih-tu k'ao* 中國歷代尺度考. Shanghai: Shang-wu, 1955.

Lu Zongli

LIST OF ABBREVIATIONS

I. Books

Bielenstein	—	Hans Bielenstein. *The Bureaucracy of Han Times.* Cambridge: Cambridge University Press, 1980.
Bodde, *Festivals*	—	Derk Bodde. *Festivals in Classical China.* Princeton: Princeton University Press, 1975.
Chang Chia-ying	—	Chang Chia-ying 張家英. *Shih chi shih-erh pen-chi yi ku* 史記十二本紀疑詁. Harbin: Hei-lung-chiang Chiao-yü Ch'u-pan-she, 1997.
Chang Lieh	—	Chang Lieh 張烈, ed. *Han shu chu-yi* 漢書注譯. 4v. Haikow: Hai-nan Kuo-chi Hsin-wen, 1997.
Chang Wen-hu	—	Chang Wen-hu 張文虎 (1808-1855). *Chiao-k'an Shih chi "Chi-chieh," "So-yin," "Cheng-yi," cha-chi* 校刊史記集解索引正義札記. 2v. Rpt. Peking: Chung-hua, 1977.
Chavannes	—	Édouard Chavannes, trans. *Les Mémoires historiques de Se-ma Ts'ien.* 5v. Paris, 1895-1905; rpt. Leiden: E. J. Brill, 1967. V. 6 Paris: Adrien Maisonneuve, 1969.
Ch'en Chih	—	Ch'en Chih 陳直. *Han shu hsin-cheng* 漢書新證. Tientsin: T'ien-chin Jen-min, 1959; second revised printing 1979.
"Cheng-yi"	—	Chang Shou-chieh 張守節 (*fl.* 730). "*Shih chi* Cheng-yi" 史記正義, as found in the *Shih chi.*
Ch'eng Shu-te	—	Ch'eng Shu-te 程樹德 (1877-1944) *Lun yü chi-shih* 論語集釋. 4v. Peking: Chung-hua, 1990.
Chiang Liang-fu	—	Chiang Liang-fu 姜亮夫. *Li-tai jen-wu nien-li pei-chuan tsung-piao* 歷代人物年里碑傳綜表. Rpt.; Hong Kong: Chung-hua, 1976.
"Chi-chieh"	—	P'ei Yin 裴駰 "*Shih chi* Chi-chieh" 史記集解, as found in the *Shih chi.*

Ch'ien Mu, *Ti-ming k'ao*	—	Ch'ien Mu 錢穆. *Shih chi ti-ming k'ao* 史記地名考. Rpt. Taipei: San-min Shu-chü, 1984.
Ch'in Han shih	—	Cheng T'ien-t'ing 鄭天挺 *et al.,* eds. *Chung-kuo li-shih ta tz'u-tien, Ch'in Han shih* 中國歷史大辭典，秦漢史. Shanghai: Shang-hai Tz'u-shu, 1990.
Ching-yu	—	*Shih chi* in *Pei Sung Ching-yu [Kuo-tzu] chien pen, Erh-shih-wu shih* 北宋景祐〔國子〕監本，二十五史, rpt of N. Sung Ching-yu [Era, 1034-1037] Academy [of the Sons of the State] Edition, in the Institute of Linguistics and History, Academia Sinica, Taiwan. Taipei: *Erh-shih wu shih* Pien-k'an Kuan 二十五史編刊館, 1955.
Dubs	—	Dubs, Homer H., trans. *The History of the Former Han Dynasty.* By Pan Ku. With the collaboration of Jen T'ai and P'an Lo-chi. V. 1. Baltimore: Waverly Press, 1938.
Fang Hsüan-ch'en	—	Fang Hsüan-ch'en 方炫琛. "*Tso chuan* jen-wu ming-hao yen-chiu" 左傳人物名號研究. Unpublished Ph. D. dissertation, Cheng-chih University, Taiwan, 1983.
Grand Scribe's Records	—	*Grand Scribe's Records, Volume 1: The Basic Annals of Pre-Han China. Volume 7: The Memoirs of Pre-Han China.* William H. Nienhauser, Jr., ed. Tsai-fa Cheng, Zongli Lu, Robert Reynolds and Nienhauser, trans. Bloomington: Indiana University Press, 1994.
Han shu	—	*Han shu* 漢書. Probably edited by Chen Chih 陳直 et al. 10v. Peking: Chung-hua, 1962.
Han shu pu-chu	—	Wang Hsien-ch'ien 王先謙 (1842-1918), ed. *Han shu pu-chu* 漢書補注. 2v. *Erh-shih-wu shih.* Rpt. Taipei: Yi-wen Yin-shu-kuan, 1955.
Hardy, *Worlds*	—	Grant Hardy. *Worlds of Bronze and Bamboo, Sima Qian's Conquest of History.* New York: Columbia University Press, 1999.
Ho Chien-chang	—	Ho Chien-chang 何建章. *Chan-kuo Ts'e chu-shih* 戰國策注釋. 2v. Peking: Chung-hua, 1990.
Ho Tz'u-chün	—	Ho Tz'u-chün 賀次君. *Shih chi shu-lu* 史記書錄. Shanghai: Shang-wu Yin-shu-kuan, 1958; rpt. Taipei: Ti-p'ing-hsien Ch'u-pan-she 地平線出版社, 1972.

Hsu and Linduff   —   Cho-yun Hsu and Katheryn M. Linduff. *Western Chou Civilization*. New Haven and London: Yale University Press, 1988.

Hucker   —   Charles O. Hucker. *A Dictionary of Official Titles in Imperial China*. Stanford: Stanford University Press, 1985.

Ho Tz'u-chün   —   Ho Tz'u-chün 賀次君. *Shih chi shu-lu* 史記書錄. Shanghai: Shang-wu Yin-shu-kuan, 1958; rpt. Taipei: Ti-p'ing-hsien Ch'u-pan-she 地平線出版社, 1972.

Hsu and Linduff   —   Cho-yun Hsu and Katheryn M. Linduff. *Western Chou Civilization*. New Haven and London: Yale University Press, 1988.

Hucker   —   Charles O. Hucker. *A Dictionary of Official Titles in Imperial China*. Stanford: Stanford University Press, 1985.

Hulsewé, *Han Law*   —   A.F.P. Hulsewé. *Remnants of Han Law, Volume 1: Introductory Studies and an Annotated Translation of Chapters 22 and 23 of the History of the Former Han Dynasty*. Leiden: E. J. Brill, 1955.

Hummel   —   Arthur W. Hummel, *Eminent Chinese of the Ch'ing Period (1644-1912)* 2v. Washington: U. S. Government Printing Office, 1943, 1944.

Ikeda   —   Ikeda Shirôjirô 池田四郎次郎 and Ikeda Eiyû 池田英雄. *Shiki kenkyû shomoku kaidai (kôhon)* 史記研究書目解題(稿本). 2v. Tokyo: Meitoku Shuppansha, 1978.

Ku and Hsü   —   Ku Chieh-kang 顧頡剛 and Hsü Wen-shan 徐文珊, eds. *Shih chi pai wen* 史記白文. 3v. Peiping: Kuo-li Pei-p'ing Yen-chiu Yüan, Shih-hsüeh Yen-chiu-hui 國力北平研究院，史學研究會, 1936.

Lau, *Analects*   —   D. C. Lau, trans. *Confucius, The Analects*. Harmondsworth, England: Penguin, 1979.

Legge   —   James Legge, trans. *The Chinese Classics*. 5v. Rpt. of 2nd rev. ed. Taipei: Southern Materials Center, 1985.

Liang Yü-sheng   —   Liang Yü-sheng 梁玉繩 (1745-1819). *Shih chi chih-yi* 史記志疑. 3v. Peking: Chung-hua, 1981.

Loewe, "Rank"   —   Michael Loewe, "The Orders of Aristocratic Rank of
                                Han China," *TP* 48.1-3 (1960): 97-174.

Loewe, *Dictionary*   —   Michael Loewe. *A Biographical Dictionary of the Qin,
                                Former Han, and Xin Periods (221 BC-AD 24)*. Leiden:
                                Brill, 2000.

Loewe, *Divination*   —   Michael Loewe. *Divination, Mythology and Monarchy
                                in Han China*. London: Cambridge University Press,
                                1994.

Lu Zongli [Lü Zongli]   —   Lu Zongli 呂宗力, *et al.* eds. *Chung-kuo li-tai kuan-chih
                                ta tz'u-tien* 中國歷代官制大辭典. Peking: Pei-ching
                                Ch'u-pan-she, 1994.

Lun heng   —   Wang Ch'ung 王充 (127-200). *Lun heng chu-shih* 論
                                衡注釋. Pei-ching Ta-hsüeh Li-shih hsi "Lun heng"
                                Chu-shih Hsiao-tsu 北京大學歷史系論衡注釋小組.
                                4v. Peking: Chung-hua, 1979.

Mizusawa, *Fu kôho*   —   Mizusawa Toshitada 水澤利忠. *Shiki kaichû koshô fu
                                kôhô* 史記會注考證附校補. Rpt with Tokyo, 1934
                                ed. of *Shiki kaichû koshô* 史記會注考證. 2v. Shanghai:
                                Shang-hai Ku-chi, 1986.

Morohashi   —   Morohashi Tetsuji 諸橋轍次. *Dai Kanwa jiten* 大漢
                                和辭典. 13v. Tokyo: Suzuki Ippei, 1955-1960.

Needham   —   Needham, Joseph *et al. Science and Civilisation in
                                China*. V. 1-. Cambridge: Cambridge University Press,
                                1957-.

Palace edition   —   *Wu Ying-tien k'an-pen Shih chi* 武英殿刊本史記. Rpt.
                                Taipei: Wen-hsiang 文馨 Ch'u-pan-she, 1978.

Panasjuk   —   V. Panasjuk. *Syma Czjan', Izbrannoe*. Mos-cow, 1956.

Pokora, "Traductions"   —   Timoteus Pokora. "Bibliographie des traductions du
                                Che ki," in Édouard Chavannes, trans. *Les Mémoires
                                historiques de Se-ma Ts'ien*. V. 6. Paris: Adrien
                                Maisonneuve, 1969, pp. 113-46.

Po-na   —   *Po-na pen Erh-shih-ssu shih* 百衲本二十四史. Rpt.
                                Taipei: Shang-wu Yin-shu-kuan, 1968.

San-fu huang-t'u   —   *San-fu huang-t'u chiao-chu* 三輔黃圖校注. Ho Ch'ing-
                                ku 何清谷, ed. Sian: San Ch'in Ch'u-pan-she, 1995.

Shen Chung — Shen Chung 沈重 et al., ed. Chung-kuo li-shih ti-ming tz'u-tien 中國歷史地名辭典. Nan-chang: Chiang-hsi Chiao-yü Ch'u-pan-she, 1988.

Shih chi — Shih chi 史記. Ku Chieh-kang 顧頡剛 (1893-1980) et al., eds. 10v. Peking: Chung-hua Shu-chü, 1963.

Shih chi p'ing-lin — Shih chi p'ing-lin 史記評林. Ling Chih-lung 凌稚隆 (fl. 1576), comp. 5v. Rpt. Taipei: Ti-ch'iu 地球 Ch'u-pan-she, 1992.

Shih chi tz'u-tien — Ts'ang Hsiu-shih 倉修食, ed. Shih chi tz'u-tien 史記辭典. Tsinan: Shan-tung Chiao-yü, 1991.

Shih Chih-mien — Shih Chih-mien 施之勉. Shih chi hui-chu kao-cheng ting-pu 史記會注考證訂補. Taipei: Hua-kang 華岡, 1976.

Shih Ting — Shih Ting 施丁. Han shu hsin-chu 漢書新注. 4v. Sian: San Ch'in Ch'u-pan-she, 1994.

SKCS — Ssu-k'u ch'üan-shu tsung-mu t'i-yao 四庫全書總目提要. 5v. Taipei: T'ai-wang Shang-wu, 1983.

"So-yin" — Ssu-ma Chen 司馬貞 (fl. 730). "Shih chi So-yin" 史記索隱, as found in the Shih chi.

SPPY — Ssu-pu pei-yao 四部備要.

SPTK — Ssu-pu ts'ung-k'an 四部叢刊.

T'ai-p'ing yü-lan — T'ai-p'ing yü-lan 太平御覽. Wang Yün-wu 王雲五, ed. 7v. Rpt. Taipei: T'ai-wan Shang-wu Yin-shu-kuan, 1968.

Takigawa — Takigawa Kametarô 瀧川龜太郎 (1865-1946). Shiki kaichû koshô fu kôhô 史記會注考證附校補. Rpt. of Tokyo, 1934 ed. with sup-plementary collation notes by Mizusawa Toshitada 水澤利忠. Shanghai: Shang-hai Ku-chi, 1986 (see also Misuzawa, Fu kôho).

T'an Ch'i-hsiang — T'an Ch'i-hsiang 譚其驤, ed. Chung-kuo li-shih ti-t'u chi 中國歷史地圖集. V. II: Ch'in, Hsi Han, Tung Han shih-ch'i 秦西漢東漢時期. Shanghai: Ti-t'u Ch'u-pan-she, 1982.

Tz'u-chih t'ung-chien — Ssu-ma Kuang 司馬光 (1019-1086). Tz'u-chih t'ung-chien 資治通鑑 Peking: Chung-hua, 1963.

Waley, *Analects* — Arthur Waley, trans. *The Analects of Confucius.* London: George Allen and Unwin, 1938.

Wang Hui — Wang Hui 王恢. *Shih chi pen-chi ti-li t'u-k'ao* 史記本紀地理圖考. Taipei: Kuo-li Pien-yi Kuan, 1990.

Wang Li-ch'i — Wang Li-ch'i 王利器, ed. *Shih chi chu-yi* 史記注譯. 4v. Sian: San Ch'in, 1988.

Wang Li-ch'i, *Jen-piao* — Wang Li-ch'i 王利器 and Wang Chen-min 王貞玟. *Han shu ku-chin jen-piao shu-cheng* 漢書古今人表疏證. Tsinan: Ch'i Lu shu-she, 1988.

Wang Nien-sun — Wang Nien-sun 王念孫 (1744-1817). "*Shih chi* tsa-chih 史記雜志," in V. 1 of Wang's *Tu-shu tsa-chih* 讀書雜志. Rpt. Taipei: Shih-chieh, 1963.

Wang Shu-min — Wang Shu-min 王叔岷. *Shih chi chiao-cheng* 史記斠證. 10v. Taipei: Chung-yang Yen-chiu Yüan, Li-shih Yü-yen Yen-chiu So, 1982. *Chung-yang Yen-chiu Yüan, Li-shih Yü-yen Yen-chiu So chuan-k'an* 中央研究院歷史語言所研究專刊, No. 87.

Watson, *Han* — Burton Watson, trans. *Records of the Grand Historian of China, from the Shih chi of Ssu-ma Ch'ien.* 2v. Rev. ed. Hong Kong and New York: The Chinese University of Hong Kong/Columbia University Press, 1993.

Watson, *Chapters* — Burton Watson, trans. *Records of the Grand Historian, Chapters from the Shih chi of Ssu-ma Ch'ien.* New York: Columbia University Press, 1969.

Watson, *Qin* — Burton Watson, trans. *Records of the Grand Historian: Qin Dynasty.* V. 3. Hong Kong and New York: The Chinese University of Hong Kong/Columbia University Press, 1993.

Watson, *Ssu-ma Ch'ien* — Burton Watson. *Ssu-ma Ch'ien, Grand Historian of China.* New York: Columbia University Press, 1958.

Wu and Lu — Wu Shu-p'ing 吳樹平 and Lu Zong-li 呂宗力, eds. and trans. *Ch'üan-chu ch'üan-yi Shih chi* 全注全譯史記. 3v. Tientsin: T'ien-chin Ku-chi, 1995.

Yang, *Li-tai*   —   Yang Yen-ch'i 楊燕起, Ch'en K'o-ch'ing 陳可青, Lai
                               Chang-yang 賴長揚, eds. *Li-tai ming-chia p'ing Shih
                               chi* 歷代名家評史記. Peking: Pei-ching Shih-fan Ta-
                               hsüeh, 1986.

Yang, *Lun-yü*   —   Yang Po-chün 楊伯峻. *Lun yü yi-chu* 論語譯注. Peking:
                               Chung-hua, 1980.

Yang, *Tso-chuan*   —   Yang Po-chün 楊伯峻. *Ch'un-ch'iu Tso chuan hui-chu*
                               春秋左傳會注. 4v. Peking: Chung-hua, 1982.

Yang, *Tz'u-tien*   —   Yang Po-chün 楊伯峻 and Hsü T'i 徐提. *Ch'un-ch'iu
                               Tso chuan tz'u-tien* 春秋左傳辭典. Peking: Chung-
                               hua, 1985.

Yang Chia-lo   —   Yang Chia-lo 楊家駱, ed. *Shih chi chin-shih* 史記今
                               釋. Taipei: Cheng-chung Shu-chü, 1971.

Yangs   —   Yang Hsien-yi and Gladys Yang. *Records of the
                               Historian.* Rpt. Hong Kong: The Commercial Press,
                               1985.

Yoshida   —   Yoshida Kenkô 吉田賢抗. *Shiki* 史記. V. 2. Tokyo:
                               Meiji Shoin, 1973.

Yüan K'o, *Shen-hua*   —   Yüan K'o 袁珂. *Chung-kuo shen-hua ch'uan-shuo tz'u-
                               tien* 中國神話傳說詞典. Hong Kong: Shang-wu,
                               1986.

II. Journals

AM   —   *Asia Major*

BIHP   —   *Bulletin of the Institute of History and Philology*
                               (Academia Sinica, Taiwan)

BMFEA   —   *Bulletin of the Museum of Far Eastern Antiquities*

BSOAS   —   *Bulletin of the School of Oriental and African Studies
                               (London University)*

CLEAR   —   *Chinese Literature: Essays, Articles, Reviews*

EC   —   *Early China*

HJAS   —   *Harvard Journal of Asiatic Studies*

JA	—	*Journal asiatique*
JAH	—	*Journal of Asian History*
JAOS	—	*Journal of the American Oriental Society*
JAS	—	*Journal of Asian Studies*
JCP	—	*Journal of Chinese Philosophy*
MS	—	*Monumenta Serica*
OE	—	*Oriens Extremus*
PFEH	—	*Papers on Far Eastern History*
Shinagaku	—	*Shinagaku* 支那學
Shu-mu chi-k'an	—	*Shu-mu chi-k'an* 書目季刊
TP	—	*T'oung Pao*
ZDMG	—	*Zeitschrift der Deutschen Morgenländischen Gesellschaft*

III. Other

adj.	—	adjective
adv.	—	adverb
ArC	—	Archaic Chinese
ed.	—	editor
m.	—	measure word
mss.	—	manuscript
n.	—	note; noun
no.	—	number
n.p.	—	noun phrase

nn.	—	notes
pn.	—	proper noun
rev. ed.	—	revised edition
rpt.	—	reprint
sv.	—	stative verb
trans.	—	translator
transl.	—	translation
v.	—	volume; verb
vi.	—	intransitive verb
v.o.	—	verb–object
vp.	—	verb phrase
vt.	—	transitive verb

The Exalted Ancestor, Basic Annals 8

[8:341] Kao-tsu 高祖 (The Exalted Ancestor, *ca.* 248-196 B.C.; r. 206-196),[1] a native of Chung-yang 中陽 Hamlet in Feng 豐 Township in P'ei 沛,[2] had the *cognomen* Liu 劉 and the *agnomen* Chi 季.[3] His father was called T'ai-kung 太公 (The Grandly Honored One or "Grandfather") and his mother was called Liu Ao 劉媼 (Mother Liu).[4] Previously,[5] Mother Liu once rested on the banks of a great marsh when she dreamed she had an encounter with a spirit.[6] At this time

---

[1]Kao-tsu 高祖 seems to be a title which combines Liu Chi's 劉季 (i.e., Liu Pang's; see n. 3 below) "temple name" (*miao-hao* 廟號) of T'ai-tsu 太祖 (Grand Ancestor) with his posthumous title, Kao-ti 高帝 (The Exalted Emperor or Emperor Kao; see Dubs, 1.145 and *Shih chi*, 10.436). Chang Yen 張晏 (a third century scholar, *agnomen* Tzu-ch'uan 子傳, a native of Chung-shan 中山, whose works are apparently cited from his *Hsi Han shu yin-shih* 西漢書音釋 in 40 *chüan*, see the biographical note in Kuo Yün-k'ai 郭雲楷, *Tseng-kuang Shang yu lu t'ung pien* 增廣尚友錄統編 [Shanghai: Chin Chang T'u-shu-chü Yin-hang 錦章圖書局印行, 1927], 7.3b) and subsequent scholars, however, have assumed this title was derived from the fact that Liu Pang's merit was "exalted" and he was the *t'ai-tsu* 太祖 or "grand ancestor" of the Liu royal clan (see *Han shu*, 1A.1). Yang Shu-ta 楊樹達 (1885-1956) argues against Chang Yen's explanation, believing that Kao-tsu was just the common form of address the people of the Han had for their first emperor, much as they referred to Ying Pu 英布 and Ch'ing Pu 黥布 ("Pu the Tattooed"; see Yang Shu-ta, *Han shu k'uei-kuan* 漢書窺管 [Shanghai: Shang-hai Ku-chi, 1984], p. 1). Although our translation of this title follows Chang Yen (see also "Chi-chieh," *Shih chi*, 8.341), another possible reading would be "Lofty Ancestor," there is at least one occasion where he was referred to as Kao-tsu while alive, suggesting that this title was either commonly used or that the passage is an interpolation (cf. *Shih chi*, 51.1995).

Although there are two suggested dates for Liu Pang's birth, 256 and 248 B.C., we believe the latter date is preferable, because it fits with subsequent events (see also n. 18, 19, and 29 below).

[2]P'ei was a Ch'in-dynasty county under the administrative control of Ssu-shui 泗水 Commandery when the latter was established in 223 B.C.; it was located a few miles northwest of modern Huai-pei City 淮北市 in Anhwei about fifty miles northeast of the commandery seat near modern P'ei-hsien in Kiangsu (T'an Ch'i-hsiang, 2:8). Although there has been much written about whether Liu Pang was from P'ei or Feng, Liu Pang himself makes it clear that he grew up in Feng: "Feng is the place where I was born and grew up. It is the last place I could forget" (*Shih chi*, 8.390); further testimony can be found in Lu Wan's biography: "Lu Wan was a native of Feng. He was from the same hamlet as Kao-tsu" 盧綰者，豐人也。與高祖同里 (*Shih chi*, 93.2637).

[3]Normally the *agnomen* and *praenomen* of a person had some semantic relationship, but Pang 邦 and Chi 季 do not. *Han shu* (1A.1) omits reference to Kao-tsu's *agnomen*. A number of scholars have suggested that Kao-tsu had but one designation, Liu Chi 季, 'Liu the Youngest' (cf. his brothers Liu Po 伯, 'Liu the Elder,' and Liu Chung 仲,'Liu the Middle Son'), until he became emperor, at which time the requisite additional appellations were added (see "So-yin," *Shih chi*, 8.342). Referring to brothers by their seniority must have been common in peasant and other families (see also Tanaka Kenji, p. 82, and Liang Yü-sheng, 6.213).

Liu Pang 劉邦, the name by which Liu Chi is usually known in subsequent writings, is not mentioned in either the *Shih chi* nor the *Han shu* (despite the "So-yin" claim that it is given in *Han shu*, see *Shih chi*, 8.342: 漢

1

書:名邦，字季). Pang appears first in Hsün Yüeh's 荀悦 (148-209) *Han chi* 漢紀 (1.2b, *SPTK* ed.). Wang Hsien-ch'ien 王先謙 (1842-1918; *Han shu pu-chu*, 1A.1b) argues that Ssu-ma Chen 司馬貞 (*fl.* 745) must have meant *Han chi* when he wrote *Han shu* in his "So-yin." Wang Shu-min (8.295) provides a citation from the *Yi-wen lei-chü* 藝文類聚 which cites the *Shih chi* itself as the source (諱邦，字季). As Wang Yün-tu 王雲度 argues, Pang was tabooed in the first years of the Han, suggesting that it was an original *agnomen* (see Wang's "Liu Pang shen-shih pien-hsi" 劉邦身世辨析, *Shan-hsi Li-shih Po-wu Kuan kuan-k'an* 陝西博物館館刊, 4 [June 1997]: 84). On the tabooing of Pang, see also Ch'en Chih, p. 1, and Jeffrey Riegel, "Eros, Introversion, and the Beginnings of *Shijing* Commentary," *HJAS* 57 (1997): 144, n. 5.

   Although Ssu-ma Ch'ien uses the name Liu Chi exclusively in this chapter, since Liu Pang is the name by which the founder of the Han is commonly known, we shall generally to him by this appellation in our apparatus. On this question in general see also Homer H. Dubs, "The Name and Ancestry of Han Kao-tsu," *TP*, 32 (1936): 59-64.

   [4]The *praenomen* of Liu Pang's father is often given in the apocryphal literature as Chih-chia 執嘉 ('To Grasp the Good," see "So-yin," *Shih chi*, 8.342). Wang Fu 王符 (*ibid.*) gives T'uan 煓. It may be that T'uan, which means 'blazing, like a fire,' was his *agnomen*; a possible link between thsee names would be that if one 'grasps the good,' his name is sure to become 'blazing' or 'illustrious.' *Ch'un-ch'iu wo ch'eng t'u*春秋握成圖 (cited in "Cheng-yi") claims that Liu Chih-chia's mother dreamed of a red bird like a dragon who sported with her before she gave birth to him. This is another attempt to link the color red to the Liu/Han line.

   Ao 媼 means an old woman, a sense that "Mother" as a general address in English conveys. Dubs (1.28) renders this "the old dame." In the apocryphal literature, cited in "So-yin," her surname is given as Wang 王 or Wen 溫 and her *praenomen* as Han-shih 含始, which means Containing or Embodying the Beginning [of the Han], as she did when she carried Liu Pang in her womb. She died at Hsiao Huang-ch'eng 小黃城 shortly after Liu Pang rebelled (see *Han yi chu* 漢儀注 as cited in "Cheng-yi," *Shih chi*, 8.342). See also Ch'eng Yü-ch'ing 程餘慶, *Shih chi chi-shuo* 史記集說 (Shanghai: Shang-hai Chiao-t'ung T'u-shu-kuan, 1918), 8.1a. A detailed account of texts related to her and the possibility that she was a second wife can be found in Lo Ch'ing-k'ang 羅慶康, *Kao-tsu hsin-chuan* 高祖新傳 (Kaifeng: Ho-nan Ta-hsüeh, 1995), p. 6. More common is the opinion that she was the primary wife and Liu Pang's father also took a concubine who bore his younger half-brother, Liu Chiao 劉交 (see Yang Tung-ch'en 楊東晨, *Han-jen mi-shih* 漢人秘史 [Sian: Shan-hsi Jen-min Chiao-yü Ch'u-pan-she, 1996], p. 8, for example).

   There are several problems with this sentence as Liang Yü-sheng (6.213) observed. Although we are not given the *praenomen* of either Liu Pang's father, T'ai-kung, or his mother, there is a small corpus of materials which grew up providing a number of contradictory accounts of their names (see the lengthy recital of texts and comments in "So-yin," *Shih chi*, 8.342). Liang Yü-sheng (*ibid.*) also rehearses these accounts and concludes that it is impossible to determine Liu Pang's parents' names. Hsü Fu-kuan 徐復觀, who approaches the question from a more general point of view in his discussion of the popularization of the *cognomen* among the common people (following the historian Ch'ien Ta-hsin 錢大昕 [1728-1804]; see Hsü's *Liang Han ssu-hsiang shih* 兩漢思想史 [Rpt. Taipei: Hsüeh-sheng, 1993], 1.321) argues convincingly that neither Liu Pang's father nor mother originally had a *cognomen*. He also believes that Liu Pang himself only took a *cognomen* after he began his political career. Tanaka Kenji (pp. 82-83) points out that the tradition that *praenomens* of Liu Pang's parents were (Liu) Chih-chia 執嘉 and (Wang) Han-shih 含始 is undoubtedly something which began after Liu Pang became emperor and that all three names given in the *Shih chi* account—[Liu] Chi (The Youngest), Grandfather, and Mother—are generic terms such as are commonly used in rural peasant villages. Thus Liu Pang may have been known simply as Chi until he began to rise in life, when like Hideyoshi, he assumed a surname (in Hideyoshi's case it was "Toyotomi") to fit his rising station (on Hideyoshi's adoption of this aristocratic-sounding surname, see Edwin O. Reischauer, *Japan: The Story of a Nation* [3ʳᵈ ed.; Tokyo: Tuttle, 1998, p. 56]).

Ironically, although Pan Ku was critical of Ssu-ma Ch'ien's acceptance of stories and folk tales, the most complete account of the legendary history of the Liu family can be found in the historian's comments following the *Han shu* version of the annals of Kao-tsu ("Kao-ti chi" 高帝紀, *Han shu,* 1B.81-83).

[5]*Ch'i hsien* 其先 is problematic. Chavannes (2:325) translates it as "auparavant." Chang Wen-hu (1.87) believes it is an interpolation (and observes that the *Han shu* version does not contain these two characters or the two following, Liu Ao 劉媼), but most extant editions of the *Shih chi* have these two graphs. Mizusawa, 8.254 notes a Northern Sung edition which has the phrase. The ancient mss. of "Kao-tsu pen-chi" held in the Kunaichô 宮内廳 in Tokyo (described by Ho Tz'u-chün 賀次君 in his *Shih chi shu-lu* 史記書錄 [Shanghai: Shang-wu Yin-shu-kuan, 1958], pp. 26-27 as a "T'ang mss.," but more likely a Sung copy of a T'ang mss.) also contains all four characters. Morever, the *Lun heng* (completed before the *Han shu* in 70-80 A.D.) contains a similar passage which reads "Kao-tsu's ancestor Liu Ao once rested on the banks of a great marsh" 高祖之先 劉媼曾息大澤之陂 (1:386). Therefore, it is more likely that this enigmatic expression puzzled Pan Ku and he, as was his wont, streamlined the passage.

Chang Chia-ying (p. 155) points out that *ch'i-hsien* is a common expression in the *Shih chi* which refers either to ancestors or to parents. Regardless of the provenance of this expression, there is an alternate reading possible that would be in line with Ssu-ma Ch'ien's general tone in this chapter. *Ch'i hsien* is used in His Honor the Grand Scribe's comments to "Ch'in pen-chi" 秦本紀 (The Basic Annals of Ch'in) as follows: "The *cognomen* of the Ch'in's ancestors was Ying. Ch'in's descendants were enfeoffed with parceled out [lands] and adopted the names of their states as their *cognomens.* There were *nomens* such as Hsü, T'an, Chü, . . . and Ch'in. Nevertheless, the Ch'in, because their ancestor [*ch'i hsien*] Tsao-fu was enfeoffed with Chao-ch'eng 趙 城, made their *nomen* Chao 趙" (*Grand Scribe's Records,* 1.123 and *Shih chi,* 5.122). This passage is a tribute to the long royal line of the Ch'in. In contrast, Ssu-ma Ch'ien realized Liu Pang, as a commoner, had no ancestry, royal or otherwise, that could be identified beyond his parents. He therefore incorporated the format he used to depict the Ch'in royal house and their *nomen* here in a sardonic description of the Lius.

[6]Dubs, 1.28, n. 1, observes that the *Book of Odes* has a similar passage and refers the reader to James Legge's translation of Mao #145, "Tse po" 澤陂. However, this poem, according to the "Hsiao hsü" 小序, alludes to Duke Ling 靈 of Ch'en 陳 (r. 613-592 B.C.), a man involved with two of his minions in a licentious affair with a woman (cf. the account in Yang, *Tso chuan,* Hsüan 9, pp. 701-702). It seems more likely that the banks of the marsh were meant to suggest the typical riverine setting in which men and women were wont to consort and extra-marital liaisons took place—as seen in any number of poems in the *Book of Odes.* This may have led the *T'ai-p'ing yü-lan* copyist (872.9b), in what is obviously a carelessly copied citation from "Kao-tsu pen-chi," to write *yu* 遊 for *hsi* 息. The *Ch'un-ch'iu wo ch'eng t'u* and the *Ti-wang shih-chi* 帝王世紀 (see "Chi-chieh" and "Cheng-yi" respectively) also record legendary stories concerning Liu Pang's mother "sporting on Lo Pond 洛池" before giving birth to the future emperor. Michael Loewe (personal communication dated 29 February 2000) raises the question of whether *tse* 澤 should be interpreted as a marsh here, preferring something like "bush, i.e., ground not purposefully cultivated, generally enriched by flooding and capable of

there was lightning, thunder, and it grew dark;[7] T'ai-kung went to look for her[8] and saw a kraken atop her.[9] Not long afterward she was with child and then gave birth to Kao-tsu.[10]

producing rich, wild vegetation." Modern residents of Feng (with wom the editor spoke in November 1998) pointed out the location of this tryst as fixed by popular tradition and it is a place that resembles that of Loewe's understanding of the term.

[7]Liang Yü-sheng (1.45) has a detailed account of the supernatural births recorded in *Shih chi.* He cites Fang Hui's 方回 (1227-1306) claim that this story and those which follow prognosticating Liu Pang's success were created to fuel Liu Pang's rise to power. Supernatural signs were part of the topos of the birth of a great leader in Chinese historiography. See also Translator's Note below.

[8]Another possible reading here is "went and saw."

[9]"Kraken" is our rendering of *chiao* 蛟, a scaly dragon which is described variously in ancient texts. Dubs points out (1:28, n. 1) that Liu Pang is supposedly descended from Liu Lei 劉累, a dragon tamer, and thus the story about his conception "would appear natural." All of this seems to be part of the myths that grew up around Liu Pang during the Han dynasty and which can be found in various commentaries as well as the Pan Ku's comment to his "Kao-ti pen-chi" 高帝本紀 (*Han shu,* 1B.81-83).

Han shu (1A.1) reads *yü shang* 於上 "above (her)" omitting *ch'i* 其 and some of the vivid intimacy of this version. *T'ai-ping yü-lan* 87.1b, citing *Shih chi,* also reads merely *yü shang,* as do two parallel accounts in *Lun heng* (1:132 and 217). *Han chi* (1.2b) reads 見蛟,龍臨之, "he saw a kraken descend upon her."

This incident is recorded in an alternate version in *T'ai-p'ing yü-lan* (87.4b, citing *Ti-wang shih-chi* 帝王世紀) in which Liu Ao dreams of "a red horse sporting like a dragon" 夢赤馬若龍戲 and then gives birth, an indication that we are dealing with oral traditions here (*Shih chi,* 8.342).

Moreover, this dragonseed tied Liu Pang to the Great Yü (whose mother had conceived after a riverside encounter with a crimson dragon) in the minds of the Han literati (see *Lun heng,* 1:217 and Kao Yu's 高誘 (*fl.* 205-212) commentary in *Huai-nan Tzu* 淮南子 (*Huai-nan Hung-lieh chi-chieh* 淮南鴻烈集解 [Rpt. Taipei: T'ai-wan Shang-wu Yin-shu-kuan, 1978; Basic Sinological Series]), 19.9a.

Liu Pang himself sired the future Wen-ti after Lady Po 薄 dreamed that a black dragon had seized her by the abdomen (據吾腹; *Shih chi,* 49.1971).

An account of these events in *Lun heng* (3:1173) adds a description of the dragon's horns as follows: 蛟龍在上,龍觩炫耀, "when the kraken was on top, the dragon's horns shone brightly."

Cross-cultural parallels to Liu Pang's birth may be seen in traditions of the birth of Alexander the Great (356-323 B.C., r. 336-323) and Augustus (63 B.C.-A.D. 14, r. 27 B.C.-A.D. 14). Alexander's mother, Olympias, had a dream about his birth before she was married, and Philipp, his father, saw a snake that lay next to his wife as she slept—see Ian Scott-Kilvert's translation, *Plutarch, The Age of Alexander* (London: Penguin, 1973), p 253. Augustus's mother Atia fell asleep late at night during the service of Apollo and a serpent glided up to her and then went away; she awoke, purified herself "as if after the embraces of her husband" and then discovered a serpent-shaped mark on her body which would not go away; ten months after this Augustus was born (Suetonius, "The Deified Augustus," in *Lives of the Caesars,* John C. Rolfe, trans. [Cambridge: Harvard University Press, 1998 (1913)], pp. 286-88).

[10]The editor was able to visit Feng County in November 1998 and found that the local people there almost universally subscribe to the idea that this dragon-human birth was a euphemistic way of covering up Liu Pang's illegitimacy. This idea is repeated by Wang Yün-tu 王雲度 in his "Liu Pang shen-shih pien-hsi," *Shan-hsi*

[342] Kao-tsu was a man[11] who had a high nose and a dragon's brow, a handsome beard,[12] and seventy-two[13] black spots on his left thigh. He was humane,[14] loved people, was fond of largesse,[15] and openhearted.[16] He usually had great plans and did not serve in the

Li-shih Po-wu Kuan kuan-k'an, 4 (June 1997): 82-83. Wang believes that Liu Ao's infidelity led to Liu's father taking a second wife (which would explain the discrepancy in the *Han shu* reporting the death of Liu Pang's mother in his fifth year of reign as well as his tenth year, see *Han shu,* 1B.52 and 67), and also to his father's poor opinion of him, something emphasized by Liu Pang reminding his father that "In the beginning you, sir, often considered me to have no prospects, unable to manage property, and not equal to [Liu] Chung in strength" (*Shih chi,* 8.387). In n. 524 below, however, the idea that Liu's mother died some time after he first rose in rebellion is refuted; see also the discussion in n. 4 above.

[11]*Wei-jen* 為人, literally "to act as a man," is used primarily to describe the behavior of powerful political figures such as the First Emperor of Ch'in or Yü the Great—see *Shih chi,* 2.51 (*Grand Scribe's Records,* 1:22): "Yü was a man both diligent and indefatigable"; *Shih chi,* 6.230 (*Grand Scribe's Records,* 1:131) [Ssu-ma Ch'ien's description of the First Emperor is here put in the words of Liao of Ta Liang]: "The King of Ch'in was born with a prominent nose, elongated eyes, the breast of a bird of prey, and the voice of a jackal; he seldom extends favor and has the heart of a tiger or wolf. When in straits, he can submit to others, but when he has his way, he can easily eat you alive"; and *Shih chi,* 87.2559-60 (*Grand Scribe's Records,* 7:353): "Furthermore, Lord Chao by his nature (*wei-jen*) is astute, incorruptible, strong-minded and forceful."

[12]*Lung yen* 龍顏 became a cliché for the imperial visage (see Chang Lieh, 1.1n.). It literally refers to the space above the eyebrows. A description recorded in the "Cheng-yi," but attributed to the *Ti wang shih-chi* 帝 王世紀, describes King Wen of Chou as having "a dragon's brow and a tiger's eyebrows" 龍顏虎眉 (*Shih chi,* 4.116).

Hsü 須 refers to the beard below the mouth, *jan* 髥 to the facial hair on the cheeks (Wu and Lu, 8.281n. based on Yen Shih-ku's 顏師古 (581-645) comments in *Han shu* [1A.2]).

[13]In Chavannes' personal copy of his translation (now housed in the Chavannes' Collection in the library of the Société Asiatique) he added a handwritten comment on the symbolic value of the number 72 which included reference to the number of Confucius' disciples (cf. *Mémoires historiques,* 6.150). Given the other references to *Wu-hsing yin-yang* numerology in this chapter, it is likely that 72 carries the cosmological ties to the Ch'ih-ti 赤帝 pointed out in "Cheng-yi" (*Shih chi,* 8.343). See also Wen Yi-to 聞一多, "Ch'i-shih-erh" 七十 二, in *Wen Yi-to ch'üan-chi* 聞一多全集 (Shanghai: K'ai-ming, 1948), pp. 207-220, and "Siebzig und zweiundziebzig: Reiche Fülle," in Franz Carl Endres and Annemarie Schimmel, *Das Mysterium der Zahl: Zahlensymbolik im Kultuvergleich* (Munich: Augen Diedrichs, 1996 [1984]), pp. 277-78. Ikeda (8.3a-b [179]) cites Tso Hsüan 左暄 (*fl.* 1811) who suggests that 72 is a part of Yin-yang numerology and used formulaically in ancient texts—like *san* 三, *chiu* 九, and *pai* 百—to indicate "a great number." See also Dubs, 1.29, n. 2.

[14]*Han shu* (1A.2) reads *k'uan jen ai jen* 寬仁愛人 "benevolent, humane and loved people" for *jen erh ai jen* 仁而愛人 here; although *T'ai-p'ing yü-lan* (87.1b) and other early texts read *jen erh ai ren,* there is some textual support for the *Han shu* reading—see Wang Shu-min, 8.298. Ironically, this chapter later depicts Hsiang Yü, in the words of Wang Ling, as one who "was humane and loved people" (*jen erh ai jen; Shih chi,* 8.381).

[15]*Hsi shih* 喜施, which we read as "fond of charitable acts, largesse" following Wu and Lu (8.281), is omitted in the *Han shu* account (1A.2).

productive enterprises of his family.[17] When he reached maturity,[18] took a test to become an officer,[19] and became Chief[20] of the Ssu 泗 River Precinct;[21] **[*343*]** there was not a single officer in the yamen that he had not slighted.[22]

[16]As is common in these *wei-jen* 為人 descriptions, here we find reference to both Kao-tsu's physical features and his character; sometimes the physical description can be omitted as in the depiction of Hsiang Yü below (*Shih chi,* 8.356).

The physical description is obviously intended to continue the association of Liu Pang and his dragon parent, as the passages cited in the "Cheng-yi" here suggest (*Shih chi,* 8.343). There is a similar description of one of the descendants of the royal house of Chao on *Shih chi,* 42.1795 (see also the discussion by John Hay, "The Persistent Dragon (*Lung*)," in Willard J. Peterson *et al.,* eds., *The Power of Culture, Studies in Chinese Cultural History* [Hong Kong: Chinese University Press, 1994], pp. 136-37). On the expression *wei-jen* in the *Shih chi* annals, see also Chang Chia-ying, pp. 156-57.

[17]I am grateful to Michael Loewe for an alternate reading of *ta-tu* 大度 as "had great plans" (personal communication dated 29 February 2000). It is also used in that sense in the passage depicting Liu Pang as the only one of the rebellious generals to be able to listen to "great plans" in Li Yi-chi's biography (*Shih chi,* 97.2692). *Ta-tu* could also mean "he looked at things from a broad perspective" and *chia-jen* 家人 might refer to "the common people" as Chang Chia-ying, pp. 177-79, has argued. Thus an alternate reading here would be: "He usually looked at things from a broad perspective and did not serve in the productive enterprises of the common people." In other words, he did not respond to calls for corvée labor or military service. This reading seems, however, less plausible. Those who understand *ta-tu* as "magnanimous" point to the claim by Kao Ch'i and Wang Ling (*Shih chi,* 8.381) that Liu Pang was able to win the empire because he "shared his gains with the world," whereas Hsiang Yü "was jealous of worthiness and envious of talent" (see also *Shih chi,* 7.331-32). The idea that Liu Pang did not participate in the agricultural work of his family also fits with the poor assessment of his prospects held by his father, T'ai-kung.

[18]*Chuang* 壯 refers to age thirty (see also n. 19 and 29 below). It was the legal minimum age for assuming a government post under Ch'in law (see Kao Heng 高恆, "Ch'in-chien chung yü chih-kuan yu-kuan te chi-ko wen-t'i" 秦簡中與職官有官的幾個問題, in *Yün-meng Ch'in-chien yen-chou* 雲夢秦簡研究, Chung-hua Shu-chü Editorial Board, eds. [Peking: Chung-hua, 1981], p. 210).

Lun heng (3:1265) records that Liu Pang became precinct chief in the year of the First Emperor of Ch'in's death, 210 B.C. Wang Yün-tu 王雲度 claims that Liu Pang's assumption of the position of precinct chief at age thirty makes it more likely this occurred in 218 B.C. (see his "Liu Pang shen-shih pien-hsi," *Shan-hsi Li-shih Po-wu Kuan kuan-k'an,* 4 [June 1997]: 82). If Liu Pang had been born in 256 B.C. (see also n. 1 above), he would have been 39 *sui* in 223 B.C., the year Ch'in completed its conquest of Ch'u, and, therefore, the earliest year he could have taken a position in the Ch'in government in Feng. Thus the later 248 B.C. birthdate could also explain why Liu Pang never served in Ch'u's army against Ch'in.

[19]Wang Shu-min (8.298) believes that this reference is to a test of his military skills, more logical in view of his subsequent position as Precinct Chief. Pan Ku also notes that "Kao-tsu did not cultivate literary studies" (*Han shu,* 1B.80). Yet a passage in Lu Wan's biography (*Shih chi,* 93.2637) specifically says that "When Kao-tsu and Lu Wan reached maturity, they studied writing (or calligraphy) together" 及高祖，盧綰壯，俱學 書 and the similarity in the stage of Liu Pang's life (also "reaching maturity") between these two passages suggests it was a test of his writing skills (see also the reference to Hsiang Yü studying writing, *Shih chi,* 7.295;

Grand Scribe's Records, 1.179).

Li Hsin-ta 李新達, *Chung-kuo k'o-chü chih-tu shih* 中國科舉制度史 (Taipei: Wen-chin, 1995), p. 18 and Huang Liu-chu 黃留珠, *Ch'in Han shih-chin chih-tu* 秦漢仕進制度 (Sian: Hsi-pei Ta-hsüeh, 1985), pp. 52-3ff. argue that there were two manners by which the Ch'in sought local officials and clerks. First, men with exemplary behavior over the age of thirty could be recommended (obviously, this means did not suit Liu Pang). Second, young men above the age of seventeen could be tested on their ability to recite texts (legal documents?) and their styles of calligraphy. It seems Liu Pang took this second course. Even after passing the examination and winning a position, however, the new official was on probation for a year (thanks to Lu Zongli for pointing out the references in Li and Huang); see also passages cited in *Ch'in hui yao ting-pu* 秦會要訂補 (Rpt. Taipei: Ting-wen, 1978), p. 248.

[20]*Chang* 長. Although we have opted to generally follow Bielenstein's translations of official titles in *Bureaucracy* for Han-dynasty titles, Bielenstein's "Chief of a Commune" for *t'ing-chang* does not seem to accurately reflect this position and we will use "precinct chief" here (see also Yang Shu-fan's 楊樹藩 claim in his "Han-tai hsiang-kuan" 漢代鄉官, *Kuo-li Cheng-chih Ta-hsüeh san-shih chou-nien chi-nien lun-wen chi* 國立政治大學三十週年記念論文集 (Taipei: Cheng-chih Ta-hsüeh, 1957), pp. 136-37, that one of the major functions of a *t'ing-chang* was dealing with bandits and that *t'ing-chang* were the equivalent of Han-dynasty police officers.

T'ing 亭 (precinct) and *li* 里 (hamlet) were the smallest units of the Ch'in government. *Li* was an civil unit subordinate to the *ling* 令 or prefect, and *t'ing* was a security unit under the command of the *wei* 尉 or commandant. A *t'ing* (precinct house) was located about every ten *li* (a little over three miles) along major land and water routes. The chief of each precinct was responsible for guests who stopped over at these houses and was also in charge of matters of safety and justice within his precinct. Many of the Han precinct chiefs had previous military training (see Ma Hung-lu 馬洪路, *Hsing-lu nan* 行路難 [Hong Kong: Chung-hua, 1990], pp. 135-6; Kao Min 高敏, "Lun Ch'in, Han shih-ch'i te 't'ing'—tu Yün-meng Ch'in chien cha-chi" 論秦漢時期的亭—雲夢秦簡札記, in Kao's *Yün-meng Ch'in chien ch'u-t'an [Tseng-ting pen]* 雲夢秦簡初探 (增訂本) [Shih-chia-chuang: Ho-pei Jen-min, 1981], pp. 269-285, esp. 273, 277, and 282-83). Studies of other bamboo slips recently discovered may help to confirm details of the research on the Yün-meng finds—see Hsieh Kuei-hua 謝桂華, "Yin-wang Han-mu chien-tu ho Hsi Han ti-fang hsing-cheng chih-tu" 尹灣漢墓簡牘和西漢地方行政制度, *Wen-wu*, 488 (1977.1): 42-48, for example—although these documents refer to conditions nearly two centuries after Liu Pang served as precinct chief.

For a general survey of village officials during the Han, see also Ma Hsin 馬新, "Liang Han te hsiang-li ts'un-lo" 兩漢的鄉里村落, in Ma's *Liang Han hsiang-ts'un she-hui shih* 兩漢鄉村社會史 (Tsinan: Ch'i-lu Shu-she, 1997), pp. 188-210; see also Yin Ta 尹達 *et al.*, *Chi-nien Ku Chieh-kang hsüeh-shu lun-wen chi* 紀念顧頡剛學術論文集 (Chengtu: Pao-Shu Shu-she, 1990), which collects many of the important articles on the scholarly debate concerning *t'ing* and *li*. On the history of the title *t'ing-chang*, see Lu Zongli, p. 621.

[21]Just east of P'ei, Liu Pang's hometown, in modern Kiangsu (Wang Li-ch'i, 8.196n).

Han shu (1A.2) has Ssu-shang 泗上 for Ssu-shui 泗水 and Wang Shu-min (8.298-99) cites a number of other texts in support of this reading. But the "Chün-kuo chih" 郡國志 in the *Hou Han shu* 後漢書 (*Chih* 志 20.3427-28), on the basis of a stele set up to Kao-tsu in P'ei, confirms the reading of Ssu-shui.

[22]*Hsia wu* 狎侮, "to slight and insult," indicates the kind of treatment Liu Pang later became known for.

He was fond of wine and women.[23] He regularly bought wine on credit from Mother Wang 王 or Old Woman Wu 武;[24] when he got drunk and lay down,[25] Old Woman Wu and Mother Wang saw that there was regularly a dragon above him and marvelled at it.[26] Whenever

We see indications of this in the passage just below when Liu Pang is visiting his future father-in-law. Wang Ling also cautions Liu Pang of this fault: 陛下慢而侮人，項羽仁而愛人. "Your Majesty was arrogant and liked to slight people. Hsiang Yü was humane and loved people" (*Shih chi*, 8.381). On at least one occasion, such behavior caused Liu Pang problems with the legal establishment: "When Kao-tsu was having some fun with [Hsia-hou Ying 夏侯嬰], he injured Ying and someone made a complaint against Kao-tsu. Since Kao-tsu at the time was the chief of the precinct, a conviction for injuring someone was considered serious. Kao-tsu stated the reasons that he did not injure Ying and Ying gave evidence to support him. Later, the verdict was reversed, and Ying was sentenced to over a year [in prison] for having Kao-tsu arrested and to be beaten with the bamboo several hundred times. By this means Kao-tsu was finally able to escape [punishment]" (*Shih chi*, 95.2664). Other passages that stress this characteristically contemptuous behavior include *Shih chi*, 55.2044, 56.2055, 89.2583, 90.2590, 96.2677, and 97.2691.

The *locus classicus* for *hsia wu* seems to be the "T'ai-shih" 泰誓 (Great Declaration) chapter in the *Shang shu* 尚書 (*Shang-shu chu-shu chi pu-cheng* 尚書注疏及補正 [Taipei: Shih-chieh Shu-chü, 1985], 11.3b) which reads: 今商王受，狎侮五常，荒怠弗敬, and which James Legge (4.294) renders: "And now Show [Chow Hsin 紂辛], the king of Shang treats with contemptuous slight the five constant virtues, and abandons himself to wild idleness and irreverence." If Ssu-ma Ch'ien had this passage in mind, he obviously meant to disparage Liu Pang by comparing him to Chow Hsin.

[23]Such tastes are those typically ascribed to the swashbuckling kind of young man Ssu-ma Ch'ien is depicting here. On Liu Pang's reputation for lasciviousness, see Fan Tseng's comments on *Shih chi*, 7.311.

See also the brief account of his visit to the "weaving rooms," a place where women who had committed offenses were confined, when he was building his harem while still in Lo-yang: 豹已死，漢王入織室，見薄姬有色，詔內後宮，歲餘不得幸 (*Shih chi*, 49.1970; "After [Wei] Pao had died, the King of Han entered the weaving rooms and, seeing that Lady Po had beauty, proclaimed that she be sent to the rear palace; for more than a year she was unable to be favored.").

[24]According to a recently recovered citation in the "Cheng-yi," Old Woman Wu was the mother of Grand Man Ru-erh 如耳 from Wei (Chang Yen-t'ien, p. 29).

There is another story, related below (see n. 28), which supports this less than magnanimous side to Liu Pang.

On the general use of *fu* 負 in Han times as an equivalent of *fu* 婦, "an older woman," see Ch'en Chih, p. 2 and Wu and Lu, pp. 282-83n.

[25]*Han shu* (1A.2) and *T'ai-p'ing yü-lan* (87.1b) citations of this *Shih chi* passage both read: *shih yin-tsui wo* 時飲醉臥.

[26]The associations between Kao-tsu's provenance from dragonseed, the dragon-shaped or variegated airs which often swirled above him, and his mandate to rule are a leitmotif in this chapter. Wang Ch'ung's 王充 (27-ca. 100) discussion of them in *Lun heng* (1:133) makes it evident they were perceived by Han readers as well. *Han shu* (1A.2), however, omits the mention of the dragon here (it reads less specifically 見其上常有怪 "saw that there were regularly marvels above him"). All important *Shih chi* editions (including *T'ai-p'ing yü-lan*, 87.1b) contain it. Moreover, it seems to be part of a larger stylistic resonance of Liu Pang's conception,

Kao-tsu bought wine and stayed to drink it, wine sales increased several fold.[27] Having seen the marvels, at the end of the year these two houses usually broke the markers and cancelled his debt.[28]

[344] When Kao-tsu was once sent as a corvée laborer to Hsien-yang 咸陽,[29] the common

when a dragon also hovered above.

A number of *Shih chi* manuscripts held in Japan add *shu* 屬 after *kuai chih* 怪之 (see Mizusawa, 8.255 and Wang Shu-min, 8.299).

[27]"So-yin" (*Shih chi*, 8.343) suggests wine was sold at a higher price due to Liu Pang's generosity to his friends; however, since he drank on credit, this really did the proprietress little benefit. Based on a similar passage in the *Han shu*, Yang Shu-ta (*Han shu k'uei-kuan*, p. 1) argues against this reading, pointing out that *ch'ou* 酬 means "requite" and that the idea here is that because of the unusual signs that surrounded Liu Pang they gave him a great deal of wine.

Tanaka Kenji (p. 85, n. 3) recalls a similar Sung-dynasty story about Lü Tung-pin and believes this anecdote to be an archetypal folk tale variations of which circulated about many famous men in traditional China.

[28]These records were kept on wooden or bamboo slips, thus they could be "broken" (see "So-yin," *Shih chi*, 8.343). Takigawa (8.6) notes that Kao-tsu's presence increasing sales has a parallel in Hsüan-ti 宣帝 (The Universal Emperor or Emperor Hsüan, r. 74-49 B.C.) who as a youth went outside the palace to buy cakes from the populace, thereby dramatically increasing the business of the cake-sellers he patronized.

Yet another account of the young Liu Pang's penchant for entertaining himself and his friends gratis can be found in "Ch'u Yüan-wang shih-chia" 楚元王世家 (*Shih chi*, 50.1987): "In the beginning when Kao-tsu was still unknown, he once went into hiding because of an incident; he often stopped by his elder sister-in-law's [Liu Po's 劉伯 wife] with his friends to eat. His sister-in-law disliked him and when he and his guests came, she would pretend that the soup was gone, rattling the ladle against the pot, so that the guests for this reason would go. After a while Kao-tsu looked in the pot and saw there was still some soup. From this time on Kao-tsu harbored resentment for his sister-in-law."

Kao-tsu's fleeing from the law is mentioned again in Jen Ao's 任敖 biography (*Shih chi*, 96.2680): "Jen Ao was formerly Warden of P'ei. Kao-tsu was once hiding from the officers [of the court], the officers arrested Empress Lü and treated her without respect. Jen Ao, who had been on good terms with Kao-tsu for a long time, got angry; he beat and wounded the officer in charge of Empress Lü." Whether the incident that caused Kao-tsu to become a fugitive was related to his accidental wounding of Hsia-hou Hou (see n. 22 above) remains unknown.

[29]Hsien-yang was the Ch'in capital, located a few miles northwest of modern Sian (T'an Ch'i-hsiang, 2:6).

Hsü Shuo-fang 徐朔方 (*Shih Han lun-kao* 史記論稿 [Nanking: Chiang-su Ku-chi, 1990], p. 84) suggests this visit to Hsien-yang took place in 220 B.C. Following the date of 248 B.C. that we accept for Liu Pang's birth, he would have been twenty-eight *sui* at this time. But other scholars suggest that Liu Pang first traveled to Hsien-yang in 212 B.C. when laborers were leveed for work on the expansion of the Shang-lin Yüan 上林苑 (Fukushima Chûrô 福島中郎, for example, in the scholarly apparatus to his *Shiki* 史記 translation [Tokyo: Gakushû Kenkyûsha, 1984], p. 403, n. 19); this date seems too late, however, if we accept the idea that Liu

people were permitted to look [at the emperor],[30] and when he looked at the Ch'in Huang-ti 秦皇帝 (The August Emperor of Ch'in) he sighed deeply and said, "Yes, a man of great ambitions should be like this!"[31]

A native of Shan-fu 單父,[32] Master Lü 呂[33] was on good terms with the Prefect of P'ei. Fleeing from an enemy, he followed him [the prefect] as a retainer, taking advantage of this to

Pang became precinct chief at age 30.

The parallel account in "Hsiao Hsiang-kuo shih-chia" 蕭相國世家 (The Hereditary House of Chancellor of State Hsiao [Ho], *Shih chi,* 53.2013) indicates Liu Pang was *in charge of* corvée laborers on this trip much as he was on the journey when he decided to revolt (cf. *Shih chi,* 8.347).

[30]This recalls the great efforts the First Emperor went to avoid being observed (see *Shih chi* Chapter 7).

Han shu (1A.3) and several other texts omit the duplicated *kuan* 觀 here, reading simply 縱觀秦皇帝 "were permitted to look at the August Emperor of Ch'in"; the *Shih chi* text may have been corrupted by dittography here (see also Wang Shu-min, 8.299). *T'ai-p'ing yü-lan* (87.1b) cites this *Shih chi* passage with a single *kuan.* Li Ching-hsing 李景星 (1876-1934) argues that the two uses of *kuan,* the first to refer to a general relaxation of rules for everyone and the second to Liu Pang himself, are essential to the "marvelous arrangement" or "order" (*shen li* 神理) of the passage which is lost in the *Han shu* version (*Ssu-shih p'ing-yi* 四史評議, Han Chao-ch'i 韓兆琦 and Yü Chang-hua 俞樟華, eds. [Changsha: Yüeh-li Shu-she, 1986]), pp. 131-32).

[31]This passage is obviously meant to call to mind Hsiang Yü's comments when he saw the First Emperor (*Shih chi,* 7.296 [*Grand Scribe's Records,* 1:180]): "When the First Emperor of Ch'in traveled to K'uai-chi, both Hsiang Liang and Hsiang Chi [i.e., Hsiang Yü] looked on as he crossed the Che River. Hsiang Chi said, 'I could take that fellow's place.' Hsiang Liang covered Chi's mouth with his hand, saying, 'Don't talk nonsense or all our clan will be executed!' But because of this, Hsiang Liang looked at Chi in a different light."

Grant Hardy, in a chapter entitled "Microcosmic Readings II," probably the best discussion of these two great antagonists in a Western language, argues that in the implicit comparison of Hsiang Yü and Liu Pang here Hsiang Yü "seems more aggressively and impetuously ambitious," whereas Liu Pang's desires "seem softer, more romantic and wistful." He then wonders aloud "Did Gaozu change during the next four years?" (Hardy, *Worlds,* p. 91). But the term *ta chang fu* 大丈夫 as used in the Han (cf. *Han shu,* 64B.2820, and *Hou Han shu,* 14.555, 27.949, 64.2121, and 66.2159) seems to suggest a man of ambition—thus our translation. Liu Pang's view of the First Emperor was more pragmatic. Whereas Hsiang Yü was thinking of the process of replacing the Ch'in emperor, i.e., rebellion, a role he proved adept in as the greatest of the insurgents, Liu Pang at his first sight of the Ch'in imperial majesty already fell to musing that ruling a huge state was the proper role for a "fellow with great ambition" like himself. Hsiang Yü played the role as the ultimate rebel right through his death scene, whereas Liu Pang began to mentally organize his administration with this glimpse of the First Emperor.

Han shu reads *ta* 大 for *t'ai* 太 and *yi* 矣 for *yeh* 也 in this sentence. The Ching-yu edition of the *Shih chi* (8.1b) also reads *ta* for *t'ai* here.

[32]Near modern Shan 單 County in Shantung (Wang Li-ch'i, 8.196n) and about forty-five miles west-northwest of P'ei (T'an Ch'i-hsiang, 2:7).

[33]In 195 B.C. he became Marquis of Lin-ssu 臨泗 and in 192 B.C. he died; in 188 B.C. Lü Hou gave him the posthumous title of King Hsüan 宣 of Lü (see "Chi-chieh," *Shih chi,* 9.395, *Han shu,* 96A.3937, and Liang Yü-sheng, 6.214). According to the *Hsiang ching* 相經 (cited here in the "Chi-chieh"), he was a native of Wei

move his family to P'ei.[34] When the officers and influential stalwarts in P'ei heard that the prefect had an important guest, they all came to offer congratulations. Hsiao Ho 蕭何 (d. 195)[35] was the chief of personnel[36] in charge of the presentation, so he issued an order to all the honorable guests saying, "Those who present less than one thousand cash,[37] I will seat beneath the hall." As the precinct chief Kao-tsu always disparaged all the other officers, so he dissembled in making up his visiting board to read: "I offer in congratulation cash in the amount of ten thousand." Actually, he did not have a single cash. When his board went in, Master Lü was greatly surprised, rose, and went to welcome him at the gate. This Master Lü was fond of reading people's faces; when he saw Kao-tsu's mien, he accordingly treated him with respect and led him in to sit down.[38] Hsiao Ho said, "Though Liu Chi has always made a lot of big talk, he has accomplished very little." Taking advantage [of Master Lü's high opinion of him], Kao-tsu, to slight the other guests, proceeded to take the place of honor without a second thought.

When the wine grew scarce, Master Lü took advantage to give Kao-tsu a look indicating that he should definitely stay. Kao-tsu finished his wine, then stayed behind. Master Lü said, "Since my youth, your humble servant has been fond of reading faces. I have read many faces, but none like yours. Please take good care of yourself. I have a daughter of my own who I wish you would accept to keep house for you as your wife.[39]

When the wine was finished, Mother Lü was very angry with Master Lü and said, "You have always wanted to make this girl special and give her to a noble man; the Prefect of P'ei is on good terms with you, sir, and has asked for her, but you would not give her [to him]. How can you be so reckless as to promise her to Liu Chi?"

and his *praenomen* and *agnomen* were Wen 文 and Shu-p'ing 叔平.

[34]On reading *pi ch'ou* 避仇 as a verb-object construction, see Chang Chia-ying, p. 158.

[35]See his biography in *Shih chi* Chapter 53.

Such congratulations normally also required the presentation of a gift (see Dubs, 1.31, n. 1).

[36]*Chu-li* 主吏 (see Lu Zongli, p. 290 and Hucker, #3489/p. 296). This title is not in *Bureaucracy*.

[37]Some indication of the value of "one-thousand cash" at this time can be seen in the contributions from Liu Pang's fellow officials of three-hundred cash for travelling expenses to Hsien-yang (only Hsiao Ho generously offered him five hundred; see *Shih chi,* 53.2013).

[38]A number of editions have variant readings here, the most common (especially among manuscripts held in Japan) is 引入坐上坐 "led him in to sit in the place of honor" (cf. Mizusawa, 8.255). This is also the text as found in *Han shu* (1A.4).

[39]This reading of Liu Pang's face, and that subsequently by the elderly father, support the idea that he has been divinely conceived and are perhaps needed, because Liu Pang never exhibits the qualities which made Hsiang Yü such an appealing figure. I am grateful to David Honey for this observation.

On face reading see also the passage where K'uai T'ung 蒯通 explains his reading of Han Hsin's 韓信 face (*Shih chi,* 92.2623) and Chu P'ing-yi 祝平一, "Huang-ti yü hsiang" 皇帝與相 in *Han-tai te hsiang-jen shu* 漢代的相人術 (Taipei: Hsüeh-sheng Shu-chü, 1990), pp. 109-118.

Chi chou ch'ieh 箕帚妾, literally "a concubine with the broom and dustpan," a common synecdoche for

Master Lü said, "This [*345*] is not the sort of thing you women can understand!"[40] Finally, he gave her to Liu Chi.[41] Master Lü's daughter became Lü Hou and she gave birth to Hsiao Hui-ti 孝惠帝 (The Filial and Kind Emperor or Emperor Hui) and Lu Yüan Kung-chu 元魯 公主 (Princess Yüan of Lu).[42]

[346] When Kao-tsu was precinct chief,[43] he once asked for home leave to go to his fields.[44] As Lü Hou 呂后 (The Empress Lü) and her two children were in the fields weeding,[45] an elderly father stopped and asked for something to drink, and Lü Hou accordingly gave him something to eat.[46] The elderly father read[47] Lü Hou's face and said, "Your ladyship will become

referring to a wife.

[40]In the 1982 edition of the Chung-hua *Shih chi* the character *tz'u* 此 is omitted at the start of this sentence (*This* is not the sort of thing . . . "). There have been many printings of the original 1959 Chung-hua *Shih chi* edition, some with minor revisions in the text (with no explanation of this in front- or back-matter), but the 1982 version seems to have been intended to incorporate many of the suggestions of reviewers and may therefore be seen as a "revised edition." The ommission of *tz'u* seems to be, however, an error, since there is no textual basis for it (cf. Mizusawa, 8.15).

[41]Lo Ch'ing-k'ang (*op. cit.*, p. 28) argues that the marriage took place in 222 B.C.

[42]Ssu-ma Ch'ien uses the posthumous titles of Liu Pang's children here out of respect. For the events relating to their careers, see *Shih chi* Chapter 9 and our translation below.

[43]Although the opening sections of the biography all focus on Kao-tsu in his early days in P'ei, this series of "When Kao-tsu was precinct chief" stories seems to form a distinct group (see also the "Translator's Note" below).

[44]This ostensibly straightforward sentence has been parsed variously. Some scholars, like Wang Li-ch'i (8.196n), read *kao-kuei* 告歸 as a compound meaning "to take home leave" and *chih* 之 as "to go." We follow his reading. Others, like Chavannes (2:329) apparently add an unexpressed object *chih* 之 to refer to the children or wife and children just mentioned (cf. "il demandait sans cesse des congés pour rentrer chez lui et aller à ses champs").

On the term *kao-kuei* and the various types of leaves it indicated, see Liao Po-yüan 廖伯源, "Han kuan hsiu-chia tsa-k'ao" 漢官休假雜考, *BIHP* 65.2 (June 1994): 221-52, especially 231-50; these requests for leave may be a type of "farming vacation" granted for a fortnight in the fifth month (see Lien-sheng Yang, "Schedules of Work and Rest in Imperial China," in Yang's *Studies in Chinese Institutional History* [Cambridge: Harvard University Press, 1963], p. 23).

If one reads *ch'ang* 常 in the preceding sentence as "often" as some commentators do, there seems to be a temporal transition needed to tie the two events—thus Chavannes adds "un jour" (2:329). Watson (1:79) understands *ch'ang* as equivalent to *ch'ang* 嘗, "once when," avoiding this problem. Since there are other occurrences in this chapter of *ch'ang* 常 being equivalent to *ch'ang* 嘗, (*Shih chi*, 8.342: 高祖常繇咸陽, for example), we follow Watson here.

[45]*Han shu* (1A.5) does not mention "weeding," saying merely that they were "in the fields." *Lun heng* (1:161) is identical.

[46]The traveler was undoubtedly hungry, too, but politely asked only for something to drink.

[47]Another physiognomist like Master Lü above.

an honored person throughout the world." When she had him read her two children's faces, he looked at [the future] Hsiao Hui and said, "The means by which your ladyship will become honored is none other than this boy." After he read [the future Princess] Yüan of Lu's face, they were indeed all to be honored.

Just after the elderly father left, Kao-tsu came back from a neighboring house.[48] Lü Hou told in great detail how a stranger had stopped by, read her face and the children's and found they were all to be greatly honored. Kao-tsu asked about him, and she said: "He cannot have gone far yet." [Kao-tsu] chased after, caught him, and questioned the elderly father. The elderly father said, "Though the lady and babies [I examined] just now all resemble you,[49] sir, your appearance is so honorable that I cannot put it into words!" Kao-tsu thanked him saying, "If it is really as you say, elderly father, I will never forget this favor!"[50] But when Kao-tsu became honored, he could not even learn the whereabouts of the elderly father.

As Kao-tsu was serving as precinct chief, he made a hat out of the outer skin of the bamboo and had his "bandit-seeker"[51] go to the district of Hsüeh 薛 to oversee this [the manufacture

[48]On p'ang-she 旁舍 we follow Wu and Lu, 8.311. Dubs (1.33) also translates "a neighboring dwelling." Lun heng (1:161) reads simply ts'ung wai lai 從外來 "came from outside" or "came from another place." The only other occurrence of the term in early historical works can be found in the T'ang-era commentary to the Hou Han shu (30B.1079); although the commentary cites the Shih chi (original on Shih chi, 6.179), modern texts of this passage read p'ang chü jen 旁居人 instead of p'ang-she.

[49]Kuo Sung-t'ao 郭嵩燾 (1818-1891), Shih chi cha-chi 史記札記 (Shanghai: Shang-wu, 1951), p. 60, points out that ssu 似, "to resemble," is written similarly to yi 以, "because of," resulting in a copyist error; the line should read: 鄉者夫人嬰兒皆以君 "[I examined] the lady and babies just now because of you, sir." Liang Yü-sheng (6.214, favors yi, too, noting that the Han shu (1A.5) also reads yi. But Ju Ch'un 如淳 (fl. 220-265) in a comment to this passage (ibid.) claims that some versions of the [Han shu] text read ssu. Moreover, as Liang Yü-sheng also points out, the Lun heng (1:161) parallel to this passage also reads ssu. Mizusawa, Fu kôho (8.15) lists no early Shih chi texts which use yi. Yoshida (8.509) keeps ssu in the text but bases his translation on the yi in the Han shu. This seems ill-advised. Although the arguments for yi have a logical basis, our text and other early versions support the reading ssu which we follow here.

[50]In a similar fashion Ssu-ma Ch'ien records Ch'en She's promise to his fellow field-hands that he will never forget them (Shih chi, 48.1949) and Han Hsin's vow to pay back the old woman who fed him when he was hungry (Shih chi, 92.2609).

[51]Ch'iu-tao 求盜, an official position not listed in Bielenstein. Dubs (1.33, n. 2, based on Ying Shao's 應劭 [fl. 200 A.D.] comments cited in "Chi-chieh") gives this title as "thief-catcher" and explains that there were two subordinates to the precinct chief: "one, called the T'ing-fu 亭父, whose duty it was to open and shut the gates, sweep and clean [streets]; the other, called the thief-catcher [ch'iu-tao 求盜] pursued and caught robbers and thieves." Yang Shu-fan, "Han-tai hsiang-kuan," p. 132 notes that it was the job of the yu-chiao 游徼 to deal with bandits at the village level. Recent discoveries suggest, however, that ch'iu-tao was a Ch'in position which was not continued in the Han local administration (see Kao Min 高敏, "Lun Ch'in, Han shih-ch'i te 't'ing'" 論秦漢時期的亭, in Kao's Yün-meng Ch'in chien ch'u-tan 雲夢秦簡初探 (Tientsin: Ho-nan Jen-min,

of this hat].[52] Sometimes he wore them. After he became honored he regularly wore them; they were none other than the so-called Liu Family Hats.[53]

[347] Kao-tsu as precinct chief escorted a group of convict-laborers to Mount Li 酈 on behalf of the county, but many of the convicts fled along the way.[54] He estimated that by the time they arrived, he would all have lost them all, so when they reached the middle of a swamp west of Feng[-yi] 豐[邑],[55] he stopped to let them drink.[56] When night fell he untied and set free all the convicts he was escorting. He said, "Gentlemen, you should all depart![57] I will also be on the run from now on."

Among the convicts were a dozen or so stalwart fellows who asked to follow him. Kao-tsu, beginning to feel his wine, followed the paths that night into the marsh, ordering one man to go ahead.[58] The one who had gone ahead returned and reported, "Ahead there is a great

1981), p. 280.

[52]Hsüeh was south of T'eng 滕 County in modern Shantung (Wang Li-ch'i, 8.196n).

According to Ying Shao (cited in the "Chi-chieh," *Shih chi,* 2.346) there was an artisan in Hsüeh who made hats. A brief history of Liu Pang's hat, later popularly known at the "magpie-tail hat" (*ch'üeh-wei kuan* 鵲尾冠) can be found in the treatise on carriages and clothing in the *Hou Han shu* (*chih* 志 30, p. 3664). These hats could be worn only by those officials above a certain rank (cf. *Han shu,* 1B.65).

[53]The punctuation here follows Wang Li-ch'i (8.196).

[54]Reading *t'u* 徒 as *hsing-t'u* 刑徒.

Mount Li was the site of the huge mausoleum the First Emperor of Ch'in was having built for himself (see *Shih chi,* 6.265 and *Grand Scribe's Records,* 1:155). Hsü Shuo-fang argues that this trip began in 212 B.C. (see Hsü's *Shih Han lun-kao,* p. 84). According to *Lun heng* (3:1265), it took place in 210 B.C. The parallels between the events which led Liu Pang to transform his group of conscript laborers into a rebel band and those which led Ch'en Sheng to form his first rebel troop in a swampy region from a similar group of laborers are striking (cf. *Shih chi,* 48.1950).

[55]*Han shu* (1A.6) adds *t'ing* 亭 "precinct station" after *tse-chung* 澤中, reading Tse-chung T'ing as a proper name: "Precinct Station in the Middle of the Swamp." Liang Yü-sheng (6.215) and Wang Shu-min (8.302) feel this is the more logical reading. Liang wonders "if the text merely says 'the middle of a swamp,' how could they stop to drink?" Yet a *T'ai-p'ing yü-lan* citation (87.2a) and other early editions of the *Shih chi* support the Chung-hua *Shih chi* reading without *t'ing.* Moreover, since Liu Pang seems to have intended to free the convicts under his charage tat this time, it is unlikely that he would do so in a place as public as a precinct station.

It is interesting to recall that Liu Pang was conceived in a swamp; now his revolt and his political career begins in very similar surroundings.

[56]A laconic account of this final meal taken with those who desired to follow him is recorded in *Hsi-ching tsa-chi* 西京雜記 ([Peking: Chung-hua, 1985; *Ku hsiao-shuo ts'ung-k'an* 古小説叢刊 ed.], 2.15, #57).

[57]*Kung teng* 公等 is also used in "Ch'en She shih-chia" 陳涉世家 (*Shih chi,* 48.1951) as a respectful way of addressing a group of men.

[58]Wu Hsün 吳恂 (1890-1973) reads the *Han shu* text, *ch'ien hsing* 前行 instead of *hsing ch'ien,* as *ch'ien hsün hsing* 前循行, "to scout around ahead," but this is merely an extended reading (following Yen Shih-ku) of

snake blocking the path. I would hope you might turn back!"

Kao-tsu drunkenly said, "When stalwart fellows are on the move, what is there to dread?" Going ahead, he drew his sword, struck and severed the snake.[59] The snake having been cut in two, the path was cleared.[60] He moved on for several *li,* became very drunk, and then lay down.

When the men from behind[61] came to the place where the snake was, there was an old crone crying in the night. A man asked her what she was crying for and the crone said, "Someone has killed my son; for this reason I am crying for him." The man said, "Why was your son

"to go first" or "go ahead" (see Wu's *Han shu chu-shang* 漢書注商. Shen Pei-tsung 沈北宗, ed. [Shanghai: Shang-hai Ku-chi, 1983], p. 2).

Another version of this story is recorded in the "Feng-shan shu" 封禪書 (Treatise on the Feng and Shan Rites), *Shih chi,* 28.1378: "When Han first arose and Kao-tsu was [still] unknown, he once killed a large snake. There was a being who said, 'The snake is the son of the White Emperor and he who killed it was the son of the Red Emperor.'" 漢興，高祖之微時，嘗殺大蛇。有物曰：「蛇，白帝子也，而殺者赤帝子。」. See also Loewe, *Divination,* pp. 31 and 50, on the role of the snake in Han religion and art.

[59]A sword with seven-colors of jewels on the hilt was later handed down as that with which Liu Pang slew this snake (see *Hsi-ching tsa-chi,* 1.3, #14). On the legends surrounding this sword see also Dubs (1.34, n. 3) and Helen Burwell Chapin, "Toward the Study of the Sword as Dynastic Talisman: The Fêng-ch'êng Pair and the Sword of Han Kao Tzu," Unpublished Ph. D. dissertation, University of California, Berkeley, 1946. On pp. 175-184 Chapin translates the story about the origin of Liu Pang's sword as recorded in the *Shih-i chi* 拾遺記 compiled by Wang Chia 王嘉 (*Han Wei ts'ung-shu* ed.; rpt. Taipei: Hsin-sheng Shu-chü, 1970, 5.1a-2b) and notes other legends connected to it. A second, more reliable translation can be found in Larry Chapin Foster, 'The *Shih-i chi* and Its Relationship to the Genre Known as *Chih-kuai hsiao-shu*," Unpublished Ph. D. dissertation, University of Washington, 1984, pp. 201-02.

[60]Liang Yü-sheng (6.215) points to two other similar accounts in Han works (*Chia Tzu* 賈子, "Ch'un-ch'iu p'ien 春秋篇" [Ch'i Yü-chang 祁玉章, *Chia Tzu Hsin shu chiao-shih* 賈子新書校釋 (Taipei: Chung-kuo Wen-hua Tsa-chih She, 1974), 6.793-94] and *Hsin hsü* 新序 "Tsa-shih" 雜事 [Chao Shan-yi 趙善詒, ed., *Hsin hsü shu-cheng* 新序疏證 (Shanghai: Hua-tung Shih-fan Ta-hsüeh, 1989), pp. 42-43]). In both narratives Duke Wen 文 of Chin (r. 636-628 B.C.) is out hunting when an outrider returns and reports a huge snake blocking the road ahead. Unlike Liu Pang, however, Duke Wen interprets this encounter as a sign that Heaven is not pleased with his rule and returns to his residence to purify himself and make offerings in a temple. Then he dreams that Heaven has killed the snake for him because it was "blocking the way of an enlightened ruler" (*Chia Tzu Hsin shu chiao-shih,* 6.793). When the duke sent someone to see about the snake, he found it rotted through, a sign that Heaven had approved his actions.

Given the parallels in the two stories, it seems possible that there is an allusion here stemming most likely from the popular storytellers who must have first passed on these tales of Liu Pang (see also n. 629 below). If this is so, this allusion casts Liu Pang's impulsive actions in a bad light, since he makes no effort to ascertain the cosmological significance of the snake's appearance, but rashly moves ahead and kills it regardless of Heaven's intent.

[61]When he impetuously went ahead to face the snake, the rest of the men seem to have lingered behind.

killed?" The crone said, "My son was the son of the Pai-ti 白帝 (The White Emperor).[62] He had changed into a snake and was blocking the way. Now he has been cut in half by the son of the Ch'ih-ti 赤帝 (The Red Emperor).[63] For this reason I cry." The man did not consider the crone to be truthful and was about to report her,[64] when the crone accordingly suddenly disappeared.

[62]Yang Shu-ta (*Han shu k'uei-kuan,* p. 3) points out that the White Emperor had been identified as a brown-colored snake blocking the road during the time of Duke Wen 文 of Ch'in (r. 765-716 B.C.) according to *Shih chi,* 28.1358.

[63]Ssu-ma Ch'ien here is playing on two of the several meanings of *chan* 斬: "to sever" and "to legally execute."

Michael Loewe in his "Water, Earth, and Fire: The Symbols of the Han Dynasty" (in Loewe, *Divination,* pp. 55-60) argues that the *Wu-hsing* element Water was adopted by the Han rulers as the dynastic symbol, but notes that Liu Pang's killing of the snake was "an incarnation of the power of Red" (p. 56). The discrepancy might be explained, however, by the different level of sources. Loewe cites elite historical records in support of Water, whereas this account (and many similar anecdotes at the start of this chapter) seem to have a popular origin. Moreover, in several unofficial histories cited in the "Cheng-yi" and "So-yin" commentaries (*Shih chi,* 8.342), Liu Pang is tied to various deities or objects associated with the color red.

Ku Chieh-kang, in his *Han-tai hsüeh-shu shih-lüeh* 漢代學術史略 (Shanghai: Tung-fang Shu-she, 1941), pp. 138-39, notes that Ch'in was associated with water and black; the symbolism in this story, red supplanting white, fire overcoming metal, seems to make sense if the stories were written from Wang Mang's point of view. Wang Mang took the earth element for his reign; earth replaced fire, and fire replaced metal. So even though Ch'in took the water element as its phase, in stories written during Wang Mang's time, it would still make sense to speak of Liu Pang's Red Emperor overcoming the White Emperor.

A number of other traditional scholars question the validity of this account of the snake's relationship to the Red Emperor. Support for their argument that this reference to the Red Emperor comes from a time much later than the final years of the Ch'in dynasty (when Liu Pang was supposed to have killed the snake) or the late-second century B.C. (when Ssu-ma Ch'ien began the *Shih chi*) can be found in Chang Shou-chieh's comments in the "Cheng-yi" on the Wu-chih 五畤, "Five Altars" (*Shih chi,* 12.453): "The Five Altars were . . . the Wu-yang 吳陽 Altar, and the Northern Altar; Duke Ling of Ch'in (r. 424-415 B.C.) made the Upper and Lower Altars at Wu-yang to sacrifice to the Red Emperor and the Yellow Emperor; Kao-tsu of Han made the Northern Altar to sacrifice to Hei Ti 黑帝 (The Black Emperor)."

The long tradition of comments on this passage makes apparent at least one thing: the *wu-hsing* tradition during the Han dynasty was a complicated issue. See also Dubs' long note (1.35-36, n. 2) and Kageyama Terukuni 影山輝国, "*Shiki* naka no 'Akatei no ko, Shirotei no ko o kiru' no kiji ni tsuite" 「史記」中の「赤帝の子、白帝の子お斬る」の記事について, in *Takeda Akira Sensei taikan kinen Higashi Ajia bunka ronsô* 竹田晃先生退官記念東アジア文化論叢 (Tokyo: Kyûko Shoin 汲古書院, 1991), pp. 49-64 [not seen].

[64]*Lun heng* (1:1265) reads: 人以嫗為妖言，因欲笞之。 "The man considered the woman['s claim] to be the words of a fey and accordingly wanted to beat her."

Lun heng follows one of two variants for *kao* 告 here: the *Han shu* (1A.7) has *k'u* 苦 (Dubs, 1.36 "to trouble her"), the *Shih chi* Po-na edition (8.6a) has *ch'ih* 笞, "to beat her." The later is very much in keeping with another well known account of an early Han figure important in the Taoist tradition (like Liu Pang), namely the biography of Mao Ying 毛盈 (*Shen hsien chuan* 神仙傳) in which Ying works magic when about to

When the men from behind reached him, Kao-tsu woke up. The men from behind reported to Kao-tsu, and Kao-tsu was secretly pleased and thought highly of himself. All of his followers were daily in more awe of him.[65]

[348] Ch'in Shih-huang-ti 秦始皇帝 (The August First Emperor of Ch'in) once said,[66] "To the southeast there is an emanation of a Son of Heaven"[67]; at this, he took advantage of a tour of inspection to the East to repress it.[68] Kao-tsu, immediately suspecting that he himself [was the source of the emanation],[69] fled and hid,[70] retreating to the area of mountains and

be beaten by his father.

Hsü Kuang 徐廣 (352-425; see also "Biographies of Commentators" in the backmatter), cited in "Chi-chieh," notes that an early *Shih chi* edition also had *k'u,* a reading shared by a *T'ai-p'ing yü-lan* (487.2a) citation of this passage.

[65]This passage is cited and analyzed in the "Chi-yao" 紀妖 chapter of Wang Ch'ung's *Lun heng* 論衡 (Huang Hui 黃暉, ed., *Lun heng chiao-shih* 論衡校釋 [Taipei: T'ai-wan Shang-wu, 1983], 2:923-4).

[66]Although the chronology of these early tales is not made explicit in the text, it seems that the various anecdotes may have been arranged in the order they occurred, from Liu Pang's drinking habits as a young man, his visit to Hsien-yang, his marriage, appointment as precinct chief, making of hats, and finally the trip with the convicts which likely took place, along with the First Emperor's travels to the east, in 210 B.C.

[67]Our translation follows Dubs (1.36) here. Just before the banquet at Hung-men, Fan Tseng also recognized that the emanations about Liu Pang indicated that he could become emperor and urged Hsiang Yü to kill him (*Shih chi,* 7:311). On such emanations and some suggestions on their possible interpretation in the Han dynasty, see also Ku T'ieh-fu 顧鐵符, "Ma-wang-tui po-shu T'ien-wen ch'i-hsiang tsa-chan chien-shu" 馬王堆帛書天文氣象雜占簡述, *Wen wu,* 1978.2:1-4. Wang Shu-min (10.3503) cites a possibly related passage recorded in the *T'ai-p'ing yü-lan* concerning the First Emperor of Ch'in searching out an emanation of a Son of Heaven to the east; the *T'ai-p'ing yü-lan* attributes the passage to the "Ch'in chi" 秦紀 (i.e., "Ch'in pen-chi"); but it is not to be found in the current version of the "Ch'in pen-chi."

[68]Although there is no specific mention of these events in the basic annals of the First Emperor, they must refer to his final eastern tour in 210 B.C. (see *Shih chi,* 6.260; *Grand Scribe's Records,* 1:151): "On the *kuei-ch'ou* day of the tenth month in his thirty-seventh year (210 B.C.), the First Emperor set out to travel."

Han shu (1A.8) omits *yin* 因 "took advantage of." The idea that the First Emperor had already planned an inspection tour to the east so that this trip did not appear out of the ordinary is lost thereby in Pan Ku's account. *Han shu* also reads *yen-tang* 厭當, "to suppress and block it," for *Shih chi's yen* 厭 "to repress."

Once again there is a sharp contrast between the basic annals of Hsiang Yü and this chapter. In *Shih chi* 7 (7.296) Hsiang Yü is in hiding when the First Emperor comes east, but he steals forth to get a look at his ruler.

[69]It seems to have been widely believed at this time that a sage-like man would arise from the Southeast (see Yang Shu-ta, *Han shu k'uei-kuan,* p. 3).

[70]*Han shu* (1A.8) omits 即自疑，亡匿 "immediately suspecting that he himself [was the source of the emanation], fled and hid." Major *Shih chi* editions all contain these five characters (cf. Mizusawa, *Fu kôho,* 8.256d). *Wang-ni* 亡匿 "fled and hid" is quite common in the *Shih chi,* occurring 10 times, most of the passages relating to situations during the first few years of the Han dynasty; it is also used to describe how Chang Liang,

marshes, cliffs and rocks between Mang 芒 and Tang 碭.[71] When Lü Hou and others went to search for him,[72] they always were able to find him. Kao-tsu found this strange and asked about it. Lü Hou said, "Because above the place where you, Chi, are staying, there is always a cloudy emanation,[73] we are able to go along following it and always find you." Kao-tsu was pleased.[74] Among the young men in P'ei, some heard about this. Many were those who wanted to attach themselves to him.[75]

[349] In the autumn of the first year of Ch'in Erh-shih 秦二世 (The Second [Emperor] of Ch'in; 209 B.C.),[76] Ch'en Sheng 陳勝[77] and his group rose up in Ch'i 蘄;[78] when they reached

later one of Kao-tsu's fellow men, hid from the First Emperor after attempting to assassinate him (*Shih chi*, 55.2034).

[71]It is likely that during this period when Liu Pang was in hiding that Empress Lü was confined and harassed by local officials until Jen Ao 任敖 went to her aid (*Shih chi*, 96.2680).

These two county seats were located a few miles north of modern Yung-ch'eng 永城 in the easternmost finger of modern Honan province, twenty miles west-northwest of Huai-pei 淮北 (modern Anhwei; T'an Ch'i-hsiang, 2:19; see also *Grand Scribe's Records*, 1:185 and n. 73). Mang lies five miles south of Tang (Wang Li-ch'i, 8.197n).

P'ei Yin adds (citing Ying Shao in "Chi-chieh," *Shih chi*, 8.349) that there was a marshy and mountainous redoubt between the two places.

[72]His hiding place was a little over fifteen miles west of P'ei, near his hometown of Feng.

[73]This seems to be an indirect reference to Liu Pang's divine patrimony, since clouds and dragons are closely associated in Chinese symbolism (see *Chou Yi Ta-chuan hsin-chu* 周易大傳新注 [Tsinan: Ch'i Lu, 1988], p. 13, for example: "Clouds come from dragons, winds come from tigers" 雲從龍，風從虎.). See also Michael Loewe's comments in "Oracles of the Clouds and Winds" (in Loewe, *Divination*, pp. 191-213, esp. p. 195).

[74]*Hsi* 喜 "to be pleased" echoes Liu Pang's sentiments at being told of the crone's claim that the snake he had just killed was actually the son of the White Emperor (see *Shih chi*, 8.347 just above).

[75]This marks the end of the first section of this chapter which gives the reader background information on Liu Pang. A number of chapters on early Han figures begin with anecdotes about their principal subject presented in an amorphous chronology. These chapters then take on the rigid chronological precision of an annals beginning with the introduction of Ch'en She and his rebellion (see, for example, *Shih chi*, Chapters 89 and 91 as well as the Translator's Note to this chapter).

Many of the *pin-k'o* 賓客 Liu Pang had supported in P'ei were no doubt among those who came to join him at this time (see also n. 24 above). Fan K'uai, for example, went into hiding with Liu Pang (*Shih chi*, 95.2651).

[76]According to *Shih chi*, 7.269, this occurred in the seventh month. See also *Shih chi*, 48.1950. *Han shu* (1A.9) reads "In autumn in the seventh month" 秋七月.

It is ironic that the first specific date given in this chapter needs further specification. Li Ching-hsing (*op. cit.*), p. 13, notes that the second section (of what he sees as five sections) of the chapter begins here.

Hsü Kuang (cited in "Chi-chieh") says that Liu Pang was forty eight *sui* at this time, but he is following the birthdate of 256 B.C.; according to the chronology we have adopted, he would be thirty-nine *sui*.

Ch'en 陳,[79] he made himself a king, designating [himself] "The One Who Claims to [Restore] Ch'u to Greatness."[80] In every commandery and county many killed the high-ranking officers in response to Ch'en She 陳涉.[81] The Prefect of P'ei was afraid and wanted to use P'ei to respond to [Ch'en] She's call. The administrator [of the jail][82] and the chief of personnel, Hsiao Ho and Ts'ao Ts'an 曹參,[83] then said, "You are an officer of Ch'in and now you want to turn your back on it and lead the young men of P'ei; we fear they will not listen to you. We hope, My Lord, that you would summon those who have fled to places outside [the county], likely obtaining a few hundred men, and, taking advantage of this opportunity, coerce the populace so that they will have to listen to you." He then ordered Fan K'uai 樊噲[84] to summon Liu Chi.[85] Liu Chi's people

[77] On Ch'en Sheng (i.e., Ch'en She) see *Shih chi* Chapter 48, *Grand Scribe's Records*, 1:158, n. 317, and Meng Ming-han 孟名漢, "Kuan-yü Ch'en Sheng ch'u-shen wen-t'i te t'ao-t'ao" 關於陳勝出身問題的探討, in *Ch'in Han wen-hua lun-ts'ung* 秦漢文化論叢 (Sian: Hsi-pei Ta-hsüeh, 1993), pp. 257-73.

[78] A county southeast of modern Su 宿 County in Anhwei (Wang Li-ch'i, 8.197n), less than fifteen miles south of Yung-ch'eng and about twenty miles south of Liu Pang's retreat.

[79] About seventy-five miles west of Ch'i, his starting point, near modern Huai-yang 淮陽 County in Honan (T'an Ch'i-hsiang, 2:19).

[80] Another possible reading is to take this expression as the title of Ch'en Sheng's revised state of Ch'u. On *Shih chi* 48.1952 the Chung-hua editors seem to read it that way (punctuating it as a proper noun there). Watson (*Han*, 1:54) translates the passage as we do, referring *chang Ch'u* 張楚 to Ch'en She himself: "When Chen She had reached the area of Chen and made himself a king with the title 'Magnifier of Ch'u' . . . ." This reading must remain tentative, however, since as Wang Li-ch'i (8.197n) points out, Ch'en Sheng elsewhere called himself simply "The King of Ch'u."

Pan Ku simplifies the text to read 至陳自立為楚王, "When he reached Ch'en he made himself King of Ch'u" (*Han shu*, 1A.9). See also the discussion of the term Chang Ch'u as it appeared in its earliest known occurence in the *Wu hsing chan* 五星占 text found with the Ma Wang-tui materials in Liu Nai-ho 劉乃和, "Po-shu so chi 'Chang Ch'u' kuo-hao yü Hsi Han fa-chia cheng-chih" 帛書所記 '張楚' 國號與西漢法家政治, *Wen-wu*, 1975.5: 35-37.

[81] Ch'en Sheng's *agnomen*.

[82] *Yüan* is often used for *yüan-shih* 掾史, administrative clerk—see Lu Zongli, p. 870 and Hucker, #8219 and #8238. Dubs (1.38) translates "chief [jailor]" based on the position of *yü-yüan* 獄掾 assigned Ts'ao in his *Han shu* biography (*Han shu*, 39.2013). Ts'ao's *Shih chi* biography (54.2021) does not give his position while in P'ei. We follow Dubs and render the position "administrator [of the jail]."

Nevertheless, there seems to be some textual problem here since the positions and those who hold them here form a chiasmus.

[83] See also his biography in *Shih chi*, Chapter 54. On the pronunciation of Ts'ao's name both Shen and Ts'an are possible. However, Shen is basically only the name of a constellation whereas Ts'an has a number of meanings, some of which ("to greet, pay respects to a superior") were related to his *agnomen*, 敬伯.

[84] On Fan K'uai, see *Grand Scribe's Records*, 1:192, n. 192. It may be that Fan K'uai felt it safe to move

already numbered nearly a hundred men.[86]

[350] At this time, Liu Chi came with Fan K'uai in his train. The Prefect of P'ei, filled with regret,[87] fearing there would be an insurrection, closed the gates in the city walls and caused the walls to be defended, intending to execute Hsiao and Ts'ao. Hsiao and Ts'ao were afraid and climbed over the wall to take refuge with Liu Chi. Liu Chi then wrote a letter on a piece of silk and shot it onto the city wall, saying to the elders of P'ei: "The world has suffered Ch'in long enough.[88] Although you elders now are defending [the walls] for the Prefect of P'ei, the 'feudal lords'[89] have risen up together and will soon put P'ei to the sword. If P'ei joins together now to execute the prefect, selects one of the young people who is worthy and installs him, thereby responding to the [call of the] feudal lords, then your families and homes could be preserved. If not, fathers and sons will all be put to the sword and there would be no benefit in doing that."[90] The elderly fathers then led the young men in concert to kill the Prefect of P'ei,

from Liu Pang's place of hiding to P'ei and back; in Fan's biography it is said that he hid out together with Liu Pang (*Shih chi*, 95.2651).

[85]In the preceding pages concerning Kao-tsu's life before the rebellion against Ch'in he is referred to by his posthumous title as "Kao-tsu," the Exalted Emperor. This suggests these passages were put into their final form some time after Kao-tsu had died. Here he is called simply by his name, Liu Chi, as the style switches to an annalistic account of current affairs. Below Liu Pang will be referred to by each of his official titles as he attains them and exercises duties related to them—from the Magistrate of P'ei (*P'ei Kung* 沛公; *kung* 公 here is the designation for "magistrate" used in the state of Ch'u, see also *Grand Scribe's Records*, 1:127, n. 17), to the King of Han, and finally to the Exalted Ancestor, Kao-tsu, again.

As the ruler of P'ei was previously referred to in this chapter as *P'ei ling* 沛令, Prefect of P'ei, this title seemingly marks a return from Ch'in designations to those of the Ch'u.

[86]*Han shu* (1A.9) reads "several hundred men," but this expression, *shu shih pai jen* 數十百人, literally "from several tens to a hundred men" (see "So-yin," *Shih chi*, 8.349) is common in the *Shih chi* (occurring eight times), especially in the accounts of the founding of the Han. It is used to depict how many men Hsiang Chi 項籍 killed at the start of the rebellion and the total Hsiang Yü slew as he was surrounded by Liu Pang's troops at the end of it (cf. *Shih chi*, 7.297 with *Grand Scribe's Records*, 1:183, and *Shih chi*, 7.335 with *Grand Scribe's Records*, 1:206). It is ironic that Liu Pang began his revolt with the same number of troops Hsiang Yü was able to slay in his final attack against it.

[87]Probably more because he summoned Liu Pang and his large band of men than because he had rebelled against Ch'in.

[88]This line becomes a formulaic slogan which recurs six times in the *Shih chi* always to justify one or the other rebellion against Ch'in (cf. *Shih chi*, 8.357, 8.362, 48.1950, 89.2574, 92.2622, and 97.2692).

[89]This term, *chu-hou* 諸侯, which earlier we translated "feudal lords," has evolved to refer to the local satraps by this time. But since Ssu-ma Ch'ien retains it, we shall, too. We have translated a related but 'new' term, *chu-hou wang* 諸侯王, however, as "noble kings" (see n. 331 below). See also *Grand Scribe's Records*, 1:xix-xx and 1:2, n. 15.

[90]Following Chang Chia-ying's (pp. 159-60) interpretation of *wu wei* 無為.

opening the gates in the city wall to welcome Liu Chi, intending to make him Prefect of P'ei.[91] Liu Chi said, "The world is in confusion, the feudal lords have risen up together; if you select a commander who is not skilled, with one defeat you will be smeared into the mud.[92] I would not dare to be concerned for my own [safety], but fear my abilities are slight and I would not be able to preserve you all, young and old. This is a great task and I would ask that again you recommend [people] among yourselves and select one who can handle it." Hsiao, Ts'ao and the others were all civil officers and concerned for their own safety; fearing that the task would not be completed, and that later Ch'in would exterminate the various kindred of their families, all yielded to Liu Chi. All the elderly fathers said, "All our lives the many extraordinary and marvelous things we have heard about Liu Chi indicate that his lot is to be honored.[93] Moreover, among the results of divinations by shell and stalks none are more auspicious than those for Liu Chi." At this point Liu Chi declined [the position] several times. But none among the group would dare to do it, so they installed Chi as the Magistrate of P'ei.[94] He worshipped Huang-ti 黃帝 (The Yellow Emperor) and offered sacrifices to Ch'ih-yu 蚩尤 in the P'ei [yamen] courtyard, and smeared the blood on

[91] According to the accounts on *Shih chi*, 18.884 and 18.962, it was Hsia-hou Ying who rallied support for Liu Pang inside the city walls and P'eng Tsu 彭祖, later Marquis Ching 敬 of Tai 戴, who opened the gates.

[92] *Yi pai t'u ti* 壹敗塗地, which we render "with one defeat you will be smeared into the mud," needs further explanation. Watson says (*Han*, 1:55) "You will be cut down in one stroke and your blood will drench the earth." Watson is inferring that it is blood that will drench the earth, perhaps based on passages like *Shih chi*, 92.2623 where K'uai T'ung 蒯通 is describing the carnage that Liu Pang and Hsiang Yü are causing: "Now Ch'u and Han divide and struggle, throughout the world causing people with no offense to have their livers and gall bladders smeared into the mud" 今楚漢分爭，使天下無罪之人肝膽塗地, Lou Ching's 婁敬 (later given the royal surname Liu 劉 for his meritorious service) similar speech to Kao-tsu (*Shih chi*, 99.2716), or the description of the King of Tai's 代 brains smeared into the mud after being assassinated (*Shih chi*, 70.2297). (Chavannes' rendition [2:334] is a bit free: "une seule défaite sera la ruine de ce pays.")

Here Liu Pang is not criticizing these people for previous carnage, however. Given the proverbial look of this phrase, it would seem to indicate something more general.

[93] Chang Wen-hu (8.89) notes that the *T'ai-p'ing yü-lan* (87.2a) cites this passage reading *ch'i-kuai* 奇怪 for *chen-kuai* 珍怪. There is a second citation of this text in *T'ai-p'ing yü-lan* (725.8b) which also reads *ch'i-kuai*, but each of these citations differs in other details from the *Shih chi* text here as well as from the *Han shu* (1A.10) parallel. The *Han shu* also reads *ch'i-kuai*. As Wang Shu-min (8.306-07) points out, the phrases are virtually identical.

Here, as above in the passage where Liu Pang's face was read, it is the *lao fu* 老父, "elderly fathers," who perceive great potential in Liu Pang.

[94] "Chi-chieh" has two interesting observations here. First, it cites Hsü Kuang that this took place in the ninth month. Second, P'ei Yin lends his support to the *Han shu yin-yi* explanation that Liu Pang was a "duke" under Ch'en Sheng, who was then King of Ch'u. Actually, *kung* was a designation for magistrate in Ch'u (see *Grand Scribe's Records*, 6.127, n. 17).

his drums and flags. The pennants were all red,[95] because the snake which was killed was the son of the Pai-ti (The White Emperor) and the one who killed it was the son of the Ch'ih-ti (The Red Emperor). For this reason red was exalted. At this time, the young bloods and stalwart officers like Hsiao, Ts'ao, Fan K'uai and the others all gathered two or three thousand of the youth of P'ei for him, attacked Hu-ling 胡陵 and Fang-yü 方與, and returned to defend Feng 豐.[96]

[95]Ch'ih-yu was the God of War, see *Shih chi*, 28.1367, 97.2695 and *Grand Scribe's Records*, 1:2, n. 17. Itano Nagahachi 板野長八 in his "Han Ko no Kan ôchô shinwa" 班固の漢王朝神話 (*Rikishigaku kenkyû* 479 [1980.4]: 1-16) notes (p. 11) that there is no mention of Kao-tsu worshipping the Yellow Emperor in the parallel passages on *Shih chi*, 28.1378 or *Han shu*, 25.1210, and suggests that Kao-tsu's reign was symbolized by the martial power of Ch'ih Yu and the color red. The military flags (*Shih chi*, 92.2616) and caducei (*Han shu*, 92.2616) of the early Han seem to have been red. Furthermore, *Shih chi*, 28.1378 relates how four years after Kao-tsu established sacrifices to Ch'ih Yu in Feng, he also had them begun in Ch'ang-an; there is again no mention of the Yellow Emperor. Yang Hsiang-k'uei 楊向奎 argues that the reference to Kao-tsu's worshipping the Yellow Emperor is a later interpolation (see his *Hsi Han ching-hsüeh yü cheng-chih* 西漢經學與政治 [Chungking: Tu-li Ch'u-pan-she, 1945], pp. 31-41).

Ying Shao cited in "Chi-chieh" (*Shih chi*, 8.351) claims that killing a sacrificial animal and smearing its blood on drums was a ritual. Dubs (1.40-41, n. 2) attempts to fix these ceremonies in the textual tradition of Confucian ritual, but concludes they were likely military rituals, possibly of local origin. Wu Hsün 吳恂 (1890-1973) reads *hsin* 釁 as "anoint" and parses this passage to read "the Magistrate of P'ei worshipped the Yellow Emperor and offered sacrifices to Ch'ih-yu 蚩尤 in the P'ei [yamen] courtyard, and anointed his drums. His flags, and pennants were all red." See Wu's *Han shu chu-shang*, pp. 3-4. Indeed, a reparsing of the *Shih chi* passage here to read "smeared the blood on his drums. The flags and pennants were all red, . . . ," seems to be preferable to the Chung-hua editors' punctuation. This latter parsing is, in fact, the punctuation given by Ku and Hsü (8.4 [154]).

A passage in the "Feng-shan shu" 封禪書 (*Shih chi*, 28.1378), 漢興，高祖之微時，嘗殺大蛇。有物曰：「蛇，白帝子也，而殺者亦帝子。」高祖初起，禱豐枌榆社。徇沛，為沛公，則祠蚩尤，釁鼓旗, suggests that both flags and drums were anointed in the sacrifices to Ch'ih-yu. It is interesting that in this parallel passage there is no reference to worshipping the Yellow Emperor.

The Fen-yü Altar mentioned here is claimed by Chang Yen 張晏 in "Chi-chieh" to be the name of a tree (*Ulmus pumila*), an altar to which was located about ten miles northeast of Feng (see also *Hou Han shu*, 110 [*Chih* 志 20].3427; Chang Yen also cites the belief that Fen-yü was the name of Kao-tsu's home village, but at the start of this chapter Liu Pang's home village was called Chung-yang). Liang Yü-sheng (6.215) notes that there is a *t'ing* 亭 in the marsh near where Kao-tsu is thought to have killed the snake.

The phrase *hsin ku* 釁鼓 "to smear blood on drums" occurs four times in *Tso chuan* (Yang, *Tso chuan*, Hsi 33, p. 500; Ch'eng 3, p. 813; Chao, 5, p. 1271; and Ting 4, p. 1535). The first three passages show that the blood smeared on the drums could have been that of a prisoner as well as an animal sacrifice. Moreover, they suggest the practice was not limited to a specific locale, as Dubs suggested. The fourth *Tso chuan* occurrence (Ting 4, p. 1535) describes the practice as part of a military ritual: "When the ruler is going to march with the army, [we] purify the altar of the land, smear blood on the drums. . . ." On the readings of *chi* 祭 "worshipped" and *tz'u* 祠 "offered sacrifices" see also Dubs, 1.40-41, n. 2.

[96]As Wang Tzu-chin 王子今 has shown in his "Shuo Ch'in Han 'shao-nien' yü 'o shao-nien'" 說秦漢少

[351] In the second year of Ch'in Erh-shih (The Second [Emperor] of Ch'in, 208 B.C.), the army of Ch'en She's general Chou Chang 周章 (d. 208 B.C.)[97] moved west to the Hsi 戲 and returned.[98] Yen, Chao, Ch'i and Wei all enthroned themselves as kings.[99] The Hsiang 項 Clan

年與惡少年 (*Chung-kuo shih yen-chiu*, 1991.4:97-106), *shao-nien* 少年 was a general term in Ch'in and Han times for a subclass of youth who usually lived in an urban setting, were at odds with the government, and were often involved in disturbances, as in "The Basic Annals of Hsiang Yü" (*Shih chi*, 7.298; translation from *Grand Scribe's Records*, 1:181): "Ch'en Ying was once the Scrivener of Tung-yang. He lived at the county seat, was always truthful and careful, and was known as a [trustworthy] elder. After the young men [*shao-nien*] of Tung-yang had killed its prefect and gathered several thousand men around them, they wanted a leader, but there was no one suitable, so they asked Ch'en Ying. Ch'en Ying declined on account of his lack of ability. They then forced Ch'en Ying to become their leader. Twenty thousand in the country followed them. The young men wanted to enthrone Ch'en Ying as king right away and rise in revolt immediately, distinguishing themselves from the other forces by wearing blue caps." Although we continue to translate *shao-nien* as "youth," these young men saw themselves as trying to emulate the *hsia* 俠 (knight-errants); their loyalty to each other and rowdy behavior, makes these young men not totally unlike the youth gangs of modern America.

Hu-ling and Fang-yü, both on or near the Ssu 泗 River, are approximately fifteen and twenty-five miles northwest of P'ei; Feng is about twenty-five miles west of P'ei. Thus the troops first headed northwest—in the direction of territory held by Ch'en Sheng—and then fell back to a position west of P'ei. Liang Yü-sheng (6.215) points out that according to *Shih chi*, 16.765 the attack on Hu-ling and Fang-yü took place in the tenth month of the *second* year of the Second Emperor—i.e., the following year (208 B.C.).

[97]Chou was also known as Chou Wen 文 and was a native of Ch'en County (modern Huai-yang County in Honan, Wang Li-ch'i, 8.198n.). He and several other commanders led their troops into the Pass and were defeated by the Ch'in general, Chang Han, in the ninth month (see *Shih chi*, 6.270, 16.764, and *Grand Scribe's Records*, 1:158 text and n. 327). Chou Chang was pursued by Chang Han, routed and finally committed suicide in the eleventh month (*Shih chi*, 48.1954 and 16.765). Thus, as Liang Yü-sheng (6.215) notes, he did not return.

[98]The Hsi River had its source on Mount Li 酈 and flowed north into the Wei 渭 (modern Shensi; Wang Li-ch'i, 8.198n.; see also *Grand Scribe's Records*, 1:158, n. 327). The fact that Chou Wen could move west into the Pass with no apparent opposition suggests the limitations of Ch'in military control at this time, explaining in part why the rebels arose East of the Mountain and were able to move about with virtual impunity in the initial months of the rebellion.

The *Han shu* reports these other revolts, which actually began in the ninth month of the first year of the Second Emperor (cf. *Shih chi*, 16.764), in a paragraph beginning "in this month" inserted just before this section. As Dubs notes (1.42, n. 2) the *Han shu* differs in the sequence of its presentation here "because the *HS* attempts to follow a strictly chronological order of events, following *SC* ch. 16." The *Han shu* not only reorders events, however, but also revises some of the content, noting that Chou Chang entered the pass and reached Hsi, but not mentioning his return. Liang Yü-sheng (6.215) points out that Chou Chang could not have returned because he was killed by Chang Han. However, the *Shih chi* text reads "Chou Chang's army . . . returned" 周章卒 . . . 還. Although *Shih chi*, 6.270 tells that Chang Han killed Chou Chang, it also notes that it put his army of several tens of thousand to flight. It was the remnants of these men who presumably returned to the P'ei region.

rose up in Wu.[100] P'ing 平,[101] the Inspector[102] of Ssu-ch'uan 泗川 [Commandery],[103] led his troops to besiege Feng; after two days, [Liu Pang] sent forth [troops] to give him battle and defeated him.[104] He ordered Yung Ch'ih 雍齒[105] to defend Feng and[106] led his troops to Hsüeh. Chuang 壯,[107] the Governor of Ssu-ch'uan, was defeated at Hsüeh 薛[108] and hastened to Ch'i 戚 ;[109] the Magistrate of P'ei's Left Marshal[110] caught Chuang, the Governor of Ssu-ch'uan, and killed him.[111] The Magistrate of P'ei returned his troops to Kang-fu 亢父;[112] he reached Fang-yü

This is impossible to see in the *Han shu* because Pan Ku has deleted the important word *chün* 軍 (army).

[99]Liang Yü-sheng (6.215-16) points out that these kings were enthroned during the eighth and ninth months of the first year of the Second Emperor (209 B.C.). He also notes that Wei Chiu 魏咎 did not enthrone himself, but was made king through the efforts of Chou Fu 周市.

[100]According to Wang Li-ch'i (8.198n.), Hsiang Liang and Hsiang Yü (the "Hsiang Clan" referred to here) had fled from Ch'u to Wu (see *Shih chi*, 7.296).

[101]His full name is unknown.

[102]*Chien* 監 inspectors were appointed by the central government to oversee the local officials in a commandery; this was one of three important commanderial posts, the other two being the *shou* 守 or governor, in charge of administrative affairs, and the *wei* 尉 or commandant, who oversaw military matters.

[103]Probably an error for "Ssu-shui" 泗水 which was a Ch'in commandery based at Hsiang 相 (a few miles northwest of modern Huai-pei 淮北 City, Anhwei; T'an Ch'i-hsiang, 2:8) encompassing most of the places involved in Liu Pang's early campaigns. Parallel passages in the *Shih chi* (54.2021, 95.2651, and 96.2676) also read Ssu-shui. Liang Yü-sheng (6.216) attributes the error to the similarity between the ancient graphs for *ch'uan* and *shui*.

[104]This took place in the tenth month (which was the first month of the Ch'in calendar, see *Shih chi*, 16.765).

[105]A man from Liu Pang's hometown of P'ei who was later enfeoffed as a marquis by Kao-tsu in the sixth year of his reign (*Shih chi*, 18.906). At this time, however, he turned on Liu Pang within a month, pledging allegiance to the newly reconstituted state of Wei (*Shih chi*, 16.765 and 767).

[106]*Han shu*, 1A.12 adds "in the eleventh month" here. *Shih chi*, 16.765 says the Magistrate of P'ei took Hsüeh in the eleventh month.

[107]His full name is unknown.

[108]A Ch'in commandery seated near modern Ch'ü-fu in Shantung (T'an Ch'i-hsiang, 2:8).

[109]About sixty miles south of Hsieh in Chuang's own Ssu-shui Commandery, some five-ten miles northeast of P'ei (T'an Ch'i-hsiang, 2:8).

[110]Ts'ao Wu-shang 曹無傷 (see *Shih chi*, 7.311 and Wang Li-ch'i, 8.199n.).

For [*tso*] *ssu-ma*[左]司馬 we use "[left] marshal" in place of Bielenstein's "major."

[111]This took place in the eleventh month. Thereafter, Liu Pang held control of the area west of Hsieh until Chou Fu arrived (see *Shih chi*, 16.765).

Han shu, 1A.12 has a different text here: 沛公左司馬得殺之 "Te, the Left Marshal of the Magistrate of P'ei, killed him [Chuang]." "So-yin" (*Shih chi*, 8.353) counters this reading and notes that the Left Marshal in question is probably Ts'ao Wu-shang 曹無傷 who appears later in this chapter in that position. Chou Shou-ch'ang

[*352*] without having given battle.[113] The King of Ch'en sent Chou Fu 周市, a native of Wei,[114] to overrun territory. Chou Fu sent a man to say to Yung Ch'ih: "Feng is where Liang [i.e., Wei] moved [its capital] in the past.[115] Now the [former] territories of Wei which have been pacified [by the new Wei rebel regime] are several dozen cities. If you now submit to Wei, Wei will make you a marquis to defend Feng. If you do not submit, we shall put Feng to the sword." Yung Ch'ih was reluctant to owe allegiance to the Magistrate of P'ei[116]; when Wei summoned him, he immediately rebelled against [the Magistrate of P'ei] and defended Feng on behalf of

周壽昌 (1814-1884) (*Han shu chu chiao-pu* 漢書注校補, 1.11a) does not believe this was Ts'ao and offers several other possibilities (see also Dubs (1.42, n. 5). Whatever the identity of this Left Marshal, it seems strange that Pan Ku would read Te 得 as a *nomen* when he does not know the *cognomen*.

[112]About fifty miles from Hsieh along the west bank of the Ssu River (T'an Ch'i-hsiang, 2:8). Wang Li-ch'i (8.199n) argues that the pronunciation of 亢 should be *kang* here.

[113]There is a textual problem here. After "reached Fang-yü," the Po-na edition (8.8b) reads: "Chou Fu 周市 came to attack Fang-yü [but Liu Pang] did not give battle." Takigawa is identical (8.19), as is the Wu-ying Tien 武英殿 "Palace Edition" (8.8b-9a). Chang Wen-hu 張文虎, who did not have the Po-na edition, does not comment on this passage. But the Chung-hua editors, apparently based on Kuo Sung-t'ao's 郭嵩燾 *Shih chi cha-chi* (1.62), decided to excise this passage. Although it is true that it is strange to have Chou Fu "sent" by the King of Ch'en after he has already arrived, the text without this passage seems syntactically awkward. The other important modern text, *Shih chi, Pai-wen chih pu* by Ku and Hsü (8.5 [155]), keeps the passage and parses the text as follows: "The Magistrate of P'ei returned his army to Kang-fu and reached Fang-yü; Chou Fu arrived to attack Fang-yü. Before they had joined in battle, the King of Ch'en sent Chou Fu, a native of Wei, to overrun territory."

Pan Ku *(Han shu,* 1A.12) has simplified the text greatly here to eliminate the problems: "The Magistrate of P'ei returned, encamped at K'ang-fu, and reached Fang-yü."

The most radical suggestion is that of Liang Yü-sheng (6.216) who rehearses several early commentators' attempts to reconcile the passage (including one which argued there must have been two Chou Fu's, one from the state of Wei!) and then rejects them all in favor of moving the line "the King of Ch'en sent Chou Fu, a native of Wei, to overrun territory" to follow the sentence "the Magistrate of P'ei returned, encamped at K'ang-fu, and reached Fang-yü." The emended text would then read: "The Magistrate of P'ei returned, encamped at K'ang-fu, and reached Fang-yü. The King of Ch'en sent Chou Fu, a native of Wei, to overrun territory. Chou Fu came to attack Fang-yü. Before they had joined battle, Chou Fu sent a man to say to Yung Ch'ih . . . ."

[114]Chou Fu had originally attempted to subdue Wei for Ch'en Sheng *(Shih chi,* 94.2643). We follow Wu and Lu's note on reading Chou's name as Fu (8.285n.).

[115]The parsing is tentative here. After Ch'in took Wei's western lands during the reign of Duke Hsiao 孝 of Ch'in (r. 361-338 B.C.), Wei moved its capital to Ta-Liang 大梁 *(Grand Scribe's Records,* 1:81, n. 270). After that time, the state of Wei was referred to as Liang. In the years just prior to Ch'in's conquest of China, Liang moved its capital a second time to Feng.

[116]Liu Pang later claimed he and Yung Ch'ih had been on bad terms for a long time *(Shih chi,* 55.2043).

Wei.[117] The Magistrate of P'ei led his troops to attack Feng, but he was not able to take it. The Magistrate of P'ei fell ill and returned to P'ei. The Magistrate of P'ei, harboring resentment for the betrayal of Yung Ch'ih and the young men of Feng, heard that Lord Ning 甯 of Tung-yang 東陽 and Ch'in Chia 秦嘉[118] had enthroned Ching Chü 景駒[119] as an acting king[120] in Liu 留,[121] so he went to follow him, intending to request troops to attack Feng.[122] At this time the Ch'in general Chang Han was pursuing Ch'en [She]; his deputy general Marshal Yi 㠯[123] led troops north to stabilize Ch'u territory, putting Hsiang 相[124] to the sword, and reaching Tang 碭.[125] Lord Ning of Tung-yang and the Magistrate of P'ei led troops west and gave him battle west of Hsiao 蕭,[126] but won no advantage. They returned to assemble their soldiers at Liu, and led their troops to attack Tang,[127] taking it after three days. They took advantage of [this defeat], to

[117]This took place in the twelfth month of 208 B.C. (actually the third month of the year in the Ch'in calendar, see *Shih chi*, 16.765).

[118]According to Ch'en Tsan 臣瓚 (in "Chi-chieh," *Shih chi*, 8.353), Ch'in Chia was a native of Kuang-ling 廣陵 and thus not the same person as Lord Ning (as some exegetes had held). Ch'en bases his argument on the text of "Ch'en She shih-chia" 陳涉世家, but the current version of that text (*Shih chi*, 48.1957) says Ch'in Chia was a man of Ling 陵."So-yin" *(ibid.)* notes that Yen Shih-ku 顏師古 believes Ning was his *cognomen* and that "lord" was merely a title given him by his own troops.

Tung-yang was distant from this area, located about fifty-five miles northwest of modern Yangchow on the Kiangsu-Anhwei border (T'an Ch'i-hsiang, 2:8). Kuang-ling 廣陵, in the vicinity of modern Yangchow, was Ch'in Chia's home place.

[119]On Ching Chü see *Grand Scribe's Records*, 1:182 and n. 36, *Shih chi*, 16.765-6 and 48.1959. "So-yin" *(Shih chi*, 16.765) says he was killed by Hsiang Liang in the eighth month.

[120]Wang Li-ch'i (8.199n.) argues that Ching was made king because the King of Ch'en, Ch'en She, had just been killed and the rebels were without a leader; but in the next few lines Ssu-ma Ch'ien shows that, at least in his chronology, Ch'en She was still alive.

[121]About ten miles southeast of P'ei on the Ssu River (T'an Ch'i-hsiang, 2:19).

[122]In the first month (*Shih chi*, 16.766 and *Han shu*, 1A.13).

[123]Probably because he believed that Ch'en She was already dead by this time, Ssu-ma Chen ("So-yin") suggests this sentence should be parsed as follows: 是時秦將章邯從陳別將司馬夷. . ., "At this time the Ch'in general Chang Han was pursuing Ch'en [She's] deputy general Marshal Yi . . . ." Ju Ch'un ("Chi-chieh") argues that Marshal Yi was Chang Han's subordinate and we have followed this reading in our translation. Wang Shu-min (8.308), among others, argues that Ssu-ma here is not a military rank, but a *cognomen*. *Pieh-chiang* 別將, our "deputy general," might also be read "deputy commander." Wu Kuo-t'ai 吳國泰, in his "*Shih chi* chieh-ku (hsia)" 史記解詁（下） *(Wen shih*, 43 [1997]: 41) also supports our reading.

[124]The Ch'in seat of Ssu-shui Commandery, see also nn. 2 and 21 above.

[125]See *Grand Scribe's Records*, 1:185, n. 73.

[126]About forty miles south of P'ei, slightly northwest of modern Hsiao County in Anhwei (Wang Li-ch'i, 8.199n.).

[127]This took place in the second month (*Shih chi*, 16.766 and *Han shu*, 1A.13).

collect troops from Tang, obtaining five or six thousand men.[128] They attacked Hsia-yi 下邑 and seized it.[129] They returned to make camp at Feng. When [Liu Chi] heard that Hsiang Liang 項梁 was in Hsüeh 薛,[130] he went with more than one hundred of his personal horse[131] to see him. Hsiang Liang increased the Magistrate of P'ei's foot soldiers by five thousand men and his commanders of the Full Grand Man [rank][132] by ten men. The Magistrate of P'ei returned and led his troops to attack Feng.[133]

[354] More than a month after Liu Chi became a follower of Hsiang Liang,[134] Hsiang Yü 項羽 had already seized Hsiang-ch'eng 襄城[135] and returned. Hsiang Liang summoned all his deputy generals[136] to [come and] stay in Hsüeh.[137] On hearing that the King of Ch'en had definitely died, he enthroned a descendant of Ch'u, [Hsiung] Hsin 熊心, the grandson of King Huai 懷 (r. 328-299 B.C.), as King of Ch'u,[138] and set his administrative seat at Hsü-yi 盱台.[139] Hsiang Liang was called Lord Wu-hsin 武信 (Valiant and Trustworthy). After several months,[140]

[128]Giving Liu Pang a total strength at this time of nine thousand men (*Shih chi*, 16.766).

[129]A county about fifteen miles north of Tang (T'an Ch'i-hsiang, 2:19). This occurred in the third month (*Han shu*, 1A.13).

[130]Not the same seat-of-a-commandery Hsüeh as mentioned just above; this was a county located about fifteen miles northeast of P'ei (T'an Ch'i-hsiang, 2:8).

[131]Although it is probable that Liu Pang's men were a ragtag group, especially in these early years, scholars have pointed out that there were two basic types of mounted soldiers under the Former Han: one on a horse of relatively small stature, with no armor, carrying a bow with a quiver of arrows on his back; the other on a larger mount, wearing partial armor, and carrying a spear-like weapon. These types could be thought of as light cavalry and heavy cavalry (see also Pai Chien-kang 白建鋼, "Hsi Han pu, ch'i-ping ping-chung ch'u-t'an" 西漢步騎兵兵種初探, in *Hsi-pei Ta-hsüeh hsüeh-pao*, 1985.1: 80.

[132]*Wu Tai-fu* 五大夫 was an aristocratic, rather than official, rank (see Loewe, "The Orders of Aristocratic Rank of Han China," *TP*, 48 (1960): 99, and Lu Zongli, 94.

[133]Liu Pang took Feng in the fourth month; Yung Ch'ih fled to Wei *(Shih chi*, 16.767).

[134]In the fifth month (*Han shu*, 1A.14).

[135]See *Grand Scribe's Records*, 1:182, n. 43.

[136]*Pieh-chiang* 別將 (see Lu Zongli, pp. 427-8).

[137]Liu Pang also went to Hsieh at this time (see *Shih chi*, 7.300).

[138]King Huai went to Ch'in in 299 B.C. and had died there in captivity in 298 B.C. Ever since then the Ch'u people had pined for him. Hsiang Liang, playing upon this sentiment, dubbed the new king "King Huai" (see *Shih chi*, 7.300 and *Grand Scribe's Records*, 1:181 and n. 52).

[139]See *Grand Scribe's Records*, 1:183 and n. 53.

[140]Wang Li-ch'i (8.199n.) is troubled by the length of time and ponders whether *yüeh* 月 could be an error for *jih* 日 "days" (probably following Liang Yü-sheng, 6.017). However, the parallel account in "The Basic Annals of Hsiang Yü" (*Shih chi*, 7.300) also reads *chü shu yüeh* 居數月.

they moved north to attack Kang-fu and went to the rescue[141] of Tung-o 東阿,[142] defeating the Ch'in army. The Ch'i army returned [to Ch'i] and Ch'u alone pursued the defeated [Ch'in troops], sending the Magistrate of P'ei and Hsiang Yü to separately attack Ch'eng-yang 城陽[143] and put it to the sword. They made camp east of P'u-yang 濮陽,[144] gave battle to the Ch'in army, and defeated it.

[355] The Ch'in army was roused again;[145] they defended P'u-yang, and encircled it with water.[146] The Ch'u army left and attacked Ting-yao 定陶; Ting-yao did not submit.[147] The Magistrate of P'ei and Hsiang Yü overran territory to the west of [the city walls of] Yung-ch'iu 雍丘,[148] gave battle to the Ch'in army, and crushed it, executing Li Yu 李由.[149] They returned to attack Wai-huang 外黃; Wai-huang did not submit.[150]

Hsiang Liang, having defeated the Ch'in army a second time, had an arrogant appearance.

[141]Ch'i troops were besieged by those of Ch'in, under Chang Han, at Tung-o; Hsiang Liang joined forces with T'ien Jung 田榮 and Lung Chü 龍且 to defeat them (see *Shih chi,* 7.301).

[142]See *Grand Scribe's Records,* 1:183, n. 57.

[143]A punitive attack against a Ch'i outpost; Hsiang Liang had had a falling out with T'ien Jung (see *Grand Scribe's Records,* 1:183-4).

[144]On P'u-yang see *Grand Scribe's Records,* 1:184, n. 62. The general movement of this campaign was to the northwest, P'u-yang located about 120 miles northwest of Hsüeh.

[145]Possibly after stragglers from the battle east of P'u-yang rejoined it as Ju Ch'un 如淳 suggests ("Chi-chieh," *Shih chi,* 8.355).

[146]Probably from the nearby Yellow River as Chang Yen believes ("Chi-chieh," *ibid.*).

[147]On Ting-yao see *Grand Scribe's Records,* 1:184, n. 63. Since the pattern "they attacked such-and-such a place; the place did not submit" seems conventional in this section, our earlier speculations about reparsing such passages (see *Grand Scribe's Records,* 1:184, n. 67) seem erroneous now.

[148]*Chih hsia* 之下, literally "beneath," occurs several times in the *Shih chi* with the implied meaning of "beneath the city walls" (*Shih chi,* 41.1748, 44.1854, 57.2065, and 69.2246). It may refer to the lands in the valley of the Sui 睢 River which flows by Yung-ch'iu to the city's northeast (T'an Ch'i-hsiang, 2:7; see also *Grand Scribe's Records,* 1:184, n. 64 and *Shih chih,* 7.302).

[149]Li Ssu's son (see also *Grand Scribe's Records,* 1:184 and n. 65).

[150]On Wai-huang see *Grand Scribe's Records,* 1:184, n. 66. This campaign began in Hsüeh, moved northwest about forty-five miles to Kang-fu, then seventy miles in the same direction to Tung-o. From there Hsiang Yü and Liu Pang moved separately southeast to Ch'eng-yang (about forty-five miles), turned west-northwest to P'u-yang (forty-five miles), returned southeast about the same distance to Ting-yao, then overran territory for about fifty-five miles to the southwest before returning the twenty miles northeast to Wai-huang. The distance covered by Hsiang Yü and Liu Pang was close to four-hundred miles. According to *Shih chi,* 16.768, this was accomplished in the seventh and eighth months of 208 B.C.

With several of the other major rebels no longer a factor (Ch'i had internal problems, Ch'en Sheng had died after driving off several of the newly enthroned kings—see *Shih chi,* Chapter 48), Hsiang Liang was in control of most of the southern part of the North China Plain.

Sung Yi 宋義[151] admonished, but he did not listen. Ch'in increased Chang Han's troops, and they struck at night with bits in their mouths [to silence them],[152] crushing Hsiang Liang at Ting-yao. Hsiang Liang died. The Magistrate of P'ei and Hsiang Yü were just about to attack Ch'en-liu 陳留,[153] when they heard that Hsiang Liang had died. They led their troops along with General Lü [Ch'en]'s 呂[臣] to the east. Lü Ch'en camped east of P'eng-ch'eng 彭城,[154] Hsiang Yü camped west of P'eng-ch'eng, and the Magistrate of P'ei camped at Tang 碭.

   After Chang Han had defeated Hsiang Liang's army, he considered the troops in the territory of Ch'u not worthy of concern; he forded the Ho, went north to strike Chao, and crushed it. In the meantime, Chao Hsieh 趙歇 [*356*] was acting as King [of Chao]; the Ch'in general Wang Li 王離[155] besieged him at Chü-lu-ch'eng 鉅鹿城[156]—this was the so-called Army North of the Ho.[157]

   In the third year of the Ch'in Erh-shih (The Second [Emperor] of Ch'in, 207 B.C.), King Huai of Ch'u, seeing that Hsiang Liang's army was defeated, was afraid, and moved his capital from Hsü-yi to P'eng-ch'eng, to bring together the armies of Lü Ch'en and Hsiang Yü and personally command them. He made the Magistrate of P'ei Governor[158] of Tang Commandery, enfeoffed him as the Marquis of Wu-an 武安,[159] in command of the troops of Tang Commandery. He enfeoffed Hsiang Yü as Marquis Ch'ang-an 長安, titling him the Duke of Lu 魯. He made Lü Ch'en Minister over the Masses[160] and his father Lü Ch'ing 呂青 became Premier.[161]

   Chao several times requested assistance. King Huai thereupon appointed Sung Yi as

[151]See *Grand Scribe's Records,* 1:185, n. 68.

[152]Chang Han used the same technique to crush Wei's armies *(Shih chi,* 94.2643). See also Dubs (1.46, n. 1) and Chavannes (2:341, n. 2).

[153]About twenty miles west-southwest of Wai-huang (T'an Ch'i-hsiang, 2:7).

[154]Modern Hsü-chou 徐州 in Kiangsu (T'an Ch'i-hsiang, 2:8).

[155]Wang Li was the grandson of the famous Ch'in general Wang Chien 王翦 whose biography appears in *Shih chi* Chapter 73. He was captured by Hsiang Yü (*Shih chi,* 7.307 and 73.2341).

[156]Also written 巨鹿, this was a Ch'in county located southwest of modern P'ing-hsiang 平鄉 County in Hopei (Wang Li-ch'i, 8.200n).

[157]On Wang Li's "Army North of the River" and Chang Han's "Army South of the River" and their movements, see Chang Ch'uan-hsi 張傳璽, "Kuan-yü 'Chang Han chün' yü 'Wang Li chün' te kuan-hsi wen-t'i" 關於章邯軍與王離軍的關係問題, in Chang, *Ch'in Han wen-t'i yen-chiu* 秦漢問題研究 (Peking: Pei-ching Ta-hsüeh Ch'u-pan-she, 1995), pp. 357-61; Chang also argues that Ssu-ma Ch'ien incorrectly identifies Ch'en Yü's 陳餘 army as the "Army North of the River" on *Shih chi,* 7.304.

[158]Wu and Lu (8.287n.) note that *chang* 長 is the Ch'u equivalent for *shou* 守, governor.

[159]Near the modern city of the same name in Hopei a few miles west of Han-tan (T'an Ch'i-hsiang, 2:9).

[160]*Ssu-t'u* 司徒. Tung Yüeh 董説 (1620-1686) in his *Ch'i-kuo k'ao ting-pu* 七國考訂補 (2v.; Shanghai: Shang-hai Ku-chi, 1987) notes this position as established much earlier in Ch'u (1.73).

[161]*Ling-yin* 令尹.

Commander in Chief, Hsiang Yü as the Lieutenant Commander,[162] and Fan Tseng as Deputy Commander,[163] and moved northward to assist Chao. He ordered the Magistrate of P'ei to overrun territory to the west and enter the Pass. He made an agreement with the various generals that whoever entered and stabilized the Land within the Passes[164] would be enthroned as king of it.

Meanwhile, the Ch'in troops were mighty, often taking advantage of a victory to pursue the defeated, [so that] none of the [Ch'u] generals considered it advantageous to be first to enter the Pass. Only Hsiang Yü harbored resentment for Ch'in defeating Hsiang Liang's army; stirred with indignation, he was willing to go west and enter the Pass with the Magistrate of P'ei. All the elder generals of King Huai said, "Hsiang Yü is a man who is brazen and crafty. When Hsiang Yü attacked Hsiang-ch'eng, he left not one of any kind [alive], burying them all, so that every place he passed by was completely destroyed. Moreover, Ch'u has several times advanced and taken [territory]; but the former King of Ch'en and Hsiang Liang were both defeated. It would be better to change and send a man of inner strengths,[165] relying on his righteousness, to head west [*357*] and make a proclamation to the elders of Ch'in. The elders of Ch'in have suffered under their rulers for a long time. Now, if we can really have a man of inner strengths go there, without imposing violence, they should submit. Now, Hsiang Yü is brazen. Now, he cannot be sent.[166] Only the Magistrate of P'ei who has all along been a sincere, generous man of inner strengths can be sent." Finally, he did not give consent to Hsiang Yü and sent the Magistrate of P'ei west to overrun territory and collect the scattered foot soldiers of King of Ch'en and Hsiang Liang. The Magistrate of P'ei took to the road at Tang and reached Ch'eng-yang[167] and Kang-li 杠里.[168] The Ch'in army, by inserting barricades between them, defeated two armies of Wei. The Ch'u army sent forth troops to strike Wang Li and crushed him.[169]

The Magistrate of P'ei led his troops west, encountered P'eng Yüeh 彭越[170] at Ch'ang-yi

---

[162]*Tz'u-chiang* 次將.

[163]*Mo-chiang* 末將.

[164]According to "So-yin" (citing the *San-fu chiu-shih* 三輔舊事) the western boundary of the Land within the Passes was the San 散 Pass and the eastern the Han-ku 函谷 Pass *(Shih chi,* 8.356).

[165]On the meaning of *ch'ang-che* 長者, "a man of great inner strengths," see also Yoshihara Hideo 吉原 英夫, "*Shiki* ni mieru 'chôsha' ni tsuite" 史記に見える「長者」について, *Kamada Tadashi Hakushi Hachijûsu kinen Kanbungaku ronshû* 鎌田正博士八十寿記念漢文学論集 (Tokyo: Daishûkan Shoten, 1991), pp. 165-81.

[166]These three "nows" (all *chin* 今 in the original text) are troubling. According to Hsü Kuang ("Chi-chieh"), an edition he saw omitted the third *chin* in this passage (今不可遷). Mizusawa (p. 29) notes that three editions he saw omit the third *chin.* This would resolve much of the problem. The *Han shu* (1A.17) omits the entire phrase with the second *chin* (今項羽慓悍) and read 項羽不可遣 for 今不可遷. But Tanaka Kenji (p. 103, n. 6) believes that this passage may represent Ssu-ma Ch'ien's attempt to replicate the animated and somewhat stilted speech of these elder generals. We have followed Tanaka's reading in our translation.

[167]For Ch'eng 成 read Ch'eng 城.

[168]Ju Ch'un claims ("So-yin," *Shih chi,* 8.357) that Kang-li is the name of the place where the second Ch'in army camped. His argument is convincing, since although several commentators, including Chang Lieh (p. 7n.), would make Kang-li a county under Ch'in, they provide no source. There is no record of such a county

in T'an Ch'i-hsiang.

[169]There is a textual problem here. Some texts read: *Ch'in chün chia-pi, p'o Wei erh chün* 乃道碭, 至成陽 與杠里. 秦軍夾壁, 破魏二軍 (the punctuation is that by Ku and Hsü, 8.7 [157]), but the Chung-hua editors parse this passage as follows: 乃道碭至成陽, 與杠里秦軍夾壁, 破魏二軍. "The Magistrate of P'ei took to the road at Tang, reached Ch'eng-yang and set up his barricades facing those of the Ch'in army at Kang-li, defeating two armies of Wei." They also adopt Chang Wen-hu's suggestion (1.90) that Wei be read Ch'in 秦. Pan Ku seems to have been similarly puzzled and simplified the text considerably here *(Han shu,* 1A.17): "The Magistrate of P'ei then took to the road at Tang and reached Ch'eng-yang and Kang-li; he attacked the Ch'in army's fortifications and defeated its two armies" 乃道碭至城陽與杠里，攻秦軍壁，破其二軍. Both Wang Li-ch'i (8.200) and Wu and Lu (8.287) keep Chung-hua's parsing. Wang Li-ch'i (8.223) translates this sentence as follows: "The Magistrate of P'ei then went from Tang and reached Ch'eng-yang, built fortifications opposing the Ch'in army stationed at Kang-li, and attacked and defeated the two Ch'in forces." This reading is possible. Wu and Lu (8.313) have a similar rendering.

The Chung-hua alterations fit Chavannes' suspicion (2:344, n. 2) that the text was corrupt here. Chavannes points out that in the chronological tables Liu Pang defeated two Ch'in armies in the tenth month of the third year of the Second Emperor of Ch'in (25 November to 23 December 208 B.C.). This text reads "[Liu Pang] attacked and defeated the Commandant of Tung-chün and Wang Li's army to the south of Ch'eng-wu" 攻破東 郡尉及王離軍 (*Shih chi,* 16.769-70) which may indicate Liu Pang defeated two armies, but might also mean he defeated two generals of the same army. Moreover, it seems unlikely that these defeats could have involved Wang Li's troops, since in the following sentence we find the armies of Ch'u attacking him.

Chang Wen-hu's objection (p. 90) to Ch'in defeating Wei armies seems to be that by this time Chang Han had defeated Wei and moved against Chao. In the final month of 208 B.C., Chang Han ordered Wang Li to besiege the Chao army at Chü-lu, while he protected Wang Li's supply lines from the south *(Shih chi,* 7.304 and 16.769). The following month (the first of 207 B.C.), Chang Han moved against Han-tan 邯鄲 *(Shih chi,* 16.769-70—*Shih chi,* 89.2578-9 records Chang first taking Han-tan and then moving to Chü-lu), while Wang Li seems to have moved south across the Ho towards Ch'eng-wu 成武 (about thirty-five miles southeast of Ch'eng-yang). Between Ch'eng-wu and Ch'eng-yang Liu Pang attacked Wang Li, finally defeating him badly at Kang-li (*Shih chi,* 54.2023). Liu Pang had been sent to this area to pacify Wei territories *(Shih chi,* 57.2066). Thus, it seems quite possible that armies of three "states" were in the Kang-li region: that of Ch'in led by Wang Li, remnants of Wei's troops, and those of Ch'u led by Liu Pang. If this were the case, Wang Li could easily have defeated *two armies* of Wei, since they would have been rather ragtag by this point. Liu Pang, who was north of this battle in Ch'eng-yang, reversed direction and moved south to Kang-li, catching Wang Li and his troops fatigued after the battle with the two Wei armies and thus was able to crush them. This interpretation would eliminate the need to alter the text as the Chung-hua editors have done and seems as sound as the others that have been proposed in terms of what we know about the movement of the various armies at this time.

Regardless of the precise readings here, Hsiang Yü's defeat of the Army North of the River was perhaps the most important blow leading to the Ch'in collapse and probably enhanced Liu Pang's ability to move west into the Land within the Passes (see also Ho Ching's 郝敬 [1558-1639] comments from his *Shih Han yü-an* 史漢 愚按 as cited in Yang, *Li-tai,* p. 416).

昌邑,[171] and together with him attacked the Ch'in army, but they fought without gaining an advantage. They returned to Li 栗,[172] encountered the Marquis Kang-wu 剛武,[173] seized [*358*] his army of some four thousand men, and united them [the two armies]. They attacked Ch'ang-yi jointly with the armies of Huang Hsin 皇欣,[174] a Wei general and Wu P'u 武蒲,[175] the Wei Edifier of the Masses,[176] but Ch'ang-yi was not seized. Heading west they stopped by Kao-yang 高陽.[177] Li Yi-chi 酈食其[178] was the gatekeeper and said, "The generals who have passed by here are many, but I see that the Magistrate of P'ei is a great man of inner strengths." Then he requested to meet and offer advice to the Magistrate of P'ei.[179] The Magistrate of P'ei was just sitting with his legs apart on a couch, having two women wash his feet.[180] Master Li did not kneel and bow

[170]See his biography in *Shih chi* Chapter 90.

[171]About thirty miles southeast of Ch'eng-yang (thirty miles east of modern Ting-yao in Shantung; T'an Ch'i-hsiang, 2:19).

[172]About sixty miles east of Ch'ang-yi near modern Hsia-yi 夏邑 County in Honan (T'an Ch'i-hsiang, 2:7); it was only ten miles northwest of Tang, Liu Pang's point of departure, thus it was a "return."

[173]Although several theories have been proposed regarding his identity, they are all without foundation, as Yen Shih-ku argues (cited in "Cheng-yi," *Shih chi*, 8.358).

[174]I.e., Huang Hsin 皇訢 (see *Shih chi*, 16.770 and 19.987).

[175]Other than a reference on *Shih chi*, 16.770, probably based on this passage, he is unknown.

[176]Wang Li-ch'i (8.201n) equates this *Shen-t'u* 申徒 with the position of *Ssu-t'u* 司徒, probably based on Hsü Kuang's note ("Chi-chieh," *Shih chi*, 55.2036) equating Chang Liang's *Shen-t'u* position in the state of Hann with *Ssu-t'u*. There is no entry on *Shen-t'u* in Lu Zongli or Hucker. Tung Yüeh (*Ch'i-kuo k'ao ting-pu*, 1.143) also has no entry on *Shen-t'u*, but gives *Ssu-t'u* as a Wei position. Our translation is based on Wang Li-ch'i's supposition.

Han shu (1A.17) reads Wu Man 武滿 for Wu P'u, does not specify his rank as *Shen-t'u*, and has the joining of these three armies against Ch'in occurring before the attack on Ch'ang-yi.

[177]Nearly one-hundred miles southwest of Ch'ang-yi, a little over twenty miles southeast of the modern city of Kaifeng in Honan (T'an Ch'i-hsiang, 2:7).

[178]See his biography in *Shih chi* Chapter 97. In the account of this meeting there (97.2692-3), Li is much more abrupt in approaching Liu Pang, probably based on the version recorded in the *Ch'u Han ch'un-ch'iu* 楚漢春秋 (*Pai-pu ts'ung-shu chi-ch'eng* 百部叢書集成 ed., 2a). Although his advice is sound here, Li is shown to be a less effective counselor in *Shih chi* Chapter 55.

[179]According to *Shih chi*, 97.2691-2, he spoke (at somewhat greater length in that passage) to one of Liu Pang's horsemen before he went to see Liu himself.

[180]Although it is normal behavior for a host surprised by a guest to straighten his clothing in respect, there seems to be either a motif in Ssu-ma Ch'ien's bag of narrative devices or a commonplace in Liu Pang's life-style, since Liu Pang received Ch'ing Pu 黥布 in a very similar fashion when the latter defected from Hsiang Yü (see *Shih chi*, 91.2602). Yet another display of a host who fails to recognize the worthiness of his guest and receives him with nonchalance can be found in the account of Yen Ying 晏嬰 and Father Yüeh-shih 越石父, *Shih chi*, 62.2135 (*Grand Scribe's Records*, 7:15). Tanaka Kenji (p. 105, n. 6) offers the interesting suggestion that this behavior may have been Liu Pang's way of testing a man's reaction to see if he could be a

his head, but bowed low and said, "Honorable Sir, if you indeed want to punish immoral Ch'in, it is not fitting to receive a man of inner strengths while seated." At this the Magistrate of P'ei stood up, straightened his clothing, apologized to him, and invited him to take the seat of honor. Yi-chi advised the Magistrate of P'ei to launch a surprise attack on Ch'en-liu 陳留[181] to obtain Ch'in's stored grain.[182] Then he made Li Yi-chi the Lord of Kuang-yeh 廣野[183] and made Li Shang 酈商[184] a general to command the Ch'en-liu troops, and, together with them, attacked K'ai-feng 開封;[185] K'ai-feng was not seized. They moved west and gave the Ch'in general Yang Hsiung 楊熊 battle at Pai-ma 白馬,[186] fighting again east of Ch'ü-yü 曲遇,[187] and crushed him. Yang Hsiung having run to Hsing-yang 滎陽,[188] the Second Emperor sent an envoy to have him executed and [the body] shown [to his troops] as a warning. The Magistrate of P'ei moved south, attacked Ying-yang 穎陽,[189] and put it to the sword. Relying on Chang Liang 張良,[190] he

loyal follower.

[181] About ten miles northwest of Kao-yang (T'an Ch'i-hsiang, 2:7).

[182] According to *Shih chi,* 7.303, Hsiang Yü and Liu Pang attacked Ch'en-liu together; there is no mention of a granary or grain-storage facility at Ch'en-liu, however. According to the parallel passage in *Ch'u Han ch'un-ch'iu* (*op. cit.,* 2a), after he was informed that a "great scholar" (*ta ju* 大儒) was waiting to see him, Liu Pang originally refused to see Li Yi-chi, provoking the latter to burst in an proclaim himself "a drinker from Kao-yang, not a great scholar!" 高陽酒徒非大儒也. For a detailed account of Master Li's first meeting with Liu Pang and his efforts to take Ch'en-liu, see *Shih chi,* 97.2692-93.

[183] Literally, "Lord of the Vast Wilds."

[184] Li Yi-chi's younger brother.

[185] About ten miles southwest of modern Kaifeng, equidistant northwest of Kao-yang (T'an Ch'i-hsiang, 2:7).

[186] T'an Ch'i-hsiang (2:7) and Wang Li-ch'i (8.201n.) concur that Pai-ma was a county near modern Hua 滑 County in northeast Honan, but this is seventy miles northeast of K'ai-feng and Liu Pang was moving steadily west at this time. Moreover, *Shih chi,* 54.2023 locates the battle at Ch'ü-yü (twelve miles northwest of Kaifeng). Thus Pai-ma is either a textual error here or it refers to a different place. These encounters took place in the third month *(Shih chi,* 16.771).

[187] About ten miles northwest of the Han K'ai-feng (T'an Ch'i-hsiang, 2:7).

[188] About forty miles west of Ch'ü-yü near the modern city of the same name (T'an Ch'i-hsiang, 2:7).

[189] Some sixty miles south of Ying-yang, a few miles west of modern Hsü-ch'ang 許昌 City in Honan (T'an Ch'i-hsiang, 2:7).

[190] Chang Liang and his troops joined Liu Pang as the latter was on his way to Huan-yüan (see also the section of Chang Liang's biography on *Shih chi,* 55.2036-7). Liu Pang employed Chang Liang here because the Chang family has served as chancellors of Hann for generations (see "Chi-chieh") and because he was the Minister of Education (*Ssu-t'u* 司徒) of the newly established King of Hann at this time (*Shih chi,* 55.2036). On Chang Liang's role under Liu Pang in general see Yoshinami Takashi 好並隆司, "Sen Kan Kôso ki ni okeru Chô Ryô no ichi" 前漢高祖期における張良の位置, *Okayama Joshi Tanki Daigaku kenkyû kiyô* 岡山女子短

then overran Huan-yüan 轘轅[191] in Han territory.

[359] Meanwhile, the Chao Deputy General Ssu-ma Ang 司馬卬[192] was on the point of crossing the Ho to enter the Pass; the Magistrate of P'ei then moved north to attack P'ing-yin 平陰[193] and block the ford across the Ho.[194] Moving south, he fought east of Lo-yang; his army gaining no advantage, he returned to Yang-ch'eng 陽城;[195] gathering together the horsemen in his army, he gave battle to [Lü] Yi 呂齮,[196] Governor of Nan-yang 南陽 [Commandery],[197] east of Ch'ou 犨[198] and defeated him.[199] When he overran Nan-yang Commandery, [Lü] Yi, the Governor of Nan-yang, fled. He took refuge within the city walls and guarded Yüan 宛.[200] The Magistrate of P'ei led his troops past and on to the west. Chang Liang admonished him saying, "Although the Magistrate of P'ei intends to hurry into the Pass,[201] the Ch'in troops are still many and they will resist from redoubts. If you do not cause Yüan to submit, Yüan will strike you from behind, and with mighty Ch'in in front, this will become a precarious way!" At this, the Magistrate of P'ei led his troops by night, following another way back, changed his flags and pennons, and in the predawn surrounded the city walls of Yüan with several rings [of soldiers].[202] The Governor of Nan-yang wanted to cut his own throat. His retainer Ch'en Hui 陳恢 said, "It is still early for dying."

Then he climbed over the wall and went to see the Magistrate of P'ei, saying, "Your subject has heard that you, Honorable Sir, have an agreement that whoever first enters Hsien-yang

---

期大学研究紀要, 19 (1996): 1-16.

[191]A strategic mountain and pass located fifty-five miles northwest of Ying-yang about fifteen miles southwest of modern Loyang on the western edge of Mount Kao 高 (T'an Ch'i-hsiang, 2:7).

[192]Hsiang Yü later made him King of Yin 殷 *(Shih chi,* 8.365).

[193]A county fifteen miles northwest of Loyang near modern Meng-chin 孟津 County (T'an Ch'i-hsiang, 2:7).

[194]In the fourth month *(Shih chi,* 16.771).

[195]Southwest about thirty-five miles from Loyang (T'an Ch'i-hsiang, 2:7).

[196]His surname is added based on the account given in the *Han chi* (1.11a; see also Wang Li-ch'i, 8.201n.).

[197]A commandery straddling the border between modern Honan and Hupei provinces centered near the modern city of Nan-yang (T'an Ch'i-hsiang, 2:7).

[198]A border-town between Ying-ch'uan 潁川 and Nan-yang commanderies, near modern P'ing-ting Shan 平頂山 City and about fifty miles south of Yang-ch'eng (T'an Ch'i-hsiang, 2:7).

[199]In the sixth month *(Shih chi,* 16.771).

[200]The seat of the commandery, about sixty miles southwest of Ch'ou, near the modern city of Nan-yang in Honan (T'an Ch'i-hsiang, 2:7). On the pronunciation of 宛 as Yüan here, see "Cheng-yi."

[201]Wu 武 Pass was about 100 miles northwest of Yüan (T'an Ch'i-hsiang, 2:7) and 125 miles from the Ch'in capital Hsien-yang.

[202]A slightly different version of this siege and surrender (in which the flags were "hidden," *ni* 匿, rather than changed, *keng* 更, appears in the *Ch'u Han ch'un-ch'iu, op. cit.,* 2a). *Han shu* (1A.19) has a similar reading, *yen* 偃, "let his flags drop."

咸陽[203] will be made king there. Now you, Sir, tarry to deal with Yüan. Yüan is the capital of a great commandery. It joins several dozen walled cities together, its populace is large, its provisions plentiful, its officers themselves [*360*] believe that to surrender would mean certain death; for this reason they have all climbed the city walls to put up a resolute defense. Honorable Sir, if you wait here all day long to attack [Yüan],[204] those of your warriors who die or suffer injury will be numerous. If you lead your troops away from Yüan, Yüan will pursue you. Honorable Sir, in what lies ahead, you will lose the agreement over Hsien-yang, in what lies behind, you will have the trouble of mighty Yüan. If I were laying plans for you, Sir, nothing would be better than to work out an agreement for surrender, enfeoff this governor, order him to stay and guard Yüan, and you lead his armored foot soldiers with yours to the west. All the walled cities which have not yet submitted, when they hear the news, will compete in opening their gates and await you, allowing you to pass through [Nan-yang] with nothing to trouble you." The Magistrate of P'ei said, "Well put!"

Then he made the Governor of Yüan the Marquis of Yin 殷[205] and enfeoffed Ch'en Hui with one thousand households. When he led his troops west, there was none which did not submit. When he reached Tan-shui 丹水,[206] [Ch'i] Sai 戚鰓,[207] the Marquis Kao-wu 高武, and Wang Ling 王陵 (d. 181 B.C.),[208] the Marquis of Hsiang 襄,[209] surrendered at Hsi-ling 西陵.[210] He

---

[203]The Ch'in capital located on the north bank of the Wei 渭 River about ten miles northwest of modern Sian (T'an Ch'i-hsiang, 2:5).

[204]On reading *chih* 止 here as "to wait" see Chang Chia-ying (pp. 163-64). An alternate parsing of this passage has been proposed by Wu Ching-jung 吳靜容 in his "Chung-hua Shu-chü pen *Shih chi* piao-tien shang-ch'üeh" 中華書局本史記標點商榷, *Shen-yang Shih-fan Hsüeh-yüan, She-hui k'o-hsüeh hsüeh-pao* 沈楊師範學院學報, 1984.2: 55 [53-56]): 今足下盡日止，攻，士死者必多. A translation based on Wu's reading would then read: "Honorable Sir, if you stop here all day long, [then] attack [Wan],[204] those of your warriors who die or suffer injury will be numerous."

[205]Although none of the usual Chinese commentaries or sources provide a location for Yin, Chavannes (2.350 n.1) says it was a prefecture near modern Nei-huang 內黃 County about fifteen miles southeast of modern An-yang in Honan. This fits Wei Chao's 韋昭 comments in "So-yin" that it is located in Ho-nei 河內.

[206]A county about seventy miles west of Nan-yang on the north side of the Tan River. Following this river valley to the northwest led one to Wu Pass and was a major route to the "land within the Passes" and the Ch'in capital, Hsien-yang.

[207]See *Shih chi*, 18.959.

[208]See *Shih chi*, 56.2059-60.

[209]As Liang Yü-sheng argues (6.219), Hsiang 襄 is probably an error for Jang 穰; Jang County is near Wang Ling's long-time base in Nan-yang 南陽 (see *Shih chi*, 56.2059-60 and T'an Ch'i-hsiang, 2:7).

[210]As Wang Li-ch'i (8.202n.) points out, the place normally called Hsi-ling is located in modern Hupei near Yi-ch'ang 宜昌, about 170 miles south of Tan-shui. It is, therefore, not a probable match for this place and situation. Partly because the *Han shu* omits this place name entirely in its parallel account, traditional scholars

returned and attacked Hu-yang 胡陽,[211] encountered Mei Hsüan 梅鋗,[212] the Lord of P'o's 番[213] Deputy General, and with them he caused Hsi 析 and Li 酈 to surrender.[214] He sent Ning Ch'ang 甯昌,[215] a native of Wei, as an envoy to Ch'in, but the one he sent did not return.[216] At this time, Chang Han had already surrendered his army to Hsiang Yü at Chao.[217]

[361] Earlier, Hsiang Yü and Sung Yi 宋義 had gone north to Chao's assistance; when Hsiang Yü killed Sung Yi, he replaced him as Commander in Chief; all the generals and Ch'ing Pu 黥布[218] put their troops under him. He defeated the army of the Ch'in general, Wang Li, caused Chang Han to surrender, and the feudal lords all attached themselves to him.[219] When Chao Kao 趙高[220] had already killed the Second Emperor, an envoy came, intending to reach agreement on dividing the Land within the Passes into kingdoms.[221] The Magistrate of P'ei considered it deception, thus he employed a plan of Chang Liang,[222] sent Master Li [Yi-chi] and Lu Chia 陸賈[223] to go and speak to the Ch'in general and, enticing him with gain, took advantage of this to launch a surprise attack on Wu 武 Pass[224] and defeat him.[225] He also gave the Ch'in

(such as Nakai Riken 中井履軒 [1732-1817; see Takigawa, 8.161c]) have also argued that Hsi-ling is an interpolation. None of the editions Mizusawa records (p. 35) omit this place name, however. Fukushima (p. 407, n. 95) notes that some Japanese scholars have tried to read *chiang* 降 here as a transitive verb, "Ch'i Sai and Wang Ling surrendered Hsi-ling" to Liu Pang, but this interpretation again fails to resolve the problem of the great distance between Hsi-ling and Tan-shui.

[211]A county forty miles south-southeast of Yüan (T'an Ch'i-hsiang, 2:7).

[212]The Lord P'o's commander, see also *Shih chi*, 7.317 and *Grand Scribe's Records*, 1:196.

[213]Wu Jui 吳芮, see *Shih chi*, 7.316 and *Grand Scribe's Records*, 1:195, n. 155.

[214]Hsi is a county about twenty-five miles northwest of Tan-shui, Li is located seventy miles east, only about fifteen miles from Yüan! (T'an Ch'i-hsiang, 2:7). Since Hu-yang, Hsi and Li are all located some distance east of Tan-shui, it is likely that Liu Pang dispatched some of his generals to attend to these encounters.

[215]Otherwise unknown.

[216]Some scholars, because of *wei* 未 "have not yet," try to link this sentence and the next, but we read the *wei* here as a simple negative (we have seen it used this way already above).

[217]See *Shih chi*, 7.309.

[218]See his biography in *Shih chi* Chapter 91.

[219]See *Shih chi*, 7.307ff.

[220]The infamous eunuch who helped to bring down the Ch'in, see also *Grand Scribe's Records*, 1:154, n. 294.

[221]One for Ch'in and one for Liu Pang.

[222]On the details of this plan see *Shih chi*, 55.2040-41.

[223]One of Liu Pang's advisors, see his biography, together with that of Master Li, in *Shih chi* Chapter 97.

[224]Located further up the Tan River Valley thirty-five miles northwest of Tan-shui just across the border of modern Shensi (T'an Ch'i-hsiang, 2:7).

[225]Liang Yü-sheng (6.220) points to several errors in this account. According to *Shih chi*, 16.773, a victory at Wu Pass took place in the eighth month of the third year of the Second Emperor (207 B.C.), about the same

armies battle south of Lan-t'ien 藍田,[226] increased the flags and banners of the decoy troops, and did not plunder any of the places he passed. The people of Ch'in were pleased. The army of Ch'in was relaxed. Taking advantage of this, he greatly defeated them. Once again he fought to its [Lan-t'ien's] north, greatly defeating them. Availing himself of this victory, he pursued and defeated them [again].[227]

[362] In the tenth month of the first year of Han (14 November–12 December 207 B.C.),[228] the troops of the Magistrate of P'ei were in the end the first among the feudal lords to

time that Chao Kao murdered the Second Emperor and Tzu Ying became king. The following month, Liu Pang also took Yao 嶢 Pass (about eighty miles northwest of Wu Pass, fifty miles southeast of Hsien-yang on the upper reaches of the Pa 灞 River in Shensi [T'an Ch'i-hsiang, 2:6]) and Lan-t'ien by means of Chang Liang's plan. This plan involved first making a demonstration of force before the Ch'in army camped at the foot of Yao Pass, then bribing the commanding general. This bribe having been accepted, Chang Liang then urged Liu Pang to attack the "relaxed" Ch'in army, routing them twice and finally forcing the final Ch'in surrender (see also *Shih chi*, 55.2037). Thus Liang Yü-sheng believes that the text should read Yao instead of Wu here. Liang also argues that the mention of Lu Chia seems to be an interpolation here.

[226]A county about twenty-five miles southeast of the Ch'in capital, Hsien-yang, and about fifteen miles southeast of modern Sian (T'an Ch'i-hsiang, 2:6).

[227]Tanaka Kenji (pp. 110-11, n. 7) points out that the repetition in the last lines of this paragraph, especially the thrice repeated verb *p'o* 破, "to defeat" or, in *ta p'o* 大破, "to crush" or "to greatly defeat," suggests both the urgency and the violent power of Liu Pang's troops at this point in the campaign. Tanaka also points out that this rhetorical effect is lost entirely in the *Han shu* (1A.22) rendition of these events.

[228]The dating throughout this second volume follows that in Hsü Hsi-ch'i 徐錫祺, *Hsi Chou (Kung-ho) chih Hsi Han li-p'u* 西周 (共和) 至西漢歷譜, 2v. (Peking: Pei-ching K'o-hsüeh Chi-shu Ch'u-pan-she 北京科學技術出版社, 1997). Hsü's dating is the result of the most recent calendric studies and differs slightly from that used by Chavannes.

The Han adopted the Ch'in calendar, thus the tenth month was the first month of the year until the calendar was changed in 104 B.C. As Derk Bodde, *Festivals,* p. 146, notes, the adoption of the Ch'in calendar may have resulted from the fact that the House of Ch'in submitted to the King of Han in the tenth month of 207 B.C., making the this a logical time to start the new year. See also "The Han Dynasty's Earlier Calendar," in Dubs, 1.154-60

Elsewhere in the *Shih chi* Ssu-ma Ch'ien has a Master Kan 甘 report that the five planets converged at this time (*Shih chi*, 89.2581); since such a conjunction of planets was an indication that a new regime had received the mandate of heaven (although as Michael Loewe has pointed out, the concept of *t'ien-ming* 天命 is one which develops somewhat later; see "The Conjunction of the Five Planets in *Tung-ching,*" in Dubs, 1.151-53), it seems strange that there is no mention of it here. The accounts in both *Han shu* (1A.22) and *Han chi* (2.1a) record it. But as David Pankenier points out, this gathering of planets in Gemini actually took place in May 205 B.C. and was "misdated in the standard *History of the Han Dynasty* to coincide with the nominal founding of the dynasty in 206 B.C." ("Astrological Origins of Chinese Dynastic Ideology," *Vistas in Astronomy,* 39 [1995], p. 511). Thus Ssu-ma Ch'ien's failure to note the conjunction here in his account of Kao-tsu, his

reach Pa-shang 霸上 (Pa Heights).[229] The Ch'in king,[230] Tzu Ying 子嬰 (d. 206 B.C.), came riding in a white chariot harnessed with white horses, a cord tied around his neck, and holding the seals, tallies and caducei of the august emperor, to surrender near the Chih 軹 Road pavilion.[231] Among the generals some spoke of executing the King of Ch'in.[232] The Magistrate of P'ei said, "When King Huai first sent me, he originally considered that I would be able to be lenient; moreover, the man has already submitted in surrender; to go further and kill him would bring bad luck." Then he entrusted the King of Ch'in to his officers[233] and finally headed west to enter Hsien-yang. He intended to stop and rest in the palaces, [but] Fan K'uai and Chang Liang admonished him, and he sealed up the storehouses of treasure and wealth and returned to camp at Pa-shang. He summoned all the elders and prominent men from the [local] counties and said, "You elders have long suffered under Ch'in's harsh laws. Those who criticized [the government] were exterminated with their three kindred.[234] Those who gathered to discuss [the *Shih* (*Songs*) and *Shu* (*Documents*)],[235] were executed and had their bodies exposed in the marketplace. I should be the King of the Land within the Passes, since I have agreed with the feudal lords that whoever enters the Pass first should rule over it as king. I will come to an agreement[236] with you elders that there will be a legal code with only three articles: those who kill a person must die, those who injure a person and steal will be punished according to the offense. I will do away

indirect presentation of the event on *Shih chi*, 89.2581, and the rather casual notice that "after Han rose, the Five Planets conversed at Tung-ching" in the "T'ien-kuan shu" 天官書 (*Shih chi*, 27.1348) may reflect Ssu-ma Ch'ien's awareness that this astronomical sign was somewhat "untimely."

[229]An elevated plain just west of the Pa River which stretched west to Hsien-yang. Because it was the last line of defense against the troops that had arrived from the southeast, it was an important strategic point (T'an Ch'i-hsiang, 2:6 and Wang Li-ch'i, 8.202n.).

[230]Chao Kao maligned Ch'in's adoption of the title "emperor" after he killed the Second Emperor; when he enthroned Tzu Ying, the son of the Second Emperor's brother, he attempted to placate the other kings of the Six States by titling Tzu Ying as "King of Ch'in" (see *Shih chi*, 6.275 and *Grand Scribe's Records*, 1:162).

[231]For an almost identical description of Tzu Ying's surrender, and several explanatory notes, see *Grand Scribe's Records*, 1:162-63.

[232]*Ch'u Han ch'un-ch'iu* 楚漢春秋 (*op. cit.*, 2b) reads: "Fan K'uai asked to kill him" 樊噲請殺之.

[233]I.e., put him under arrest; cf. the use of *shu li* 屬吏 on *Shih chi*, 87.2551. Tzu Ying was subsequently killed by Hsiang Yü after he arrived in Hsien-yang about a month later (*Shih chi*, 6.275).

[234]This severe punishment, in which the relatives of the convicted person's father, mother and wife were all killed with him ("three kindred") was begun by Ch'in in 739 B.C. (see *Shih chi*, 5.179, *Grand Scribe's Records*, 1:91, and n. 46 on 1:91; see also A. F. P. Hulsewé, *Remnants of Han Law* [Leiden: Brill, 1955], pp. 112f.).

[235]Cf. Li Ssu's speech to the First Emperor, *Shih chi*, 6.255 and *Grand Scribe's Records*, 1:147.

[236]"Cheng-yi" (as cited in Takigawa, 8.35) says the word *yüeh* 約 here means "to reduce"; thus the line could also be parsed without the break to read: "I shall reduce the laws to three articles for you elders." Wang Shu-min (10.316) favors this reading as does Hulsewé (*Remnants of Han Law*, pp. 368-72).

with all the rest of Ch'in's laws.[237] All the officers and people will live in peace as before.[238] Do not be afraid—I have come to do away with that which causes you elders harm, not to impose tyranny! The reason I have returned my army to Pa-shang is to await the arrival of the feudal lords and to reach a decision on the agreement." Then he sent men together with the Ch'in government officers to make rounds of inspection in the counties, districts and towns, and proclaim these things. The people of Ch'in were greatly pleased and strove to bring oxen, sheep, wine, and food to feast the officers in his army. The Magistrate of P'ei refused to accept them, saying, "The grain in the granaries is plentiful, there is nothing we lack and I do not want to cause the people expense." The people were even more pleased and only feared that the Magistrate of P'ei would not become King of Ch'in.

[364] Someone[239] advised the Magistrate of P'ei, saying, "Ch'in is richer by tenfold than the rest of the world and its topography makes it mighty. Now I have heard that Chang Han has surrendered to Hsiang Yü and Hsiang Yü titled him King of Yung 雍,[240] making him King of the Land within the Passes. If he comes, the Magistrate of P'ei, I fear, will not be able to possess this place.[241] You should quickly send troops to defend Han-ku 函谷 (Contained Valley) Pass[242] and not allow the armies of the feudal lords to enter, while gradually levying troops from within the Passes to increase your own and resist them." The Magistrate of P'ei agreed with his plan and followed it.

In the middle of the eleventh month (13 December 207–11 January 206 B.C.),[243] Hsiang Yü as expected led the troops of the feudal lords west, intending to enter the Pass, but the gates to the Pass were closed. When he heard that the Magistrate of P'ei had already stabilized the Land within the Passes, he was enraged and sent Ch'ing Pu and others to attack and break

---

[237]Liang Yü-sheng notes (6.220) that a number of the more harsh of the Ch'in laws were not rescinded until years later under later emperors. For a more detailed study, see Chang Wei-hua 張維華, "Lun Hsi Han ch'u-nien tui-yü hsing-lü te hsiu-cheng" 論西漢初年對於刑律的修正, Wen-shih-che, 1982.5: 12-18, esp. p. 14.

[238]On reading an tu 案堵 as an chü 安居 see Chang Chia-ying (pp. 164-65) and the translation in Wu and Lu (8.314).

[239]According to the Ch'u Han ch'un-ch'iu (cited in "So-yin") this was a Master Hsieh 解. Shih chi, 7.311 says it was Tsou-sheng 鄹生 which we interpreted as "a mean fellow" (Grand Scribe's Records, 1:191).

[240]Yung was the traditional name for the area about modern Feng-hsiang 鳳翔 in Shensi (cf. Grand Scribe's Records, 1:93, n. 71, and T'an Ch'i-hsiang, 2:6).

[241]Not only because he was appointed by Hsiang Yü, but also because he was a native of Ch'in whose behavior had not antagonized the Ch'in people.

[242]Northeast of Ling-pao 靈寶 County on the border between modern Honan and Shensi about 120 miles east of Sian (T'an Ch'i-hsiang, 2:6).

[243]Liang Yü-sheng (6.220-21) argues that according to the chronological tables (Shih chi, 16.774-75) Liu Pang issued his three articles of law in the eleventh month, but since Hsiang Yü led his troops west only in the twelfth month, this seems unlikely.

through Han-ku Pass.[244] In the middle of the twelfth month (12 January–10 February 206 B.C.), he finally reached Hsi. The Left Marshal of the Magistrate of P'ei, Ts'ao Wu-shang 曹無傷,[245] heard that Hsiang Yü was angry and intended to attack the Magistrate of P'ei; he sent a man to say to Hsiang Yü, "The Magistrate of P'ei intended to be King of the Land within the Passes, to make Tzu Ying his prime minister, and as for the precious treasures, he will take possession of them all." He wanted through this to seek a fief [from Hsiang Yü]. Ya-fu 亞父[246] urged Hsiang Yü to launch an attack on the Magistrate of P'ei. Then he feasted his officers, [intending] to join battle when the next day dawned. At this time Hsiang Yü's troops numbered 400,000, but [Hsiang Yü] claimed them to be "a million." The Magistrate of P'ei's troops numbered 100,000, but [the Magistrate] claimed them to be "the 200,000"—not enough to match him. It happened that Hsiang Po 項伯,[247] intending to keep Chang Liang alive, went to see him that night, and the Magistrate of P'ei took the opportunity to clarify things in writing for Hsiang Yü[248]; Hsiang Yü then desisted. The Magistrate of P'ei, followed by more than one hundred horsemen, hastened to Hung-men 鴻門 (Goose Gate)[249] to see Hsiang Yü and apologize. Hsiang Yü said, "This is what Ts'ao Wu-shang, the Left Marshal of the Magistrate of P'ei, told me. Were it not so, how could I have come up with this [idea]?" The Magistrate of P'ei, because of Fan K'uai and Chang Liang, was able to get away and return [to his camp].[250] After he returned, he immediately had Ts'ao Wu-shang executed.[251]

[244] According to the *Ch'u Han ch'un-ch'iu* (*op. cit.*, 2b) it was Fan Tseng (see n. 246 below) who arrived at the Han-ku Pass and when he was not allowed to enter, realized that Liu Pang was in rebellion. He then threatened to burn down the gate and the gate was opened.

[245] See n. 110 above.

[246] Fan Tseng 范增 whom Hsiang Yü called "Second Father" (Ya-fu) to express his close feelings for him (see also *Grand Scribe's Records*, 1:191-2 and n. 125 on p. 192).

[247] Hsiang Yü's uncle (*praenomen* Ch'an 纏) who later was enfeoffed under the Han (see *Shih chi*, 7.311, n. 118 in *Grand Scribe's Records*, 1:190, and *Shih chi*, 7.338). He was indebted to Chang Liang for hiding him after he had killed a man when they were both knights-errant in Hsia P'ei (see *Shih chi*, 55.2036). He also protected Liu Pang from Hsiang Chuang 項莊 when Chuang tried to kill the King of Han at Hung-men (cf. *Shih chi*, 7.312-13).

[248] According to the parallel passage in *Shih chi*, 7.312, there is no mention of any written document; there we read Liu Pang explained things to Hsiang Po who then reported (*pao* 報, presumably orally) to Hsiang Yü.

[249] See *Grand Scribe's Records*, 1:164, n. 372.

[250] The famous (and extremely detailed) account of this meeting at Hung-men can be found on *Shih chi*, 7.312-4; *Grand Scribe's Records*, 1:191-3). There is a passage in *Ch'u Han ch'un-ch'iu* (*op. cit.*, 3a) which parallels the account in "The Basic Annals of Hsiang Yü" in which Fan Tseng reports on the emanations his spies have observed surrounding the King of Han and urges Hsiang Yü to allow him to kill the king. The *Ch'u Han ch'un-ch'iu* version varies in details, but tells essentially the same story about how Hsiang Yü is reluctant to have Liu Pang killed; Fan K'uai eventually shields Liu Pang from Fan Tseng allowing him to escape.

[251] According to the *Ch'u Han ch'un-ch'iu* (*op. cit.*, 3b), after Liu Pang escaped from Hung-men, he sent Chang Liang and Han Hsin, the Marquis of Huai-yin, to pay a formal visit to Hsiang Yü. They presented him

[365] Hsiang Yü then moved west, putting Hsien-yang and all the Ch'in palaces to the sword and the torch, so that wherever he passed there was nothing which was not destroyed. Though the people of Ch'in had lost hope, they still feared him and did not dare to resist Hsiang Yü sent a man to return and report to King Huai. King Huai said, "It should be as agreed." Hsiang Yü harbored resentment for King Huai because he was not willing to allow him to go west into the Pass together with the Magistrate of P'ei, but caused him to go north to Chao's assistance, thereby leaving him behind in the agreement [as to whom] would rule the world. Thus he said, "This King Huai was merely enthroned by my family's Hsiang Liang and has won no merit on campaign. How can he be able to act as master of the agreement? Those who originally stabilized the world are the various generals and I." He then feigned respect by making King Huai "Yi-ti" 義帝 (The Righteous Emperor or Emperor Yi),[252] but did not actually employ his orders.

In the first month (11 February–11 March 206 B.C.),[253] Hsiang Yü enthroned himself as the Hegemon-King of Western Ch'u 西楚霸王, ruling the nine commanderies of [former] Liang and Ch'u[254] with his capital at P'eng-ch'eng. Turning his back on the agreement, he changed the investment of the Magistrate of P'ei to King of Han 漢,[255] ruling Pa 巴, Shu 蜀, and Han-chung 漢中[256] with his capital at Nan-Cheng 南鄭.[257] He divided the Land within the Passes into three parts, enthroning three Ch'in generals: Chang Han became the King of Yung, with his capital at Fei-ch'iu 廢丘,[258] Ssu-ma Hsin 司馬欣[259] became King of Sai 塞,[260] with his capital at Yüeh-yang

with a jade disc and a jade dipper. Fan Tseng, in his anger, took the dipper and smashed it on the ground, breaking it.

[252]Wang Li-ch'i (8.203n.) records the two arguments that have been presented to explain Yi here as "false" or "famous"; the former is in all likelihood merely an extension of the *Shih chi* text which tells us that Hsiang Yü was only feigning respect. If the term were read in its normal sense as "Righteous" or something close to this, it could still be understood ironically. See also *Grand Scribe's Records*, 1:194, n. 139.

[253]Literally *cheng-yüeh* 正月, "prime month" or "first month." There is a problem with the calendar here. As we have seen just above (n. 228), the tenth month remained the "prime month" under the early Han.

[254]After a lengthy consideration of the various sources (pp. 166-170), Chang Chia-ying concludes that the nine commanderies were Tung-hai 東海, K'uai-chi 會稽, Ssu-shui 泗水, Hsüeh-chün 薛郡, Tung-chün 東郡, Tang-chün 碭郡, Ying-ch'uan 潁川, Ch'en-chün 陳郡, and Nan-yang 南陽.

[255]A parallel, but more detailed, account of whom, how, and why these generals were enfeoffed is found on *Shih chi*, 7.316 (see also *Grand Scribe's Records*, 1:194-96).

[256]Shu, Pa and Han-chung approximated the Ch'in commanderies of the same names (T'an Ch'i-hsiang, 2:11).

[257]Near modern Han-chung City in southwest Shensi (T'an Ch'i-hsiang, 2:5). Although it is not that distant from Sian, Han-chung is cut off from the Wei River Valley by the Ch'in-ling 秦嶺 Mountains.

[258]About thirty miles west of modern Sian on the north bank of the Wei River (T'an Ch'i-hsiang, 2:6).

[259]Chang Han was one of the major Ch'in generals; on his activities to put down the rebellions against

櫟陽;²⁶¹ Tung Yi 董翳²⁶² became King of Ti 翟, with his capital at Kao-nu 高奴.²⁶³ The Ch'u general Shen Yang 申陽 of Hsia-ch'iu 瑕丘²⁶⁴ became King of Ho-nan 河南,²⁶⁵ with his capital at Lo-yang. The Chao general Ssu-ma Ang became King of Yin 殷, with his capital at Chao-ko 朝歌.²⁶⁶ Chao Hsieh 趙歇,²⁶⁷ King of Chao, was moved to rule Tai 代. The Prime Minister of Chao, Chang Erh 張耳,²⁶⁸ became the King of Ch'ang-shan 常山,²⁶⁹ with his capital at Hsiang-kuo 襄國.²⁷⁰ The Lord of Tang-yang 當陽,²⁷¹ Ch'ing Pu, became the King of Chiu-chiang 九江,²⁷² with his capital at Liu 六.²⁷³ Kung Ao 共敖,²⁷⁴ the Pillar of State²⁷⁵ under King Huai, became King of Lin-Chiang 臨江, with his capital at Chiang-ling 江陵.²⁷⁶ Wu Jui 吳芮, the Lord of P'o, became King of Heng-shan 衡山,²⁷⁷ with his capital at Chu 邾.²⁷⁸ The Yen general **[*366*]** Tsang T'u 臧

Ch'in see *Shih chi*, 6.270 and Chapters 7 and 8, *passim.*

²⁶⁰See *Grand Scribe's Records*, 1:195, n. 143.

²⁶¹About thirty-five miles northeast of modern Sian (T'an Ch'i-hsiang, 2:6). Yüeh-yang had become the Ch'in capital in 383 B.C. (see *Shih chi*, 5.201); it was replaced by Hsien-yang in 350 B.C. (*Shih chi*, 5.203).

²⁶²On *Shih chi*, 7.316 it is explained that Ssu-ma Hsin was enthroned because he had dropped a legal case involving Hsiang Liang when he (Hsin) had been Warden of Yüeh-yang (*Shih chi*, 7.296).

²⁶³Just north of modern Yen-an in Shensi (T'an Ch'i-hsiang, 2:6).

²⁶⁴See *Grand Scribe's Records*, 1:195, n. 145.

²⁶⁵See *Grand Scribe's Records*, 1:78, n. 243.

²⁶⁶On the north bank of the Yellow River near modern Ch'i 淇 County in Hopei (T'an Ch'i-hsiang, 2:6).

²⁶⁷On *Shih chi*, 7.316 we read that Tung Yi was enthroned because it was he who first urged Chang Han to surrender.

²⁶⁸See his biography in *Shih chi* Chapter 89.

²⁶⁹This state seems to have been based on the Ch'in commandery of the same name (T'an Ch'i-hsiang, 2:9).

²⁷⁰The Han-dynasty name of the county Ch'in called Hsin-tu 信都, near modern Hsing-t'ai 邢台 City in Hopei (T'an Ch'i-hsiang, 2:6).

²⁷¹The name may be associated with the Han county of the same name located a few miles south of Ching-men 荊門 City in Hupei (T'an Ch'i-hsiang, 2:22).

²⁷²Probably approximating the size and location of the Ch'in commandery of that name (T'an Ch'i-hsiang, 2:12).

²⁷³North of Lu-an 六安 County in modern Anhwei (T'an Ch'i-hsiang, 2:12).

²⁷⁴Some of his previous accomplishments are recounted on *Shih chi*, 7.316; he ruled Lin-Chiang for thirty-one years until his death in 176 B.C. *(Shih chi, 16.791).*

²⁷⁵*Chu-kuo* 柱國.

²⁷⁶Near the modern city of the same name in Hupei (T'an Ch'i-hsiang, 2:22).

²⁷⁷Approximating the Ch'in commandery of the same name (T'an Ch'i-hsiang, 2:12).

²⁷⁸Near modern Huang-kang 黃岡 in Hupei (T'an Ch'i-hsiang, 2:12).

荼[279] became King of Yen with his capital at Chi 薊.[280] The former King of Yen, Han Kuang 韓廣,[281] was moved to rule Liao-tung 遼東.[282] Kuang would not obey and Tsang T'u attacked and killed him at Wu-chung 無終.[283] He enfeoffed the Lord of Ch'eng-an 成安,[284] Ch'en Yü 陳餘,[285] with three counties in Ho-chien 河間,[286] his residence in Nan-p'i 南皮.[287] He enfeoffed Mei Hsüan with 100,000 households.

[367] In the fourth month (10 May–8 June 206 B.C.), the troops were dismissed[288] from the lower reaches of the Hsi 戲,[289] and the feudal lords each headed for their own states. When the King of Han went to his state, King Hsiang sent thirty thousand foot soldiers to follow him[290] and the men from Ch'u and the other feudal lords who [also] admired and followed him were several tens of thousands; [they all] entered into Li 蝕 [Valley][291] from south of Tu 杜.[292]

[279]He had gone with Hsiang Yü to assist Chao, before following him into the Pass *(Shih chi*, 7.316).

[280]A few miles southwest of modern Peking (T'an Ch'i-hsiang, 2:9).

[281]On Han Kuang's background, see also *Shih chi*, 48.1955-6.

[282]Located approximately where the Ch'in commandery of the same name had been (T'an Ch'i-hsiang, 2:10).

[283]Wu-chung was the seat of the Ch'in commandery Yu Pei-p'ing 右北平, located near modern Chi 薊 County in Hopei (T'an Ch'i-hsiang, 2:10).

According to *Shih chi*, 16.783, this occurred in the eighth month.

[284]See *Grand Scribe's Records*, 1:196, n. 168.

[285]Ch'en Yü had refused to go with Hsiang Yü into the Pass, thus his fief is less impressive (see *Shih chi*, 7.317 and his biography in Chapter 89).

[286]Ho-chien was a country located about 120 miles south of modern Peking in Hopei; according to T'an Ch'i-hsiang (2:26), the administrative seat of Ho-chien was at Yüeh-ch'eng 樂成, a few miles northwest of Chiao-ho 交河 County, also in Hopei. Nan-p'i was about twenty-five miles east of Yüeh-ch'eng and about fifteen miles southwest of the modern city of Ts'ang-chou 滄州; in Ch'en's biography only Nan-p'i is mentioned (*Shih chi*, 89.2581).

[287]See *Grand Scribe's Records*, 1:196, n. 170.

[288]Dismissed by Hsiang Yü to return to the command of their own kings. Another reading would be "the troops withdrew [to go home] from below Hsi."

[289]The "Cheng-yi" cites Hsü Shen 許慎 [d. ca. 120 A.D.],, the Han exegete and the author of the *Shuo-wen* 説文,that "hsi" 戲 here was *ta-ch'i* 大旗, "large flags," which presumably flew over the armies of each of the newly enthroned kings. This is supported by the editors of the Chung-hua *Han shu* (1A.29) and Yen Shih-ku's comment cited there. But given the proximity of the Hsi River to Hung-men (only several miles separate them), it seems more likely this is a place name (as Ku and Hsü understand it, 8.11 [161]). See also *Grand Scribe's Records*, 1:196, n. 174.

[290]The restrictions placed on the strength of Liu Pang's army—which was 100,000 strong when he entered the Pass—are not mentioned in "The Basic Annals of Hsiang Yü" (*Shih chi*, 7.316-17).

[291]The reading "Li" here comes from "Chi-chieh" (*Shih chi*, 8.367). Wang Li-ch'i (8.204n) believes this

Once the King of Han left [a place], he quickly burned the plank roadways[293] at once as a precaution against bandit troops from the feudal lords launching a surprise attack on him and also to show Hsiang Yü that he had no thoughts of the East.[294] Reaching Nan-Cheng, [he found] many of his generals, officers and men had fled for home along the way; the [remaining] officers and men all sang of their longing to return to the East.[295] Han Hsin 韓信[296] advised the King of Han: "Hsiang Yü has made kings of those generals who had merit and made Your Majesty alone live in Nan-Cheng. This is a banishment.[297] The officers and foot soldiers are all men from east

was the important and ancient route from the Land within the Passes to Han-chung; it is also called the Tzu-wu 子午 Valley.

[292]A county about fifteen miles southwest of modern Sian (T'an Ch'i-hsiang, 2:6).

[293]*Chan-tao* 棧道 "covered way" or a "way built of planks" constructed along a precipitous trail and supported by wooden piles. Our translation follows the gloss given in "So-yin" *(Shih chi,* 8.367).

[294]Once again this was in accord with Chang Liang's advice (see *Shih chi,* 55.2039).

[295]To bolster his armies, it is likely that Liu Pang followed the advice of Fan Mu 范目 to enlist a number of soldiers from the Ts'ung 賨 tribes of Szechwan (see An Tso-chang 安作璋 and Meng Hsiang-ts'ai 孟祥才, *Liu Pang p'ing-chuan* 劉邦評傳 [Tsinan: Ch'i Lu Shu-she, 1988], p. 136, and Feng Sui-p'ing 馮歲平, "Lun Pa-jen tsai Han-wang Liu Pang pei ting San Ch'in chung te tso-yung" 論巴人在漢王劉邦北定三秦的作用, *Liu Pang yen-chiu,* 1993.3: 48-49).

[296]There are two men with the identical name, Han Hsin, who figure in this annals. This Han Hsin was born a commoner in Huai-yin 淮陰. He first served Hsiang Yü and then, when Liu Pang was ruling in Han, went over to him. He became a great general-advisor and was rewarded for his successes by being named King of Ch'i, then King of Ch'u, and finally Marquis of Huai-yin. In the end, however, he rebelled against the Exalted Emperor, was defeated and executed. His biography is *Shih chi* Chapter 92.

The second Han Hsin (first mentioned in the translation of *Shih chi,* 8.369 below) figures less frequently in the narrative and therefore will be referred to as "Hann Hsin" (following Burton Watson). Since these two men have exactly the same names (in Chinese as in English romanization), they are easily confused. A longer speech similar to this one is found in Han Hsin's biography (*Shih chi,* 92.2611-12), but another oration even closer to this speech is recorded in Hann Hsin's biography (*Shih chi,* 93.2632). Hann Hsin is not shown to be an advisor in any other passage (such as in his biography in Chapter 93). Takigawa (8.41-42) believes Hann Hsin could not have made this speech and argues that Ssu-ma Ch'ien has mistakenly reduplicated a version of this speech on *Shih chi,* 93.2632.

[297]Cf. *Grand Scribe's Records,* 1:194, translation of *Shih chi,* 7.316: "King Hsiang and Fan Tseng had suspected that the Magistrate of P'ei might gain the world. But since there had been a reconciliation on this matter, and since they were loathe to break the agreement made with Yi-ti for fear that the feudal lords might rebel against them, they plotted in secret: 'The roads to Pa and Shu are steep. When Ch'in *banished* people, it sent them to live in Shu.'

So they said: 'Pa and Shu, too, are lands within the Pass."

For these reasons King Hsiang enthroned the Prefect of P'ei as the King of Han to rule over Pa, Shu and Han-chung, with Nan-Cheng as his capital" [emphasis ours].

Ch'ien 遷 is often used to indicate a change in position (sometimes even a promotion), but here it clearly seems to mean a change for the worse (see also Wei Chao's note in "Chi-chieh").

of the Mountain; night and day they stand on tiptoe gazing towards the way back. If you can take advantage of this keenness[298] and employ it, you shall have great merit. Once the world is already stable, the people all at peace with themselves, you will not be able to use them again. It would be best to decide on a plan for heading east and struggling for control of the world."

[368] When Hsiang Yü came out of the Pass, he sent a man to move Yi-ti [from P'eng-ch'eng], saying: "The emperors of ancient times ruled over one thousand *li* [on a side] of territory and invariably lived on a river's upper reaches." Thus he sent an envoy to move Yi-ti to Ch'en 郴 County in Ch'ang-sha 長沙,[299] urging Yi-ti on his way. [The emperor's] vassals showed considerable disloyalty to King Hsiang. He thus secretly ordered the kings of Heng-shan and Lin-chiang to attack him, cutting down Yi-ti South of the Chiang.[300]

Hsiang Yü harbored resentment for T'ien Jung 田榮,[301] and enthroned the Ch'i general T'ien Tu 田都 as King of Ch'i.[302] T'ien Jung was angry and accordingly enthroned himself King

---

[298] *Feng* 鋒 here refers to the mood of the soldiers, not as Watson has it (1:94), to Liu Pang's "lance" ("If you take up your lance now and use it, ... "). There is some similarity between the situation of Liu Pang's men who are about to desert him here and that of his first band of convicts who were fleeing him along the road. In both cases, moreover, Liu Pang was able to cleverly reassess his position and, through his daring, to win the hearts of men who were about to abandon him.

[299] Near modern Ch'en-chou 郴州 City in Hunan, about six-hundred miles from P'eng-ch'eng on the upper reaches of what was then the Feng 豐 River; this was the furthermost frontier of southern Ch'u (T'an Ch'i-hsiang, 2:12).

[300] In Ch'ing Pu's biography there is a different account *(Shih chi,* 91.2599) which claims that Yi-ti was moved to Ch'ang-sha and in the eighth month–the tenth month according to *Shih chi,* 16.783-84–Ch'ing Pu and others were ordered to pursue and kill him. They caught up with him in Ch'en County and he died there. *Shih chi,* 7.320 says he died *Chiang chung* 江中, "on the Chiang." But our text here agrees with Hsiang Yü's original intent that Yi-ti should live "on a river's upper reaches" and the expression South of the Chiang is repeated below *(Shih chi,* 8.370), seemingly confirming the text here.

The verb *shih* 弒 is used when a person or persons of a lower station kills someone of a higher station and is sometimes translated as "to assassinate." We have tried to use "cut down" or "fell."

[301] T'ien Jung and his elder cousin T'ien Tan 田儋 revolted shortly after Ch'en Sheng. They reestablished the state of Ch'i, but were surrounded by the Ch'in general Chang Han at Tung-o 東阿. Hsiang Liang came to their aid. T'ien Jung then went back to Ch'i and made T'ien Tan's son, T'ien Fu 田市, King of Ch'i, chasing off T'ien Chia 田假 who had laid claim to the throne. T'ien Chia escaped to Hsiang Liang. When Hsiang Liang faced the Ch'in armies at Ting-yao, T'ien Jung refused to come to his aid and Hsiang Liang was killed in battle. This was the basis of the bad feelings between T'ien Jung and Hsiang Yü (see details in T'ien Tan's biography, *Shih chi* Chapter 94).

[302] Hsiang Yü actually divided Ch'i into three parts. T'ien Tu, who had been a general under T'ien Fu and had gone into the Pass with Hsiang Yü, was made king of a reduced state of Ch'i. T'ien An 田安, descendant of the King of Ch'i-pei 齊北 (Northern Ch'i), was made King of Northern Ch'i, and T'ien Fu was changed to become King of Chiao-tung 膠東. T'ien Jung then killed T'ien Fu and T'ien An and drove off T'ien Tu,

of Ch'i, killed T'ien Tu,[303] and rebelled against Ch'u; he gave P'eng Yüeh the seal of a general and ordered him to rebel in the [former] Liang territory. Ch'u ordered Chüeh 角, Magistrate of Hsiao 蕭,[304] to attack P'eng Yüeh; P'eng Yüeh crushed him. Ch'en Yü harbored resentment for Hsiang Yü's not having made him a king, and ordered Hsia Yüeh 夏説 to advise T'ien Jung, requesting troops to attack Chang Erh. Ch'i gave Ch'en Yü troops and Ch'en struck at and defeated Chang Erh, the King of Ch'ang-shan; Chang Erh fled and went over to Han [i.e., Liu Pang]. Ch'en Yü went to welcome the [former] King of Chao, [Chao] Hsieh, from Tai, restoring him to the throne as King of Chao.[305] The King of Chao accordingly enthroned Ch'en Yü as King of Tai. Hsiang Yü was enraged and moved north to strike at Ch'i.

In the eighth month (5 September–4 October 206 B.C.), the King of Han employed Han Hsin's plan,[306] and, following the Old Road[307] back [to the Land within the Passes], launched a surprise attack against the King of Yung, Chang Han.[308] Chang Han met the King of Han's attack at Ch'en-ts'ang 陳倉 (Ch'en Granary).[309] Yung's troops were defeated, turned and fled, stopping to fight at Hao-chih 好畤,[310] were defeated again, and fled to Fei-ch'iu.[311] The King of Han then stabilized the territory of Yung. He moved east to Hsien-yang, led his troops to surround the King of Yung at Fei-ch'iu, and dispatched various generals to overrun and stabilize Lung-hsi 隴西 (West of Lung), Pei-ti 北地 (The Northern Territories), and Shang-chün 上郡 (The Upper Commandery).[312] He ordered Generals Hsüeh Ou 薛歐[313] and Wang Hsi 王吸[314] to go out through

reuniting Ch'i. For details see *Shih chi* Chapter 94.

[303] As Wang Shu-min (8.320) points out, T'ien Tu was not killed but fled to Ch'u.

[304] About fifteen miles west of P'eng-ch'eng (modern Hsü-chou) near modern Hsiao 蕭 County in Anhwei (T'an Ch'i-hsiang, 2:8).

[305] Chao Hsieh was at the time King of Tai, see also *Han shu,* 1A.32.

[306] Han Hsin's plan, given in detail on *Shih chi*, 92.2612, in essence urged Liu Pang to return to the Land within the Passes, which should be rightfully his according to the agreement reached under Yi-ti earlier.

[307] *Ku-tao* 故道 a road through a pass near the modern Kansu-Shensi border, abut ten miles southwest of modern Ku-tao hsien (T'an Ch'i-hsiang, 2:5).

[308] Chang Han was based in Fei-ch'iu north of Nan-Cheng.

[309] About ten miles northwest of Ku-tao and seventy miles upstream from Chang Han's capital at Fei-ch'iu on the north side of the Wei River (T'an Ch'i-hsiang, 2:5).

[310] About twenty miles northwest of Fei-ch'iu. In familiar terrain, Chang Han seems to have tried to elude Liu Pang by leaving the Wei River Valley for the hills northwest of Hsien-yang (cf. T'an Ch'i-hsiang, 2:6).

[311] Chang Han's capital.

[312] Three large commanderies which made up much of what is now modern Shensi—Lung-hsi was in the southwest, Pei-ti to the northwest, and Shang-chün in the northeast (T'an Ch'i-hsiang, 2:5-6).

[313] Hsüeh Ou was made *Tien-k'o* 典客 (Director of Guests) in 202 B.C. (*Han shu,* 19B.747), then became Marquis of Ching 敬 in 201 B.C. (*Shih chi,* 18.886), and was later appointed Marquis of Kuang-p'ing 廣平 ("Chi-chieh," *Shih chi,* 96.2685). He died in 188 B.C. (*Han shu,* 16.536).

[314] Wang Hsi later became Marquis of Ch'ing-yang 清陽 ("So-yin," *Shih chi,* 8.369); according to *Han shu* (16.534) he was Marquis Ting 定 of Ch'ing-ho 清河, appointed in 201 B.C.; he died three years later.

Wu Pass and take advantage of Wang Ling's 王陵 troops being at Nan-yang 南陽 [Commandery] to go and meet T'ai-kung and Lü Hou at P'ei and escort them back. Ch'u heard of this, and sent forth troops to resist them at Yang-chia 陽夏,[315] so that they were unable to go forward. Hsiang Yü ordered the former Prefect of Wu 吳, Cheng Ch'ang, 鄭昌, to be King of Hann 韓, and resist Han's 漢 troops.[316]

[369] In the second year (205 B.C.), the King of Han moved east overrunning territory and [Ssu-ma] Hsin, the King of Sai, [Tung] Yi, the King of Ti, and Shen Yang, the King of Ho-nan, all surrendered.[317] [Cheng] Ch'ang, the King of Hann, would not obey [the order to surrender] and the King of Han sent Hann Hsin 韓信[318] to strike at and defeat him. At this point he set up Lung-hsi, Pei-ti, Shang-chün, Wei-nan 渭南 (South of the Wei), Ho-shang 河上 (On the Ho) and Chung-ti 中地 (Central Territory) commanderies;[319] outside the Passes he set up Ho-nan

[315]Yang-chia (reading of "chia" follows Wang Li-ch'i, 8.205n) was located about fifteen miles north of Ku-ling 固陵 near the modern county of T'ai-kang 太康 in southeastern Honan (T'an Ch'i-hsiang, 2:7).

This point of interception raises the question of roads during the Ch'in-Han interregnum. A direct line from Nan-yang Commandery to P'ei would move northeast from Nan-yang. The modern roads seem to follow closely what we can assume to have been Wang Ling's route. In this case, roads given by T'an Ch'i-hsiang (2:7) seem not as reliable as those given on "World Cart" map of China issued by American Map but printed by RV Reise- und Verkehrsverlag (Berlin, 1994-95; hereafter referred to as China Map). On the China Map the main road from modern Nan-yang runs northeast through modern Xuchang then turns east directly through Taikang (i.e., Yang-chia).

[316]Cheng Ch'ang had been Prefect of Wu when Hsiang Liang rebelled and chose to follow Hsiang Liang. "The Basic Annals of Hsiang Yü" (Shih chi, 7.321) notes that Cheng Ch'ang was, along with several other commanders, ordered to attack P'eng Yüeh, but they were defeated. In his biography (Shih chi, 93.2632) Hann Hsin is said to have defeated Cheng at Yang-ch'eng 陽城 and subsequently been made King of Hann as a reward. See text immediately below.

[317]Liang Yü-sheng (6.223) points out that both of these kings surrendered in the eighth month of the first year of Han. Yang Shu-ta notes (Han shu k'uei-kuan, p. 11) that it was Liu Chia 劉賈 who conquered Sai (Shih chi, 51.1993).

[318]This is the second of the two men named Han Hsin who figure in this chapter; he will be referred to as "Hann Hsin." Hann Hsin was of royal blood, a descendent of the Hann 韓 kings of the Warring States Era. He had led his troops to follow Liu Pang into the Land within the Passes. When Liu Pang began his march east, he made Hann Hsin his King of Hann. Hsiang Yü countered by appointing Cheng Ch'ang 鄭昌 his King of Hann (Shih chi, 93.2632). Hann Hsin defeated Cheng Ch'ang, ruling as King of Hann for a short time. Liu Pang then moved him to be King of T'ai-yüan, a region where Hsiung-nu incursions were common. In 200 B.C. Hann Hsin was attacked by the Hsiung-nu and surrendered to them. For the next several years he fought with the Hsiung-nu against the Han, but was finally killed by Han troops in 196 B.C. His biography can be found in Shih chi, 93.2631-6.

[319]These three commanderies in the capital area were later incorporated into the Ching-chao Yin 京兆尹 (Wang Li-ch'i, 8.206n.).

河南 (South of the Ho) Commandery. He enthroned his Grand Commandant, [Hann] Hsin as the King of Hann in [Cheng Ch'ang's] place. Those generals who had led ten thousand or caused a commandery to surrender, he enfeoffed with ten thousand households. He repaired the fortifications of Ho-shang.[320] As for all the former Ch'in [imperial] reserves, grounds, gardens, and ponds,[321] he ordered that the people be able to farm them.

In the first month (31 January–28 February 205 B.C.), he captured the younger brother of the King of Yung, Chang P'ing 章平. He broadly pardoned those who had committed offenses.

[370] The King of Han, having gone out of the Pass as far as Shan 陝,[322] comforted the elders outside the Pass, returned, and, when Chang Erh came seeking audience, the King of Han treated him generously.

In the second month (29 February–29 March 205 B.C.), he ordered that Ch'in's altars of soil and grain be abolished, and established Han altars of soil and grain in their place.

In the third month (30 March-28 April 205 B.C.), the King of Han crossed [the Ho] at Lin-Chin 臨晉 (Overlooking Chin);[323] [Wei] Pao 豹, the King of Wei 魏, commanded his troops and accompanied him. They subdued Ho-nei 河內 (Within the Ho),[324] captured the King of Yin, and set up Ho-nei Commandery. He moved south to cross the Ho at P'ing-yin 平陰 Ford,[325] reaching Lo-yang. At Hsin-ch'eng 新城[326] Master Tung 董, the *San-lao* 三老,[327] intercepted the

---

[320]Probably destroyed or damaged in the battles with Ch'in and later with Chang Han.

[321]There are various explanations of *yüan* 苑 and *yu* 囿, "ranges and grounds," but commentators generally agree that they were lands where various kinds of animals were raised; on that basis, it may be possible that *yüan* 園 and *ch'ih* 池, "gardens and ponds," may here refer to places where vegetables and fish were cultivated. On the expanded number of such ranges and grounds in third-century Ch'in, see Wu Shu-p'ing 吳樹平, "Yün-meng Ch'in chien so fan-ying te Ch'in-tai she-hui chieh-chi chuang-k'uang" 雲夢秦簡所反映的 秦代社會階級狀況, in *Yün-meng Ch'in chien yen-chiu* 雲夢秦簡研究 (Peking: Chung-hua, 1981), p. 82.

[322]A county just west of San-men Hsia 三門峽 City in Honan on the south side of the Yellow River (T'an Ch'i-hsiang, 2:6).

[323]Located in modern Shensi a few miles west of the Yellow River and about ten miles north of where the river bends to the north; it was on the major route from what was then Ch'in (Shensi) to the former area of Chin (Shansi) and was thus the homeland of Wei Pao (cf. T'an Ch'i-hsiang, 2:6).

[324]The seat of this commandery was located about twenty-five miles northwest of modern Chengchow on the north side of the Yellow River; the commandery was a narrow band of land on the north bank of the river stretching west from its seat about fifty miles and northeast to modern An-yang (T'an Ch'i-hsiang, 2:9).

[325]About ten miles northwest of modern Lo-yang (T'an Ch'i-hsiang, 2:7).

[326]About twenty miles south of modern Lo-yang (T'an Ch'i-hsiang, 2:43); the news of Yi-ti's death was spreading north from Ch'u, so Master Tung heard it earlier than the people in Lo-yang.

[327]*San-lao* 三老, was a position at the *hsiang* (village) level held by elders (usually over the age of 50) who were seen to have reached an advanced age because of their tripartite understanding of heaven, earth and man; they were appointed to oversee local education and customs in administrative entities up to county size. See Lu Zongli, p. 17, Yang Shu-fan 楊樹藩, "Han-tai hsiang-kuan" 漢代鄉官, *Kuo-li Cheng-chih Ta-hsüeh san-shih chou-nien chi-nien lun-wen chi* 國立政治大學三十週年紀念論文集 (Taipei: Cheng-chih Ta-hsüeh,

King of Han to tell him about the causes of Yi-ti's death.[328] The King of Han heard this, bared his [left] arm, and wailed.[329] Then he proclaimed a mourning period for Yi-ti, and held memorial services for three days. He sent out envoys to inform the feudal lords, saying: "All the world together enthroned Yi-ti, facing the north and serving him. Now Hsiang Yü has exiled and killed Yi-ti South of the Chiang; this is treasonous and unprincipled. The lonely one, I, have personally proclaimed a mourning period for him, so the feudal lords should all wear plain white garments. We will send forth all the troops within the Passes, gather the warriors of the San Ho 三河 (Three Ho) [Commanderies],[330] and float south on the Han and the Chiang [rivers] in the hopes to follow the noble kings[331] to assault the one in Ch'u who killed Yi-ti."

At this time Hsiang Yü had gone north to strike at Ch'i, and T'ien Jung gave him battle at Ch'eng-yang. T'ien Jung was defeated, and fled to P'ing-yüan 平原[332]; the people of P'ing-yüan killed him. All of Ch'i surrendered to Ch'u. Ch'u took advantage of this [*371*] to burn its city walls and ramparts and take its women and children captive. The people of Ch'i turned against him [Hsiang Yü]. T'ien Jung's younger brother, Heng 橫, enthroned Jung's son, Kuang 廣, as King of Ch'i. The King of Ch'i revolted against Ch'u at Ch'eng-yang. Although Hsiang Yü had heard that Han was moving east, he had already engaged the Ch'i troops in battle and wanted to completely defeat them and then strike at Han. The King of Han for this reason appropriated the troops of five feudal lords,[333] finally entering P'eng-ch'eng.[334] Hsiang Yü heard of this, then led

1957), pp. 137-44, Ch'üan Hsi-kang 全晰綱, "Ch'in Han hsiang-kuan li-li k'ao" 秦漢鄉官里吏, *Shan-tung Shih-ta hsüeh-pao: She-k'o pan (Chi-nan)* 山東師大學報社科板 (濟南), 1995.6: 77, Chi Shu-shih 吉書時, "Lüeh-lun Han-tai te san-lao" 略論漢代的三老, in *Pei-ching Shih-fan Ta-hsüeh hsüeh-pao*, 1983.6: 59-65, and Liu Hsiu-ming 劉修明, "Hsi Han hsiang-kuan 'san-lao' ch'ien-t'an" 西漢鄉官三老淺探, *Wen-shih-che*, 1984.5: 32-34.

[328]Master Tung, a recluse from the Ch'in era who was 82 *sui* when he met Liu Pang, was appointed Marquis Ch'eng 成 for this service (according to the *Ch'u Han ch'un-ch'iu* [*op. cit.*, 3b]).

[329]*Tso t'an* 左祖, "to bare the left arm," was a gesture which indicated a sign of respect or loyalty (see Hsü Chia-lu, p. 235; see also Wang Li-ch'i, 8.206n.).

[330]Ho-nei, Ho-nan, and Ho-tung—the commanderies between the Land within the Passes and Lo-yang along both sides of the Yellow River (T'an Ch'i-hsiang, 2:43).

[331]This term, *chu-hou wang* 諸侯王 "noble kings," was originally used to indicate those kings appointed by Hsiang Yü as opposed to the kings descended from the feudal states which Ch'in had eliminated (see *Shih chi*, 8.370 and 89.2580). It then referred to those kings made from Liu Pang's generals (see "Han hsing yi-lai Chu-hou-wang nien-piao" 漢興以來諸侯王年表, *Shih chi* Chapter 17). Finally, it came to distinguish kings who were born into the royal Liu family as opposed to those appointed to their thrones by Lü T'ai-hou (see Ts'ai Yung's 蔡邕 [133-192] comments cited in "Chi-chieh," *Shih chi*, 9.406). There were from ten to twenty "noble kings" in the early Han, who "enjoyed a higher degree of nobility than the *hou* or marquises" (see Michael Loewe, "The Orders of Aristocratic Rank of Han China," *TP*, XLVII [1960]: 110).

[332]Near modern P'ing-yüan on south bank of the Yellow River in Shantung (T'an Ch'i-hsiang, 2:7-8).

[333]There are various lists of these five lords, see *Grand Scribe's Records*, 1:198, n. 192. A thorough

his troops away from Ch'i and, traveling through Lu, went [by the roundabout way] through Hu-ling 胡陵 to reach Hsiao 蕭; he gave Han a great battle on the banks of the Sui 睢 River east of Ling-pi 靈壁 near P'eng-ch'eng.[335] He crushed the Han army, killing many officers and soldiers, so that because of this [the great number of corpses] the Sui River could not flow.[336] Then he took the father, mother, wife and children of the King of Han at P'ei,[337] placing them in his camp as hostages. Meanwhile, the feudal lords could see that Ch'u was mighty and Han was defeated, and they all left Han and were again for Ch'u. The King of Sai, [Ssu-ma] Hsin fled to enter Ch'u.

The elder brother of Lü Hou, Marquis Lü [Tse 澤] of Chou commanded the troops for Han, and was stationed at Hsia-yi 下邑. The King of Han followed him, gathering little by little the officers and men [who had fled],[338] and camped at Tang.[339] The King of Han then moved west, passing through Liang territory, reaching Yü 虞.[340] He sent the Internuncio[341] Sui Ho 隨何 to go to the place where [Ch'ing] Pu, King of Chiu-chiang, was and say: "If you, Sir, are able to make [Ch'ing] Pu raise troops and rebel against Ch'u, Hsiang Yü will have to stay and attack him. If you are able to make him stay for several months, my taking the world will be assured." Sui Ho went to advise [Ch'ing] Pu, the King of Chiu-chiang, and Pu indeed did turn his back on Ch'u. Ch'u had Lung Chü 龍且 go and strike at him.

modern study by Yen Tung-yang 嚴冬陽 concludes that these five lords were those of Ch'ang-shan 常山 (i.e., Chang Erh 張耳), Ho-nan 河南 (Shen Yang 申陽, who had been enfeoffed King of Ch'ang-shan by Hsiang Yü and had just surrendered to Liu Pang [*Shih chi,* 8.369]), Yin 殷 (Ssu-ma Ang 司馬卬, whose troops had just been captured by Liu Pang [*Shih chi,* 8.370]), Wei 魏 (Wei Pao 魏豹) and Han 韓 (Han Hsin 韓信; see Yen's "Han-wang Liu Pang 'ch'üeh wu chu-hou ping' ju P'eng-ch'eng k'ao" 漢王劉邦閻劫五諸侯兵入彭城考, *Kuo-li Pien-i Kuan kuan-k'an,* 12.1 (June 1983): 35-49, esp. p. 49.

[334]See also the parallel account in "The Basic Annals of Hsiang Yü" (*Shih chi,* 7.321-22).

[335]The Sui flowed through modern Shantung from Kaifeng, north of Ling-pi (southwest of modern Huai-pei 淮北 City in Anhwei [Wang Li-ch'i, 7.177n.]), to join with the Ssu 泗 River near modern Sui-ning 睢寧 (T'an Ch'i-hsiang, 2:7-8).

[336]More than 100,000 bodies were pushed into the river according to the parallel account on *Shih chi,* 7.322.

[337]According to the parallel account in "The Basic Annals of Hsiang Yü" (*Shih chi,* 7.322), Liu Pang, as he fled this defeat, had pushed his children out of his carriage in order to lighten the load, thereby allowing their capture by Hsiang Yü.

[338]*Shih chi,* 7.324 notes that additional forces were raised by Hsiao Ho from the Land within the Passes and then sent to Hsing-yang; these new troops were primarily men above and below the age limits of normal Ch'in enlistment, 17 and 60 (see also Yü Hao-liang 于豪亮 and Li Chün-ming 李均明, "Ch'in-chien so fan-ying te chün-shih chih-tu" 秦簡所反映的軍事制度, in *Yün-meng Ch'in-chien yen-chiu,* p. 154).

[339]His base of operations before he started west.

[340]A little over ten miles east of Sui-yang 睢陽 (Tang-chün 碭郡) near modern Yü-ch'eng 虞城 in eastern Honan (T'an Ch'i-hsiang, 2:7).

[341]*Yeh-che* 謁者.

[372] Having been defeated at P'eng-ch'eng, the King of Han moved west,[342] as he went, sending someone in search of his family; but his family had indeed fled and they were not able to find each other. After the defeat he was only able to find [future emperor] Hsiao Hui[343] and in the sixth month (15 July–13 August 205 B.C.) he installed him as the Heir Apparent, and broadly pardoned those who had committed offenses. He ordered the Heir Apparent to defend Yüeh-yang 櫟陽[344] and the sons of the feudal lords in the Land within the Passes all gathered in Yüeh-yang as guards.[345] He led water [from the Wei River] to flow into Fei-ch'iu, Fei-ch'iu surrendered, and Chang Han committed suicide. He changed the name of Fei-ch'iu to Huai-li 槐里 (Acacia Hamlet).[346] Thereupon, he ordered the officials in charge of offerings to sacrifice to Heaven, earth, the four directions, Shang-ti 上帝 (The Supreme Deity), the mountains, and the rivers; the sacrifices were to be made according to the proper times.[347] He roused the foot soldiers within the Passes to take up positions along the barrier fortifications.

At this time, [Ch'ing] Pu, King of Chiu-chiang, battled with Lung Chü, was not victorious, and together with Sui Ho returned by backroads to [the King of] Han.[348] The King of Han little by little regathered his officers and men, and together with his generals, strengthened by foot soldiers from the Land within the Passes; because of this his troops were greatly invigorated at Hsing-yang and defeated Ch'u between Ching 京 and So 索.[349]

---

[342]There is an interesting account in *Ch'u Han ch'un-ch'iu* (*op. cit.*, 4a) which augments what we know of Liu Pang's personality. As Liu Pang was fleeing from the defeat at P'eng-ch'eng, he was pursued by a man of Hsüeh 薛, Ting Ku 丁固 (see Loewe, *Biographical Dictionary*, p. 62). When Liu Pang asked Ting why he was pressing him so, Ting turned his horse and left. After Liu Pang took the throne, he blamed Ting Ku for Hsiang Yü's defeat and had him whipped to death because of his disloyalty.

[343]The son of Lü Hou and Kao-tsu, Liu Ying 劉盈, was controlled by his mother and ruled in name only from 195-188 B.C. (see *Shih chi* Chapter 9 below).

[344]Since this was within the Passes, it was a relatively safe area.

[345] The Heir Apparent, although "in charge" of Yüeh-yang, was only five years old at the time (*Ch'in Han shih*, p. 241, gives his dates as 210 B.C.; the date of birth of 206 B.C. given in the *Cambridge History*, p. xxxix is obviously an error).

[346]According to the "Ti-li chih" 地理志 (Treatise on Geography) in the *Han shu* (28.1546), Huai-li was called Ch'üan-ch'iu 犬丘 during the Chou dynasty and King Yi of Chou took it as his capital; the name was changed to Fei-ch'iu during the Ch'in dynasty, and Kao-tsu renamed it Huai-li.

[347]For a succinct introduction to the Han gods and some of the actual practices of worship, see Michael Loewe, "The Gods," in Loewe, *Chinese Ideas,* pp. 17-24. On sacrifices in general in early China, see also Terry F. Kleeman, "Licentious Cults and Bloody Victuals: Sacrifice, Reciprocity, and Violence in Traditional China," *AM,* Third Series, 7.1 (1994): 185-211.

[348]According to *Shih chi,* 16.790, Ch'ing Pu returned to Han in the twelfth month of the third year, not the second year.

[349]So 索 was a place (hamlet?) less than ten miles southwest of Hsing-yang, and Ching was a county about

In the third year (204 B.C.), [Wei] Pao, the King of Wei, asked for leave to return home and visit his sick parents; on reaching [the Ho] he immediately blocked the ford across the Ho and returned [his allegiance] to Ch'u.[350] The King of Han sent Master Li [Yi-chi] to persuade Pao, but Pao would not listen. The King of Han dispatched General Han Hsin; he struck at and crushed him, taking Pao prisoner.[351] Then he stabilized the territories of Wei, setting up three commanderies called Ho-tung 河東 (East of the River), T'ai-yüan 太原 (The Great Plain), and Shang-Tang 上黨 (Upper Tang).[352] The King of Han then ordered Chang Erh and Han Hsin to move east, subdue Ching-hsing 井陘 (Well Gorge), and strike at Chao; they executed Ch'en Yü and [Chao] Hsieh, the King of Chao.[353] The next year (203 B.C.), [the King of Han] enthroned Chang Erh as King of Chao.

The King of Han camped south of Hsing-yang and constructed a walled way[354] connecting

fifteen miles south of Hsing-yang in modern Honan; the battle took place about twenty miles west of modern Chengchow (T'an Ch'i-hsiang, 2:7). Chavannes (2:367) reads this line: "C'est ainsi qu'il se trouva avec ses soldats dans une situation très prospère à Yong-yang [our Hsing-yang]."

There is a popular account recorded in a text which originally belonged to the *Feng-su t'ung-yi* 風俗通義 (*Feng-su t'ung-yi chu-tzu so-yin* 風俗通義逐字索引, *A Concordance to the Feng su tong yi* [Hong Kong: The Commercial Press, 1996], pp. 154-55), which tells that Liu Pang fled into some dense undergrowth after being defeated by Hsiang Yü. Hsiang Yü pursued him, but when a dove (*chiu* 鳩) in a tree just above Liu Pang began to sing, the pursuers thought their could be no one there and left off the chase. Later, after Liu Pang became emperor, he created a "dove staff" (*chiu chang* 鳩杖) to be presented to venerable old men in order to honor the bird. Ch'en Chih (p. 7) believes this tradition could be historically accurate and ties it to the Han linkage of doves and phoenixes. See also the discussion of these staffs and other pigeon/dove lore in Michael Loewe, "The Wooden and Bamboo Strips Found at Mo-chü-tzu (Kansu)," *JRAS,* 1965, pp. 17f., and the discussion of the decree that granted elderly men this staff in Loewe, "Han Administrative Documents, Recent Finds from the Northwest," *TP,* LXXII (1986): 306.

[350]Grant Hardy has a fascinating discussion of what he terms "the multiple narrations" of this incident in his *Worlds of Bronze and Bamboo* (New York: Columbia University Press, 1999), pp. 75-81. He shows that in the four or five more extensive treatments of this disaffection Ssu-ma Ch'ien has attributed quite different motives to Wei Pao. Hardy concludes that "Sima Qian is willing to tell different stories in which all the different motivations have full narrative force, even if these tales are not strictly compatible. In short, the *Shiji* replicates some of the confusions and uncertainties presented by our evidence of the past . . . [p. 81]."

[351]According to Han Hsin's biography (*Shih chi,* 92.2613), the chronological tables (*Shih chi,* 16.788), and the parallel passage in *Han shu* (1A.38), Wei was captured during the second year of Han, 205 B.C.

[352]Ho-tung Commandery was located just east of the Yellow River in what is now southwestern Shansi (T'an Ch'i-hsiang, 2:15-16); Shang-tang Commandery was southeast of Ho-tung centered on the modern city of Ch'ang-tzu 長子 in Shansi (T'an Ch'i-hsiang, 2:18); T'ai-yüan Commandery was located east of Ho-tung centered on its namesake city in Shansi (T'an Ch'i-hsiang, 2:18).

[353]This took place in the tenth month of 204 B.C. (*Shih chi,* 16.789). For details of the complicated story of the relationship between Chang Erh and Ch'en Yü see their biographies in *Shih chi* Chapter 89.

[354]*Yung-tao* usually means "a raised way," but here refers to a "raised way between earthen walls."

to the Ho, so he could get [rations] from the Ao 敖 Granary.[355] He and Hsiang Yü kept each other at bay for more than a year. Hsiang Yü several times raided Han's walled [*373*] way, so that the Han armies were short of rations; then he surrounded the King of Han. The King of Han requested a peace, ceding [lands] west of Hsing-yang for Han. Hsiang Yü did not heed him. The King of Han was dismayed by this and employed a plan of Ch'en P'ing 陳平[356]; he gave Ch'en P'ing forty thousand catties of gold, with which to estrange the [King of Ch'u] from his ministers. As a result of this [plan], Hsiang Yü began to have doubts about Second Father [Fan Tseng]. Second Father at this time had been urging Hsiang Yü to cause Hsing-yang to submit, but when he was doubted by Hsiang Yü, he became angry and resigned [his commission] because of old age, hoping that his old bones might be allowed to return to the ranks of the foot soldier, but before he reached P'eng-ch'eng he died.[357]

The Han army had exhausted its rations, so by night [the King of Han] sent more than two thousand women out of the eastern gate; as they were wearing armor, Ch'u accordingly assaulted them from four sides. General Chi Hsin 紀信[358] rode in the royal chariot, pretending he was the King of Han, to deceive the Ch'u [soldiers]. The Ch'u [soldiers] all shouted "Hurrah!"[359] and went to the eastern city walls to look on. Because of this, the King of Han along with several dozen horsemen were able to go out of the western gate and escape. He ordered the Grand Master of the Imperial Scribes,[360] Chou K'o 周苛,[361] Wei Pao, and Master Ts'ung 樅[362] to defend Hsing-

---

[355]The Ao Granary had been built by Ch'in a few miles north of Hsing-yang on the southern bank of the Yellow River (T'an Ch'i-hsiang, 2:7); it took its name from nearby Mount Ao and was of strategic importance, as was Hsing-yang, to any army hoping to control the North China Plain.

[356]Ch'en P'ing's plan is laid out in his biography (*Shih chi* Chapter 56). In part he wrote to various commanders in the Ch'u army reminding them that they had not received territory or become kings; in part he arranged for a bogus feast which was supposedly for Fan Tseng and allowed an envoy from Hsiang Yü to see it, further arousing Hsiang Yü's suspicions (*Shih chi*, 55.2055).

[357]*Shih chi*, 7.325 claims he died of an ulcer which broke out on his back.

Wang Li-ch'i (8.208n.) notes that *tsu* 卒 and *wu* 伍 are small communal units and that this phrase indicates Fan Tseng wanted to return to the life of a commoner.

[358]Chi Hsin had been one of the four attendants who guarded Liu Pang when he escaped from Hsiang Yü at Hung-men (*Shih chi*, 7.314); for a parallel account of these events, see *Shih chi*, 7.326, where Chi Hsin suggests the idea of impersonating the King of Han.

[359]According to Wang Li-ch'i (8.208n.), *wan sui* 萬歲 was a kind of general cheer at this time and did not mean "long live [the king]."

[360]*Yü-shih tai-fu* 御史大夫. We use "Grand Master of the Imperial Scribes" based on parallels with other translated titles in place of Bielenstein's "Grandee Secretary." On the duties and importance of this position, one of the most powerful during the Han dynasty, see Bielenstein, pp. 8-10.

[361]See his biography, *Shih chi*, 96.2576-77.

[362]Otherwise unknown.

yang.[363] Those generals and foot soldiers who were not able to follow him all remained within the city walls. Chou K'o and Master Ts'ung said to each other: "A king who has rebelled against his state—it would be difficult to defend the city with him." Accordingly, they killed Wei Pao.

The King of Han, having gotten out of Hsing-yang and entered the Pass, gathered troops with the intention to head east again. Master Yüan 袁[364] advised the King of Han, saying: "Han and Ch'u have held each other at bay at Hsing-yang for several years[365] and Han has often been in straightened circumstances. I would ask that My Lord King go out through the Wu Pass; Hsiang Yü will have to lead his troops and flee southward. Your Majesty can dig deep trenches and allow [the troops at] Hsing-yang and Ch'eng-kao 成皋[366] a little time to get some rest. Send Han Hsin and others to appease [those] north of the Ho in Chao territory, join with Yen and Ch'i, and then, My Lord King, if you run again to Hsing-yang it will not be too late. If you do this, the places Ch'u must defend will be many, its strength divided, and Han will be able to rest, to again give them battle, and the defeat of Ch'u will be certain!" The King of Han followed his plan; he sent out troops between Yüan 宛 and She 葉,[367] joined [his army] with Ch'ing Pu, and gathered [more] troops as they moved.[368]

[374] When Hsiang Yü heard that the King of Han was in Yüan, as expected he led his

[363]Wang Li-ch'i (8.324n.) notes that Hann Hsin was also ordered to defend Hsing-yang (see parallel account in Hann's biography, *Shih chi*, 93.2632).

[364]Otherwise unknown. He does not appear in the parallel account in "The Basic Annals of Hsiang Yü" (*Shih chi*, 7.327).

[365]Liang Yü-sheng (6.226) points out that the Han armies occupied Hsing-yang in the fifth month of the second year and left in the fifth month of the third year spending a little over a year there. He argues that the expression "several years" (*shu sui* 數歲) here in 漢與楚相距滎陽數歲, "Han and Ch'u have held each other at bay at Hsing-yang for several years" should be altered to read *sui yü* 歲餘 "a little over a year," as in the text above (*Shih chi*, 8.372; 漢王軍滎陽南... 與項羽相距歲餘; "The King of Han camped south of Hsing-yang . . . . He and Hsiang Yü kept each other at bay for more than a year."

[366]About ten miles west of Hsing-yang on the main route west leading to Kung 鞏 County (T'an Ch'i-hsiang, 2:7).

[367]Yüan was the county in which the seat of Nan-yang Commandery was located near the modern city of Nan-yang in southwest Honan; She 葉 was a neighboring county, almost fifty miles to the northeast near the modern county of the same name (T'an Ch'i-hsiang, 2:7).

[368]Here the parallel passage in "The Basic Annals of Hsiang Yü" (*Shih chi*, 7.327) is much different. It reads: "After the King of Han left Hsing-yang, he fled south to Yüan and She and gained the support of Ch'ing Pu, the King of Chiu-chiang; as he marched he regrouped his troops and returned to defend Ch'eng-kao (a few miles west of Hsing-yang)." According to this version, Liu Pang did not return within the Pass, but fled south to Yüan and She (about 90 and 125 miles southwest of Hsing-yang respectively), there receiving Ch'ing Pu who had left Hsiang Yü's service to come over to the Han cause. According to the account in Ch'ing Pu's biography (*Shih chi*, 91.2602), Ch'ing Pu had very few troops with him but Liu Pang was forced to divide his forces with Ch'ing. This supports the version in "The Basic Annals of Hsiang Yü." Moreover, there seems to have been no road "between Yüan and She" to allow Liu Pang to send out troops as is claimed here. This version may be one in which the effect of the defeat at Hsing-yang was attenuated by scribes loyal to the King of Han.

troops south. The King of Han secured his fortifications and did not offer battle. At this time P'eng Yüeh crossed the Sui 睢 River[369] and gave battle to Hsiang Sheng 項聲[370] and the Magistrate of Hsüeh 薛[371] at Hsia-p'ei 下邳 (Lower P'ei)[372]; P'eng Yüeh crushed the Ch'u army.[373] Hsiang Yü thus led his troops east to assault P'eng Yüeh. The King of Han also led his troops north to camp at Ch'eng-kao. Hsiang Yü had already defeated and run off P'eng Yüeh, when he heard that the King of Han had again encamped at Ch'eng-kao; thus he again led his troops west, seizing Hsing-yang, executing Chou K'o and Master Ts'ung, capturing the King of Hann 韓, [Hann] Hsin, and then besieging Ch'eng-kao.

The King of Han made a run for it.[374] With only the Magistrate of T'eng 滕[375] sharing his

[369]The Sui flows from south of modern Kaifeng in Honan across Anhui into Kiangsu to join the Ssu 泗 River about ten miles of the modern city of Sui-ning 睢寧 in Kiangsu (T'an Ch'i-hsiang, 2:8). Han shu (1A.41) says this took place in the fourth month of the third year.

[370]One of Hsiang Yü's generals active at this time (see Shih chi, 91.2602 and 95.2670). According to the latter reference, he was defeated by Kuan Ying north of the Huai River in 204 B.C.

[371]The Magistrate of Hsüeh (Hsüeh 薛 was a county about twenty five miles northeast of P'ei County in modern Shantung [T'an Ch'i-hsiang, 2:8]) was mentioned in "The Basic Annals of Hsiang Yü" (Shih chi, 7.327); this text claims that P'eng Yüeh killed the Magistrate of Hsüeh who was commanding Ch'u's forces near Tung-o in 204 B.C. In Kuan Ying's biography (Shih chi, 95.2670) it is claimed that he was executed by Kuan Ying.

[372]Hsia-p'ei was located about fifteen miles southwest of modern P'ei (normally pronounced P'i) 邳 County in Kiangsu (T'an Ch'i-hsiang, 2:8) and about twenty miles northwest of the confluence of the Sui and Ssu rivers; to reach Hsia-p'ei, therefore, P'eng Yüeh would have had to cross both the Sui and the Ssu rivers.

[373]There are a number of inconsistencies (some commented upon in the notes immediately preceding this) between this account and those parallel versions which appear in other chapters of the Shih chi. According to his biography, P'eng Yüeh had moved north in 204 B.C. to station his troops on the Yellow River (Shih chi, 90.2592, see especially the "Cheng-yi" here and on Shih chi, 90.2592 which further locates his camp at Hua-chou 滑州—also called Po ma 白馬—a few miles east of modern Hua 滑 County in Honan [T'an Ch'i-hsiang, 2:7]). It is difficult to see how he could have moved over one-hundred miles south and east, through Ch'u territory, to enable him to cross the Sui River and attack Hsia-p'ei. In his biography (Shih chi, 90.2592) he is said to have moved north in 205 B.C. and this is more likely. In 203 B.C. P'eng Yüeh operated behind Hsiang Yü's lines on the upper reaches of the Sui River, taking Wai-huang, Sui-yang (in modern Honan, see T'an Ch'i-hsiang, 2:8) and some seventeen cities in all. This area was near P'eng's home town of Ch'ang-yi 昌邑. Thus it seems more likely that P'eng would have crossed the Ssu River from the west, possibly in conjunction with Kuan Ying, to attack the Ch'u army under the Magistrate of Hsüeh and Hsiang Sheng. The Han shu parallel passages do not resolve these inconsistencies. Han shu, 1A.41 claims that P'eng Yüeh killed the Magistrate of Hsüeh (echoing Shih chi, 7.327 and Han shu, 30.1814). According to Kuan Ying's biography (Shih chi, 95.2670), Kuan killed him. P'eng's biography in the Han shu (34.1879) records these events, but gives no date for P'eng Yüeh taking the seventeen cites.

[374]Tanaka Kenji (pp. 130-31, n. 1) notes that parallel passage in Shih chi, 7.327 reads t'ao 逃 for the t'iao

chariot, he went out through Ch'eng-kao's Yü 玉 (Jade) Gate,[376] headed north to cross the Ho, and hastened to Hsiu-wu 脩武 (Cultivate the Martial) where he spent the night. Calling himself an envoy, at dawn he rushed into the fortifications of Chang Erh and Han Hsin and seized their armies.[377] Then he sent Chang Erh north to gather more troops in Chao territory and sent Han Hsin east to assault Ch'i.[378] When the King of Han obtained Han Hsin's army, his vigor was restored. He led his troops along the Ho, faced them south, and feasted his army south of Hsiao Hsiu-wu 小脩武 (Minor Cultivate the Martial),[379] intending to do battle again. The Palace

跳 here. He points out that *t'iao* 跳 as used here suggests more clearly the panic of Liu P'ang's escape. *T'iao* does not often occur in the *Shih chi,* but the passage on *Shih chi,* 51.1997 may be instructive in reading our text; it depicts Liu Tse's 劉澤 actions as follows: 至梁，聞漢遣灌將軍屯滎陽，澤還兵備西界，遂跳驅至長安。 Watson (1:344) translates: "He had gotten as far as Liang when he received news that the Han court had dispatched Guan Ying with an army, which was camped at Xingyang, whereupon he led his troops back to defend the western border of his territory. Finally, *he marched by forced stages* to Chang'an . . ." [italics ours]. But there seems to be little basis for reading *t'iao ch'ü* as "march by forced stages." The reading offered in "So-yin," *t'o du ch'ü* 脫獨去, "to escape alone and go to," seems to fit the context in Liu Tse's case as well as here for Liu Pang. Our translation, nevertheless, attempts to suggest the confusion Tanaka believes is suggested by the change from *t'ao* in "The Annals of Hsiang Yü" to *t'iao* here.

[375]I.e., Hsia Hou-ying 夏侯嬰, a native of Liu Pang's hometown, had been Magistrate of T'eng (near modern T'eng County in Shantung and about twenty miles north of P'ei, T'an Ch'i-hsiang, 2:8).

[376]"Chi-chieh" says the Jade Gate is the northern gate; *Shih chi,* 7.327 reads Pei-men 北門 (Northern Gate).

[377]Hsiu-wu was about ten miles west of modern Hsin-hsiang 新鄉 City in Honan (T'an Ch'i-hsiang, 2:7).

A more detailed account of this "coup" can be found in Han Hsin's biography (*Shih chi,* 92.2619): "The King of Han came out [from Hsing-yang] toward the south and went to a point between Yüan and She. He obtained Ch'ing Pu['s support] and they raced into Ch'eng-kao. The Ch'u forces once again pressed him and surrounded him. In the sixth month, the King of Han came forth from Ch'eng-kao, moved east and crossed the Ho, together only with the Magistrate of Teng, following [the route] Chang Erh took to encamp at Hsiu-wu. When he arrived, he spent the night in the post house. At dawn, claiming himself to be an envoy from the King of Han, he raced into the [King of] Chao's [i.e., Chang Erh's] fortifications. As Chang Erh and Han Hsin had not yet arisen, he went straightaway to their quarters and seized their seals and tallies [of command].With these he summoned all their generals, reassigning them to new posts. Only when Han Hsin and Chang Erh arose did they realize to their astonishment that the King of Han had come. The King of Han seized both men's armies . . . ."

In the *Han shu* (1A.42) these events took place in the sixth month.

[378]*Han shu* (1A.42) also dates Chang Erh's mission to the sixth month.

[379]According to Chin Cho 晉灼 (Chin dynasty; cited in "Chi-chieh," *Shih chi,* 8.374), Little Hsiu-wu was to the east of Hsiu-wu.

The parsing of the text here is suggested by the *Tzu-chih t'ung-chien* (10.338) which reads: 八月，引兵臨河，南鄉，軍小修武，欲復與楚戰。 "He led his troops to overlook the Ho, faced them south, encamped at Little Hsiu-wu, intending to again give Ch'u battle."

Attendant[380] Cheng Chung 鄭忠 persuaded the King of Han to stop, cause the earthworks to be raised higher and the moats dug deeper, and not to offer battle.[381] The King of Han listened to his plan and sent Lu Wan 盧綰 and Liu Chia 劉賈 in command of twenty thousand foot soldiers and several hundred horsemen[382]; they crossed [the Ho] at Pai-ma 白馬 Ford,[383] entered Ch'u territory, and, together with P'eng Yüeh, again struck at and defeated the Ch'u army west of the outer walls of Yen 燕 County,[384] further causing more than ten walled cities in Liang territory to submit.[385]

[375] [The Marquis of] Huai-yin 淮陰 [i.e., Han Hsin] had already received the order to move east, but had not yet crossed [the Ho] at P'ing-yüan. The King of Han had Master Li [Yi-chi] go persuade the King of Ch'i, T'ien Kuang; Kuang turned against Ch'u, concluded a peace with Han, and together with it attacked Hsiang Yü. Han Hsin, employing a plan of K'uai T'ung 蒯通,[386] then launched a surprise attack on Ch'i and defeated it.[387] The King of Ch'i

[380]*Lang-chung* 郎中.

[381]There is nothing further known about Cheng Chung other than his mention in the parallel account in "The Basic Annals of Hsiang Yü" (*Shih chi,* 7.327). That parallel account varies slightly and claims that Cheng Chung dissuaded Liu Pang from "crossing the Ho and marching south."

[382]Liu Chia's biography (*Shih chi,* 51.1993) says that Liu Pang sent Liu Chia alone in command of twenty-thousand soldiers and several hundred cavalry "to enter Ch'u territory and burn its accumulated stores"; Lu Wan's biography (*Shih chi,* 93.2637) says Liu Chia joined Lu Wan only in the winter of 202 B.C.; the account in "The Basic Annals of Hsiang Yü" (*Shih chi,* 7.327) reads: "The King of Han sent Liu Chia to lead troops to assist P'eng Yüeh and set fire to Ch'u's stores." Lu Wan was a childhood friend of Liu Pang, the two having been born in the same hamlet on the same day (*Shih chi,* 93.2637).

[383]This ford was about sixty miles northeast of Hsiu-wu and a few miles northeast of modern Hua 滑 County in Honan (T'an Ch'i-hsiang, 2:7).

[384]Yen County was about thirty miles southwest of Pai-ma Ford and about sixty miles northeast of Hsing-yang near modern Ch'ang-yüan 長垣 County in Honan (T'an Ch'i-hsiang, 2:7).

[385]According to P'eng Yüeh's biography (*Shih chi,* 90.2592), during the winter of 203 B.C. P'eng was forced by Hsiang Yü to move his army north to Ku-ch'eng 觳城 ("Cheng-yi," *Shih chi,* 91.2593, states this city was located about ten miles east of Tung-o; T'an Ch'i-hsiang gives it as 谷城 [2.7]). Since Ku-ch'eng is nearly one hundred miles northeast of Pai-ma Ford, P'eng's retreat suggests his cooperation with Liu Chia, and indeed the entire campaign, must therefore have been shortlived. See also Liang Yü-sheng (6.226-27) on various questions connnected to this passage.

[386]A rhetorician from Fan-yang 范陽 who had studied in Ch'i; he gradually became an important advisor for Han Hsin at this time (see also *Shih chi,* 92.2620, where K'uai T'ung's advice is given in more detail, *Shih chi,* 94.2649, where Ssu-ma Ch'ien heaps scorn on K'uai T'ung in his comments, and *Grand Scribe's Records,* 7:260-61, n. 36).

[387]Han Hsin was angry that what he had been sent to do militarily was being undermined by a diplomatic mission led by Li Yi-chi and thought about holding up his attack. But K'uai T'ung persuaded him to continue his

boiled Master Li alive and fled eastward to Kao-mi 高密.[388] When Hsiang Yü heard that Han Hsin had already raised troops north of the Ho and defeated Ch'i and Chao, and was on the point of assaulting Ch'u, he sent Lung Chü and Chou Lan 周蘭[389] to go and attack him. Han Hsin gave them battle; the Cavalry General Kuan Ying 灌嬰 attacked and crushed the Ch'u armies, killing Lung Chü. [T'ien] Kuang, the King of Ch'i, fled to P'eng Yüeh.[390] Meanwhile, P'eng Yüeh was in command of the troops stationed in Liang territory, going back and forth to harass the Ch'u troops, cutting off their provisions.[391]

In the fourth year (203 B.C.), Hsiang Yü said to the Marquis of Hai-ch'un 海春, the Grand Marshal[392] Ts'ao Chiu 曹咎, "Defend Ch'eng-kao with care. If Han challenges you to battle, take heed and do not give him battle, simply do not allow him to be able to move eastward. I will certainly stabilize the Liang territories within fifteen days, and will then join you again." Thus he set out to attack Ch'en-liu, Wai-huang, and Sui-yang 睢陽,[393] and cause them to submit. Han as expected challenged the Ch'u army several times, [but] the Ch'u army did not come out; [but] when Han sent men to revile them for five or six days, the Grand

campaign against Ch'i. T'ien Kuang 田廣, the King of Ch'i, was holding negotiations with Li Yi-chi and had relaxed the defenses originally prepared against the Han forces, so that Han Hsin was able to conquer much of Ch'i easily (*Shih chi*, 92.2620). He subsequently fought a battle with the Ch'u general Lung Chü 龍且 near Kao-mi, routing and eventually capturing all the Ch'u forces and killing Lung Chü (see also the accounts on *Shih chi*, 54.2027 and 95.2669-79). But this campaign led to mistrust and ill feeling between Han Hsin and Liu Pang that finally led to Han Hsin's downfall.

As Wang Shu-min (8.327) points out, however, Han Hsin's attack on Ch'i took place in the fourth year, not the third year.

[388]About 135 miles east-southeast of modern Tsinan near modern An-ch'iu 安丘 County in Shantung (T'an Ch'i-hsiang, 2:8). *Shih chi*, 54.2027 records the battle site as Shang-chia-mi 上假密, but a parallel account on *Shih chi*, 95.2669 also gives Kao-mi as the location.

[389]Chou Lan was one of Lung Chü's commanders. He was captured alive during these battles (*Shih chi*, 54.2027).

[390]Ts'ui Shih (p. 62) also notes that this must be Heng 橫 who fled to P'eng Yüeh since Kuang 廣 had been captured by Han Hsin.

[391]An almost identical description of P'eng Yüeh's activities at this time appears in his biography (*Shih chi*, 90.2592).

[392]*Ta Ssu-ma* 大司馬. Bielenstein uses "Commander-in-Chief." On this position see also Yoshimura Masayuki 吉村昌之. "Zen Kan no Taishiba" 前漢の大司馬, *Shisen* 史泉, 84 (1996).

In *Han shu* (1A.41) this took place in the fifth month of the third year.

[393]Located just south of the modern city of Shang-ch'iu 商丘 in Honan on what was then the north bank of the Sui River (T'an Ch'i-hsiang); it was about 120 miles from Hsing-yang. Wai-huang and Ch'en-liu were about halfway between Hsing-yang and Sui-yang on the northern and southern sides of the Sui respectively (T'an Ch'i-hsiang, 2:7). Thus Hsiang Yü proposed to travel at least 300 miles and subdue three cities in the space of a little over two weeks; in the parallel account on *Shih chi*, 7.329, it seems that more than three cities surrendered to him.

Marshal grew angry and had his troops cross the Ssu River.[394] When the officers and men were half way across, Han attacked them, crushing the Ch'u army, obtaining all of the gold, jade goods and wealth and property of the Ch'u state. The Grand Marshal [Ts'ao] Chiu and the Senior Scribe [Ssu-ma] Hsin both slit their throats on the banks of the Ssu River.[395] When Hsiang Yü reached Sui-yang, he heard of the Marquis of Hai-ch'un's defeat, and thus led his troops back. The Han army had just surrounded Chung-li Mo 鍾離眛[396] east of Hsing-yang, [but] when Hsiang Yü arrived, they all fled to the hills.[397]

[376] When Han Hsin had already defeated Ch'i, he sent a man to speak to [the King of Han], saying: "Ch'i borders Ch'u, and my power [here] is small; if I am not made acting king, I fear I will not be able to bring calm to Ch'i." The King of Han wanted to attack him. The Marquis of Liu 留[398] [Chang Liang] said, "It would be better to take advantage [of his request] and enthrone him, to cause him to defend it for himself." Thus he dispatched Chang Liang carrying the seal and cords [of authority] to enthrone Han Hsin as King of Ch'i.[399] When Hsiang Yü heard that Lung Chü's army had been defeated, he was fearful and sent Wu She 武涉, a native of Hsü-yi 盱台,[400] to go and offer Han Hsin advice.[401] Han Hsin did not heed him.

[394]*Han shu* (1A.43) dates this in the tenth month.

[395]Senior Scribe is our rendition of *Chang-shih,* 長史.

Ts'ao Chiu had been an acquaintance of Hsiang Liang and Warden of Ch'i 蘄. When Hsiang Liang was imprisoned at Yüeh-yang 櫟陽, he asked Ts'ao to write a letter to the warden there, Ssu-ma Hsin, and as a result was released (see *Shih chi,* 7.295 and *Grand Scribe's Records,*1:179). There are parallel passages on this attack on *Shih chi,* 7.330 and 90.2592.

[396]One of Hsiang Yü's generals originally from Yi-lu 伊廬 Village in Ch'ü 朐 County near what was then the seacoast (see *Shih chi,* 92.2627 and T'an Ch'i-hsiang, 2:45). After Ch'u was defeated, he sought Han Hsin's protection, commiting suicide when Han considered turning him over to Liu Pang (*Shih chi,* 55.2055 and 92.2627)

[397]Although we have translated *hsien-tsu* 險阻 above variously as "defiles and obstacles" (*Shih chi,* 6.252; *Grand Scribe's Records,* 1:145) and "defiles and mountains" (*Shih chi,* 7.330; *Grand Scribe's Records,* 1:203), it literally means "places where there are obstacles to travel" and fits the English expression "to take to the hills" well here.

[398]A country about fifteen miles southeast of P'ei (Liu Pang's hometown) in modern Kiangsu (T'an Ch'i-hsiang, 2:19).

[399]Here again Grant Hardy has provided an insightful analysis of Ssu-ma Ch'ien's various accounts of Han Hsin becoming King of Ch'i (in *Shih chi* chapters 7, 55, 56, and 92) in his *Worlds of Bronze and Bamboo,* pp. 93-6.

[400]Near modern Hsü-yi County in Kiangsu (T'an Ch'i-hsiang, 2:8).

[401]The advice was, of course, to return his allegiance to Hsiang Yü. *Shui* 說 here could also be understood as "to persuade." The *Ch'u Han ch'un-ch'iu* (*op. cit.,* 4a-b) records Han's response, recalling that when he had served Hsiang Yü, his position was low, but when he joined Liu Pang, he was feasted and presented with

For a long time Ch'u and Han held [their positions] without a decisive battle, their able-bodied men suffering from camp living, their old and weak exhausted from transporting field rations.[402] The King of Han and Hsiang Yü spoke to each other as they stood overlooking Kuang-wu 廣武 Ravine which divided them.[403] Hsiang Yü wanted to challenge the King of Han to do battle with him, man to man.

The King of Han enumerated Hsiang Yü's [faults], "In the beginning when I first received orders from King Huai together with Hsiang Yü,[404] we said that whoever could first enter and stabilize the Land within the Passes would be made king of it, but Hsiang Yü turned his back on the agreement and made me King of Shu and Han. This is his first offense. Hsiang Yü falsified an order to kill the Excellent Scion, Head of the Army,[405] and promoted himself.[406] This is his second offense. After Hsiang Yü had rescued Chao, he should have returned and reported [to King Huai], but without authority he forced the troops of the feudal lords to enter the Pass.[407] This is his third offense. King Huai had us agree whoever entered Ch'in would do so without brutalizing and plundering, [but] Hsiang Yü burned the Ch'in palaces, dug up the Ch'in Shih-huang's grave,[408] and selfishly gathered their wealth. This is his fourth offense. Further, he used his might to slay the surrendered King of Ch'in, Tzu Ying. This is his fifth offense. He fraudulently buried two hundred thousand of the young men of Ch'in at Hsin-an 新安, and made kings of

gifts. See also *Shih chi*, 92.2622.

[402]*Hsiang* 餉 has the meaning of lunches taken to farmers working their fields; here it presumably refers to meals brought to the men manning the trenches, fortifications, and outposts both armies had set up. According to the *Han shu* (1A.43) account, as soon as Liu Pang was able to take Ch'eng-kao and camp at Kuang-wu, he was able to access the Ao Granary.

[403]During one of these exchanges, Hsiang Yü threatened to boil Liu Pang's father alive (*Shih chi*, 7.327-8; *Grand Scribe's Records*, 1:202). Probably because Liu Pang pretended to be willing to allow this to happen, it is not mentioned here. *Shih chi*, 7.327 reads: "Hsiang Yü built a raised chopping block [*kao tsu* 高俎] and placed T'ai-kung atop it." The account in *Ch'u Han ch'un-ch'iu* (*op. cit.*, 4a) seems more logical: "King Hsiang built a high pavilion (or platform?, *kao ko* 高閣) and put T'ai-kung atop it."

According to *Shih chi*, 7.327-28, however, these events took place *before* Han took Ch'eng-kao. *Han shu* (1A.43) agrees with the chronology here; Liu Pang took Ch'eng-kao and then encamped at Kuang-wu. The problem in dating may allow speculation as to the historicity of these events.

[404]By addressing Hsiang Yü in the third person in this harangue Liu Pang adds to the disrespect he intends to show his adversary. It is difficult to believe that Hsiang Yü would have allowed Liu Pang to finish his speech before shooting him. *Han shu* (1A.44) has Liu Pang directly address his rival as "Yü" 羽.

[405]I.e, Sung Yi. His title was *Ch'ing-tzu kuan-chun* 卿子冠軍–see also *Grand Scribe's Records*, 1:186, n. 86.

[406]Cf. *Shih chi*, 7.304-5.

[407]This is Liu Pang's interpretation of events which are narrated on *Shih chi*, 7.307-310.

[408]Wang Li-ch'i (8.210n) points out that the archaeological teams working on the pits surrounding the First Emperor's tomb have found no evidence that any grave-robbers were successful in breaking in.

their generals.[409] This is his sixth offense. Hsiang Yü made kings of his generals in excellent territory and moved or drove out the former rulers, causing their subjects to struggle to rebel [against these new rulers]. This is his seventh offense. Hsiang Yü expelled Yi-ti from P'eng-ch'eng, taking it for his own capital, and seized the territory of the King of Hann 韓, ruling as king of Liang and Ch'u, providing too much for himself. This is his eighth offense. Hsiang Yü sent a man to secretly cut down[410] Yi-ti South of the Chiang. This is his ninth offense. To be a man who was a vassal and yet felled his ruler, who killed those who already surrendered, who in administering was not fair, who though in charge of an agreement was not trustworthy, is something the world cannot forgive, it is treasonous and unprincipled. This is his tenth offense. With my righteous troops I joined with the feudal lords to execute this cruel thief. I could have those men who committed offenses and have been punished strike and kill Hsiang Yü; why should I trouble myself to do battle with you, sir?"[411]

Hsiang Yü was enraged and shot the King of Han [with a crossbow] from hiding.[412] The King of Han was wounded in the chest, yet rubbed his foot and said, "The brigand[413] has shot me in the toe!" The King of Han [*377*] because of his wound lay down; Chang Liang forcibly implored the King of Han to get up, to inspect and encourage his army, to ease the concern of his officers and men, and to prevent Ch'u from taking advantage of this to gain a victory over Han. The King of Han emerged to inspect his army, but as the pain grew more severe, he accordingly hastened into Ch'eng-kao.

When the wound had healed, he moved west into the Pass, reaching Yüeh-yang, presenting his greetings to the elders,[414] setting out wine,[415] and suspending the head of the former King of

---

[409]Hsin-an was a Ch'in county about forty miles west of modern Lo-yang in Honan; modern Hsin-an County is about twenty miles east of the Ch'in county (T'an Ch'i-hsiang, 2:7).

On the battle and burial of these soldiers, about which there has been much debate—burying 200,000 soldiers would have been a difficult affair—see also *Shih chi*, 7.310 and *Grand Scribe's Records*, 1:189.

The generals made kings were Ssu-ma Hsin and Tung Yi (see *Shih chi*, 7.316 and *Grand Scribe's Records*, 1:195).

[410]On *shih* 弑 see also n. 300 above.

[411]We read this sentence based on Wang Li-ch'i's (8.210n.) interpretation.

[412]The parallel passage in "The Basic Annals of Hsiang Yü" (*Shih chi*, 7.328) emphasizes Hsiang Yü's bravery in staring down a skilled archer from the Han camp just prior to one of Hsiang Yü's archers striking Liu Pang.

[413]*Lu* 虜 is an epithet used for enemies, much like *fei* 匪 in modern Chinese.

[414]*Ts'un-wen* 存問 "to present greetings" or "to make polite inquiries" suggests Liu Pang sent forth messengers to inquire about conditions and thereby comfort the elders.

[415]*Chih chiu* 置酒, "to set out wine," was probably a part of the ancient rite of Village Wine Drinking (see "Hsiang-yin chiu-yi" 鄉飲酒義, in Sun Hsi-tan 孫希旦 [1736-1784], *Li-chi cheng-yi* 禮記正義 [Peking: Chung-hua, 1989], v. 3, *chüan* 59, pp. 1424-1436). As described so eloquently by Frederick Mote in his *The Poet Kao Ch'i (1336-1374)* (Princeton: Princeton University Press, 1962), p. 216, "the purpose of this ceremony was to

Sai, [Ssu-ma] Hsin, in the marketplace at Yüeh-yang.[416] He stayed four days and returned to his army; they camped at Kuang-wu. The troops from the Land within the Passes increasingly came forth.

Meanwhile, P'eng Yüeh was in command of the troops stationed in Liang territory, going back and forth and harassing the Ch'u troops, cutting off their provisions.[417] T'ien Heng 田橫 went to submit to him.[418] Hsiang Yü attacked P'eng Yüeh and his associates several times, and the King of Ch'i, [Han] Hsin, also advanced to strike at Ch'u. Hsiang Yü was fearful, and came to an agreement with the King of Han to divide the world in half, ceding that which was

honor old men of the community, who were the guests of honor, and to make a public display of forms of etiquette; a complementary purpose was to instruct the people in the laws which affected them. The reading of the laws, normally an abbreviated version of the penal code, was the first order of business after the officals had arrived and the old men were all seated, ranked according to their age. Then followed a feast, in which the niceties of deferring to others for their seniority in age or accomplishment were carried to great lengths . . . . There would be a solid wall of observers ringing them about, all of whom would be greatly moved by the scene" (see also *Ch'in hui yao ting-pu* 秦會要訂補 [Rpt. Taipei: Ting-wen, 1978], pp. 73-74 and Yao Wei-yüeh 姚偉鈞, "Chung-kuo ku-tai yin-shih li-su yü hsi-kuan lun-lüeh" 中國古代飲食禮俗與習俗論略, *Chiang Han lun-t'an*, 1990.8: 53; Wang Kuan-shih 王關仕, "T'an Hsiang-yin chiu-li" 談鄉飲酒禮, in *K'ung Meng yüeh-k'an*, 21.9 [May 28, 1983]: 28; and the detailed study by Yang K'uan 楊寬, "'Hsiang-yin chiu-li' yü 'Hsiang-li' hsin-t'an" 鄉飲酒禮與饗禮新探, in *Chung-kuo wen-shih lun-ts'ung*, 4:1-31). Thus "setting out wine" was not unlike the traditional ancient banquet in the West, with both eating and drinking (deipnon and symposium).

Moreover, it should be noted that although there is a great deal of discussion of Liu Pang's fondness for wine in the early sections of this chapter, the Han had followed the Ch'in dynasty in its restrictive laws concerning the production and drinking of alcoholic beverages (see Han Yang-min 韓養民, "Yin shih" 飲食, in Han's *Ch'in Han wen-hua shih* 秦漢文化史 [Rpt. Taipei: Li-jen, 1986], pp. 133-43, especially p. 139) and also Han Yang-min and Chang Lai-pin 張來斌, "Yin-chiu" 飲酒, in their *Ch'in Han feng-su* 秦漢風俗 [Taipei: Po-yüan 博遠, 1989], pp. 82ff.). Thus these occurrences of "setting out wine" were particularly welcomed by the recipients. Mu-choo Poo, "The Use and Abuse of Wine in Ancient China," *Journal of the Economic and Social HIstory of the Orient* 42.2 (1999): 123-51, also depicts the Village Wine Drinking (pp. 136-7), but views the consumption of wine as a common daily event in the early Han. Poo's ideas admittedly fit better with Liu Pang's predilection for wine as depicted in the early pages of this chapter.

[416]Ssu-ma Hsin had committed suicide after he was defeated by the Han troops at the Ssu Rivers (*Shih chi*, 7.330). Liu Pang brought back his head to Yüeh-yang, since this was Ssu-ma Hsin's capital after Hsiang Yü had named him King of Sai 塞.

[417]In his attempt to weave the many subplots together, Ssu-ma Ch'ien has here repeated the sentence informing us of P'eng Yüeh's actions at this time (cf. *Shih chi*, 8.375 and our translation above).

[418]T'ien Heng was the younger brother of T'ien Jung 田榮 and a member of the Ch'i ruling family. Hsiang Yü was distracted from defeating him by Liu Pang, while the Ch'u and Han armies held each other off at Hsing-yang, T'ien Heng retook many Ch'i cities (*Shih chi*, 7.321 and 325). Later, after he was defeated by Kuan Ying, he fled first to P'eng Yüeh and then to an island in the sea. Liu Pang considered him too great a danger to his control of Ch'i, however, and summoned him. Once in the hands of Han troops, T'ien Heng slit his own throat (*Shih chi*, 94.2644-48).

west of Hung-kou 鴻溝 (Hung Canal)[419] to Han, that which was east of Hung-kou to Ch'u. [*378*] King Hsiang returned the King of Han's father, mother, wife and children, as those in the camp all cried out "Hurrah!" Then they parted to return home.

Hsiang Yü disengaged and returned to the east. The King of Han intending to lead [his troops] and return west, employed a plan of Marquis of Liu [i.e., Chang Liang] and Ch'en P'ing[420] and advanced troops to pursue Hsiang Yü; reaching a place south of Yang-chia they halted, made camp,[421] and arranged with the King of Ch'i, [Han] Hsin, and the Marquis of Chien-ch'eng 建成,[422] P'eng Yüeh, to meet at a certain time and attack the Ch'u army. When he reached Ku-ling 固陵,[423] no one met him. Ch'u struck at the Han army and crushed it. The King of Han again entered behind fortifications, deepened his moats and defended them. He put a plan by Chang Liang into use and accordingly both Han Hsin and P'eng Yüeh moved out.[424] When Liu Chia entered Ch'u territory, he besieged Shou-ch'un 壽春[425]; the King of Han was defeated at Ku-ling[426] and sent an envoy to summon the Grand Marshal [of Ch'u], Chou Yin 周

[419]Also known as the Lang-t'ang Ch'ü, 狼湯渠, this canal ran north from the Yellow River about twenty miles northwest of modern Chengchow east to modern Kaifeng, then south finally ending in the Ying 穎 River near modern Shen-ch'iu 沈丘 County, all in today's Honan (see T'an Ch'i-hsiang, 2:7-8). It essentially gave Liu Pang control of lands west of the Ying River and Hsiang Yü control of those east of it. See also the slightly variant account on *Shih chi*, 7.330-31.

[420]On this plan see also *Shih chi*, 7.331 and 90.2593.

[421]Liang Yü-sheng (6.227) argues that these movements took place in the winter of the fifth year (202 B.C.), not during the fourth year. The account on *Shih chi*, 7.331 supports this dating. The chronological tables offer no help with this, but *Shih chi*, 16.795 says Hsiang Yü returned Liu Pang's father in the ninth month of the fourth year (i.e., late in 203 B.C.), supporting the supposition that the following events took place in 202.

[422]Just south of modern Yung-ch'eng 永城 County in extreme eastern Honan, about twenty miles southwest of the modern Huai-pei 淮北 City in Anhwei (T'an Ch'i-hsiang, 2:18).

[423]Ku-ling was located a little over sixty miles south-southeast of modern Kaifeng (Honan), about ten miles south of Yang-chia (T'an Ch'i-hsiang, 2:7).

[424]Chang Liang's plan, which involved recognizing the previous service of Han Hsin and P'eng Yüeh by promising them additional fiefs, is presented in detail in the parallel passage on *Shih chi*, 7.331-32.

Indeed, although Liang Yü-sheng (6.227-28) correctly points out that there are various conflicting accounts of these events (cf. *Shih chi*, 51.1993, 55.2042, 90.2593, 91.2602-3, and 92.2626), Ssu-ma Ch'ien seems to indicate his preference for the version given in "The Basic Annals of Hsiang Yü" (7.331-32) by referring the reader to that passage on *Shih chi*, 55.2042.

[425]Located a few miles west of the modern city of Huai-nan 淮南 on the south bank of the Huai River in Anhwei (T'an Ch'i-hsiang, 2:12).

[426]This line, as it now reads, simply repeats information given just above in the text, suggesting it is out of place or the text is corrupt here.

殷, to raise troops in Chiu-chiang and to welcome [Ch'ing Pu].[427] The King of Wu [i.e., Ch'ing-pu] marched to Ch'eng-fu 城父,[428] put it to the sword, and followed Liu Chia and the feudal lords of Ch'i [Han Hsin] and Liang [P'eng Yüeh] into a grand assembly at Kai-hsia 垓下.[429] [The King of Han] enthroned [Ch'ing] Pu, King Wu 武, as the King of Huai-nan 淮南.[430]

In the fifth year (202 B.C.), the troops of Kao-tsu and the feudal lords together struck at the Ch'u army and had a decisive battle with Hsiang Yü at Kai-hsia.[431] The Marquis of Huai-yin commanded 300,000 and personally matched up to Hsiang Yü, with General K'ung 孔 occupying the left and General Pi 費 on the right, and the emperor to the rear.[432] The Marquis Chiang 絳 [433]

[427]Both the Chung-hua editors and Ku and Hsü (8.19 [169]) believe that the *chih* 之 here—乃使使者召大 司馬周殷舉九江兵而迎之武王行屠城父隨何劉賈齊梁誅侯皆大會垓下—is an error and want to delete it. Although the *chih* appears in many other traditional texts (see Po-na edition, 8.27b, for example), this fits other accounts of these events (*Shih chi*, 51.1993-94, for example). Chou Yin, whom Liu Chia was besieging at his capital, Shou-ch'un, was invited by agents of the King of Han to join Ch'ing Pu. In the passage on *Shih chi*, 91.2602-03, it is Ch'ing Pu who is said to have incited Chou Yin to revolt.

The Chung-hua editors have also deleted the *ho* 何 following *sui* 隨 midway through this passage. Although most editions retain the *ho*, the text then makes no sense, and we follow Chung-hua's excised version.

[428]Located southeast of modern Po 亳 County in Anhwei, about eighty-five miles north of Shou-ch'un (Wang Li-ch'i, 7.181n.). It was near Ch'eng-fu that Chang Han had killed Ch'en Sheng (*Shih chi*, 6.270).

[429]Kai-hsia was located about 20 miles east of modern Ku-chen 固鎮 County in Anhwei a little over 20 miles north of the Huai River (T'an Ch'i-hsiang, 2:8). It was some 65 miles northeast of Shou-ch'un and about 130 miles east-southeast of Ku-ling. Thus Han Hsin approached Hsiang Yü from the northeast, the King of Han from the west, and P'eng Yüeh from the south, thereby surrounding the King of Ch'u and his forces.

[430]According to Ch'ing Pu's biography (*Shih chi*, 91.2602), this took place in the seventh month of the fourth year. It therefore preceded any "assembly at Kai-hsia." Thus the last section of this paragraph, beginning with the repetition of Liu Pang's defeat at Ku-ling (see n. 423), and extending through the questionable pronoun *chih* 之 (see n. 427), seems corrupt. Wu was Ch'ing Pu's posthumous title (cf. *Shih chi*, 17.807).

[431]As Chüan Ah 卷阿 pointed out in his "Ch'ien *Shih* so-yen" 遷史瑣言, *Hsüeh-hai yüeh-k'an* 學海月刊, 1944.1 (as cited in Yang, *Li-tai*, p. 421), Liu Pang should still be referred to here, in Ssu-ma Ch'ien's scheme, as the King of Han, not as "Kao-tsu." Chüan infers that the text here may be interpolated.

[432]Many scholars have puzzled over the identity of these two otherwise unknown generals—K'ung and Pi. The "Cheng-yi" (*Shih chi*, 8.379) maintains that they were two of Han Hsin's commanders, K'ung Hsi 孔熙 and Ch'en Ho 陳賀, respectively, who were later enfeoffed with the counties of Liao 蓼 (northeast of modern Ku-shih 固始 County in Honan) and Pi 費 (modern Pi County in Shantung; see also Wang Li-ch'i, 8.211n.). The *Hsi-ching tsa-chi* 西京雜記 (4.2a, *SPTK*) argues they are made-up names, but *Han shu pu-chu* (16.17a-b) supports their authenticity.

Whatever the reliability of these names, Liang Yü-sheng (6.228) observes that Ssu-ma Ch'ien's usual careful correspondence of referring to persons by the rank they held at the time of the event depicted is not followed in this passage: Kao-tsu should be the King of Han, the Marquis of Huai-yin (Han Hsin) was still King of Ch'i, and Chou Po would not be made Marquis Chiang until the following year.

As we have seen above, as Liu Pang's rank increases from magistrate, to king, and finally to emperor, so does Ssu-ma Ch'ien's method of reference to him. Here, however, he is anticipatory, since Liu Pang is not and General Ch'ai 柴 were to the rear of the emperor. Hsiang Yü's foot soldiers numbered perhaps 100,000. [The Marquis of] Huai-yin first joined [in battle], gained no advantage and [*379*] withdrew. General K'ung and General Pi loosed their troops and the Ch'u troops could find no advantage, the Marquis of Huai-yin returned to avail himself of this opportunity and inflicted a great defeat at Kai-hsia. When Hsiang Yü's foot soldiers heard the Ch'u songs of the Han army, they believed that Han had taken all of Ch'u territory. Hsiang Yü thus was defeated and fled and, because of this, his troops suffered a great defeat. Han caused its Cavalry General Kuan Ying to pursue and kill Hsiang Yü at Tung-ch'eng 東城,[434] cutting off 80,000 heads and finally overrunning and stabilizing the territory of Ch'u. Lu 魯 strengthened its defenses on behalf of Ch'u and would not submit. The King of Han lead the troops of the feudal lords north, showed the head of Hsiang Yü to the elders of Lu, and Lu then surrendered. Then with the title of Duke of Lu he buried Hsiang Yü at Ku-ch'eng 穀城.[435] He returned to Ting-yao, rushed into the King of Ch'i's fortifications, and seized his army from him.[436]

In the first month (28 January-25 February 202 B.C.), the feudal lords, generals and ministers together jointly requested that the King of Han be elevated to become emperor.[437] The King of Han said, "I have heard that the imperial position should be held by those who are worthy. This empty talk and vain speeches are not what I sought; I dare not take the position of emperor."

made emperor until the following paragraphs. See also n. 432 above.

[433]Chou Po was not made Marquis of Chiang until the following year (on the *ping-wu* 丙午 day of the prime month 正月 of the sixth year, i.e., 6 March 201; see *Shih chi,* 18.894). Chiang was a county in Ho-tung 河東 Commandery near modern Hou-ma 侯馬 City in Shansi (T'an Ch'i-hsiang, 2:16); it had been one of the early capitals of the state of Chin (cf. *Shih chi,* 5.188); Chou Po's fief included 8,100 households.

[434]Located about twenty miles south of the Huai River, about sixty miles northwest of modern Nanking in Anhwei (T'an Ch'i-chiang, 2:12).

[435]Wang Li-ch'i (8.211-212n.) locates Ku-ch'eng in modern P'ing-yin 平陰 County in Shantung.   A parallel account (*Shih chi,* 7.337-38) explains that the King of Han buried Hsiang Yü in Lu because King Huai of Ch'u had appointed Hsiang Yü as Duke of Lu early in the rebellion (*Shih chi,* 7.304) and because Lu was the last to submit to him. Liu Pang's decision may also have been both an attempt to win over Lu and to diffuse Hsiang Yü's popularity in the south.

[436]He obviously did so because he did not trust Han Hsin. As Tanaka Kenji (p. 140, n. 4) points out, this is the third time Liu Pang seized one of his general's armies: he first took the Marquis Kang-wu's men (*Shih chi,* 8.357-58) and then, after fleeing Ch'eng-kao, seized the armies of Chang Erh and Han Hsin (*Shih chi,* 8.374). These acts reflect the arrogance attributed to Liu Pang by Kao Ch'i and Wang Ling (*Shih chi,* 8.381); they may also cause the reader to reflect on Han Hsin's failure to oppose Liu Pang (K'uai T'ung had urged him not to ally himself with Liu Pang [*Shih chi,* 92.2623-24]), and may even resonate with the famous story of Han Hsin's failure to accept the challenge made by a butcher in his youth (*Shih chi,* 92.2610).

[437]B. J. Mansvelt Beck, in his "The True Emperor of China," in *Leyden Studies in Sinology,* W. L. Idema, ed. (Leiden: E. J. Brill, 1981), p. 26, claims that Liu Pang "created emperorship at the request of his army."

The assembled vassals all said, "Great King, you rose up from humble circumstances, you have executed the brutal and treasonous, you have brought peace and stability to [the land within] the four seas; for those who gained merit, you immediately divided up territory and enfeoffed them as marquis and kings. Great King, if you do not elevate your title, all [titles] will be suspect and unreliable. We vassals will hold to [our demand] until death."

The King of Han renounced it three times, before he realized he was unable to put it to an end and said, "If you lords insist that doing this would be advantageous, then it must be advantageous for the state." On the *chia-wu* 甲午 day[438] he then took the position of emperor on the north bank of the Fan 氾 River.[439]

[380] The emperor said that Yi-ti had no descendants. The King of Ch'i, Han Hsin, was well versed in the customs and practices of Ch'u, so he moved him to become King of Ch'u, with his capital at Hsia-p'ei. He enthroned the Marquis of Chien-ch'eng, P'eng Yüeh, as King of Liang, with his capital at Ting-yao. The former King of Hann, [Hann] Hsin, was made King of Hann[440] with his capital at Yang-ti 陽翟.[441] He moved the King of Heng-shan, Wu Jui, to become King of Ch'ang-sha, with his capital at Lin-hsiang 臨湘.[442] The Lord of P'o's [i.e., Wu Jui's] general Mei Hsüan had achieved merit and had accompanied [the King of Han] into Wu Pass, therefore he paid back the Lord of P'o. [Ch'ing] Pu, King of Huai-nan, Tsang T'u, King of Yen, and [Chang] Ao 張敖,[443] King of Chao, all remained as before.[444]

The world was grandly stable. Kao-tsu[445] put his capital at Lo-yang, and the feudal lords all acknowledged themselves as vassals subordinate to him. The former King of Lin-chiang,

---

[438]As Chavannes points out (2:381, n. 1, following the comments of Hsü Kuang recorded in the "Chi-chieh") there was no *chia-wu* day in the first month. This must refer to that day in the second month (28 February 202 B.C.). See also Liang Yü-sheng (6.229).

[439]The Fan River (not the Ssu as Chavannes, 2:381, has it) flowed from near Ts'ao 曹 County in modern Shantung through the northern part of Ting-yao County into the Ku-ko Tse 古渮澤 (Wang Li-ch'i, 8.212n.). However, the location where Liu Pang became emperor is traditionally assumed to have been northwest of the county seat of Ting-yao (see *Shih chi*, 89.2722).

[440]There is a question as to why Hann Hsin would need to be named King of Hann again (he had been appointed in 205 B.C., see *Shih chi*, 8.369). Liang Yü-sheng (6.229) believes this sentence must be an interpolation. But Hsiang Yü had captured Hann Hsin in 204 B.C. (*Shih chi*, 8.374), presumably interrupting his reign. Watson's understanding that this was a reconfirmation of Hann's title (*Han*, 1.75), therefore, seems correct.

[441]Near the seat of modern Yü 禹 County (about forty miles south of Chengchow) in Honan (T'an Ch'i-hsiang, 2:19).

[442]Modern Changsha city in Hunan (T'an Ch'i-hsiang, 2:23).

[443]Chang Erh's son. Although Chang Ao's royal title suggests that his father had died, according to *Shih chi*, 16.798 Chang Erh died later, in the seventh month of this year. *Han shu*, 32.1839 supports this dating. Perhaps Ao is an error for Erh?

[444]For further details on these appointments see Liang Yü-sheng (6.229-30).

[445]Since the King of Han has now been made emperor, Ssu-ma Ch'ien refers to him as Kao-tsu from this point on.

Huan 驩,[446] had revolted against Han on Hsiang Yü's behalf; Kao-tsu ordered Lu Wan and Liu Chia to lay siege to him, but he did not submit. After a few months he surrendered, and Kao-tsu had him killed at Lo-yang.

In the fifth month (26 May-23 June 202 B. C.), the troops were all dismissed and returned home. The sons of the feudal lords who remained in the Land within the Passes received exemption from taxes and corvée labor for twelve years, those who returned home received exemption for six years, and a food allowance for a year.

Kao-tsu set out wine in the Southern Palace[447] at Lo-yang. Kao-tsu said, "Marquises and generals, do not dare to hide things from me, but all speak forth what is in your hearts. What is the reason I was able to gain the world? [*381*] What is the reason that the Hsiang Clan [i.e., Hsiang Liang and Hsiang Yü] lost the world?"

Kao Ch'i 高起[448] and Wang Ling responded: "Your Majesty was arrogant and liked to slight people. Hsiang Yü was humane and loved people.[449] But when Your Majesty sent someone to attack cities and overrun territory, those [cities and territories] which surrendered, you accordingly gave to him, sharing your gains with the world. Hsiang Yü was jealous of worthiness and envious of talent, and would hate those who achieved merit, and doubt those who were worthy. If someone won a victory, he would not accord him merit, if someone gained territory, he would not give him the profits. This was why he lost the world."

Kao-tsu said, "You gentlemen have understood the first [reason], but you still do not understand the second. As for setting schemes and devising strategies from within a field tent which lead to decisive victories beyond a thousand *li,* I am not as good as Tzu-fang 子房 [i.e., Chang Liang]. As for guarding a country, calming its people, providing provisions and field rations, and not allowing supply lines to be cut, I am not as good as Hsiao Ho. As for joining an

---

[446]Although the chronological tables also read Huan (*Shih chi,* 16.213), Liang Yü-sheng (6.229) points out that this is a mistake for Kung Wei 共尉, who succeeded his father, Kung Ao 共敖, as King of Lin-chiang (see also *Shih chi,* 50.1994 and 93.2637). Liang also argues that Kung Wei was captured in the twelfth month of the fifth year, but his basis for this is the chronological tables (16.213) that he has already shown to be in error regarding the name. Both "The Hereditary House of the Kings of Ching and Yen" and Lu Wan's biography (*Shih chi,* 50.1994 and 93.2637) clearly relate the campaign and capture of Kung Wei as something which took place after Hsiang Yü's death.

[447]This was apparently a Ch'in palace (see "Cheng-yi").

[448]Wang Li-ch'i (8.212-3n) argues that Kao Ch'i had nothing to do with this exchange and his name should be deleted here. The basis for his argument can be found in Ch'en Chih (p. 10): the *T'ai-p'ing yü-lan* (445.3a-b) cites the parallel passage to this in the *Han shu* without mention of Kao Ch'i; this also fits with the record in *Han chi* (3.6b, *SPTK*).

Han Hsin viewed Hsiang Yü's love for people and his humaneness as a kind of "women's humaneness" (*fu-jen chih jen* 婦人之仁, see Han's comments as recorded in his biography [*Shih chi,* 92.2612]).

[449]Ironically, Ssu-ma Ch'ien used exactly this language, 仁而愛人, "he was humane and loved people," when he first characterized Liu Pang at the start of this chapter (*Shih chi,* 8.342).

army of a million men, winning victory whenever one fights, taking [lands] whenever one attacks, I am not as good as Han Hsin. These three are all heroes among men and I was able to employ them—this is the reason why I was able to take the world. Hsiang Yü had Fan Tseng but he was not able to employ him, this is the reason why he was captured by me."[450]

Kao-tsu had intended to keep the capital at Lo-yang forever, [but] Liu Ching 劉敬, a native of Ch'i, [tried to] persuade him [to move it].[451] When the Marquis of Liu [i.e., Chang Liang] urged the sovereign to move the capital into the Land within the Passes, on that very day Kao-tsu set out by carriage and moved the capital into the Land within the Passes.[452]

In the sixth month (24 June-23 July 202 B.C.), he granted a general amnesty throughout the world.[453]

In the tenth month,[454] the King of Yen, Tsang T'u, rebelled, attacking territories in Tai and causing them to submit.[455] Kao-tsu took personal command and struck at him, and caught the King of Yen, Tsang T'u. He immediately enthroned his Grand Commandant[456] Lu Wan as King of Yen.[457] He had the Chancellor[458] [Fan] K'uai command troops to attack Tai.[459]

---

[450]This seems to be Ssu-ma Ch'ien's view of why Liu Pang was able to vanquish Hsiang Yü and reunite the country. It echoes several other speeches including Han Hsin's assessment of Liu Pang (*Shih chi*, 92.2611-12).

[451]Liu Ching's arguments are given on the first few pages of his biography (*Shih chi*, 99.2715-16). His advice met with resistance, since most of Liu Pang's followers were from the south or east and did not want to move to the far west.

[452]Because of the opposition to Liu Ching's (originally named Lou Ching, see n. 91 above) suggestion, and the fact that he was not a courtier, it was actually Chang Liang's persuasion (see *Shih chi*, 55.2043-44) that convinced Liu Pang to move. The palace was first moved to Yüeh-yang, later to Ch'ang-an (Ho Ch'ing-ku 何清谷, ed., *San-fu huang-t'u chiao-chu* 三輔黃圖校注 [Sian: San Ch'in, 1995], pp. 101, n. 1 and 2).

[453]To celebrate the moving of the capital.

[454]As Chavannes pointed out (2:384, n. 5), the tenth month (十月) should not come after the sixth month. He suspects "ten" (*shih* 十) is a scribal error for seven" (*ch'i* 七), these characters being very similar in Han-dynasty script. According to *Shih chi*, 93.2637, Lu followed Kao-tsu to attack Tsang T'u in the seventh month and became King of Yen in the eighth month. The chronological tables (*Shih chi*, 16.799) say Kao-tsu attacked Tsang T'u in the eighth month and captured Tsang in the ninth. Thus the revolt would have taken place earlier, probably in the seventh month (24 July–21 August 202 B.C.).

[455]Tsang T'u had been made King of Yen by Hsiang Yü (*Shih chi*, 7.316) and was left in that position by Liu Pang after he became emperor (*Shih chi*, 8.380).

[456]*T'ai-wei* 太衛; the Grand Commandant was in charge of military affairs, but the position was filled only from 205-202 B.C., 196-195, 189-177, and 154-140. In 119 B.C. the title was changed to Ta Ssu-ma 大司馬, Grand Marshal, see Bielenstein, pp. 10-11.

[457]On Lu Wan's appointment see also *Shih chi*, 93.2637.

[458]*Ch'eng-hsiang* 丞相; the title of Chancellor, probably the second highest official (following the *T'ai-fu* 太府, the Grand Tutor), was changed to *Hsiang-kuo* 相國, Chancellor of State, in 196 B.C. From 189-178 B.C., a *Yu Ch'eng-hsiang* 右丞相 (Chancellor of the Right) and a *Tso Ch'eng-hsiang* 左丞相 (Chancellor of the Left) shared duties, the former being senior (Bielenstein, pp. 7-8).

That fall, Li Chi 利幾 rebelled, and when Kao-tsu took personal command of troops to strike at him, Li Chi fled. This Li Chi was a general of the Hsiang Clan. When the Hsiang Clan was defeated,[460] Li Chi was Magistrate of Ch'en 陳,[461] but did not follow Hsiang Yü, escaping to surrender to Kao-tsu; Kao-tsu made him Marquis of Ying-ch'uan. When Kao-tsu reached Lo-yang, he summoned all those who attained [the rank of] marquis[462] according to the registry, but Li Chi was fearful,[463] and for this reason he revolted.

[382] In the sixth year (201 B.C.), Kao-tsu paid his respects once every five days to T'ai-kung, as was the custom between father and son in a family.[464] T'ai-kung's Household Prefect[465] said to T'ai-kung: "Heaven does not have two suns, earth does not have two kings.[466] Now although Kao-tsu is your son, he is the ruler of men; although T'ai-kung is the father, he is the subject of a man. How can it be that the ruler of men is made to kneel down and bow to the subject of a man! If it goes on like this, then he will not enact prestige and respect [in others]." Later when Kao-tsu came one morning to pay his respects, T'ai-kung, clasping a broom, met him at the gate and walked backwards.[467] Kao-tsu was greatly surprised, got down from his carriage,

---

[459]Although Fan K'uai was later active in putting down rebellions in the Tai region, this campaign is not mentioned in his biography (*Shih chi*, 95.2631ff.).

[460]This refers to Hsiang Liang's defeat and death.

[461]Ch'en County, also the seat of Ch'en Commandery, was located near modern Huai-yang 淮陽 County in Honan (T'an Ch'i-hsiang, 2:7).

[462]*T'ung-hou* 通侯 seems to be equivalent to *lieh-hou* 列侯 (ranking marquises), the highest twenty noble ranks at the start of the Han dynasty (a system inherited from the Ch'in; see Loewe, "Aristocratic Ranks," pp. 98-99). In the parallel passage to this in *Han shu* (1B.56) we read *lieh-hou chu-chiang* 列侯諸將 for the *t'ung-hou chu-chiang* 通侯諸將 we have here. Both terms derive from the original called *ch'e-hou* 徹侯 (freely paraphrased, following Ying Shao's explanation [*Han shu*, 1b.56], as "those whose virtue and merit are so great they extend all the way to the royal house"). *Ch'e* was Emperor Wu's *praenomen* and was thus subsequently tabooed (see the comments by Ying Shao and Chang Yen, *Han shu*, 1B.56, and Wang Li-ch'i, 8.213n.). Chavannes (2:385, n. 1) argues that the *t'ung-hou* were those marquises with no fief who were dependent on the emperor, but *Han shu*, 7.739 (in the "Tables of One Hundred Officials, Excellencies, and Ministers") shows clearly that *t'ung-hou* were intended to have fiefs and were the top twenty ranks of nobility in the Ch'in system. Despite the equivalance with *lieh-hou*, our translation attempts to reflect the slight difference in terms. See also Lu Zongli, pp. 349 and 716.

[463]Fearful that as a former supporter of Hsiang Yü he would be arrested once he reported to the court.

[464]On the interpretation of *chia-jen* here see Chang Chia-ying, p. 177.

[465]*Chia-ling* 家令.

[466]In *Meng Tzu*, 5A.4 (*Meng Tzu Chao chu* 孟子趙注, 9.7b [*SPPY*]) we read: "Confucius said, 'Heaven does not have two suns and the people do not have two kings.'" The *Li chi* (5A.23, *SPPY*) reads: "Confucius said, 'Heaven does not have two suns, earth does not have two kings.'"

[467]Receiving a guest with a broom in hand, like walking backwards so as not to turn the back, is a sign of

and went to support T'ai-kung. T'ai-kung said, "The emperor is the ruler of men. How could he disrupt the codes of the world because of me?" From this point on Kao-tsu elevated T'ai-kung to become T'ai-shang Huang" 太上皇 (His Most Honored Majesty)[468] In his heart he was pleased with the words of the Household Prefect and granted him five hundred catties of gold.

In the twelfth month (17 January-14 February 201 B.C.), someone submitted a report of seditious affairs, accusing [Han] Hsin, the King of Ch'u, of plotting rebellion; the sovereign asked his ministers in attendance, and his ministers in attendance contended [with each other] intending [him] to attack [Han Hsin].[469] Employing Ch'en P'ing's plan, he pretended to be taking a pleasure trip to Yün-meng 雲夢,[470] gathered the feudal lords at Ch'en 陳, and when [Han] Hsin, King of Ch'u came to welcome him, he immediately took the opportunity to seize him.[471] On this day he granted a general amnesty throughout the world.[472] T'ien K'en 田肯[473] congratulated him and took the opportunity to offer Kao-tsu advice: "Your Majesty has obtained Han Hsin and also set your capital within the Lands of Ch'in.[474] Ch'in was a state with a victorious topography, bordered by the strongholds of the Ho and the mountains,[475] separated by a thousand *li* [from the feudal lords][476]; if an army of one-million men bearing halberds [approached], with two men for every hundred Ch'in could hold them off. Sending troops down from a terrain so advantageous upon the feudal lords could be compared to sitting on top of a tall building and letting water pour down a tile drainspout.[477] As for Ch'i, to its east there is the

respect to a guest (see also the reception given Master Tsou 騶 in Yen, *Shih chi,* 74.2345, *Grand Scribe's Records,* 7:181)

[468]*T'ai-shang Huang* 太上皇 is the same title the First Emperor of Ch'in gave his father (see *Shih chi,* 7.236 and *Grand Scribe's Records,* 1:136).

[469]A parallel passage in Han Hsin's biography (*Shih chi,* 92.2627) explains that the suspicions of revolt were aroused by Han Hsin taking along troops as he made a tour of inspection of district towns on first arriving in Ch'u.

[470]The large swamp north of modern Yüeh-yang 岳陽 City in modern Hupei (T'an Ch'i-hsiang, 2:12).

[471]Ch'en P'ing's attempts to persuade Kao-tsu are related in detail in his biography (*Shih chi,* 56.2056-57).

[472]On such amnesties see also Satake Akira 佐竹昭, "Chûgoku kodai no teii keishô to onsha, kaigen" 中国古代の帝位継承と恩赦、改元, *Chiiki bunka kenkyû* 地域文化研究 (Hiroshima Daigaku Sôgô Kagakubu), 22 (1996): 137-72.

[473]*Han shu pu-chu* (1b.8a) notes an alternate tradition which reads T'ien Hsiao 宵 for T'ien K'en.

[474]Ch'in-chung 秦中; as Ju Ch'un points out in "Chi-chieh" *(Shih chi,* 8.383), this was the term people from the east used to refer to Kuan-chung 關中, the Land within the Passes.

[475]Ku and Hsü (8.22 [172]) read both Ho and Shan as place names, apparently reading Shan as Mount Hua 華 which helps form the natural defenses for attacks from the east. The passage could also be read as a general reference to "rivers and mountains."

[476]Our translation here follows "Chi-chieh" in reading 縣 as 懸. Dubs (1.110) believes the one-thousand *li* refers to the length of Ch'in's borders with the feudal lords. Several interpretations of this difficult passage are summarized in Tanaka Kenji (pp. 149-50, n. 3).

[477]This is the source of the modern idiomatic expression, *kao-wu chien-ling* 高屋建瓴, which means

bountifulness of Lang-ya 琅邪 and Chi-mo 即墨, **[*383*]** to the south the fastness of Mount T'ai 泰, to the west the border of the Turbid Ho, to the north the benefits of the Po-hai 勃海. Its lands two thousand *li* [on a side], if an army of one-million men bearing halberds [approached], with two men for every ten Ch'i could hold them off. For this reason there is an east Ch'in and a west Ch'in. No one but one of your sons or brothers should be allowed to rule Ch'i." Then Kao-tsu said, "Well spoken." He granted him five hundred catties of yellow gold.

[384] More than ten days later, he enfeoffed Han Hsin as the Marquis of Huai-yin, dividing his territory into two states. Kao-tsu said, "General Liu Chia has several times achieved merit and, because of it, should be King of Ching 荆, to rule over lands east of the Huai.[478] My younger brother [Liu] Chiao 交 will become King of Ch'u, to rule over lands west of the Huai.[479] My son [Liu] Fei 肥 will become King of Ch'i, to rule over more than seventy walled cities[480]; those people who were able to speak the Ch'i language all are to belong to Ch'i."[481] Having thus arbitrated their merit, he split tallies with the various marquises to effect their enfeoffment. He moved the King of Hann 韓,[482] [Hann] Hsin, to T'ai-yüan 太原.[483]

literally "to erect tile shoots or pentroughs on a steep roof," used to suggest a strategically advantageous position.

[478]In Liu Chia's biography (*Shih chi*, 51.1994) is it made clear that this appointment and the following were made to divide up Ch'u which had been recently taken back from Han Hsin. Liu Chia was given the new Kingdom of Ching which contained fifty-two cities.

[479]His kingdom was made up of thirty-six cities (*Shih chi*, 51.1994).

[480]As T'ien K'en had advised, Kao-tsu gave the strategic state of Ch'i to one of his sons, Liu Fei, who was then twenty-one years old (see also n. 601 below).

[481]This is not given as a direct quotation in the Chung-hua edition (cf. also *Shih chi*, 52.1999).

As the "So-yin" notes, the allotment of all "those people who were able to speak the Ch'i language" to Liu Fei's state may have been an attempt to induce the former residents of Ch'i, many of whom had fled the region in the recent fighting, to return to their hometowns.

[482]This was the final move to weaken the power of the kingdoms under Kao-tsu. He moved Hann Hsin from his homeland and power base in Hann to T'ai-yüan to become King of Tai (see the more detailed account of his reasons for this move in Hann Hsin's biography, *Shih chi*, 93.2633), which would place him near the Hsiung-nu, a menace Kao-tsu had yet to consider. In the passage which follows, Hann Hsin is immediately faced with the problem of confronting his powerful northern neighbors and finally decides to join them against Kao-tsu. As Liang Yü-sheng points out (6.233), Hann Hsin's decision to revolt is dated in his biography to the sixth year (201 B.C.).

[483]T'ai-yüan was a commandery surrounding the modern city of the same name in Shansi (T'an Ch'i-hsiang, 2.9). Its seat was Chin-yang 晉陽 (see also *Shih chi*, 93.2633). In the seventh year of Kao-tsu (200 B.C.), Hann Hsin requested to move his capital to Ma-yi 馬邑, ostensibly in order to be closer to his border defenses, but probably because he had already decided to rebel and wanted to be nearer the Hsiung-nu on whom he would then become dependent.

In the seventh year (200 B.C.),[484] the Hsiung-nu attacked [Hann] Hsin, the King of Hann, at Ma-yi 馬邑,[485] and Hsin took advantage of this to join them and plot a revolt against T'ai-yüan.[486] Wan-ch'iu Ch'en 曼丘臣[487] of Pai-t'u 白土[488] and Wang Huang 王黃[489] enthroned the former Chao general Chao Li 趙利[490] [*385*] as king [of Chao] in order to rebel, and the Kao-tsu personally went to attack them.[491] When the weather turned cold, those of his officers and men who lost fingers were two or three out of every ten; finally they reached P'ing-ch'eng 平城.[492] The Hsiung-nu surrounded us at P'ing-ch'eng and withdrew only after seven days. He ordered Fan K'uai to stay and stabilize the territory of Tai.[493] He enthroned his elder brother, Liu Chung 劉仲, as King of Tai.[494]

[484]This took place in the autumn of the sixth year, according to Hann Hsin's biography (*Shih chi*, 93.2633).

This chapter omits the detailed description of the audience held at court in the tenth month—cf. *Shih chi*, 99.2713.

[485]Ma-yi was located about one hundred miles north of Chin-yang (modern T'ai-yüan) near modern Shuo 朔 County in Shansi (T'an Ch'i-hsiang, 2:9).

[486]See the parallel account in Hann Hsin's biography (*Shih chi*, 93.2633-34)

[487]Wang Li-ch'i (8.214n.) gives his *cognomen* as Wan-ch'iu. He was originally a merchant (*Shih chi*, 93.2641) and was later involved with the Tai general, Ch'en Hsi 陳豨, when the latter revolted in 197 B.C. (*Shih chi*, 93.2641). He and Wang Huang were eventually captured in the twelfth month of 195 B.C. (*ibid.*).

[488]A county in what is now northern Shensi about 125 miles southwest of modern Huhetot (T'an Ch'i-hsiang, 2:17).

[489]Wang Huang's name is linked closely with Wan-ch'iu Ch'en, another merchant turned general (see n. 487 above). After rebelling, Wang was captured by Liu Tse 劉澤 (*Shih chi*, 51.1995).

[490]Although there are several references to Chao Li in parallel accounts (*Shih chi*, 57.2070, for example), nothing further known of descendants of the Chao royal house (*Shih chi*, 93.2632).

[491]A rather different version of these events is presented in the chapter on the Hsiung-nu (*Shih chi*, 110.2894). After the Hsiung-nu surrounded Hann Hsin, he surrendered. This brought a Han army led by Liu Pang to the scene; through a ruse, Liu was trapped with a small number of men by a huge Hsiung-nu force on Pai-teng 白登 Mountain (near P'ing-cheng). Liu Pang was able to negotiate an escape and then abandoned the campaign.

[492]Located just north of the modern city of Ta-t'ung 大通 in Shansi (T'an Ch'i-hsiang, 2:9).

[493]See also the account in Fan K'uai's biography (*Shih chi*, 95.2657).

[494]Liu Chung was the eldest surviving male in the Liu family; his older brother, Liu Po 劉伯, having passed away early in his life (*Shih chi*, 50.1987). Hsü Kuang ("Chi-chieh," *ibid.*), gives Liu Chung's *agnomen* as Hsi 喜 (see also *Han shu*, 1B.61).

Liu Chung was made King of Tai as a result of the rebellion by the previous king, Hann Hsin. Kao-tsu hoped thereby to replace another general with a family member, but Liu Chung proved unable to deal with the Hsiung-nu, fled to Lo-yang, and was deposed (*Shih chi*, 106.2821). Liang Yü-sheng (6.232) believes the enthronement of Liu Chung took place in the first month of the sixth year along with other similar appointments.

In the second month (5 Mar.-3 Apr. 200 B.C.)[495] Kao-tsu went from P'ing-ch'eng past Chao[496] and Lo-yang[497] to reach Ch'ang-an 長安.[498] As the Ch'ang-lo 長樂 (Ever Joyful) Palace was completed,[499] officials from the chancellors on down moved to govern from Ch'ang-an.[500]

[495]Liang Yü-sheng (6.233) notes that according to the *Han shu* (1B.63) Liu Pang passed through Chao in the twelfth month of the preceding year and reached Ch'ang-an in the second month.

[496]I.e., the capital of the state of Chao located near modern Han-tan (T'an Ch'i-hsiang, 2:16).

[497]This route—southeast, then southwest, and finally west—was circuitous; the more direct route southwest along the Chih 治 and Fen 汾 river valleys was probably not feasible because of the Hsiung-nu being active in this area (cf. T'an Ch'i-hsiang, 2:9).

[498]This is the first mention of Ch'ang-an in the *Shih chi;* according to a commentary to the *Han yi* 漢儀 cited in the "So-yin," the capital was changed from Hsien-yang, on the north bank of the Wei River, to the new city of Ch'ang-an on the south bank, in the sixth year of Kao-tsu (201 B.C.). According to Ho Ch'ing-ku 何清谷, ed., *San-fu huang-t'u chiao-chu* 三輔黃圖校注 (Sian: San Ch'in, 1995), pp. 101, nn. 1 and 2, however, Liu Pang moved the capital from Lo-yang to Yüeh-yang in 205 B.C., and then decided to move to Ch'ang-an three years later in 202 B.C. (his fifth year). Other sources (*Shih chi*, 55.2043-44, for example) claim it was the sixth year of Kao-tsu's reign (201 B.C.) before Lou Ching 婁敬 and Chang Liang convinced Liu Pang to move the capital within the Pass (see our translation of *Shih chi*, 8.381 and nn. 451 and 452 above). Dubs, 1.179, n. 3, cites several other sources which speculate on the dating of the walls' construction.

Like any new capital city, for the first few years Ch'ang-an was no doubt a maze of muddy paths and newly arrived townspeople. Although the Ch'ang-le and Wei-yang palaces were completed in 200 and 198 B.C. respectively (*Shih chi*, 8.385 and 386), the city walls were not constructed until after Liu Pang's death (192-189 B.C., see *Shih chi*, 9.398). Ssu-ma Chen ("So-yin," *Shih chi*, 8.398) gives details on the building of the walls and cites the *San-fu chiu-shih* 三輔舊事 to the effect that these first walls were shaped like the Big Dipper; thus this was perhaps only a partial walling of the city. Given the unfinished nature of the city and its defenses, Li Tse-fen 李則芬 speculates that Liu Pang may have actually resided in Hsien-yang, the former Ch'in capital (see Li's "Ch'ang-an ts'ang-san shih" 長安滄桑史, in Li's *Sui T'ang Wu-tai li-shih lun-wen chi* 隋唐五代歷史論文集 (Taipei: T'ai-wan Shang-wu, 1989): p. 255 [pp. 255-286]. On the construction of Han Ch'ang-an see also Koga Noboru 古賀登, "Kandai Chôan no kenchiku puran" 漢代長安の建築プラン, *Tôyôshi kenkyû*, 31.2 (1972): 182-215; Stephen Hotaling, "The City Walls of Han Ch'ang-an," *TP*, 64 (1978): 1-46; Ch'en Li 陳力, "Kandai Chôan no kensetsu puran no hensen to sono shisôteki haikei" 漢代長安の建寫設プランの変遷とその思想的背景, *Hannan Ronshû–Jinbun shizen kagakuhen* 31.3 (1996): 1-8; Wang Zhongshu, "Changan, The Capital City of Western Han," in Wang's *Han Civilization*, K. C. Chang et al., trans. (New Haven: Yale University Press, 1982), pp. 1-3; and the useful introduction and excellent bibliography provided in Nancy Shatzman Steinhardt, *Chinese Imperial Planning* (Honolulu: University of Hawai'i Press, 1990), pp. 55-68.

[499]Located in the southwest portion of the modern city of Ch'ang-an near modern Ma Chia hao ts'un 馬家豪村 (Wang Li-ch'i, 8.215n.), the Ch'ang-le Palace was a restoration of the Ch'in Hsing-le 興樂 Palace (Chavannes, 2:390, n. 2). Its walls were about seven miles in circumference, occupying about nearly five square miles or one-sixth of the area of the Han city in its southeastern corner) at this time (Steinhardt, *Chinese*

In the eighth year (199 B.C.),[501] Kao-tsu moved east to strike at the bandits remaining from the rebellion of the King of Hann, [Hann] Hsin, at Tung-yüan 東垣.[502]

As Chancellor Hsiao was constructing the Wei-yang 未央 (Eternal) Palace,[503] he erected an eastern gate-tower,[504] a northern gate-tower, the front hall, the armory, and a great granary. When Kao-tsu returned, he saw that the palace and gate-towers were imposing in the extreme and he was angry; he said to Hsiao Ho: "The world has been in an uproar and suffered through fighting for several years; whether we will accomplish [our goal] or be defeated still cannot be known. In this situation, how could you go to such excess in managing the building of palaces and residences?" Hsiao Ho said, "It is because the world is still not stable [*386*] that we should take advantage to complete palaces and residences. Moreover, the Son of Heaven takes

Imperial Planning, p. 56). It became Kao-tsu's residence from 200 B.C. until his death. Lü Hou also often lived in this palace; beginning with Hui-ti, however, the emperors lived in the Wei-yang Palace (Ho Ch'ing-ku, *San-fu huang-t'u chiao-chu*, p. 101-02 and 105). There are suggestions that some government business was also conducted in this early imperial residence (see, for example, *Shih chi*, 99.2723).

[500]There is a conflict between this passage and that in Shu-sun T'ung's 叔孫通 biography. There (*Shih chi*, 99.2723) we read that in the tenth month of the seventh year the nobles and officials came to court and viewed the new court rites that Shu-sun had made for Kao-tsu. The only mention of a similar gathering in these annals is that in the ninth year after the completion of the Wei-yang Palace (*Shih chi*, 8.386); it is possible the two events have been confused.

[501]According to *Shih chi*, 93.2641, Kao-tsu set out on this campaign in the twelfth month; he returned from Tung-yüan later that same year to Ch'ang-an (*Shih chi*, 89.2583).

[502]Near modern Shih-chia-chuang 石家莊 city in Hopei (T'an Ch'i-hsiang, 2:9).

Hann Hsin was living among the Hsiung-nu (he was defeated and killed by a Han army in 196 B.C., see *Shih chi*, 93.2635); these bandits may have been men formerly in his service.

[503]This palace was located in the southwest corner of Han Ch'ang-an and was almost as large as the Ch'ang-le palace, occupying about four square miles (Steinhardt, *Chinese Imperial Planning*, p. 56). The name of the palace, Wei-yang or "Eternal," was supposed to suggest longevity for the Liu Clan's reign. It alludes to the "Li-sao" 離騷 attributed to Ch'ü Yüan (*Ch'u-tz'u pu-chu* 楚辭補注, 1.30b, SPPY; Hawkes translates the lines: "Gather the flower of youth before it is too late, / While the fair season is still not yet over" 乃年歲之未晏兮，時亦猶其未央 [*Ch'u Tz'u, The Songs of the South* (Oxford: Clarendon Press, 1959), p. 32]). Liang Yü-sheng points out that other sources claim it was completed in the second month of the seventh year (200 B.C.) and two years later began to be the site where the emperor entertained all official court gatherings. Wang Shu-min (8.342) counters this argument by noting it was possible that the palace was under construction in both the seventh and eighth years (200 and 199 B.C.), and was only completed in 198 B.C.

The walls were about nine miles in circumference and construction of gates and buildings within the palace walls went on until Wu-ti's 武帝 (The Martial Emperor or Emperor Wu) reign (141-86 B.C.; see Ho Ch'ing-ku, *San-fu huang-t'u chiao-chu*, pp. 105-07). See also *Han Ch'ang-an Wei-yang Kung* 漢長安未央宮, Institute of Archaeology of the Chinese Academy of Social Sciences, ed. 2v. (Peking: Chung-kuo Ta-pai-k'o Ch'üan-shu 中國大百科全書, 1996).

[504]*Ch'üeh* 闕. Chavannes (2:391, n. 1) speculates that there were no gatetowers to the south and the west because of Kao-tsu's reproach about excess.

the [lands within the] four seas as his home; without a magnificent and beautiful [dwelling], there will be no way to emphasize his majesty; this will also prevent later generations from having a more [magnificent and beautiful building] than this." Kao-tsu was thus pleased.

Kao-tsu went to Tung-yüan and passed by Po-jen 柏人[505]; the Prime Minister of Chao, Kuan Kao 貫高, and others plotted to fell Kao-tsu, [but] Kao-tsu sensed something and accordingly did not stay there.[506] The King of Tai, Liu Chung, abandoned his state and fled, returning by himself to Lo-yang.[507] He was deposed and made the Marquis of Ho-yang 合陽.[508]

In the ninth year (198 B.C.), the affairs of the Prime Minister of Chao, Kuan Kao, and the

[505] About sixty miles south of Tung-yüan 東垣 (modern Shih-chia-chuang city in Hopei) on the road to Han-tan 邯鄲 (T'an Ch'i-hsiang, 2:9).

Ch'en Chih (p. 11-12) believes the original name was Po-jen 柏仁 and that the place was famous for producing seeds (jen 仁) of the po-tree (cypress) which played a role in Chinese traditional pharmacy (see G. A. Stuart, *Chinese Materia Medica* [rpt.; New York: Gordon Press, 1977], p. 432).

[506] The most detailed account of these events can be found in the biographies of Chang Erh 張耳 and Ch'en Yü 陳餘 (*Shih chi*, 89.2583-84). There Liu Pang is said to have asked the name of the place he had arrived at and, upon learning it was *po-jen*, 柏 [=迫] 人, interpreted it to mean he was being pursued. Thus he did not stay. The *Han shu* (1B.65) account adds more detail here.

The background for this assassination attempt can also be found in Chapter 89. After Chang Erh died in 202 B.C., his son Chang Ao 張敖 succeeded him as King of Chao. Kao-tsu's daughter, Princess Yüan of Lu, was married to Chang Ao. But when Kao-tsu was returning from dealing with Hann Hsin's rebellion (in 200 B.C., not from the campaign against Ch'en Hsi, as *Shih chi*, 104.2775-76 argues), he passed through Chao. Although Chang Ao treated the emperor with the greatest respect and courtesy, Liu Pang sat with his legs sprawled (*chi chü* 箕踞) and cursed his son-in-law, reminiscent not only of Liu Pang's receptions of Li Yi-chi (*Shih chi*, 8.358) and of Ch'ing Pu (*Shih chi*, 91.2602), but also the criticism offered by Kao Ch'i and Wang Ling shortly after Liu Pang became emperor (*Shih chi*, 8.381). The expression "sat with sprawled legs" also appeared in two other chapters of the *Shih chi*, both in accounts of knight-errants. In Ching K'o's 荊軻 biography, after his assassination attempt had failed and he was wounded, "he leaned against and pillar and laughed; his legs spread before him, he cursed the king" (*Shih chi*, 86.2535 and *Grand Scribe's Records*, 7.332). In Kuo Hsieh's biography the expression *chi chü* is used to depict a man who dared to show his lack of respect for Kuo (*Shih chi*, 124.3186). Ssu-ma Ch'ien may be trying to suggest that Liu Pang shared some of the spirit of the knight-errant.

Whatever the case, Liu Pang's behavior angered the King of Chao's retainers. The following year (199 B.C.), as Liu Pang was returning from Tung-yüan through Chao lead by Kuan Kao 貫高, Chao's prime minister, a man had been hidden within the walls of the post station at Po-jen. After Liu Pang escaped, the plot was uncovered, and he had the king and the conspirators arrested.

[507] Liu Chung fled from the Hsiung-nu (see also *Shih chi*, 106.2821). Liang Yü-sheng (6.233) believes the dating of this to the twelfth month of the seventh year by the *Han shu* (1B.63) is correct.

[508] Also known as Ho-yang 郃陽, it was a county located in modern Shensi in the southeastern portion of the modern county with the same name (Wang Li-ch'i, 8.215n.).

others came to light. He and his three kindred were exterminated.[509] [Kao-tsu] deposed the King of Chao, [Chang] Ao, and made him Marquis Hsüan-p'ing 宣平.[510] This year, he moved the noble families Chao 召, Ch'ü 屈, Ching 景, and Huai 懷 of Ch'u and the T'ien 田 Clan of Ch'i to the Land within the Passes.[511]

The Wei-yang Palace[512] was completed. Kao-tsu held a great court gathering for the feudal lords and the assembled ministers, setting out wine in the front hall of the Wei-yang [Palace].[513] Kao-tsu lifted his jade scyphus,[514] and stood up to offer [his father] the T'ai-shang Huang a toast, saying: [*387*] "In the beginning you, sir, often considered me to have no prospects, unable to manage property, and not equal to [Liu] Chung in ability.[515] Now seeing those tasks which I have accomplished, whose have been more numerous, Chung's or mine?"[516] The assembled ministers in the hall all shouted "Long life!" and roared in their pleasure.[517]

In the tenth month of the tenth year (5 November-3 December 198 B.C.), Ch'ing Pu, the King of Huai-nan,[518] P'eng Yüeh, the King of Liang,[519] Lu Wan, the King of Yen,[520] Liu Chia, the

---

[509]According to one account (*Shih chi*, 104.2775-76), when faced with arrest, all of the conspirators except for Kuan Kao committed suicide; Kuan then allowed himself to be taken to Ch'ang-an so he could exonerate Chang Ao with his testimony. The most detailed account of these events (*Shih chi*, 89.2583), however, argues that all the conspirators were taken to Ch'ang-an. After Kuan Kao's testimony assured the emperor that Chang Ao was not involved, Kuan slit his throat. All the other conspirators were rewarded for their bravery with official positions. There is no mention of his execution.

[510]According to Wang Li-ch'i (8.215n.), this was a title only with no fief. But *Han shu pu-chu* (16.46a) records Chang Ao's title as "Marquis Wu of Hsüan-p'ing" and suggests he indeed was enfeoffed with Hsüan-p'ing; T'an Ch'i-hsiang lists no such place.

[511]This move was suggested by Liu Ching and involved over 100,000 people (*Shih chi*, 99.2719-20).

[512]On the dating of the palace's construction see n. 503 above.

[513]It seems that this gathering took place in the tenth month (that is to say at the New Year) of the ninth year (cf. *Han shu*, 1B.66).

[514]According to Ying Shao 應邵 (cited in "Chi-chieh") this was one of the vessels used in the Village Wine Drinking ceremony (see also n. 415 above). On scyphus (skyphos) and its similarity to a *chih* 卮 see the paintings on the Greek vase "Harvard 1960.346" displayed on the Perseus Project Website (www.perseus.tufts.edu).

[515]Following Wang Li-ch'i's (8.231) reading of *li* 力 as *neng-li* 能力.

[516]This question had an edge to it since only a year earlier Liu Chung had fled the Hsiung-nu and been deposed for his cowardice (*Shih chi*, 8.386).

[517]Tanaka Kenji (p. 157, n. 3) cites this passage as an example of Ssu-ma Ch'ien's ability to create a dramatic scene from the simplest of situations. Part of Liu Pang's triumph in these first days in the new capital must have been the satisfaction he received from proving to his father that he was not the ne'er-do-well most people in P'ei must have considered him to be in his early years.

[518]According to Ch'ing Pu's biography (*Shih chi*, 91.2603), he attended court in the seventh, eighth, and ninth years of Kao-tsu's reign; there is no mention of this visit to Ch'ang-an.

[519]There is a record of P'eng Yüeh attending court in Ch'ang-an in the ninth and tenth years in his

King of Ching,[521] Liu Chiao, the King of Ch'u, Liu Fei, the King of Ch'i,[522] and Wu Jui, the King of Ch'ang-sha, all came to pay homage at court in the Ch'ang-lo Palace.[523] In spring and summer there were no incidents.

In the seventh month (28 July-25 August 197 B.C.), the T'ai-shang Huang passed away in the Yüeh-yang 櫟陽 Palace.[524] The kings of Ch'u and Liang both came to take part in the funeral procession.[525] Those who were confined in Yüeh-yang were granted pardons.[526] The name

biography (*Shih chi*, 90.2594).

[520]There is no record in Lu's biography (Chapter 93) of him attending court at this time.

[521]There is no record in Liu Chia's biography (Chapter 51) of him attending court at this time.

[522]No court visits are mentioned in the short biography for Liu Fei in Chapter 52. On Liu Fei see also n. 601 below.

[523]The chronological tables (*Shih chi*, 17.810) also record this court visit of the seven kings at New Year.

[524]This was the palace that Liu Pang and his family lived in while waiting for the Ch'ang-le Palace-Residence in Ch'ang-an to be completed.

The *Han chi* (4.2b) records Liu Pang's father's death in the fifth month and his interment on the *kuei-mao* 癸卯 day of the seventh month (9 August 197). This dating seems to have won approval by many scholars and it is that which Ssu-ma Kuang 司馬光 (1019-1086) follows in the *Tzu-chih t'ung-chien*, 12.386. Ch'ien Ta-chao 錢大昭 (1744-1813) in his *Liang Han shu pien-yi* 兩漢書辨疑 (Kuang-ya Shu-chü, 1887), 1.6b-7a, points out that another passage in the *Han shu* supports the dating of T'ai-shang Huang's death in the seventh month ("Lu Wan chuan" 盧綰傳, *Han shu*, 34.1892). He also believes the *Han shu* (1B.67) reference to the death of the "T'ai-shang Huang-hou" 太上皇后 (The Grand Empress, Liu Pang's mother) in the fifth month of this year is an interpolation. Dubs (1:124-25, n. 1) shows this would have been impossible, since she died at the time Kao-tsu first rose in rebellion. Ch'en Chih (p. 12) argues that there were two mothers involved, but it seems improbable that a step-mother who was not Liu Pang's birth mother would have been so honored. Moreover, there is no record of Liu Pang's birth mother having the title T'ai-shang Huang-hou. She was first honored as "Chao-ling Fu-jen 昭靈夫人 (*Han shu*, 1B.52), and later titled "Chao-ling Hou" 昭靈后 and "T'ai-shang Huang-fei" 太上皇妃 (*Han shu*, 3.99).

Based on all the evidence, it seems that (1) the *Shih chi* account of Liu Pang's father passing in the seventh month is correct; (2) there was no one named "T'ai-shang Huang-hou" and the *Han shu* claim that she died in the fifth month must be an error or an interpolation; and (3) Hsün Yüeh, puzzled by the statement in *Han shu* claiming the "T'ai-shang Huang-hou" died in the fifth month—夏五月，太上皇后崩, deleted the word *hou* 后 from the *Han shu* account resulting in his claim in the *Han chi* that Liu Pang's father died in the fifth month—夏五月，太上皇崩.

[525]It may be of interest that only Liu Chia and P'eng Yüeh came to the funeral. In the fall of the same year P'eng Yüeh refused to join Liu Pang in fighting Ch'en Hsi and was eventually accused of treason and executed (*Shih chi*, 90.2594).

[526]Tanaka Kenji (p. 158, n. 2) believes this was to allow them to work on the mausoleum for Liu Pang's father.

of Li-yi 酈邑[527] was changed to Hsin Feng 新豐 (New Feng).[528]

In the eighth month (26 August-24 September 197 B.C.),[529] Ch'en Hsi 陳豨,[530] the Minister of State[531] of Chao, revolted in Tai territory.[532] The sovereign said, "Hsi was once an envoy for me, he really had my trust. The Tai territory is of critical importance to me; for this reason I enfeoffed Hsi as a ranking marquis,[533] to serve as Minister of State [of Chao] and guard against Tai. Only now has he joined with Wang Huang and the others in plundering and robbing Tai territory! The officers and people in Tai territory have committed no offense. Let the officers and people of Tai be pardoned."

In the ninth month (25 September-23 October 197) [*388*], the sovereign personally went east to assault them. When he reached Han-tan, the sovereign was pleased and said, "As Hsi did not come south to occupy Han-tan and oppose us at the Chang 漳 River,[534] I understand that there is nothing he can do!" When he heard that Hsi's generals were all former merchants,[535] the sovereign said, "I know the means by which I can deal with them."[536] Then he enticed Hsi's

[527]A little over twenty miles due east of modern Sian in Shensi (T'an Ch'i-hsiang, 2:6).

[528]According to the *K'uo-ti chih* 括地志 (compiled under the supervision of Li T'ai 李泰 (618-652), this adminstrative geography was presented to the throne in 642, listing the adminsitrative divisons of China according to a 639 register; later lost and constructed by Sun Hsing-yen 孫星衍 (1753-1818) into the modern 8 *chüan* versions) cited in "Cheng-yi," Liu Pang moved many of the townsfolk from Feng Township to Yüeh-yang because his father had missed them and the lifestyle he led in Feng. As "Cheng-yi" suggests, however, it would have been more logical to rename Yüeh-yang "Hsin Feng" when this happened, not after Liu Pang's father died. According to a note in the *Hsi-ching tsa-chi* 西京雜記 (Peking: Chung-hua, 1985, pp. 11-12), what Liu Pang's father missed most were the cockfights, gambling, drinking and the like and such were the companions who populated Hsin Feng and gave it a reputation as a wide open town.

[529]Liang Yü-sheng (6.234) notes that the dating of this revolt varies considerably in the various accounts in the *Shih ch;* Liang concludes Ch'en revolted in the ninth month of the tenth year (197 B.C.).

[530]See his biography in Chapter 93. Ch'en Hsi was a native of Yüan-ch'ü 宛句 (southwest of modern Ho-tse 菏澤 County in Shantung, Wang Li-ch'i, 8.216n.). He gained merit for his service under Liu Pang in the campaign against Hann Hsin and was put in charge of most of the troops on the Hsiung-nu border.

[531]*Hsiang-kuo* 相國. Bielenstein suggests "Chancellor of State."

[532]This perhaps as a result of Liu Pang deposing the King of Chao, Chang Ao, the previous year (*Shih chi,* 8.386).

[533]*Lieh-hou* 列侯. Bielenstein has "Full Marquis." See also n. 462 above.

[534]West of Han-tan the Chang flows south creating an arc around the city before it swings north again a few miles further east (T'an Ch'i-hsiang, 2:9). This natural fortification was often defended by Chao armies in earlier times against troops moving from the south.

[535]In Ch'en Hsi's biography (*Shih chi,* 93.2641) he is told this by an unidentified party.

[536]*Yü* 與 here has been read variously by traditional commentators. In support of our reading, "to deal with," see Wu Hsün, *Han shu chu-shang,* pp. 10-11.

On Kao-tsu's relations with merchants see also Hayashi Hideki 林英樹. "Zenkan Gôso no akibito shihai" 前漢高祖の商人支配, *Tôyô gakuhô,* 79.1 (1997).

generals with gold many times and many of Hsi's generals surrendered.[537]

In the eleventh year (196 B.C.), with the matter of Kao-tsu being in Han-tan to execute Hsi and the others still unfinished, Hsi's general Hou Ch'ang 侯敞, in command of more than ten thousand men, was marauding about, Wang Huang was camped at Ch'ü-ni 曲逆,[538] and Chang Ch'un 張春 crossed the Ho to strike at Liao-ch'eng 聊城.[539] Han sent General Kuo Meng 郭蒙[540] together with a general of Ch'i to assault them and they crushed them.[541] The Grand Commandant Chou Po 周勃 took the road by way of T'ai-yüan to enter and stabilize the territory of Tai. When he reached Ma-yi, Ma-yi would not submit, and he immediately attacked and put it to the sword.[542]

Hsi's general Chao Li defended Tung-yüan; Kao-tsu attacked him, but he did not submit.[543] After more than a month, his foot soldiers reviled Kao-tsu and Kao-tsu became angry. After the city surrendered, he ordered that those who had reviled him should be sent out and he would execute them, those who did not [*389*] revile him, he would pardon.[544] At this point he subdivided the land north of the Chao mountains,[545] enthroned his son, Heng 恆, and with the

[537]In the various parallel accounts of these actions there is no mention of any general surrendering because he had accepted gold or other property.

[538]About twenty miles west of modern Pao-ting 保定 City in Hopei (T'an Ch'i-hsiang, 2:9).

[539]About seventy five miles east of Han-tan near the modern county of the same name in Shantung (T'an Ch'i-hsiang, 2:8).

[540]Nothing further is known of Kuo.

[541]In Kuan Ying's biography (Shih chi, 95.2672) Kuan is said to have defeated and executed Hou Ch'ang. Hou and Wang Huang were captured and put to death after fighting below Ch'ü-ni; Chang Ch'un was defeated by Han troops at Liao-ch'eng (Shih chi, 93.2641).

[542]See also the notice in Chou Po's biography (Shih chi, 57.2070).

[543]The accounts of this campaign against Ch'en Hsi in other chapters of the Shih chi are numerous and varied. The date for the start of the campaign is also listed as autumn of the tenth year (Shih chi, 90.2594); Shih chi, 93.2628 claims the rebellion began a year later. In the winter of the eleventh year several of Ch'en's generals were taken (Shih chi, 93.2641). Liu Tse 劉澤 also participated in the campaign during the eleventh year (Shih chi, 51.1993). In the spring of the eleventh year Ch'en Hsi's armies were defeated (Shih chi, 10.413). Finally, in Chou Po's biography (no date given; see Shih chi, 57.2070) Liu Pang is said to have attacked the forces of Hann Hsin, Ch'en Hsi, and Chao Li at Lou-fan 樓煩 (near modern Ning-wu in Shansi about one-hundred miles north-northwest of T'ai-yüan [T'an Ch'i-hsiang, 2:9]).

[544]The parallel account on Shih chi, 93.2641 reads 不罵者黥之, "those who did not revile him, he would have tatooed."

[545]Lü Tsu-ch'ien 呂祖謙 (1137-1181) notes that this passage reveals the wide geographical knowledge that Ssu-ma Ch'ien presumably gained in his travels (from Lü's Ta-shih chi-chieh t'i 大事記解題 as cited in Yang, Li-tai, p. 415). The "Chao mountains" probably refer to the Ch'ang Shan 常山 (Ch'ang Mountains, see also the following note).

land made him King of Tai, with his capital at Chin-yang 晉陽.[546]

In the spring, Han Hsin, the Marquis of Huai-yin, plotted rebellion in the Land within the Passes; he and his three kindred were exterminated.[547]

In the summer,[548] P'eng Yüeh, the King of Liang plotted rebellion; he was deposed and moved to Shu; he again plotted rebellion, and finally he and his three kindred were exterminated.[549] [Kao-tsu] enthroned his son [Liu] Hui 恢 as King of Liang,[550] and his son [Liu] Yu 友[551] as King of Huai-yang 淮陽.[552]

In the fall, in the seventh month (16 August-13 September 196), Ch'ing Pu, the King of Huai-nan, rebelled[553]; to the east he annexed territory of Liu Chia, the King of Ching, to the

[546]Liu Heng was the future Wen-ti 文帝 (The Cultured Emperor, r. 180-157 B.C.).

Chin-yang is located near modern T'ai-yüan in Shansi (T'an Ch'i-hsiang, 2:6). Liang Yü-sheng (6.234) points out that both Chin-yang and Chung-tu 中都 are listed in related accounts as the capital; Liang speculates that Chin-yang was the official capital, but the king preferred to live in Chung-tu.

The account of these events on *Shih chi,* 93.2641 differs somewhat: "Liu Pang returned to Lo-yang and said, 'Tai is located north of the Ch'ang Mountains and we consider it too distant for Chao to control from south of the mountains.' He made its capital at Chung-tu with [former] Tai and Yen-men 雁門 both belonging to Tai."

[547]According to Han Hsin's biography (*Shih chi,* 92.2628-29), after Han Hsin had been removed as King of Ch'u, he made an agreement with Ch'en Hsi, that if the latter revolted, Han would support him. When Ch'en rebelled and Liu Pang left to lead the troops in the east, Han made plans to move against Lü Hou and the Heir in the capital. The empress heard of this and devised a scheme with Hsiao Ho to pretend that Ch'en Hsi had been captured and killed, summoning all the nobles to offer their congratulations. Han Hsin was ill, but Hsiao Ho pressed him and he came, only to be arrested and executed along with his family.

[548]Liang Yü-sheng (6.234) points out that Liu Hui and Liu Yu were made kings in the third month of the eleventh year, thus P'eng Yüeh's rebellion must have taken place before that, not *in the summer.* Although Liang makes a small error here—the chronological tables (*Shih chi,* 17.811) tell us Liu Hui was made King of Liang in the *second* month and Liu Yu in the third—his point is well taken.

[549]Details are provided in P'eng's biography (*Shih chi,* 90.2594): after being assigned to Shu as a commoners, P'eng met Empress Lü, who was on her way to Lo-yang, on the road and begged to be allowed to return to his home, Ch'ang-yi 昌邑 (about thirty-five miles southwest of modern Chi-ning 濟寧 in Shantung [T'an Ch'i-hsiang, 2.7]). The empress agreed and accompanied him to Lo-yang, but then denounced P'eng falsely to Kao-tsu resulting in P'eng's execution.

[550]Liu Pang's fifth son who later became King Kung 共 of Chao (cf. *Shih chi,* 8.393).

[551]Liu Pang's sixth son who later became King Yu 幽 of Chao (cf. *Shih chi,* 8.393).

[552]A small state of about 5,500 square miles centered around the area of modern Huai-yang City in eastern Honan about 100 miles southeast of Chengchow (T'an Ch'i-hsiang, 2.19); its capital was at Ch'en 陳 County to which Liu Pang summoned the nobles in 201 B.C. in order to depose Han Hsin (*Shih chi,* 8.382).

[553]Here, as in the case of most of the "rebellions" of Liu Pang's former generals, although there was talk about rebellion in Ch'ing Pu's camp, it was a disaffected member of Ch'ing Pu's staff who accused him of plotting to rebel out of spite (*Shih chi,* 91.2603-4).

north he crossed the Huai 淮 and [Liu] Chiao, the King of Ch'u, fled to Hsüeh 薛.[554] Kao-tsu personally went to assault him.[555] He enthroned his son, [Liu] Ch'ang 長, as King of Huai-nan.[556]

In the tenth month of the twelfth year (12 November-11 December 196 B.C.), Kao-tsu had already struck at [Ch'ing] Pu's army at K'uai-chui 會甀[557]; Pu fled and [Kao-tsu] ordered his deputy generals to pursue him.[558]

As Kao-tsu returned [to the capital], he stopped by P'ei and stayed on.[559] He set out wine at the Palace of P'ei 沛, summoning all his old acquaintances, the elders, and the youth to

[554]In the more detailed account given in Ch'ing Pu's biography (*Shih chi*, 91.2603-6) it is said that Ch'ing Pu pursued Liu Chia and killed him. Hsüeh County was located about forty-five miles southeast of modern Chi-ning in Shantung (T'an Ch'i-hsiang, 2:8). Ch'ing Pu had assured his generals that the emperor was too old to lead the army in person this time, but had been wrong. Ch'ing's plan of attack, moreover, was predicted by one of Liu Pang's advisors and generally considered to be a weak one.

[555]Tanaka Kenji (p. 161-62, n. 2) points out that this is the fourth place Ssu-ma Ch'ien records Kao-tsu personally leading troops out of the capital on a campaign. Ssu-ma Ch'ien earlier tells us he also led troops against Tsang T'u 臧荼, the King of Yen (*Shih chi*, 8.381-82: 十月，燕王臧荼反，攻下代地。高祖自將擊之，得燕王臧荼), against Li Chi 利幾 (*Shih chi*, 8.381-82:其秋，利幾反，高祖自將兵擊之，利幾走), and against Chao Li 趙利 (*Shih chi*, 8.384-85: 曼丘臣、王黃立故趙將趙利為王以反，高祖自往擊之). He believes that Ssu-ma Ch'ien's retention of this repetition from what were probably the original records of the campaigns by early Han scribes was intentional and designed to show that despite the claims that Liu Pang was "humane and loved people, fond of largesse, and openhearted" 仁而愛人，喜施，意豁如也 (*Shih chi*, 8.342), he had become suspicious by nature in his later years." To support this contention, Tanaka points to the conversation between Liu Pang and the Marquis of K'uai-ch'eng 蒯成, Chou Hsieh 周A, on *Shih chi*, 98.2712: "When the sovereign was about to personally attack Ch'en Hsi, the Marquis of K'uai-ch'eng wept and said, 'When Ch'in first attacked and defeated the world, he never personally went [on campaign]. Now Your Highness often personally goes on campaign—is this because there is no one who can be sent?' The sovereign considered [Chou Hsieh] loved him too much and granted that when he entered the [imperial] hall he did not have to take small quick steps [as prescribed by ritual] and that he would not be put to death if he killed someone." The point is that Liu Pang in fact no longer trusted anyone to undertake such campaigns as Chou Hsieh's question suggested.

[556]This was Liu Pang's seventh son (*Shih chi*, 8.394). On this appointment, see also *Shih chi*, 17.811. Chavannes (8.396, n. 1) points out that Liu Ch'ang was a child of three *sui* at the time. See also n. 606 below.

[557]A village about fifteen miles south of modern Su-chou 宿州 City in Anhwei (T'an Ch'i-hsiang, 2:19).

[558]Ch'ing Pu escaped across the Huai with one hundred of his cavalry, much like Hsiang Yü. He made it further than Hsiang Yü, however, crossing the Yangtze. But finally he was tricked into going to P'o-yang 鄱陽 (about ten miles southwest of modern Ching-te-chen 景德鎮 City in in modern Kiangsi [T'an Ch'i-hsiang, 2:12]) where he was killed by locals at Tzu 茲 Township (*Shih chi*, 91.2606).

[559]K'uai-chui was about one-hundred miles south of P'ei (T'an Ch'i-hsiang, 2:19) and thus the stopover in Liu Pang's hometown involved only a short detour on his way back to the capital.

indulge in wine,[560] he had over 120 children from P'ei sent to him, to teach them to sing. When he was in his cups, Kao-tsu struck the dulcimer, and sang a song he had composed himself:

> A great wind arose, clouds flew up!
> My prestige increasing within the seas, I return to my hometown.
> But where will I find valiant warriors to hold the four directions![561]

[560]There is irony here, since Liu Pang couldn't even pay for the wine he drank when he first lived in P'ei. This occasion was surely related to the ceremony of Village Wine Drinking which is described at some length above in n. 415.

[561]This poem should be read in the context of the song Hsiang Yü sang just before he died, the latter as a lament for Hsiang's failure, the former as a victory song. Hsiang Yü's song reads: "My strength lifted mountains, my vigor overshadowed the world. / But the times are not favorable, and Piebald can no longer fly. / Piebald cannot fly, but nothing can be done about it? / And Yü, oh Yü! what can I do about you?" 力拔山兮氣蓋世，時不利兮騅不逝。騅不逝兮可奈何，虞兮，虞兮，奈若何！ (*Shih chi*, 7.333; the translation is slightly revised from that in *Grand Scribe's Records*, 1:205).

It is obvious that both poems are written in the *sao*-meter of the *Ch'u tz'u*. The language of Hsiang Yü's lament reflects that collection somewhat. The ending of "Ta ssu ming" 大司命, for example, a poem which is also a lament over the imminent parting of lovers, ends: 愁人兮奈何，願若今兮無虧。固人命兮有當，孰離合兮可為？ (Chin Kai-ch'eng 金開誠 *et al.*, *Ch'u Yüan chi chiao-chu* 屈原集校注 [2v., Peking: Chung-hua, 1996], p. 243), which in David Hawkes' translation becomes: "It pains my heart, but what can I do? / I only wish the present could always stay the same. / But all man's life is fated; / Its meetings and partings not his to arrange" (*Ch'u Tz'u*, p. 40). It also fits Mark Edward Lewis' claim that the *Ch'u tz'u* poems "provided a language for the assertion of private worth in the face of political failure" (in Lewis' *Writing and Authority in Early China* [Albany: State University of New York Press, 1999], p. 7).

Liu Pang's poem seems to depict his own rise (as symbolized by the clouds that are often associated with the dragon of his supposed patrimony) in the midst of the great winds of rebellion at the end of the Ch'in (this interpretation owes much to Yoshikawa Kôjirô 吉川幸次郎 and his "Kan Kô So no Daifûka ni tsuite" 漢高祖の大風歌似ついて, in *Yoshikawa Kôjirô zenshû* 吉川幸次郎全集 [Tokyo: Tsukuma Shobô, 1969], 6:23-42) in the first line (大風起兮雲飛揚). The second line depicts the present and echoes the Chinese sentiment that it is useless to become rich and famous unless you can go home to show it off (威加海內兮歸故鄉). The final line is concerned with the future and suggests Liu Pang's rising suspicion of his subordinates (安得猛士兮守四方).

It also contains imagery and language suggestive of the *Ch'u tz'u*. The expressions *feng ch'i* 風起 and *fei yang* 飛揚 from the first line, for example, frame the opening section of the "Ho Po" 河伯 in the *Ch'u tz'u*: 與女遊兮九河，衝風起兮橫波。乘水車兮荷蓋，駕兩龍兮驂螭。登崑崙兮四望，心飛揚兮浩蕩。(Chin Kai-ch'eng, *Ch'u Yüan chi chiao-chu*, p. 267). In Hawkes' rendition these lines become: "I wander with you by the Nine Mouths of the river / When the storm wind rises and lashes up the waves. / I ride a water chariot with a canopy of lotus; / Two dragons draw it, betweeen two water-serpents. / I climb the K'un-lun mountain and look over the four quarters, / And my heart leaps up in me, beating wildly" (*Ch'u Tz'u*, p. 42). It is not too difficult to find other resonances here: like the persona of the "Ho Po" Liu Pang too has recently metaphorically ascended Mount K'un-lun to look down upon the four quarters of his reign; the dragons in harness are also appropriate.

He had the children all practice the song with him. Kao-tsu then got up to dance, his emotions ran high until they overcame him and streams of tears flowed down his face. He said to the elders of P'ei, "The traveler sorrows for his old village. Although my capital is in the Land within the Passes, after my long span of years my soul will still draw pleasure from thinking about P'ei.[562] Moreover, since I came from being Magistrate of P'ei, executing the brutal and faithless, to finally obtain the world, let P'ei be made my bath-town![563] I exempt you from taxes and corvée labor, and for generation after generation there will be nothing that you have to provide [the state]." The elders and older women of P'ei, all old acquaintances, day after day drank to their hearts' content and told stories of former times, having a good time poking fun [at each other]. After more than ten [*390*] days, Kao-tsu wanted to leave, but the elders of P'ei insisted that Kao-tsu to stay longer. Kao-tsu said, "My people are too numerous, you elders can not keep them supplied." Only then did he go. [The people of] P'ei emptied the county-seat going to the west of the town to offer [wine and food]. Kao-tsu was again brought to stay longer and in tents that were set up they drank for three days. The elders of P'ei all knocked their foreheads against the ground and said, "P'ei has been fortunate to have its taxes and corvée labor exempted, but Feng 豐[564] has not yet had an exemption. Would that Your Majesty take pity on it." Kao-tsu said, "Feng is the place where I was born and grew up. It is the last place I could forget. But I singled it out for the reason that it rebelled against Us under Yung Ch'ih on Wei's behalf." Only after the elders of P'ei implored did he also exempt Feng as he had P'ei. At this time, he appointed the Marquis of P'ei, Liu P'i 劉濞 (215-154 B.C.), as King of Wu.[565]

Whether or not these poems evoke particular passages of the *Ch'u tz'u,* they suggest its style as would be appropriate for two great leaders with ties to the state of Ch'u. Were these songs actually written by Hsiang Yü and Liu Pang? More likely they were composed by the same person, intending them to be read as a pair—either the author of one of Ssu-ma Ch'ien's sources for this chapter or the Grand Scribe himself.

Another reading of Liu Pang's poem, featuring the song's role in early Han music and dance, can be found in Wang Wen-ch'ing 王文清, "Liu Pang yü Han ch'u yin-yüeh ko-wu" 劉邦與漢初音樂歌舞, *Liu Pang yen-chiu,* 3 (1993): 39-47, especially p. 43.

[562]These four lines have been read as a folksong by modern critics such as T'ang Yüeh (see his "Chiu-shu chung te hsin-shih" 舊書中的新詩, *Hsiao-shuo yüeh-pao* 小説月報, 13.10-12 (10 Dec. 1922), pp. 1-2.

[563]*T'ang-mu yi* 湯沐邑 or "bath-towns" were originally located in the royal domain and granted to feudal lords as a place to bathe before their audience with the king (see also *Grand Scribe's Records,* 7:219, n. 17). By Han times they had evolved into towns in any location which had been exempted from paying taxes to the government, their revenues going to supply "bath water," i.e., private funds, for their lord. The idea here is that this would be both a way for Liu Pang to honor his home town as well as to except them from taxes. See also Watson, *Han,* 1:84, n. 24.

[564]The township (now a county) located about twenty miles west of P'ei (T'an Ch'i-hsiang, 2:8).

[565]Liu P'i was the son of Liu Pang's elder brother, Liu Chung (see Liu P'i's biography in *Shih chi* Chapter 106). The kingdom of Wu was revived after Ch'ing Pu killed Liu Chia 劉賈 (*Shih chi,* 17.812), who had been

The Han generals separately struck at [Ch'ing] Pu's army south and north of the T'ao 洮 River,[566] and all crushed it; they pursued, caught, and executed Pu at P'o-yang 鄱陽.[567]

Fan K'uai separately commanded troops to stabilize Tai,[568] and executed Ch'en Hsi at Tang-ch'eng 當城.[569]

King of Ching 荊 (*Shih chi*, 91.2606); see also Chavannes, 2:398, n. 3).

[566]The location of the T'ao River is problematic. Wang Li-ch'i (8.216n.) believes the T'ao is north of what was then the seat of Ling-ling 零陵 Commandery, almost fifty miles west of modern Ling-ling in Hunan. This location raises a problem, however, since it is about 650 miles southwest of the K'uai-chui battlefield from which Ch'ing Pu fled and over 350 miles southwest of Po-yang where Ch'ing Pu was supposedly killed after the battles on the T'ao. The T'ao is not in T'an Ch'i-hsiang, although T'ao-yang 洮陽, a county-seat presumably on the north bank of a river named T'ao is (2:23). Chavannes (2:398, n. 5), following Hsü Kuang's claim in "Chi-chieh," fixes it between the Huai and Chiang rivers. Although this is a more logical location, it would mean Ch'ing Pu was able to move nearly 100 miles south before he was captured, since Po-yang is over 60 miles south of the Yangtze (T'an Ch'i-hsiang, 2:12). Liang Yü-sheng (6.234-35) in a long note proposes that T'ao is an error for Pi 沘 which is written similarly. The Pi is moreover about 80 miles south of K'uai-chui (Ch'ing Pu would have logically fled southward after his defeat), and between the Huai and Chiang rivers (it flows north into the Huai through the countyseat, Liu hsien 六縣, Ch'ing Pu's hometown; see T'an Ch'i-hsiang, 2:8 and 2:24), and is within Ch'ing Pu's state of Chiu-chiang. All this fits so well we are inclined to support Liang Yü-sheng's argument in favor of Pi.

Most commentators have focussed on the question of the location of these events. We know that Ts'ao Ts'an aided in the campaign againts Ch'ing Pu (*Shih chi*, 54.2028), but we can only speculate that the other generals were Ch'en P'ing 陳平 (see *Shih chi*, 56.2058), Li Shang 酈商 (*Shih chi*, 95.2662), Shen-t'u Chia 申屠 嘉 (*Shih chi*, 96.2682), and Liu P'i 劉濞 (*Shih chi*, 106.2821). The parallel passage in the *Han shu* (1B.75) reads *pieh-chiang* 別將 (deputy general) for the *chiang pieh* 將別 (generals separately) here in the *Shih chi* passage; although this fits better with the preceeding accounts (see *Shih chi*, 8.389: 十二年，十月，高祖已擊布軍會甄， 布走，令別將追之。), it still does not make clear who this (these?) *pieh-chiang* was (were).

[567]P'o-yang is about ten miles south of modern Ching-te-chen 景德鎮 City in modern Kiangsi (T'an Ch'i-hsiang, 2:12).

According to Ch'ing Pu's biography, he was killed near P'o-yang by local people (*Shih chi*, 91.2606), not by the Han army.

[568]Wang Li-ch'i (8.217n. argues there is no record in Fan K'uai's biography (*Shih chi* Chapter 95) of him stabilizing Tai; Ch'en Hsi's biography records (*Shih chi*, 93.2642) that Chou Po stabilized Tai during the winter of the eleventh year (196 B.C.). But Fan's biography (*Shih chi*, 95.2657) does claim that Fan defeated and captured a number of Ch'en Hsi's generals and brought order to seventy-three villages in Tai. There is also an account in Ch'en's biography which relates that Fan K'uai captured and executed Ch'en (*Shih chi*, 93.2642).

[569]Tang-ch'eng is located about 80 miles west-northwest of modern Peking in Hopei (T'an Ch'i-hsiang, 2:18). There is also an account of Fan K'uai capturing and executing Ch'en Hsi in the latter's biography (*Shih chi*, 93.2642); in this version Fan executed Ch'en in the winter of the twelfth year (195 B.C.) at Ling-ch'iu 靈 丘, near modern Ling-ch'iu County in Shansi (T'an Ch'i-hsiang, 2:18); Ling-ch'iu is 110 miles west-southwest of Peking, about 50 miles southwest of Tang-ch'eng. Liang Yü-sheng (6.235) brings in a second variable (besides the location), pointing out that in Chou Po's 周勃 biography (*Shih chi*, 57.2070) he is said to have

[391] In the eleventh month (12 December 196-9 January 195), Kao-tsu went from [Ch'ing] Pu's army to Ch'ang-an.[570]

In the twelfth month (10 January-8 February 195), Kao-tsu said, "The First Emperor of Ch'in, King Yin 隱 of Ch'u, Ch'en She,[571] King An Hsi 安釐 of Wei (r. 276-243),[572] King Min 緡 of Ch'i (r. *323-284),[573] and King Tao Hsiang 悼襄 of Chao (r. 244-236)[574] all were cut off without descendants; I confer on each of them ten families[575] to attend to their graves—for the First Emperor of Ch'in twenty families and for Wu-chi 無忌 (d. 243), the Noble Scion of Wei,[576] five families." He pardoned the officers and people of the Tai territory who had been robbed and plundered by Ch'en Hsi and Chao Li, he pardoned all of them.[577] The generals of Ch'en Hsi who had surrendered said that when he rebelled, Lu Wan, the King of Yen, sent a man to Hsi's place and plotted secretly with him. The sovereign sent the Marquis of Pi-yang 辟陽[578] to call Wan in, but Wan claimed he was ill. The Marquis of Pi-yang returned, and said there were signs that Wan would rebel.[579] In the second month (10 March-8 April 195), he sent Fan K'uai and Chou Po commanding troops to strike at [Lu] Wan, King of Yen.[580] He pardoned the officers and people

executed Ch'en. Since both Chou Po and Fan K'uai were active in supressing rebellious activities in Tai during this period, it is possible that a force with both of them in command positions was responsible for Ch'en Hsi's defeat and death. They served together a little later in the campaign against Lu Wan (see *Shih chi*, 8.391).

[570]This counterdicts the text just above which relates that on his way back from fighting Ch'ing Pu's forces Liu Pang stopped off at P'ei (cf. our translation of *Shih chi*, 8.389 just above).

[571]Ch'en She's biography makes up *Shih chi* Chapter 48. Wang Li-ch'i (8.217n.), following Liang Yü-sheng (6.236) points out that Liu Pang is careful to refer to all these rulers except Ch'en She by their posthumous title and believe that Ch'en She was probably originally a note of gloss which was erroneously copied into the text.

[572]See the account of King An Hsi in "The Hereditary House of Wei" (*Shih chi*, 44.1853ff.).

[573]See the description of his reign, *Shih chi*, 46.1895-1901.

[574]See the account of his reign in "The Hereditary House of Chao" (*Shih chi*, 43.1830-31).

[575]In Ch'en She's biography (*Shih chi*, 48.1960) it is said that Kao-tsu had thirty families attend to Ch'en's grave.

[576]His biography makes up *Shih chi* Chapter 77.

[577]As in the English formulation here, the Chinese syntax is unusual. Wang Li-ch'i (8.217n.) suggests that the first *she* 赦 "pardon" is an error and should be excised.

[578]This was Shen Yi-chi 審食其. Pi-yang 辟陽 was a county located southeast of modern Chi County in Hopei (Wang Li-ch'i, 8.217n.). Shen had received this appointment through Lü Hou who prized him highly, in part for the role he played as her protector when she was captured by Hsiang Yü (*Shih chi*, 7.321). Later, under her rule, he became chancellor of the left (*Shih chi*, 9.400).

[579]We follow Wang Li-ch'i (8.217n.) in reading *tuan* 端 as *chi-hsiang* 跡象, "signs" or "indications."

[580]The military details of this campaign are given in Chou Po's biograpy (*Shih chi*, 57.2070). In the parallel account in Lu Wan's biography, the suspicions about Lu Wan's loyalty are dismissed as a plot by Emperess Lü. Lu eventually fled to join the Hsiung-nu, but died about a year later (*Shih chi*, 93.2638-39). There

of Yen who rebelled with him. He enthroned the imperial son [Liu] Chien 建 as King of Yen.[581]

When Kao-tsu had struck at [Ch'ing] Pu, he had been hit by a errant arrow and along the road [back] he fell ill.[582] His illness got worse, and Lü Hou called in an excellent physician. When the physician entered to examine him, Kao-tsu asked him about treatments. The physician said, "The illness can be treated."[583] At this Kao-tsu contemptuously said to him: "With the status of a commoner I carried a three-foot sword to take the world, was this not the will of Heaven? Fate lies with Heaven—even P'ien Ch'üeh 扁鵲[584] could not help!"[585] In the end he did not allow him to treat his illness, but granted him fifty catties of gold and dismissed him. In a short while, Lü Hou asked, "After your majesty's hundred years are up, if Chancellor of State Hsiao dies, who should be allowed to replace [*392*] him?" The Sovereign said, "Ts'ao Ts'an would do."[586] She asked about who would be next, and the sovereign said, "Wang Ling would do. But Ling is a bit outspoken and Ch'en P'ing could assist him. Ch'en P'ing has more than enough intelligence, but can hardly be relied on by himself.[587] Chou Po is respectful and loyal, but lacks refinement, but the one who could pacify the Liu Clan would certainly be Po. He could be allowed to be Grand Commandant."[588] Lü Hou again asked about who would be next, and the

is a record of this campaign in Fan K'uai's biography (*Shih chi*, 95.2657).

[581]This was Liu Pang's eighth son (*Shih chi*, 8.393). See also *Shih chi*, 17.812.

[582]There are various accounts of this illness. In the hereditary house devoted to Chang Liang the text claims that Kao-tsu was ill before Ch'ing Pu's revolt and had originally intended to send the Heir at the head of his troops (*Shih chi*, 55.2045). In the following chapter it is said that Kao-tsu was ill all the way back to the capital after putting down the revolt (*Shih chi*, 56.2059), suggesting that the illness was longterm and not merely the result of his wound.

[583]As Wang Li-ch'i (8.218n.) argues, the physician probably believes the Kao-tsu will not recover, so he simply says "The illness can be treated." Liu Pang understands the nature of the doctor's response and therefore becomes angry and refuses treatment.

Yang Yen-ch'i 楊燕起 reads this as Ssu-ma Ch'ien's condemnation of the idea of *T'ien-ming* 天命, see his "Ssu-ma Ch'ien yü Tung Chung-shu" 司馬遷與董仲舒, *Shih-hsüeh shih yen-chiu* 史學史研究, 1986.4: 31.

[584]A legendary Chinese healer of antiquity, see his biography in *Shih chi* Chapter 105.

[585]This is reminiscent of Hsiang Yü's refusal of the offer made by chief of Wu-chiang's precinct to ferry Hsiang Yü across the Yangtze ahead of the closing troops of Liu Pang. Hsiang Yü replied, "Since Heaven is causing me to perish, why should I bother to cross the river?" 天之亡我，我何渡為 (*Shih chi*, 7.336; revised translation from *Grand Scribe's Records*, 1.207).

[586]Although Ts'ao Ts'an did replace Hsiao as Chancellor of State on the later's death in 193 B.C., both accounts of this event claim that although Hsiao Ho and Ts'ao Ts'an had had a falling out, when Hui-ti asked Hsiao Ho on his deathbed who should replace him, Hsiao himself recommended Ts'ao Ts'an (cf. *Shih chi*, 53.2019 and 54.2023).

[587]In 189 B.C., a year after Ts'ao Ts'an died, the chancelloship was divided, Wang Ling becoming Chancellor of the Right and Ch'en P'ing the Chancellor of the Left (*Shih chi*, 56.2059).

[588]Chou Po first filled the position of Grand Commandant in 184 B.C. (*Shih chi*, 9.403); according to Chou's biography (*Shih chi*, 57.2071-72) this took place in 189 B.C. Various critics have argued for the

sovereign said, "The events which transpire after these even you will not be able to know about."[589]

Lu Wan with several thousand horsemen was located beneath the border fortifications waiting and reconnoitering, hoping that the sovereign's illness would improve and he could personally come in to apologize.[590]

In the fourth month on the *chia-ch'en* 甲辰 day (6 June 195), Kao-tsu passed away in the Ch'ang-lo Palace. For four days no mourning was announced. Lü Hou plotted with Shen Yi-chi 審食其: "All the generals and the emperor were commoners of registered households.[591] Now [the generals] all face the north as subjects, [but] they have often been discontented [with this]; now that they must serve a young ruler, if we do not completely eradicate these people and their kindred, the world will not remain settled." Someone heard of this and talked to General Li 酈 about it.[592] General Li went to see Shen Yi-chi and said: "I have heard that the emperor has already passed away, that after four days no mourning has been announced, and that [Lü Hou] intends to execute all the generals. If things are really like this, the world is in peril. Ch'en P'ing and Kuan Ying are in command of ten thousand defending Hsing-yang, Fan K'uai and Chou Po are in command of twenty thousand stabilizing Yen and Tai. If these men heard that the emperor has passed away and that all generals are to be executed, they will certainly join their troops together and turn their direction in order to attack the Land within the Passes. With the great ministers turning against us within and the feudal lords rebelling

correctness of one of these dates based on passages in the *Han shu, Han chi,* and *Tzu-chih t'ung-chien.* Yet there may be a third date to consider, since on *Shih chi,* 8.388 above, the text reads: The Grand Commandant Chou Po took the road by way of T'ai-yüan to enter and stabilize the territory of Tai." *Shih chi,* 22.1122 also claims Chou Po attacked Tai as a Grand Commandant, but the position of *T'ai-wei* was later abolished. Thus when Chou Po became *T'ai-wei* in either 189 or 184 B.C., he did so for the second time (see also *Han shu,* 19.751). He was subsequently (179 B.C.) made Chancellor of the Right (*Shih chi,* 10.418) to reward his service against the Lüs.

[589]Liu Pang's entire final speech is by way of both suggestion and prediction, since everything he suggests in fact comes to be. This despite other sources claiming that he had nothing to do with Ts'ao Ts'an replacing Hsiao Ho, for example (see n. 586 above). In the final line Liu Pang suggests he can foresee even when Empress Lü will pass on. Since there is no possibility anyone could have overheard such a conversation, and given the perfect correlation between Liu Pang's predictions and the way things turned out in reality, it seems likely that this speech was created by Ssu-ma Ch'ien.

[590]A parallel account of Lu Wan's vigil is given in his biography (*Shih chi,* 93.2639) where he is said to have waited "beneath the Great Wall."

[591]*Pien-hu min* 編戶民. Ch'in law required that commoners register for tax, military service and corvée labor, a requirement not made of nobles.

[592]As Hsü Kuang points out in "Chi-chieh," the *Han shu* (1B.79) identifies this general as Li Shang 酈商, who had served Liu Pang since 207 B.C. (see *Shih chi,* 8.358). Li Shang was the younger brother of Li Yi-chi, but there is no mention of this conversation in his biography (*Shih chi,* 95. 2660-63).

against us without, our fall can be awaited on tiptoe."[593] Shen Yi-chi went in and spoke to her, and, on the *ting-wei* 丁未 day [of the fourth month] (9 June 195), the mourning period was announced. A general amnesty was granted throughout the world.

When Lu Wan heard that Kao-tsu had passed away, he finally fled to the Hsiung-nu.[594]

On the *ping-yin* 丙寅 day (28 June 195), Kao-tsu was buried. On the *chi-ssu* 己巳 day (1 July 195), the Heir was enthroned [as emperor] and he went to the Ancestral Temple of His Most Honored Majesty.[595] The assembled ministers all said, "Kao-tsu[596] rose from humble circumstances[597] to dispel the chaos of the world and return it to the correct [path], to pacify and stabilize the world; he was the grand ancestor of the Han with merit which was the highest." They offered respectfully that he be titled Kao Huang-ti 高皇帝 (The Exalted August Emperor)." The Heir succeeded to the title of emperor and became [posthumously] Hsiao Hui-ti 孝惠帝 (The Filial and Kind Emperor or Emperor Hui). He ordered that the feudal lords from the commanderies and states each erect Exalted Ancestor temples and select proper times of the year for sacrifice.[598]

[393] When Hsiao Hui[-ti] was in his fifth year [190 B.C.], he thought about how Kao-tsu had sorrowed for and enjoyed P'ei, and he made the P'ei Palace into the Original Funerary Temple for Kao-tsu.[599] All of the 120 children that Kao-tsu had taught to sing, he had play music there;[600] later whenever there was an opening [in the group], it was immediately filled.

[593]In other words, our fall will be imminent.

[594]Lu Wan had already acknowledged that he believed Lü Hou intended to do away with all the non-Liu kings, see *Shih chi*, 93.2638-39. Thus he waited until Kao-tsu was dead before breaking with the Han to join the Hsiung-nu.

[595]This was the temple to Liu Pang's father.

[596]As Wang Li-ch'i notes (8.218n.), it would be improper for the assembled ministers to call Liu Pang by his temple name before that was determined.

[597]Cf. the similar passage on *Shih chi*, 8.379, beginning "Great King, you rose up from humble circumstances . . . ."

[598]On imperial shrines see also Michael Loewe, "The Imperial Cults," in Loewe's *Chinese Ideas*, pp. 127-43, esp. 140-1. Liu Pang's shrine was built within the capital city (see Loewe, *ibid.*, p. 280f.; see also Ho Ch'ing-ku, *San-fu huang-t'u chiao-chu*, pp. 291-93). On the services performed at his shrine, see Loewe, *ibid.*, pp. 282-83. Shrines were also built within the compound surrounding the imperial tomb (p. 285).

[599]In contrast to the standard Funerary Temple that was set up in the capital. Although Hsü Kuang ("Chi-chieh") and other traditional commentators argue that *yüan* 原 here means "secondary" or "other," their arguments seem tautological and unconvincing.

A much different motive for Hui-ti's actions are given in Shu-sun T'ung's biography (*Shih chi*, 99.2725-26). There it is said that that the emperor had ordered an elevated walkway built between his residence and that of Lü Hou so that he could pay respects to her without causing the palace streets to be cleared first. However, the walkway crossed the way that was taken monthly to bring Kao-tsu's robes and caps from his tomb to his funerary temple. As a means to avoid the degradation of having the first emperor's descendants walk above the path to his temple, Shu-sun T'ung suggested that a second temple north of the Wei River be set up.

[600]Or "perform the song to the accompaniment of wind instruments" as Watson (*Han*, 1:118) has it.

Kao-ti 高帝 (The Exalted Emperor or Emperor Kao) had eight sons: the eldest was the son of a concubine,[601] [Liu] Fei, King Tao Hui 悼惠 of Ch'i; the next was Hsiao Hui[-ti] 孝惠[帝] (The Filial and Kind Emperor or Emperor Hui)],[602] Lü Hou's son; the next, [Liu] Ju-yi 如意, King Yin 隱 of Chao and the son of Lady Ch'i 戚;[603] the next [Liu] Heng, King of Tai, who has already been enthroned as Hsiao Wen-ti 孝文帝 (The Filial and Cultured Emperor or Emperor Wen), a son of Po T'ai-hou 薄太后 (Empress Dowager Po);[604] the next was [Liu] Hui, King of Liang, who during the time of Lü T'ai-hou 呂太后 (Empress Dowager Lü) was moved to become King Kung 共 of Chao;[605] the next was [Liu] Yu 友, King of Huai-yang, who was moved during the time of Lü T'ai-hou to become King Yu 幽 of Chao;[606] the next was [Liu] Ch'ang 長, King Li 厲 of

[601] Actually, all Liu Pang's sons except Hui-ti were born to concubines or other women. Liu Fei was born *ca.* 222 B.C. to a woman who was apparently Liu Pang's mistress from the Ts'ao 曹 family (see "So-yin," *Shih chi*, 9.396, Hu Tzu-chieh 胡子杰, "Liu Pang pa-tzu chien-piao" 劉邦八子簡表, *Liu Pang yen-chiu*, 2 [1992]: 71, and Liu Fei's biography on *Shih chi*, 52.1999). The parallel passage in *Han shu* (37.1987) also claims that Lady Ts'ao 曹夫人 was Fei's mother; later on that same page, however, it says he was born to a *wai-fu* 外婦, an expression Yen Shih-ku (*ibid.*) takes to refer to an adulterous relationship with a neighbor.

[602] This was Liu Ying 劉盈 (210-188 B.C.) who became Heir in 205 and Imperial Heir (*Huang T'ai-tzu* 皇太子) in 202 B.C. On him see also the first half of the translation of Chapter 9 below.

[603] Liu Ju-yi (205-195 B.C.) became King of Tai 代 in 200 B.C. (*Shih chi*, 17.809) before his transfer to King of Chao in 198 B.C. Shortly after Kao-tsu's death, he was summoned to court and poisoned by Lü T'ai-hou—see the opening pages of Chapter 9 below.

[604] Liu Heng (203-157 B.C.) served as King of Tai (196-181 B.C.; *Shih chi*, 17.811) prior to ascending the imperial throne (posthumously titled Hsiao Wen 孝文帝; see his annals in *Shih chi* Chapter 10).

His mother, Po 薄 T'ai-hou, was the illegitimate daughter of a man from Wu named Po and a woman from the former royal house of Wei. She was taken into Wei Pao's palace when Wei was revived and then captured by Liu Pang in 204 B.C. after Wei Pao rebelled (*Shih chi*, 8.372). Her biography can be found on *Shih chi*, 49.1970-71.

[605] Liu Hui was made King of Liang in 196 B.C. (*Shih chi*, 17.811) and moved to become King of Chao in 181 B.C., a position which troubled him, since its last two occupants had been killed by Lü T'ai-hou. Like his brother Liu Yu (see the following note), he was also tied by marriage to the Lü Clan, his wife being the daughter of Lü Ch'an himself. Also like Liu Yu, Liu Hui was in love with a concubine. When this unfortunate woman was poisoned by Lü Ch'an's daughter, Liu Hui wrote a song lamenting her death and shortly thereafter committed suicide (*Shih chi*, 9.404).

[606] Liu Yu was appointed King of Huai-yang 淮陽 by Kao-tsu in 196 B.C. (*Shih chi*, 8.389 and 17.811) and moved to become King of Chao in 194 B.C. (*Shih chi*, 9.397); shortly thereafter he was slandered by his wife, a member of the Lü Clan who was jealous of another palace woman, and was ordered to come to the capital. After he arrived, Empress Lü had him confined in the official capital residence of the King of Chao, ordered that food be denied him, and caused him to starve (see *Shih chi*, 9.403-4). The similarity between the lives and deaths of Liu Hui (see preceeding note) and Liu Yu raises suspicions of duplication, either intentional, as an archetypical depiction of the wiles of the Lü Clan, or unintentional, involving confusion between records of the

Huai-nan;[607] and the next was [Liu] Chien 建, King of Yen.[608]

His Honor the Grand Scribe says: "The administration of the Hsia [dynasty] was sincere. The deterioration of this sincerity generated a vulgar manner among the petty folk. For this reason the people of the Yin [dynasty] received [this sincere administration of the Hsia] respectfully. The deterioration of [this] respect generated superstition among the petty folk. For this reason the people of the Chou received [the respect of the Yin] within refined norms and institutions. The deterioration of this refinement generated an insincere manner among petty folk. For this reason, to relieve this lack of refinement, nothing could be better than sincerity.[609]

The way of the Three Kings [Yü of Hsia, T'ang of Shang, and Wen of Chou] is like the turning of a circle—when the end is reached it begins again. [*394*] Between Chou and Ch'in it could be said that refined norms and institutions deteriorated. The Ch'in administration made no reforms [towards restoring sincerity], but rather made more severe the punishments and laws--how could this not have been an error? For this reason, when the Han arose it reformed the deterioration which it received and, to prevent the people from the fatigue [of severe punishments and laws],[610] it obtained the succession from Heaven.

two brothers.

[607]Liu Ch'ang (199-174 B.C.) received the posthumous title of King Li 厲 of Huai-nan; he was appointed king while in his infancy, following Ch'ing Pu's rebellion in 196 B.C. (*Shih chi*, 17.811). He was a powerful rogue who led an exciting life (see his biography in *Shih chi*, Chapter 118), but he plotted rebellion against Wen-ti in 174 B.C., and, although he was pardoned, died of illness soon after (*Shih chi*, 10.426). Wang Yün-tu 王雲度 argues that Liu Ch'ang may not have been Liu Pang's natural son, but a son he adopted, in his "Liu Ch'ang fei Liu Pang chih tzu p'ei-hsi" 劉長非劉邦之子剖析, *Chung-kuo shih yen-chiu*, 1996.1: 166-67.

[608]Liu Chien is posthumously known as King Ling 靈 of Yen; he passed away in 181 B.C. (*Shih chi*, 9.404) and his heir (by a palace beauty) was killed by an agent of his jealous empress (*Han shu*, 38.1991).

A similar list is given a few lines later in the text (at the start of Chapter 9—*Shih chi*, 9.396). This passage does not seem to fit the context of Chapter 8, as Pan Ku may have concluded, since he omitted it from his account of Kao-tsu (*Han shu*, 1B.80).

[609]This passage certainly owes something to Tung Chung-shu's 董仲舒 (*ca.* 179-*ca.* 104 B.C.) discussion of the way of government that he presented to Wu-ti (r. 141-87 B.C.), cf. *Han shu*, 56.2518-19. Tung advised the emperor to reject the refinement of the Chou (周之文) and return to the sincerity of the Hsia (夏之忠). Since Tung's point was that the Han government had strayed from the sincerity of Liu Pang's time largely because of Wu-ti's politics, Ssu-ma Ch'ien may intend this commentary to be his own criticism of Wu-ti. Regardless of Ssu-ma Ch'ien's intentions, it is remarkable that these comments say so little about the man to whose annals they are affixed.

On Ssu-ma Ch'ien's indebtedness to Tung Chung-shu, see also Yang Yen-ch'i 楊燕起, "Ssu-ma Ch'ien yü Tung Chung-shu" 司馬遷與董仲舒, *Shih-hsüeh shih yen-chiu* 史學史研究, 1986.4: 23-32 and Chang Ta-k'o 張大可, *Shih chi yen-chiu* 史記研究 (Lanchow: Kan-su Jen-min, 1985), pp. 370-75.

[610]The idea of avoiding overtaxing the people when ruling is an old one, expressed in the "Hsi-tz'u (hsia)" 繫辭下 of the *Book of Changes* (*Zhou Yi chu-tzu so-yin* [Hong Kong: The Commerical Press, 1995], p. 82): 神農氏沒，黃帝、堯、舜氏作。通其變，使民不倦。 "When Shen-nung died, Huang-ti, Yao and Shun

Kao-tsu set the date for the feudal lords to come to court as the tenth month.[611] He set the standards for his vehicles and vestments, rode in a chariot with a yellow silk canopy and a pheasant-feather [ornament] on its left side. He was buried in Ch'ang-ling 長陵(Long Tumulus).[612]

       *   *   *   *   *

[Hsiang] Tzu Yü 子羽 was violent and tyrannical, while the [King of] Han practised merit and virtue. To vent his pent up anger,[613] the King of Han marched forth from Shu and Han, returning to stabilize the three kingdoms of Ch'in. He executed Chi [Hsiang Yü] and accomplished the enterprise of becoming emperor, and all the world found repose. He reformed the regulations and changed the customs of the people.[614] Thus I made "The Basic Annals of the Exalted Ancestor."[615]

served. They thoroughly understood his changes and kept the people from fatigue." Ssu-ma Ch'ien has penned a similar passage on the founders of the Yin and Chou dynasties in his commentary following the "P'ing-chun shu" 平準書 (Treatise on Measurements, *Shih chi,* 30.1442): 湯武承弊易變，使民不倦。 "[Kings] T'ang and Wu accepted what had deteriorated and changed it, so that the people would be kept from fatigue."

[611]As Tanaka Kenji (p. 178, n. 9) points out, this final section of these comments have been held up as spurious by a number of traditional scholars. Nakai Riken (Takigawa, 8.176b) argues that there is text missing here.

[612]Located northeast of modern Hsien-yang 咸陽 in Shensi (Wang Li-ch'i, 8.219n.); see also the map of the imperial tombs of the eleven former Han emperors in Michael Loewe, "The Imperial Tombs of the Former Han Dynasty and Their Shrines," in *Divination,* p. 275. Loewe notes (*ibid,,* p. 279) that "Kao-ti's tomb was placed directly north of Ch'ang-an city and almost centrally between the limits of the northern wall." For further details on Liu Pang's tomb see Ho Ch'ing-ku, *San-fu huang-t'u chiao-chu,* pp. 348-50, Liu Ch'in-chu 劉慶柱 and Li Yü-fang 李毓芳, "Kuan-yü Hsi Han ti-ling hsing-chih chu wen-t'i t'an-t'ao" 關於西漢帝陵形制諸問題探討, *K'ao-ku yü wen-wu,* 1985.5: 102-09, and Yang Tung-ch'en, *Han-jen mi-shih,* p. 75 (which also gives the tomb's dimensions).

[613]*Fen fa* 憤發, translated here as "to vent his pent up anger," retains the connotation of an anger justified by some wrong; it often makes the angered person strong enough to accomplish some great deed. Here it denotes Liu Pang's anger at Hsiang Yü for ignoring their agreement about the first through the Pass being made king.

[614]Referring, no doubt, to Liu Pang's simplification of Ch'in's legal system and its effect on society.

[615]This is Ssu-ma Ch'ien's account of why he wrote this chapter from his postface, *Shih chi,* 130.3301.

Translators' Note

What is striking about Ssu-ma Ch'ien's comments on the last pages of the chapter just above is that they say almost nothing about Liu Pang, the subject of these annals. Rather they reflect Tung Chung-shu's 董仲舒 (*ca.* 179-*ca.* 104 B.C.) ideas of the evolution of government from Hsia to Yin to Chou (see also n. 608 above) and may very possibly be intended as an indirect criticism of the Han government—as shaped by Emperor Wu—in Ssu-ma Ch'ien's own day.[616]

Such indirection is indeed the method employed by Ssu-ma Ch'ien in the text of these annals to depict Liu Pang's rise and fall, one of the main themes of this chapter.[617] In the list of Liu Pang's characteristics given at the beginning of the annals, Liu Pang is said to have been "openhearted" and "magnanimous" (*ta tu* 大度).[618] It was these characteristics that can be seen in Liu Pang's skillful employment of his subordinates throughout the chapter as well as in the emperor's claim that he was able to capture the world because he was able to employ its heroes better than Hsiang Yü (see *Shih chi*, 8.381). It was also his generosity that Kao Ch'i and Wang Ling suggested as the reason Liu Pang was able to capture the world:

> Kao-tsu said, "Marquises and generals, do not dare to hide things from me, but all speak forth what is in your hearts. What is the reason I was able to gain the world? What was the reason that the Hsiang Clan lost the world?"
>
> Kao Ch'i and Wang Ling responded: "Your Majesty was arrogant and liked to insult others. Hsiang Yü was humane and loved others. But when Your Majesty sent someone to attack cities and overrun territory, those [cities and territories] which surrendered you accordingly gave to him, sharing your gains with the world. Hsiang Yü was jealous of worthiness and envious of talent, and would hate those who achieved merit, and doubt those who were worthy. If someone won a victory, he would not accord him merit, if someone gained territory, he would not give him the profits. This was why he lost the world." (*Shih chi*, 8.380-81).

---

[616]See also Grant Hardy's note on this commentary following "The Basic Annals of Kao-tsu" (Hardy, *World*, p. 246, n. 51).

[617]Although we have identified several themes for these annals, Wu Ju-lun 吳汝綸 (1840-1903) in his *T'ung-ch'eng Hsien-sheng tien-k'an Shih chi* 桐城先生點勘史記, chapter 8 (quoted in Yang, *Li-tai*, pp. 418-19) argues that there is only one: "'The Exalted [Ancestor's] Annals' takes pacifying the world as its theme. The first half of the piece is [an account of] contesting for the world with Hsiang Yü; the second half of the piece is [a description of] wiping out rebels in order to stabilize the world. Other matters which are not tied to the establishing or losing [of the state] are not recorded."

[618]See n. 17 above on the possibility of reading *ta-tu* as "magnanimous."

Liu Pang's success is so dependent on his subordinates, most old comrades who fought with him beginning in P'ei, that he is not even present for Hsiang Yü's final defeat and death. Yet after becoming emperor, the gradual erosion of Liu Pang's ability to employ others and the diminution of his generous spirit is evident. In reacting to one rebel after another—Tsang T'u (*Shih chi,* 8.381), Li Chi (*Shih chi,* 8.381-82), Chao Li (*Shih chi,* 8.384-85), Ch'en Hsi (*Shih chi,* 8.387-90), and Ch'ing Pu (*Shih chi,* 8.389)—Liu Pang personally commands his troops. Not only does his inability to trust subordinates with this task place the emperor under the repeated stress of long campaigns, but it also causes a kind of chain reaction as one after the other of his former commanders turn against a man who seems incapable of putting his trust in anyone. This change in Liu Pang was noted by his subordinates as the following exchange between Chou Hsieh, Marquis of K'uai-ch'eng, and Liu Pang reveals:

> When the sovereign was about to personally attack Ch'en Hsi, the Marquis of K'uai-ch'eng wept and said, "When Ch'in first attacked and defeated the world, he never personally went [on campaign]. Now Your Highness often personally goes on campaign—is this because there is no one who can be sent?' The sovereign considered [Chou Hsieh] loved him too much and granted that when he entered the [imperial] hall he did not have to take small quick steps [as prescribed by ritual] and that he would not be put to death if he killed someone" (*Shih chi,* 98.2712).

And it is revealed clearly in Liu Pang's own victory song:

> A great wind arose, clouds flew up!
> My prestige increasing within the seas, I return to my hometown.
> But where will I find valiant warriors to hold the four directions?

Surrounded by those who helped him *take* the four directions in the first place, this is a strange query.

Aside from the message of the importance of trust between the ruler and his government, a message Ssu-ma Ch'ien surely felt held a personal relevance given his relationship with Emperor Wu, the structure of these annals, differing greatly from the pre-Ch'in annals, invites comment. In this chapter we have a bifurcated account of Liu Pang's rise to power, a prologue consisting of anecdotes focussing on revealing aspects of his character and personality, the main section depicting the rebellions against the Ch'in, Liu Pang's victory over Hsiang Yü, and then the subsequent rebellions against the Han itself. As the first part focuses on characterization of its hero, is largely achronological, and is personal in nature, the second is driven by an impersonal chronology which pays considerable attention to the actions of those around Liu Pang, especially as they impact upon the winning of the world and the suppression of the early Han rebels. This structure differs considerably from the first six *pen-chi* (annals), although it bears an affinity to the form of "The Basic Annals of Hsiang Yü" (*Shih chi,* Chapter 7). More importantly, it parallels many of the biographies of early Han generals.

Those biographies mirror this chapter, for example, in the use of anecdotes designed to characterize a subject then punctuated by references to Ch'en She's rebellion[619] and include "The Basic Annals of Hsiang Yü" (*Shih chi*, 7.297), "The Hereditary House of the Marquis of Liu [Chang Liang]" (*Shih chi*, 55.2036), "The Hereditary House of Chancellor Ch'en" [Ch'en P'ing] (*Shih chi*, 56.2052), "The Memoirs of Chang Erh and Ch'en Yü" (*Shih chi*, 89.2572), "The Biography of Ch'ing Pu" (*Shih chi*, 91.2598), "The Memoir of the Marquis of Huai Yin" [Han Hsin] (*Shih chi*, 92.2610),[620] "The Memoirs of Master Li [Li Yi-chi] and Lu Chia" (*Shih chi*, 97.2691), and "The Biography of Shu-sun T'ung" (*Shih chi*, 99.2720). While the prologues of some of these accounts (that of Shu-sun T'ung, for example) are too brief to contain anecdotal material, many closely resemble the presentation of Liu Pang in this chapter. In *Shih chi* Chapter 55, for example, Chang Liang's ancestors are first presented, explaining the origins of his hatred for Ch'in. Then there is a story about him journeying to Huai-yang to study ritual, an account of his attempt to cut down the First Emperor, and finally his encounters with the old man who transmitted to him the book of tactics which supposedly allowed Chang to become such an effective military advisor. At this point the personal narrative breaks off abruptly with the announcement that "Ten years later, Ch'en She and the others began their military uprisings . . . ." The biography of Ch'en P'ing is even more similar to the account of Liu Pang, beginning with a description of his good looks and an anecdote about how Ch'en refrained from the agricultural tasks the entire family was expected to undertake. It then depicts his poverty, his apparently poor prospects, his marriage arranged by a woman who could detect the potential in Ch'en, and his excellent work in a minor official position he then won. This parallels in essence the information we are given on Liu Pang in his annals.

Thus, whether this structure is a result of sources Ssu-ma Ch'ien consulted,[621] perhaps a combination of oral narratives about these various individuals with a written *shih chi* writ small for the interregnum between Ch'in and Han which began with Ch'en She's rebellion, or whether it is a "biographical model" of Ssu-ma Ch'ien's own creation, we cannot be sure. But whatever its provenance, it does seem to have been the standard structure for a number of these

---

[619]Grant Hardy gives Ch'en She's rebellion as an example of what he calls a "trigger event," something that has significance much greater than would normally be expected because it works in conjunction with important, long-term developments (Hardy, *World*, p. 92).

[620]The anecdotal beginning to this account of Han Hsin ends not with a reference to Ch'en She's rebellion, but with the mention of Hsiang Liang's crossing the Huai River, another symbol of open revolt in the East.

[621]Wu Chien-ssu 吳見思 (*fl.* 1680-90) points out that the same events are depicted in two chapters by Ssu-ma Ch'ien, the annals of Hsiang Yü and those for Liu Pang, but argues that in the account of Hsiang Yü each separate event constitutes a section, whereas in that of Liu Pang the events are woven together so that "in the midst of order there is chaos [of the many rebellions at the start of the Han], in the mist of chaos there is order [provided by Ssu-ma Ch'ien's narrative structure], all without seams, so that the events are even more difficult [to understand?]" 整中見亂，亂中見整，絕無痕跡，更為難事. Wu's comments point both to the power of Ssu-ma Ch'ien's brush and to the relatively primitive state of his sources.

early Han "lives."[622]

The underlying theme of a ruler who becomes incapable of trust was discussed earlier in this note. There are, however, two more salient themes in these annals. First, Ssu-ma Ch'ien wants to demonstrate how the Han dynasty, under Liu Pang, came to the Mandate of Heaven. Second, he intends to record the events of Liu Pang's life as rebel against the Ch'in, and rival to Hsiang Yü.

The first task is accomplished by appeals to two realms, the legendary and the human. The stylistic changes in the chapter are a key. The first eight sections (as parsed by the Chung-hua editions, *Shih chi*, 8.341-8), a kind of introduction, are episodic in structure, anecdotal in form, and fabulous in content. The mode is more dramatic than usual—there are several extended scenes (such as when Liu Pang visits Master Lü and is betrothed to the Master's daughter) and considerable dialogue (such as that between Liu Pang and the prisoners he has just released). The result is a kind of "Kao-tsu wai-chuan" 高祖外傳 (Unofficial Biography of Kao-tsu) in which the reader is offered a series of tales testifying to Liu Pang's uniqueness.[623]

The overall effect is that of matching the archetype of a true first emperor. He was divinely conceived by a kraken, bore signs of this conception in his extraordinary face (which amazed two physiognomists) and the seventy-two black spots on his left thigh, as well as in his magnanimous and courageous (albeit sometimes wine-inspired) behavior. He exudes pneumas or emanations. And although there are attempts to link these characteristics to traditional modes of authority such as the First Emperor of Ch'in's sensing the "emanation of a Son of Heaven to the southeast," the major thrust of these first eight sections is to devise an authority for the Founder of the Han Dynasty based on supernatural forces. As Michael Loewe has observed:

[622]The later synoptic versions of Liu Pang's annals found in the *Shih chi ching-hua lu* 史記菁華錄 (originally edited by Yao Ning-t'ien 姚蘋田 [*fl.* 1721] and punctuated by the modern editors Wang Hsing-k'ang 王興康 and Chou Yen-chia 周旻佳), begins its text with the description of Kao-tsu's character and the list of his personal attributes, includes only the anecdotes about Kao-tsu's early days, and then concludes with the story of his visit to his hometown in the tenth month of his twelfth year (195 B.C.) (Shanghai: Shang-hai Ku-chi, 1988), pp. 22-25.

[623]The corpus of popular tales about Liu Pang may be not dissimilar to those the elders and old women of P'ei told when they were drinking with Kao-tsu on his visit home in the late fall of 196 B.C. (cf. our translation of *Shih chi*, 8.389 above). These tales could possibly also be expanded to include the accounts of Hsia-hou Ying taking the blame for a court case and the wife of Liu Pang's elder brother, Liu Po, trying to trick Liu Pang and his cronies into leaving her house by pretending to have run out of food (see details on *Shih chi*, 50.1987 and 95.2665 as well as in nn. 22 and 28 above). Other references to "the time when Kao-tsu was still unknown" can be found in the memoirs of Wang Ling (*Shih chi*, 56.2059) and Jen Ao (*Shih chi*, 96.2680)

The popularity of descendants of these stories in vernacular literature of the T'ang through Ming dynasties has been explored in great detail by W. L. Idema in an article titled "The Founding of the Han Dynasty in Early Drama: The Autocratic Suppression of Popular Debunking," in Idema and E. Zürcher, eds., *Thought and Law in Qin and Han China, Studies Dedicated to Anthony Hulsewé on the Occasion of His Eightieth Birthday* (Leiden: E. J. Brill, 1990), pp. 183-207. Idema points out that "the saga of the founding of the Han was far more popular than the tale of its downfall" (i.e., the San-kuo stories) from the late T'ang to the early Ming.

In the account of the first Ch'in emperor's adoption of his title, we read solely of his successful conquest of his enemies, but by the time of Han Kao-ti there is a perceptible change. For it is acknowledged that such achievements depend on something more than human proficiency, and that the strength of the victor is derived from heaven . . . ("The Authority of the Emperors of Ch'in and Han," in Loewe, *Divination*, p. 90).

It would seem that since Liu Pang lacked the human pedigree of the First Emperor of Ch'in, there was no choice but to seek out and craft together a divine ancestry for him.[624]

Yet the tone of this first part of the narrative does not fit divine origins. Rather than the high tragic tone that Northrop Frye and others have argued is appropriate for ruling class figures, "The Annals of Kao-tsu" is closer to comedy in its opening, as in the accounts of Liu Pang's drinking, his creation of a unique type of hat, and his chasing after the soothsayer after the latter had examined his wife and children. All of this, as well as Liu Pang's slaying of the Red Emperor in a snake's form while drunk, could be seen to mock the standard sacral character of kingship.[625]

Still, Ssu-ma Ch'ien does portray Liu Pang as a capable, sometimes brilliant general. When he was defeated and driven from Hsing-yang, for example, he refuses to retreat and, like Ulysses S. Grant in the Wilderness Campaign, outflanks his great adversary Hsiang Yü by moving away from his power base in the west towards Hsiang Yü's ally Ch'i. In the depictions of so many campaigns of so many armies, moreover, we should not lose sight of one of Liu Pang's qualities which Ssu-ma Ch'ien must have understood well—the love of travel, the desire to keep on the move. Scholars have estimated that Goethe traveled about 25,000 miles in his life, but it is likely that Liu Pang easily exceeded this total.[626] Liu Pang was truly a man of the

---

[624] Although Liu Pang was in many ways the antithesis of the First Emperor of Ch'in, the materials on his life must have been shaped in the popular mind by the only imperial archetype available, that of the First Emperor. Liu Pang himself admired his predecessor, ordering families to attend his grave shortly after taking the throne (*Shih chi*, 8.391) and giving his father the same title bestowed on the First Emperor of Ch'in's father (see n. 468 above). Moreover, when Liu Pang is depicted as "a man who had a high nose and a dragon's brow, a handsome beard, and seventy-two black spots on his left thigh: he was humane and loved people, fond of largesse, and openhearted" (*Shih chi*, 8.342), it may well be that Ssu-ma Ch'ien had his own depiction of the First Emperor of Ch'in in mind (*Shih chi*, 6.230; *Grand Scribe's Records*, 1:131): "The King of Ch'in was born with a prominent nose, elongated eyes, the breast of a bird of prey, and the voice of a jackal; he seldom extends favor and has the heart of a tiger or wolf. When in straits, he can submit to others, but when he has his way, he can easily eat you alive."

Was this comparison an implicit criticism of Liu Pang? Possibly, but not likely a criticism that came originally from Ssu-ma Ch'ien himself.

[625] Indeed, it is not hard to find a different Liu Pang in the events of the opening pages of this chapter from the man Ssu-ma Ch'ien tells us was "humane, loved people, was fond of largesse, and openhearted." In these stories of his early years, we see rather a petty, selfish, irresponsible, superstitious, uncooperative, and arrogant individual.

[626] An estimate taking into consideration at least one trip from P'ei-hsien to Hsien-yang under Ch'in rule,

roads. We often see him on some out-of-the-way track in this chapter. Hsiang Yü, on the other hand, lacked the ability to negotiate backroads. When, after his defeat at Kai-hsia he is forced to flee through unfamiliar territory, he encounters a number of cul de sacs that quickly lead to his demise. Liu Pang, however, seems to have had an excellent sense of direction. More than once his mastery of byways was instrumental in his success: his ability to find his way through the swamp led to his execution of the Red Emperor in the form of a snake, his escape from the gathering at Hung-men, his return to Ch'in from Han over the dangerous passes of the Ch'in-ling 秦岭, and finally his ability to infiltrate Chang Erh and Han Hsin's armies at Hsiu-wu are only the most outstanding examples of this skill. This ability to find his way may have been honed during his early trip(s) to Hsien-yang,[627] or it may have been a natural gift. In all of the offensives against Hsiang Yü, however, there is no climactic battle. Although this may have led Hsiang Yü to claim "fate" as the arbiter of his struggle with Liu Pang, it fits with Ssu-ma Ch'ien's understanding that Liu Pang won the empire by relying on a number of advisors and generals and that each battle gradually contributed to Hsiang Yü's downfall.

The second theme draws parallels between Hsiang Yü and Liu Pang not only in their military movements, but also their distinct reaction to the First Emperor of Ch'in: Hsiang Yü seeing the man as a challenge to his manhood, Liu Pang admiring the prestige of the station itself (cf. *Shih chi,* 7.296 and 8.344 respectively). It also contrasts their emotional comments on their fates in the songs each left: Hsiang Yü concerned with his beloved Yü 虞 and claiming his defeat was due to the "times not favoring him" (*Shih chi,* 7.333; *Grand Scribe's Records,* 1:205); Liu Pang worrying already that he would not be able to rely on the generals who helped him win the throne to defend it (*Shih chi,* 8.389). Hsiang Yü is shown to win many victories, but none decisive. Liu Pang is consistently the aggressor. Hsiang Yü seems reluctant to exploit his early success. When advised to move into the Land within the Passes, he refuses. Faced with the same choice, Liu Pang listens to his advisors and moves his capital to Ch'ang-an. If the Hung-men banquet is the key scene in "The Basic Annals of Hsiang Yü," the confrontation between these two generals at Kuang-wu dominates this chapter. The results of these two meetings are interesting. At Hung-men Liu Pang is threatened and escapes; overlooking Kuang-wu, Hsiang Yü becomes frustrated and acts in a cowardly manner, having Liu Pang shot from ambush.

The sources Ssu-ma Ch'ien had for this transitory period between Ch'in and Han include the *Ch'u Han ch'un-ch'iu* 楚漢春秋 (see the historian's comments to Pan Ku's biography of Ssu-ma Ch'ien in *Han shu,* 62.2737-38), a text which has been carefully compared to this annals (see nn. 178, 182, 202, and 232, for example), and various other archival materials (see Juan Chih-sheng 阮芝生, "T'ai-shih-kung tsen-yang sou-chi ho ch'u-li tzu-liao" 太史公怎樣搜集和處理資料, *Shu-mu chi-k'an* 書目集刊, 7.4 [March 1974]: 22). But the origins of these first eight episodes may have been popular and religious in nature. Perhaps oral traditions. Evidence

---

Liu Pang's march west with all its twists and turns, and his numerous campaigns after becoming emperor, might be 30,000 miles.

[627]It is ironic that Ch'in's harsh legal system required agents like Ch'en She and Liu Pang to bring conscript laborers from the "lands east of the Mountain" to the capital region, since after they revolted both Ch'en and Liu were able to lead their troops over some of the same routes they had taken with their conscripts.

of a growing corpus of such materials can be found in the citation of texts like *Ch'un-ch'iu wo ch'eng-t'u* 春秋握成圖 or *Ch'en Liu feng-su chuan* 陳留風俗傳 cited in the notes to these sections (see "Cheng-yi," *Shih chi,* 8.342-3) which provide detailed, if anachronistic, information about Liu Pang's ancestry. The complexity of possible sources here suggests that further study of the "strata" of this chapter—along the lines of David Hawkes' similar work on Ch'ü Yüan's biography[628]—could produce interesting insights into the compilation methods of the *Shih chi.* It might be argued that this chapter is composite in nature, drawing on at least four sources: the anecdotal beginning possibly of oral origin, in which several of the stories were aligned under the formulaic exposition "when Kao-tsu was precinct chief" (could this be called "O"?),[629] the annalistic base narrative which takes over immediately after the introductory anecdotes (A), the *Ch'u Han ch'un-ch'iu* (source C—possibly in its original form close to A??), and the archives or *tang-an* 檔案 that may have yielded stories interspersed in the annalistic section such as Liu Pang first receiving Li Yi-chi (source T). Whether or not these hypothetical sources can be considered viable, these eight introductory episodes from Liu Pang's youth reveal both a human side to the first Han emperor which is more vivid than most portrayals in the *lieh-chuan* and also the historian's sympathy, if not total admiration, for this character. In addition, they also point to the brevity of Ssu-ma Ch'ien's "natural breath patterns" in composition, often building on the anecdote, the form that some scholars have claimed was the basis of so much early historical narrative.[630]

[628]Hawkes, "General Introduction," in Hawkes, *The Songs of the South, An Anthology of Ancient Chinese Poems by Qu Yuan and Other Poets* (Harmondsworth: Penguin, 1985), pp. 51-60.

[629]Robert W. Funk's description of how stories began to grow up around Jesus may be relevant here: "In the absence of hard information, scholars theorize that the New Testament gospels were composed during the last quarter of the first century by third-generation authors on the basis of folk memories preserved in stories that had circulated by word of mouth for decades. The oral stories the four evangelists recorded had been shaped, reshaped, augmented, and edited by numerous storytellers for a half century or more before achieving their final written forms."

"The followers of Jesus no doubt began to repeat his witticisms and parables during his lifetime. They soon began to recount stories about him, perhaps about his encounters with critics or about his amazing way with the sick and demon-possessed. At time went by, the words were gathered into compounds and clusters suggested by common themes or by catchwords to make them easier to remember and quote" (Robert W. Funk and the Jesus Seminar, *The Acts of Jesus, The Search for the Authentic Deeds of Jesus* [San Francisco: Harper, 1998], p 2).

The reasons behind compiling (or inventing) these stories, Funk argues, were the following: 1) to fulfill a prophecy or to match scriptural languages; 2) to assist in marketing the messiah to the larger world; 3) to give expression to their own convictions about who Jesus was and what he did and said; 4) to justify practices adopted by themselves or their communities; 5) to make claims on their own behalf or on behalf of their leaders. Once again, these reasons could possibly apply to Liu Pang's followers compiling the stories about him which begin this chapter.

[630]See, for example, Al Dien's comments in his review of Richard B. Mather's *Shih-shuo hsin-yü: A New*

The second part of this annals, which records the events of Liu Pang's deeds and words related to the imperial enterprise, begins on *Shih chi,* 8.349. The text is carefully punctuated by dates and temporal transitions such as *erh-nien* 二年 (in the second year) or *tang shih-shih* 當 是時 (in the meantime). This is a narrative in which proper names of people and places overwhelm, a text which inundates the reader, carrying him beyond these annals to the more detailed and often more comprehensible accounts in other sections of the *Grand Scribe's Records.* Although it may lack the drama of Hsiang Yü's annals (for there the style remains more consistently dramatic), it supplements that chapter by presenting new details and perspectives about the interregnum between Ch'in and Han.

The Liu Pang of this second narrative section is more pragmatic than prescient. It is not by accident that one character after another advises (*shui* 說) or presents a plan (*chi* 計) which he then puts to effective use. This ability to select between men and their plans and proposals is one of the major differences Ssu-ma Ch'ien draws between Kao-tsu and Hsiang Yü. Although the mold was set in the divine clay of the early episodes in Liu Pang's life, the figure which emerges there and moves through the annals year by year is totally human, more conscious of his foibles than Hsiang Yü (whom the Grand Historian derides for blaming his fate on Heaven in Chapter 7!), especially as he approaches that most human action, death.

Two of the most striking aspects of Ssu-ma Ch'ien's Kao-tsu are his feel for matters of space and of time. With regard to space, Kao-tsu realized that by assigning his most trusted vassals their own territory, he was making his own empire stronger (recall again the speech by Kao Ch'i and Wang Ling, *Shih chi,* 8.381, and the emperor's response). He understood that to overly esteem his homeland (as Hsiang Yü did) was to render himself a provincial satrap at best. And since he was always ready to lead out troops himself, to cross thousands of *li* to quell a rebellion, he ruled effectively from Ch'ang-an. With regard to time, although Hsiang Yü held the reputation as the great warrior, it was Liu Pang who outdid him repeatedly in timing—reaching the Ch'in capital first, leaving the banquet at Hung-men at just the right second, and escaping in similar ways from his enemy at other crucial moments.

The chapter is also, however, important in considering issues beyond that of the Founder of the Han himself. It provides the basis for considering two larger questions.

First, the relationship between the *Han shu* and the *Shih chi.* Pan Ku was often critical of Ssu-ma Ch'ien's penchant for the unusual, his predilection for esoteric thought. Yet in Pan's account of Kao-tsu he retains all of the anecdotal episodes which open the *Shih chi* annals, indicating that Pan realized that these texts were a part of the necessary legend to support the founder of his dynasty. Other differences between the two accounts, however, suggest that Pan Ku emended Ssu-ma Ch'ien's original text and provide support for the argument that the *Han shu* is generally derivative of the *Shih chi* in parallel passages (as argued in detail in the

Account of Tales of the World by Liu I-ch'ing with Commentary by Liu Chün (*HJAS,* 37.2 [December 1977], pp. 425-6): "Chinese traditional historiography was in large measure anecdotal. Without resource to a narrative technique, characteristically the flow of history moved from one anecdote to another in episodic fashion. Standard histories would intersperse there anecdotes with details of the individual's career, but it was the anecdote, a self-contained account of some interaction between two or more individuals, which gave insight into the actors and events."

"Introduction" to this volume).

Second, we find that The Grand Scribe's comments here are philosophical, discussing the dynasty of the Han, not the man Liu Pang. It is HAN writ large, Han as a house, not a man. Liu Pang appears in the comments only to be buried. This is in sharp contrast to the lively account of Liu Pang in the annals themselves. This might indicate that the comments were penned by Ssu-ma T'an, or it could suggest the subtext criticizing Emperor Wu that we have postulated above.

This chapter features a technique seen often in the *Shih chi:* a defamiliarization involving characters of obscure origin (like Fan Sui or Ching K'o) who are placed in new socio-political realms. THE great story in *The Grand Scribe's Records,* one might argue, is how a ragtag group of southern rebels won China, overcoming a Northwest Culture that had dominated the region for over a millennium. If that is the case, this chapter must play an important role as the narrative backdrop to its deservedly famous dramatic bookend, "The Basic Annals of Hsiang Yü."

For all that is expressed in this chapter, one aspect of Liu Pang's life remains unexplained. Feng 豐, Liu Pang's hometown, had been a part of the state of Sung until Ch'i destroyed it in 287 B.C. Shortly thereafter Ch'u took the area from Ch'i and Liu Pang was born a "man of Ch'u." Yet in Ch'u's battle against Ch'in, Liu Pang, despite being of an age to bear arms (26 *sui* according to our dating when Ch'in conquered Ch'u in 223 B.C.), was not involved in this fighting.

Bibliography

I. References

Ch'u Han ch'un-ch'iu 楚漢春秋. *Shih-chung Ku yi-shu* 十種古逸書 ed. Ch'en Chih 陳直, *et al.*, eds. *Han shu* 漢書. 12v. Peking: Chung-hua, 1962.

II. Translations

Chavannes, Édouard. *Les Mémoires historiques de Sseu-ma Ts'ien.* 5v. Paris: Ernest Leroux, 1895-1905; v. 6, Paris: Adrien Maisonneuve, 1969, 2:324-405.

Yoshida Kenkô 吉田賢抗. *Shiki* 史記. Tokyo: Meiji Shoin, 1973, 2.504-87.

Viatkin, Rudolf V. *Istoricheskie zapiski ("Shi tszi").* 7v. Moscow: Nauka, 1972- ; 2:157-99, notes 412-43.

Watson, Burton. *Records of the Grand Historian: Han Dynasty 1*. Rev. ed. New York: Columbia University Press, 1993, 1:51-86.

III. Studies

An Tso-chang 安作璋. *Han Kao-ti ta chuan* 漢高帝大傳. Chengchow: Ho-nan Jen-min, 1997.

An Tso-chang and Meng Hsiang-ts'ai 孟祥才. *Liu Pang p'ing-chuan* 劉邦評傳. Tsinan: Ch'i Lu Shu-she, 1988.

Chang Ch'uan-hsi 張傳璽. "Han Kao-tsu Liu Pang hsin-p'ing" 漢高祖劉邦新評, in Chang, *Ch'in Han wen-t'i yen-chiu* 秦漢問題研究. Peking: Pei-ching Ta-hsüeh Ch'u-pan-she, 1995, pp. 375-88.

Han Chao-ch'i 韓兆琦. "'Kao-tsu pen-chi' shang-hsi" 高祖本紀賞析, in Han's *Shih chi p'ing-yi shang-hsi* 史記評議賞析 (Hohetot: Nei Meng-ku Jen-min, 1985), pp. 176-94.

Hardy, Grant. "Microcosmic Reading II," in Hardy, *Worlds of Bronze and Bamboo, Sima Qian's Conquest of History.* New York: Columbia University Press, 1992, pp. 86-113.

Hsü Shuo-fang 徐朔方. "Liu Pang, ssu-t'i" 劉邦四題, in Hsü's *Shih Han lun-kao* 史漢論稿. Nanking: Chiang-su Ku-chi, 1984, pp. 81-7.

Hu Ta-kang 胡大岡. *Han Kao-tsu Liu Pang* 漢高祖劉邦. Peking: Chung-hua, 1985.

Hulsewé, A. F. P. "Founding Fathers and Yet Forgotten Men: A Closer Look at the Tables of the Nobility in the *Shih chi* and the *Han shu*," *TP* LXXV (1989): 43-126.

Li Chen-yü 李真瑜. "*Shih chi* yü *Ch'u Han ch'un-ch'iu*" 史記與楚漢春秋, *Ch'ü-ching Shih-chuan hsüeh-pao* 曲靖師專學報 3 (1983.2): 13-21.

Liu Pang yen-chiu 劉邦研究. Journal published for three years beginning in 1992 after a conference on Liu Pang held in Feng 豐 County in 1992.

Lo Ch'ing-k'ang 羅慶康. *Liu Pang hsin chuan* 劉邦新傳. Kaifeng: Ho-nan Ta-hsüeh, 1995.

Loewe, Michael. *Divination, Mythology and Monarchy in Han China.* Cambridge: Cambridge
　　University Press, 1994, especially "The Authority of the Emperors of Ch'in and Han"
　　(pp. 85-111).

___. "Liu Bang 劉邦," in Loewe, *Dictionary,* pp. 253-59.

Shiki shô Kenkyûkai 史記抄研究会. "*Shiki* Tôgen shô 'Kôso honki' shakukai (1)" 史記桃源抄
　　高祖本紀釋解, *Ritsumeikan bungaku,* 249 (1966): 41-69 (275-303).

Sukhu, Gopal. "Early Han Images of Chu: Chu Remembers Chu" (in "Monkeys, Shamans, Emperors
　　and Poets: The *Chuci* and the Han Dynasty") in *Defining Chu: Image and Reality in
　　Ancient China.* Constance A. Cook and John S. Major, eds. Honolulu: University of
　　Hawaii Press, 1999, pp. 146-51.

Wang Yün-tu 王雲度. "Liu Pang shen-shih pien-hsi" 劉邦身世辨析, *Shan-hsi Li-shih Po-wu
　　Kuan kuan-k'an* 陝西博物館館刊, 4 (June 1997): 81-85.

Wu Ju-yü 吳汝煜. *Shih chi lun-kao* 史記論稿. Nanking: Chiang-su Chiao-yü, 1986, pp. 98-104.

Zaisen (Chôgen Zaisen) 瑞仙 (挑源瑞仙, 1430–1489). "Kôso honki" 高祖本紀, in *Shiki shô* 史
　　記抄. 3v. Mike Kôkô 三ケ尻浩, editor and collator 校訂. Kyoto: Shosha Hagyô 緒者発
　　行, Shôwa 13 (1938). (A commentary, both general and interlineal, on this chapter
　　including frequent references to the *Han shu*).

Empress Dowager Lü, Basic Annals 9

[9.395] Lü T'ai-hou 呂太后 (Empress Dowager Lü),[1] a consort from the time when Kao-tsu was [still] unknown,[2] gave birth to Hsiao Hui-ti 孝惠帝 (The Filial and Kind Emperor or Emperor Hui the Filial, r. 195-188 B.C.)[3] and had a daughter who was Queen Dowager Lu Yüan T'ai-hou 魯元太后 (Queen Dowager Yüan of Lu).[4]

When Kao-tsu became King of Han,[5] he acquired Beauty Ch'i 戚 of Ting-yao 定陶,[6]

[1]Her *agnomen,* according to *Shih chi,* 49.1969, was O-hsü 娥姁. "Chi-chieh" (*Shih chi,* 9.395) gives her *praenomen* as Chih 雉. But, as with the names of Liu Pang and his parents (see the notes to our translation of Chapter 8 above), this is all conjecture and it is likely that these names, if reliable, were given only after Liu Pang had gained power and position.

It is possible that Liu Pang had taken a 'mistress' prior to his marriage to Empress Lü, since the mother of his eldest son, Liu Fei 劉肥, was a Lady Ts'ao 曹 (*Shih chi,* 52.1999). Since she was a *wai fu* 外婦 (mistress), her son was never eligible to succeed his father.

Much of the traditional criticism on this chapter focuses on Ssu-ma Ch'ien's decision to allow a woman a basic annals (Yang, *Li-tai,* pp. 421-3). Pan Ku shifts much of the material in this chapter to other chapters and allows Empress Lü only a brief biography in his *Han shu* (97A.3937-40).

[2]*Wei-shih* 微時, an epithet commonly used by Ssu-ma Ch'ien to describe Liu Pang's youth (cf. also *Shih chi,* 28.1378, 50.1987, and 56.2059), suggesting both his obscurity and his humble beginnings.

[3]Liu Ying 劉盈 (210-188 B.C.). On his birthdate and age, see Wu Hsün 吳恂, *Han shu chu-shang* 漢書注商 (Shanghai: Shang-hai Ku-chi, 1983), p. 13. As Yang Shu-ta (*Han shu k'uei-kuan,* p. 30) points out, the designation *hsiao* 孝 (filial) was first given posthumously to Emperor Hui and was intended to reflect the emperor's dutiful observance of the sacrifices in the Tsung miao 宗廟 (Temple of the Royal House).

[4]The princess was the wife of Chang Ao 張敖, Chang Erh's 張耳 son. Chang Ao became King of Chao and took the princess for his consort in 202 B.C., but was involved in a plot against Kao-tsu and removed from the throne (*Shih chi,* 89.2582ff.). Where her title originates is debated (see Chavannes, 2:299-300, n. 5 and the various comments in "Chi-chieh," *Shih chi,* 9.398). According to Liang Yü-sheng (7.240-41), her husband Chang Ao was posthumously titled King Yüan 元 of Lu in 187 B.C. (see *Shih chi,* 9.404) and her son made King of Lu because of her title and position! That confusion existed in Ssu-ma Ch'ien's mind concerning this problem is evident from his reference three times in this chapter to Chang Yen 張偃 as "King Yüan of Lu" (*Shih chi,* 9.405 and 407). In fact, Chang Yen received no posthumous title because in 179 B.C., owing to his close relationship to the Lüs, his state was abolished and his position reduced to marquis (*Shih chi,* 17.826).

Her daughter, Chang Yen 張嫣 (see "So-yin," *Shih chi,* 49.1969), became Emperor Hui's empress; having no son, she took one from one of the other palace women and tried to pretend he was her own; this "son" later became Shao-ti 少帝 (The Youth Emperor or Emperor Shao) for a short time after Emperor Hui's death (see the text in the translation of this chapter below [*Shih chi,* 9.402-3], as well as *Shih chi,* 49.1969 and Chavannes, 6:31-32).

[5]206 B.C.

In the Chung-hua edition this section is not made into a new paragraph.

105

loved and favored her, and begot [Liu] Ju-yi 如意,[7] King Yin 隱 of Chao 趙. Hsiao Hui[-ti] was a man who was humane and weak,[8] and Kao-tsu thought "He is not like me," often intending to remove the Heir and to install the son of Beauty Ch'i, Ju-yi; "Ju-yi resembles me," [he thought].[9]

[6]A county near the modern county of the same name in western Shantung (T'an Ch'i-hsiang, 2:7). Liang Yü-sheng (7.238) notes that if Beauty Ch'i was from Ting-yao she must be a native of Chi-yin 濟陰 (the Han commandery for which Ting-yao was the seat, see T'an Ch'i-hsiang, 2:19). He also points out that the *Shui-ching chu* 水經注 (27.889) claims she was from Yang-ch'uan 洋川, and opines that she probably had moved to Yang-ch'uan to avoid the fighting in her home area (the troops of Hsiang Liang and Hsiang Yü seem to have first come through Ting-yao after defeating a Ch'in army in the eighth month of 208 B.C., see *Shih chi*, 16.768). Liang argues it was there in Yang-ch'uan that Liu Pang met her. Yang-ch'uan does not seem to have been a Han-dynasty place name, but rather the name of a commandery of the Northern Dynasties, particularly the Pei Chou, and was seated near modern Hsi-hsiang 西鄉 about forty miles east of Han-chung 漢中 City in south-central Shensi (T'an Ch'i-hsiang, 4:68). The entire text of the *Shui-ching chu* account, however, makes it clear that Yang-ch'uan was her hometown. It relates how she longed for Yang-ch'uan to the point that Liu Pang ordered relay stations set up along the road from Yang-ch'uan to Ch'ang-an. If this account in *Shui-ching chu* is reliable, it would be strange indeed for Beauty Ch'i to feel such nostalgia for a place other than her hometown. The Yang-ch'uan location would also fit the timing here, since it was when Liu Pang was in Han-chung as the King of Han (206 B.C.) that he met Beauty Ch'i. Another possibility is that her family moved from Ting-yao to Yang-ch'uan before she was born, making her a 'native' of Ting-yao who had actullay been born in Yang-ch'uan. This is all, however, but speculation, and the *Shui-ching chu* reference does not seem basis enough to believe that her birthplace was someplace other than Ting-yao.

On the title *chi* 姬, "beauty, belle," we follow Ju Ch'un's 如淳 comments in "Chi-chieh" that this was a general designation for the non-ranked women of the harem (he notes that it should be pronounced *yi* 怡). Bielenstein's "Ladies of the Harem" (pp. 73-74) treats the Han harem in its systematic later form and is not useful here.

[7]Ju-yi as *praenomen* is not consistent with the names of his brothers: Liu Ying, Liu Fei, etc., all of whom had single-syllable *praenomens*. Ju-yi 如意, literally "As One Would Wish," seems rather to reflect Liu Pang's hopes for the boy as his successor. Wang Shu-min (9.356) points out that in the "Wai-ch'i chuan" 外戚傳 (Memoir on the Maternal Relatives) in the *Han shu* there is the character *tzu* 字 (*agnomen*) before his name. This seems logical, but unfortunately neither mention of Liu Ju-yi in this chapter (*Han shu*, 97A.3937 and 3938) indicates his *agnomen*.

[8]*Jen-jo* 仁弱; this term is used only once in *Shih chi*, to describe Emperor Hui. It should be read in conjunction with the subsequent description of the emperor's mother, Empress Dowager Lü, as *kang yi* 剛毅, "obstinate and resolute." On this point see also Lo Shih-lieh 羅世烈, "Liu-Lü chih cheng p'ing-yi" 劉呂之爭平議, *Chin-yang hsüeh-k'an*, 18 (1983.3): 67.

[9]The use of the first-person pronoun *wo* 我 twice here, without indication from the Chung-hua editors or other commentators that this is direct speech, is puzzling. Chavannes renders this in the third person (2:407); Watson translates the first occurrence in third-person, the second in the first-person: "For Ju-yi is just like me," he would say (Watson, *Han*, 1:267). Our translation is tentative. Pan Ku apparently found the use of *wo* 我 here unusual as well. In the parallel passage (*Han shu*, 97A.3937) his rendition of these events substitutes *chi* 己 for

While Beauty Ch'i was in favor,[10] she often followed the sovereign to Kuan-tung 關東 (East of the Pass),[11] weeping and whimpering day and night, intending to cause her son to be installed in place of the Heir. Empress Lü was old, and often left to guard [the capital], rarely seeing the sovereign, [so] they became more estranged. After Ju-yi was enthroned as King of Chao,[12] he almost replaced the Heir several times.[13] [The Heir] relied on the great ministers to dispute this, and when the Marquis of Liu 留 employed his stratagem,[14] the Heir was able to avoid removal.[15]

[396] Lü T'ai-hou was a person who was obstinate and resolute;[16] she assisted Kao-tsu in stabilizing the world,[17] and many of the great ministers who had been executed [owed their demise] to Empress Lü's power.[18] Empress Lü had two elder brothers and both were generals. The

wo in the first usage. For the second, the Chung-hua editors believe he indicated a direct citation.

[10]There is a story that Beauty Ch'i was a skilled singer and dancer and often sang the nostalgic "Ch'u sai, ju sai"出塞入塞 (Out of the Frontier Pass, Into the Frontier Pass; see *Hsi-ching tsa-chi* 西京雜記 [Miscellaneous Notes on the Western Capital], *SPTK*, 1.2a).

[11]These trips, primarily to deal with rebellions, are described in *Shih chi* Chapter 8 above (see also the Translator's Note to Chapter 8). Chavannes (2:407, n. 2) limits her travels to the expedition in 197-196 B.C. against Ch'en Hsi.

[12]Ju-yi was enthroned in 198 B.C. as King [posthumous title Yin 隱] of Chao (r. 198-194 B.C.)–*Shih chi*, 17.809. *Shih chi*, 96.2678, tells us that when Ju-yi was ten years old Kao-tsu was concerned about the boy's fate after his own death. This was probably in 196 B.C., suggesting Ju-yi's date of birth was about 205 B.C. Thus Liu Ying, his great rival as the Heir and later Hui-ti, was five years older than his half-brother Ju-yi.

[13]There are several narratives depicting efforts to dissuade Kao-tsu from changing the Heir. The first involved Shu-sun T'ung 叔孫通 arguing against the move in 198 B.C. (*Shih chi*, 99.2724-5), the second featured Chou Ch'ang 周昌 (*Shih chi*, 96.2677). Fan K'uai was also accused of wanting to execute Beauty Ch'i and Liu Ju-yi shortly before Liu Pang's death (see *Shih chi*, 95.2659). See also the reference in the text just below to Marquis Liu's plan.

[14]See the narration of this plan conceived by Chang Liang in *Shih chi*, 55.2046-47.

[15]In previous chapters of the *Shih chi* there are several antecedents of rulers intending to overthrow their royal spouses and heirs in favor of a beautiful young rival and her son, but the most famous is King Yu 幽 of Chou (r. 781-771 B.C.) and his fateful infatuation with Lady Pao 褒 of Ssu 姒 (see *Shih chi*, 4.147 and *Grand Scribe's Records*, 1:73; see also *Shih chi*, 5.177, and 5.181).

[16]This term, *kang-yi* 剛毅, was also used to describe the First Emperor of Ch'in's government (*Shih chi*, 6.136, *Grand Scribe's Records*, 1:136): 剛毅戾深，事皆決於法 "His government was obstinate and resolute, perverse and unfathomable." The line might also be understood as "He [the First Emperor] was obstinate and resolute, perverse and unfathomable." Ssu-ma Ch'ien here seems to imply a kindred spirit between Empress Lü and the First Emperor.

[17]This is confirmed by a Master T'ien 田 in "Ching Yen shih-chia" 荊燕世家 (*Shih chi*, 51.1995) who points out the merit of the Lüs on Kao-tsu's behalf. See also Lo Shih-lieh, "Liu-Lü chih cheng p'ing-yi," p. 67.

[18]As Chavannes notes (2:407-98, n. 4) Han Hsin and P'eng Yüeh were put to death as a result of Empress Lü's machinations (see *Shih chi*, 92.2628 and 90.2594, respectively). Wang Li-ch'i (8.235n.) adds a third person to this list, arguing that Ch'ing Pu was also a victim of Empress Lü, but Ch'ing's revolt and death

eldest brother, the Marquis of Chou-Lü 周呂, died in service [of his state],[19] and [Kao-tsu] enfeoffed his son, Lü Yi 呂台 as Marquis of Li 酈[20]; his son, Ch'an 產, became Marquis of Chiao 交.[21] Her next eldest brother, Lü Shih-chih 呂釋之, was the Marquis of Chien-ch'eng 建成.[22]

On the *chia-ch'en* 甲辰 day of the fourth month in the twelfth year of his [reign] (1 June 195 B.C.), Kao-tsu passed away in the Ch'ang-lo 長樂 Palace, and the Heir inherited his title and became emperor. At this time Kao-tsu had eight sons: the eldest male was [Liu] Fei 肥 Hsiao Hui[-ti's] eldest brother from a different mother[23]; [Liu] Fei became the King of Ch'i 齊;

can only be seen as indirectly arising from Empress Lü's actions in the deaths of Han Hsin and P'eng Yüeh (see *Shih chi*, 91.2603). *Han shu*, 97A.3937, does not include this reference to Empress Lü's guilt in these men's death.

[19]As Liang Yü-sheng (7.238) notes, Lü Tse 呂澤, the elder brother, served as Marquis of Chou-Lü 周 呂 from 201 B.C. until his death in 199 B.C. (*Shih chi*, 18.888). Our reading of Chou-Lü as an honorific title follows Liang Yü-sheng and Wu and Lu (9.326): the Lü clan originally had the *cognomen* Chiang 姜, thus the appellation Chou-Lü suggested the Han House was assisted by the Lü in a manner similar to that which the Chou House was aided by Chiang Tzu-ya 姜子牙, also known as Lü Shang 呂尚 (The Most Esteemed of the Lüs), the original Duke of Ch'i (see the account at the beginning of *Shih chi* Chapter 32). Wang Li-ch'i (9.235n.) argues that both Chou and Lü are place names.

Takigawa (9.183) speculates that "the service" referred to here may have been during Hann Hsin's rebellion in 199 B.C. Wu and Lu (8.326n.) note that the circumstances of Lü Tse's death are unknown, but it must have come as a result of efforts either in military or other "public business" (*kung shih* 公事). Chavannes (2.408, n. 1) comments on the unusual expression, *ssu shih* 死事. With the concordances and on-line texts of the *Shih chi* available today, however, it is easier to locate other similar uses of the expression. On *Shih chi*, 107.2845, for example, we read: "According to military law, when a father and son are together on a military campaign, if one of them happens to die in service, the other is able to return home with the corpse" 軍法，父子俱從軍，有死事，得與喪歸 (see also Watson's translation [*Han*, 2:102]). A second example can be found on *Shih chi*, 120.3109: "In your vassal's unworthy opinion, all those Tartars that Your Majesty subjugates and captures should be considered slaves to be granted to the families of those who died in service on the campaign" (see also Watson, *Han*, 2:313) 臣愚以為陛下得胡人，皆以為奴婢以賜從軍死事者家.

[20]Liang Yü-sheng (7.238) believes this holding should be Fu 酈 County (located about one-hundred miles north-northeast of Ch'ang-an (T'an Ch'i-hsiang, 2:15), not Li which is in Nan-yang 南陽 Commandery (modern Hupei, T'an Ch'i-hsiang, 2:22).

[21]This appointment took place under Empress Lü's reign according to Liang Yü-sheng (7.238-9). Liang also corrects the name of the fief to Hsiao 沒, located near Empress Lü's home area of P'ei. *Shih chi*, 19.980-81 further specifies the date as the fourth month of the first year (28 April-26 May 194 B.C.).

[22]Lü Shih-chih was appointed Marquis of Chien-ch'eng in the sixth year of Kao-tsu's reign (201 B.C.). He died three years later (*Shih chi*, 18.889-90).

There were three Chien-ch'eng counties under the Western Han, but as Wu and Lu (9.326n.) point out, this must refer to the county in P'ei 沛 Commandery located southeast of modern Yung-ch'eng 永城 County in Ho-nan.

[23]A woman with the *cognomen* Ts'ao 曹 according to "So-yin" (see n. 1 above).

This list of Liu Pang's sons seems out of place, especially since a similar list has been provided just the remaining [sons] were all Hsiao-hui's younger brothers: the son of Beauty Ch'i, [Liu] Ju-yi became King of Chao; the son of Lady Po 薄,[24] [Liu] Heng 恆 became King of Tai; [as for] the sons of the various [court] beauties, his son [Liu] Hui 恢 became King of Liang 梁; his son [Liu] Yu 友 became King of Huai-yang 淮陽; his son [Liu] Chang 長 became King of Huai-nan 淮南; and his son [Liu] Chien 建 became King of Yen 燕. Kao-tsu's younger brother [Liu] Chiao 交 became King of Ch'u 楚, the son of his elder brother, [Liu] P'i 濞, became King of Wu 吳. [Wu] Ch'en 臣, son of Wu Jui, the Lord of P'o, who was not of the Liu family but a vassal with merit, became King of Ch'ang-sha 長沙.

[397] Empress Lü, harboring the greatest resentment for Lady Ch'i and her son the King of Chao, ordered the Long Lane [officials][25] to confine Lady Ch'i[26] and summoned the King of Chao. The envoys returned three times. The Prime Minister of Chao, Chou Ch'ang 周昌, Marquis of Chien-p'ing 建平,[27] said to the envoys: "Kao-ti 高帝 (The Exalted Emperor or Emperor

above at the end of "Kao-tsu pen-chi" (*Shih chi*, 8.393); it does not appear in the parallel account in the *Han shu* (97A.3937). However, as becomes evident below, this catalogue becomes a kind of "hit list" for Empress Lü.

[24]See the notice on her in *Shih chi*, 49.1970-72. She escaped Empress Lü's recriminations following Kao-tsu's death, because she had not been a favorite. Her son, Liu Heng 劉恆, became Emperor Wen 文 (r. 179-157 B.C.).

On these sons of Liu Pang see notes 601-608 in our translation of "Kao-tsu pen-chi" above. On Wu Jui see n. 277 to this same translation.

[25]*Yung-hsiang* 永巷, the Long Lane, was a way in a detached palace along which the palace ladies had originally resided, but came to be the name for the harem until Emperor Wu changed it to Yeh-t'ing 掖庭 in 104 B.C. (see also *Han shu*, 19A.731-32); the Long Lane could also be used to confine women who had committed some offense as in this passage; see also the "Chi-chieh" and "So-yin" comments on this passage as well as *Shih chi*, 79.2406. Wang Li-ch'i's reading is that *yung-hsiang* stands for *Yung-hsiang ling* 令 (Prefect of the Long Lane) and he explains that the Long Lane was overseen by a prefect and other minor officials (9.236n–see also Lu Zongli, p. 296). This is possible, but *yung-hsiang* may also just refer to the institution as a whole (including all of its officials) here. *Shih chi*, 49.1971 tells that all of Kao-tsu's favorites were confined at this time.

[26]Liang Yü-sheng (7.239) points to the more detailed account of Beauty Ch'i's confinement in *Han shu* (97A.3937-8). First "commanded to pound grain" (*ling ch'ung* 令舂), a standard punishment for women which usually involved a four-year sentence (see Ying Shao's comments, *Han shu*, 2.87 and Hulsewé, *Han Law*, p. 129), Beauty Ch'i composed a song about her plight which, although it seemingly was a simple lament, was actually seditious (see also the discussion by Donald Holzman in his "Les premiers vers pentasyllabiques datés dans la poésic chinoise," *Mélanges de Sinologie offerts à Monsieur Paul Demiéville* [Paris: Presses Universitaires de France, 1974], pp. 81-83). It was at this point that Empress Lü had her mutilated.

[27]Liang Yü-sheng (7.239) notes that in his biography Chou Ch'ang was named Marquis of Fen-yin 汾陰 (about 110 miles northeast of Ch'ang-an in modern Shansi, T'an Ch'i-hsiang, 2:16) in 201 B.C. (*Shih chi*, 96.2677) but in the chronological tables (*Shih chi*, 18.896) he is referred to as the Marquis of Chien-p'ing (in modern Shantung about 35 miles southeast of Shang-ch'iu 商丘 City and 75 miles southwest of P'ei, T'an Ch'i-hsiang, 2:19); Liang suspects that his fief was changed to Chien-p'ing during the reign of Emperor Hui.

Kao) entrusted the King of Chao to me[28] and the King of Chao is [still] young. I have privately heard that the T'ai-hou harbors resentment for Lady Ch'i and wants to summon the King of Chao and execute them together. Your subject does not dare to send the king. Moreover, the king is also ill, so he cannot receive your decree." Empress Lü was enraged and sent someone to summon the Prime Minister of Chao. After the Prime Minister of Chao had been called in to Ch'ang-an, she sent someone to again summon the King of Chao. [At the time,] the King of Chao was on his way, but had not yet arrived. Hsiao Hui-ti 孝惠帝 (The Filial and Kind Emperor or Emperor Hui the Filial) was compassionate and humane, and knew that the T'ai-hou was angry, so he personally met the King of Chao at Pa Shang 霸上 (Pa Heights) and entered the palace with him, taking him under his protection, resting, rising, eating, and drinking with him.[29] The T'ai-hou intended to kill him [the King of Chao], but she was not able to find an opportunity.[30]

In the twelfth month of the first year of Hsiao Hui[-ti] (31 December 195–28 January 194 B.C.), the emperor went out early shooting;[31] the King of Chao was young and not able to rise early. When the T'ai-hou heard he had been left alone, she sent someone to take serpent-eagle [wine][32] and cause him to drink it.[33] At dawn,[34] when Hsiao Hui[-ti] returned, the King of Chao

Pan Ku includes no title other than *hsiang* 相 in his account (*Han shu*, 97A.3938).

[28]See *Shih chi*, 96.2678.

[29]The fact that Emperor Hui had a male favorite named Hung 閎 who always "lay down with and rose together with the sovereign" and a number of courtiers who seem to have aspired to such a relationship (see *Shih chi*, 125.3191 and Bret Hinsch, *Passions of the Cut Sleeve, The Male Homosexual Tradition in China* [Berkeley: University of California Press, 1990], pp. 35-36 and 47) may have caused Empress Lü to be more concerned about the growing affection between her son and Ju-yi and the political implications such a relationship would have.

[30]The parallel passage on *Han shu*, 97A.3938 makes no mention of Empress Lü's premeditation.

[31]This passage is not separated as a distinct paragraph by the Chung-hua editors, but is attached to that above. As is our standard policy where a new date (and/or narrative begins), we break the text into a new paragraph.

A citation of this section as recorded in the *T'ai-p'ing yü-lan* 太平御覽 adds *chih* 雉 after *she* 射 ("went out to shoot pheasant"; 87.9a, *SPTK*).

[32]The *Chen* 鴆 or Chinese Serpent Eagle (*Haematornis cheela*) was a bird that fed on poisonous snakes; it gained a reputation for being venomous itself, and wine steeped in its feathers was considered a deadly potion in ancient China (see also Edward Schafer, *The Vermilion Bird, T'ang Images of the South* [Berkeley and London: University of California Press, 1967], p. 245, and Wang Li-ch'i, 9.236n).

[33]In another account of this murder in the *Hsi-ching tsa-chi* (1.2b, *SPTK*), a strong man strangled Ju-yi in his bed for the empress and was later rewarded greatly. When Emperor Hui learned the details, he had the man executed without the Empress's knowledge. Liang Yü-sheng (7.239-40) prefers this version, because he believes that it is unlikely that Emperor Hui did not seek to find out how and by whom Ju-yi had been killed. Actually, however, it must have been evident to all that Empress Lü was behind the murder. Moreover, *Shih chi*, 96.3679 also says Ju-yi drank a drug (*yin-yao* 飲藥) and died.

had already died.[35] At this point, she transferred [Liu] Yu, the King of Huai-yang, to be King of Chao. In the summer she issued a decree granting the father of the Marquis of Li[36] the posthumous title of Marquis Ling-wu 令武. The T'ai-hou then cut off Lady Ch'i's hands and feet, removed her eyes, cauterized her ears, caused her to drink a drug that rendered her mute, and sent her to live in the privy, calling her "the human hog."[37] After several days, [the T'ai-hou] summoned Hsiao Hui-ti to view "the human hog." When Hsiao Hui[-ti] saw her, he had to ask before he realized that this was Lady Ch'i. Then he wept so hard that he became ill; it was over a year before he was able to get up. He sent someone to say to[38] Lü Hou: "This is not something that a human being would do. As the son of the T'ai-hou, I will never be able to rule the empire." Because of this, Hsiao Hui[-ti] drank and engaged himself in excessive pleasures day after day, not attending to the administration of the government; for this reason he became ill.

[398] In the second year (193 B.C.), King Yüan 元 of Ch'u (r. 201-179 B.C.) and King Tao Hui 悼惠 of Ch'i (r. 201-189 B.C.)[39] both came to court.[40]

[34]Wang Nien-sun (3A.80) believes li-ming 犁明 "at dawn" is not logical here (how could the young emperor have gone hunting and still returned by dawn?) and suggests emending the text to read li 犁 [=pi 比]: "When Hui the Filial returned, ..." See also Wang Shu-min (9.359). Han shu (97A.3938) reads simply: 遲帝 還 . . ., "when the emperor returned . . . ."

[35]According to Shih chi, 49.1969, Empress Lü also killed all members of Beauty Ch'i's clan and other harem favorites of Kao-tsu. A passage on Han shu, 41.2073 suggests Beauty Ch'i and her son had a group of followers and supporters.

Han shu records two dates for his death, the twelfth month of Emperor Hui's first year (31 December 195–28 January 194 B.C.; Han shu, 2.88) and the twelfth year of Kao-tsu (195 B.C.; Han shu, 14.404). Given the sequence of events, it seems impossible that Ju-yi was killed before the onset of 194 B.C., however.

[36]The Marquis of Li was Lü Yi , his father Lü Tse 呂澤.

[37]Jen-chih 人彘 is rendered "the human hog" here because chih indicates a large pig (Morohashi, 4:4182, gloss1), similar to the meaning of "hog." Han chi (4.2a) reads simply jen shih 人豕 "human pig"; etymologically the graph suggests a pig with its hind feet lame or mutilated (see Tuan Yu-ts'ai 段玉裁 (1735-1815), Shuo wen chieh-tzu chu 說文解字注 [Shanghai: Shang-hai Ku-chi, 1981], p. 456) which may be part of why Beauty Ch'i was referred to by this term.

Although this passage claims Beauty Ch'i was forced to live in the privy (where pigs were often kept), Han shu (97A.3938) and Han chi (4.2a) claim respectively she was placed in the chü yü 鞠域 or chü shih 鞠室, a walled-in rectangular "field" in which balls were kicked (see the detailed description in Ch'in Han shih-tai 秦漢時代, in Chung-kuo wen-ming shih 中國文明史 [Taipei: Ti-ch'iu, 1991], 3:024-27). Liang Yü-sheng (7.240) believes that it is more likely that Beauty Ch'i was put in the ball field rather than the privy. Tzu-chih t'ung-chien (12.410) also records that Beauty Ch'i was held in the privy. This variance suggests in all probability that several accounts of Beauty Ch'i's treatment had circulated. Dub's idea that she was "thrown out into the gully through which ran the sewer" (1.169) seems to be a misreading.

[38]Wang Shu-min (9.360) argues, by means of textual variants, that ch'ing 請 has the meaning of kao 告 "to announce, inform, tell," here.

[39]I.e., Liu Chiao and Liu Fei, respectively.

In the tenth month (20 November-19 December 194 B.C.), Hsiao Hui[-ti] and the King of Ch'i feasted and drank together in front of the T'ai-hou; Hsiao Hui[-ti], considering that the King of Ch'i was his elder brother, placed him in the honored seat as was the custom of family members.[41] Hsiao Hui[-ti], considering that the King of Ch'i was his elder brother, placed him in the honored seat, as was the custom among family members.[42] The T'ai-hou was angry[43] and ordered two scyphi of serpent-eagle [wine] to be poured and placed before them; she ordered the King of Ch'i to rise and toast her. The King of Ch'i rose. Hsiao Hui[-ti] also rose and, taking a scyphus, he intended to join in the toast. The T'ai-hou became afraid, rose herself, and overturned Hsiao Hui[-ti]'s scyphus. The King of Ch'i found this strange and accordingly dared not drink; feigning drunkenness he left. When he inquired and learned it was serpent-eagle [wine], the King of Ch'i grew afraid, and thinking to himself that he would not be able to escape Ch'ang-an, he became worried. Ch'i's Scribe of the Capital, Shih 士,[44] advised the king: "The T'ai-hou only has Hsiao Hui[-ti] and Princess Yüan of Lu.[45] Now Your Majesty has more than seventy walled

[40]This clause seems to have added meaning when one consults the chronological tables which show that although annual visits were the norm, neither king had appeared at court for three years (*Shih chi*, 17.811-814). None of the other kings had come to court during this period (196-194 B.C.), either. The visit by Liu Chiao and Liu Fei, Liu Pang's younger brother and eldest son, respectively, were intended to show their acceptance of Liu Ying as emperor and perhaps also to encourage their younger counterparts (most of the other kings were Emperor Hui's brothers) to do the same.

[41]Here again we have created a paragraph break that is not indicated by the Chung-hua editors.

Yen-yin 燕飲 suggests a lack of formality that disturbed the Empress Dowager; for years she had hoped to gain respect through her son, and now she saw one of Liu Pang's sons by a different mother flout that respect.

[42]As Chang Chia-ying (p. 177) points out, the parallel passage in Liu Fei's biography (*Shih chi*, 52.1999) reads: "Emperor Hui and the King of Ch'i feasted and drank together observing the ritual of common family members with equal status" [*k'ang li ju chia-jen* 亢禮如家人]. Liu Pang had also honored his father by treating him "as a family member" in 201 B.C. (see the translation of this passage from *Shih chi*, 8.382 above). There is a parallel passage in *Han shu* (37.1987-88) which amplifies the text to explain that Hui-ti gave his elder brother the best seat according to their family rank. The Empress took offense here because, by thinking in family terms, that is as members of the royal Liu House, both the Emperor and his mother were denied their political rank, and probably also because this treatment reminded her that she was actually still an "outsider" in matters which concerned the Liu family.

[43]She was angry because instead of family etiquette the social codes of the court should have taken precedence; the King of Ch'i's relaxed acceptance of the exalted position could also have been viewed as an indirect slight to the Empress Dowager herself.

[44]Otherwise unknown; Liang Yü-sheng (7.239) believes Shih was his *cognomen* and Hsün 勛 his *praenomen*, probably based on the parallel account on *Shih chi*, 52.1999.

[45]As Ts'ui Shih (*Shih chi t'an-yüan* 史記探源 [Rpt. Peking: Chung-hua, 1986], 3.63) points out "Emperor Hui" and "Princess Yüan of Lu" are used anachronistically here. But such is the practice throughout the annals of the first two Han rulers.

cities and the princess has [only] several walled cities as places to provide her with provisions.[46] If Your Majesty would really take a commandery to present to the T'ai-hou as the princess's bath-town,[47] the T'ai-hou would certainly be pleased and Your Majesty would certainly have no more worries." At this the King of Ch'i presented the commandery of Ch'eng-yang 城陽[48] and honored the princess as the "Queen Dowager."[49] Empress Lü was pleased and allowed it. She had wine set out in the Ch'i Residence;[50] they had music played and drank, and when it ended, she allowed the King of Ch'i to return home.[51]

In the third year (192 B.C.), they began to build Ch'ang-an's city walls; in the fourth year (191 B.C.), they completed half [of them]; and in the fifth and sixth years the walls were finished.[52] The feudal lords[53] came to an assize.[54] In the tenth month (29 October–27 November

[46]Reading *shih* 食 as "taking a place as a fief manor," i.e., "taking it for one's provision."

[47]See n. 563 to our translation of *Shih chi* Chapter 8 above.

[48]This commandery with its capital near modern Chü 莒 County in eastern Shantung (T'an Ch'i-hsiang, 2:20) later became a Han kingdom (*kuo* 國) of the same name.

[49]Liang Yü-sheng (6.240-41) points out that the King of Ch'i was treating the princess, who was actually his half-sister, as his mother, in order to curry favor with Empress Lü. He was allowed to do this since his mother, Lady Ts'ao, was Liu Pang's mistress and therefore not the king's legal mother. These unnaturally complicated familial relationships illustrate for Liang the absurdity of Empress Lü's reign.

[50]Each of the feudal lords and governors of commanderies was expected to keep a residence (*ti* 邸) in Ch'ang-an which would then house any important visitors from that state.

[51]For two other accounts of this incident, see *Shih chi,* 52.1999 and *Hsin hsü shu-cheng* 新序疏證, Liu Hsiang 劉向, compiler, Chao Shan-yi 趙善詒, ed. (Shanghai: Hua-tung Shih-fan Ta-hsüeh Ch'u-pan-she, 1989), p. 295. In the *Hsin hsü* account Hui-ti learns that the wine is poisoned and in effect spoils Empress Lü's plans. Moreover, in this account there is a dialogue between the Scribe of the Capital and the King of Ch'i. It is possible that an earlier version of the more elaborate account given in the *Hsin hsü* was Ssu-ma Ch'ien's source here.

The paragraph which follows is included with this one in the Chung-hua edition.

[52]The northwestern side of the city wall was begun in 194 B.C. according to *Shih chi,* 22.1122. However, the notice for 192 B.C. in the same chapter (*ibid.*) says that the city walls were first begun in that year. These construction projects were perhaps seen as separate undertakings. Liang Yü-sheng (7.241) dismisses the *Shih chi* references, and based primarily on the *Han shu,* concludes the walls were begun in 194 B.C. and completed in 190 B.C. (as do Wu and Lu, 9.328n.: they refer to *Han shu* "Hui-ti chi" 惠帝紀 [2.88-91] and note that the construction in the sixth year was not on the city wall, but to build the Western Market 西市 and repair the Ao 敖 Granary). This passage in the *Han shu* provides other interesting details: In the spring, 146,000 men and women from within 600 *li* of Ch'ang-an were dispatched to wall the city. Within 30 days their work was finished; in the sixth month 20,000 convicts and slaves of the noble kings and full marquises were sent forth to work on walling Ch'ang-an. Finally another levy of 145,000 men and women in the first month of the fifth year brought the walls to completion in the ninth month (2.91).

Hsü Shuo-fang 徐朔方 in his "Tu *Shih chi* "Lü Hou pen-chi" 讀史記呂后本紀 (in Hsü's *Shih Han lun kao* 史漢論稿 [Nanking: Chiang-su Ku-chi, 1984], p. 89) argues that Yang-ch'eng Yen 陽城延 (who was

192 B.C.), they came to court to offer congratulations.[55]

[399] On the *wu-yin* 戊寅 day of the eighth month, in the autumn of the seventh year (26 September 188 B.C.), Hsiao Hui-ti passed away.[56] When the mourning was announced, the empress wailed but no tears fell.[57] Chang Pi-ch'iang 張辟彊, the son of the Marquis of Liu, was a

made Marquis of Wu-ch'i 梧齊侯 in 179 B.C. [or of Wu-ch'i 梧齊 according to *Han shu*, 16.619]) should be given credit for supervising the construction of the Wei-yang and Ch'ang-le palaces as well as the city walls. This is confirmed by *Shih chi*, 19.981-82. See also Dubs, 1:179, n. 3.

[53]Some later printings of the Chung-hua edition have misprinted *ch'ing* 請 for *chu* 諸 here.

[54]Rendering *hui* 會 as "assize" here. By coming, they recognized the power of Emperor Hui.

[55]As other scholars have noted, the tenth month under the calendar at this time began the new year. Thus the congratulations at court. But by listing the tenth month *after* the six month, the text here seems to take a perspective from the era after the calendar reforms of 104 B.C.

Han Chao-ch'i 韓兆琦 claims this is the end of the first section of this chapter, the end of Empress Lü's campaign against the Liu family sons (see his *Shih chi hsüan-chu chi-shuo* 史記選注集說 [Nanchang: Chiang-hsi Jen-min, 1982], p. 73).

It might also be noted that for the following four years, 192-188 B.C., the *Shih chi* account of Emperor Hui records no events. The parallel sections of the *Han shu* (2.90-92) and *Han chi* (6.6a-14b, *SPTK*), on the other hand, are filled with portents, including two solar eclipses in the seventh year just before Hui-ti's death. The *Hsi-ching tsa-chi* (2.5b-6a) also notes that in the seventh month, shortly before the emperor passed away, lightning shook the Southern Mountains and started a fire which burned several thousand trees to the ground. When people went to the area several months later they found the remains of a dragon and two *chiao* 蛟. It is possible that Pan Ku crafted his annals for Emperor Hui out of the same portentous source that the *Hsi-ching tsa-chi* employed. Grant Hardy points out that this is not the only case where Ssu-ma Ch'ien may have been selective in his recording of eclipses, since he only noted twenty three of the thirty six eclipses that appear in the text of the *Ch'un ch'iu* for the the corresponding years in his "Shih-erh chu-hou nien-piao" 十二諸侯年表 (Chronological Table of the Twelve Feudal Lords; Hardy, *Worlds*, p. 239, n. 32).

[56]According to the *Han shu* (2.92) and *Han chi* (5.14b, *SPTK*) he died in the Wei-yang Palace. Takigawa (9.8) cites Wang Ming-sheng's 王鳴盛 (1722-1798) argument that Emperor Hui died at 23 *sui*, not 24 as claimed in the *Han shu* commentary (2.93).

[57]The section on "tears" (*ch'i* 泣) in the *Yi-wen lei-chü* 藝文類聚 (Wang Shao-ying 汪紹楹, ed., 2nd edition; Shanghai: Shang-hai Ku-chi, 1982 [1965], 35.623) cites the *Ch'u Han ch'un-chiu* as follows: "When Empress Lü was intending to make a high grave mound for Hui-ti, she caused it [to be built at such a height] that it could be seen when sitting in the Wei-yang Palace. The Marquis of Tung-yang [Chang Hsiang-ju 張相如, see *Shih chi*, 18.951] wept and said, 'Your Majesty day and night looks at Emperor Hui's grave, you sorrow and shed tears without end. This will harm your health. Your servant is humbly saddened by this.' Only then did the Empress Dowager stop." 呂后欲為惠帝高墳，使從未央宮坐而見之。東陽侯垂泣曰：陛下日夜見惠帝冢，悲哀流涕無已，是傷生也。臣竊哀之。太后乃止。

Ssu-ma Ch'ien, in his attempts to chastise Lü Hou, would probably not have used this account even if he had seen it.

palace attendant and aged fifteen; he said to the chancellor,[58] "The T'ai-hou has only [one son],
Hsiao Hui[-ti]. Now he has passed away, [but] in her wailing there is no sorrow. Do you, sir,
know an explanation?" "What explanation [can there be]?" said the chancellor. Pi-ch'iang said,
"The emperor had no fully grown son and the T'ai-hou is in awe of you, sir, and your colleagues.
If you now request that Lü Yi, Lü Ch'an, and Lü Lu 呂祿 be appointed generals, to command the
troops stationed in the Northern and Southern armies[59] and allow all the Lüs to move into the
palace, and remain within to take power, the T'ai-hou in this way will feel secure and you and
your colleagues will have the good fortune to avoid disaster." The chancellor then followed
Pi-ch'iang's stratagem. The T'ai-hou was pleased and her wailing then became mournful. The
power of the Lü Clan originated from this. Then she granted a general amnesty throughout the
empire.

On the *hsin-ch'ou* 辛丑 day of the ninth month (19 October 188 B.C.) [the Emperor]
was buried.[60] The Heir ascended the throne as emperor[61] and paid a visit to the Temple of the
Exalted [Ancestor].[62]

In the first year (187 B.C.), verbal orders originated solely from the T'ai-hou.

[400] The T'ai-hou caused [her orders] to be called decrees[63] and caused the question

---

[58]Given Wang Ling's strong opposition to the Lüs in the passage which follows, this was very likely
the Chancellor of the Left, Ch'en P'ing 陳平 (see Liang Yü-sheng, 7.242). According to Wang Shu-min
(9.364), the *Fa-yen* 法言 (*Han Wei ts'ung-shu* 漢魏叢書 ed., in *Pai-pu ts'ung-shu,* 7.5a) explicitly names the
chancellors as [Ch'en] P'ing 平 and [Chou] Po 勃.

[59]The Southern Army, its troops conscripted from the commanderies outside the capital, was stationed
south of the Wei-yang and Ch'ang-le palaces and designed to protect the south of the city. As Bielenstein (pp.
114 ff.) notes, the soldiers of this army were rotated annually and were therefore not veteran troops. The
Northern Army, with troops levied from the capital city, was based north of the two palaces and could be
considered an army made up primarily of professional soldiers; it was considered the main force in any defense
of the capital (see Wu and Lu, 9.329n. and *Ch'in Han shih,* pp. 312 and 117 respectively). See also Hamaguchi
Shigekuni 浜口重国, "Sen Kan no Nanboku gun ni tsuite" 前漢の南北軍に就いて, *Shin Kan Zui Tô shi no
kenkyû* 秦漢隋唐史の研究 (Tokyo: Tokyo Daigaku Shuppankai, 1998 (1966), pp. 251-266, and Dubs' useful
note on these armies (1:206-7, n. 4).

[60]Hui-ti was buried at An-ling 安陵 (Peaceful Tumulus) located about ten miles northeast of modern
Hsien-yang (*Han shu,* 2.92; *Han chi,* 5.15a, *SPTK;* see also Chang Lieh, 1:58n. and *Hsi-an shih-ch'ü ti-t'u tse* 西
安市區地圖冊, Chu Yi-ch'ün 朱伊群 and Shih Jui-chü 施瑞菊, eds. [2nd printing; Sian: Hsi-an Ti-t'u Ch'u-
pan-she], 1991 [1989], pp. 57-58).

[61]This was Emperor Shao 少, the boy that the empress of Hui the Filial had taken from another palace
woman (see n. 4 above). Since he never received a posthumous title, he is known simply as the "Youth
Emperor." He was deposed and killed in 184 B.C. (see *Shih chi,* 9.403 and 22.1124; see also Dubs, 1:209, n. 3),
Liu Yi succeeding him (see nn. 85 and 103 below).

[62]On Hui-ti's having two temples for his father, Kao-tsu, constructed, see *Shih chi,* 99.2725-26, and
Patricia Ebrey, "Portrait Sculptures in Imperial Ancestral Rites in Song China," *TP* LXXXIII (1997): 55.

[63]On the expression *ch'eng chih* 稱制 see also Chang Chia-ying, p. 179, Yen Shih-ku's comments

of whether to enthrone the Lüs as kings to be deliberated, questioning the Chancellor of the Right, Wang Ling 王陵 (d. 181 B.C.).[64] Wang Ling said, "The vow we all made when Kao-ti slaughtered a white horse read,[65] 'If someone who is not of the Liu Clan is made king, the world will join together to attack him.' To now make kings of the Lü Clan would be to go against the covenant."[66] The T'ai-hou was not pleased. She questioned Ch'en P'ing 陳平 (d. 178 B.C.),[67] the Chancellor of the Left, and Chou Po 周勃 (d. 169 B.C.),[68] the Marquis of Chiang 絳.[69] [Chou] Po and the others replied, "When Kao-ti stabilized the world, he made kings of his younger brothers and sons. Now that the T'ai-hou has announced [that she would issue] the [imperial] decrees, there is nothing wrong with her making kings of her brothers and the [other] Lüs." The T'ai-hou was happy with this and dismissed the court. Wang Ling upbraided Ch'en P'ing and the Marquis

(*Han shu,* 3.95), and Dubs (1:192). Dubs translates this term as "announced [that she would issue] the [imperial] decrees." But *ch'eng* seems to mean simply "called" her orders edicts, referring back to the First Emperor of Ch'in's adoption of this term for imperial orders (*Grand Scribe's Records,* 1:136: "The king is to be called 'His Primeval Majesty.' His orders are to be called 'decrees,' and his ordinances, 'edicts' [*Shih chi,* 6.236: 王為【泰皇】，命為【制】，令為【詔】.]) Yang Lien-sheng also supports this reading by providing example of how Empress Lü maintained here control of imperial decrees (see his "Female Rulers in Imperial China," in *Studies of Governmental Institutions in Chinese History,* John L. Bishop, ed. [Cambridge, Mass.: Harvard University Press, 1968], pp. 53-54). There are two other occurrences of *ch'eng chih* in the *Shih chi,* that make clearer the denotations and connotations of this term. The first concerns the use of the term by Chao T'o 趙佗, the ruler of Yüeh 越 during the reigns of Kao-tsu and Empress Lü: 迺乘黃屋左纛，稱制，與中國侔 (*Shih chi,* 113.2969); "Then [Chao T'o] rode about in a carriage with a yellow top, decorated with plumes on the left side, called his orders 'edicts,'[demonstrating] he was an equal of [the ruler of] the Central States." The second comes in the biography of the King of Huai-nan 淮南, Liu Ch'ang 劉長, who rebelled against the Han under Emperor Wen: "[Liu Ch'ang] did not employ the Han laws; when he left and entered he caused [attendants] to call out 'Pay attention! Clear the way!' and called his commands 'decrees,' making up his own laws and orders, in imitation of the Son of Heaven"; 不用漢法，出入稱警蹕，稱制，自為法令，擬於天子 (*Shih chi,* 118.3076). These passages suggest *ch'eng* should be read simply as "to call"; moreover, they illustrate that this later association with female usurpers postdates the *Shih chi* and that Ssu-ma Ch'ien intended the term to be applied to only to those who openly opposed the Han rule, regardless of their sex.

[64]See Wang's biography in *Shih chi* Chapter 55.

[65]The use of horses (and cattle) for oaths involving kings is a practice begun in the Warring States era (cf. Su Ch'in advocating the sacrifice of a white horse to validate an anti-Ch'in oath on *Shih chi,* 69.2249). See also the translation of this passage in *Grand Scribe's Records,* 7:102, especially n. 37 on that page which discusses the use of various animals in covenants, and Mark Edward Lewis, *Sanctioned Violence in Early China* (Albany: SUNY Press, 1990), pp. 43-50.

[66]In Wang Ling's biography (*Shih chi,* 56.2060), he simply replies, "It cannot be done" (不可). In that same passage Ch'en P'ing then responds "It can be done" (可).

[67]See Ch'en's biography in *Shih chi* Chapter 56.

[68]See Chou's biography in *Shih chi* Chapter 57.

[69]A county near what is now Hou-ma 侯馬 City in modern Shansi (T'an Ch'i-hsiang, 2:16).

of Chiang: "When we first sipped blood and swore an oath with Kao-ti, can it be that you, sirs, were not present? Now that Kao-ti has passed away, and the T'ai-hou as a female ruler wants to make kings of the Lü Clan, you, sirs, if you indulge her to pander to her intentions, you turn your backs on the covenant. How will you be able to face up to Kao-ti in the underworld?" Ch'en P'ing and the Marquis of Chiang said, "Just now, in criticizing and opposing [the T'ai-hou] face to face in court, we do not measure up to you, Milord. With regard to maintaining the altars of soil and grain, securing the posterity of the Liu Clan, you surely do not measure up to us!"[70] Wang Ling had no reply for them.

In the eleventh month (13 December 188–11 January 187 B.C.), the T'ai-hou wanted to remove Wang Ling,[71] so she appointed him Grand Tutor to take away his power as chancellor. Wang Ling then resigned because of illness and went home. Then she made Chancellor of the Left, [Ch'en] P'ing, Chancellor of the Right, and Shen Yi-chi 審食其, Marquis of Pi-yang 辟陽, Chancellor of the Left.[72] She caused the Chancellor of the Left to be free from regulating affairs, [but] to supervise [things] in the palace, like the Prefect of the Palace Attendants.[73] [Shen] Yi-chi for this reason gained favor with the T'ai-hou; and often exercised power, so that the honored ministers all relied on him in deciding affairs. Then she posthumously honored the father of the Marquis of Li 酈[74] as King Tao Wu 悼武, intending to use him as the starting point towards making kings of the Lüs.

In the fourth month (10 May–7 June 187 B.C.), the T'ai-hou, intending to make marquises of the Lüs, first enfeoffed [Feng] Wu-tse [馮]無擇, Prefect of the Palace Attendants, an official with meritorious service to Kao-tsu, as the Marquis of Po-ch'eng 博城.[75] Princess Yüan of Lu

[70]Ch'en P'ing was able to overcome Empress Lü's suspicions which had been aroused by her younger sister, Lü Hsü (see *Shih chi*, 56.2059).

[71]Here, again, we indicate a paragraph break (because of the date given here) that is not in the original Chung-hua version.

[72]Shen Yi-chi was a favorite. He had been captured together with Empress Lü and T'ai-kung by Hsiang Yü and no doubt won favor by protecting the empress during this time (cf. *Shih chi*, 7.322) and *Grand Scribe's Records*, 1.199, n. 203.

[73]Bielenstein renders *Lang-chung ling* 郎中令 as "Prefect of the Gentlemen-of-the-Palace" (p. 23).

[74]I.e., Lü Tse who had died in 198 B.C. (see the translation of *Shih chi*, 9.396 and n. 18 above).

[75]According to *Shih chi*, 19.983, Feng had been palace attendant to Lü Tse, King Tao-wu, but also served meritoriously since early in Liu Pang's uprising. Po-ch'eng is also written 博成 (see Wu and Lu, 9.330n., *Shih chi*, 19.983, *Han shu*, 68.2957, and"Cheng-yi," *Shih chi*, 9.401). T'an Ch'i-hsiang (2.19) refers to it simply as Po County and locates it in T'ai-shan 泰山 Commandery (a few miles southeast of modern T'ai-an 泰安 in Shantung).

Here we can see at work the strategy Empress Lü employed repeatedly in bringing the Lüs to power: first enfeoff a member of the Liu Family or one of their supporters (like Feng) to appease the great ministers and other Lius, then appoint members of her own clan. This pattern is repeated in the appointment of the various "sons" of Emperor Hui in the paragraph immediately following this one, and the paired appointments of Lü Ch'an as King of Lu and Liu Tse as King of Lang-ya (see *Shih chi*, 51.1995-96).

passed on, and she granted her the posthumous title of Queen Dowager Yüan of Lu. Her son, [Chang] Yen became King of Lu. The King of Lu's father was Chang Ao, Marquis Hsüan-p'ing 宣平. She enfeoffed the son of King Tao Hui 悼惠 of Ch'i, [Liu] Chang 章, as Marquis of Chu-hsü 朱虛,[76] [*401*] and married Lü Lu's daughter to him. She made [Ch'i] Shou [齊]壽, the Chancellor of Ch'i, Marquis of P'ing-ting 平定.[77] She made [Yang-ch'eng] Yen [陽成] 延, the Privy Treasurer,[78] Marquis of Wu 梧.[79] And she enfeoffed Lü Chung 呂種 as Marquis of P'ei 沛,[80] Lü P'ing 呂平 as Marquis of Fu-liu 扶柳,[81] and Chang Mai 張買 as Marquis of Nan-kung 南宮.[82]

   The T'ai-hou intending to make kings of the Lü Clan, first installed [Liu] Ch'iang 彊, a son from the harem [women] of Hsiao Hui[-ti], as the King of Huai-yang 淮陽,[83] [another] son,

[76]A county located about one-hundred miles east-southeast of modern Tsinan in Shantung (T'an Ch'i-hsiang, 2:20).

[77]The seat of Hsi-ho 西河 Commandery in what is extreme northwest Shensi today (T'an Ch'i-hsiang, 2:18).

[78]Shao fu 少府.

[79]A county about sixty miles south of Liu Chi's hometown of P'ei, a few miles northeast of the modern city of Huai-pei 淮北 in Anhwei (T'an Ch'i-hsiang, 2:19).

[80]Hsü Kuang points out that Lü Chung was the son of the empress's elder brother, Lü Shih-chih 呂釋之 ("Chi-chieh"). This appointment of a Lü family member to hold the fief where Liu Pang began his career must have been particularly noisome for the Liu loyalists.

[81]Lü P'ing, according to Hsü Kuang ("Chi-chieh") was the son of Empress Lü's elder sister.

   Fu-liu was a county in what is now southeast Honan, about fifty-five miles southeast of Shih-chia-chuang 石家莊; it was located in the Han state of Hsin-tu 信都 (T'an Ch'i-hsiang, 2:26). Liang Yü-sheng (7.243) points out that Lü P'ing was given the fief of Fu 邟 County in Lang-ya 瑯邪 and that Lü Ch'an was also made Marquis of Hsiao 洨 at this time (see Shih chi, 19.980). See also n. 20 above.

[82]Hsü Kuang ("Chi-chieh") says he was the son of a cavalry commander from Yüeh who served Liu Pang.

   Nan-kung was a county about twenty miles southwest of the Han county of Fu-liu (see note immediately above) in modern Hopei (T'an Ch'i-hsiang, 2:26).

[83]Although the Empress Dowager was intending to make kings of the Lü Clan, she first made these supposed sons of Emperor Hui, therefore members of the Liu Clan, kings (on this technique, see also n. 75 above). Dubs (1:193-94) identifies all these sons of Hui-ti as members of the Lü Clan (Lü Ch'iang, Lü Pu-yi, etc.), presumably because although they were all children of Emperor Hui's consorts, they had been claimed as sons by Hui-ti's empress, Chang Yen 張嫣 (see Wang Li-ch'i, 9.243n). Watson (1:272, n. 6) refuses to label them either Lius or Lüs (1:272, n. 6): "We are told later that these were not really sons of Emperor Hui but the children of other men whom the empress dowager attempted to pass off as the emperor's sons. I have therefore given only their personal names and omitted the surname Liu; no surname is given in the original." Watson is here referring to the claims made by the great ministers on Shih chi, 9.410. But it seems also possible that the great ministers in attempting to remove all vestiges of the Lü rule maligned these sons of the emperor. Nevertheless, all these men are listed as "Lius" in the Shih chi jen-ming so-yin and we follow their identification. The Han shu distinguishes the king-making of the Lü Clan (3.95) clearly from these appointments (3.96).

[Liu] Pu-yi 不疑, as King of Ch'ang-shan 常山,[84] a son, [Liu] Shan 山, as Marquis of Hsiang-ch'eng 襄城,[85] a son, [Liu] Ch'ao 朝, as Marquis of Chih 軹,[86] and a son, [Liu] Wu 武, as Marquis of Hu-kuan 壺關.[87] The T'ai-hou insinuated her meaning to the great ministers and the great ministers requested that Lü Yi, the Marquis of Li, be made King of Lü. The T'ai-hou approved it. [Lü] Shih-chih [呂]釋之, Marquis K'ang 康[88] of Chien-ch'eng, expired. His eldest son had committed an offense and he was set aside; she established his younger brother, Lü Lu, as the Marquis of Hu-ling 胡陵,[89] to continue the line of Marquis K'ang.

In the second year (186 B.C.), when the King of Ch'ang-shan passed on, she made his

Huai-yang was a statelet surrounding the modern city of the same name (in Honan; T'an Ch'i-hsiang, 2:19).

[84]Pu-yi 不疑 (No Doubt) seems to be a moniker not unlike Ju-yi (see n. 7 above). It suggests he was a legitimate son of Hui-ti in an era when Empress Dowager Lü considered male children in the harem to be chess pieces. He died shortly thereafter, still in the first year of Empress Lü's reign (see *Shih chi*, 17.816; Chin Cho's 晉灼 comments on *Han shu*, 3.98, place his death the following year).

Ch'ang-shan was a small state surrounding the modern city of Shih-chia-chuang in Hopei (T'an Ch'i-hsiang, 2:47-48).

[85]Liu Shan later changed his name to Liu Yi 義 and then again to Liu Hung 弘. He succeeded his brother Pu-yi as King of Ch'ang-shan in the second year of Empress Dowager Lü's reign (*Shih chi*, 17.818). Following the death of the first Shao-ti 少帝 (The Youth Emperor), he was appointed emperor on the *ping-chen* day of the fifth month of the fourth year of the Empress Dowager (15 June 184 B.C.) and also known as Shao-ti (*Shih chi*, 9.403 and 17.818). It was he whom Liu Hsing-chü took captive and whom Chou Po subsequently executed after Empress Lü's death (see *Shih chi*, 9.411).

Yang Shu-ta, *Han shu k'uei-kuan*, p. 32, argues that Liu Hung was actually a member of the Lü Clan. His argument is primarily based on a sentence found on *Han shu*, 27.1330: 更立呂氏子弘為少帝 "They replaced him and made Hung, a son of the Lü Clan, Emperor Shao). Yang (p. 33) also cites a comment by Ju Ch'un in his *Han shu* commentary (*Han shu*, 3.96) which claims that Liu Hung and all his brothers were all sons of Lü Clan, but the sentence 皆呂氏子 in question cannot be found in the current version of *Han shu*. One of Emperor Wen's letters to the King of Nan-Yüeh cited on *Han shu*, 95.3849 says they were sons with other *cognomens*: 乃取它姓子為孝惠皇帝嗣 . In the *Shih chi*, the evidence is contradictory. On *Shih chi*, 9.401 Ssu-ma Ch'ien claims that Hung and his brothers "were sons of Emperor Hui the Filial's harem [women]" 孝惠 后宮子, whereas on *Shih chi*, 9.410 the "great ministers" argue they are "sons of other people." Ssu-ma Ch'ien, living in a time closer to the reign of Emperor Shao, perhaps had heard several versions of these boy's provenance. Serving the mercurial Emperor Wu, he may have felt less comfortable in claiming they were members of the Lü Clan and couched this claim in the words of the great ministers.

Hsüan-ch'eng was a county located near the present city (in Honan) of the same name, about sixty miles south of modern Chengchow (T'an Ch'i-hsiang, 2:19).

[86]A county about twenty-five miles north of modern Lo-yang (T'an Ch'i-hsiang, 2:16).

[87]A county just north of the modern city of Ch'ang-chih 長治 in Shansi (T'an Ch'i-hsiang, 2:18).

[88]K'ang was his posthumous title.

[89]A county about ten miles north-northwest of P'ei in modern Shantung (2:8).

younger brother, [Liu] Shan, the Marquis of Hsiang-ch'eng, King of Ch'ang-shan, and changed his *praenomen* to Yi 義.

In the eleventh month (3 December–31 December 187 B.C.), [Lü] Yi, King of Lü, passed away and was posthumously titled King Su 肅; his heir, Chia 嘉, was enthroned in his place [*402*] as king.

In the third year (185 B.C.), there were no incidents.[90]

In the fourth year (184 B.C.), she enfeoffed Lü Hsü 呂嬃[91] as Marquise of Lin-kuang 臨光,[92] Lü T'o 呂他 as Marquis of Yü 俞,[93] Lü Keng-shih 呂更始 as Marquis of Chui-chi 贅其,[94] Lü

[90]Wang Shu-min (9.366) points out that under the third year, both the *Han shu* (3.98) and *Han chi* (6.2b, *SPTK*) record the appearance of a comet that was visible during the day throughout the autumn. *Han shu* also notes that the Chiang 江 and 漢 Han rivers flooded during the summer of this year, displacing more than four-thousand families. It appears Ssu-ma Ch'ien either did not have the source which Pan Ku and Hsün Yüeh used for their many references to portents during the reigns of Emperor Hui and Empress Lü, or that he chose not to employ this information in his text. The only other occurrence of the expression *wu shih* 無事 "there were no incidents" to describe an entire year is in the thirtieth year of the First Emperor of Ch'in (217 B.C.; *Shih chi*, 6.251). Perhaps Ssu-ma Ch'ien chose to omit events from one year of Empress Lü's dominance to suggest parallels between her reign and that of the First Emperor's. Whatever his motives, this record of 'nothing happening' must certainly have drawn many readers' attention. Strangely enough, the section for the third year of Empress Lü's reign in the most complete traditional account of events for each year in the Han dynasty, Wang Yi-chih's 王益之 (Southern Sung) *Hsi Han nien-chi* 西漢年紀 (An Annual Record of the Western Han), edited by the modern scholar Wang Ken-ling 王根林 ([Chengchow: Chung-chou Ku-chi, 1993], Preface p. 4 and text p. 66) has been lost.

This paragraph and the two immediately above are considered to be part of the paragraph beginning "The Empress Dowager intending to make kings of the Lü Clan . . ." in the Chung-hua edition. Once again we have broken them out because of the specific dating.

[91]Lü Hsü was he wife of Fan K'uai and Empress Lü's younger sister, see *Shih chi*, 9.404 and Wei Chao's comments in "So-yin."

[92]Liang Yü-sheng (7.240) argues that Lin-kuang 臨光 is not a placename, but points out that in both "So-yin" (*Shih chi*, 9.404) and "Chi-chieh" (*Shih chi*, 10.416) she was referred to as the Marquise of Lin-kuang 林光. This argument is supported by Wang Shu-min (9.366). Lin-kuang 林光 was the name of a Ch'in palace in Yün-yang 雲陽 (see "Chi-chieh," *Shih chi*, 10.424) and Liang Yü-sheng believes that Lü Hsü was put in charge of this palace with Yün-yang (a county about thirty-five miles north-northwest of Ch'ang-an; T'an Ch'i-hsiang, 2:15) as her fief manor.

[93]Lü T'o was the son of Lü Ying 呂嬰, one of Kao-tsu's followers (*Shih chi*, 19.989).

I.e., Yü 郁, a county two-hundred miles south of modern Peking (in Shantung, T'an Ch'i-hsiang, 2:20).

[94]Chui-chi was located in modern Kiangsu about seventy-five miles west-southwest of Yangchow (T'an Ch'i-hsiang, 2:20).

As Chavannes (2:418, n. 5) points out, according to the chronological tables (*Shih chi*, 19.986), Lü Sheng 呂勝, the empress' nephew (see "Chi-chieh," *Shih chi*, 9.402), was Marquis of Chui-chi, and Lü Keng-shih was Marquis of T'eng 滕 (*Shih chi*, 19.990) until their deaths four years later. See also Wang Shu-min (9.366).

Fen 呂忿 as Marquis of Lü-ch'eng 呂城,[95] and five chancellors of the feudal lords [as marquises].[96]

When the Marquis of Hsüan-p'ing's daughter was the empress of Hsiao Hui[-ti], she had no sons, but pretended to be with child, and took the son of a [palace] beauty, claimed it, killed his mother, and established the son she had claimed as the Heir. When Hsiao Hui[-ti] passed away, the Heir was enthroned as emperor. While the emperor was growing up,[97] he once heard that his mother had died and he was not truly the empress's son, he vented [his feelings] in words: "How was the Empress[98] able to kill my mother and claim [*403*] me? I am not fully grown yet, but when I am fully grown I will cause trouble." The T'ai-hou heard of it and worried about it; fearing that he would cause rebellion, she confined him in the Long Lane, saying that the emperor's illness was serious and his attendants would not be able to see him.[99] The T'ai-hou

[95]Lü Fen was also Empress Lü's nephew (Wang Li-ch'i 9.239n.).

Lü-ch'eng is west of modern Nan-yang 南陽 City in Honan (Wang Li-ch'i, 9.239n.).

[96]Liang Yü-sheng (7.245) argues that it was six men, not all former chancellors to the noble lords, who were enfeoffed in the fourth month of the fourth year. Liang's list includes Chu T'ung 朱通, who was appointed Marquis of Chung-yi 中邑 (see also *Shih chi*, 19.987), Wei Wu-tse 衛無擇, the new Marquis of Le-p'ing 樂平 (see also *Shih chi*, 19.987), Chou Hsin 周信, who became Marquis of Ch'eng-t'ao 成陶 (see also *Shih chi*, 19.988), Wang T'ien-k'ai 王恬開, the Marquis of Shan-tu 山都 (see also *Shih chi*, 19.987), Hsü Li 徐厲, the Marquis of Sung-tzu 松茲 (see also *Shih chi*, 19.988; some texts read Chu-tzu 祝茲, but this is incorrect, Lü Jung 呂榮 was appointed to the new fief of Chu-tzu four years later [*Shih chi*, 19.993]), and a certain Yüeh 越, who was made Marquis of Li-ling 醴陵 (see also *Shih chi*, 19.990). Liang notes that Ssu-ma Ch'ien errs here, since two of these six were never chancellors–Wei Wu-tse and Chou Hsin. Although this is true, Ssu-ma Ch'ien was correct, since in all eleven marquises were created at this time (see also Wu and Lu, 9.331n.) and the five who had been chancellors listed by Hsü Kuang in the "Chi-chieh": Chu T'ung, former chancellor of the state of Lu, Wang T'ien-k'ai, who was chancellor in Liang, Hsü Li, who served in Ch'ang-shan, Lü Keng-shih, chancellor to the King of Ch'u, and Yüeh, who had been chancellor in Ch'ang-sha.

Once again this is not a separate paragraph in the Chung-hua edition.

[97]Because he says below he is *not yet* grown, Wang Li-ch'i (9.240) believes that *chuang* 壯, here translated as "grew up," is an interpolation. This is also the opinion of Chang Wen-hu (1.99).

[98]Many readers of this passage have assumed this *hou* 后 must be an error for *t'ai hou* 太后 and refer to the Empress Dowager Lü. Empress Hui, Chang Yen, could not have been born until *ca.* 201 B.C. (her father, Chang Ao, became King of Chao and took Princess Yüan of Lu for his consort in 202 B.C.). Moreover, there is no doubt that Empress Lü was behind the murder of Emperor Shao's mother. Pan Ku 'corrects' *hou* to *t'ai hou* in the parallel passage on *Han shu*, 97A.3940. However, there is another possibility that seems plausible and would retain the Chung-hua text—namely, that Emperor Shao knew full well Empress Lü had killed his mother, but also realized that if he confronted her with this fact face to face he would be risking death himself; thus he cunningly claimed that it was Empress Hui who had murdered his mother. This also fits the description of Empress Lü "worrying about it" in the text just below. Although the young emperor had not accused her directly, his intent was obvious and Empress Lü was eventually forced to kill him.

[99]In the parallel account in the *Han shu* (3.98), Shao-ti is only said to have "uttered words of resentment" 出怨言, without citing his exact speech. Moreover, Empress Lü's speech in our text becomes an imperial decree in the *Han shu*.

said, "He who has the mandate to possess the world and manage the myriad people should cover them like Heaven, hold them like Earth. The sovereign must have a cheerful heart to bring contentment to the people, before the people can joyously serve their sovereign. When cheer and joy flow back and forth [between the sovereign and the people],[100] then the world is managed. Now with the illness of the August Emperor untreatable for so long, he has fallen into delusion and confusion, and cannot succeed to the throne and offer sacrifices in the ancestral temple [of the royal house]. The world cannot be entrusted to him. Let Us replace him!"[101] The assembled ministers struck their foreheads on the ground and said, "The Huang T'ai-hou 皇太后 (The August Empress Dowager)'s stratagem on behalf of the common people of the world, thereby to stabilize the ancestral temple and the altars of soil and grain, is formidably profound. We assembled ministers strike our foreheads on the ground and accept your decree." The emperor was removed from the throne, and the T'ai-hou had him confined and killed.[102]

On the *ping-ch'en* 丙辰 day of the fifth month (15 June 184 B.C.), she enthroned Yi 義,[103] the King of Ch'ang-shan, as emperor and changed his *praenomen* to Hung 弘. There was no declaration of the first year [of the reign], because the T'ai-hou regulated the affairs of the world. She made [Li] Ch'ao 朝, the Marquis of Chih, King of Ch'ang-shan. She established the office of Grand Commandant,[104] and Po, the Marquis of Chiang, became Grand Commandant.

In the eighth month of the fifth year (22 August–20 September 183 B.C.), the King of Huai-yang passed away, and she made his younger brother, Wu, Marquis of Hu-kuan, King of Huai-yang.

In the tenth month of the sixth year (19 November–17 December 183 B.C.), the T'ai-hou said the life-style of Chia, the King of Lü, was extravagant and dissipated, and she deposed him.[105] She made Lü Ch'an 呂產, the younger brother of [Lü] Yi, King Su, King of Lü.[106]

In the summer, there was an pardon for everyone in the world. She enfeoffed [Liu]

[100]On the meaning of *chiao-t'ung* 交通 here, see Chang Chia-ying, pp. 182-83.

[101]In the *Han shu* (3.96) the text reads "May you discuss replacing him!" 其議代之。

[102]*Han shu* omits the sentence about Emperor Shao being killed in the annals for Empress Kao (3.98), moving it to the "Wai-ch'i chuan" 外戚傳 (Memoir on the Maternal Relatives, 97A.3940).

[103]Liu Yi, originally Liu Shan 山 (see text above, *Shih chi*, 9.401 and n. 85). Like his predecessor (see n. 61 above), he was given no posthumous title, he became known simply as "Shao-ti" 少帝, the "Youth Emperor."

In the Chung-hua edition, this paragraph and the following three were part of the paragraph above which begins: "When the Marquis of Hsüan-p'ing's daughter was the empress of Hui the Filial . . . ."

[104]*T'ai-wei* 太尉. This position was established and abolished several times during the early years of the Han dynasty (see Wang Li-ch'i, 9.239n., and Bielenstein, pp. 10-11).

[105]Wang Shu-min (9.367) understands this as direct speech: "The life-style of Chia, the King of Lü, is extravagant and dissipated; We shall depose him."

[106]According to *Shih chi*, 51.1995-96, this enthronement was the result of a plan by Master T'ien 田, a native of the state of Ch'i.

Hsing-chü [劉]興居,[107] the son of King Tao Hui 悼惠 of Ch'i, as Marquis of Tung-mou 東牟.[108]

In the first month of the seventh year (5 February–4 March 181 B.C.), the T'ai-hou summoned [Liu] Yu 友, the King of Chao. Yu had made one of the Lü women his queen, but did not love her; he loved another beauty, and the daughter of the Lüs was jealous. In her anger, she left him and slandered him to the T'ai-hou, falsely accusing him of committing an offense in saying, "How can the Lü Clan be kings! After the T'ai-hou has lived out her span, I will certainly attack them." The T'ai-hou was angry and for this reason summoned the King of Chao. When the King of Chao arrived, she placed him in his [capital] residence and would not see him. She ordered that guards surround it and did not give him anything to eat. When some of his assembled ministers[109] sent him food in secret, she had them arrested and sentenced forthwith. As the King of Chao starved,[110] he composed a song which went:

> In power are the Lüs, imperiled the Lius; [*404*]
> They coerce kings and marquises, force a consort on me;
> My consort grown jealous, falsely accuses me of a wrong;
> A slandering woman disorders the state,[111] the sovereign after all unaware.
> I have no loyal vassals, for what reason did I abandon my state?
> If I put an end to myself midst the fields, would blue heaven do what is just?[112]
> Alas! too late for regrets, I should have made a decision earlier.[113]
> To be a king and starve to death–who will pity him?
> The Lü Clan has broken with reason, I trust to Heaven to repay my enemies!

[107]See his biography in *Shih chi* Chapter 52.

[108]This is a remote holding located about ten miles southeast of the modern resort city of Yen-t'ai 煙台 on the northeast coast of Shantung (T'an Ch'i-hsiang, 2:20).

[109]Wang Li-ch'i (9.240n) argues that this *ch'i* 其 refers to the King of Chao's ministers who came to the capital with him. Thus when the king sings that "I have no loyal vassals," he means they have been imprisoned, too.

[110]The maximum time Liu Yu could have been in confinement was from the time he arrived in the capital until 21 February when he passed away. However, since he was not summoned until 5 February or later (the first day of the first month that year), and since it would have taken him some time to go from Chao to Ch'ang-an, leaving perhaps only a week between the time of his arrival and that of his death, it seems that either the time frame or the cause of his death has not been recorded correctly.

[111]Referring here to Liu Yu's queen, a member of the Lü Clan, and to the state of Chao (see Wang Li-ch'i, 9.240n.).

[112]Reading *chü* 舉 as "to put into effect."

[113]Reading *ts'ai* 財 as *tsai* 裁, "to judge" or "make a decision." The king seems here to regret his decision to support the Empress Dowager. On the expression *tzu ts'ai* 自財, see also Chavannes, 2:422, n. 2. Another reading for *tzu ts'ai* 自財 would be 'to commit suicide' (cf. Wang Shu-min, 9.368 and Wang Li-ch'i, 9.240n.); the line would then end "Alas, too late for regrets, it would have been better to take my own life earlier!"

On the *ting-ch'ou* 丁丑 day (21 February 181 B.C.), the King of Chao died in confinement and was buried with the rites of a commoner next to the graves of the common people of Ch'ang-an.[114]

On the *chi-ch'ou* 己丑 day (4 March 181 B.C.), the sun was eclipsed and during the day it became dark. The T'ai-hou abhored this and was not pleased; she said to her attendants, "This is because of me."

In the second month (5 March–3 April 181 B.C.), she moved Hui, the King of Liang, to be King of Chao. Ch'an, King of Lü, was moved to be King of Liang, but the King of Liang did not go to his state, becoming the Grand Tutor for the emperor. She enthroned the imperial son, [Liu] T'ai [劉] 太, Marquis of P'ing-ch'ang 平昌,[115] as King of Lü. She changed the name of [the state of] Liang to Lü; Lü was called Chi-ch'uan 濟川 (Chi River). Lü Hsü, the T'ai-hou's younger sister, had a daughter who became the wife of Liu Tse 劉澤, Marquis of Ying-ling 營陵[116]; Tse became Grand Commander.[117]

After the T'ai-hou made kings of the Lüs, she was afraid that after she passed away they would be harmed by General Liu [Tse], thus she made Liu Tse the King of Lang-ya 琅邪[118] to set his mind at ease.

[Liu] Hui, the King of Liang, having been moved to be King of Chao, harbored some unhappiness about it.[119] The T'ai-hou made the daughter of Lü Ch'an the King of Chao's queen. The queen's suite of officials were all from the Lüs and they acted on their own authority, spying from hiding on the King of Chao, so that the King of Chao was not able to do as he pleased. The King had a beauty whom he loved, and the queen sent someone with serpent-eagle [wine] to kill her. The King then composed an ode in four strophes, and ordered his musicians to sing it. The king despaired and in the sixth month (1 July–30 July 181 B.C.) he committed suicide. When the T'ai-hou heard of it, she considered it to be a case of a king abandoning the rites of the ancestral temple because of a woman,[120] and removed the rights of inheritance from

[114]There is a parallel account in *Han shu* (38.1989).

[115]In the "Hui, Ching chien hou-che nien-piao" 惠景閒侯者年表 (Chronological Tables of the Marquises of the Reigns of Emperors Hui and Ching, *Shih chi,* 19.986), Liu T'ai is referred to as the Marquis of Ch'ang-p'ing 昌平. Both places are actual locations–there are two P'ing-ch'ang counties, one in P'ing-yüan 平原 Commandery (about 50 miles north of modern Tsinan in Shantung [T'an Ch'i-hsiang, 2:19]), the other in Hsü-chou 徐州 Commandery (about 135 miles east-southeast of Tsinan [T'an Ch'i-hsiang, 2:20]). Ch'ang-p'ing was located a few miles north of modern Peking (T'an Ch'i-hsiang, 2:27).

[116]Located in Pei-hai 北海 Commandery about ten miles southwest of modern Wei-fang 濰坊 City in Shantung (T'an Ch'i-hsiang, 2:20).

[117]Bielenstein (p. 116) has General-in-Chief for *Ta Chiang-chün* 大將軍.

[118]Located about forty miles southwest of modern Tsingtao on the southeastern coast of Shantung (T'an Ch'i-hsiang, 2:20).

[119]This is not surprising, since Liu Ju-yi and Liu Yu, both sons of Kao-tsu, had been made King of Chao before the Empress Dowager had them killed! See the accounts of their deaths in the translation above.

[120]Since by committing suicide he could no longer perform sacrifices to his ancestors. See also Chavannes,

his successors.

Chang Ao, Marquis of Hsüan-p'ing, expired, and she made his son, Yen, King of Lu; the posthumous title of King Yüan 元 of Lu was conferred upon Ao.[121]

In the autumn, the T'ai-hou sent an envoy to tell the King of Tai that she intended to move him to be King of Chao. The King of Tai declined, professing his wish to guard the border region of Tai.[122]

[Lü] Ch'an, the Grand Tutor, [Ch'en] P'ing, the Chancellor, and others said that Lü Lu, Marquis of Wu-hsin, should be the highest marquis, his position ranked number one,[123] and requested that he be enthroned as King of Chao. The T'ai-hou allowed it, posthumously [*405*] honoring [Lü] Lu's father, Marquis K'ang, as King Chao 昭 of Chao.

In the ninth month (28 September–26 October 181 B.C.),[124] [Liu] Chien [劉]建, King Ling 靈 of Yen, passed on; he had a son by one of his beauties. The T'ai-hou sent a man to kill him. There being no descendants, the state was abolished.

In the tenth month of the eighth year (27 October–25 November 181 B.C.), she enthroned Lü T'ung 呂通, Marquis of Tung-p'ing 東平[125] and the son of King Su of Lü, as King of Yen, and enfeoffed, Lü Chuang 呂莊, T'ung's younger brother, as Marquis of Tung-p'ing.[126]

In the middle of the third month (24 March–22 April 180 B.C.), Empress Lü performed the purgation rites;[127] on her return, as she passed the Chih 軹 Road[128] she saw a being which

2:424, n. 2.

[121]Wang Shu-min (9.369) cites various sources, including Shih chi, 18.950 and 89.2586, in support of his argument that Chang Ao died a year earlier in the sixth year.

[122]This was Liu Heng 劉恆, later Hsiao Wen-ti 孝文帝 (The Filial and Cultured Emperor), who through this clever refusal was able to stay alive. He was keenly aware that the last three kings of Chao were killed directly or indirectly by the Empress Dowager (see also n. 119 above).

[123]Earlier Liu Pang had ranked his marquises according to their merits; under Kao-tsu, Hsiao Ho 蕭何 had been the highest ranking marquis, Ts'ao Ts'an 曹參 number two, and so forth. But with these men now mostly dead, Empress Lü decided to re-rank the marquises (see Wu and Lu, 9.333n.).

[124]Here again this paragraph and the following do not follow the parsing in the Chung-hua edition.

[125]Southeast of the modern county of the same name in Shantung (Wang Li-ch'i, 9.240n.).

Liang Yü-sheng (7.246-47) argues that Lü T'ung was at this time Marquis of Ch'ui 錘, not T'ung-p'ing and his praenomen was P'i 庀. Wang Shu-min, citing Shih chi, 19.991, concurs.

[126]The chronological tables (Shih chi, 19.993) record Lü Chuang's appointment at Marquis of Tung-p'ing in the fifth month of the eighth year (22 May–20 June 180 B.C.). He was not, as implied here, replacing Lü T'ung (see n. 125 and the text just above).

[127]The fu 祓, a kind of "ritual purgation," was mentioned above (see Shih chi, 4.132: 周公乃祓齋; Grand Scribe's Records, 1:64: "The Duke of Chou purified himself to perform an exorcism."). It was usually performed in the first or third month of the year at the temple of the royal ancestors or at altars, but especially near bodies of water (for purification); it became associated with the festivities of the third day of the third lunar month. According to the "Wu-hsing chih" 五行志 in the Han shu (27B.a.1397) the Empress Dowager performed this fu at Pa Heights; she had been worried about portents such as the eclipse which troubled her

looked like a blue-green dog. It seized[129] Kao-hou 高后 (The Exalted Empress or Empress Kao)[130] under her arm and, suddenly, it was not to be seen. When they divined by shells and bones about it, the result read: "Ju-yi the King of Chao is casting his evil influence." Kao-hou subsequently became ill from the wound under her arm.

Because her maternal grandson, [Chang] Yen, King Yüan of Lu,[131] was young, had lost his father and mother early, and was alone and weak, Kao-hou enfeoffed two sons by former beauties of Chang Ao; [Chang] Ch'ih [張]侈 was made Marquis of Hsin-tu 新都[132] and [Chang] Shou [張]壽 was made Marquis of Yüeh-ch'ang 樂昌,[133] to provide support for Yen, King Yüan of Lu. And she enfeoffed Chang Shih 張釋,[134] the Regular Grand Internuncio,[135] as Marquis of

about a year earlier and this was no doubt intended to exorcise such evil influences and replace them with good; see also Chapter XII: "The Lustration Festival," in Bodde, *Festivals,* pp. 273-88.

[128]See *Grand Scribe's Records,* 7:100, n. 22.

[129]Watson (1:331) and Chavannes (2:425) both read *chü* 據 as "bit"; Wang Li-ch'i (9.241n.) glosses it as *chuang* 撞, "to run into." "Chi-chieh" says *chü* should be read chi 戟 here; Wang Shu-min (9.369-70) points out that the parallel passage in the *Han shu* "Wu-hsing chih" (27B.a.1397) reads *chi* 撠, "to seize" (also noting that the animal which attacked Empress Lü was the spirit of Liu Ju-yi).

[130]As in other chapters, Ssu-ma Ch'ien changes his manner of reference to the main figure—here Empress Lü. Above he has called her Empress Lü, then T'ai Hou 太后, Empress Dowager, and finally, after she has her fatal encounter with the dog, she becomes Kao-hou 高后, The Exalted Empress or perhaps the Empress of the Exalted [Emperor]. Ying Shao 應劭 explains this title in the commentary on *Han shu,* 3.95, as follows: 禮，婦人從夫謚，故稱高也. "According to the ritual code, a woman should follow the posthumous title of her husband; for this reason she was called 'exalted.'"

[131]As Wang Shu-min (9.370) points out Chang Yen's father Chang Ao had been posthumously titled King Yüan of Lu (see our translation of *Shih chi,* 9.404, just above). Yüan is an error here, later in this sentence, and on *Shih chi,* 9.407 later in this chapter. See also n. 4 above.

[132]This appointment was made in the fourth month (*Shih chi,* 19.992).

Hsin-tu 新都 is a county in Nan-yang 南陽 Commandery thirty miles south of the modern city of Nan-yang in Honan (T'an Ch'i-hsiang, 2:22). However, *Shih chi,* 19.992 and 89.2586 both read Hsin-tu 信都, a county located in near modern Chi 冀 County in Hopei (Wu and Lu, 9.333n.). It seems the text here is in error.

[133]Chang Shou, written 受 in the chronological tables (*Shih chi,* 19.992), was also appointed in the fourth month. He was involved in a crime during the first year of Emperor Wen (179 B.C.) and his state was abolished.

Yüeh-ch'ang was a county 120 miles south of modern Peking in Hopei (T'an Ch'i-hsiang, 2:26).

[134]Chang Shih is written Chang Tse 張澤 in the chronological tables (*Shih chi,* 19.993) and later in this chapter (*Shih chi,* 9.411). Liang Yü-sheng (7.247-48) notes that he is also referred to as Chang Tzu-ch'ing 張子卿, Chang Ch'ing 張卿, and Chang Shih-ch'ing 張釋卿 in various chapters of the *Shih chi* and *Han shu.* Liang concludes that his *praenomen* was probably Shih 釋 and his *agnomen* Tzu-ch'ing 子卿. Tse 澤 seems to have been interchangeable with Shih at this time (see n. 198 below). See also a detailed discussion of the variants of Chang's name by Wang Shu-min, 9.370-71.

[135]*Chung ta yeh-che* 中大謁者. The position of *Chung yeh-che* 中謁者 had formerly been held by

Chien-ling 建陵[136] and Lü Jung 呂榮 as Marquis of Chu-tzu 祝茲.[137] All those prefects of eunuchs and assistants of eunuchs,[138] she made Marquises of the Land within the Passes,[139] with fief-manors of five hundred households.

[406] In the middle of the seventh month (20 July–18 August 180 B.C.), Kao-hou's illness grew worse, and she ordered Lü Lu, the King of Chao, to become Commander in Chief, in command of the Northern Army;[140] [Lü] Ch'an, the King of Lü, assumed the post of [Commander of] the Southern Army. Lü T'ai-hou cautioned Ch'an and Lu: "When Kao-ti had already stabilized the world, he made a covenant with his great ministers which read: 'If someone who is not of the Liu Clan is made king, the world will join together to attack him.' Now the Lü Clan have been made kings and the great ministers are not at peace with this. As I am about to pass away[141] and the emperor is young, the great ministers, I fear, will try to cause changes [after my death].[142] You must hold your troops firmly in hand, guard the palace, be cautious, and do not accompany the funeral procession. Do not be restrained by others."

On the *hsin-ssu* 辛巳 day (18 August 180 B.C.), Kao-hou passed away, leaving an edict granting the noble kings[143] each one thousand *chin*; the generals, prime ministers, ranking marquises, attendants and clerks were granted gold, each according to his rank. She granted a general amnesty to everyone in the world. She made [Lü] Ch'an, King of Lü, Chancellor, and Lü Lu's daughter the empress.[144]

Kuan Ying. The addition of the character *chung* 中 to the title suggests that many of its occupants were palace eunuchs (see "Chi-chieh" and Wu and Lu, 9.333n.).

[136]A county 125 miles northwest of modern Yangchow in Kiangsu (T'an Ch'i-hsiang, 2:20).

[137]This place has not been located. "So-yin" (*Shih chi*, 19.992) points out that the chronological tables in the *Han shu* say he was Marquis of Lang-ya 琅邪.

[138]On the interpretation of *ling ch'eng* 令丞 here see Wu and Lu, 9.333n.

[139]*Kuan-nei hou* 關內侯, a noble rank nineteenth on the list of the twenty feudal ranks of the Ch'in and early Han dynasties (see Wu and Lu, 9.333n., and Loewe, "Aristocratic Rank," p. 99). Loewe also points out (p. 121) that the *Han shu* (3.100) records Empress Lü conferring the rank on a group of officials in the eunuchs' offices at about this same time.

[140]Liu Tse 劉澤 had commanded the Southern Army until he was made King of Lang-ya in 181 B.C. (see the translation of *Shih chi*, 9.405 above). The Northern Army had been led by Lü Lu 呂祿 since 186 B.C. when he succeeded Lü Yi 呂台 (d. 186) in the position (Liang Yü-sheng, 7:248).

[141]Here Empress Lü uses the honorific *peng* 崩 to refer to her own imminent death, a final act of hubris.

[142]*Wei-pien* 為變, translated here as "to cause changes," could also be understood as "to cause an incident, trouble."

[143]See n. 331 to our translation of "Kao-tsu pen-chi" above on *chu-hou wang* 諸侯王 noble kings."
This paragraph break does not follow the parsing of the Chung-hua editors.

[144]Han Chao-ch'i, *op. cit.*, p. 78, sees this description of Empress Lü's passing as the end of the second section of this chapter.

Although this edict is consistent with Empress Lü's desire to strengthen her clan's hold on power, it is

After Kao-hou had been buried,[145] Shen Yi-chi, the Chancellor of the Left, was made Grand Tutor to the emperor.

Liu Chang, the Marquis of Chu-hsü, was energetic and strong[146]; [Liu] Hsing-chü, the Marquis of Tung-mou, was his younger brother. They were both younger brothers of King Ai 哀 of Ch'i[147] and lived in Ch'ang-an. In the meantime, the Lüs exercised power and acted on their own authority; wanting to make rebellion; they were in awe of the former great ministers of Kao-ti, [the Marquis of] Chiang,[148] Kuan [Ying], and others, and did not dare to set forth. The wife of the Marquis of Chu-hsü, as the daughter of Lü Lu, secretly learned of their plot. Fearing that he would be killed, [the Marquis of Chu-hsü] secretly ordered someone to tell his older brother, the King of Ch'i, wanting him to order troops sent westward, to execute the Lüs and enthrone [himself]. The Marquis of Chu-hsü and the great ministers were expected to respond from within the capital. The King of Ch'i wanted to send out troops, but his prime minister would not listen to him.[149]

On the *ping-wu* 丙午 day of the eighth month (12 September 180 B.C., the King of Ch'i was about to send someone to execute the Prime Minister [of Ch'i]. Thus the Prime Minister, Shao P'ing 召平, rebelled and gathered troops, intending to surround the king. The king took this opportunity to kill his prime minister, then he sent out troops to the east, by deception [*407*] seized the troops of the King of Lang-ya, joined them to his own, and led them to the west. An account can be found in the accounts of the "Kings of Ch'i."[150]

The King of Ch'i then sent the various noble kings a letter which read, "When Kao-ti pacified and stabilized the world and made kings of his sons and younger brothers, he made

difficult to see why she would not have made Lü Ch'an Chancellor *before* passing away. Thus this edict seems dubious. Liang Yü-sheng's (7.249) argument that Lü Ch'an was made Chancellor in the seventh month of the seventh year when Shen Yi-chi was dismissed seems more logical. Ssu-ma Ch'ien obviously had a different view of these appointments since in the next sentence he still has Shen Yi-chi as Chancellor of the Left.

[145]She was buried at Ch'ang-ling 長陵, like Kao-tsu, but separately from her husband's tomb a little to the southeast (see Ch'in Po 秦波, "Hsi Han huang-hou yü-hsi ho kan-lu erh-nien t'ung fang-lu te fa-hsien" 西漢皇后玉璽和甘露二年銅方爐的發現, *Wen-wu*, 1973.5: 26-29.

[146]For a detailed account of how Liu Chang, though only twenty years old at the time, was able to defy Empress Lü and her clan, thereby becoming one of her main opponents, see his biography in *Shih chi*, 52.2000-01.

[147]I.e., Liu Hsiang 劉襄, the eldest son of Liu Fei 劉肥. He had been appointed King of Ch'i in 188 B.C. and died in the tenth year of his reign in 179 B.C. (*Shih chi*, 17.815 and 826).

[148]I.e., Chou Po 周勃.

[149]In this paragraph the plans of both sides are revealed; the language reflects here the mood–Ssu-ma Ch'ien uses the word *yü* 欲 "wanting, wanted, intending, intended" four times to indicate the optative nature of these intentions.

The following parargraph is joined to this in the Chung-hua edition.

[150]I.e., "Ch'i Tao Hui Wang shih-chia" 齊悼惠王世家 (Hereditary House of King Tao Hui of Ch'i), *Shih chi*, 52.2001-02. In that account, Shao P'ing commits suicide.

King Tao Hui King of Ch'i. When King Tao Hui passed on, Hsiao Hui-ti sent [Chang] Liang [張] 良, the Marquis of Liu, to enthrone me as King of Ch'i. When Hsiao Hui[-ti] passed away, Kao-hou exercised power, [but] her years had mounted up and she listened to the Lüs, acting on her own to depose and re-enthrone emperors. Further, she killed three kings of Chao in succession, annihilated Liang, Chao and Yen so as to make kings of the Lüs,[151] and divided Ch'i into four parts.[152] The loyal ministers presented admonitions, but the sovereign had fallen into delusion and confusion and did not listen to them.[153] Now Kao-hou has passed away and the emperor, with his [future] years so abundant,[154] is not yet able to manage the world; he certainly needs to rely upon the great ministers and marquises. Yet the Lüs have further acted on their own to exalt their positions, raised troops to lend severity to their majesty, coerced the ranking marquises and loyal ministers, forged decrees so as to issue orders to the world, thereby endangering the ancestral temple. I, the Lonely One, lead troops into [the capital] to execute those who should not be kings."

When the Han [court][155] heard of this, [Lü] Ch'an, the Chancellor, and others sent Kuan Ying, the Marquis of Ying-yin 潁陰, to command the troops to attack him. When Kuan Ying reached Hsing-yang 滎陽, he thought to himself of a plan: "The Lüs hold military power in the Land within the Passes. They intended to imperil the Liu Clan and establish themselves. Now if I defeat Ch'i, return and report it, this will increase the resources of the Lüs." So he stopped and set up camp at Hsing-yang, sending an envoy to make clear to the King of Ch'i and the various marquises that he would join with them to wait for the Lü Clan to make their move, [then] jointly execute them. When the King of Ch'i heard this, he returned his troops to the western border [of Ch'i] to await a meeting.[156]

Lü Lu and Lü Ch'an wanted to start a rebellion in the Land within the Passes, but they dreaded the Marquises of Chiang and Chu-hsü and others inside the capital, and were awed by the troops of Ch'i and Ch'u outside the capital. They also feared Kuan Ying would turn against them, and, intending to wait for Kuan Ying's troops to meet [those of] Ch'i before they started, they hesitated and made no decision.

In the meantime, [Liu] T'ai 太, King of Chi-ch'uan, [Liu] Wu 武, King of Huai-yang,

[151]In some cases it was the kings rather than the states that were annihilated (see Wang Li-ch'i, 9.243n).

[152]Lü 呂, Lang-ya 琅邪, Ch'eng-yang 城陽, and Ch'i 齊.

[153]The phrase *Shang huo luan* 上惑亂, "the sovereign has fallen into delusion and confusion," is taken from the Empress Dowager Lü's decree in 184 B.C. asking that Emperor Shao 少 be deposed (*Shih chi,* 9.403).

[154]A circumlocution which projects a long life for the emperor, this expression simply put means he is still young.

[155]Chavannes (2:431, n. 1) suggests there may be irony in the use of the term "Han 漢," since the court at this time was dominated by the Lü family.

There is no paragraph break here in the Chung-hua text.

[156]*Yüeh* 約 here could mean "a meeting" or might refer to "an agreement," something only suggested by Kuan Ying's envoy.

and [Liu] Ch'ao 朝, King of Ch'ang-shan, nominally the younger brothers of Emperor Shao,[157] and the maternal grandson of Lü T'ai-hou, King Yüan of Lu, were young and had not yet gone to their states, [but] were living in Ch'ang-an; [Lü] Lu, King of Chao, and [Lü] Ch'an, King of Liang, each commanded troops stationed in the Southern and Northern Armies; they were all men of the Lü Clan. The ranking marquises and assembled ministers themselves could not guarantee their own fates.

[408] The Grand Commandant [Chou] Po, the Marquis of Chiang, was unable to enter the army camp and take charge of the troops. Li Shang 酈商,[158] the Marquis of Ch'ü-chou 曲周,[159] was old and sick and his son, [Li] Chi [酈]寄, was on good terms with Lü Lu. The Marquis of Chiang then plotted with the Chancellor, Ch'en P'ing, to send someone to coerce Li Shang to order his son, Chi, to go and trick Lü Lu by advising him as follows: "Kao-ti and Empress Lü stabilized the world together. The Liu Clan has enthroned nine kings, the Lü Clan has enthroned three kings; all were deliberated by the great ministers and when these matters had been announced to the various marquises, the various marquises all considered them fitting. Now the Empress Dowager has passed away, the emperor is young, and you, Honorable Sir, though you wear at your waist the seal of the King of Chao, have not hurried to your state to guard the barriers,[160] but have become Commander in Chief;[161] by commanding the troops and remaining here, you have made the great ministers and various marquises suspicious. Why don't you, Honorable Sir, return the commander's seal and entrust the troops to the Grand Commandant? If you can request that the King of Liang return the seal of the Chancellor and together with him take an oath with the great ministers and go to your states, the Ch'i troops will certainly be dismissed, the great ministers will gain peace of mind, and you, Honorable Sir, can sit back and rule as king [a domain] of one thousand *li* [on a side]; this will bring advantages for a myriad generations."

Lü Lu trusted in and agreed with his plan,[162] and was about to return his commander's seal and entrust his troops to the Grand Commandant. When he sent someone to report to Lü Ch'an and the various Lü elders, some found it advantageous, some said it was not advantageous. In planning, they hesitated and could not make a decision. Lü Lu trusted Li Chi and once went

[157]These kings were all children of Emperor Hui's consorts, but had been claimed as sons by his empress, Chang Yen 張嫣 (see Wang Li-ch'i, 9.243n).

There is no paragraph break here in the Chung-hua edition.

[158]The younger brother of Li Yi-chi 酈食其, advisor (as Chancellor of the Right) and general under Kao-tsu (Wang Li-ch'i, 9.243n).

[159]A county northeast of the modern county by the same name in Hopei (Wang Li-ch'i, 9.243n.).

[160]*Fan* 藩, literally "fence, hedge, or barrier" was used metaphorically to indicate those states which surround the lands within the Passes.

[161]The text reads *Shang chiang* 上將 here, but the intent is *Shang chiang-chü* 上將軍, the position to which Lü Lu was just appointed (see *Shih chi*, 9.406). Lu Zongli (p. 55) gives *Shang chiang* as equivalent to *Shang chiang-chün*.

[162]There is no paragraph break in the Chung-hua edition.

out hunting with him. When they stopped by to see Lü Hsü, his aunt,[163] Hsü was enraged and said, "You are a general, but you abandon your army. Now the Lü Clan has no place to turn." Then she took out all the jewels and precious vessels[164] and scattered them about below the hall, saying: "I will not safekeep these for others any more."

[409] The Chancellor of the Left, [Shen] Yi-chi was dismissed.[165]

On the morning of the *keng-shen* 庚申 day of the eighth month[166] (26 September 180 B.C.), [Ts'ao] Chu [曹] 窋,[167] the Marquis of P'ing-yang, who was provisionally attending to the affairs of the Grand Master of the Imperial Scribes, went to see [Lü] Ch'an, the Chancellor, to plan matters. The Prefect of Palace Attendants, Chia Shou 賈壽, who had come back from being an envoy to Ch'i, took the opportunity to upbraid Ch'an: "Your Majesty did not go to your state earlier and now, even if you wanted to go, how could you still be able to?" He told Ch'an in detail how Kuan Ying had united with Ch'i and Ch'u, intending to execute the Lüs, then urged Ch'an to hurry into the palace. The Marquis of P'ing-yang heard most of their conversation, then hastened to tell the Chancellor and the Grand Commandant. The Grand Commandant wanted to enter the Northern Army, but he was not able to enter. [Chi] T'ung [紀]通,[168] the Marquis of Hsiang-p'ing 襄平, was in charge of tallies and caducei;[169] [the Grand Commmandant] ordered

[163]Lü Hsü was the younger sister of the Empress Dowager Lü.

[164]Apparently she had possession of the "royal treasures."

[165]Just after Empress Lü's death Shen Yi-chi had been transferred from his position as Chancellor of the Left to Grand Mentor to the emperor (see *Shih chi*, 9.406 above). Liang Yü-sheng (7.249) believes this took place a year earlier, in the seventh month of the seventh year of Empress Lü. He further argues (7.250) that this passage recording Shen Yi-chi's dismissal from the position of Chancellor of the Left is an error, since Shen did not take up the position of Chancellor of the Left again until the ninth month, after the suppression of the Lü Clan (see also *Shih chi*, 22.1125).

[166]There was no such day in the eighth month; scholars are nearly unanimous in emending "eighth" to "ninth" here; our dating is based on this emendation.

[167]Ts'ao Ts'an's 曹參 son.

Yü-shih tai-fu 御史大夫 had formerly been a Ch'in position; when reinstituted by the Han, the Grand Master of the Imperial Scribes was subordinate only to the Chancellor; the positions of Chancellor, Grand Master of the Imperial Scribes, and Grand Commandant were referred to as the *San kung* 三公 (Three Honorable Positions or Three Eminences).

As Yang Shu-ta (*Han shu k'uei-kuan*, p. 35) points out Ts'ao Chu was been involved in some difficulties after the Lüs had been killed and was dismissed (to be replaced by Chang Ts'ang 張蒼); thus he is said here to be "provisionally attending to the affairs of the Grand Master of the Imperial Scribes."

[168]According to Chang Yen ("Chi-chieh") Chi T'ung was Chi Hsin's 紀信 son and the Prefect of Tallies and Caducei (*Fu-chieh ling* 符節令). But a number of scholars have pointed out that this is an error and that as the chronological tables point out his father as Chi Ch'eng 紀成 (*Shih chi*, 18.947; see also *Han shu pu-chu*, 3.6b-ua and Takigawa, 9.30). See also Loewe, *Dictionary*, pp. 182-83.

[169]On *fu* 符 and *chieh* 節, tallies and caducei, see Lao Kan, "The Early Use of the Tally in China," in *Ancient China*, pp. 91-98. Much of this article describes various types of tallies, but on p. 97 Lao Kan explains

him then to carry a caduceus and a forged order to allow him [the Grand Commandant] entry to the Northern Army. The Grand Commandant again ordered Li Chi together with the Director of Guests,[170] Liu Chieh 劉揭, to first persuade Lü Lu by saying, "The emperor has ordered the Grand Commandant to take care of the Northern Army and wants you, Honorable Sir, to go to your state, returning the commander's seal and taking your leave forthwith. If you do not, disaster will occur." Lü Lu believed Li K'uang 酈兄[171] would not deceive him and thus took off the seal and entrusted it to the Director of Guests; he handed over his troops to the Grand Commandant. The Grand Commandant took it [the seal] and entered the camp gate, issuing an order to those in the camp: "Those for the Lü Clan, bare your right arm; those for the Liu Clan, bare your left arm."[172] Those in the camp all bared their left arms for the Liu Clan. When the Grand Commandant was about to arrive, General Lü Lu had also already taken off the seal of the Commander in Chief and the Grand Commandant finally commanded the Northern Army.[173]

But there was still the Southern Army. When the Marquis of P'ing-yang heard [the conversation between Chia Shou and Lü Ch'an],[174] he told [Ch'en] P'ing, the Chancellor, of Lü Ch'an's plot. [Ch'en] P'ing, the Chancellor, then summoned the Marquis of Chu-hsü to assist the Grand Commandant. The Grand Commandant ordered the Marquis of Chu-hsü to hold the

the *chieh* as "a tassled staff given to an imperial messenger to show his authorization." See also Li Chün-ming 李均明, "Han chieh so-chien ch'u-ju fu, chuan yü ch'u-ju ming-chi" 漢簡所見出入符，傳與出入名籍, *Wen shih,* 19 (1981): 27-35.

[170]*Tien-k'o* 典客.

[171]Hsü Kuang argues ("Chi-chieh") that his *agnomen,* 兄, should be pronounced K'uang and says his *praenomen* was Chi 寄.

[172]*Yu t'an* 右袒 "bearing the right arm" is done to indicate a readiness to accept punishment (as might be expected of followers of the Lüs, *tso t'an* 左袒 "to bare the left arm" indicated a sign of respect or loyalty (Hsü Chia-lu, p. 235). Thus Chou Po put his question cleverly so that the soldiers would naturally bear their left arms to avoid incriminating themselves by bearing the right.

[173]Wang Li-ch'i (9.243n.) suggests this last sentence was originally part of the subtext which was erroneously copied into the main text. However, since the *Han shu* (3.102) account contains reference to "Po finally commanding the Northern Army," Wang Li-ch'i's concerns are questionable.

[174]It was intially unclear what the antecedent of *chih* 之 is here (*what* did the marquis hear?). Liang Yü-sheng (7.250) points out that in the paragraph just above we were told "The Marquis of P'ing-yang heard a little of their words, then hastened to tell the Chancellor and the Grand Commandant" (*Shih chi,* 9.409), thus this sentence not only seems out of context, but is redundant; Liang believes it should be considered an interpolation. The sentence, as Liang points out, does not appear in the *Han shu.*

However, it is possible that Ssu-ma Ch'ien was narrating two incidents here, one concerning what happened inside the Northern Army camp and the other focusing on the fight in the palace. He might have chose accounts of these incidents from two distinct sources, both of which began by stating that "the Marquis of P'ing-yang heard about Lü Ch'an's plan . . . ." I am grateful to Cao Weiguo for this reading. Another possibility, related to but not dependent on the two-source hypothesis, is that Ssu-ma Ch'ien repeated this sentence as a means of tying together two original accounts of different events. In any case, it seems clear that the *chih* must refer to "the conversation betwen Chia Shou and Lü Ch'an."

gate to the camp. He ordered the Marquis of P'ing-yang to tell the Commandant of the Guards:[175] "Do not let the Chancellor, [Lü] Ch'an, enter the gate to the [residence] halls."[176] Lü Ch'an did not know that Lü Lu had already left the Northern Army and he [Lü Ch'an] entered the Wei-yang Palace, intending to make rebellion, but at the gate to the [residence] halls he was not allowed to enter and paced back and forth. The Marquis of P'ing-yang, fearing they could not overcome them [the Lüs], hastened to talk to the Grand Commandant. The Grand Commandant still feared they could not overcome the Lüs and did not dare to publically announce [*410*] they were to be executed.[177] Then he sent the Marquis of Chu-hsü and told him, "Hurry and enter the palace to guard the emperor." The Marquis of Chu-hsü asked for foot soldiers and the Grand Commandant gave him more than one thousand foot soldiers. They entered the gate to the Wei-yang Palace. They then saw [Lü] Ch'an in the courtyard. As the sun was low in the west, they then attacked Ch'an. Ch'an ran. A heavenly wind rose up strongly and for this reason the officials accompanying him were thrown into chaos, none daring to fight. They pursued Ch'an and killed him in the privy of the functionaries in the Office of the Palace Attendants.[178]

After the Marquis of Chu-hsü had killed [Lü] Ch'an, the emperor ordered an internuncio bearing a caduceus to thank the Marquis of Chu-hsü for his service. The Marquis of Chu-hsü wanted to seize his caduceus and credentials,[179] but the internuncio was not willing and the Marquis of Chu-hsü thus followed and rode [in the same chariot] with him. Taking advantage of the caduceus and credentials, they went at a gallop and cut off the head of Lü Keng-shih 呂更始, the Commandant of the Ch'ang-lo 長樂 Palace Guard. They returned, galloping into the Northern Army, to report to the Grand Commandant. The Grand Commandant rose [onto his haunches], kneeled, bowed his head, and congratulated the Marquis of Chu-hsü saying, "The only one who distressed me was Lü Ch'an. Now that he has already been executed, the world will be stabilized." Then [the great ministers[180]] sent men divided into groups to arrest all of the men and women of

[175] *Wei-wei* 衛尉.

[176] Reading *tien* 殿 as the halls where the emperor resided (see Watson, 1:337, where he renders the term "imperial apartments," and Chavannes, 2:436 and his translation: "bâtiment impérial"). This is confirmed by Wu and Lu (9.337n.) who recognize that this was to prevent Lü Ch'an from absconding with Shao ti 少帝. They point out that after Kao-tsu had held court primarily in the Ch'ang-lo Palace, Emperor Hui had moved it to Wei-yang Palace, which also was the imperial residence. Dubs (1:207, n. 2) has "front hall" and explains that it was "a hall of audience in the Wei-yang Palace; the imperial apartments were there."

[177] Hsü Kuang (cited in "Chi-chieh") notes that one edition reads *kung* 公 for *sung* 訟. Wang Shu-min (9.374) argues that these graphs were interchangeable and the parallel passage in *Han shu* (3.102) reads *sung yen* 誦言, suggesting that the the meaning here may be "to make a public announcement" (see also *Han shu pu-chu*, 3.7b). This is the reading both Wu and Lu (9.337n.) and Wang Li-ch'i (9.243n.) also prefer.

[178] Wang Li-ch'i (9.244n) points out this office was located just inside the palace.

[179] On the use of *hsin* 信 as "seal," cf. Ch'ing K'o's comments on *Shih chi*, 86.2532.

[180] It is also possible that 'Chou Po' or 'the Grand Commandant' could be the subject of this sentence and the several which follow in sequence. In support of this reading Chou's biography in *Han shu* (40.2048) reads "In the Grand Commandant [Chou] Po personally using troops to execute the Lüs, his merits were many."

the Lüs, and, regardless of their age, behead them all.

On the *hsin-yu* 辛酉 day (27 September 180 B.C.),[181] they arrested and beheaded Lü Lu and had Lü Hsü beaten to death. They sent men to execute Lü T'ung 呂通, King of Yen, and deposed [Chang] Yen, King of Lu.

On the *jen-hsü* 壬戌 day (28 September 180 B.C.), they made the emperor's Grand Mentor, [Shen] Yi-chi, Chancellor of the Left again.[182]

On the *wu-ch'en* 戊辰 day (4 October 180 B.C.), they moved the King of Chi-ch'uan to be King of Liang and enthroned [Liu] Sui [劉]遂, the son of King Yu 幽 of Chao, as the King of Chao.[183] They despatched [Liu] Chang, the Marquis of Chu-hsü, to tell the King of Ch'i the events in which the Lüs had been executed and to order him to dismiss his troops. Kuan Ying's troops were also dismissed at Hsing-yang and he returned [to the capital].[184]

The great ministers plotted secretly together: "Neither Emperor Shao nor the kings of Liang,[185] Huai-yang or Ch'ang-shan are true sons of Hsiao Hui[-ti]. Empress Lü as a stratagem to fradulently claim sons of other people, kill their mothers, cause them to be raised in the harem, order Hsiao Hui[-ti] to treat them as sons,[186] and to establish them as his descendants and as various kings, in order to add to the might of the Lü Clan. Having already wiped out all of the Lüs, were we to set up [as emperor] one whom they had [*411*] enthroned,[187] when he grows up

Later in the same chapter (*Han shu*, 40.2054), however, Pan Ku contradicts himself by claiming that "[Chou] Po joined together with the Chancellor [Ch'en] P'ing and [Liu] Chang, Marquis of Chu-hsü to execute the Lüs." This order of execution seems to have included Liu Chang's wife, the daughter of Lü Lu (see *Shih chi*, 9.400-01), who originally learned of the Lüs' plan to revolt and informed Liu Chang (*Shih chi*, 9.406).

[181]The Chung-hua edition does not indicate a paragraph break here, or for the following two brief paragraphs in our translation.

[182]Shen Yi-chi had just recently been dismissed from this position (*Shih chi*, 9.409). He was a trusted follower of Empress Lü, however, and these changes no doubt reflect more the uncertainty of the political situation than Shen's loyalty to the empress.

[183]Liu Sui, the son of Liu Yu 劉友, ruled Chao for twenty-six years, committing suicide after taking part in the rebellions of 156 B.C. (see also his biography in *Shih chi*, 50.1989-90). According to the "Hsiao Wen pen-chi" 孝文本紀 (Basic Annals of Emperor Wen, *Shih chi*, 10.423), Emperor Wen himself installed Liu Sui in the second year of his reign (178 B.C.).

[184]The record of the victory of the Liu Family forces marks the end of the third section of this chapter according to Han Chao-ch'i (*op. cit.*, p. 84).

[185]*Han shu* (40.2054) reads King of Chi-ch'uan 濟川 for King of Liang here; according to the *Shih chi* (in the passage just above, 9.410) the King of Ch'i-ch'uan had just been moved to become King of Liang.

[186]Wang Li-ch'i, 9.244n. observes that the text earlier in this chapter we are told that these were sons of various "beauties" or "belles" (*mei-jen* 美人) of Emperor Hui whom Empress Chang 張 took as her own. This may be, as Wang Li-ch'i suggests, merely a pretext for the strong action the "great ministers" take against the Lüs.

[187]I.e., Shao ti 少帝.

and exercises power, there will be none of [our] kind left [alive].[188] It would be better to examine which of the various [noble] kings is most worthy and enthrone him."

Someone spoke forth:[189] "King Tao Hui of Ch'i was Kao-ti's eldest son; now the eldest son of his principal wife is King of Ch'i. Speaking from the point of view of examining [their] origins, he is Kao-ti's eldest grandson by blood and should be enthroned."

The great ministers all said, "It was the evil of the maternally related Lü Clan that nearly imperiled ancestral temple and caused chaos among the meritorious ministers. Now the King of Ch'i's maternal family are the Ssu [i.e., *cognomen* Ssu 駟] and Ssu Chün 駟鈞[190] is an evil man. If you enthrone the King of Ch'i, then they [the Ssu family] will become another 'Lü Clan.'" Some wanted to enthrone the King of Huai-nan, but he was considered too young, and his mother's family was also evil. Then they said, "The King of Tai is the eldest of those sons of Kao-ti still alive; he is humane, filial, tolerant, and kind.[191] The Queen Dowager's family, the Po 薄 Clan, are prudent and good [people]. Moreover, to enthrone the eldest has always been fitting, and as his humaneness and filiality is known throughout the world, it will

---

[188]In other words, "we will all be put to death." On the phrase *wu lei* 無類, see Wang Li-ch'i, 9.244n. and Chang Chia-ying, pp. 185-86. A similar expression, *wu yi lei* 無遺類 can be found in "Kao-tsu pen-chi" (*Shih chi*, 8.356: "When Hsiang Yü attacked Hsiang-ch'eng, he left not one of any kind [alive] . . . " 項羽嘗攻 襄城，襄城無遺類).

[189]This and the following three paragraphs are all part of the paragraph above in the Chung-hua edition.

[190]There are two versions of the text reflected in various editions, one which reads 今齊王母駟鈞，駟 鈞惡人也 (see, for example, Taikigawa, 9.35 [279], the Palace edition [殿本], 9.14a, *Shih chi p'ing-lin*, 9.8b, or Ku and Hsü, 9.12 [p. 192]), and the text as emended here by Chang Wen-hu (1.101), which omits the first *chün* 鈞 (Mizusawa, 9.285a, notes other early editions which support Chang's deletion of *chün*). Wang Shu-min (9.375) takes this a step further, arguing that the repetition of *Ssu Chün* is a case of dittography and believes the text originally read simply 今齊王母駟鈞惡人也, "Now Ssu Chün, who belonged to the family of the mother of the King of Ch'i, was an evil man." This view is supported by a more detailed parallel passage on *Shih chi*, 52.2003, and followed by Wu and Lu (9.337n.).

Shortly after the great ministers maligned Ssu Chün, who was the King of Ch'i's maternal uncle, the newly enthroned Emperor Wen enfeoffed him as Marquis of Ch'ing-kuo 清郭 (*Shih chi*, 10.421). The account of Ch'i's reaction to the Lü plot to take over the government following the empress' death suggests Ssu Chün was loyal to the Lius (*Shih chi*, 52.2001), but intended to make his own lord, Liu Hsiang 劉襄, King Ai 哀 of Ch'i, emperor. On *Shih chi*, 19.995, however, Ssu Chün is said to have committed an offense six years earlier and it could be this unknown offense that caused the great ministers to doubt him. According to *Shih chi*, 52.2003, however, it was the King of Lang-ya, Liu Ts'e 劉測, then the eldest living Liu family member, who denounced Ssu Chün and caused the great ministers to reject Liu Hsiang as a candidate for emperor. Liu Ts'e did so because he had just been deceived and held captive by Ch'i as a part of the machinations of Ssu Chün (then the prime minister of Ch'i) and others to elevate the king to the imperial throne (see *Shih chi*, 52.2001 ff.)

[191]*K'uan-hou* 寬厚, "tolerant and kind," was also used to describe the Four Lords of *Shih chi* Chapters 75-78, see *Shih chi*, 6.279 and *Grand Scribe's Records*, 1:166.

be an advantage."

Then they came to terms with each other and together sent someone in secret to summon the King of Tai. The King of Tai sent someone to decline. Only when [their envoy] returned a second time, did he finally take six relay carriages [to the capital].[192]

On the *chi-yu* 己酉 day, the last day of the intercalary month after the ninth [month] (14 November 180 B.C.),[193] he reached Ch'ang-an and took lodging in the Tai Residence. The great ministers all went to pay him a visit, offered the seals of the Son of Heaven to the King of Tai, and together raised him up to be enthroned as the Son of Heaven. The King of Tai declined several times and, only when the assembled ministers implored him, did he heed them.

[Liu] Hsing-chü, the Marquis of Tung-mou, said, "Although in executing the Lü Clan I had no merit, I request to be able to cleanse the palace." Then together with the Magistrate of T'eng 滕,[194] Marquis of Ju-yin 汝陰, and the Grand Servant,[195] he entered the palace. They advanced and said to Emperor Shao, "Honorable Sir, you are not of the Liu Clan and should not have been enthroned."[196] Then he turned his head and waved his hand towards those attendants holding halberds [signalling] to put down their weapons and leave. There were several men who were unwilling to part with their weapons. When the Prefect of the Eunuchs,[197] Chang Tse 張澤,[198] made things clear to them, they also parted with their weapons. The Magistrate of T'eng then summoned the emperor's equipage to take Emperor Shao out [of the palace]. Emperor Shao said, "Where are you placing me?" The Magistrate of T'eng said, "After we leave the palace, we shall find you lodging." He lodged him in the Office of Privy Treasuries.[199] Then he presented the ceremonial Model Equipage[200] for the Son of Heaven and went to meet the King of Tai at his

---

[192]"For further details on the King of Tai's summons and arrival, see also *Shih chi,* 10.413-14 and *Han shu,* 4.105-6.

[193]In the early Han calendar the ninth month was the last of the year; intercalary months were inserted "after" this last month of the year. Ku Chieh-kang records this passage in his personal notes as an example of the disorderly state of the calendar in the early Han period (see Ku's *Ku Chieh-kang tu-shu pi-chi* 顧頡剛讀書筆記 [Taipei: Lien-ching, 1990], 6:4288). Thus Emperor Wen arrived on Ch'u-hsi 除夕 or New Year's Eve.

[194]Hsia-hou Ying 夏侯嬰 who, like Liu Pang, had come from P'ei and had been the Magistrate of T'eng County (southwest of modern T'eng County in Shantung [Wu and Lu, 9.338n.] under the Ch'in (Wang Li-ch'i, 9.245n). He was originally a stable master in P'ei and drove Liu Pang's carriage, but after Liu Pang came to power, he served him, Emperor Hui, Empress Lü, and Emperor Wen as Grand Servant until his death in 172 B.C. (see his biography, *Shih chi,* 95.2663-67).

[195]*T'ai-p'u* 太仆.

[196]This was Liu Shan 山 (also known by his later *praenomen* of Yi 義 and Hung 弘). He was ostensibly a son of Emperor Hui (see *Shih chi,* 9.401 and nn. 85 and 103 above).

[197]*Huan-che ling* 宦者令.

[198]I.e., Chang Shih 張釋 (see n. 134 and the translation of *Shih chi,* 9.405 above); Wu and Lu (9.338n.) point out that Shih 釋 and Tse 澤 were used interchangeably in antiquity.

[199]*Shao-fu* 少府.

[200]"Chi-chieh" cites Ts'ai Yung's explanation that *Fa-chia ch'e* 法駕車 "Model Equipage" was an

residence. He reported: "The palace has been carefully cleansed." As evening approached the King of Tai entered the Wei-yang Palace. There were ten internuncios holding halberds and guarding the main gate.[201] They said, "The Son of Heaven is in residence. What are you, Honorable Sirs, doing that you would enter?"[202]

The King of Tai then spoke to the Grand Commandant. The Grand Commandant went and made things clear [to them] and the ten internuncios all [*412*] put down their weapons and left. The King of Tai then entered and [began to] administer government affairs. By nightfall the authorities divided up to execute the kings of Liang,[203] Huai-yang and Ch'ang-shan, along with Emperor Shao in their [respective] residences.

The King of Tai was enthroned as the Son of Heaven. In the twenty-third year [of his reign] (157 B.C.), he passed away and was posthumously titled the Hsiao Wen-ti 孝文帝 (The Filial and Cultured Emperor or Emperor Wen the Filial, r. 180–157 B.C.).[204]

His Honor the Grand Scribe says: "During the time of the Hsiao Hui Huang-ti 孝惠皇帝 (The August Emperor Hui the Filial) and Kao-hou, the black-haired [common] people were able to part from the suffering of the Warring States, and lords and vassals all intended to rest in non-action.[205] For this reason, Hui-ti let fall his robes and folded his hands,[206] Kao-hou as a female ruler announced [she would issue] the imperial decrees and managed to govern without going out of her chambers, and the world was peaceful, punishments and penalties were rarely employed, and those who had committed offenses then became rare. The people devoted themselves to planting and harvesting, and [as a result] clothing and food became increasingly abundant.[207]

entourage of thirty-six vehicles, one of three types of entourages used by the emperor (*Shih chi*, 9.412).

[201]On *tuan men* 端門 as "main gate" see Wu and Lu, 9.338n. Yen Shih-ku's comments to the parallel passage on *Han shu*, 40.2055 read: 端門，殿之正門; "The *Tuan* Gate was the main gate to the hall."

[202]Liang Yü-sheng (7.251) is troubled that these guards could still be in palace *after* Liu Hsing-chü had "cleansed" the palace. There is no paragraph break here in the Chung-hua text.

[203]Once again *Han shu* (40.2055) reads King of Chi-ch'uan for King of Liang (see n. 185 above).

[204]In Han Chao-ch'i's analysis, this is the end of the fourth and final section of this chapter (*op. cit.*, p. 87).

[205]*Wu-wei* 無為 or "non-action" sounds the first note of an evaluation of Empress Lü and Emperor Hui the Filial as continuing the Huang-Lao government of Kao-tsu. Whoever wrote this evaluation—Ssu-ma T'an is certainly a possible author—strongly approved of this means of governing.

[206]*Ch'ui-kung* 垂拱 appears first in the *Shang shu* depicting King Wu's method of reigning after he conquered the Shang: 垂拱而天下治 "He let his [robes] fall and folded [his hands] across his chest, and the empire was managed" (see "Wu-ch'eng" 武成, in *Shang shu chi-shih* 尚書集釋, Ch'ü Wan-li 屈萬里, ed. [Taipei: Lien-ching, 1986], p. 322]). Subsequently, it became a tenet of Huang-Lao politics, the ideal means for the ruler to handle the administration of his state. See also Mark Csikszentmihalyi, "Chapter One: Huang Lao during the Western Han," in his dissertation, "Emulating the Yellow Emperor: The Theory and Practice of Huang Lao, 180-141 B.C." (Stanford University, 1994), pp. 7-57.

[207]The historian's comments to "Kao-hou chi" 高后紀 in the *Han shu* (3.104) are essentially the same

*   *   *   *   *

Hui-ti passed away at an early age and the Lü family did not support [the Liu family succession]. When they heaped honor and position on Lü Lu and Lü Ch'an, the feudal lords began to plot against them, and when they murdered Liu Ju-yi and Liu Yu, [both] kings of Chao, the high ministers were filled with fear and distrust. In the end disaster fell on the house of Lü. Thus I made "The Basic Annals of Empress Dowager Lü."[208]

as those here, with some minor, mostly stylistic changes. Although these final two sentences of the historian's comment seem totally positive in their assessment of Empress Dowager Lü's reign, Ssu-ma Ch'ien clearly criticizes her attempts to establish the Lü Family in his comment to "Wai-ch'i shih-chia" 外戚世家 (The Hereditary House of the Maternal Families) on *Shih chi,* 49.1969 and his comments in his postface (cited just below in the text).

[208]This is Ssu-ma Ch'ien's account of why he wrote this chapter from his postface, *Shih chi,* 130.3301.

Translator's Note

This is not a standard "basic annals." Perhaps there was no such thing until the Pan 班 Family complied their *Han shu*.[209] This chapter is not standard most obviously because its subject is a woman. It is also not standard because in describing the Grand Dowager Lü, it subsumes the rule of her son, Emperor Hui (r. 195-188 B.C.), and two subsequent puppets. It is not a female biography either. Suzanne E. Cahill has reconstructed a standard biography of women: it begins with names and titles of the subject, turns then to information about her lineage and birthplace, often includes a depiction of her marriage, mentions her teachers and associates, and finally narrates her deeds, often in the context of some larger meaning intended for the text (see Cahill's *Transcendence and Divine Passion, The Queen Mother of the West in Medieval China* [Stanford: Stanford University Press, 1993], p. 67). Such information about Grand Dowager Lü was either given above in the annals of Kao-tsu, or is, because of her common origins, unknown. This leaves Ssu-ma Ch'ien with no alternative but to introduce her anachronistically, placing her, in the opening lines of this chapter, into history by means of her posthumous title and the eventual titles her children would attain.

Then, before any other information is provided about the Grand Empress, the 'other woman' appears. This is Beauty Ch'i who captivated Kao-tsu in his final years. There are several stories about her, each of which reveals more about the cruelty of the Empress than about Liu Pang's new paramour. The heartless poisoning of the child-king Ju-yi and the disfigurement of Beauty Ch'i come first to mind. These stories conclude in an ironic result—when Emperor Hui views Beauty Ch'i's transmogrification into "the human hog" he is overcome by the sight, takes to debauchery, and falls ill, unable and unwilling to rule for the rest of his short life. Whether this is the author's means of blaming Empress Lü for her son's failure to maintain his father's legacy, or an accurate portrayal of events, it foreshadows the heavenly condemnation that will eventually undo the Lüs in the late 180s. They, like Empress Lü, went too far in their evil designs.

Though neither annals nor female biography, this chapter is structured not unlike that

---

[209]See Dubs' comments on "Lü T'ai-hou pen-chi" (Dubs, 1:167): "The *SC* puts this material into one chapter ["Lü T'ai-hou pen-chi"]; Pan Ku divides it into two because there were two rulers. Pan Ku furthermore has transferred into his 'Memoirs' the more sensational stories given in the *SC*, seemingly because he felt that these accounts concerned the private lives of the actors, rather than their public acts. Thus he has left in these 'Annals' only the bare mention of Liu Ju-yi's death and that of Liu Yu, and has said nothing about the Empress's treatment of the Lady *née* Ch'i. Concerning the attempted assassination of Liu Fei, he mentions only its administrative result. He gives those accounts in full in his 'Memoir of the Imperial Relatives by Marriage' and the 'Memoir of the Five Kings who Were Sons of Kao-tsu.' Thus Pan Ku seems to have conceived of the 'Annals' as chronicles properly devoted to the official acts of the ruler and the important events of the reign, rather than as an attempt to give in full an account of the period."

of "Kao-tsu pen-chi": it begins with a series of anecdotes about Empress Lü and then shifts to an annalistic account of her reign—the general form Ssu-ma Ch'ien seems to have preferred for his early Han biographies (see the Translator's Note for "Kao-tsu pen-chi"). Indeed, a volume prepared towards the end of the Cultural Revolution, *Shih chi hsüan-yi* 史記選譯, subtitles "Lü T'ai-hou pen-chi" as "Lü Chih chuan" 呂雉傳, "Lü Chih's Memoir," in its table of contents.[210] Yet the annalistic section of this chapter seems derived from a livelier account of the Empress' reign, than was the source(s) for the similar section in "Kao-tsu pen-chi," for here the narrator is often able to overhear conversations or to impute motives for various actions (as he does with Lü Ch'an and Lü Lu in the section where they are contemplating open rebellion [*Shih chi,* 9.407], for example).

Although the total effect is to render Grand Empress Lü a hateful figure, a few lines by Ssu-ma Ch'ien depicting the empress' reaction to her son's death are the most poignant. The Grand Scribe tells us that Empress Lü was performing the wailing rites of the funeral, but could not shed real tears until she was satisfied that her own coterie had been allowed to enter the palace and take control—only then did "her wailing become sorrowful" (*Shih chi,* 9.399). It seems she could not have a genuine emotion even for her own son. Heaven realizes this and she departs this world not through illness or old age or political intrigue, but after being bitten by an otherworldly cur.

As suggested above, these annals are dominated by the feminine. Not only the protagonist, but also her choice of weapons–poison, potions, and plots–speaks to the traditions of the innermost bowers of the palace. Moreover, the manner is which she deals with her enemies is often confinement (Beauty Ch'i, the first Emperor Shao, and Liu Yu come immediately to mind), a particularly effective method that is normally employed to hold women in check.[211] Whatever we think of Empress Lü, she is a prototype for some of the strong women (not always evil) who play such an important role in later Chinese fiction. Even among the secondary players in this chapter women are often dominant: the scene in which Lü Hsü realizes that Lü Lu and Lü Ch'an are not going to be able to sustain the Lü cause and then scatters her valuables before the hall is one of the most memorable (*Shih chi,* 9.408).

After Empress Dowager Lü's death, which takes place barely half-way through this narrative, the reader is allowed to view enough of the machinations of the surviving Lü family members that he can feel but little remorse when they are put to the sword in the process of reinstating a ruler from the Liu Clan.

Although this may not be one of Ssu-ma Ch'ien's most memorable chapters, it can contribute to the discussion of the relationship between the *Han shu* and the *Shih chi.* "Lü T'ai-hou pen-chi" seems clearly to have been the older text here (as discussed in the "Introduction" above). Pan Ku may have disliked the idea of a female annals so much that he dismantled this chapter into five separate chapters of the *Han shu* (2, 3, 38, 40 and 97–see also Wu Fu-chu 吳福助, *Shih Han kuan-hsi* 史漢關係 [Taipei: Wen-shih-che, 1975], p. 10), including a separate annals for Emperor Hui. Some critics have extolled Pan's honoring Emperor Hui so, but Ch'en

---

[210]Edited by a group of cadre in Wei-mao 衛戍 District, Peking (Peking: Chung-hua, 1976).

[211]I thank David Honey for pointing out the repeated imagery of confinement in this chapter.

Jen-hsi 陳仁錫 (1581-1636) supports Ssu-ma Ch'ien's decision to treat Hui-ti together with his mother in this chapter:

> For what reason was Emperor Hui not given an annals? Because Hui lost the reigns of government. Power lay with his mother, the Empress. Why is it that power lay with his mother, the Empress? If she wanted someone to live, then she let him live. If she wanted to execute someone, then she executed him. Hui was not able to participate in this. In this way he was without constancy. For what reason should an annals be made for him? His Honor the Grand Scribe did this as a warning for men of later ages against lords who lost the reigns of government. His intentions [in not having an annals for Hui] were subtle indeed![212]

Indeed, the reactions of traditional scholars to according Empress Lü an annals have varied greatly. Cheng Ch'iao 鄭樵 (1104-1162) claimed that by depicting these years in an annals for Empress Lü rather than for her son, Emperor Hui, Ssu-ma Ch'ien "rewarded a bandit."[213] It seems rather that Ssu-ma Ch'ien wanted to focus attention on the Empress in order to show her actions and thoughts to be "obstinate and resolute," in the manner of the First Emperor of Ch'in, as Liu Chih-chi 劉知幾 (661-721) has argued: "[Ssu-ma Ch'ien] wanted to say that he executions of the great ministers after the world was pacified were due to Empress Lü's power, thus he first characterized her as 'obstinate and resolute.' This is that which is called foreshadowing the [subsequent] narration of events."[214]

A reading of the Grand Scribe's comments at the end of this account again raises the question of whether the same author could have written both the commentary and the chapter itself. The contradictions here are even greater than in "Kao-tsu pen-chi": following a clearly condemnatory narrative the comments are generally positive, praising the Huang-Lao political techniques of Emperor Hui and Empress Lü.[215] It may be that Ssu-ma T'an 司馬談 (d. 110 B.C.) attempted to impose his ideas about schools of thought in the early Han (see *Shih chi* Chapter 130) on these annals, ideas which his son was unable to follow in tracing the horrors of the Lü family, for despite what His Honor the Grand Scribe has to say in his closing remarks, this is a narrative distinctive for its condemnation of the Lüs and their great matriarch, a narrative which through semi-fictional accounts brings many of these players to life.

---

[212]These comments are recorded in the *mei-p'i* 眉批 (headnotes) to *Shih chi p'ing-lin* 史記評林 (Taipei: Ti-ch'iu, 1992), 1:9.1a-1b (pp. 333-334) and probably based on Ch'en's *Shih p'in ch'ih-han* 史品赤函, see *Ssu-k'u ch'üan-shu tsung-mu* 四庫全書總目 (rpt. Taipei: T'ai-wan Shang-wu, 1983), *chüan* 65, fol. 18a (2:40).

[213]This in the headnotes to *Shih chi p'ing-lin*, 9.1a (p. 333).

[214]As cited in the headnotes to *Shih chi p'ing-lin*, 9.1b (p. 334).

[215]The historian's comments on Empress Lü in the "Wai-ch'i shih-chia" 外戚世家 (*Shih chi*, 49.1969) are extremely critical and it may be that Ssu-ma Ch'ien is following a principle he often employs of criticizing a man or woman in a chapter not specifically devoted to that person.

Bibliography

I. Editions, References

"Lü Hou pen-chi, Ti chiu" 呂后本紀，第九. MSS. copy of a Sung-dynasty (or earlier) text held
in the Kunaichô 宮内庁 Library. Tokyo: Koten Hozonkai 古典保存會, 1935.

      Contains a preface by Yamada Takao 山田孝雄 dated Showa 10 (1935) etc. This a
a reproduction of a MSS known as the Tokyo Mao-li Shih Lü-hou pen-chi 東京毛利氏
呂后本紀.There is a collophon dated Enkyû 延九 5 (1073 A.D.). This text seems to be a
part of a manuscript to which belong two other early handwritten MSS (of "Hsiao Wen
pen-chi" and "Hsiao Ching pen-chi") held in Japan. This annals is from a *Shih chi
Chi-chieh* edition, but the copyist, a certain Ôe Iekuni 大江家國, has added some of
the "So-yin" commentary interlineally and/or in the top margin.

II. Translations

Chavannes, 2:406-42.
Watson, *Han,* 1:267-84.
Yoshida, 2:588-623.
Viatkin, 2:200-220, notes 443-51.

III. Studies

An Tso-chang 安作璋. "Lun Lü-hou" 論呂后, *Shan-tung Shih-yüan Hsüeh-pao* 山東師院學報,
    1962.1 [not seen].

Chou Hsiu-mu 周修睦. "Lü-hou p'ing-chuan" 呂后評傳,*Shang-hai Shih-yüan hsüeh-pao,* 1980.2
    [not seen].

Cutter, Robert Joe. "Palace Women in the Early Empire," in Cutter and William Gordon Crowell,
    Empresses and Consorts, Selections from Chen Shou's Records of the Three States
    with Pei Songzhi's Commentary. Honolulu: University of Hawai'i Press, 1999, pp.
    9-25.

Feng Hui-min 馮惠民. "Ch'ung-p'ing Lü-hou" 重評呂后, *Shan-tung Shih-yüan hsüeh-pao,*
    1980.2 [not seen].

Fujita Katsuhisa 藤田勝九.*"Shiki* 'Ro Go honki' ni mieru Siba Sen no rekishi shisô" [史記」呂
    后本紀に見える司馬遷の歴史思想, *Tôhôgaku,* 86 (1993): 21-35.

Hsü Shuo-fang 徐朔方. "Tu Shih chi 'Lü Hou pen-chi'" 讀史記呂后本紀 in *Shih Han lun-kao* 史
    漢論稿. Nanking: Chiang-su Ku-chi, 1984, pp. 88-90.

Lo Shih-lieh 羅世烈. "Liu-Lü chih cheng p'ing-yi" 劉呂之爭平議, *Chin-yang hsüeh-k'an,* 18
    (1983.3): 66-71.

Loewe, "Lü Zhi 呂雉," in Loewe, *Dictionary,* pp. 426-29.

Kasuga Harunan 春日春南. "Môri Hon '*Shiki* 'Ro Go honki' oboegaki" 毛利本史記呂后本紀覺
え書, *Bungaku ronshû* 文学論集 2 (1954): 18-31.

Mikami Jun 三上順. "Shiba Sen no shisô to *Shiki* no kôsei (ue)—'Shikaku retsuden' to 'Ro Go
honki' o chûshin ni" 司馬遷の思想と史記の構成（上）―「刺客列伝」と「呂后本
紀」を中心に, *Hijiyama Daigaku Hijiyama Joshi Tanki Daigaku, Josei Bunka Kenkyû
Sento̵ nenpô* 比治山大学、比治山女子短期大学、女性文化研究センター年報, 11
(1996): 1-28 [not seen].

Nitta Kôji 新田幸治. "Tu 'Lü-hou pen-chi'" 讀呂后本紀, *Tôhôgaku ronsô, Tôhô Daigaku
Bungakubu kiyô* 東洋學論叢，東洋大學文學部紀要, 35 (1982): 77-94.

Noguchi Sadao 野口定男 (1917-1979). "'Ro Go honki' o yomu" 呂后本紀を読む, in Noguchi's
Shiki o yomu 史記を読む. Tokyo: Kenbun Shuppan 研文出版, 1980, pp. 77-96.

Raphals, Lisa. "Empress Lü," in Raphals, *Sharing the Light, Representations of Women and
Virtue in Early China.* Albany: State University of New York Press, 1998, pp. 70-78.

Shen Tieh 沈颶. "Tu 'Lü-hou' sui-pi" 讀呂后隨筆. *Chung-hua wen-shih lun-ts'ung, ti erh chi* 中
華文史論叢，第二輯.

Tsukamoto Terukazu 塚本照和. "*Shiki*—'Ro Taigo honki' o yomu" [史記] ―呂太后本紀世を
読む, *Tenri Daigaku gakuhô, Bessatsu,* 4 (1993): 83-109.

The Filial and Cultured [Emperor], Basic Annals 10

[10. 413] The August Emperor Wen 文 the Filial (r. 180–157 B.C.) was a middle son[1] of Kao-tsu 高祖 (The Exalted Ancestor, r. 206–195 B.C.).[2] In the spring of the eleventh year of Kao-tsu (196 B.C.), after [Kao-tsu] defeated[3] the army of Ch'en Hsi 陳豨[4] and stabilized the territory of Tai 代,[5] [Kao-tsu] enthroned him [Liu Heng] as the King of Tai, making Chung-tu 中都[6] the capital. He was the son of Queen Dowager Po 薄.[7] He reigned there seventeen years until, in the seventh month of the eighth year of Kao-hou 高后 (The Exalted Empress)[8] (180 B.C.), Kao-hou passed away. In the ninth month, Lü Ch'an 呂產[9] and the other Lüs[10] intended to cause rebellion, thereby endangering the Liu Clan. The great ministers in concert had them executed and plotted to summon and enthrone the King of Tai. These incidents are recorded in the

[1] His *praenomen* was Heng 恆. Wen the Filial was his posthumous title. Kao-tsu had eight sons, Liu Heng was his fourth. See *Shih chi*, 8.393 and the translation above.

[2] Kao-tsu (The Exalted Ancestor) was Liu Pang 劉邦, the founder of the Han Dynasty. He was also called the Exalted Emperor (Kao-ti 高帝). See *Shih chi*, 8.341-94 and the translation of Chapter 8 above.

[3] The parallel passage in *Han shu* (4.104) reads "executed Ch'en Hsi," but according to *Shih chi*, 8.390 and 93.2642, it was not until the winter of the twelfth year of Kao-tsu that Fan K'uai 樊噲 killed Ch'en Hsi.

[4] Ch'en Hsi was made Chancellor of the State of Chao 趙 and commanded troops of Chao and Tai in 200 B.C. He rebelled and proclaimed himself King of Tai in 197 B.C. See his biography (*Shih chi*, 93.2639-42).

[5] In parts of modern Hopei, Shansi, and Inner Mongolia (Wang Li-ch'i, 10.253). *Shih chi*, 22.1122 and 93.2641 both claim that Chou Po 周勃, the Grand Commandant, attacked and stabilized Tai in that year.

[6] Chung-tu was located a few miles southwest of the seat of modern P'ing-yao 平遙 County, Shansi (T'an Ch'i-hsiang, 2:18). *Shih chi*, 8.389 says the capital was Chin-yang 晉陽, which was about forty miles northeast of Chung-tu (T'an Ch'i-hsiang, 2:18). Ju Ch'un 如淳 (in "Chi-chieh," *Shih chi*, 8.389) points out it is possible that the capital of Tai was moved from Chin-yang to Chung-tu. Liang Yü-sheng (6.224) suggests that the capital was Chin-yang, while the King of Tai lived in Chung-tu. See also Wang Hui, p. 453.

[7] She was called Po Chi 薄姬 (Beauty Po) and was one of Kao-ti's consorts. According to her biography (*Shih chi*, 49.1970-71), she dreamed of a black dragon and then became pregnant with Emperor Wen, an account similar to the story surrounding the birth of Liu Pang (cf. *Shih chi*, 8.341 and our translation above).

[8] That is, Empress Lü 呂. See "Lü T'ai-hou pen-chi" 呂太后本記 (*Shih chi*, 9.395-412).

[9] He was Empress Lü's nephew and was made King of Liang 梁 in 181 B.C. After Empress Lü died, he struggled for power with the Han ministers and was eventually killed. See *Shih chi*, 9.404, 410.

[10] Empress Lü made five members of the Lü Clan kings and six marquises. They were called "the Lüs" (*chu Lü* 諸呂). See also n. 21 below.

"account of the Empress Lü."[11]

The Chancellor, Ch'en P'ing 陳平,[12] the Grand Commandant, Chou Po 周勃,[13] and the others sent a man to invite the King of Tai.[14] The King of Tai questioned Chang Wu 張武,[15] his Prefect of the Palace Attendants, and other courtiers [about this]. Chang Wu and the others discussed it and said, "The great ministers of Han were all great generals in the time of the late Kao-ti 高帝 (The Exalted Emperor). They are versed in the art of war and well supplied with plots and deceptions. This indicates that their ambition does not stop at this [stage]. They were only fearful of the awesome power of Kao-ti and Empress Dowager Lü. Now they have already executed the Lüs and newly sipped blood[16] in the great metropolis.[17] This [invitation] is to welcome you, Great King, in name, in reality it cannot be trusted. We hope you, Great King, will plead illness and not go there so as to watch how the situation develops."

Sung Ch'ang 宋昌,[18] the Commandant of the Capital,[19] put forward his idea, saying, "The ministers' discussions are all incorrect. When Ch'in failed in its government, the feudal lords and stalwarts rose up together; those who believed they themselves could obtain [the world] can be counted in tens of thousands. Yet in the end it was a man of the Liu Clan who ascended the throne of the Son of Heaven and all [the rivals for] the world have given up their

[11]This refers to "Lü T'ai-hou pen-chi" 呂太后本記 translated above.

[12]See his biography on *Shih chi*, 56.2051-63.

[13]See his biography on *Shih chi*, 57.2065-73.

[14]The parallel account in *Shih chi*, 9.411 did not mention who sent an envoy to meet the King of Tai. Moreover, it reads 陰使人召代王 "secretly sent a man to summon the King of Tai" for 使人迎代王 "sent a man to invite the King of Tai." It is strange that the ministers could "summon" their ruler. The different accounts of the great ministers' action in Chapters 9 and 10 suggest that there may indeed have been intrigue on their side. See further discussion of this issue in the "Translator's Note."

[15]He served as the Prefect of the Palace Attendants for the imperial court once Liu Heng was enthroned as the emperor. Later he became a general who fought against the Hsiung-nu (see *Shih chi*, 22.1128-29, 110.2901).

[16]*Sha-hsüeh* 喋血 means to sip blood as part of an oath. The parallel passage in *Han shu* reads *tieh-hsüeh* 喋血, meaning "to tread bloody [ground]" or to create a bloodbath. Most commentators and modern translators follow the opinion of "So-yin" (in *Shih chi*, 10.414) and believe that *tieh-hsüeh* should be the correct reading since there is no other record to show that the Han ministers made a covenant after they executed the Lüs. See Chang Chia-ying, pp. 180-81, and Wang Shu-min, 10.379.

[17]The original word is *ching-shih* 京師. According to *Kung-yang chuan* 公羊傳 (cited in "Chi-chieh," *Shih chi*, 10.414), *ching* means "great," *shih* means "multitude." *Ching-shih* is thus the great metropolis where the Son of Heaven dwelled. Here, the great metropolis refers to the Han capital Ch'ang-an 長安, which was located slightly northwest of modern Sian 西安, Shensi (T'an Ch'i-hsiang, 2:12).

[18]He was appointed as General of the Guards on the night when Emperor Wen entered the imperial palace. Later he was enfeoffed as Marquis of Chuang-wu 壯武 (see *Shih chi*, 19.995). According to *Tung-kuan Han chi* 東觀漢紀 (cited in "So-yin," in *Shih chi*, 10.414), he was a descendant of Sung Yi 宋義.

[19]*Chung-wei* 中尉.

aspirations. This is my first point. Kao-ti enfeoffed his sons and younger brothers as kings. Their territories [interlock] like the teeth of a dog and thus control each other. This is the so-called '[royal] house as solid as a great rock.' [*414*] The world has submitted to its might. This is my second point. After Han arose, it abolished the harsh government of the Ch'in, simplified the laws and ordinances, spread virtue and kindness.[20] Everyone feels at ease, and it will be difficult to sway them. This is my third point. Empress Dowager Lü, by means of her prestige, established [some of] the Lüs as the 'Three Kings.'[21] They dominated power and monopolized control; however, the Grand Commandant used a single caduceus to enter the Northern Army,[22] and with a single call, all the officers bared their left arms.[23] They acted for the Liu Clan and turned against the Lüs, thereby eventually destroying them.[24] This [power] is bestowed by Heaven, not due to human strength.[25] Now even if the great ministers intend to

[20] After Kao-ti defeated Ch'in and entered its capital, he announced to the commoners that he intended to do away with all the harsh laws of Ch'in and to replace them with a legal code with only three articles. As a result, people of Ch'in were greatly pleased and hoped that he would be their ruler (see *Shih chi*, 8.362).

[21] The "Three Kings" refer to Lü Ch'an 呂產, King of Liang 梁, Lü Lu 呂祿, King of Chao 趙, and Lü T'ung 呂通, King of Yen 燕. Wang Li-ch'i (10.254n.) observes that four of the Lüs were made kings and, since Lü T'ung 呂通 succeeded his father, Lü Yi 呂台, they were referred to as the "Three Kings." However, based on *Shih chi*, 17.816-25 and 9.401-5, there are clearly *five* Lüs who served as kings: Lü Yi, King of Lu 魯, Lü Chia 呂嘉, who succeeded his father as King of Lu, Lü Ch'an, King of Liang, Lü Lu, King of Chao, and Lü T'ung, King of Yen. However, by the time the Great Ministers opposed the Lüs openly, Lü Yi had died (187 B.C.) and Lü Chia had been deposed (182 B.C.), so that there were only "Three Kings" remaining among the Lüs.

[22] The Northern Army was stationed north of the capital. Its responsibility was to guard the city, while the Southern Army guarded the palace. For a discussion of the Northern and Southern Armies, see Bielenstein, p. 114, and n. 59 in our translation of Chapter 9 above.

[23] The officers bared their left arms to show their loyalty to the Liu Clan. According to Chao Yi 趙翼, *Kai yü ts'ung k'ao* 陔餘叢考 (Shanghai: Shang-wu Yin-shu-kuan, 1957), pp. 370-71, the action of baring an arm to indicate choice came from an ancient custom. Chao notes that according to *Yi li* 儀禮, when one participates in auspicious or funerary ceremonies, he bares his left arm; when one receive punishment, he bares his right arm. Chao also cited two more examples of "baring one's arm" in the early historical works. The first Chao claimed was in the *Shih chi*, but it actually seems to have been recorded only in the *Chan-kuo ts'e* 戰國策 (see Ho Chien-chang, p. 450): after Nao-ch'ih 淖齒 killed King Min 湣 of Ch'i (r. *323-284 B.C.), Wang-sun Chia 王孫賈 entered the marketplace and shouted, "Those who want to follow me and kill Nao-ch'ih, bare your right arm!" The second can be found on *Han shu*, 31.1781: after Ch'en Sheng 陳勝 rose in rebellion, his people also bared there right arms. See also n. 172 to our translation of Chapter 9 above.

[24] For a detailed account of this incident, see *Shih chi*, 9.409.

[25] As Takigawa (10.4) and Wang Shu-min (10.380) both point out, this sentence may have come from a popular saying at that time. In *Shih chi*, 55.2036, Chang Liang 張良 said, "The [power of] the Magistrate of P'ei 沛 is probably bestowed by Heaven." In *Shih chi*, 92.2628, Han Hsin 韓信 said to Kao-tsu, "[The power of] Your Majesty is said to have been bestowed by Heaven, it is not due to human's strength." This may

cause trouble, the populace will not allow themselves to be ordered about. How can their partisans unite as one? Right now[26] inside the capital there are your relatives such as [the Marquis of] Chu-hsü 朱虛[27] and [the Marquis of] Tung-mou 東牟;[28] outside the capital [the ministers] fear the power of [the kings of] Wu 吳,[29] Ch'u 楚,[30] Huai-nan 淮南,[31] Lang-ya 瑯邪,[32] Ch'i 齊,[33] and Tai 代. Right now of the sons of Kao-ti, only you, Great King, and the King of Huai-nan[34] remain. Moreover, you, Great King, are the elder. Your worthiness, sagacity, benevolence, and filial piety are known all over the world.[35] Therefore the great ministers, conforming to the

indicate that this a widely held opinion at that time.

[26]Takigawa (10.4) points out that the original term *fang chin* 方今 here seems to be redundant, since the sentence immediately below also starts with *fang chin.* Pan Ku deleted this word in his parallel passage in *Han shu.*

[27]Chu-hsü was located about 15 miles southeast of modern Lin-ch'ü 臨朐 County, Shantung (T'an Ch'i-hsiang, 2:20). The Marquis of Chu-hsü was Liu Chang 劉章, son of Liu Fei 劉肥, Liu Pang's eldest son by a concubine, who became King Tao Hui 悼惠 of Ch'i 齊. He was among the first to plot with the great ministers against members of the Lü Clan.

[28]Tung-mou was located in modern Mou-p'ing 牟平 County, Shantung (T'an Ch'i-hsiang, 2:20). The Marquis of Tung-mou was Liu Hsing-chü 劉興居, younger brother of Liu Chang.

[29]The state of Wu occupied parts of modern Anhwei, Kiangsu, and Chekiang. Its capital was Kuang-ling 廣陵 (northwest of modern Yangchow 揚州, Kiangsu; T'an Ch'i-hsiang, 2:20). The King of Wu was Liu P'i 劉濞. He was the son of Liu Chung 劉仲, Liu Pang's second eldest brother (see *Shih chi,* 106.2821).

[30]The state of Ch'u occupied parts of modern Anhwei and Kiangsu. Its capital was P'eng-ch'eng 彭城 (modern Hsü-chou 徐州, Kiangsu; T'an Ch'i-hsiang, 2:20). The King of Ch'u was Liu Chiao 劉交. He was Liu Pang's younger brother (see *Shih chi,* 50.1987).

[31]The state of Huai-nan occupied the central part of modern Anhwei. Its capital was Shou-ch'un 壽春 (modern Shou 壽 County, Anhwei; Wang Li-ch'i, 10.254). The King of Huai-nan was Liu Ch'ang 劉長. He was the seventh son of Liu Pang (see *Shih chi,* 118.3075).

[32]The state of Lang-yeh occupied the southern part of the Shantung Peninsula. Its capital was Tung-wu 東武 (modern Chu-ch'eng 諸城 County, Shantung; T'an Ch'i-hsiang, 2:20). The King of Lang-yeh was Liu Tse 劉澤. He was a cousin of Liu Pang (see *Shih chi,* 51.1995).

[33]The state of Ch'i occupied northern and eastern parts of modern Shantung. Its capital was Lin-tzu 臨淄 (northwest of modern Lin-tzu County; T'an Ch'i-hsiang, 2:20). The King of Ch'i was Liu Hsiang 劉襄, he was the son of Liu Fei 劉肥, Liu Pang's eldest son by concubine (see *Shih chi,* 52.1999).

[34]See his biography on *Shih chi,* 118.3075-80.

[35]Although Sung Ch'ang convincingly listed a number of good reasons why the great ministers intended to enthrone the King of Tai, he missed one important reason. According to *Shih chi,* 9.411, the great ministers had considered the King of Ch'i and King of Huai-nan as candidates to be emperor. They abandoned these two men mainly because their mothers' families were both "evil." In other words, the great ministers had learned a lesson from Empress Lü and did not want a maternal family to take control of the government. Emperor Wen was finally chosen because his mother's family was said to be "prudent and good." See the further discussion in the "Translator's Note."

common will of the world, intend to invite you, Great King, to take the throne. Your Majesty should not be suspicious."

The King of Tai reported to the Queen Dowager and they considered it [the offer], but still hesitated and could not decide. He divined the matter by tortoise-shell. The sign he obtained[36] was "Great Transversal." The divination read,

> "The Great Transversal indicates change.[37]
> I shall be the Heavenly King.
> Like Ch'i 啟 of Hsia,[38]
> I shall thereby glorify [my ancestors]."

The King of Tai said, "We have already become a king. How can We become a king again?" The diviner said, "The so-called Heavenly King is the Son of Heaven."[39]

At this, the King of Tai dispatched Po Chao 薄昭,[40] the younger brother of the Queen Dowager, to go and see the Marquis of Chiang 絳.[41] The Marquis of Chiang and others explained in detail to [Po] Chao the reason why they intended to invite the king to take the throne.[42] Po

[36]*Han shu* (4.106) reads *chao* 兆 for *kua chao* 卦兆. Ying Shao 應邵 in his commentary says, "Divination by tortoise shell is called *chao*; divination by stalks of plants is called *kua*." See also Dubs, 1:225, n. 1.

[37]Following Chang Yen's 張晏 interpretation (in "Chi-chieh"), which says *keng* 庚 is similar to *keng* 更 "change," indicating that the King of Tai should leave his position as a feudal lord and ascend the throne.

[38]Ch'i was the son of Yü 禹, the founder of the Hsia dynasty. "Chi-chieh" says, "Earlier, when the Five Emperors ruled the world, each yielded his position to a worthy man when he became old. When it came to Ch'i, he was the first to inherit his father's rank thus enabling him to glorify his deceased lord's basic enterprise. Emperor Wen also succeeded to his father's achievements. Thus it was said he was like Ch'i of Hsia." According to *Shih chi*, 2.83, after Yü passed away, he yielded the world to Yi 益, but people of the world shunned Yi and paid homage to Ch'i. Subsequently Ch'i ascended the throne of the Son of Heaven (see also *Grand Scribe's Records*, 1:36). The succession of Ch'i may be seen as a parallel to that of Liu Heng. It is noteworthy that *ch'i* was also the *praenomen* of Emperor Wen's heir, the future Emperor Ching 景 (r. 156-141 B.C.).

[39]As Chavannes (2:447) points out, in *Tso chuan*, the term "Heavenly King" always refers to the Son of Heaven. Examples can be found in Yin 1, 3, and 7; Yang 16, 24, and 53; etc.

[40]Po Chao became General of Chariots and Cavalry and was enfeoffed as Marquis of Chih 軹 in the first year of Emperor Wen's reign (180 B.C.). He committed suicide in the tenth year of his reign (171 B.C., see *Shih chi*, 19.994, and *Han shu*, 18.683).

[41]The Marquis of Chiang was Chou Po; Chiang was located northeast of modern Hou-ma 侯馬, Shansi (T'an Ch'i-hsiang, 2:16).

[42]The parallel sentence in *Han shu* (4.106) reads *ying li wang che* 迎立王者 "to invite and enthrone the king" for *ying li wang yi* 迎立王意 "the intention to invite and enthrone the king." As Wang Hsien-ch'ien 王先謙 (1842-1918) points out, the *Shih chi* reading is preferable, because not only does it fit the context better,

Chao returned and reported, saying, "They are trustworthy. There is nothing to suspect." The King of Tai then smiled and told Sung Ch'ang, "It is indeed as you said, sir." Then he ordered Sung Ch'ang to be his third man on the chariot, and Chang Wu and others, six men in all, to ride in post chariots[43] to reach Ch'ang-an. When he came to Kao-ling 高陵[44] he stopped to rest, sending Sung Ch'ang to gallop ahead to Ch'ang-an to observe how the situation developed.

[415] When [Sung] Ch'ang came to the Wei 渭 Bridge,[45] the chancellor and all officials below him welcomed him. Sung Ch'ang returned to report. The King of Tai galloped to Wei Bridge. All the ministers knelt and bowed their heads to pay homage, declaring themselves his ministers. The King of Tai alighted from the chariot, knelt and bowed. The Grand Commandant, Chou Po, came forward and said, "I wish to speak [with you] alone." Sung Ch'ang said, "If what you say concerns public interests, then say it publicly. If what you say is a private matter, one who is king does not receive private requests." The Grand Commandant then knelt and submitted the seal and tallies of the Son of Heaven. The King of Tai declined and said, "Let us go to the Tai

but the word *yi* also appears in Yen Shih-ku's commentary, suggesting the version of *Han shu* Yen had seen also reads *ying li wang yi*. See Wang Hsien-ch'ien, *Han shu pu chu* 漢書補註, 4.2b.

[43]The parallel passage in *Shih chi*, 9.411 reads *ch'eng liu sheng-chuan* 乘六乘傳 "to ride in six post chariots" for *liu jen sheng chuan* 六人乘傳 "six men riding in the post chariot." *Han shu* (4.106) reads, "Chang Wu and others, six men in all, ride in *six* post chariots." Wang Shu-min (10.380) notices that an ancient manuscript of *Shih chi* has "to ride in six post chariots." Mizusawa (10.298) also points out that the Yen-chiu 延 久 and T'ao 桃 editions read "to ride in six post chariots." According to Ju Ch'un 如淳 (in *Han shu*, 1.57), there were three kinds of post chariots at that time, the one pulled by four fine horses was called *chih-chuan* 置傳; the one pulled by four average horses was called *ch'ih-chuan* 馳傳; the one pulled by four inferior horses was called *sheng-chuan* 乘傳. See also Chao K'o-yao 趙克堯, "Han-tai te chuan, sheng-chuan, yü chuan-she" 漢 代的傳,乘傳與傳舍, *Chiang-Han lun t'an*, 1984.12: 70-71, and Chang Chia-ying, pp. 187-88. It may appear strange to readers that the King of Tai should come to the capital by the slowest chariot. On the other hand, he may have deliberately chosen to do so in order to take some time to "observe how the situation developed."

[44]Kao-ling was located twenty miles northeast of Ch'ang-an (T'an Ch'i-hsiang, 2:15); Liu Pang's mausoleum was located there.

[45]There were three bridges over the Wei River (T'an Ch'i-hsiang, 2:15). They were called Central Wei Bridge (*Chung Wei* 中渭), Eastern Wei Bridge and Western Wei Bridge. Wang Li-ch'i (10.254) claims that the Wei Bridge in question was the Central Wei Bridge which was located north of the capital and about fifteen miles southwest of Kao-ling where the King of Tai was waiting. According to "So-yin," the bridge was built by King Chao 昭 of Ch'in (r. 306-251 B.C.), who intended to connect the palaces along the north and south sides of the Wei River through this bridge. However, it seems the bridge here may refer to the Eastern Wei Bridge, since according to "So-yin" (*Shih chi*, 102.2755), it was the Eastern Wei Bridge which was on the road to Kao-ling, a little over five miles southwest of Kao-ling. Although some modern scholars claim the Eastern Wei Bridge was not built until the reign of Emperor Ching (see *Shih chi tz'u-tien*, p. 566), according to "Cheng-yi" (*Shih chi*, 69.2246), the Ch'in troops went over the Eastern Wei Bridge to launch an attack against Hann, thus it is possible that the Eastern Wei Bridge may also have been built in the pre-Han period. Ho Ch'ing-ku 何清谷 in his *San-fu huang-t'u chiao-chu* 三輔黃圖校註 (Sian: San Ch'in, 1995, pp. 340-42) suggests that the Eastern Wei Bridge was built during the reign of the First Emperor of Ch'in and was rebuilt during the

Residence and discuss it."[46] Then he galloped off and entered the Tai Residence.[47] All the ministers followed him and arrived there. The Chancellor, Ch'en P'ing, the Grand Commandant, Chou Po, the Commander-in-chief, Ch'en Wu 陳武,[48] the Grand Master of the Imperial Scribes, Chang Ts'ang 張蒼,[49] the Director of the Imperial Clan, Liu Ying 劉郢,[50] the Marquis of Chu-hsü, Liu Chang 劉章, the Marquis of Tung-mou, Liu Hsing-chü 劉興居, and the Director of Guests, Liu Chieh 劉揭, all knelt and bowed their heads twice and said, "None of the [putative imperial] sons, [Liu] Hung 弘 and company, are sons of Emperor Hui 惠 the Filial (r. 195-188 B.C.).[51] They do not deserve to make offerings at the ancestral temple [of the imperial house]. Your ministers have respectfully asked the Marquise of Yin-an 陰安,[52] the ranking marquise Queen of King Ch'ing 頃,[53] **[416]** together with the King of Lang-ya,[54] members of the imperial clan, great

reign of Emperor Ching.

[46]According to *Shih chi chi-shuo* 史記集説 (10.2a), the Grand Commandant was unwise in both begging to speak to the king privately and bluntly submitting the imperial seal at Wei Bridge. By contrast, Sung Ch'ang established the prestige of his master by deflating Chou Po, then a celebrated minister.

[47]The King of Tai reached the Tai Residence on the *chi-yu* 己酉 day, the last day of the intercalary month after the ninth [month] (14 November 180 B.C.; *Shih chi*, 9.411). Dubs (1:227, n. 2) notes that this was forty-eight days after the Lü Clan was wiped out.

[48]Fu Ch'ien 服虔 (cited in Takigawa, 10.6) says the name should be Ch'ai Wu 柴武 instead of Ch'en Wu. According to *Shih chi*, 10.425 and 22.1126, Ch'en Wu was the Marquis of Chi-p'u 棘蒲 and he was not made the Commander-in-chief until 177 B.C. Liang Yü-sheng (7.251) found the same person was called both Ch'en Wu and Ch'ai Wu in *Shih chi* and *Han shu*, thus he suspects that this person had two *cognomen*s. *Han shu yin yi* 漢書音義 (cited in "Chi-chieh," *Shih chi*, 8.358) also maintains that both Ch'en and Ch'ai were his *cognomen*s. Ch'ien Ta-chao 錢大昭 (1744-1813, as quoted in *Han shu pu chu*, 4.3a) argues that the Commander-in-chief here must refer to Kuan Ying 灌嬰, not Ch'en Wu or Ch'ai Wu, since the relevant chapters in *Shih chi* and *Han shu* all indicated Kuan was the Commander-in-chief at that time, whereas Ch'en or Ch'ai did not become Commander-in-chief until 177 B.C.

[49]See his biography on *Shih chi*, 96.2675-85.

[50]He was a son of Liu Chiao 劉交, King Yüan 元 of Ch'u. Liang Yü-sheng (7.251) and Wang Nien-sun in his *Han shu tsa-chih* 漢書雜誌 (1.21a) argue the name should be Liu Ying-k'o 劉郢客. According to *Shih chi*, 50.1988 and *Han shu*, 4.108, Liu Chiao's son was Liu Ying. But according to *Shih chi*, 19.985, *Han shu*, 15.429, 19.753, and 36.1923, his *praenomen* was Ying-k'o. Perhaps this person had two *praenomen*s.

[51]Emperor Hui the Filial was Liu Ying 劉盈, the second son of Liu Pang. He became the emperor after Liu Pang died. Liu Hung was born to Emperor Hui's concubine. Empress Lü invested him as Emperor and he (and a predecessor) were both known as Shao Ti 少帝 (The Young Emperor). He was eventually killed by the great ministers on the first evening Emperor Wen entered the imperial palace.

[52]Yin-an was located about ten miles southwest of modern Nan-lo 南樂 County, Honan (T'an Ch'i-hsiang, 2:26).

[53]According to *Shih chi*, 18.967, King Ch'ing was Liu Chung 劉仲, Liu Pang's second eldest brother. Some commentators say that the Marquis of Yin-an and the Queen of King Ch'ing were the same person. Others argue that the Marquis of Yin-an was the wife of Liu Po 劉伯, Liu Pang's elder brother. Liang Yü-sheng (7.251) points out that it is not proper to put two women at the top of the official list and argues that

ministers, ranking marquises, officers of the rank of two thousand *shih*[55] to discuss this; they said, 'You, Great King, are the eldest [living] son of Kao-ti and are suitable to be the successor of Kao-ti.' We hope you, Great King, will ascend the throne of the Son of Heaven." The King of Tai said, "To make offerings at the ancestral temple of Kao-ti is a heavy responsibility. We are incompetent and not suitable to [make offerings at] the ancestral temple. We hope you will ask the King of Ch'u[56] to consider who is suitable. We dare not undertake this." All the ministers prostrated themselves and implored persistently. The King of Tai, facing west, declined three times, and then facing south, declined twice.[57] Chancellor [Ch'en] P'ing and the others all said, "Your ministers have humbly considered it. You, Great King, are the most suitable person to make offerings at the ancestral temple of Kao-ti. Even though the feudal lords and numerous commoners of the world regard you as suitable, your ministers consider this is for the sake of the ancestral temple and the altars of soil and grain and thereby do not venture to be remiss. We hope you, Great King, will favorably listen to your ministers. Your ministers respectfully hold the imperial seals and tallies of the Son of the Heaven, bow our heads twice, and submit [them to you]." The King of Tai said, "The imperial clan, generals, ministers, kings, and ranking marquises believe that no one is more suitable than We. We dare not decline." Then he ascended the throne of the Son of Heaven.

[417] All the ministers arranged themselves in attendance according to the social code of precedence. They sent the Grand Coachman, [Hsia-hou] Ying [夏侯]嬰,[58] and the Marquis of Tung-mou, Liu Hsing-chü, to clear the palace.[59] They led the standard equipage of the Son of Heaven[60] and welcomed him at the Tai Residence. At sunset of this day the emperor entered the

this may reflect vestiges of the customs of Empress Lü. Wu Shu-p'ing and Lu Zongli (10.350), on the other hand, argue that they are on the top of the list because they are the eldest among the members of the imperial house.

[54]See his biography on *Shih chi*, 51.1995-97.

[55]The officials of the rank of two-thousand *shih* constituted the highest rank at that time. The rank of ten-thousand *shih* was not created until 8 B.C. See Bielenstein, pp. 4-5.

[56]"So-yin" says the King of Tai wanted to consult with Liu Chiao, the King of Ch'u, because he was the most senior member in the imperial clan.

[57]As "Chi-chieh" (*Shih chi*, 10.417) points out, according to ancient social codes, the host should face west in receiving a guest, while the emperor should face south when he met his subjects. When the King of Tai received the great ministers, he first faced west, then faced south, indicating his change of status.

[58]See his biography on *Shih chi*, 95.2663-67.

[59]According to "Chi-chieh," when an emperor was to visit a place, he would send officers to go first and inspect it to make sure everything was in order. Here, clearing the palace was especially necessary because the Young Emperor (Shao-ti 少帝) and his guards were still living there. They had to be driven out before the King of Tai came. Actually, the king was still stopped by several armed internuncios when he was about to enter the palace. See the parallel account on *Shih chi*, 9.412, and our translation above.

[60]According to "So-yin," the Son of Heaven had two kinds of equipage: the Grand Equipage (*Ta chia* 大駕) and the Standard Equipage (*Fa chia* 法駕). The Grand Equipage was accompanied by eighty-one carriages, while the Standard Equipage was accompanied by thirty-six carriages. For a detailed description of

Wei-yang 未央 Palace,[61] and that night he appointed Sung Ch'ang as General of the Guards to control and calm the Southern and Northern Armies. He made Chang Wu Prefect of the Palace Attendants, to walk through the halls [of the palace]. He returned and took his seat[62] in the Front Hall.[63] That very night[64] he issued an edict, saying, "Recently the Lüs exercised power and arrogated authority to themselves. They plotted to commit high treason, intending thereby to endanger the Ancestral Temple of the Liu Clan. Thanks to the generals, ministers, ranking marquises, imperial clan, and great ministers, they have been executed, and have all accounted for their crimes. We have just ascended the throne. Let Us issue an amnesty throughout the world, grant one degree [increase] in noble rank to each commoner,[65] and oxen and wine[66] to women of every hundred households.[67] Let there be a bacchanal for five days."[68]

the Son of Heaven's equipage, see *Hou Han shu*, 29.3648-50.

[61]The Wei-yang Palace was located southwest of Ch'ang-an. This was the place where the Han emperors usually held court. For a description of this palace, see Wang Chung-shu, *Han Civilization* (New Haven: Yale University Press, 1982), pp. 4-5.

[62]According to the punctuation of Chung-hua editors (*Shih chi*, 10.417), the subject of the phrase *hsing tien chung* 行殿中 "to walk through the halls of the palace" is Chang Wu. Chang was appointed as the Prefect of the Palace Attendants, with the duty of patroling the palace. However, Dubs (1:230) proposed another reading which makes the subject of *hsing tien chung* the Emperor. According to this reading, it was the emperor who walked through the halls of the palace, then returning to the Front Hall.

[63]According to Wang Chung-shu (*Han Civilization*, p. 4), the Front Hall (*ch'ien-tien* 前殿) was actually located at the center of the Wei-yang Palace. Its foundation still remains.

[64]*Shih chi p'ing-lin* 史記評林 (10.3a) points out that in the narrative of this incident, Ssu-ma Ch'ien used the word *ch'ih* 馳 "to gallop" two times: 1) "the king of Tai galloped to the Wei Bridge;" and 2) "[the king] galloped off to the Tai residence." He used the word *yeh* 夜 (night) twice: 1) "[he] appointed Sung Ch'ang as General of the Guards on that night;" and 2) "[he] issued an edict on that night." This is because the situation was very critical and brooked no delay. This also shows he was amazingly quick in response to emergencies. It seems Ssu-ma Ch'ien may have deliberately used these two words to create a certain literary effect while he narrated this exciting and somewhat alarming historical moment. By contrast, Pan Ku only retained the word *yeh* in one instance and deleted the rest of the words in his parallel account in *Han shu*, 4.107-8, making his narrative less dramatic.

[65]During the time of Han, there were twenty degrees of noble rank. These were originally designed as rewards for services rendered to the state. Occasionally there were general grants of one degree of noble rank as an imperial bounty—on great imperial ceremonies such as accessions, the nomination of an imperial consort, or the investment of an imperial heir. The benefits of the noble rank include exemption from state services and mitigation of some punishments. See Loewe, "Rank."

[66]Although "So-yin" claims that Emperor Wen granted "one ox and ten *shih* of wine" to the commoners according to the "Feng Shan shu" 封禪書 (*Shih chi* Chapter 28), in the current version of "Feng Shan shu" there is no such record.

[67]"So-yin" says the oxen and wine were given to women without husbands or sons. But Yen Shih-ku (*Han shu*, 4.110) says they were given to wives of men who received an increase of degree in noble rank.

[68]According to the Han statutes (cited here in "Chi-chieh"), when three or more people gathered

[418] On the *keng-hsü* 庚戌 day of the tenth month of the first year of Emperor Wen the Filial (15 November 180 B.C.),[69] [Liu] Tse 劉澤, the previous King of Lang-ya, was transferred to be enthroned as King of Yen 燕.[70]

On the *hsin-hai* 辛亥 day (16 November 180 B.C.), the emperor ascended the Eastern Steps[71] and paid his homage at the Temple of Kao-ti.[72] The Chancellor of the Right, Ch'en P'ing, was transferred to the position of the Chancellor of the Left.[73] The Grand Commandant, Chou Po, was transferred to the position of the Chancellor of the Right.[74] The Commander-in-chief, Kuan Ying 灌嬰,[75] was made the Grand Commandant. The territories in Ch'i and Ch'u previously seized by the Lüs were returned to their rightful owners.[76]

On the *jen-tzu* 壬子 day (17 November 180 B.C.), [the emperor] dispatched the General of Chariots and Cavalry, Po Chao, to escort the Empress Dowager from Tai. The emperor said, "Lü Ch'an set himself up as the Chancellor of State,[77] and Lü Lu became the Senior General.

together to drink without a reason, they would be fined four taels of gold. Only with the permission of the state could people hold a bacchanal. See also *Grand Scribe's Records,* 1:134, n. 118.

[69]The tenth month was still the first month of the year (it remained so until 104 B.C., see Bodde, *Festivals,* pp. 145ff.).

[70]The state of Yen was in the northern part of modern Hopei. Its capital was Chi 薊 (about five miles southwest of modern Peking). According to *Han shu,* 4.110, this transfer took place in the twelfth month. It seems very unlikely that Emperor Wen would transfer the position of a king before he ascended the throne.

[71]According to Wu Shu-p'ing and Lu Zongli (10.351), the Eastern Steps of the ancestral temple were called *tso* 阼. Only the ruler of the country or the head of a clan could ascend such steps. Paying homage at the ancestral temple was an important ceremony when an emperor was about to ascend the throne.

[72]Liang Yü-sheng (7.252) argues the account here may be mistaken. Since Emperor Wen entered the capital on the last day of the intercalary month after the ninth [month], it would have been proper for him to ascend the throne on the next day (*keng-hsü* day), which was the first day of the tenth month and the beginning of the year according to the early Han calendar. Then he paid homage to the ancestral temple on the third (*hsin-hai*) day.

[73]The Chancellor of the Right was considered to be a higher position than the Chancellor of the Left (see Bielenstein, p. 7).

[74]Liang Yü-sheng (7.252) argues the change of the positions of Ch'en P'ing, Chou Po, and Kuan Ying did not take place in the tenth month, since according to *Shih chi,* 22.1125, these changes occurred in the eleventh month. Moreover, in the following edict, the emperor still called Chou Po "Grand Commandant Chou Po," indicating his position was not yet changed.

[75]See his biography on *Shih chi,* 95.2667-73.

[76]According to Takigawa (10.11), Empress Lü 呂 made Lü Yi 呂台 the King of Lu, and seized land from Ch'u and Ch'i so as to enlarge Lu's territory. According to *Han shu* (4.110), this event took place in the twelfth month.

[77]Wu Shu-p'ing and Lu Zongli (10.351) say *hsiang-kuo* 相國 and *ch'eng-hsiang* 丞相 were the same position. Fu Chü-yu 傅舉有 argues that *hsiang-kuo* was a higher position. See Fu Chü-yu, "Han-tai hsiang-kuo ch'eng-hsiang wei liang kuan" 漢代相國丞相為兩官, *Wen shih,* 26 (1986): 347-50. Miao Wen-yüan

They presumptuously falsified an order and dispatched General Kuan Ying to command troops and assault Ch'i, intending to replace the Liu Clan. Kuan Ying remained at Hsing-yang 榮陽[78] and did not attack. He plotted jointly with the feudal lords to execute the Lü Clan. As Lü Ch'an was up to no good, Chancellor Ch'en P'ing and Grand Commandant Chou Po plotted to seize the troops of Lü Ch'an and the others. The Marquis of Chu-hsü, Liu Chang, first arrested Lü Ch'an and the others. The Grand Commandant personally guided the Marquis of Hsiang-p'ing 襄平,[79] [Chi] T'ung [紀]通, to carry the caduceus, bear the imperial edict, and enter the Northern Army. The Director of Guests, Liu Chieh, personally seized the seal of the King of Chao 趙,[80] Lü Lu.[81] Now let there be added to the fief of the Grand Commandant Chou Po ten thousand households, and grant him five thousand *chin* of gold;[82] to the fiefs of Chancellor Ch'en P'ing and General Kuan Ying three thousand households and two thousand *chin* of gold each; to the fiefs of the Marquis of Chu-hsü, Liu Chang, the Marquis of Hsiang-p'ing, Chi T'ung, and the Marquis of Tung-mou, Liu Hsing-chü, two thousand households and one thousand *chin* of gold each; let the Director of Guests Liu Chieh be enfeoffed as Marquis of Yang-hsin 陽信,[83] and grant him one thousand *chin* of gold."

In the twelfth month (13 January-11 February 179 B.C.), the sovereign said,[84] "The laws are the rectification of administration and the means of restraining violence and guiding good men. Today though a man who violates the law is already sentenced, still we cause his

---

繆文遠 in his *Ch'i-kuo k'ao ting pu* 七國考訂補 (Shanghai: Shang-hai Ku-chi, 1987) argues that *hsiang-kuo* was originally called *hsiang-pang* 相邦 under Ch'in. He claims that the name was changed to *hsiang-kuo* in the Han period because of the taboo of Liu Pang's name. He also notes that the name of *ch'eng-hsiang* first appeared during the reign of the First Emperor of Ch'in (Miao Wen-yüan, pp. 2-5). Bielenstein (p. 7) notes that the title *ch'eng-hsiang* was in use from the beginning of the Han dynasty. It was changed to *hsiang-kuo* in 196 B.C., and in 189 B.C. the earlier title was restored.

[78]Northeast of modern Hsing-hsiang County, Honan (T'an Ch'i-hsiang, 2:16). According to *Shih chi*, 9.407, after Kuan Ying reached Hsing-yang, he sent an envoy to the King of Ch'i, informing him that he planned to ally with the feudal lords to execute the Lüs.

[79]According to T'an Ch'i-hsiang (2:28), it was in modern Liao-yang 遼陽, Liaoning. But Wang Li-ch'i (10.256) follows "So-yin" and locates it northwest of modern Hsü-yi 肝眙, Kiangsu.

[80]It seems inappropriate for Emperor Wen to call Lü Lu "King of Chao" in his edict. Liang Yü-sheng (7.252), based on a parallel text in *Han shu*, 4.110, argues that the words "King of Chao" should be deleted.

[81]For a detailed account of the struggle between the great ministers and the Lü Clan, see *Shih chi*, 9.407-10.

[82]One *chin* of gold (= 245 g) was nominally worth 10,000 cash in copper coins (see *Cambridge History of China*, 1:589).

[83]Northeast of modern Yang-hsing County, Shantung (T'an Ch'i-hsiang, 2:27).

[84]Pan Ku moved the following long discussion concerning the laws of the prosecution and enslavement of criminals' relatives to *Han shu*, 23.1104-5. *Han shu* also dated this event in the second year of Emperor Wen's reign. Ch'ien Ta-chao 錢大昭 (in *Han shu pu chu* 漢書補註, 23.17b) lists a number of pieces of evidence to show that the *Han shu* dating was incorrect.

innocent parents, wife, children, and siblings [born] of the same father or mother[85] also to be prosecuted for it, and take them as slaves.[86] We surely cannot accept this. Let this be discussed."[87]

The authorities concerned[88] all said, "The commoners are unable to administer themselves. Therefore we make laws to restrain them. [*419*] To be prosecuted for another's crimes and to take [as slaves] those who are prosecuted for their being related to criminals[89] are ways to encumber the people's minds and make them weigh the consequences of breaking the law. This [practice] came into being a long time ago. To do as before will be advantageous."

The sovereign said, "We have heard that if the laws are rectified, then the commoners will be prudent and respectful. If crimes are punished properly, then the commoners will follow [the law]. Furthermore, he who shepherds the commoners and guides them toward the good is a

---

[85]The original term is *t'ung-ch'an* 同產. Wang Li-ch'i (10.256) says this refers to brothers and sisters born by the same mother. Recently T'ao T'ien-yi 陶天翼 examined a number of occurrences of this term in Han texts and defined it as "brothers and sisters of same parents or of the same father but a different mother." See T'ao T'ien-yi, "Shih t'ung-ch'an" 釋同產, in Hsü Cho-yün 許倬雲, *et al.*, eds. *Chung-kuo t'u-shu wen-shih lun-chi* 中國圖書文史論集 (Peking: Hsien-tai Ch'u-pan-she, 1992), pp. 351-75.

[86]The practice of prosecuting the relatives of a criminal originated in Ch'in law. According to *Shih chi*, 68.2230, when the Lord of Shang 商 (ca. 390-338 B.C.) introduced institutional reform in Ch'in, he put commoners in groups of five and ten households with each member of the group guiding and watching the others and each responsible for the others' crimes. By the time of the Second Emperor of Ch'in, the law was made more severe by having those who had committed crimes implicate each other in their punishment and include their entire clan (*Shih chi*, 87.2553). See also A. F. P. Hulsewé, "Ch'in and Han Law," in *Cambridge History of China*, 1:523.

[87]*Shih chi p'ing-lin* (10.4a) points out that neither Ssu-ma Ch'ien's account of Kao-ti nor his account of Emperor Ching recorded the emperor's edicts. Only in this chapter are the texts of the edicts and claims "the sovereign said" (*shang yüeh* 上曰) given. This is to show that the edicts stemmed from the emperor's true feelings. According to *Han shu*, 51.2335, the virtue of the emperor transformed the commoners so successfully that even old men would lean on their sticks to listen to the imperial edicts. It is noteworthy that the parallel edicts in *Han shu* usually begin with the phrase "the edict said" (*chao yüeh* 詔曰); Pan Ku never uses the phrase "the sovereign said" to begin an edict. On the other hand, the "Basic Annals of Emperor Wu" of *Shih chi* also uses "the edict says" to begin an edict. Dubs (*History of Former Han*, 1:234) likewise noticed in one instance *Shih chi* has *shang yüeh* for *chao yüeh* and he believes this indicates a speech by the emperor. It seems Ssu-ma Ch'ien's use of "the sovereign said" may be intended to add a personal touch to his narrative, whereas Pan Ku's "the edict said" renders his version in an impersonal, historical mode.

[88]In *Han shu* (23.1104), it was Chou Po and Ch'en P'ing who submitted the memorial to the emperor.

[89]*Tso shou* 坐收 is difficult to interpret here. Wang Shu-min (10.383) suggests this phrase may be an error and he argues *chi shou* 及收 "and take them as slaves" in *Han shu* (23.1104) may be the correct reading. On the other hand, Chang Chia-yin argues that the word *tso shou* means "to imprison those who are prosecuted for their relationship with the criminals." See Chang Chia-ying, pp. 190-91. The fact that the *Shih chi* variant presents a more difficult reading may suggests *tso shou* was likely from the original *Shih chi* text and Pan Ku may have simplified the *Shih chi* wording in his *Han shu*.

government officer. If he not only cannot guide them, but also uses unrectified laws to punish them, he will, on the contrary, do harm to commoners and cause violence himself. How can you restrain them? We have not yet seen its advantage. Let this be carefully considered."

The authorities concerned all said, "Your Majesty exerts great kindness. Your virtue is so grand that your ministers could never attain it. We beg to act on your edict and abolish the statutes and ordinances concerning prosecuting and enslaving criminals' relatives." [90]

In the first month (12 February-12 March 179 B.C.), the authorities concerned proposed, "To establish the Heir early is the way to honor the ancestral temple. We beg you to install the Heir."

The sovereign said, "We already are without virtue. The Supreme Deity and other deities have not partaken of Our offerings. The people of the world have not fulfilled their desire. Now even if We cannot extensively seek the world's [most] worthy, sagacious, and virtuous man and yield the world to him, to say 'establish the Heir beforehand' is to double our being without virtue. How shall we explain this to the world? Let this be laid aside."

The authorities concerned said, "To establish the Heir beforehand is the way by which to give weight to the ancestral temple and the altars of soil and grain and not to forget about the world."[91]

The sovereign said, "The King of Ch'u is our younger uncle. He is advanced in years and has seen much of the righteousness and principles of the world. He is clear about the cardinal tenets of the country. The King of Wu[92] is an elder brother to Us. He is kind, benevolent and fond of virtue.[93] The King of Huai-nan is a younger brother to Us. He embraces virtue to assist Us. How can they not be consulted beforehand? The noble kings, members of the imperial clan, our elder and younger brothers, and meritorious ministers, many of them are worthy and possess virtue and righteousness. If you recommended a man of virtue to assist Us for what We could not accomplish [alone], it would be a blessing to the altars of soil and grain and the fortune of the world. Now you do not choose to recommend them, instead you say the Heir must

[90]Although Emperor Wen abolished this law, it seems the law was either restored later or it could still have been applied to certain people whose crimes were regarded as the most heinous, as in the case when Hsin-yüan P'ing 新垣平 was found guilty of deceiving the Sovereign and his clan wiped out (*Shih chi*, 10.430). In another case, the Emperor intended to wipe out the clan of a person who had stolen a jade ring from the ancestral temple of Kao-ti (*Shih chi*, 102.2755). Ch'ü T'ung-tsu argues this law was abolished only for a short period and remained in effect throughout the rest of the Han dynasty. See Ch'ü T'ung-tsu, *Han Social Structure* (Seattle: University of Washington Press, 1972), p. 136.

[91]As Lü Tsu-ch'ien 呂祖謙 (1137-1181, cited in *Shih chi p'ing-lin*, 10.4b) pointed out, Emperor Ching (then Emperor Wen's eldest son) was only ten years old in the first year of Emperor Wen. The reason the great ministers urged him to establish the Heir was that Kao-ti's hesitation in establishing his successor had led the Lü Clan to usurp power.

[92]The King of Wu was actually a cousin of Emperor Wen.

[93]As Watson (1: 291) points out, the parallel passage in *Han shu* (4.111) omits the sentence "he is kind, benevolent, and fond of virtue," probably because the King of Wu later revolted in the reign of Emperor Ching. Thus, the presence of the sentence here strongly speaks for the authenticity of the speech.

be Our son. People will consider We have forgotten those worthy and virtuous men and care only for [Our] son. This is not the way to be concerned about the world. We surely cannot accept this."

The authorities concerned all implored him, saying, "In ancient times, when Yin and Chou possessed the state, both administered it peacefully for over one thousand years.[94] That no dynasty in ancient times which possessed the world lasted longer than them is because they [Yin and Chou] employed this way.[95] That it must be a son who is installed as successor is a practice that came into being a long time ago.[96] Kao-ti, in personally leading knights and great officers, was the first to pacify the world and establish the feudal lords, and he became the grand ancestor of the emperors. The noble kings and ranking marquises who first received their states also all became the ancestors of their states. To have sons and grandsons continue in succession from generation to generation without end is the great principle of the world. Therefore, Kao-ti set up [this practice] to placate the land within the Four Seas. Now if we renounce the person who is suitable to be installed and instead [*420*] choose someone else from the feudal lords or the imperial clan, this will not be Kao-ti's intention. It is not fitting to discuss this issue again. Son so-and-so[97] is the eldest. He is pure, honest, benevolent and lenient. We beg you to establish him as the Heir."

The sovereign then consented to them and accordingly granted to every commoner due to succeed his father one degree of noble rank. He enfeoffed General Po Chao as Marquis of Chih 軹.[98]

[94]As Ch'ien Ta-hsin 錢大昕 (1728-1804, *Nien-erh shih k'ao yi* 廿二史考異 [Rpt. 2v. Taipei: Chung-wen Ch'u-pan-she, 1980], 1:1.10-11) points out, neither Yin or Chou possessed the world more than one thousand years. Thus, "over one thousand years" was a loose term and it may include the period of the ancestors of Chou and Yin. *Han shu* (4.111) reads "both administered it peacefully for nearly one thousand years," attempting to make the statement much precise.

[95]That is, the way of establishing the heir.

[96]As Ch'en Shu-kuo 陳戍國 points out, this statement is actually not true, since during the Yin dynasty, the successor to the throne was not necessarily the son of the ruler. The younger brother could also inherit the throne from his elder brother. See Ch'en Shu-kuo, *Ch'in Han li-chih yen-chiu* 秦漢禮制研究 (Changsha: Hu-nan Chiao-yü, 1993), p. 89.

[97]This refers to Liu Ch'i 劉啟, the eldest living son of Emperor Wen. He later became Emperor Ching 景 (r. 156-141 B.C.). The historian employed the character *mou* 某 "so-and-so" to avoid the taboo on using the *praenomen* of an emperor. On the other hand, the parallel passage in *Han shu* (4.111) directly supplies Ch'i 啟. In *Shih chi* (10.422), the text reads, 以告朕, whereas the parallel in *Han shu* (4.116) reads 以啟告朕. In both cases, *Shih chi* employed the taboo of an emperor's *praenomen* whereas *Han shu* did not. *Han shu pu chu* (4.6b) suggests this may be due to the reason that Pan Ku did not have to use the taboo for an emperor of the remote past. Ch'ien Ta-hsin (op. cit., 1:1.11) also points out that even in *Shih chi* the rule for taboos is not consistent. The *praenomen* of Emperor Wen appears in the "Basic Annals of Kao-tsu," and the *praenomen* of Emperor Wu appears in the "Basic Annals of Emperor Ching."

[98]Chih is located southeast of modern Chi-yüan 濟源 County in Honan (T'an Ch'i-hsiang, 2:16). According to "Chi-chieh" (in *Shih chi*, 10.420), this appointment took place in the first month, but *Shih chi*,

In the third month (12 April-10 May 179 B.C.), the authorities concerned begged the emperor to install an empress. The Empress Dowager Po said, "Since the feudal lords all have the same *cognomen* [as that of the emperor],[99] let the Heir's mother be installed as empress." The *cognomen* of the empress was Tou 竇.[100] Because the sovereign installed the empress, he granted to each of the world's widowers and widows, orphans and childless,[101] and the poor and distressed, along with those who were over eighty years old, and orphans who were below nine, a certain amount of cloth, silk, grain and meat.[102] The sovereign came from Tai.[103] Soon after he ascended

19.994, indicates that it happened in the fourth month.

[99]Another reading of this sentence is proposed by "So-yin," which interprets *t'ung hsing* 同姓 as "to be born by the same mother." Thus, the sentence became, "since the feudal lords [referring to the emperor's sons] are all born by the same mother, let the Heir's mother be installed as empress." This reading is problematic. First, it seems strange that the term *chu-hou* 諸侯, usually a general collective noun for the leaders of all the states or kingdoms, can be used here to refer specifically to only the imperial sons. Secondly, it is incorrect to state that the imperial sons were all born by the same mother. Actually, Empress Tou 竇 only gave birth to two of the imperial sons (*Shih chi*, 49.1972). Both Ku Yen-wu 顧炎武 (1613-1682) and Ho Ch'o 何焯 (1661-1722, cited in Takigawa, 10.16-17) rejected this reading. They argued that the Son of Heaven was previously supposed to take his queen from a family of the feudal lords, according to the old custom of the Chou, but in Han times the situation has changed: since all the feudal lords had the same *cognomen* as the imperial house, it was impossible for the emperor to select an empress from the families of the feudal lords. It should also be pointed out that Empress Tou was from humble origins (*Shih chi*, 49.1973). Her younger brother was sold at an early age because her family was poor. Thus, it seems there may have been some debate at that time as to who should be chosen as the empress. The Empress Dowager's statement here was probably meant as an argument against some of the great ministers' proposals, which may have suggested that the empress should be chosen from a noble family. The *Han shu* (4.113) deleted this sentence, probably because it is hard to understand without the proper context. See further discussion in the "Translator's Note."

[100]She was called Tou Chi 竇姬 (Beauty Tou). See her biography on *Shih chi*, 49.1972-75.

[101]I.e., *kuan kua ko tu* 鰥寡孤獨. It seems Mencius first raised the idea that a virtuous ruler should take care of these people, "The old and wifeless are called widowers; the old and husbandless are called widows; the old and childless are called solitaries; the young and fatherless are called orphans: —these four classes are the most destitute of the people, and have none to whom they can tell their wants, and King Wen, in the institution of his government with its benevolent action, made them the first objects of his regard" (translation from Legge, *The Chinese Classics*, 2:162).

[102]The parallel passage in *Han shu* (4.113) includes an edict by Emperor Wen concerning this grant. As Liang Yü-sheng (7.253) points out, the edict in *Han shu* did not mention giving food and clothes to the orphans under the age of nine. This seems to provide further support that the current *Shih chi* text of this chapter was not copied from *Han shu*. If a scribe or scholar were to have used the *Han shu* as the base text, there would be no account of giving food and clothes to orphans in the *Shih chi* version, since this does not appear in the *Han shu*. Since the *Han shu* relies on the edict, it seems most probable that Ssu-ma Ch'ien did not have this edict at hand (NB: there are other edicts copied verbatim into the text), but used another source or sources, when he compiled this chapter; Pan Ku, realizing this, added the edict to his account.

[103]Before Emperor Wen became the emperor, he had been the King of Tai for seventeen years

the throne, he spread favor and kindness to the world and placated the feudal lords. The Barbarians of the Four Directions were all harmonious and elated. Then he glorified those meritorious ministers who followed him from Tai.[104] The sovereign said, "At the time when the great ministers executed the Lüs and invited Us, We were as suspicious as a fox,[105] and all [the officials] detained Us [from going]. Only the Commandant of the Capital, Sung Ch'ang, encouraged Us [to go]. We thereby are able to protect and make offerings at the ancestral temple. We have already honored him by making him the General of the Guards, now let Us enfeoff [Sung] Ch'ang as Marquis of Chuang-wu 壯武.[106] As for those six men who followed Us [to the capital], all their official positions will reach the rank of the Nine Ministers."[107]

[421] The sovereign said, "To each of the fiefs of all those sixty-eight ranking marquises

(*Shih chi,* 10.413). The sentence "the sovereign came from Tai" seems abrupt here in the narrative. On the other hand, Ssu-ma Ch'ien may have intended this sentence to give pause in his narrative as well as to comment on Emperor Wen's achievements during the first months of his reign. In fact, the sentence "Emperor Wen came from Tai" is repeated in the following passage (10.433), echoing the sentence here. It is followed by Ssu-ma Ch'ien's long summary of Emperor Wen's virtuous rule. Pan Ku obviously did not admire this peculiar style of Ssu-ma Ch'ien and hence did not record the sentence in both instances. It is interesting to note that the parallel passage on *Han shu,* 4.114, gives an account of negative portents such as earthquakes, landslides, and floods. Ssu-ma Ch'ien may have omitted these accounts in his attempt to bolster the image of a virtuous ruler, as will be discussed in detail in the "Translator's Note."

[104]The original sentence is 乃循從代來功臣. The meaning of the word *hsün* 循 in this sentence seems obscure. Liang Yü-sheng (7.253) cited two readings from previous scholars. The first, by Yü Yu-ting 余有丁 (1527-1584) cited in *Shih chi p'ing-lin* 史記評林, argues that the word *hsün* here means "to make [rewards] reach each person in proper order." Ho Ch'o 何焯 (1611-1722) in his *Yi-men tu-shu chi* 義門讀書記 notes that the parallel passage in *Han shu* reads *hsiu* 脩 for *hsün,* and argues that the *Han shu* reading is more likely from the original *Shih chi* text. Liang Yü-sheng believes Ho Ch'o's reading is better. He points out that in the ancient script 脩 and 循 were similar and this similarity probably caused the word *hsiu* to be miscopied as *hsün* in the text here. He further cited two other passages in the *Shih chi* with similar problems in support of his reading. On *Shih chi,* 26. 1260, the original text should be 朕唯未能脩明 也, but the current text was corrupted and became 朕唯未能循明也. In *Shih chi,* 22.1126, the name of the Marquis of Shen-tse 深澤 should be Hsiu 脩, but the current text was also corrupted and became Hsün 循. Wang Shu-min (10.386), Wang Hsien-ch'ien (*Han shu pu chu,* 4.8a), and Chang Wen-hu (1.103) all support this reading. Mizusawa (10.300) notices that several ancient Japanese editions read *hsiu* for *hsün* here. It is noteworthy that a similar sentence occurs in *Shih chi,* 6.290: 脩先王功臣, "[King Chuang-hsiang 莊襄 of Ch'in] glorified the meritorious vassals of the Late King." The sentence has exactly the same structure as the above sentence, but the verb here is *hsiu.* This further confirms Liang's idea that the original word was *hsiu* instead of *hsün.*

[105]On *hu yi* 狐疑, Yen Shih-ku (in *Han shu,* 4.115) notes that the fox was suspicious by nature.

[106]Chuang-wu was located about twenty miles northwest of modern Chi-mo 即墨 County in Shantung (T'an Ch'i-hsiang, 2:20).

[107]This refers to the senior officers of the nine most important central government offices. Their rank was surpassed only by the Three Excellencies (*san kung* 三公; see Bielenstein, p. 17).

who followed Kao-ti to enter Shu 蜀[108] and Han-chung 漢中,[109] three hundred households will be added. Tsun 尊,[110] Governor of Ying-ch'uan 穎川,[111] and nine other former officers who were above the rank of two thousand *shih* will be given a fief manor of six hundred households; Shen-t'u Chia 申徒嘉,[112] the Governor of Huai-yang 淮陽,[113] and nine other men, five hundred households; And Ting 定[114] the Commandant of the Guards, and nine other men, four hundred households. Let Us enfeoff Chao Chien 趙兼, the King of Huai-nan's maternal uncle, as Marquis of Chou-yang 周陽,[115] Ssu Chün 駟鈞, the King of Ch'i's maternal uncle,[116] as Marquis of Ching-kuo 清郭."[117] In the autumn, he enfeoffed Ts'ai Chien 蔡兼, the previous Chancellor of Ch'ang-shan 常山,[118] as Marquis of Fan 樊.[119]

[108]Shu was a commandery located in central modern Szechwan with its seat at Ch'eng-tu 成都 (modern Chengtu; T'an Ch'i-hsiang, 2:11).

[109]Han-chung was a commandery located in the southern part of modern Shensi with its seat at Nan-Cheng 南鄭 (modern Han-chung City in Shensi; T'an Ch'i-hsiang, 2:11). After Ch'in collapsed, Liu Pang was made the King of Han 漢, governing the Shu and Han-chung regions (*Shih chi*, 8.365). Therefore, those officers who had followed him to those areas were regarded as the senior meritorious vassals at the time of Emperor Wen.

[110]Otherwise not mentioned in *Shih chi*.

[111]Ying-ch'uan was a commandery located in the central part of Honan with its seat at Yang-ti 陽翟 (modern Yü 禹 County in Honan; T'an Ch'i-hsiang, 2:19).

[112]See his biography on *Shih chi*, 96.2682-84. In *Han shu*, 4.115, his name is given as Shen-t'u Chia 申屠嘉. Wang Nien-sun (1.23a-b) argues *t'u* 徒 and *t'u* 屠 were interchangeable in antiquity.

[113]Huai-yang was a commandery located in the eastern part of Honan with its seat at Ch'en 陳 County (modern Huai-yang County in Honan; T'an Ch'i-hsiang, 2:19).

[114]Otherwise not mentioned in *Shih chi*. In *Han shu*, 4:115, the name is written as Tsu 足.

[115]Chou-yang was located southwest of modern Chiang 絳 County in Shansi (T'an Ch'i-hsiang, 2:16).

[116]Ssu Chün was regarded as an evil person by the great ministers (*Shih chi*, 9.411). At that time he probably held the position of chancellor in the state of Ch'i (*Shih chi*, 52.2001). Thus, it seems this enfeoffment was to weaken his control over the state of Ch'i. See also n. 190 to our translation of Chapter 9 above.

[117]"Chi-chieh" says the word 清 should be pronounced *ching* 靜. In *Han shu*, 4.115, the name is Ching-kuo 靖郭. In the "Hui Ching chien hou-che nien-piao" 惠景閒侯者年表 (Yearly Table of the Marquises from Emperor Hui through Emperor Ching, *Shih chi*, 19.995), the name of the place is Ching-tu 清都. Liang Yü-sheng (7.254) argued Ching-kuo 靖郭 should be the correct reading. Since Ssu Chün was the maternal uncle of the King of Ch'i, he must have been enfeoffed at a place in that state, and Ching-kuo was located in Ch'i, whereas Ch'ing-tu is never given as a place-name elsewhere in *Shih chi* or *Han shu*. Ch'en Chih 陳直 (*Shih chi hsin cheng*, p. 34) examined the clay impressions of official seals of the Han era and concluded the name should be Ch'ing-kuo 請郭. Wang Shu-min (10.387) says the words 清, 靖, and 請 were all interchangeable in antiquity. Wang Li-ch'i (10.258) suggests that it was Ching-kuo-yi 靖郭邑 of the Warring States period, which was located in modern T'eng 滕 County in Shantung.

[118]The state of Ch'ang-shan occupied parts of Hopei and Shansi with its seat at Yüan-shih 元氏

Someone admonished the Chancellor of the Right, saying, "Originally you executed the Lüs and invited the King of Tai. Now you are boastful of your merits, receive the sovereign's rewards and occupy an honorable position. Misfortune is about to befall you." The Chancellor of the Right, [Chou] Po, then pleaded illness and was removed from his office.[120] The Chancellor of the Left, Ch'en P'ing, acted alone as the chancellor.

[422] In the tenth month of the second year (5 November-3 December 179 B.C.), the Chancellor, Ch'en P'ing, expired. The emperor again made the Marquis of Chiang, Chou Po, the chancellor.[121] The sovereign said, "We have heard that in antiquity, feudal lords established over one thousand states.[122] Each guarded his own territory and entered [the court] to pay tribute at the proper time. Thus the commoners were not overworked. Both the sovereign and his subjects were elated and there was no virtue which was neglected. Now most of the ranking marquises reside in Ch'ang-an. Their fiefs are far away. Their officers and soldiers are put to expense and hard labor transporting supplies for them. Moreover, the ranking marquises do not have a chance to teach and instruct their commoners. Let the ranking marquises be ordered to go to their states. Those who are acting as court officers or who are retained by imperial edicts will send their heirs [to their states]."

On the last day of the eleventh month (2 January 178 B.C.), there was an eclipse of the sun. On the fifteenth day of the twelfth month (17 January 178 B.C.), there was again an eclipse of the sun.[123] The sovereign said, "We have heard this: Heaven begot the multitude of commoners, and for them sets up a lord to nourish and govern them.[124] If the ruler of men is not virtuous, and if his administration of government is not fair, then Heaven will show him disasters so as to warn him of his bad administration. Now on the last day of the eleventh month, there was an eclipse of the sun. Condemnation has appeared in Heaven. What disaster can be greater than that? We were chosen to protect the ancestral temple. With an insignificant body, We are entrusted with a position above the millions of commoners, lords, and kings. The order or disorder of the world depends on Us, a single man, with only those two or three ministers holding [the powers

(northwest of modern Yüan-shih County in Shansi; See T'an Ch'i-hsiang, 2:26).

[119]Fan was located about ten miles southwest of modern Yen-chou 兗州 in Shantung (T'an Ch'i-hsiang, 2:19).

[120]According to "Chi-chieh," this took place in the middle of the eighth month. A parallel account of this event can be found in *Shih chi,* 57.2072, and *Han shu,* 40.2055. For a discussion of Ssu-ma Ch'ien's accounts of Chou Po's resignation, see Grant Hardy, *Worlds,* pp. 74-75.

[121]According to *Shih chi,* 22.1125, Chou Po's position was not restored until the eleventh month.

[122]The original text reads "the feudal lords established states for over one thousand years" 諸侯建國 千餘歲. On *Han shu,* 4.115, there is no character *sui* 歲 "year." Wang Nien-sun (1.23b) argues the word *sui* is redundant. The Chung-hua editors have also deleted the character *sui.*

[123]It is impossible for a solar eclipse to occur in the middle of the lunar month. A solar eclipse can take place only on the day of new moon when the Moon lies between the Sun and the Earth. Chang Wen-hu and others (Takigawa, 10.19) suggested the word "sun" may be a mistake for "moon." For a detailed discussion of these two eclipses, see Dubs, 1:284.

[124]This sentence is based on *Tso chuan* (Yang, *Tso chuan,* Hsiang 14, p. 1016).

of] the government like Our legs and arms. Below, We cannot govern and rear the living creatures; above, [We] obstruct the brilliance of the Three Lights.[125] So great is Our lack of virtue.[126] After this order arrives, let all consider Our faults, as well as what We cannot come up to in understanding, vision, and thinking. We beg you to tell Us these things and to recommend worthy, good, straight, and upright men,[127] who are able to speak straightforwardly and admonish Us unflinchingly. By this means, you can remedy Our shortcomings. Everyone should take this opportunity to overhaul his official duties and endeavor to reduce corvée and expenses so as to benefit the commoners. Since We are not able to extend Our virtue far, [We] thereby are anxiously concerned that there might be misconduct among the foreigners. Because of this, We cannot cease our preparations [against the enemy]. Now even though [We] cannot dismiss the frontier garrisons, how can [We] further overhaul the troops and strengthen the palace guards? Let the troops of the General of the Guards be dismissed.[128] As for the horses currently in the Grand Coachman's Office, let enough be kept and all the rest be sent to the post stations."

[423] In the first month (1 February-2 March 178 B.C.),[129] the sovereign said, "Agriculture is the basis of the world.[130] Let Us open up the Chi 籍 Field.[131] We will personally lead the

[125]The Three Lights refer to the sun, the moon, and the stars.

[126]Takigawa (10.20) pointed out that beginning with Emperor Wen, people related celestial phenomena to the secular, especially political, events. Since that time, moreover, emperors would issue edicts to criticize themselves whenever a solar eclipse occurred.

[127]The original text here reads: *hsien-liang fang-cheng* 賢良方正 "worthy, good, straight and upright." Wang Li-ch'i (10.258) says that beginning from this edict of Emperor Wen, Han set up the recommendatory system called *Hsien-liang fang-cheng* to select talented people and make them officials (see also Bielenstein, p. 133).

[128]Below (10.425), Emperor Wen is said to have put the Capital Commandant's crack soldiers under the control of the General of the Guards in 177 B.C. Thus his troops were either not totally disbanded in 178 B.C. or were restored the following year with the infusion of the new soldiers from the Capital Commandant.

[129]The parallel passage in *Han shu* (4.117) has "on the *ting-hai* 丁亥 day of the first month" instead of "in the first month."

[130]As *Shih chi p'ing-lin* (10.8b) points out, the reason that Emperor Wen started to attach importance to agriculture may be that he was influenced by Chia Yi 賈誼 (200-168 B.C.), who submitted a memorial urging him to encourage people to be engaged in agriculture soon after he ascended the throne (see *Han shu*, 24.1127-30).

[131]Although commentators generally agree that the Chi Field (*Chi T'ien* 籍田) was cultivated by the emperor so as to offer sacrifices to the altar of soil and grain, they have different ideas about the meaning of the word *chi*. One reading (cited in "Chi-chieh") maintains *chi* means "to borrow," because the emperor mainly borrows the commoner's labor to till the land; the other reading (also cited in "Chi-chieh") claims it means "to step," since the emperor personally stepped on the land to cultivate it. This institution stemmed from the pre-Ch'in period. *Kuo yü* 國語 (1. 11a) records a speech in which a minister admonished King Hsüan 宣 of Chou (r. 827-782 B.C.) to cultivate the Chi field. Wei Chao 韋昭 in his commentary says it was an old institution for the Son of Heaven to have a Chi Field of one thousand *mu*, and for the feudal lords to have a Chi Field of one hundred *mu*. Hsu Cho-yun claims by issuing this edict Emperor Wen revived a tradition of semireligious

ploughing so as to provide the ancestral temple with millet and grain to be held in sacrificial utensils."[132]

In the third month (1-30 April 178 B.C.), the authorities concerned requested [the emperor] to enthrone imperial sons as noble kings.[133] The sovereign said, "King Yu 幽 of Chao[134] died in confinement.[135] Our pity for him is extreme. We have already enthroned his eldest son [Liu] Sui 遂[136] as King of Chao. [Liu] Sui's younger brother [Liu] P'i-chiang 辟彊, and the sons of King Tao Hui 悼惠 of Ch'i–the Marquis of Chu-hsü, [Liu] Chang, and the Marquis of Tung-mou, [Liu] Hsing-chü–have all gained merits and can be made kings." Then he enthroned King Yu of Chao's younger son [Liu] P'i-chiang as the King of Ho-chien 河間,[137] used the Commandery of Ch'i which required heavy administrative work[138] to enthrone the

and semipolitical ritual in the Han imperial house. From this time on, emperors would symbolically push the plow three times in the spring, in the ancient rite specifically advocated by Confucian scholars. He further points out that the rite of cultivating the ceremonial field can be traced as far back as the Western Chou dynasty or even to the Shang period. Some early Chou bronze inscriptions bear the term *chi-t'ien.* See Hsu Cho-yun, *Han Agriculture* (Seattle: University of Washington Press, 1980), p. 24. Derk Bodde argues the word *chi* means "to cultivate" since the graph for *chi* in bronze inscriptions show a very graphic representation of a man holding an agricultural implement, with turned soil under his feet. He also points out this ceremony has continued through the twentieth century and has often been cited to exemplify the tremendous Chinese emphasis on agriculture (Bodde, *Festivals,* pp. 223, 232-33).

[132]As Liang Yü-sheng (7.258) notes, the parallel edict in *Han shu* (4.117) has an additional line of eighteen characters, "Those commoners who are punished [and made to work] for the county officials, together those who have borrowed seed and food, and have not paid it back, and those who have not paid in full, let them all be pardoned."

[133]Liang Yü-sheng (7:258) observes that according to the "Chronological Tables" on *Shih chi* 17.827 and *Han shu,* 14.406, Emperor Wen enthroned noble kings in the second month, not the third month. But according to these basic annals here and the corresponding passage in *Han shu* (4.117), this event took place in the third month.

[134]The state of Chao was in the southern part of Hopei. Its capital was Han-tan 邯鄲 (modern Han-tan in Hopei).

[135]King Yu of Chao was Liu Yu 劉友. He was the sixth son of Liu Pang (see also n. 606 to our translation of "Kao-tsu pen-chi" above. On his death, see the detailed account in *Shih chi,* 9.403-4 and our translation above.

[136]Liu Sui was made King of Chao in the tenth month of the first year of Emperor Wen's reign. See his biography on *Shih chi,* 50.1989-90.

[137]The state of Ho-chien was located southwest of Hopei. Its capital was Lo-ch'eng 樂成 (southeast of modern Hsien 獻 County in Hopei; see T'an Ch'i-hsiang, 2:26).

[138]Following Wang Li-ch'i's (10.259) interpretation, which reads *chü-chün* 劇郡 as "a large commandery which was important and required heavy administrative work." This is the sole occurrence of this term in the *Shih chi.* The word occurs on *Han shu,* 76.3219, 自請治劇郡, in which case it can also be interpreted as "heavy administrative work"—"[He] personally asked to govern the commandery which required heavy administrative work." Watson (3:296) is most probably mistaken in stating *chü-chün* was the name of a

Marquis of Chu-hsü as the King of Ch'eng-yang 城陽,[139] enthroned the Marquis of Tung-mou as the King of Chi-pei 濟北,[140] and [enthroned] the imperial sons [Liu] Wu 武[141] as the King of Tai, [Liu] Ts'an 參[142] as the King of T'ai-yüan 太原,[143] and [Liu] Yi 揖[144] as the King of Liang 梁.[145]

The sovereign said, "In ancient times, as for administering the world, the court had banners for presenting good advice[146] and boards[147] for criticism. This is the way to open administrative channels and to cause those who would admonish to come forth. Under present law there are [*424*] the crimes of criticism and evil speech.[148] This causes ministers not to venture to express their feelings in full and the sovereign to have no way to hear about his faults. How can We make the worthy and good men of faraway regions come? Let these [laws] be abolished. Some commoners imprecate the sovereign[149] and pledge alliance to each other, yet after a while they betray each other.[150] The officers regard this as great treason. If they say some

Ch'i commandery. The parallel passage on *Han shu*, 4.117, does not have the word *chü chün*.

[139]The state of Ch'eng-yang was located in the southwest part of modern Shantung. Its capital was Chü 莒 (modern Chü County in Shantung; see T'an Ch'i-hsiang, 2: 20).

[140]The state of Chi-pei was in modern Shantung. Its capital was Lu 盧 County (twenty miles southwest of modern Ch'ang-ch'ing 長清 County in Shantung; T'an Ch'i-hsiang, 2:19).

[141]He was the second son of the emperor. Later he was transferred to be the King of Huai-yang 淮陽 and King of Liang. See his biography in *Shih chi* Chapter 58.

[142]The third son of the emperor. Later he became the King of Tai, see *Shih chi*, 58.2081.

[143]The state of T'ai-yüan was in the central part of modern Shansi. Its capital was Chin-yang 晉陽 (southwest of modern T'ai-yüan City; T'an Ch'i-hsiang, 2:18).

[144]The fourth son of the emperor. According to *Shih chi*, 58.2081-82, his *praenomen* is Sheng 勝 instead of Yi 揖.

[145]The state of Liang occupied the eastern part of modern Honan and the northwestern part of Anhwei. Its capital was Sui-yang 睢陽 (south of modern Shang-ch'iu 商丘 County in Honan; T'an Ch'i-hsiang, 2:19).

[146]According to "Chi-chieh," the ancient sage Yao 堯 set up banners along the major roads. People presented proposals under the banners.

[147]According to "Chi-chieh," Yao set up pillars beside bridges and attached a wooden board to them. People vented their criticisms on them.

[148]*Han shu*, 3.96, records that Empress Lü had abolished the crime of evil speech earlier. Yen Shih-ku (*Han shu*, 4.118) suspects it had been restored. For a discussion of the crimes of "evil speech" (*yao-yen* 妖言) and "criticism" (*fei-pang* 誹謗), see Ch'ü T'ung-tsu, *Han Social Structure*, p. 264.

[149]According to other chapters in *Shih chi*, "to imprecate the sovereign" (*chu-tsu shang* 祝詛上) was regarded as "treasonous and unprincipled" (*ta-ni wu-tao* 大逆無道). A marquis who committed such a crime was usually punished by being deprived of his state (cf. *Shih chi*, 18.930, 962; 19.1019-20). For a discussion of this crime, see Loewe, *Crisis*, pp. 88-89, and Hulsewé, *Han Law*, pp. 168ff. See also Kobayashi Madoka 小林 円, "'So' no kôzô to kinô" 詛の構造と機能, *Taishô Daigaku daigakuin kenkyû ronshû* 大正大学大学院論集, 20 (1996).

[150]Ku Yen-wu 顧炎武 (cited in Takigawa, 10.23) says the commoners falsely accused each other in

other [calumnious] words, the officers will consider them to be criticism. Such is the petty commoners' foolishness and ignorance which cause them to face death. We surely cannot accept this. From now on, whoever violates these laws will not be brought to trial."[151]

In the ninth month (13 October-11 November 178 B.C.), the emperor first gave governors of the commanderies and ministers of states the bronze tiger-[shaped] tallies[152] and bamboo diplomatic tallies.

On the *ting-yu* 丁酉 day of the tenth month of the third year (22 December 178 B.C.), the last day of the month, there was an eclipse of the sun.

In the eleventh month (23 December 178 B.C.-21 January 177 B.C.), the sovereign said, "Previously, [We] issued an edict dispatching all the ranking marquises to go to their states. Some of them have made excuses and not yet left. The chancellor [*425*] is the person to whom We give weight. Let him lead the marquises to go to their states for Us." The Marquis of Chiang, [Chou] Po, was removed from his chancellor's position and proceeded to his state. [153] [The Emperor] used the Grand Commandant, [Kuan] Ying, the Marquis of Ying-yin 穎陰,[154] as the chancellor.[155] [The Emperor] did away with the position of the Grand Commandant, its duties being assumed by the chancellor.

In the fourth month (19 May-16 June 177 B.C.), [Liu] Chang, the King of Ch'eng-yang, passed away. [Liu] Ch'ang, the King of Huai-nan, and his attendant, Wei Ching 魏敬, killed Shen Yi-chi 審食其,[156] the Marquis of P'i-yang 辟陽.[157]

reports to the local officials.

[151]As *Shih chi p'ing-lin* (10.6b) points out, Emperor Wen might have abolished the crimes of criticism and evil speech because the prosecution of these crimes was associated with the fall of Ch'in. The First Emperor of Ch'in is said to have once executed over 460 scholars because they committed the crimes of criticism and evil talk (see *Shih chi*, 6.258). When Kao-ti first entered the land of Ch'in, he singled out "wiping out the clan of those who criticized" as one of the harsh laws of Ch'in (*Shih chi*, 8.362).

[152]According to Ying Shao as cited in the "Chi-chieh," when the state was about to marshal troops, it sent envoys to the commanderies to match tallies. If the tallies were matched, then the officers of the commanderies would obey the order.

[153]As *Shih chi chi-shuo* (10.4b) points out, this edict of Emperor Wen was meant to be a hidden attack against Chou Po. He ordered the marquises to go to their states so that he could remove the power of Chou Po. The Emperor may have been suspicious of him as early as when he first entered the capital from Tai. According to *Shih chi*, 57.2072, after Chou Po went to his state, he constantly feared that the Emperor might want to execute him, thus he wore armor whenever he met the local officials. He was subsequently accused of conspiracy against the state and was put into prison. Only after the Empress Dowager appealed on his behalf was he released.

[154]Ying-yin was in modern Hsü-ch'ang 許昌 in Honan (T'an Ch'i-hsiang, 2:19).

[155]According to *Shih chi*, 22.1126, and a parallel passage in *Han shu* (4.119), Kuan Ying was made chancellor in the twelfth month, not the eleventh month.

[156]Shen Yi-chi was a man from P'ei 沛. He always accompanied Empress Lü during the years when Liu Pang fought to seize the world. He was made the Chancellor of the Left during the Empress Lü's reign and was removed from his position when Emperor Wen ascended the throne. See also n. 72 to our translation of

In the fifth month (17 June-16 July 177 B.C.), the Hsiung-nu entered Pei-ti 北地,[158] remaining in Ho-nan[159] as raiders. The Emperor for the first time favored the Kan-ch'üan 甘泉 [(Sweet Springs) Palace] with a visit.[160]

In the sixth month (17 July-14 August 177 B.C.), the Emperor said, "The Han agreed to an alliance of brotherhood with the Hsiung-nu, [hoping] this would keep them from doing harm to our borders. [The Han] transported and gave gifts to the Hsiung-nu generously.[161] Now the Worthy King of the Right[162] leaves his state and commands his troops to stay in the subjugated area of Ho-nan. There is no proper reason for that. They come and go near our fortresses, capturing and killing our officers and soldiers, driving away the Man 蠻 and Yi 夷 peoples on the ramparts[163] and the fortresses, and keeping them from being able to stay at their old [residences]. They trample down the frontier officers, enter [Our land] and rob. They are very arrogant and unreasonable. All these [acts] broke our agreement. Let Us send out 85,000[164] frontier horsemen and officers to Kao-nu 高奴[165] and dispatch Chancellor Kuan Ying, the Marquis of Ying-yin, to

"The Basic Annals of Empress Dowager Lü" above.

[157]P'i-yang was located southeast of modern Chi 冀 County in Hopei (T'an Ch'i-hsiang, 2:26). In 196, Liu Ch'ang's mother was put into prison and subsequently killed herself. Although Shen was asked to speak to Empress Lü and to plead for mercy for Ch'ang's mother, he did so halfheartedly. Therefore, Liu Ch'ang held a grudge against Shen. For a detailed account of this incident, see *Shih chi*, 118.3076.

[158]Pei-ti was a commandery located in the northeastern part of modern Kansu and the southeastern part of modern Ningsia. Its seat was at Ma-ling 馬岭 (about twenty miles northwest of modern Ch'ing-yang 慶 陽 County in Kiangsu; T'an Ch'i-hsiang 2:17).

[159]This refers to the area south of the Yellow River in modern Inner Mongolia.

[160]The Kan-ch'üan (Sweet Spring) Palace was built on Kan-ch'üan Mountain, about fifteen miles northwest of modern Ch'un-hua 淳化 County in Shensi (T'an Ch'i-hsiang, 2:15). This is the place where the Han emperors offered sacrifices to Heaven. For an account of the historical remains of this place, see Yao Sheng-min 姚生民, "Han Kan-ch'üan Kung yi-chih k'an-ch'a chi" 漢甘泉宮遺址勘查記, *K'ao-ku yü wen-wu*, 1980.2: 51-60.

[161]After the Han first stabilized the empire, Kao-ti personally led troops to attack the Hsiung-nu, but was besieged at Po-teng 白登 (northeast of modern Ta-t'ung 大同, Shansi; T'an Ch'i-hsiang, 2:18) for seven days. Since that time, the Han had sent imperial princesses as well as food and clothes to the Hsiung-nu in order to make peace (*Shih chi*, 110. 2894-95).

[162]I.e., *Yu hsien-wang* 右賢王. This is one of the highest positions among the Hsiung-nu. The Hsiung-nu confederacy was divided into left (east) and right (west) administrative regions, the left having precedence over the right. The Worthy King of the Left and the Worthy King of the Right ruled the respective regions and answered only to the Shan-yü, who acted as supreme ruler. See Loewe, *Cambridge History of China*, 1:384-85.

[163]The original word *pao* 保 has been interpreted by many commentators as "to protect," Chavannes (2:468-69), based on a parallel passage in *Shih chi*, 110.2895, convincingly argues that *pao* is interchangeable with *pao* 葆 here, which means "rampart."

[164]In the parallel passage in *Han shu* (94.3756), the number is 80,000, not 85,000.

[165]Kao-nu was a county located northeast of modern Yen-an 延安 City, Shensi (T'an Ch'i-hsiang, 2:

assault the Hsiung-nu." When the Hsiung-nu left, [the emperor] sent out the Skill Soldiers[166] of the Commandant of the Capital and put them under the command of the General of the Guards. They garrisoned Ch'ang-an.

On the *hsin-mao* 辛卯 day (12 August 177 B.C.), the emperor went from Kan-ch'üan to Kao-nu. He took the opportunity to favor T'ai-yüan[167] with a visit and saw his previous ministers, granting favors to all of them and dispensing rewards according to merit. He granted oxen and wine to commoners in the hamlets and exempted commoners of Chin-yang 晉陽 and Chung-tu[168] from taxes and corvée for three years. He remained at T'ai-yüan and toured it for over ten days.

[Liu] Hsing-chü, the King of Chi-pei, heard that the emperor had gone to Tai, intending to go and assault the Hsiung-nu. He then revolted[169] and sent out his troops, intending to raid Hsing-yang. At this [the emperor] issued an edict to dismiss the chancellor's troops. He dispatched the Marquis of Chi-p'u 棘蒲,[170] Ch'en [*426*] Wu,[171] as Commander-in-chief, commanding 100,000 men to go and assault him. The Marquis of Ch'i 祁, Ho 賀,[172] acted as a general and encamped at Hsing-yang.

On the *hsin-hai* 辛亥 day of the seventh month (1 September 177 B.C.), the Emperor went from T'ai-yüan to Ch'ang-an. He then issued an edict to the authorities concerned, saying, "The King of Chi-pei has turned his back upon virtue and revolted against his sovereign, leading his officers and commoners into error. He is committing great treason. As for those officers, soldiers, and commoners of Chi-pei who have stabilized themselves before [our] troops arrive, and those who surrender with their armies, lands, and towns, [We] shall pardon them all

17).

[166]*Ts'ai-kuan,* 材官. Bielenstein (p. 114) says when people reached the age of twenty-three, they were trained as Skilled Soldiers in their home commanderies for one year.

[167]After Emperor Wen ascended the throne, the state of Tai was divided into two states and T'ai-yüan was one of them, with its capital at Chin-yang (see n. 143 above and Wang Hui, *Shih chi pen-chi ti-li k'ao,* p. 489). Thus, the emperor was visiting the place which he had previously administered when he was the King of Tai.

[168]Both cities were previous capitals of Tai.

[169]According to *Shih chi,* 52.2010, at the time when the great ministers of Han planned to execute the Lüs, they promised to enfeoff Liu Hsing-chü with the entire territory of Liang, and enfeoff Liu Chang, his brother, with the entire territory of Chao, in order to reward their support. However, after Emperor Wen ascended the throne, he enfeoffed each of the two brothers with a single commandery Ch'i, having heard that they originally intended to enthrone the King of Ch'i, their elder brother Liu Hsiang 劉襄, as the emperor. Thereafter Liu Hsing-chü and Liu Chang harbored resentment against Emperor Wen. Liu Chang died early, and Liu Hsing-chü eventually rose in rebellion.

[170]Wang Li-ch'i (10.260), following the "Cheng-yi," believes Chi-p'u was P'ing-chi 平棘, located in modern Chao 趙 County in Hopei. Wu Shu-p'ing and Lu Zongli (10.357) argue that Chi-p'u and P'ing-chi are different places and that Chi-p'u was located somewhere near the Wei 魏 Commandery in the Han dynasty. Its seat was at Yeh 鄴 County (southwest of modern Lin-chang 臨漳 in Hopei).

[171]In *Han shu,* 4.120, Ch'en Wu is called Ch'ai Wu 柴武.

[172]According to *Shih chi,* 18.916, his *cognomen* was Tseng 繒. The parallel passage in *Han shu*

and reinstate their official positions and ranks. As for those who had contact with [Liu] Hsing-chü, the king, [We] shall also pardon them."[173] In the eighth month, [the Han] defeated Chi-pei's army and captured its king.[174] All the officers and commoners of Chi-pei who had revolted along with the king were pardoned.

In the sixth year (175-174 B.C.),[175] the authorities concerned reported that [Liu] Ch'ang, the King of Huai-nan, had abandoned the laws of the previous emperors and did not listen to the edicts of the Son of Heaven. His residence defied proper standards,[176] and the mode of his coming and going imitated that of the Son of Heaven.[176] He arrogatingly made laws and ordinances, plotted to revolt with [Ch'en] Ch'i 陳奇, the Heir of the Marquis of Chi-p'u, and dispatched men on diplomatic missions to Min-Yüeh 閩越[177]and the Hsiung-nu, [asking them] to send out their troops, intending thereby to endanger the ancestral temple and the altars of soil and grain. The ministers discussed this, and all said, "[Liu] Ch'ang should be executed and his corpse exposed in the marketplace." The emperor could not bear to apply the law to a king. He pardoned his crime, but deposed him as a king. The ministers begged to place the [former] king to the area of Yen-tao 嚴道[178] and Ch'iung-tu 邛都[179] in Shu. The Emperor gave his consent. Before [Liu] Ch'ang arrived at the place where he was supposed to stay, he fell ill and died on the way.[180] The sovereign pitied him. Later, in the sixteenth year of his reign (164 B.C.), he posthumously honored Liu Ch'ang, the King of Huai-nan, with the title of King Li 厲. He enthroned his three sons as the King of Huai-nan, the King of Heng-shan 衡山,[181] and the King of Lu-chiang 廬江.[182]

(4.120) reads Tseng Ho.

[173]Wu Kuo-t'ai 吳國泰 suggests another reading of this sentence. He argues that the original sentence should be parsed as, 與王興居去，來，亦赦之. Thus, the meaning of the sentence becomes "For those who have gone along with Hsing-chü, the King, to rebel, if they come back [to our side], they should also be pardoned." See Wu Kuo-t'ai, "*Shih chi* chieh ku," 史記解詁, *Wen shih*, 43 (1997): 42.

[174]According to *Han shu*, 4.120, the king was captured and committed suicide.

[175]The affairs of the fourth and fifth years are missing. *Han shu* (4.120-1) has recorded these affairs. *Shih chi*, 22.1126 also records several events during these two years, some of them overlapping with the *Han shu* records.

[176]This mainly refers to the equipages he used in coming and going.

[177]Min-Yüeh was one branch of the ancient Yüeh Clan. They lived in the southern part of modern Chekiang and throughout most of Fukien. Liu Pang enthroned the head of the clan, Wu-chu 無諸, as the King of Min-Yüeh in 202 B.C., making Tung-yeh 東冶 (modern Foochow, Fukien) the capital. See *Shih chi*, 114. 2979.

[178]Modern Hsing-ching 滎經 County in Szechwan (T'an Ch'i-hsiang, 2:29).

[179]Ch'iung-tu was located southeast of modern Hsi-ch'ang 西昌 County in Szechwan (T'an Ch'i-hsiang, 2:32). According to *Shih chi*, 118.3079, and *Han shu*, 44.2143, the name of this place is Ch'iung-yu 邛郵, which was about fifteen miles southeast of Yen-tao (T'an Ch'i-hsiang, 2: 29).

[180]According to *Shih chi*, 118.3080, he refused to eat and thereby died in Yung 雍 (modern Feng-hsiang 鳳翔 county in Shensi).

[181]The state of Heng-shan occupied parts of modern Honan, Anhwei, and Hupei. Its capital was Chu 邾 (north of modern Huang-kang 黃崗 in Hupei; Wang Li-ch'i, 10.261).

[427] In the summer of the thirteenth year (167 B.C.),[183] the sovereign said, "[We] have heard that according to the way of Heaven, misfortune rises from resentment, while fortune springs up through virtue. The wrongdoings of the hundred officers should be of Our own responsibility. Now the officials [known as] the secret invocators[184] shift blame onto the subjects. In this way, Our lack of virtue is made even clearer. We surely cannot accept this. Let this office be abolished."[185]

In the fifth month (29 May-26 June 167 B.C.), [186] the Prefect of the Grand Granary of Ch'i, Master Ch'un-yü 淳于,[187] committed an offense and deserved to be punished. The Officer of the Imperial Prison[188] arrested him and moved him to Ch'ang-an for imprisonment. The Master of the Grand Granary had no sons, but five daughters. When the Master of the Grand Granary was just being arrested and was about to leave, he reviled his daughters, saying, "In begetting children, I did not beget sons. In a time of emergency they are of no help!" T'i-ying 緹縈, his youngest daughter, was hurt and wept. She then followed her father to reach Ch'ang-an and submitted a letter [to the Emperor], saying, "Your servant's father acted as an officer. People in Ch'i all praised him for his purity and impartiality. Now he is being prosecuted according to the law and is facing punishment. Your servant feels grieved that those who are dead cannot return to life, those who have been punished [by mutilation] cannot be restored [to their original bodies]. Even if they intend to correct their faults and make a fresh start, there is no path they can take. Your servant is willing to be taken as a government slave so as to atone for her father's crime and allow him to be able to make a fresh start." The letter was presented to the Son of Heaven. The Son of Heaven sympathized with and was moved to sorrow by her intention. Then he issued an edict, saying, "[We] have heard in the time of the Yu-yü 有虞 clan,[189] people

[182]The state of Lu-chiang was in the southern part of modern Anhwei and the eastern part of Hupei, with its capital at Shu 舒 (about ten miles southwest of Lu-chiang 廬江 in Anhwei; T'an Ch'i-hsiang, 2:24). The King of Huai-nan was Liu An 劉安. The King of Heng-shan was Liu Po 劉勃. The King of Lu-chiang was Liu Tz'u 劉賜. See their biographies in *Shih chi,* 118.3081-98.

[183]The affairs of Emperor Wen from the seventh year to the spring of the thirteenth year are missing in the *Shih chi* text. *Han shu* recorded these affairs. See *Han shu,* 4.122-125, and the reconstructed account in Wang Yi-chih 王益之 (Southern Sung), *Hsi Han nien-chi* 西漢年紀, Wang Ken-lin 王根林, ed. (Chengchow: Chung-chou Ku-chi, 1993), pp. 100-32.

[184]According to "Chi-chieh," the secret invocators shift blame onto the subjects; the state closely guarded this activity in secret, thus they were called "secret invocators." According to *Shih chi,* 28.1377, this office originated in the Ch'in dynasty. Whenever a natural disaster occurred, the secret invocators would pray that the blame be put on the lower-ranking officials and commoners.

[185]A parallel edict can be found in *Han shu*, 25.1212, but the *Han shu* version of this edict is much shorter and only contains part of the last sentence.

[186]According to *Shih chi,* 105.2795, the following event took place in 176 B.C., not 167 B.C.

[187]He was Ch'un-yü Yi 意, a famous physician of the time. See his biography on *Shih chi,* 105.2794-2817.

[188]*Cha-yü* 詔獄. See Bielenstein, pp. 38-39.

[189]A legendary clan in ancient times. Shun 舜, one of the Five Emperors, was the head of this clan. See *Shih chi,* 1.45.

regarded it as shameful if their clothes and hat were painted and if they were distinguished from others by dress which was marked.[190] Yet the commoners did not violate the laws. Why was that? It was [because of] the best administration. Now under our law there are three kinds of corporal punishments,[191] yet crime has not ceased. Where does the defect lie? Is it not that Our virtue is insufficient and Our instruction is not clear? We are deeply ashamed of Ourselves. [*428*] Therefore, if the ruler does not teach and guide properly, foolish commoners will fall into error. The *Odes* says, 'Affable and amiable is the lord. Father and mother of the common people.'[192] Now if a man has faults, before instruction is applied, punishment is imposed. If someone intends to change his conduct and do good, there is no path for him to take. Our pity for him is extreme. The punishment has gone to such extremes as to cut off limbs and carve the skin and flesh, so that victims cannot recover for the rest of their lives. How painful and immoral is this. Can this be called the intention of father and mother of the common people? Let the corporal punishments be abolished."[193]

The sovereign said, "Agriculture is the basis of the world. No endeavor is greater than that. Right now [some] diligently engage in it, yet they have to bear the imposition of land

[190]"Cheng-yi" cites a passage from "The Treatise on Punishment and Law" in the *Chin shu* 晉書 (30.917), which reads: "During the time of Five Emperors, if a criminal was sentenced to suffer the punishment of tattooing the face, people dyed his scarf black instead; if a criminal was to suffer cutting off the nose, people dyed his clothes red instead. For castration, people had the criminal wear a pair of different-sized shoes." Actually, a similar idea can also be found in the following passage in *Hsün Tzu* 荀子 ("Cheng-lun" 正論, 18.3, Wang Hsien-ch'ien 王先謙, comm., *Hsün Tzu chi-chieh* 荀子集解, Shen Hsiao-huan 沈嘯寰 and Wang Hsing-hsien 王星賢, eds. [Peking: Chung-hua, 1988], 12.326-7): "In well-ordered periods of antiquity corporal punishments were not employed; rather, there were only symbolic punishments. For black-branding they had the offender wear a black hood over his face, for cutting off the nose, he wore a bleached cap-string; for amputation of the feet, he wore hemp sandals; for castration, he wore an apron with a piece cut off; and for the death penalty, he wore colorless garments dyed with red ocher." See John Knoblock, trans. *Xunzi, A Translation and Study of the Complete Works* (Stanford: Stanford University Press, 1988), 3:36-37.

[191]Most commentators believe the three types of corporal punishments were tattooing, cutting off the nose, and cutting off the heels. Liang Yü-sheng (7.259-60) and others argue that Emperor Wen also abolished castration. Recently Han Kuo-p'an 韓國磐 suggested the character *san* 三 "three" here may be a mistake for "four," since the ancient writing of the character "four" (with four horizontal strokes) was similar to that of "three" and could easily have been confused. See "Han Wen-ti ch'u jou-hsing k'ao" 漢文帝除肉刑考 in *Chung-kuo shih yen-chiu*, 1991.2: 104-6.

[192]These lines are from the *Book of Odes*, Mao, #251 (Legge, 1:489).

[193]All these punishments were restored in some form in later generations. See Han Kuo-p'an, 106-11.

A parallel account can be found in *Shih chi*, 105.2795. In the parallel passage in *Han shu* (4.125), Pan Ku abbreviated his account of this event, moving it into his "Treatise on Punishment and Law" (*Han shu*, 23.1097-99). Ssu-ma Ch'ien, having personally suffered the cruel punishment of castration himself, may regarded this event as a perfect example of Emperor Wen's virtuous rule and thereby recorded the more detailed account found here.

taxes and other levies. In this way no distinction between those who work at the essential and those who work at the nonessential is made.[194] This indicates our way of encouraging agriculture is not perfect. Let the land taxes be abolished."[195]

In the winter of the fourteenth year (167-166 B.C.), the Hsiung-nu plotted to enter the frontier as raiders. They attacked Chu-na 朝邪[196] and the 'Fortress,'[197] killing [Sun] Ang [孫]卬, the Chief Commandant of Pei-ti. The sovereign then dispatched three generals[198] to encamp at Lung-hsi 隴西,[199] Pei-ti, and Shang-chün 上郡.[200] [He] made the Commandant of the Capital, Chou She 周舍, the General of Guards; and the Prefect of the Palace Attendants, Chang Wu, General of Chariots and Cavalry. They were encamped north of the Wei [River], with 1,000 chariots and 100,000 horsemen and foot soldiers. The emperor personally took greetings and gifts to the army. He exercised control over the troops, gave instructions and ordinances, and made grants to officers and soldiers of the army. The emperor intended to command troops himself to strike at the Hsiung-nu. All the ministers remonstrated him, [but] he listened to none. Only when the empress dowager insistently held him, back did the emperor [*429*] stop. At this point he made the Marquis of Tung-yang 東陽,[201] Chang Hsiang-ju 張相如,[202] the Commander-

---

[194]"Chi-chieh" says, "The essential is agriculture. The nonessential is commerce. It says that both farmers and merchants bear the tax and there is no distinction made between them. Thus the land tax was abolished."

[195]The rate of the land tax was one-fifteenth of the yield at the beginning of the Han (*Han shu*, 24.1127). According to *Han shu*, 4.118, Emperor Wen issued an edict and reduced the land tax by one half in 168 B.C. This edict is not recorded in *Shih chi*. Both *Shih chi* and *Han shu* (24.1135) recorded the above edict in which Emperor Wen abolished the land tax in 167 B.C. In 156 B.C. Emperor Ching levied the land tax at the rate of one-thirtieth of the yield (*Shih chi*, 11.439, *Han shu*, 5.140; *Han shu*, 24.1135 dated this event to 155 B.C.). Previously scholars believed that from 167 to 156 B.C. the land tax was totally abolished (Hsu Cho-yun, *Han Agriculture*, p. 72; *Cambridge History of China*, 1:596-97), but recently some scholars have been debating whether the land tax was abolished by Emperor Wen for the single year 167 B.C. See Huang Chin-yen 黃今言, "Han-tai t'ien-shui cheng-kuo chung jo-kan wen-t'i te k'ao-ch'a" 漢代田稅征課中若干問題的考察 in *Chung-kuo shi yen-chiu*, 1981.2:23-27 and Tseng Wei-hua 曾維華, "Yeh t'an Han Wen-ti mien-ch'u tsu-shui te nien-tai wen-t'i" 也談漢文帝免除租稅的年代問題, *Shang-hai Shih-yüan hsüeh-pao*, 1982.3: 94-7.

[196]Southeast of modern Ku-yüan 固原 County in Ningsia (T'an Ch'i-hsiang, 2:34).

[197]According to "Cheng-yi," 'The Fortress' refers to the Hsiao 蕭 Pass located just north of Chu-na (see n. 196 above) and about 165 miles northwest of Ch'ang-an in the Ningsia Hui Autonomous Region (T'an Ch'i-hsiang, 2:34). According to Shih *chi*, 110.2901, and *Han shu*, 94.3761, the *Shan-yü* of the Hsiung-nu led 140,000 horsemen to enter Chu-na and the Hsiao Pass. Their vanguard reached as far as Kan-ch'üan Palace.

[198]For detailed information about these three generals, see *Shih chi*, 110.2901.

[199]Lung-hsi was a commandery located in the southeastern part of modern Kansu, with its seat at Ti-tao 狄道 (modern Lin-t'ao 臨洮 County in Kansu; T'an Ch'i-hsiang, 2:34).

[200]Shang-chün was a commandery located in the northern part of Shensi and the southern part of Inner Mongolia, with its seat in Fu-shih 膚施 (southeast of modern Yü-lin 榆林 County in Shensi; T'an Ch'i-hsiang, 2:17-18).

[201]Northeast of modern Wu-ch'eng 武城 in Shantung (Wu Shu-p'ing and Lu Zongli, 10.360).

in-chief; the Marquis of Ch'eng 成,[203] Ch'ih 赤,[204] was made the Clerk of the Capital;[205] and Luan Pu 樂布[206] was made a general. They struck at the Hsiung-nu and the Hsiung-nu withdrew and fled.

In the spring, the sovereign said, "From the time We obtained the opportunity to hold the sacrificial victims, jade utensils, and silks to serve the Supreme Deity and the ancestral temple, it has been fourteen years. The days that have passed have been very long. With neither wisdom nor brilliance, [We] have pacified and administered the world for a long time. We are deeply ashamed of Ourselves. Let [Us] extensively increase the sacrificial mounds and level ground,[207] jade utensils and silks. In the past, the former kings spread favor widely, yet did not seek repayment, [they] performed the Wang望 Sacrifice,[208] yet did not pray for their own blessings. They put worthy men above their own relatives, and put commoners first and themselves second. They were brilliant to the utmost. Right now I have heard that when the sacrificial officials pray for fortune, they make all the blessings befall upon Us, not the populace. We are deeply ashamed of this. With Our lack of virtue, We alone enjoy the blessings, and the populace has no share in them. This will double Our lack of virtue. Let the sacrificial officials be ordered not to pray [for Us] when they pay their homage."[209]

At that time the Marquis of Pei-p'ing 北平,[210] Chang Ts'ang, was the Chancellor. He had just made clear the pitch-standards and calendar.[211] Kung-sun Ch'en 公孫臣, a man of Lu 魯,

[202]For more information on Chang Hsiang-ju, see *Shih chi*, 18.952.

[203]In modern Pao-ting 保定 in Hopei (Wu Shu-p'ing and Lu Zongli, 10.360).

[204]According to *Shih chi*, 22.1128, his *cognomen* was Tung 董.

[205]According to *Shih chi*, 110.2901, Tung Chih was made the General of the Van (*Ch'ien Chiang-chün* 前將軍). The parallel passage in *Han shu* (94.3761) says that Tung Chih was made a general. However, another passage in *Han shu* (4.125) reads "Tung Ho 董赫, the Marquis of Chien-ch'eng 建成, and Luan Pu, the Clerk of the Capital, were both made generals." Liang Yü-sheng (7.260) points out both *Shih chi*, 22.1128, and *Han shu*, 4.126, indicate that Luan Pu, instead of Tung Chih, was the Clerk of the Capital at that time. Yet he also notes that according to *Han shu*, 19.758, Tung Ch掂h was made the Clerk of the Capital. Wang Shu-min (10.398) further argues the sentence should be read as "The Marquis of Ch'eng, Tung Chih, and the Prefect of the Capital, Luan Pu, were made generals."

[206]See his biography on *Shih chi*, 100.2733-34.

[207]In *Shih chi*, 28.1381, and *Han shu*, 4.126, the word is *t'an-ch'ang* 壇場 instead of *shan-ch'ang* 墠場. Wang Shu-min (10.399) says that *t'an* and *shan* were originally interchangeable. According to Yen Shih-ku (*Han shu*, 1.30), piling up earth makes a *t'an*, leveling the ground makes a *ch'ang*.

[208]The Wang Sacrifice, literally "The Sacrifice of Gazing at [Mountains] from Afar," was made to the famous mountains and rivers from a distance (see *Grand Scribe's Records*, 1:9, n. 103).

[209]A parallel edict can be found in *Shih chi*, 28.1381. But in *Shih chi* Chapter 28, the edict was issued in 167 B.C. rather than 166 B.C. The language of that edict differs greatly from the text given here. On the other hand, the parallel edict in *Han shu*, 4.126 is much closer to this edict.

[210]North of modern Man-ch'eng 滿城 in Hopei (T'an Ch'i-hsiang, 2:26).

[211]For an account of Chang Tsang's work on the pitch-standards and calendar, see *Shih chi*, 96.2681.

submitted a memorial to set forth the matter of the revolution of the cyclic Five Essences.[212] He said that the present was the time of the earth essence,[213] and that in the time of the earth essence a yellow dragon[214] should appear, so it was necessary to change the standards concerning the beginning of the year and the official color of the vestments. The Son of Heaven handed the matter down to the chancellor for deliberation. The chancellor reckoned and believed that the time was of the water essence,[215] thus making it clear that the tenth month should be the annuary month and that the color of black should be exalted. [The chancellor] thought his [Kung-sun Ch'en's] opinion was incorrect and asked that he be dismissed.

[430] In the fifteenth year (166-165 B.C.), a yellow dragon appeared in Ch'eng-chi 成 紀.[216] The Son of Heaven then again summoned Kung-sun Ch'en of Lu and made him an Erudite, letting him explain the matter of the earth essence. At this, the sovereign issued an edict, saying, "A supernatural being appeared in Ch'eng-chi. That will do no harm to the commoners. This year there will accordingly be a good harvest. We will personally offer the Suburban Sacrifice to the Supreme Deity and the other deities. Let the ritual officials discuss it. Let them not cover up things for fear of laboring Us." The ritual officials concerned all said, "In ancient times, the Son of Heaven in the summer personally paid salutation and offered sacrifices in the suburbs to the Supreme Deity. Therefore, this was called the Suburban Sacrifice." At this the emperor for the first time favored Yung 雍 with a visit[217] and paid homage to the Five Emperors[218]

[212]The theory was first raised by Tsou Yen 鄒衍 (305-240 B.C.), a *yin-yang* scholar in the Warring States period. It holds that all things develop in accordance with the cyclic revolution of the five basic essences of the world. See *Shih chi*, 74.2344, and *Grand Scribe's Records*, 7:180, n. 22.

[213]In his memorial, Kung-sun Ch'en stated that the Ch'in had obtained the water essence. Now that the Han replaced the Ch'in, it should take the earth essence, since it is the earth essence that overcomes water essence (see *Shih chi*, 28.1381 for his detailed argument).

[214]In the *yin-yang* theory of correspondences, the color yellow is associated with the earth essence.

[215]According to *Shih chi* 28.1381, Chang Ts'ang believed in the water essence because he saw the sign of the Yellow River bursting the solid bank, which indicated the water essence had come to power.

[216]North of modern Ch'in-an 秦安 County, Kiangsu (T'an Ch'i-hsiang, 2:34).

[217]Wang Li-ch'i (10.263) says Yung 雍 is P'i-yung 辟雍, a ritual hall where the emperor performed the state sacrifices. This is probably not true, since the P'i-yung Hall of the Han was not built until the end of the Western Han (Wang Chung-shu, *Han Civilization*, p. 10). Wu Shu-p'ing and Lu Tsung-li (10.361) argue Yung was located south of modern Feng-hsiang 鳳翔 County in Shensi. Emperor Wen was the first of the Han emperors to pay his respects at Yung (*Cambridge History of China*, 1:151). Michael Loewe says Yung had been the most important religious site since the pre-Ch'in period and that it was located in an area that was much later to be designated as the Han metropolitan division of the *Yu-fu-feng* 右扶風. For a discussion of the importance of Yung as a religious center, see Loewe, *Crisis*, pp. 167-68.

[218]There are different theories with regard to who these emperors are. One claims they are T'ai-hao 太昊, Yen-ti 炎帝, Huang-ti 黃帝, Shao-hao 少皞, and Chuan-hsü 顓頊. Another theory says that they are the Blue Emperor of the East, the Red Emperor of the South, the Yellow Emperor of the Center, the White Emperor of the West, and the Black Emperor of the North (see Wang Li-ch'i, 10.263; see also *Grand Scribe's Records*, 1:1, n. 1). According to *Shih chi*, 28.1378, the Ch'in had already established the temples of the White,

through a Suburban Sacrifice. He performed the rites in response [to the auspicious Heavenly signs][219] in the fourth month, the first month of summer (6 May-4 June 165 B.C). Hsin-yüan P'ing 新垣平, a man of Chao, had an audience by virtue of having observed an emanation.[220] He took the opportunity to advise the sovereign to establish a temple to the Five [Emperors][221] in Wei-yang 渭陽,[222] intending to make the Tripods of Chou[223] come out. The jade quintessence [224]

Blue, Yellow and Red emperors, and Kao-ti in addition established the temple of the Black Emperor.

[219]The original term is *ta li* 答禮. Most modern translators and annotators tend to ignore the meaning of the word *ta* (Watson translates this sentence as "The ceremony was performed in the fourth month, the first month of summer" [1:303] and Chavannes renders it "ce fut au quatrième mois [6 mai-4 juin 165], qui était le premier mois de l'été, qu'il accomplit ces rites" [2:481-2]). Chang Ta-k'o 張大可 (*Shih chi ch'üan-pen hsin chu* 史記全本新註 (Sian: San-ch'in, 1990, p. 245) claims that *ta li* is to "respond to the harvest of the year." It seems the emperor not only responded to the harvest, but also to the deities. From the context of the sentence, we find that before the first *ta li* a yellow dragon appeared, and there was accordingly a harvest, and before the second *ta li*, Hsin Yüan-p'ing numerated various auspicious signs and suggested to the emperor that he should sacrifice to the Supreme Deity so as to act in accord with these signs (see *Shih chi*, 28.1382). Thus, *ta* here seems to carry the meaning "to respond to the Heavenly auspicious signs." Such a reading of *ta* can be supported by a sentence in the "Treatise on the Suburban Sacrifice" (*Han shu*, 25.1252), *yi ta chia jui* 以答嘉瑞 "to respond to the auspicious omen." Yen Shih-ku indicated that *ta* here means "to respond." Michael Loewe (*Crisis*, p. 187) found that in several Han edicts the emperor worshiped the deities to "give thanks for incidents of a felicitous nature" or "in response to these happy signs." It seems such practice may start from the time of Emperor Wen. Another reading of this sentence, as suggested by Martin Kern in personal correspondence, is the emperor "performed the rites in accordance to the season of summer."

[220]Hsin-yüan P'ing claimed he had observed an emanation of a deity northeast of the capital. For a more detailed account of this event, see *Shih chi*, 28.1382.

[221]The original text reads "five temples of Wei-yang" (*Wei-yang wu miao* 渭陽五廟). Wang Shu-min (10.400) quotes several relevant passages and argues the text should be *Wei-yang Wu-ti Miao* 渭陽五帝廟 ("Temple of the Five Emperors"). According to *Shih chi*, 28.1382, the five emperors were actually put under one temple and each occupied one hall. They faced the five doors, and each door had the same color as that of its corresponding emperor.

[222]Northeast of modern Hsien-yang, Shensi (Wang Li-ch'i, 10.263).

[223]This refers to the nine precious tripods of the Chou dynasty. According to "Cheng-yi" (in *Shih chi*, 5.218), they were made by Yü of Hsia. The term *chiu ting* 九鼎 first appears in *Tso chuan* (Yang, *Tso chuan*, Hsüan 3, p. 670). There the description of what was represented on the tripods is rather vague: "(During the time of Hsia), people of remote lands presented pictures of objects. The Nine Shepherds paid tribute in metal. The tripods were cast to represent objects. Because of this one hundred objects were all provided [with representations], thereby causing the people to know the deities and evils." A parallel passage appears on *Shih chi*, 40.1700; Wang Li-ch'i (40.1260) indicates that the "objects" (*wu* 物) mentioned there refer to "many states and all kinds of strange creatures." It seems likely that the one hundred objects referred pars pro toto to the myriad things, i.e., the world; thus possession of these tripods signified that one had the right to rule the world (see also K.C. Chang's discussion in his *Art, Myth, and Ritual: The Path to Political Authority in Ancient China* [Cambridge: Harvard University Press, 1983], pp. 95-97). After the Ch'in conquered the Chou, it seized these

would be manifest.[225]

In the sixteenth year (165-164 B.C.), the sovereign personally paid homage through the Suburban Sacrifice in the Temple of the Five Emperors in Wei-yang. He also performed the rites in response [to the auspicious Heavenly signs] in the summer and exalted the color red.[226]

In the seventeenth year (164-163 B.C.), a jade cup was obtained[227] and it was carved with the characters "The Ruler of Men will live a long life."[228] At this the Son of Heaven for the first time changed the reign year count[229] to the first year.[230] He ordered the people of the world

tripods, but they were subsequently lost in the Ssu River (see also *Shih chi*, 28.1365 and *Grand Scribe's Records*, 1:62, n. 81).

[224]The jade quintessence could supposedly make people live forever. A line from *Ch'u tz'u* 楚辭 reads, "Ascend Mount K'un-lun 崑侖 and eat the jade quintessence; share the same longevity as the heaven and earth, and share the same brightness as the sun and moon" See Chiang Liang-fu 姜亮夫, *Ch'ung-ting Ch'ü Yüan fu chiao-chu* 重訂屈原賦校註 (Tientsin: T'ien-chin Ku-chi, 1987), p. 428. According to *Sung shu* 宋書, 27.766, the mother of Kao-ti [of Han] once met a jade bird which held a red pearl with the inscription, "Jade quintessence; swallow it and become a king." She swallowed it and later gave birth to Kao-ti.

[225]As Takigawa (10.33-34) points out, it seems Ssu-ma Ch'ien missed one important event in this year. According to *Han shu*, 4.127, in the ninth month of this year, the emperor issued an edict asking the feudal lords and governors of commanderies to recommend those worthy and good men who were able to admonish the sovereign straightfowardly. The emperor would personally question them by written examination. Dubs (1:259) believes this event signifies one of the beginnings of the Chinese examination system and quotes Chou Shou-ch'ang 周壽昌 (fl. 1845) as saying, "This was the first time the Han court set literary exercises for the [prospective] officials . . . and Ch'ao Ts'o 晁錯 (200-154 B.C.), because he had the highest grade, was promoted from the position of the Heir-apparent's Household Steward to Palace Grandee." Pan Ku gives a more detailed account of the event of the Examination of Worthy and Good Men in his "Memoir of Ch'ao Ts'o" (*Han shu*, 49.2290). Ssu-ma Ch'ien surprisingly made no mention of this here or in his biography of Ch'ao Ts'o; he may not have recorded this event because he disliked Ch'ao.

[226]Wu Shu-p'ing and Lu Tsung-li (10.361) say that according to the Theory of the Five Essences, summer corresponds to fire and the color of red. Since Emperor Wen performed the sacrifice in summer, he exalted the color red.

[227]According to *Han shu*, 4.128, the jade cup was obtained in the ninth month of the sixteenth year. Liang Yü-sheng (7.261) argues the *Han shu* dating is correct. However, both *Shih chi*, 28.1383, and *Han shu*, 25.1214, date this event in the seventeenth year. It seems Ssu-ma Ch'ien was at least consistent in his dating concerning this event, whereas Pan Ku was not.

[228]According to *Shih chi* 28.1383, this seems to have been another of Hsin-yüan P'ing's schemes. He asked someone to carry the jade cup and present it to the emperor, having told the emperor beforehand that he had discovered someone who was going to come to court with "the emanations of precious jade."

[229]*Shih chi*, 28.1383 records another "magic performance" by Hsin-yüan P'ing. After the sun had risen to the medidian once, he told the emperor, "I expect the sun to rise to the meridian twice [in one day.]" After a while, the sun really rose to the meridian again. Liang Yü-sheng argues it was this incident that made Emperor Wen change the calendar.

[230]Since Emperor Wen changed his seventeenth year to the first year, historians have called the

to hold a great bacchanal. In this year, Hsin-yüan P'ing's fraud came to light. His clan was wiped out.

[431] In the second year of his Later Reign (163-162 B.C.), the sovereign said, "Since We are not brilliant at all, [We] are not able to spread virtue afar. This has caused some states outside our border to be restless. The people of the four remote quarters do not live a peaceful life; the people around Our royal region are hard-working and cannot rest at ease. The responsibility for these two things all comes from Our lack of virtue and Our being unable to extend it afar. Recently, year after year the Hsiung-nu have continuously ravaged Our frontier and killed many officers and commoners. Moreover, the frontier ministers, troops and officers are unable to express Our inner intentions [to the Hsiung-nu], thereby doubling Our lack of virtue. For a long time disasters and military actions have come one after another. How can the states in the center and those beyond be at rest? Right now We rise early and retire late,[231] working diligently for the world and worrying about all the commoners. [We] feel sad, alarmed and uneasy for them and have never forgotten about them in Our mind for a single day. Therefore, [We] have dispatched so many envoys that their caps and carriage canopies are within sight of each other and their carriage ruts cross on the road. By these means [We] want to express Our intentions to the Shan-yü 單于. Right now the Shan-yü is returning to the old ways. He considers the security of the altars of soil and grain and facilitates the interests of all the commoners. Together with Us, he personally abandons all the [previous] trivial offenses. We both go along the great way and swear to the principle of brotherhood so as to preserve the good commoners of the world. The marital alliance has been concluded. It will start from this year."[232]

In the sixth year of the Later Reign (159-158 B.C.), in the winter, thirty thousand of the Hsiung-nu's men entered Shang-chün, and thirty thousand men entered Yün-chung 雲中.[233]

following years "the latter reign period" (hou yüan 後元).

[231] These words come from a line in Book of Odes, Mao #196 (Legge, 1:335).

[232] Ho-ch'in 和親, which prior to the Han dynasty was primarily used to describe conditions of peace and intimacy between states, clans, and their members (see Yang Po-chün, Tso chuan, Hsiang 23, p. 1074). Although the policy of reinforcing political alliances through marriage between various Chou ruling houses and non-Chinese groups had been practiced since high antiquity (see Hsu and Linduff, Western Chou Civilization, pp. 48-49, 55-59 and 193-94 for discussion and references), it was not until 198 B.C. that the expression ho-ch'in was applied to such an alliance, when Lou Ching 婁敬 concluded a treaty with the Hsiung-nu Federation following the disastrous Chinese defeat at P'ing-ch'eng 平城 (see Shih chi, 99.2719). During the Han dynasty, ho-ch'in policy was carried out extensively with the Hsiung-nu (see the relevant passages on the development of this policy in the "Hsiung-nu lieh-chuan," Shih chi, 110.2894-96, and modern discussions by Pan Yihong, "Marriage Alliances and Chinese Princesses in International Politics from Han through T'ang," Asia Major, 10 (1997): 95-126; Chang Chun-shu, "War and Peace with the Hsiung-nu in Early Han China," in Essays in Commemoration of the Eightieth Birthday of Professor T'ao Hsi-sheng [Taipei, 1979], pp. 611-98; Ying-shih Yü, Trade and Expansion in Han China [Berkeley: University of California Press, 1967], pp. 10-12 and 36-51; and Dubs, 1.195-96).

For a parallel account of this marital alliance, see Shih chi, 110. 2902-4.

[233] Yün-chung was a commandery located east and north of the place where the Yellow River bends

The Palace Grandee, Ling Mien 令勉,[234] was made General of Chariots and Cavalry, encamping at Fei-hu 飛狐 [Pass];[235] [*432*] the previous Chancellor of Ch'u, Su Yi 蘇意, was made a general, encamping at [Mount] Kou-chu 句注;[236] General Chang Wu garrisoned Pei-ti; the Governor of Ho-nei 河內,[237] Chou Ya-fu 周亞夫,[238] was made a general, staying at Hsi-liu 細柳;[239] the Director of the Imperial Clan, Liu Li 劉禮,[240] was made a general, staying at Pa-shang 霸上 (Pa Heights);[241] the Marquis of Chu-tzu 祝茲[242] encamped at Chi-men 棘門.[243] With this they took preparation against the barbarians. After several months, when the barbarians left, [the troops] were also dismissed.

There were droughts and plagues of locusts in the world. The emperor granted more favor [to the people]. He ordered that the feudal lords should not enter court to pay tribute. He

to the south, stretching to the west and south of modern Hu-ho-hao-te 呼和浩特 City in what is now Inner Mongolia (T'an Ch'i-hsiang, 2:18).

[234]The original reads *chung ta fu ling mien* 中大夫令勉. "So-yin" proposed another reading, which took *chung ta fu ling* as an official title (Prefect of the Palace Grandee) and *mien* as the person's *praenomen*. The parallel passages in *Shih chi*, 22.1129, and *Han shu*, 4.130, read *ling mien* 令免 for *ling mien* 令勉. As Liang Yü-sheng (7.261) points out, according to the parallel passage in *Han chi* 漢紀 (8.15a, *SPTK*), his name was Li Mien 李勉.

[235]Fei-hu was an important pass located south of modern Wei 蔚 County and north of Lai-yüan 淶源 County in Hopei. It was a strategic point which connected the interior commanderies to the northern frontier (Wu Shu-p'ing and Lu Zongli, 10.362).

[236]Kou-chu was also called Mount Yen-men 雁門. One of the nine famous fortresses at that time, it was located northwest of modern Tai 代 County, Shansi (Wang Li-ch'i, 10.264).

[237]Ho-nei was a commandery which covered the area north of Yellow River in modern Honan Province, with its seat in Huai 懷 County (southwest of modern Wu-chih 武陟 in Honan; Wang Li-ch'i, 10.264).

[238]Chou Ya-fu was a son of Chou Po, the Marquis of Chiang. The parallel passage in his biography records an anecdote in which Emperor Wen, after inspecting his troops at Hsi-liu, recognized his military talent and called him "a true general." The emperor thereupon promoted him to be the commandant of the capital. Later, Chou Ya-fu played an important role in putting down the rebellion of the seven states. See his biography on *Shih chi*, 57.2073-80.

[239]Southwest of modern Hsien-yang in Shensi on northern side of the Wei River (T'an Ch'i-hsiang, 2:15).

[240]He was a son of Liu Chiao 劉交, King Yüan 元 of Ch'u. Later he became King Wen 文 of Ch'u (*Shih chi*, 50.1988-89).

[241]East of modern Hsien-yang in Shensi and west of the Pa River (T'an Ch'i-hsiang, 2:15).

[242]According to *Shih chi*, 57.2074, and *Han shu*, 4.131, the Marquis of Chu-tzu was Hsü Li 徐厲. But according to *Shih chi*, 19.988, Hsü Li was Marquis of Sung-tzu 松兹, not Chu-tzu. The Marquis of Chu-tzu was Lü Jung 呂榮 (*Shih chi*, 19.993). Liang Yü-sheng (7.262) argues that both *Shih chi* and *Han shu* made mistakes here and that the person in question should be the Marquis of Sung-tzu, Hsü Tao 徐悼, who was the son of Hsü Li.

[243]Northeast of modern Hsien-yang in Shensi (Wang Li-ch'i, 10.264).

lifted the ban on mountains and lakes,[244] reduced imperial robes, carriages, horses and dogs, cut down on the number of palace attendants and officers, and opened the granaries and enclosures to relieve the poor commoners. Commoners were allowed to sell their ranks.

[433] Emperor Wen came from Tai. It had been twenty-three years since he ascended the throne. As for his palaces and halls, enclosures and parks, dogs and horses, and robes and carriages, he increased none of them. If something did not benefit [the commoners], he immediately got rid of it so as to profit the commoners. Once he intended to build an open-air terrace. He summoned artisans to draw up estimates for it. Its cost was one hundred *chin*. The sovereign said, "One hundred *chin* is equal to the properties of ten middle-income families. I have received the palaces and halls of the late emperors, and am often afraid that I will bring disgrace to them. Why should I have this terrace?" The sovereign often wore robes of thick, crude silk.[245] As for Lady Shen 慎,[246] whom he favored, he ordered that her robe not be allowed to drag on the ground, and that her curtains not be allowed to have embroidered decorative patterns. By these means he showed simplicity and set a leading example for the world. Upon building the Pa 霸 Mausoleum,[247] he only used implements of baked clay, forbidding the use of gold, silver, copper or tin to decorate it and [forbidding] the raising of a mound for the tomb. He intended to save expenses and not to trouble the commoners. 'Commandant' T'o 佗,[248] the King of Nan-Yüeh 南越, enthroned himself as Emperor Wu 武. Yet the sovereign summoned and honored 'Commandant' T'o's brothers, using his favor to repay him. [Chao] T'o thus abandoned the title of emperor and proclaimed himself a subject. [The Emperor] formed a marital alliance with the Hsiung-nu, yet the Hsiung-nu turned their back on the agreement and entered [the frontier] to pillage. [The Emperor,] however, ordered the frontier officers to guard and prepare against the

[244] I.e., to allow people to hunt and fish freely.

[245] The parallel passage in *Han shu*, 4.134 reads *yi-t'i* 弋綈 "thick, black silk" for *t'i-yi* 綈衣 "thick, crude silk"; "Chi-chieh" also cites Chia Yi 賈誼, which read: "[Emperor Wen] wore clothes of thick, black silk."

[246] Lady Shen was a woman from Han-tan 邯鄲. It was said that because Empress Tou had lost her eyesight, the emperor began to favor Lady Shen. When the emperor amused himself in the palace, he often took her with him and made her sit in the seat normally accorded the empress, an action which went against the social codes. Only when Yüan Ang 袁盎, the Gentleman of the Household, presented an admonition, did she stop doing that. See *Shih chi*, 49.1974 and 101.2740.

[247] The Pa Mausoleum was for Emperor Wen. It was located on the western bank of the Pa River, in modern Pao-ch'i-chai 鮑旗寨 Village, an eastern suburb of Sian. See Tu Pao-jen 杜葆仁, "Hsi-Han chu-ling wei-chih k'ao" 西漢諸陵位置考 *K'ao-ku yü wen-wu*, 1980.1: 30. Emperor Wen began to construct the Pa Mausoleum in 171 B.C. (*Shih chi*, 22.1127). According to *Shih chi*, 102.2753, he once intended to build it quite handsomely, but probably because of the the advice of his Gentleman of the Household, Chang Shih-chih 張釋之, he gave up the idea.

[248] I.e., Chao T'o 趙佗, a Commandant of Nai-hai 南海 Commandery during the Ch'in dynasty. After the fall of the Ch'in, he seized three commanderies in the southern region. In 196 B.C., Kao-ti enthroned him as the King of Nan-Yüeh. In Empress Lü's reign, he further claimed himself Emperor Wu of Nan-Yüeh. See his biography on *Shih chi*, 113.2967-70.

Hsiung-nu, but not to send troops deep into [Hsiung-nu territory], because he detested causing the populace trouble and suffering. The King of Wu[249] feigned sickness and did not come to court. The Emperor granted him an armrest and a cane[250] right away. Although many ministers such as Yüan Ang 袁盎[251] spoke sharply and straightforwardly, he was often tolerant of them and used their ideas. Ministers such as Chang Wu accepted bribes of gold and cash. When the facts came to light, the sovereign opened the imperial storehouse and granted them gold and cash, thereby causing them to feel ashamed. He did not hand them over to the [prison] officers. He solely endeavored to use virtue to transform the commoners. Because of this, all the lands within the seas became abundant and wealthy. Propriety and righteousness prevailed. [252]

On the _chi-hai_ 己亥 [day] of the sixth month of the seventh year of the Later Reign (1 July 156 B.C.), the emperor passed away in the Wei-yang Palace. He left a testamentary edict, which read: "We have heard that of all the creatures in the world, none will not die after they are born. Death is the law of Heaven and earth, and a natural phenomenon of beings. How can this be lamentable? In present times, the people of the world all praise life and detest death. They bury in a lavish manner and thereby ruin their estates. They engage in deep mourning and thereby injure [*434*] their own lives. We surely cannot accept this. Furthermore, We already lack virtue and have no means to aid the populace. Now We are passing away. If We cause people to observe deep mourning and lamentation for a long time, thereby causing them to encounter extremes of cold and heat, afflicting fathers and sons, hurting the feelings of old and young, leading them to reduce their food and drink, suspending the sacrifices to spirits and deities, it will double Our lack of virtue. What shall we say to the world? We have obtained the opportunity to protect the ancestral temple. With an insignificant body, [We] have been entrusted with a position above the lords and kings of the world for over twenty years. Relying on the spirits of Heaven and earth and the blessing of the altars of soil and grain, it is peaceful and tranquil within the country, and there is no war. Since We are unwise, [We] have often feared that our faulty activities would bring disgrace to the virtuous legacy of the late emperors. For a long time, We have been afraid that We would not end well. Right now [We] are fortunate that having fulfilled the span of life assigned by Heaven, [We] are allowed to be enshrined in the Temple of

[249]The King of Wu is Liu P'i. His heir was killed by Emperor Wen's heir in an accident. Liu P'i thereby harbored resentment and did not go to court thereafter (see _Shih chi_, 106.2823).

[250]The armrest was for elderly people to lean on. Granting the armrest and cane shows respect. With these gifts Emperor Wen indicated Liu P'i did not have to come to court. According to _Shih chi_, 106. 2823, the emperor at first arrested several envoys from Wu because Liu P'i did not pay homage to the court. Later, an envoy from Wu told the emperor that Liu P'i was frightened and was plotting rebellion. The emperor then pardoned those envoys and granted the armrest and cane to Liu P'i.

[251]See his biography on _Shih chi_, 101.2737-45.

[252]The general style of dynastic histories is to put the historian's comments at the end of the chapter. Thus, Ssu-ma Ch'ien's long comment on Emperor Wen seems out of place here. As _Shih chi p'ing-lin_ (10b-11a) points out, this may be because he admired Emperor Wen's virtuous rule so much that he wanted to give a general summary of his achievements in medias res. _Shih chi chi-shuo_ (10.7a) points out Ssu-ma Ch'ien altogether listed ten virtuous deeds of Emperor Wen in this summary.

Kao-ti. While We are not brilliant, We regard this [ending] a good thing.[253] How can it be sad? Let Us issue an order to the officers and commoners of the world: after the order arrives, people should hold a memorial service for three days, then all should take off their mourning apparel. Do not forbid those who wish to take a wife, marry off a daughter, offer sacrifices, drink wine or eat meat. For those who should arrange mourning affairs, wear mourning apparel, and hold memorial services, none of them need to wear unhemmed mourning apparel.[254] The circumference of their hemp ribbons[255] should not exceed three *ch'un*. Do not display chariots and weapons [in the funeral ceremony]. Do not send men and women from the commoners to wail and hold memorial services in the palace. As for those in the palace who should hold memorial services, all should raise their voices fifteen times each morning and evening. After the ceremony they should stop [crying]. Except for morning and evening memorial services, people are not allowed to cry without permission. After internment, let the people concerned wear 'Deep Mourning' for fifteen days, 'Light Mourning' for fourteen days, and 'Thin Hemp'[256] for seven days; after that they should take off their mourning apparel. As for other affairs not addressed in this order, all should be handled in the sense of this order. [257] The order should be proclaimed all over the

[253]The passage sentence 朕之不明與嘉之 is read as a complete sentence by the Chung-hua editors. Wang Shu-min (10.405) cites Yen Shih-ku's opinion and suggests that the word *yü* 與 can be equivalent to *yü* 歟. Thus the passage can be parsed as 朕之不明與？嘉之. "Am I not brilliant? [Yet I received such a good ending.] I regard this [ending] a good thing." Takigawa (10.41) also believes that this sentence should be parsed between 朕之不明與 and 嘉之. But he argues that *chia chih* 嘉之 means "the ministers should regard this as a good thing." Wang Nien-sun 王念孫 (1.23b [81]) quoted "Chi-chieh" and concluded that *yü* was an expletive and an auxiliary word. Wang Li-ch'i (10.265) also follows this opinion.

[254]According to Fu Ch'ien 服虔 cited in "Chi-chieh," the word *chien* 踐 was interchangeable with *chien* 翦, which means to cut out mourning apparel with no hem. Such mourning apparel was called *chan-ts'ui* 斬衰 and it formed the most severe among the Five Degrees of Mourning Apparel (*Wu fu* 五服; see also Dubs, 1:269, n. 1). Meng K'ang 孟康 (ca. 180-260) says *chien* just means "to bare one's feet." Wang Li-ch'i (10.265) follows Meng K'ang's interpretation and says that to bare the feet in mourning is to express deep sorrow.

[255]The hemp ribbons are applied to both the head and the waist. According to the social codes, in wearing the mourning apparel with no hem (*chan-ts'ui*), the circumference of the ribbon around the head should be nine *ts'un*, while the ribbon around the waist should be four-fifths of that (see Wu Shu-p'ing and Lu Zongli, 10.364).

[256]The "Deep Mourning" (*Ta-kung* 大功 or *Ta-kung* 大紅), "Light Mourning" (*Hsiao-kung* 小功 or *Hsiao-kung* 小紅), and "Thin Hemp" (*Hsien* 纖 or *Ssu-ma* 緦麻) are all names from the Five Degrees of Mourning Apparel. According to traditional social codes, people should wear "Deep Mourning" for nine months, "Light Mourning" for five months, and "Thin Hemp" for three months. The institution of mourning apparel originated from the Chou period and was recorded in the *Yi li* 儀禮. For a detailed discussion of this system, see Ch'ü T'ung-tsu, *Han Social Structure*, pp. 313-15; Li Yü-chieh 李玉潔, *Hsien Ch'in sang-tsang chih-tu yen-chiu* 先秦喪葬制度研究 (Chengchow: Chung-chou Ku-chi, 1991), pp. 70-83.

[257]As Mu-chou Poo points out, lavish burials were very popular during the Ch'in-Han period. The Han Emperors usually enjoyed handsome funerals. Thus, the edict of Emperor Wen shows he tried to change

world, so that everyone will be clear about Our intentions. The mountains and rivers around Pa Mausoleum should be kept as they are, and nothing should be changed. Send back imperial consorts ranking from Lady to Junior Maid."[258]

[The Emperor] ordered that the Commandant of the Capital, Chou Ya-fu, be made the General of Chariots and Cavalry; the Director of Dependent States, Han 悍,[259] be made General of Encampment; and the Prefect of the Palace Attendants, [Chang] Wu, be made the General of Replacing the Earth. He sent out sixteen thousand soldiers on active service from nearby counties and fifteen thousand soldiers of the Clerk of the Capital. [These men would] bury the coffin, digging out and replacing the earth under the command of General [Chang] Wu.

[435] On the *yi-ssu* 乙巳 day (7 July 157 B.C.),[260] all the ministers struck their foreheads against the ground and offered the honored title "Emperor Wen the Filial."

[436] The Heir ascended the throne in the temple of Kao-ti. On the *ting-wei* 丁未 day (9 July 157 B.C.), he succeeded to the title of "Emperor."

In the tenth month of the first year of Hsiao Ching-ti 孝景帝 (The Filial and Luminous Emperor or Emperor Ching the Filial, r. 156-141 B.C.), he issued a decree and an edict to the Grand Master of the Imperial Scribes:[261] "[We] have heard that in ancient times, the ancestor

this custom and to lead the world to practice more frugal burial. See Mu-chou Poo, "Ideas Concerning Death and Burial in Pre-Han and Han China," *Asia Major* 3rd series, 3.2 (1990): 25-40. Li Yü-chieh says during the pre-Ch'in era ministers were expected to observe a mourning period of three years for his ruler. It is this edict by Emperor Wen that ended such practice. See Li Yü-chieh, *Hsien Ch'in sang tsang chih-tu yen-chiu*, p. 96.

[258]According to "Chi-chieh," below the rank of Lady, there were Beautiful Ladies, Sweet Ladies, Eighth Rank Ladies, Seventh Rank Ladies, Senior Maids, and Junior Maids (see also Bielenstein, p. 73, and Dubs, 1:271, n. 1).

[259]According to "Chi-chieh," his *cognomen* is given as Hsü 徐. On *Shih chi*, 22.1129, the name was given as Han 捍. "So-yin" says he was actually Hsü Li, the Marquis of Sung-tz'u 松兹. Takigawa (10.42 and 22.13) argues that Hsü Li died one year before Emperor Wen passed away, thus he believes that this was Hsü Tao 徐悼, the son of Hsü Li.

[260]According to *Han shu*, 4.132, Emperor Wen was buried in the Pa Mausoleum on that day.

[261]In the *Han shu*, the following edict by Emperor Ching, as well as the great ministers' discussion of Emperor Wen's merits, were all moved to the "Basic Annals of Emperor Ching" (*Han shu*, 5.137-38). Takigawa (10.44) argues that it is reasonable to put the following section in Chapter 11 ("The Basic Annals of Emperor Ching") and he believes that the "original text" of the *Shih chi* must have been so structured. He claims some later scholar copied this section from the *Han shu* and attached it to the end of the current version of *Shih chi* Chapter 10, since the original version of *Shih chi* Chapter 11 had been lost. On the other hand, Liang Yü-sheng (7.264) believes Ssu-ma Ch'ien had his reasons to put this section in Chapter 10, instead of Chapter 11. He points out that this section thematically continues the previous passage in Chapter 10 concerning the merits and virtue of Emperor Wen. *Shih chi p'ing chu* 史記評註 (in *Erh-shih-wu shih san pien* 二十五史三編, Chang Shun-hui 張舜徽, ed. [Changsha: Yüeh-lu Shu-she, 1994], p. 665) also points out Ssu-ma Ch'ien put this edict into the current chapter in order to summarize Emperor Wen's virtuous deeds, and this serves as a perfect ending for his chapter; whereas Pan Ku shows he only "knows how to write historical works, but does not know how to write literary works" (知作史而不知作文) when he moved this edict to the next chapter. Ssu-ma Ch'ien

achieved merit and the patriarch possessed virtue.[262] As for formulating social codes and music, each had their own cause. [We] have heard that songs are the means to elucidate virtue, and that dances are the means to clarify merit. When a libation[263] is offered in the Temple of Kao-ti, the Dances of Military Virtue, the Civilized Beginning and the Five Essences[264] are performed. When a libation is offered in the Temple of Hsiao Hui-ti, the Dances of the Five Essences and the Civilized Beginning are performed. When Hsiao Wen-ti governed the world, he opened up the passes and bridges,[265] making the remote areas no different [from areas near the capital]. He did away with laws concerning criticism, removed corporal punishment, granted rewards to the elders, and compensated orphans and the childless. By these means he nurtured all the living creatures. He restrained his desires, accepted no gifts[266] and did not seek his own selfish interests. He did not take criminals' relatives as slaves, and did not execute innocent people. He abolished the punishment of castration, and sent away the beauties, because he realized the severity of cutting off family lines.[267] We are unwise and unable to understand [all these things]. Even the ancients could not measure up to this, yet Hsiao Wen-ti practiced it personally. His virtue was as profound as that of Heaven and earth. His kindness and favor spread over the four seas. No one failed to obtain his blessing. His brilliance was like that of the sun and moon. Yet the music of the temple does not match it. We are extremely apprehensive about that. Let the Dance of

is showing his particular fascination with Emperor Wen's virtuous government here (see also "Translator's Note" below).

[262]According to "Chi-chieh," the person who first seized the world was called "the ancestor," the person who first administered the world was called "the patriarch." Wang Ch'i-yüan 王啟原 (cited in Takigawa, 10.44) says although K'ung-tzu chia yü 孔子家語 claimed these were the words of Confucius, there is no way to verify this. Wang also finds that the commentary to Hou Han shu (1.1) cited this sentence and said it was from the Li 禮 (The Classics of Rites). He suspects it to be from a lost passage in the Li. Actually, a sentence in the Han shu (48.2231) also seems to confirm that this is from the Li (see also Dubs, 1:304, n. 4).

[263]The original character is chou 酎. "Chi-chieh" says that people started to make this particular wine at the beginning of the year and that in the eighth month it was completed. The word chou literally means "pure wine."

[264]According to Han shu, 22.1044, the Dance of Military Virtue was composed in the fourth year of Kao-ti's reign (203 B.C.). It was to symbolize that the commoners of the world were happy because Kao-ti had used military force to bring peace to the world. The Dance of the Civilized Beginning originated from the Shao 招 Dance in the time of Shun. In the sixth year of Kao-ti's reign (201 B.C.) the name was changed to "The Civilized Beginning" to indicate the change of dynasties. The Dance of the Five Essences originated from the Military Dance of the Chou Dynasty. In the twenty-sixth year of the First Emperor of Ch'in's reign (221 B.C.), the name was changed to the Dance of Five Essences

[265]According to Han shu, 4.123, in the twelfth year of his reign (168 B.C.), Emperor Wen ordered that people no longer needed a pass to go through the passes and over the bridges. This order was not recorded elsewhere in Shih chi.

[266]In Han shu, 10.114, it says that in the sixth month of the first year of Emperor Wen (179 B.C.), he ordered that those who governed commanderies and states should not come to the court to present gifts. This order was also not recorded elsewhere in Shih chi.

Illustrious Virtue be performed at the Temple of Emperor Wen the Filial so as to make clear his moral excellence. After that, the merit and virtue of our ancestor and patriarch can be written down on bamboo and silk. They will be handed down from generation to generation, for ever and ever, without end. We praise this exceedingly. Let the chancellor, ranking marquises, officials ranking fully two thousand *shih,* and ritual officials draw up the ritual and ceremonial codes and then submit a memorial."

The Chancellor [Shen-t'u] Chia and other ministers said, "Your Majesty always thinks of filial duty. You established the Dance of Illustrious Virtue to make clear the abundant virtue of Hsiao Wen-ti. These are things to which your foolish ministers cannot measure up. Your ministers propose: as for the generational merit,[268] no one has been greater than Kao-ti; as for virtue, no one had it more abundantly than Hsiao Wen-ti. The Temple of Kao-ti should be the temple of the emperors' Grand Ancestor; the Temple of Hsiao Wen-ti should be the temple of the emperors' Grand Patriarch. The Son of Heaven should offer sacrifices at the temples of his ancestor and patriarch from generation to generation. Each commandery and feudal state should establish a 'Temple of the Patriarch' for Hsiao Wen-ti. Envoys of noble kings and ranking marquises should attend upon the Son of Heaven to offer sacrifices at the temples of the ancestor and the patriarch every year. We beg to have this written down on bamboo and silk and have it announced to the world." The emperor replied with the decree: "It is approved."

[437] His Honor the Grand Scribe says, "Confucius said, 'There must be one generation before the benevolence [prevails]. If good men administer the state for one hundred years, they will surely overcome tyranny and do away with killing.'[269] These words are indeed true! After Han arose, there had been over forty years up to the time of Hsiao Wen-ti His virtue was the most abundant. He was gradually approaching the point of changing the beginning of the year and the official color of the vestments, and offering the *Feng* 封 and *Shan* 禪 Sacrifices.[270] It was

---

[267]As seen above, Emperor Wen sent his palace women back home upon his death, here the reason is given—he wanted those women to bear children so as to continue their family lines.

[268]The term *shih-kung* 世功 comes from *Tso chuan* (Yang, *Tso chuan,* Ying 8, p. 62); Yang Po-chün notes that "generational merit" means the forefathers [of a clan] accumulated such merit that their official title became the *cognomen* of the clan. Wang Shu-min (10.408) and Dubs (1:308) argue the word *shih* is an interpolation, because it is does not seem to fit in the text here.

[269]These words are from the *Analects* (8.12): "If good men were to govern a country for a hundred years, they would certainly be able to overcome tyranny and do away with killing . . . . If a king were to arise, there would have to be a generation before there would be benevolence" (our translation, revised slightly from Legge, 1:267. Wang Shu-min (10.409) points out that the *Analects* reads *wei pang* 為邦 for *chih kuo* 治國. Ssu-ma Ch'ien changed the word *pang* to *kuo*, undoubtedly in order to avoid the taboo of Liu Pang's name. This fact may help to confirm the passage's authenticity.

[270]For the *Feng* Sacrifice, the emperor ascended Mount T'ai 泰 and offered sacrifices to Heaven. For the *Shan* Sacrifice, the emperor offered sacrifices to earth on Mount Liang-fu 梁父 (see *Grand Scribe's Records,* 1:138, n. 158). See also Chavannes, "Textes relatifs aux sacrifices fong et chan," in Édouard Chavannes,

only due to his modesty that up to now the task was not accomplished. Alas! Was he not [*438*] benevolent?"[271]

*   *   *   *   *

After the Han newly arose, the successor [to the throne] was unclear. The King [of Tai] was invited to ascend the throne, and people of the world submitted to him wholeheartedly. [The emperor] abolished corporal punishment, and opened up the passes and bridges. He extensively spread favor and kindness, thus he was called the Grand Patriarch. So I wrote Chapter 10, "The Basic Annals of Emperor Wen the Filial."[272]

LeT'ai Chan, essai de monographie d'un culte chinois (Paris: Leroux, 1910), pp. 158-261, and Chavannes translation of "Feng-shan shu" 封禪書 from the *Shih chi* published in 1890 as *Le Traité sur les Sacrifices Fong et Chan*, Extrait du *Journal of the Peking Oriental Society* (Peking: Pei-T'ang, 1890).

[271] As Takigawa (10.47) points out, if one ponders these comments carefully, it seems Ssu-ma Ch'ien was expressing his grievances against Emperor Wu (see further discussion in the "Translator's Note").

[272] This is Ssu-ma Ch'ien's account of why he wrote this chapter from his Postface, *Shih chi*, 130.3303.

Translator's Note

Questions have been raised as to the authenticity of this chapter. Ts'ui Shu 崔適 (1852-1924) pointed out that the records of the fifth, and seventh to twelfth years of the Emperor Wen's former reign period and the third to fifth years of the Later Reign period were missing, while in the *Han shu* records of the events of these years could be found. Ts'ui further argued that the original text of the *Shih chi* "Hsiao Wen pen-chi" 孝文本紀 had been lost and that the current text was a forgery copied back from the *Han shu*.[273] In a careful comparison of the annals of Emperor Wen in the *Shih chi* and the *Han shu*, the modern Korean scholar Park Jae-Woo 朴宰雨 pointed out that eight edicts had been added in these annals in the *Han shu*, but also noted that Pan Ku omitted some materials found in these *Shih chi* annals, transferring them to other relevant chapters in the *Han shu*.[274] If we examine those affairs and edicts which were not recorded in *Shih chi*, we can find they were primarily brief accounts of minor events; nonetheless, some among them are important. For example, on *Shih chi*, 10.436, an edict from Emperor Ching mentioned that Emperor Wen "had opened up passes and bridges" and "accepted no gifts," yet in the preceding pages there was no record of such affairs. The *Han shu*, by contrast, records both of these items.[275] Ssu-ma Ch'ien actually mentioned Emperor Wen's "opening up the passes and bridges" in his "Postface by His Honor the Grand Scribe" ("T'ai-shih kung tzu-hsü" 太史公自序),[276] which suggests he attached much importance to the matter.

From the above, readers may wonder why Ssu-ma Ch'ien did not record this event in his basic annals of Emperor Wen and suspect that part of the original chapter was lost. Another possibility is that Ssu-ma Ch'ien may just have omitted some minor events when he wrote his extensive work in haste, while Pan Ku, with Ssu-ma Ch'ien's book at hand, could unhurriedly check imperial archives and supplement and revise the latter's original work.

Moreover, it seems that Ts'ui Shih's contention that the chapter was a forgery is still untenable. If this text were a forgery and supposedly taken from the *Han shu*, then the forger should have had both time and material to make the chapter well organized. Why did he unwisely delete many of the *Han shu* materials to allow the text to look like a possible forgery? The translator has attempted to make close comparisons between the *Shih chi* and the *Han shu* in this chapter. In a number of instances it seems that the *Shih chi* variants either give a preferable reading or they show such distinct qualities that one can only identify them as following the

[273]Ts'ui Shih, *Shih chi t'an yüan* 史記探源 (Peking: Chung-hua, 1986), p. 65. It should be added that records of the fourth year of the former reign were also missing.

[274]Park Jae-woo, *Shih chi Han shu pi-chiao yen-chiu* 史記漢書比較研究 (Peking: Chung-kuo Wen-hsüeh Ch'u-pan-she, 1994), p. 80; see also Dubs, 1:214-15.

[275]See nn. 265 and 266 to the translation of this chapter.

[276]See *Shih chi*, 130.3303.

original writing of Ssu-ma Ch'ien, not that of a forger or copyist.[277] (For further discussion, see the "Introduction" to this volume).

Textual questions aside, this chapter seem to be an integral part of Ssu-ma Ch'ien's view of early Han history. As Michael Loewe points out, imperial stability faced a stern test following the death of Empress Lü and the subsequent expulsion of the Lüs by the great ministers.[278] Fundamental questions affected the imperial succession. In the beginning of this chapter, Ssu-ma Ch'ien indicates that the great ministers "sent a man to invite the King of Tai" in order to enthrone him. However, the parallel passage in "The Basic Annals of Empress Dowager Lü" (*Shih chi,* 9.411) reads: "[The great ministers] secretly sent a man to summon the King of Tai." It is strange that the ministers could "summon" the man they wanted to make emperor.[279] Moreover, the fact that they summoned the king in a secret manner arouses suspicion. A close look at the parallel account in Chapter 9 reveals that the idea of enthroning the King of Tai resulted from the great ministers' "secret plots" (*yin mou* 陰謀). The term yin mou occurs ten times in the *Shih chi* and in most cases it carries a negative connotation. For example, on *Shih chi,* 6.264 it is said that Chao Kao "secretly plotted" with Li Ssu to forge a letter they claimed had been written by the First Emperor of Ch'in in order to invest Hu Hai as the Heir.[280] As the first pages of this chapter show, the King of Tai was aware that the great ministers may have been scheming against him and therefore was reluctant to go to the capital. Most of his courtiers advised him not to go because of their mistrust of the great ministers.[281] Although Sung Ch'ang enumerated a number of reasons why the great ministers intended to enthrone the King of Tai, Sung missed the most important reason: that unlike the irrepressible Liu Chang, or his brother the King of Ch'i,[282] the great ministers must have suspected that the King of Tai would have been easier to control.

Thus from the first day that the King of Tai entered the capital there was an underlying tension between the great ministers and the king.[283] This tension is evident in Ssu-ma Ch'ien's description of their first encounter at the Wei Bridge: Chou Po, the most prominent figure among the great ministers, requested to speak with the king privately, but Sung Ch'ang bluntly

[277]See nn. 42, 64, 84, 87, 88, 93, 99, 261, 274, and 279.

[278]See *Cambridge History of China,* 1:136-7.

[279]Notice that the parallel passage on *Han shu,* 3.104 reads *tsun li Wen ti* 尊立文帝 "to honor and enthrone Emperor Wen" in place of "secretly sent a man to summon the King of Tai," suggesting that Pan Ku tried to emend the wording of the *Shih chi* text to dignify the passage.

[280]See *Grand Scribe's Records,* 1:154-5.

[281]*Shih chi,* 10.420 claims that all his officials except for Sung Ch'ang wanted to dissuade him from leaving Tai.

[282]Michael Loewe points out that the King of Ch'i was actually in the strongest position to inherit the throne, see *Cambridge History of China,* 1:137.

[283]As Hsü Shuo-fang points out, Emperor Wen's arrival at the capital did not mean the question of who would succeed Emperess Lü had been resolved, rather it indicated that events were nearing a crisis (see Hsü's *Shih Han lun-kao* 史漢論稿 [Nanking: Kiangsu Ku-chi, 1984], pp. 114-6, and Wang Han-ch'ang 王漢昌 "Han Wen-ti ch'u-cheng" 漢文帝初政, *Ho-pei Ta-hsüeh hsüeh-pao,* 1991.3: 79-80).

rejected his proposal. Shortly after the king ascended the throne as emperor, Chou Po mysteriously gave up his position as Chancellor of the Right. Grant Hardy points out there are conflicting versions of this story.[284] In one account, it seems Chou Po resigned because he was unable to answer Emperor Wen's specific questions, such as how many judicial cases there were each year. Another account relates that someone warned Chou that "misfortune is about to befall you," as a result of Po's boasting and his many awards.[285] Hardy wonders whether it was Chou Po's inability to respond to Emperor Wen's queries or his fear of the pendulum swings of fortune at the early Han court. It seems more likely that Chou Po's resignation followed from his sense that Emperor Wen wanted him gone. The emperor seems to have purposely put him in an awkward position by posing difficult questions; he may also have sent the person who warned Chou of impending trouble. It is noteworthy that although Chou Po was briefly restored to the position of chancellor, thereafter he was removed from this high office again and sent to his own fief where he spent his remaining years in constant fear that the emperor might decide to have him executed.[286]

Another incident which reveals the tension between the great ministers and the emperor was the rebellion of Liu Hsing-chü. Although the current chapter does not give the reasons why Liu rebelled, on *Shih chi*, 52.2010 there is a clear link between the rebellion and the "secret plots" of the great ministers. They had made a deal with Liu Hsing-chü and his brother Liu Chang to the effect that once the Lüs were all dead, Liu Hsing-chü would acquire the entire territory of Liang and Liu Chang would be given the kingdom of Chao. However, after Emperor Wen ascended the throne, he learned of the plan to enthrone the King of Ch'i and thereby only enfeoffed Hsing-chü and Chang with commanderies. Liu Chang and Chou Po were the two major figures in the great minister's overthrow of the Lüs and Liu Hsing-chü was also a force to be reckoned with. Yet within three years after ascending the throne, Emperor Wen was fortunate to witness Liu Chang's death, the failure of Liu Hsing-chü's rebellion, and the removal of Chou Po's from power. At this point Emperor Wen can be said to have secured his hold on the throne.

The rivalry between the great ministers and Emperor Wen is not openly discussed in this chapter. Any negative actions by the emperor in his attempt to secure power must be sought—as is often the case—in other chapters of the *Shih chi*. The modern scholar Chang Ta-k'o 張大可 rightly pointed out that Ssu-ma Ch'ien gave prominence to "virtue" (*te* 德) in his description of Emperor Wen in these annals.[287] The character *te* occurs forty-three times in his biography of Emperor Wen. By contrast, in the annals for Kao-tsu this word occurs only twice, in both cases it with a meaning other than "virtue;" in the biography of Empress Lü, there is no character *te*; in the biography of Emperor Ching, *te* occurs twice, but one of these occurrences was actually praising the virtue of Emperor Wen. In other chapters of the *Shih chi*, Ssu-ma Ch'ien constantly described Emperor Wen as a virtuous ruler. For example, on *Shih chi*, 25.1243, he said Emperor Wen was what Confucius called a virtuous gentleman.[288] On *Shih chi*, 113.2970,

---

[284]Hardy, *Bronze and Bamboo*, pp. 74-5.

[285]See *Shih chi*, 10.421, 56.2061, and 57.2072.

[286]See also the discussion in n. 153 above.

[287]Chang Ta-k'o, *Shih chi ch'uan-pen hsin-chu*, p. 250.

[288]In his comments on Chapter 10, Ssu-ma Ch'ien also cited Confucius to praise Emperor Wen.

he said that Emperor Wen made the feudal lords and four barbarian tribes understand his great virtue. In portraying Emperor Wen's virtue, Ssu-ma Ch'ien created an image of the ideal ruler, who was benevolent, modest, frugal and eager to care for the well being of the commoners. As scholars suggest, Ssu-ma Ch'ien's praise for Emperor Wen's virtue can actually be linked to his political concept of "virtuous rule" (*te chih* 德治),[289] it also served as a tool for satirizing Emperor Wu, who not only possessed none of Emperor Wen's virtue, but also went to the opposite extreme by engaging in violence, cruelty, and far-ranging military exploits. Shen Tso-che 沈作喆(fl. 1147) stated that like the "Hsiao Wu pen-chi" 孝武本紀 (Basic Annals of Emperor Wu the Filial) and "Feng Shan shu" 封禪書 (Treatise on the Feng and Shan Sacrifices), this chapter was also intended to satirize Emperor Wu.[290] In his comments at the end of this chapter, Ssu-ma Ch'ien said that Emperor Wen's virtue was so great that he deserved to perform the Feng and Shan sacrifices, and that it was only due to his modesty that he did not attempt them. This is in sharp contrast to Emperor Wu, who possessed no virtue but nonetheless was eager to perform these sacrifices. Thus, Ssu-ma Ch'ien's comments on Emperor Wen were actually on another level aimed at Emperor Wu.[291] Wu Chien-ssu 吳見思 (fl. 1680-90) further argued the whole chapter was in a sharp contrast to the annals of Emperor Wu and was therefore implicitly critical of Emperor Wu.[292]

It may be due to Ssu-ma Ch'ien's work that for a long time Emperor Wen was recognized by Chinese literati as representing the worthy ruler, and his reign the symbol a time of peace and propriety.[293] However, scholars have questioned whether Emperor Wen was as virtuous as

---

[289]For a discussion of Ssu-ma Ch'ien's concept of "virtuous rule," see Ch'en T'ung-sheng 陳桐生, *Chung-kuo shi-kuan wen-hua yü Shih chi* 中國史官文化與史記 (Taipei: Wen-chin Chu-pan-she, 1993), pp. 218-21.

[290]Cited in Yang, *Li-tai,* p. 363.

[291]See *Li-tai ming-chia p'ing Shih chi,* p. 424. Takigawa (10.47) and Dubs (*History of Former Han,* 1:275) express similar ideas. It is interesting to note that although the accounts of Emperor Wen in the *Shih chi* and the *Han shu* have great similarities, Ssu-ma Ch'ien's praise of Emperor Wen, which was regarded by many commentators as a hidden attack against Emperor Wu, was basically not repeated in Pan Ku's *Han shu*, a fact that further suggests this chapter was not copied from *Han shu*.

[292]Wu Chien-ssu, *Shih chi lun-wen* 史記論文 (Taipei: T'ai-wan Chung-hua Shu-chü, 1967), 1:94b.

[293]It seems as early as the end of the Former Han, the image of Emperor Wen as a sagacious ruler was common among Chinese literati. A passage from Ying Shao's 應劭 (ca. 140-ca. 206) *Feng su t'ung* 風俗通 reads: "Emperor Ch'eng 成 the Filial (r. 32-1 B.C.) asked Liu Hsiang 劉向 (77-6 B.C.), 'Later generations all said that Emperor Wen in administering the world almost reached the Great Peace. His virtue can be compared to that of the Duke of Chou 周'" (Wu Shu-p'ing 吳樹平, ed., *Feng-su t'ung-yi chiao-chu* 風俗通義校註 [Tientsin: T'ien-chin Ku-chi, 1979], 1:2.74). The famous poet Wang Ts'an 王粲 (177-217), facing the collapse of the Han empire, could only turn to the tomb of Emperor Wen at Pa-ling 霸陵 to express his yearning for a peaceful state: "In the south I climb the Pa-ling Ridge, / Turning my head I gaze towards Ch'ang-an" 南登霸陵岸，回首望長安 ("Ch'i ai shih 七哀詩, #1, in Ting Fu-pao 丁福保, ed., *Ch'üan Han San-kuo Chin Nan-pei ch'ao shih* 全漢三國晉南北朝詩 [Rpt. Taipei: Kuang-wen, 1968], 1:257; cf. Ronald Miao, *Early Medieval Chinese Poetry, the Life and Verse of Wang Ts'an* [Wiesbaden: Steiner, 1982], p. 132).

Ssu-ma Ch'ien portrayed him. Liang Yü-sheng pointed out that although Emperor Wen had abolished laws prosecuting the criminals' relatives, later he wiped out the clan of Hsin-yüan P'ing. In another instance he intended to wipe out the clan of another man simply because he stole a jade ring from the ancestral temple of the imperial clan. Liang further reminded readers that the "Hsing fa chih" 刑法志 (Record of Punishments and Laws) in the *Han shu* had already criticized his punishments as too severe.[294] Modern scholars have pointed out that the reign of Emperor Wen was not a period without problems and that Emperor Wen was not as virtuous as had been generally thought.[295] For example, although Emperor Wen appeared very frugal, he once granted Teng T'ung 鄧通, one of his male favorites, millions in cash.[296] In the present chapter, it seems that he was very strict with Lady Shen, his favorite consort. But on *Shih chi*, 101.2740, it is said that when he amused himself in the palace, he often took Lady Shen with him and let her sit on a seat of the same rank as that of the empress, an act which went against the social codes. Thus it seems that Ssu-ma Ch'ien carefully organized his source materials in order to create an image of an ideal ruler. That is to say, he selected only what he considered to be virtuous acts to include in "The Basic annals of Emperor Wen," relegating any less positive behavior to other chapters. The image of Emperor Wen was thereby "purified," even at the expense of 'historical truth.' Ssu-ma Ch'ien may be condemned for his skill in creating and adhering to the theme of Emperor Wen as a virtuous emperor—a demonstration that the Grand Scribe valued literary values as well as historical—but this literary manipulation of events should also undermine the likelihood that this chapter is from the pen of a forger.

[294]See Liang Yü-sheng, 7.261. In the "Hsing fa chih" 刑法志 (Record of Punishments and Laws; *Han shu*, 23.1099), Pan Ku relates that after Emperor Wen abolished corporal punishment, those who formerly would have had the toes on their right foot cut off, now received the death penalty; those who formerly would have had the toes on their left foot cut off, now received five hundred lashes, and those who formerly would have had their noses cut off, now received three hundred lashes—most of whom later died. Thus, Pan Ku concluded, "In name [this abolition] mitigated punishments, [but] in reality it killed people."

[295]For discussion of the defects of Emperor Wen and his reign, see Hsü Shuo-fang 徐朔方, "Lun Wen Ching chih chih" 論文景之治 in *Shih Han lun-kao* 史漢論稿, pp. 114-18; Ch'ien Mu 錢穆, *Ch'in Han shih* 秦漢史 (Taipei: Lian-ching, 1994), pp. 68-69; Li Ch'ang-chih 李長之 (1910-1978), *Ssu-ma Ch'ien chih jen-ko yu feng-ko* 司馬遷之人格與風格 (Rpt. Peking: San-lien, 1984 [1948]), pp. 126-27.

[296]See *Shih chi*, 125.3192.

Bibliography

I. Translations

Chavannes, 2:443-495.
Watson, *Han,* 1:285-310.
Viatkin, 2:221-46, notes 451-67.
Yoshida, 2: 624-73.

II. Studies

Ch'ien Mu 錢穆. "Wen Ching liang-ch'ao chih cheng-chih" 文景兩朝之政治, in *Ch'in Han shi* 秦漢史, 67-70.

Han Kuo-p'an 韓國磐. "Han Wen-ti ch'u jou-hsing k'ao-hsi" 漢文帝除肉刑考析 *Chung-kuo shih yen-chiu* 1991.2104-11.

Hsü Shuo-fang 徐朔方. "Lun Wen Ching chih chih" 論文景之治, in *Shih Han lun kao* 史漢論稿, 114-18.

Liu, Kuang-sheng. "Shih lun Han Wen-ti te kai-ko" 試論漢文帝的改革, *T'ien-chin she-hui k'o-hsüeh* 1985.4: 88-93.

Loewe, "Liu Heng 劉恆," *Dictionary,* pp. 306-11.

Yen Ying-ch'ing 閻應清. *Han Wen-ti* 漢文帝. Peking: Chung-hua Shu-chü, 1981.

Wang Han-ch'ang. "Han Wen-ti ch'u-cheng" 漢文帝初政, *Ho-pei Ta-hsüeh hsüeh-pao* 1991.3: 79-84.

The Filial and Luminous [Emperor], Basic Annals 11

[11.439] Hsiao Ching Huang-ti 孝景皇帝 (The Filial and Luminous August Emperor or The Filial Emperor Ching, r. 156–141 B.C.)[1] was a middle son of Hsiao Wen[-ti] 孝文帝 (The Filial and Cultured Emperor or Emperor Wen).[2] His mother was Tou T'ai-hou 竇太后 (Empress Dowager Tou).[3] At the time Hsiao Wen[-ti][4] was in Tai 代,[5] his former queen had three sons. When Tou T'ai-hou gained favor, the former queen died, and then the former queen's three sons died one after the other.[6] For these reasons, Hsiao Ching[-ti] was able to be established [as the Heir].

On the *yi-mao* 乙卯 day of the fourth month of the first year (20 May 156 B.C.), [the Emperor] granted an amnesty throughout the world.

On the *yi-ssu* 乙巳 day (8 May 156 B.C.) he granted the commoners an increase of one rank.[7]

---

[1]The new emperor ascended the throne on the *ting-wei* 丁未 day of the sixth month of the seventh year of the Later Reign of Emperor Wen, i.e., 9 July 156 B.C. (see *Shih chi*, 10.436 and *Han chi*, 9.1a).

[2]Liu Ch'i 劉啟 (188-141 B.C., *agnomen* K'ai 開 according to Hsün Yüeh's 荀悅 [148-209] comment cited in the commentary on *Han shu*, 5.137) was a son of Liu Heng 劉恆 (203-157 B.C.) ruled from 180-157 B.C. and was posthumously titled Emperor Hsiao Wen 孝文. Thus he was Kao-tsu's grandson. Although Liang Yü-sheng (7.265) argues that Liu Ch'i's three half-brothers by the former queen of Tai should not figure in Liu Ch'i's familial rank, it seems that he was a 'middle son' as here stated. Neither the *Han shu* nor the *Han chi* mentions his birth order. Michael Loewe, *Dictionary,* p. 338, in his entry on Liu Ch'i notes he "was born in 188 as one of the two sons of Wendi and the Empress Dou 竇, surviving the death of three other sons born to the emperor by other women." Aside from the fact that all three were born to Liu Heng's former queen—one woman—Loewe's is perhaps the best statement of Liu Ch'i's familial rank (see also n. 6 below and *Shih chi,* 11.439 and 58.2081).

[3]After Emperor Ching ascended the throne Empress Tou was honored as the Empress Dowager (Wang Li-ch'i, 11.275n.). See her biography on *Shih chi*, 49.1972.

[4]Emperor Wen the Filial was enthroned as the King of Tai during the eleventh year of the reign of Kao-tsu (196 B.C.; see *Shih chi* 10.413).

[5]Tai was a kingdom at the beginning of the Han in the region of modern Hopei, Inner Mongolia and the northeast part of Shansi (Wang Li-ch'i, 11.275n.).

[6]According to *Shih chi,* 49.1972 and *Han shu*, 97A.3943, she had four sons. Wu and Lu (11.377) also note this discrepancy.

[7]According to Chavannes, this date is incorrect. The *yi-ssu* day is the forty-second day of the cycle, and here it follows the *yi-mao* day, which is the fifty-second day of the cycle (Chavannes, 2:497, n. 1). Liang Yü-sheng (7.265) also notes this discrepancy and argues that this *yi-ssu* is an interpolation, since according to

In the fifth month (27 May–24 June) he exempted one half of the land tax.[8] For Hsiao Wen[-ti] he erected the T'ai-tsung Miao 太宗廟 (Grand Patriarch Temple). He ordered that the assembled ministers need not come to court to congratulate [him]. The Hsiung-nu entered Tai, and he agreed with a marital alliance.[9]

In the spring of the second year (155 B.C.), he enfeoffed Hsi 係, the grandson of the former Minister of State, Hsiao Ho 蕭何, as the Marquis of Wu-ling 武陵.[10] Young men twenty years old registered [for conscription].[11]

Han custom, the general amnesty and the granting of increases of rank normally took place on the same day. Wu and Lu (11.377) offer a similarly detailed argument that *yi-ssu* should be deleted.

[8]During the thirteenth year of his reign (167 B.C.), Emperor Wen had entirely abolished agricultural taxes. Here his successor reestablishes one half of the ancient taxes. Chavannes quotes the *T'ung-chien kang-mu* 通鑒綱目 in assessing this value to be one-thirtieth of the land's yield (Chavannes, 2:497, n. 3). See also n. 195 to the translation of Chapter 10 above.

[9]Although *Han shu*, 5.140 claims this treaty was concluded by Yen Ch'ing-ti 嚴青翟, the commentary there notes that Yen lived later during Emperor Wu's reign and T'ao Ch'ing 陶青 was the man who represented the Han in these negotiations. Yen Shih-ku in a note to the *Han shu* passage concurs, noting that *ti* 翟 seems to be an interpolation.

On *ho-ch'in* see also n. 232 to our translation of *Shih chi* Chapter 10 above. The terms of this treaty are revealed in a letter of complaint sent by the Hsiung-nu *Shan-yü* to the Han in response to demands the former felt were not part of the original treaty: "In the old agreement, Han often sent princesses, and provided silks and foodstuffs of various grades in order to conclude a marital alliance; and the Hsiung-nu also did not trouble the border" (*Han shu*, 94A.3773; cf. 94A.3780).

[10]See Hsiao Ho's biography in *Shih chi* Chapter 53. His appointment to the position of Minister of State is mentioned on *Shih chi*, 53.2017. According to Hsü Kuang in the "Chi-chieh," Hsiao's grandson Hsi is also referred to in the *Han shu* (in both the "Table of Meritorious Vassals," 16.543, and the "Memoir of Hsiao Ho," 39.2012) as Hsiao Chia 嘉. Hsü believes that he had two *praenomina*. Liang Yü-sheng notes that the *Han shu* (16.543) records that Hsiao Chia was enfeoffed as the Marquis of Wu-yang 武陽, not Wu-ling.

Wu-ling was a commandery originally known as Ch'ien-chung 黔中 during the Ch'in, occupying a region in modern southwest Hunan and northeast Kueichow. Wu-yang, on the other hand, was a county about thirty miles south of modern Chengtu in Szechwan (T'an Ch'i-hsiang, 2:22–3, 29–30). Wang Hui lists the fief as Wu-yang (p. 525, entry 776). Which place Hsiao was actually enfeoffed with remains unclear. *Han shu* (5.141) and *Han chi* (9.2a) avoid the problem by simply noting that "he became a ranking marquis" (*wei lieh-hou* 為列侯) without mentioning his fief. Liang Yü-sheng (7.265), however, argues convincingly that a commandery was much too large to serve as a fief. Liang also notes that the *Han chi* records this event as occurring in the sixth month of summer, rather than the second month of spring, but the current *Han chi* (9.2a) clearly dates it to "the eighth month of fall."

[11]This registration was for both military service as well as corvée labor (on *fu* 傅 see the comments by Ju Shun and Yen Shih-ku on *Han shu*, 1.37-8). Elsewhere Yen Shih-ku claims that the age should be twenty-three (*Han shu*, 5.141). Takigawa (11.3) argues that fifteen was the age for young men to register and that Emperor Ching was liberally lifting the age limit to twenty. *Ch'in Han shih* (p. 494) is similar, noting that the

On the *jen-wu* 壬午 day of the fourth month (9 June 155 B.C.), the Hsiao Wen T'ai-hou 孝文太后 (Empress Dowager of the Filial and Cultured [Emperor]) passed away.[12] The kings of Kuang-ch'uan 廣川[13] and Ch'ang-sha 長沙[14] both went to their states. Chancellor Shen-t'u Chia 申屠嘉 expired.[15]

In the eighth month he made Grand Master of the Imperial Scribes T'ao Ch'ing 陶青, the Marquis of K'ai-feng 開封,[16] the Chancellor. A comet appeared in the northeast.[17]

age under the Ch'in dynasty was seventeen, raised to twenty by Emperor Ching.

[12]See the short biography of Empress Dowager Po in *Shih chi* Chapter 49.

[13]Kuang-ch'uan was originally called Hsin-tu 信都, the name being changed by Emperor Ching in the early part of his reign. Its seat was in Hsin-tu, which was in Chi 冀 county in modern Hopei. The King of Kuang-ch'uan at this time was Liu P'eng-tsu 劉彭祖, the eighth son of Emperor Ching (Wang Li-ch'i, 11.275n.).

[14]Ch'ang-sha corresponds to modern Changsha in Hunan. The King of Ch'ang-sha at this time was Liu Fa 劉發, the tenth son of Emperor Ching (Wang Li-ch'i, 11.275n.); see also Liu Fa's biography in *Shih chi* Chapter 59.

[15]Chavannes notes that the *Han shu* (5.141) indicates this death occurred in the sixth month (Chavannes, 2:498, n. 1).

[16]T'ao Ch'ing held this fief until 150 B.C. and was posthumously titled Marquis Yi 夷. His father, T'ao She 陶舍, had originally been enfeoffed with K'ai-feng (posthumously titled Marquis Min 閔) in 196 B.C. for his meritorious service during the reign of Kao-tsu (see *Shih chi*, 18.952-3 and n. 9 above); he died the following year.

K'ai-feng was county about fifteen miles south of the modern city of Kaifeng in Honan (Wang Hui, p. 432, entry 608).

[17]As Liang Yü-sheng (7.266) points out, both the "Ching-ti chi" 景帝紀 and the "T'ien wen chih" 天文志 of the *Han shu* have records of a comet in the second year which differ with this account. The "Ching-ti chi" (*Han shu*, 5.141) reads: 二年冬十二月，有星孛于西南; "In the twelfth month of winter of the second year there was a comet in the southwest." The "T'ien-wen chih" (*Han shu*, 26.1303) reads: 是歲彗星出西南; "During this year a comet appeared in the southwest." The *Han chi* (9.1b) reads: 二年冬十一月，有星孛于西南; "In the eleventh month of winter of the second year there was a comet in the southwest." In his comment on the text in this chapter, Dubs notes (1.312n.): "This is comet no. 18 in John Williams, *Chinese Observations of Comets* (London, 1871). Williams' date is incorrect; this month was Jan. 18–Feb. 15, 155 B.C. The *Han chi*, 9.1b erroneously dates this comet in the eleventh month; the *Tzu-chih T'ung-chien* reads as the present text does." Dubs obscures, however, the fact that the *Tzu-chih t'ung-chien* (16.512 and 513) preserves records of these two comets as two separate events, an understanding shared by Wang Shu-min (11.413).

According to *Shih chi*, 27.1348-9, the appearance of this comet, along with some of the following portents, is associated with the imminent Rebellion of the Seven Kingdoms (see text below and *Han shu*, 26.1303-4). However, the pattern formed by the portents, peaking at the beginning and the end of Emperor Ching's reign, leads Wolfram Eberhard to suggest that the Scribes of these annals and its parallels wanted to criticize Emperor Ching personally (see "The Political Function of Astronomy and Astronomers in Han China," in *Chinese Thought and Institutions*, ed. John K. Fairbank [Chicago: University of Chicago Press, 1957], p. 58). For a recent study of comets in the Han, see Michael Loewe, "The Han View of Comets," in *Divination*, pp.

In the autumn hail fell in Heng-shan 衡山,[18] the large ones [hailstones] measured five
ts'un, the deep ones [penetrating to] two *ch'ih.*[19] Mars moved in retrograde and guarded the
North Star. The moon appeared in the vicinity of the North Star.[20] Sui Hsing 歲星 (Jupiter)
[*440*] retrograded amid the constellation T'ien-t'ing 天廷 (Heaven's Court).[21] [the Emperor]

61–84.

[18]Heng-shan was a state occupying the modern area corresponding to eastern Hupei, southern
Honan, and western Anhwei. Heng-shan took its name from a mountain which is now called Huo-shan 霍山 (in
modern Anhwei) within its boundaries. Its seat was at Chu 邾, which is north of Huang-kang 黃岡 county in
modern Hupei (Wang Li-ch'i, 11.275n.).

[19]The original text reads 大者五寸深者二尺, but Wang Nien-sun (2.24b [p. 82]) claims that the *che*
者 following the character *shen* 深 is an interpolation. He bases this on quotations of this passage in the *Ch'u
hsüeh chi* 初學記 and the *T'ai-p'ing yü-lan* which do not have this character (Takigawa, 11.4). In light of
Wang's claims, as well as the physical improbability of a hailstone penetrating the ground to a *depth* of two
ch'ih, a more likely reading of this passage would be "the large ones [hailstones] measuring up to five *ts'un* in
diameter, [piled up] to a depth of two *ch'ih.*"

[20]Mars is associated with chaos in general and with the presence of armies in particular (see *Shih
chi,* 27.1332 and 1371, respectively), as well as with times when Wu or Ch'u were mighty (see *Shih chi,*
27.1346). *Ying-huo* 熒惑, the term employed here for Mars, is also used in a rare occurrence in the *Shih chi* by
one of the rebellious King of Wu's officials in its other sense to describe Ch'ao Ts'o (see n. 34 below) as
"misleading (*ying-huo*) the Emperor, encroaching on and seizing [the lands of] the feudal lords . . . who all have
intentions of rebelling" (see *Shih chi,* 106.2826).

[21]Heaven's Court (*T'ien-t'ing* 天廷 or 天庭) is the alternative designation for the constellation Grand
Tenuity (*T'ai-wei* 太微; see Fang Hsüan-ling 房玄齡 [578-648], *et al., Chin shu* 晉書 [Peking: Chung-hua
shu-chü, 1974], 11.291-2). Liang Yü-sheng (7.266) believes that these movements of two planets and the moon
are not in keeping with astronomical probability and cites the *Han shu* "T'ien-wen chih" 天文志 (26.1303) as
containing more relevant information on the movement of the planets. David Pankenier (in personal correspondence
dated 25 September 2000) has offered the following comments (the romanization has been changed to Wade-Giles
for consistency): "The problem is essentially that, if *pei-ch'en* (the pole-star asterism) and *t'ien-ting (San-t'ai*
asterism) are given their usual attested meanings, the positional observations involving Mars, the Moon and
Jupiter become physically impossible. The orbital inclination of Mars and Jupiter of 1.8 and 1.3 degrees
respectively means that neither is ever seen farther than that from the ecliptic. There is simply no way any of
them could ever be observed in the vicinity of the north polar region to which *pei-ch'en* and *t'ien-t'ing* both
refer. The same is true of the Moon. The translation 'constellations north of the ecliptic' [which was our original
rendering here—Editor] for *pei-ch'en* is not acceptable, even if understandable as an attempt to reconcile the
irreconcilable. Even if this did solve the problem for Mars and the Moon, the problem of Jupiter's purported
position remains unresolved. Comparison with *Han shu,* 26.1303, and reconstructing the actual locations of the
planets during the early years of Ching-ti suggests the following: (1) *Han shu* is correct in placing Me, Ma, Ve,
Ju in lunar mansion #26 Chang (Hya) in summer 156 B.C., or Ching I; (2) In the following year (Ching II) Ma
retrograded in Gem and was extremely close to the full Moon (< 1 deg) on 12/21 near Beta Gem (LM #22
Tung-ching), but these positions do not shed light on the strange record on *Shih chi,* 11.440, except perhaps for

established Nan-ling 南陵 (Southern Mausoleum) and Tui-hsü 祋祤 of Nei-shih 內史 as counties.[22]

On the *yi-ssu* 乙巳 day of the first month of the third year (27 February 154 B.C.), [the Emperor] granted an amnesty throughout the world.[23] An elongated star appeared in the west.[24] Heavenly fire burned the walls and chambers of the Great Hall in the Eastern Palace in Lo-yang.[25]

the mention of the Moon in close proximity to Mars. (3) The same year (Ching II = 155), according to *Han shu,* Ma and Me were in conjunction in lunar mansion #8 Nan-tou. This is correct for 154 = Ching III, *not* 155. So *Han shu erh nien* 二年 is an obvious copyist's error for *san nien* 三年. (4) Both *Shih chi* and *Han shu* record the appointments of several kings in Ching II and the appearance of a comet (in the West according to *Shih chi* in the SW according to *Han shu*)."

"Conclusion: Since we now know the *Han shu* Ching II record actually dates from Ching III, the events recorded in *Han shu* under Ching II = 155 actually occurred in Ching III = 154, including the cometary apparition and probably also the kingly appointments as well. The *Shih chi,* 11.440 record is undoubtedly corrupt but probably also originally recorded events of Ching III = 154. The locations given for Ma, Moon and Ju in *Shih chi* are quite impossible for those bodies, but very reasonable for the comet sighted in 154, which is mentioned in both *Shih chi* and *Han shu.* I suspect what happened is that the two positional records (Ma, Ju and Moon on the one hand, and comet on the other) have somehow been confused and conflated. In any case, I cannot believe *Shih chi,* 11.440 originally contained the problematic sentence as it now stands, as neither Ssu-ma T'an nor Ssu-ma Ch'ien could have made such a gross error."

[22]Nei-shih was the capital district (Wang Hui, p. 533, entry 788), a title first given by the Ch'in and reinstated by Liu Pang for the Han in 198 B.C. Tui-hsü was located about forty miles north of modern Sian near modern Yao 耀 County; Nan-ling was the settlement which had naturally begun to grow around the worksite of the mausoleum intended for Emperor Wen's Empress Po 薄 who had died earlier in the year (see *Shih chi,* 49.1972 and T'an Ch'i-hsiang, 2:15).

[23]*Han shu,* 5.142 dates this amnesty after the beginning of the Revolt of the Seven Kingdoms which follows in the text here.

[24]Wen Ying 文穎 (*fl.* 200) distinguishes three types of comets (*po* 孛, *hui* 彗 and *ch'ang* 長)—"bushy," "broomlike," and "long"—and notes that *po* and *hui* often suggest the implementation of something new, while *ch'ang* suggest a potential military revolt (*Han shu,* 4.122). Michael Loewe, in his "The Han View of Comets" (p. 73), points out that it would be difficult to apply these distinctions to all Han-dynasty records of comets.

In the "T'ien-kuan chih" and Liu An's biography, a comet visible in this year was clearly associated with the Rebellion of the Seven Kingdoms (see *Shih chi,* 27.1348 and 118.3082 respectively).

[25]*T'ien-huo* 天火 probably refers to *ignis fatuus.* This is the only reference to this phenomenon in the *Shih chi.* On *ignis fatuus* in general, see William H. Nienhauser, Jr., "A UFO in Ancient China: A Comparative Study of the *Pi-fang* 畢方 (Fire Crane) and Its Western Analogues," *Asian Culture Quarterly,* XVII (Winter 1989): 67-79.

The *Han shu* (5.142) has a variant reading here: 春正月，淮陽王宮正殿災; "In the first month in spring, the main hall of the palace of the King of Huai-yang burned." Wu and Lu (11.378n.) argue that this referred to the palace of the King of Huai-yang, Liu Yü 劉餘 (d. 128 B.C.), Emperor Ching's son (brief biography on *Shih chi,* 59.2095 and an expansive entry in Loewe, *Dictionary,* p. 402).

However, it would seem more likely that this reference is to the eastern palace Kao-tsu built in

[Liu] P'i 濞, the King of Wu 吳[26]; [Liu] Wu 戊, the King of Ch'u 楚[27]; [Liu] Sui 遂, King of Chao 趙[28]; [Liu] Ang 卬, the King of Chiao-hsi 膠西[29]; [Liu] Pi-kuang 辟光, the King of Chi-nan 濟南[30]; [Liu] Hsien 賢, the King of Tzu-ch'uan 菑川[31]; and [Liu] Hsiung-ch'ü 雄渠, the King of Chiao-tung 膠東[32] revolted and sent out troops heading west.[33] The Son of Heaven, for them,

Lo-yang (he also had southern and northern palaces built there) while it was his capital and that both the comet and this heavenly fire were omens which foretold the Rebellion of the Seven Kingdoms against the Han. It seems rather uncommon to record fires in the various states or commanderies of the Han empire in the annals. The *Tzu-chih t'ung-chien* (16.516) follows the *Shih chi* text and records a fire in the Eastern Palace in Lo-yang. See also Chavannes, 2:498-9, n. 6.

[26]Liu P'i was the son of Kao-tsu's second oldest brother, Liu Chung 劉仲. Under Emperor Wen's reign, Liu P'i's son and Heir, Liu Hsien 劉賢, had been killed by the imperial Heir, Liu Ch'i, while they were drinking. Although Emperor Wen did not punish his son, he was extremely tolerant of Liu P'i, who increasingly acted in a manner which indicated his disregard from the Han court. Liu P'i's revolt—which became known as the Rebellion of the Seven Kingdoms—against Liu Ch'i, now emperor, was in part provoked by the arguments put forth by Ch'ao Ts'o to restrict Liu P'i's actions and reduce the power of the Kingdom of Wu. See his biography in *Shih chi* Chapter 106. For an excellent map of the Han kingdoms, see Loewe, *Dictionary*, p. 810.

[27]The grandson of Kao-tsu's younger half-brother Liu Chiao 劉交, King of Ch'u. He had also been attacked by Ch'ao Ts'o and accused with immoral behavior (*Shih chi*, 106.2825).

[28]Liu Sui was Kao-tsu's grandson, son of Liu Yu 劉友, King Yu 幽 of Chao (see his biography, *Shih chi*, 50.1989-90). His kingdom was also reduced in size as a result of his 'crimes' (*Shih chi*, 106.2825).

[29]Kao-tsu's grandson, son of Liu Fei, 劉肥, King Tao-hui 悼惠 of Ch'i 齊; he had been the Marquis of P'ing-ch'ang 平昌 until he was made King of Chiao-hsi in 164 B.C. (see his biography on *Shih chi*, 52.2011-2). Liu Ang at first did not want to join the rebellion, but was persuaded by Liu P'i's minister Ying Kao 應高, and finally by a personal visit from Liu P'i himself (*Shih chi*, 106.2825-26). Liu Ang was killed by the Han troops.

[30]This was another of the sons of King Tao-hui of Ch'i. He received his appointment as king in 164 B.C. and was brought into the conspiracy by his brother, Liu Ang. See Liu Pi-kuang's biography on *Shih chi*, 52.2010.

[31]Another of Liu Ang's brothers, Liu Hsien had also been given his kingdom in 164 B.C. after serving as Marquis of Wu-ch'eng 武城, and he too fell in the rebellion. See his biography on *Shih chi*, 52.2011.

[32]Yet another son of King Tao-hui of Ch'i, Liu Hsiung-ch'ü had been made king in 164 B.C. after serving as Marquis of Pai-shih 白石. After his death following the rebellion, Chiao-tung was made into a commandery. See his biography on *Shih chi*, 52.2011.

Liu Chih 劉志 (d. 129 B.C.), the final brother of this group of sons of Liu Fei, had agreed to join the conspiracy, but could not complete his preparations in time to send out troops with the other rebels. As a result, he was able to avoid recriminations following the suppression of the rebellion, although he was transferred to the smaller kingdom of Tzu-ch'uan (he was posthumously titled King Yi 懿 of Tzu-ch'uan; see his biography on *Shih chi*, 52.2011, and the relevant passage in Liu P'i's biography on *Shih chi*, 106.2827).

[33]This refers to the seven kingdoms that revolted ostensibly in order to force the execution of Ch'ao Ts'o (on Ch'ao see the note immediately below).

executed Ch'ao Ts'o 晁錯[34] and sent Yüan Ang 袁盎 (d. 148 B.C.)[35] to inform and instruct them; they did not stop, moving west and besieging Liang 梁.[36] The sovereign thereupon sent Commander in Chief Tou Ying 竇嬰 (d. 131 B.C.)[37] and the Grand Commandant Chou Ya-fu 周亞夫 (d. 143 B.C.)[38] to lead troops to execute them.

On the *yi-hai* 乙亥 day of the sixth month (27 July 154 B.C.), [the Emperor] pardoned the troops that had fled and Yi 蓺, the son of King Yüan 元 of Ch'u 楚,[39] and others who had participated in plotting rebellion.[40] He enfeoffed the Commander in Chief Tou Ying as the Marquis of Wei-chi 魏其.[41] He established the son of King Yüan of Ch'u, [Liu] Li 禮,[42] the Marquis of P'ing-lu 平陸,[43] as the King of Ch'u.

[34]Ch'ao Ts'o (200-154 B.C.; biography in *Shih chi*, Chapter 101) was a native of Ying-ch'uan 潁川 (a commandery centered around modern Hsü-ch'ang 許昌 in Honan [T'an Ch'i-hsiang, 2:19]) and had served as Scribe of the Capital and Grand Master of the Imperial Scribes; he advocated policies that emphasized agriculture and suppressed trade. He also advocated fortifying the borders with troops to stop the advancing Hsiung-nu and seizing fiefdoms from marquises in order to strengthen the power of the central government. When the Seven Kingdoms revolted, the emperor finally heeded Tou Ying and Yüan Ang, and had Ch'ao don his imperial robes and appear in the eastern market of the capital, there to be cut in half (*Shih chi*, 101.2747).

[35]Yüan Ang held several important positions at court, and was on notoriously bad terms with Ch'ao Ts'o. It was he who suggested to the Emperor to have Ch'ao Ts'ao executed so as to assuage the feudal lords. See his biography in *Shih chi* Chapter 101.

[36]Located near the border of modern Honan and Anhwei (Wang Li-ch'i, 11.276n.).

[37]The nephew of Empress Tou. See his biography in *Shih chi* Chapter 107.

[38]Chou Ya-fu 周亞夫 (d. 143 B.C.) was a native of P'ei 沛 (near modern P'ei County in Kiangsu [T'an Ch'i-hsiang, 2:19]) and a son of Chou Po 周勃. He was originally enfeoffed as the Marquis of T'iao 條. He also served as a general. During the time of Emperor Ching, he served as the Grand Commandant and as Chancellor. He was the most important general in the pacification and stabilization of Wu, Ch'u and the Seven Kingdoms. Afterward he was imprisoned and starved to death (Wang Li-ch'i, 11.276n.), the details of which are given in his biography in *Shih chi* Chapter 57. *Han shu*, 5.142 details the deaths of the rebelling kings and relates that in crushing the rebellion Chou Ya-fu and Tou Ying cut off more than 100,000 heads. On *T'ai-wei* 太尉 or Grand Commandant see n. 456 to our translation of Chapter 8 above.

[39]King Yüan of Ch'u, Liu Chiao 劉交, was one of Kao-tsu's younger brothers from a different mother, thus a half-brother. Yüan was his posthumous title (Wang Li-ch'i, 11.276n.). See also his biography in *Shih chi* Chapter 50.

[40]See n. 32 above. *Han shu*, 5.142-3 contains an edict which outlines this pardon.

[41]Southeast of Lin-yi 臨沂 County in modern Shantung (Wang Li-ch'i, 11.276n.).

[42]This appointment was made with the approval of Empress Dowager Tou who rejected at the same time a proposal to appoint Liu P'i's younger brother, Liu Kuang 劉廣, King of Wu (*Shih chi*, 50.1988-9).

[43]Wang Li-ch'i (11.276n.) and Wang Hui (p. 518, entry 755) locate P'ing-lu in the northeast part of Wei-shih 尉氏 County in modern Honan. T'an Ch'i-hsiang (2:8) indicates P'ing-lu as a county under the Ch'in near modern Tung-p'ing 東平 in Shantung, but he gives no location for a P'ing-lu during the Han dynasty.

[The Emperor] enthroned the imperial son [Liu] Tuan 端[44] as the King of Chiao-hsi 膠西 and his son [Liu] Sheng 勝[45] as the King of Chung-shan 中山.[46] He transferred [Liu] Chih 志,[47] the King of Chi-pei 濟北,[48] to be the King of Tzu-ch'uan 菑川[49]; [Liu] Yü 餘,[50] the King of Huai-yang 淮陽, to be the King of Lu 魯[51]; and [Liu] Fei 非,[52] King of Ju-nan 汝南, as the King of Chiang-tu 江都.[53] [Liu] Chiang-lu 將廬,[54] the King of Ch'i, and [Liu] Chia 嘉,[55] the King of Yen

[44]Liu Tuan (d. 108), Emperor Ching's son by Beauty Ch'eng 程, had a reputation as a cruel but clever man (see Loewe, *Dictionary,* pp. 293-4). Despite controversies with a number of advisors and courtiers, he ruled Chiao-hsi for forty-seven years until his death in 108 B.C. He was posthumously titled King Yü 于 of Chiao-hsi (see his biography on *Shih chi,* 59.2097).

[45]Liu Sheng, Emperor Ching's son by Beauty Chia 賈, ruled for forty-two years until he died in 112 B.C. For most of his reign, he indulged himself in pleasure; he left a large number of sons. He was posthumously titled King Ching 靖 of Chung-shan (see his biography on *Shih chi,* 59.2099).

[46]Located west and south of modern Paoting City in Hopei, its capital was at modern Ting 定 County (T'an Ch'i-hsiang, 2:26).

[47]On Liu Chih see n. 32 above.

[48]Located southwest of modern Tsinan in Shantung (and to the south west of the state of Chi-nan; T'an Ch'i-hsiang, 2:44).

[49]According to the "Cheng-yi" (*Shih chi,* 11.440) its capital was at Chü-ch'eng 劇城, about ten miles south of modern Shou-kuang 壽光 in north-central Shantung (see also T'an Ch'i-hsiang, 5:45).

[50]Liu Yü was posthumously titled King Kung 共 of Lu, Emperor Ching's son by Beauty Ch'eng 程 (see *Shih chi,* 59.2095).

[51]Huai-yang was a state situated in what is now Honan, north and east of the modern city of Huai-yang. Lu was located about one hundred miles northeast of Huai-yang, in the southern part of modern Shantung east of the modern city of Chi-ning 濟寧 (T'an Ch'i-hsiang, 2:19-20).

[52]Liu Fei (168-127 B.C.) was a son of Emperor Ching by Beauty Ch'eng and the elder brother of Emperor Wu; he was posthumously titled King Yi 易 of Chiang-tu (see his biography on *Shih chi,* 59.2096).

[53]Ju-nan was located in the area of modern Ju-nan in southeastern Honan; T'an Ch'i-hsiang (2:19) shows Ju-nan Commandery. Chiang-tu was located about five miles southwest of modern Yangchow 揚州 in Kiangsu (T'an Ch'i-hsiang, 2:20). On the scope of the Kingdom of Chiang-tu, see *Han shu pu-chu,* 28B(2).40b-41a (pp. 848-49).

[54]Liu Chiang-lü 劉將閭 (sometimes written 將廬), was a brother of Liu Wu, Liu Sui, Liu Ang, etc., but he resisted their pressure to join the Rebellion of the Seven Kingdoms; nevertheless fearing reprisals after the rebellion was put down, he poisoned himself. According to "So-yin," he was King Tao-hui of Ch'i's grandson; he was posthumously titled King Hsiao 孝 of Ch'i (see *Shih chi,* 19.998-99, 52.2005, and 106.2827).

[55]Liu Chia, mentioned in passing on *Shih chi,* 51.1997, was the son and successor to Liu Tse 劉澤, King Ching 敬 of Yen. He was made king in 177 B.C. (*Shih chi,* 17.829) and implicated as one of the rebels in a letter Liu P'i wrote to the conspirators (*Shih chi,* 106.2828). Since Liu Chia died two years later, it seems unlikely that he committed suicide, like Liu Chiang-lü. He was posthumously titled King K'ang 康 of Yen.

燕,[56] [*441*] both passed on.[57]

[442] In the summer of the fourth year (153 B.C.) [the Emperor] established the Heir.[58] He enthroned the imperial son [Liu] Ch'e 徹[59] as King of Chiao-tung 膠東.[60]

On the *chia-hsü* 甲戌 day of the sixth month (20 July 153 B.C.), [the Emperor] granted an amnesty throughout the world.

In the intercalary month after the ninth month (18 October-16 November 152 B.C.), [the Emperor] changed Yi-yang 易陽 to Yang-ling 陽陵.[61] He reestablished the fords and passes, and the use of travel permits for exit and entry.[62]

In the winter[63] [the Emperor] made the State of Chao into Han-tan 邯鄲 Commandery.[64]

[56]Located in the northeast part of the Han empire approximating modern Liao-ning, see Loewe, *Dictionary*, p. 810.

[57]Hsü Kuang ("Chi-chieh," *Shih chi*, 11.442) points out that the chronological tables (see *Shih chi*, 17.844) record the King of Yen's death in the fifth year of Emperor Ching, 152 B.C.

[58]This was Liu Jung 劉榮, Prince Li 栗, son of Beauty Li (see *Shih chi*, 59.2094 and n. 82 below).

[59]The use of Ch'e 轍 here poses a problem; as Emperor Wu's *praenomen*, it would have been taboo during Ssu-ma Ch'ien's time.

[60]Liu Ch'e succeeded his father in 141 B.C. (see the translation of Chapter 12 below) and became posthumously known as Hsiao Wu-ti 孝武帝 (The Filial and Martial Emperor or Emperor Wu the Filial).

Chiao-tung was located north of modern Tsingtao in the central part of the Shantung peninsula (T'an Ch'i-hsiang, 2:20).

[61]The "Cheng-yi" cites the *K'uo ti chih* 括地志 as saying that this was the tomb of Emperor Ching (see *Shih chi*, 11.442). It was located about ten miles northeast of Hsien-yang on the northern side of the Wei River in modern Shensi (see the insert map on T'an Ch'i-hsiang, 2:15). Chinese archaeologists found twenty-nine tombs of the prisoner-laborers of Yang-ling in 1972 in which thirty-nine skeletons of the shackled convict-laborers had been buried. See the original report of this excavation: Ch'in Chung-hsing 秦中行, "Han Yang-ling fu-chin ch'ien-t'u mu te fa-hsien," 漢陽陵附近鉗徒墓的發現 *Wen-wu* 文物 2 (1972): 51–3. See also Shan-hsi sheng K'ao-ku Yen-chiu-so Han ling K'ao-ku-tui 陝西省考古研究所漢陵考古隊, "Han Ching-ti Yang-ling nan-ch'ü ts'ung tsang-k'eng fa-chüeh ti-i hao chien-pao" 漢景帝陽陵南區從葬坑發掘第一號簡報, *Wen wu* 4 (1992), pp. 1-13. and Shan-hsi Sheng K'ao-ku Yen-chiu-so Han-ling K'ao-ku-tui 陝西省考古研究所漢陵考古隊, "Han Ching-ti Yang-ling nan-ch'ü ts'ung tsang-k'eng fa-chüeh ti-erh hao chien-pao" 漢景帝陽陵南區從葬坑發掘第二號簡報, *Wen wu* 6 (1994), pp. 4-23. *Han shu*, 5.143 says that in the first month of the fifth year Emperor Ching "made [or 'built'] Yang-ling Township" 作陽陵邑 (see also Wang Shu-min, 5.414n.)

[62]As noted by Chang Yen in the "Chi-chieh" (*Shih chi*, 11.442) these "travel permits" (*chuan* 傳) were later referred to as *kuo-so* 過所. They were typically made of wood and approximately five inches long, with proof of identity written on top and affixed with the seal of an Imperial Censor. According to Ying Shao (*ibid.*), during the twelfth year of Emperor Wen (168 B.C.) frontier-gates were eliminated and travel permits (*chuan*) were no longer used; thus the practice was reestablished here.

[63]Under the Han calendar winter was the first season of the year (the tenth month was the first of the year); thus a record of winter events here, following the ninth or last month of the year, violates normal

[443] In the third month of the fifth year (12 April to 11 May 152 B.C.) the Yang-ling (Yang Mausoleum) and the bridge over the Wei 渭 River were under construction.[65]

In the fifth month (11 June to 10 July 152 B.C.) [the Emperor] enlisted [people] to move to Yang-ling, providing 200,000 cash [for the move]. In Chiang-tu 江都 a squall came in from the west, destroying twelve *chang* of the city wall.[66]

On the *ting-mao* 丁卯 day (8 July 152 B.C.), [the Emperor] enfeoffed [Ch'en] Chiao 蟜, the son of the Elder Princess, as the Marquis of Lung-lü 隆慮.[67] He transferred the King of Kuang-ch'uan to be the King of Chao.[68]

In the spring of the sixth year (151 B.C.), [the Emperor] enfeoffed the Capital Commandant [Wei] Wan [衛] 綰[69] as Marquis of Chien-ling 建陵;[70] [Ch'eng 程] Chia 嘉 (d. 133),[71] Chancellor

---

chronology. The *Han shu* annals of Emperor Ching does not mention this event. *Han shu,* 28B.1630 says that the state of Chao was turned into Han-tan Commandery in the third year (153 B.C.) of Emperor Ching's reign and was restored in the fifth year (151 B.C.). Given the achronological placement here, it seems probable that this change took place a year earlier in 153 B.C.

[64]Both Chao and the resulting commandery of Han-tan encompassed a small area north and west of modern Han-tan City in Hopei (T'an Ch'i-hsiang, 2:26). Chao was eliminated as a kingdom because its king, Liu Sui, had joined the Rebellion of the Seven States and committed suicide when Chao fell (see *Shih chi,* 50.1989-90).

[65]The Yang Mausoleum was begun in this year; intended for Emperor Ching, it was located about ten miles northeast of Ch'ang-an on the north bank of the Wei River (T'an Ch'i-hsiang, 2:15). Both the *Han shu* (5.143) and the *Tzu-chih t'ung-chien* (16.531) mention only the construction of the Yang Mausoleum. The bridge in question here seems to be the Eastern Wei Bridge (Wang Shu-min, 11.414). It would have provided access from Ch'ang-an to the Yang Mausoleum on the opposite side of the river. This bridge was probably first built under the Ch'in, then rebuilt or repaired at this time (see Ho Ch'ing-ku 何清谷, *San-fu huang-t'u chiao-chu* 三輔黃圖校註 [Sian: San Ch'in, 1995], pp. 340-42, and n. 45 to the translation of *Shih chi* Chapter 10 above).

[66]Wang Li-ch'i (11.414n.) points out that this storm was not recorded in the *Han shu* or the *Han chi.*

[67]Ch'en Chiao (also known as Ch'en Jung 陳融, see Loewe, *Dictionary,* p. 38) was the son of Liu P'iao 劉嫖 (also known as the Kuan-t'ao 館陶 Princess, d. 116 B.C., see *Shih chi,* 49.1972, *Han shu,* 45.2177, 65.2853, 97A.3943, 3945ff.), the elder sister by Empress Tou of Emperor Ching, and Ch'en Wu 陳午 (d. 129), who became Marquis of T'ang-yi 堂邑 in 177 B.C. (*Shih chi,* 18.887). Ch'en Wu's daughter became Emperor Wu's Empress Ch'en 陳.

Lung-lü was a county located near modern Lin 林 County in Honan (Wang Li-ch'i, 11.276n.).

[68]I.e., Liu P'eng-tsu 劉彭祖 (d. 92 B.C.) was a son of Emperor Ching; he had been made King of Kuang-ch'uan in 155 B.C. He ruled as King of Chao for over sixty years, effectively thwarting the attempts of the Han court to limit his control through the appointment of high officials of Chao in Ch'ang-an (see *Shih chi,* 52.2008, 59.2098, 112.2962, and 118.3094).

[69]Although the Chin-ling (11.2b) and Po-na (11.3a) editions both have "Chao Wan" here, the man referred to here is Wei 衛 Wan (see Liang Yü-sheng, 7.268, *Shih chi,* 19.1014, Wu and Lu, 11.381 n., Wei Wan's brief biography on *Shih chi,* 103.2768-2770, and Loewe, *Dictionary,* p. 577). On Chao Wan, see *Shih chi,* 12.452 and the second paragraph of our translation of *Shih chi* Chapter 12 below as well as the entry in Loewe, *Dictionary,* pp. 711-12.

of Chiang-tu, as Marquis of Chien-p'ing 建平;[72] Hun-yeh 渾邪,[73] the Governor of Lung-hsi 隴西,[74] as the Marquis of P'ing-ch'ü 平曲[75]; [Su 蘇] Chia 嘉 (d. 147),[76] Chancellor of Chao, as the Marquis of Chiang-ling 江陵;[77] and the former General [Luan 欒] Pu 布[78] as the Marquis of Shu 郰.[79] The kings of Liang and Ch'u both passed on.[80]

In the intercalary month after the ninth month, they cut trees along the Speedway to shore up Lan-ch'ih 蘭池 (Orchid Lake).[81]

[70]A county northwest of Shu-yang 沭陽 county in modern Kiangsu (Wang Li-ch'i, 11.277n.).

[71]Ch'eng Chia was rewarded for his service as a general against the Seven Kingdoms (*Shih chi*, 19.1014).

[72]A county southwest of Yung-ch'eng 永城 County in modern Honan (Wang Li-ch'i, 11.277n.).

[73]I.e, Kung-sun 公孫 Hung-yeh who was descended from a unspecified Tartar people (see *Shih chi*, 111.2941). He was later tried for some offense and deprived of his marquisate.

[74]Lung-hsi was a commandery based near modern Lin-t'ao 臨洮 County in southeastern Kansu (T'an Ch'i-hsiang, 2:34).

[75]According to Wang Li-ch'i (11.277n.), P'ing-ch'ü was a town east of Pa 霸 County in modern Hopei. T'an Ch'i-hsiang (2:20) locates it as a county in what was then Tung-hai 東海 Commandery a few miles southeast of modern Tung-hai 東海 County in Kiangsu. Wang Hui (p. 521, entry #761) concurs with T'an Ch'i-hsiang.

[76]Su Chia was also appointed in acknowledgment of his service as a general against the rebellion of 154 B.C. (*Shih chi*, 19.1015).

[77]Chiang-ling was a county northwest of modern Chiang-ling County in Hopei (Wang Li-ch'i, 11.277n.). Su Chia's fief is incorrectly identified as Chiang-yang 江陽 on *Shih chi*, 19.1015.

[78]Luan Pu was a native of Liang who had been friends with P'eng Yüeh 彭越 (the King of Liang) when P'eng was still a commoner. His relationship with P'eng involved him in many interesting events (see his biography on *Shih chi*, 100.2733-35).

[79]Shu was a county southwest of P'ing-yüan 平原 county in modern Shantung (Wang Li-ch'i, 11.277n.).

[80]King Hsiao 孝 of Liang, Liu Wu 劉武, ruled Liang from 168 B.C. until his death in the sixth year of the Middle Reign of Emperor Ching (145-144 B.C., cf. *Shih chi*, 11.446). This is corroborated in Liu Wu's biography (*Shih chi*, 58.2086) and a number of other sources. Liang Yü-sheng (7.269) observes this report of his death in 151 B.C. to be an error. On Liu Wu see also n. 106 below.

The King of Ch'u, Liu Li 劉禮, was a son of Liu Chiao 劉交, the King of Ch'i from 201 to 179 B.C. He ruled Ch'u until his death in 150 B.C. Wang Li-ch'i (11.277n.) believes the text should read simply "King Wen of Ch'u passed on."

[81]The text here literally reads "they cut trees along the Speedway (see *Grand Scribe's Records*, 1:138, n. 155) and planted trees at Orchid Lake." It may be that this refers to two separate activities. However, Wang Li-ch'i (11.277n.) notes that this area was located northeast of modern Hsien-yang and was later known as "Orchid Lake Slope" 蘭池陂. Thus the variant noted by Hsü Kuang in the "Chi-chieh" (*Shih chi*, 11.443)—*t'ien* 填 "to fill up" or "fill in," for *chih* 殖 "to plant"—seems to merit serious consideration. Using the logs cut from around the Speedway to construct a dam of sorts would quite plausibly create a sloping terrain. Mizusawa

In the winter of the seventh year, [the Emperor] removed Heir Li 栗 and made him the King of Lin-chiang 臨江.[82]

On the last day of the eleventh month (22 January 150 B.C.), there was a solar eclipse.[83]

In the spring, [the Emperor] dismissed conscript-laborers who were building Yang-ling. Chancellor [*444*] [T'ao] Ch'ing [陶]青 was dismisseed.[84]

In the second month, on the *yi-ssu* 乙巳 day (7 April 150 B.C.), he made Chou Ya-fu, the Grand Commandant, and the Marquis of T'iao 條, the Chancellor.

On the *yi-ssu* 乙巳 day of the fourth month (6 June 150 B.C.), he established the Queen Dowager of Chiao-tung 膠東 as the Huang Hou 皇后 (August Empress).[85]

On the *ting-ssu* 丁巳 day (18 June 150 B.C.), he set up the King of Chiao-tung as the Heir. His *praenomen* was Ch'e 徹.[86]

In the first year of the Middle Reign (150-149 B.C.), [the Emperor] enfeoffed [Chou] P'ing [周]平,[87] the grandson of the former Grand Master of the Imperial Scribes, Chou K'o 周苛, as the Marquis of Sheng 繩, and [Chou] Tso-ch'e [周]左車, the grandson of the former Grand

Toshitada (Takigawa, 11.312) cites a note by Liu Po-chuang 劉伯莊 (*fl.* 627) that reads: 此時蘭池壞溢故堰填; "At this time Orchid Lake was damaged and flooding, therefore they filled in the dikes." The expression *yen-t'ien* 堰填, "fill in the dikes," supports both the variant noted by Hsü Kuang and the idea that these two activities (cutting trees and building dikes) were related, much as the repair work on the Eastern Wei Bridge and the construction of the Yang Mausoleum were joined (see the translation of *Shih chi,* 11.443 and n. 65 above). Thus our translation follows Hsü Kuang's variant. Other readings indicate that they were actually filling the lake up with the logs (see Chavannes, 2:164, n. 1).

[82]Li Jung 栗融 was the son of Beauty Li 栗姬, one of Emperor Ching's favorite palace women. When Li Jung was made Heir in 151 B.C., it was expected that his mother would become Empress. Through the machinations of a rival, Wang Chih 王åZ (d. 126), Beauty Li was supplanted in the Emperor's affections. Li Jung was removed as Heir, Wang Chih's son Liu Ch'e 劉轍 (the future Emperor Wu) was installed in his place, and Wang Chih herself soon became Empress (see text below and also the entry on Wang Chih, in Loewe, *Dictionary,* p. 565, as well as n. 5 on Chavannes, 2:501-2).

Lin-chiang was located at modern Chung 忠 County in eastern Szechuan (T'an Ch'i-hsiang, 2:30).

[83]Wu and Lu (11.382n.) argue based on parallels in the *Han shu* that this should be the twelfth month.

[84]According to *Han shu,* 19B.763, T'ao Ch'ing was dismissed as Chancellor on the *yi-ssu* 乙巳 day in the sixth month when Chou Ya-fu was appointed the new Chancellor (see text below).

[85]I.e., Wang Chih 王åZ (see n. 82 above).

[86]The future Emperor Wu 武 (r. 141-87 B.C.; see also n. 82 above).

[87]Wang Li-ch'i notes that this should be Chou Ying 周應 instead of Chou P'ing, presumably based upon Hsü Kuang's note of a variant in the "Chi-chieh." He cites the "Kao-tsu kung-ch'en hou-che nien-piao" 高祖功臣侯者年表 as saying that it was Chou K'o's great grandson Chou Ying who was enfeoffed, not Chou P'ing; Chou P'ing was the son of Chou Ying and the great great grandson of Chou K'o. The location of Sheng is unclear, although it is thought to be in modern Shantung (Wang Li-ch'i, 11.277n.).

Master of the Imperial Scribes, Chou Ch'ang 周昌, as the Marquis of An-yang 安陽.[88]

On the *yi-ssu* day of the fourth month (31 May 149 B.C.), he granted an amnesty throughout the world and bestowed an increase of one rank. He abolished the restrictions and restraints [on serving as officials].[89] The earth quaked. It hailed in Heng-shan 衡山 and Yüan-tu 原都,[90] with the large [stones] measuring one *ch'ih* eight *ts'un*.

In the second month of the second year of the Middle Reign (20 March-17 April 148 B.C.), the Hsiung-nu entered Yen, and as a result there was no marital-alliance.

In the third month (18 April-17 May 148 B.C.), [the Emperor] summoned the King of Lin-chiang to come [to the capital]; he then died shortly after in the office of the Capital Commandant.[91]

In the summer, [the Emperor] enthroned the Imperial Son [Liu] Yüeh 越 as the King of Kuang-ch'uan, and his son [Liu] Chi 寄 as the King of Chiao-tung. He enfeoffed four marquises.[92] On the *chia-hsü* 甲戌 day of the ninth month (22 October 148 B.C.), the sun was eclipsed.

[445] In the winter of the third year of the Middle Reign, [the Emperor] abolished the Palace Assistant Secretaries[93] among the feudal lords.

In the spring, two kings of the Hsiung-nu led their followers in to surrender, and they were both enfeoffed as ranking marquises.[94] [the Emperor] enthroned the Imperial Son [Liu]

[88]Located south and west of modern An-yang City in Honan (Wang Li-ch'i, 11.277n.).

[89]*Chin ku* 禁錮 were the restrictions which during the Han dynasty banned merchants, husbands who lived with their wives' families, and officials who had taken bribes from serving in office (see Wu and Lu, 11.382n.). Many more examples, and a detailed discussion of what Hulsewé calls "exclusion from office" can be found in his *Han Law*, pp. 135-40.

[90]T'an Ch'i-hsiang offers no location for Yüan-tu, but Wang Li-ch'i (11.277n.) locates it within the borders of modern Kansu.

[91]This was the former Heir Liu Jung, who was posthumously known as King Min 閔 of Lin-chiang. For details surrounding his suicide see *Shih chi*, 59.2094.

[92]These four new marquises were sons of officials from the states of Chao and Ch'u who had resisted their ruler's decisions to revolt in 155 B.C.: Chang Tang-chü 張當居, son of Chang Shang 張尚, the former Ch'u Chancellor, became Marquis of Shan-yang 山陽 on the *yi-ssu* 乙巳 day of the fourth month (26 May 148 B.C.); on the same day, Chao Chou 趙周, son of Chao Yi-wu 趙夷五, Ch'u's Grand Tutor, became Marquis of Shang-ling 商陵; Chien Heng 建橫, son of Chien Te 建德, the former Chancellor of Chao, became Marquis of Chü 遽; and Wang Ch'i 王棄, son of Wang Han 王悍, the former Scribe of the Capital of Chao, became Marquis of Hsin-shih 新市 (*Shih chi*, 19.1016-8).

[93]*Yü-shih chung-ch'eng* 御史中丞.

[94]Here the basic annals seem to be in conflict with the chronological tables of both the *Shih chi* and the *Han shu*. The "Cheng-yi" cites the *Han shu* chronological tables as a source that lists the names of seven men who were enfeoffed as ranked marquises as a result of the surrender of the two Hsiung-nu kings. Liang Yü-sheng delves deeper into the matter, noting that the tables in both histories corroborate the case that seven men were enfeoffed due to the Hsiung-nu surrender. He also notes that the "Cheng-yi" listed the names

Fang-ch'eng 方乘 as the King of Ch'ing-ho 清河.[95]

In the third month (18 April-17 May 147 B.C.), a comet appeared in the northwest.[96] Chancellor Chou Ya-fu was dismissed,[97] and the Grand Master of the Imperial Scribes and Marquis of T'ao 桃, Liu She 劉舍,[98] was made Chancellor.

In the fourth month (18 May-15 June 147 B.C.) the earth quaked.

On the last day of the ninth month, the *wu-hsü* 戊戌 day (10 November 147 B.C.), there was a solar eclipse. The army camped outside the Tung-tu Men 東都門 (East Metropolis Gate).

In the third month of the fourth year of the Middle Reign (8 April-6 May 146 B.C.), [the Emperor] established the Te-yang Kung 德陽宮 (Palace of Virtue and Solar Potency).[99] There was a plague of locusts.

In the autumn, he pardoned the conscript-laborers building Yang-ling.[100]

In the summer of the fifth year (145 B.C.) of the Middle Reign, he enthroned the Imperial Son, [Liu] Shun 舜, as the King of Ch'ang-shan 常山.[101] [The Emperor] enfeoffed ten marquises.[102]

On the *ting-ssu* 丁巳 day of the sixth month (21 July 145 B.C.), [the Emperor] granted

---

incorrectly and erred in the times of some of the enfeoffments (Liang Yü-sheng, 7.271-72).

[95]Loewe (*Dictionary,* p. 282) notes that his name was Liu Ch'eng 劉乘. Takigawa (11.10) and Wang Shu-min (11.418) also observe that other editions and parallels do not include the character *Fang* 方.

Ch'ing-ho was a state that had its seat east of Ch'ing-ho county in modern Hopei (Wang Li-ch'i, 11.278n.).

[96]*Han shu* (5.147) dates this to the ninth month.

[97]The Chin-ling edition (11.3b) has *ssu* 死 (died) for *mien* 免 (was dismissed). Chang Wen-hu (1:108), probably basing his decision on Liang Yü-sheng's arguments (7.271), claims that *mien* is the correct reading. The Chung-hua editors have subsequently revised the Chin-ling edition here. An account of Chou Ya-fu's falling out with the Emperor can be found on *Shih chi,* 57.2078-9.

[98]Liu She was the son of Hsiang Hsiang 項襄, a member of Hsiang Yü's clan who had been made Marquis of T'ao and granted the imperial surname Liu (see *Shih chi,* 7.338, and *Grand Scribe's Records,* 1:208)

[99]This was a temple that Emperor Ching established for himself, but out of propriety called a palace. It was located in what is now the northeast part of modern Hsien-yang in Shensi (Wang Li-ch'i, 11.278n.).

[100]As mentioned above (see n. 61), the tombs at Yang-ling were excavated in 1972. Over ten thousand prison-laborers were buried in an area of about eighty thousand square meters. See Ch'in Chung-hsing 秦中行, "Han Yang-ling fu-chin ch'ien-t'u mu te fa-hsien," 漢陽陵附近鉗徒墓的發現, *Wen-wu,* 1972.2: 51–3; see also Wang Zhongshu (Wang Chung-shu) *Han Civilization,* tr. K. C. Chang *et al.* (New Haven and London: Yale University Press, 1982), pp. 212–3.

[101]Ch'ang-shan was located in the region along the modern borders of the central part of Hopei and the eastern part of Shansi (Wang Li-ch'i, 11.278n.).

[102]According to the "Hui, Ching chien hou-che nien-piao" 惠景間侯者年表 (*Shih chi,* 19.1021-3), there were only five marquises enfeoffed during this period. Wu and Lu (11.383-4n.) argue that *shih* 十 "ten" is an error for *wu* 五 "five."

an amnesty throughout the world and bestowed an increase of one rank. There were heavy rains in the world. He changed the title of chancellors of the feudal lords to prime ministers.

In the autumn the earth quaked.[103]

[446] On the *chi-mao* 己卯 day of the second month of the sixth year of the Middle Reign (9 April 144 B.C.), [the Emperor] favored Yung 雍 with a visit,[104] performing the *Chiao* 郊 (Suburban) Sacrifice to the Five Emperors.[105]

In the third month there was a hailstorm.

In the fourth month (14 May-12 June 144 B.C.), King Hsiao 孝 of Liang,[106] King Kung 共 of Ch'eng-yang 城陽,[107] and the King of Ju-nan 汝南[108] all passed on. [The Emperor] enthroned [Liu] Ming 明, the son of King Hsiao of Liang, as the King of Chi-ch'uan 濟川; [King Hsiao's] son [Liu] P'eng-li 彭離 as the King of Chi-tung 濟東; [Hsiao's] son [Liu] Ting 定 as the King of Shan-yang 山陽; and [Hsiao's] son [Liu] Pu-shih 不識 as the King of Chi-yin 濟陰.[109] Liang was divided into five. He enfeoffed four marquises.[110] He changed the title of Commandant of Justice[111]

[103]Neither the heavy rains nor this earthquake are recorded in the *Han shu* account of this year (5.148).

[104]Yung here refers to Yung-chih 雍畤, where the early Han emperors performed their sacrifices to the Five Emperors (see *Hou Han shu*, 28.989–90). According to the *Han shu* (5.148), these rites took place during the New Year in the tenth month (18 November-17 December 145 B.C.).

[105]According to the "Cheng-yi" (*Shih chi*, 12.453) the Five Emperors were Pai-ti 白帝 (The White Emperor), Ch'ing-ti 青帝 (The Green Emperor), Ch'ih-ti 赤帝 (The Red Emperor), Huang-ti 黃帝 (The Yellow Emperor), and Hei-ti 黑帝 (The Black Emperor).

[106]I.e., Liu Wu 劉武, the younger brother of Emperor Ching by Empress Tou (see *Shih chi*, 58.2081 and 2087-91). He was known for his patronage of writers of *fu* 賦 (rhapsodies) as well as for his loyalty to the his brother, the emperor, during the Rebellion of the Seven Kingdoms.

Liang corresponded to the area that is now the border region of Honan and Anhwei, with its capital at Sui-yang 睢陽 near modern Shang-ch'iu 商丘 City (T'an Ch'i-hsiang, 2:19).

[107]This was Liu Hsi 劉喜, the son of Liu Chang 劉章, the former King of Ch'eng-yang and the grandson of Liu Fei 劉肥, King Tao-hui 悼惠 of Ch'i 齊. Ch'eng-yang was located in the region around modern Yi-nan 沂南 County in Shantung (Wang Li-ch'i, 11.278n.).

[108]The date of death of the King of Ju-nan, Liu Fei 劉非, seems to be an error here. According to the "Han hsing yi-lai chu-hou-wang nien-piao" 漢興以來諸侯王年表, Ju-nan was established as a Han state in 156 B.C. with Liu Fei as its first king (*Shih chi*, 17.838-9), but Liu Fei was moved to be King of Chiang-tu 江都 in 153 B.C. (*Shih chi*, 17.842) and no successor was established. Liu Fei died more than twenty years later in 128 B.C. (*Shih chi*, 17.858-9 and 57.2096). The *Han shu* (5.149) mentions only the King of Liang's death at this time.

[109]The only other biographical mention of these four men is made on *Shih chi*, 58.2086-7.

[110]According to the "Ching-ti chi" in the *Han-shu* (5.149), when the King of Liang died, the Emperor divided Liang into five states. He enthroned each of the five sons of King Hsiao as kings, rather than the four we see mentioned here. The *Han shu* does not list the names of the sons. Liang Yü-sheng notes that [Liu] Mai 買, the Marquis of Ch'eng-shih 乘氏, inherited the position of the King of Liang, and [Liu] Ming had already been

to Grand Judge,[112] Privy Treasurer of Architecture[113] to Court Architect,[114] Palace Commandant over the Nobility[115] to Capital Commandant,[116] Supervisor of the Household[117] of the Ch'ang-hsin 長信 Palace to Privy Treasurer[118] for the Ch'ang-hsin Palace, Empress's Usher[119] to Grand Prolonger of Autumn,[120] Grand Usher[121] to Usher,[122] Upholder of Ceremonies[123] to Grand Master of Ceremonies,[124] Director of Guests[125] to Grand Usher, and Clerk of the Capital for Directing Grain[126] to Minister of Agriculture.[127] [Officials of the] Grand Inner Palace Office[128] became [a rank of] 2,000 *shih*,[129] and a left and right inner official were established, belonging to the Grand Inner Palace Office.

On the *hsin-hai* 辛亥 day of the seventh month (8 September 144 B.C.), there was a solar eclipse.

In the eighth month (9 September-8 October 144 B.C.) the Hsiung-nu entered Shang-chün 上郡.[130]

enfeoffed as the Marquis of Huan-yi 桓邑. Only the remaining three had not previously been enfeoffed as marquises. He notes that the *Han shu* passage which says, "he divided Liang into five states, enthroning the five sons of King Hsiao as kings," is the more correct record (Liang Yü-sheng, 7.273).

[111]*T'ing-wei* 廷尉.

[112]*Ta-li* 大理.

[113]*Chiang-tso shao-fu* 將作少府.

[114]*Chiang-tso ta-chin* 將作大匠.

[115]*Chu-chüeh chung-wei* 主爵中尉.

[116]*Tu-wei* 都尉.

[117]*Chan-shih* 詹事.

[118]*Shao-fu* 少府.

[119]*Chiang-hsing* 將行.

[120]*Ta ch'ang-ch'iu* 大長秋.

[121]*Ta-hsing* 大行.

[122]*Hsing-jen* 行人.

[123]*Feng-ch'ang* 奉常.

[124]*T'ai-ch'ang* 太常.

[125]*Tien-k'o* 典客.

[126]*Chih-su nei-shih* 治粟內史. Not in Bielenstein.

[127]*Ta-nung* 大農. Not in Bielenstein.

[128]*Ta-nei* 大內.

[129]On officials of this rank see *Ch'in Han shih*, pp. 1-2 and 73.

[130]Located in modern northern Shensi and the area south of modern Ho-t'ao 河套 in Inner Mongolia (Wang Li-ch'i, 11.278n.).

In the *Han shu* (5.150) parallel account this invasion began in the sixth month.

[447] During the winter of the first year of the Later Reign, [the Emperor] changed the title of Palace Grand Masters[131] to Commandant of the Guards.[132]

On the *ting-yu* 丁酉 day of the third month (22 April 143 B.C.), he granted an amnesty throughout the world and bestowed an increase of one rank. [Officials] of 2,000 *shih* and prime ministers of various lords were given the rank of Right Chief of Staff.[133]

In the fourth month (4 May-1 June 143 B.C.) there was a great bacchanal.[134]

On the *ping-hsü* 丙戌 day of the fifth month (10 June 143 B.C.), the earth quaked, and during the morning meal there was an aftershock. The earth quaked for twenty-two days in Shang-yung 上庸,[135] destroying the city walls and ramparts.

On the *yi-ssu* 乙巳 day of the seventh month (28 August 143 B.C.), there was a solar eclipse. Chancellor Liu She 劉舍 was dismissed.

On the *jen-ch'en* 壬辰 day of the eighth month[136] [the Emperor] made Grand Master of the Imperial Scribes, [Wei] Wan [衛]綰, Chancellor and enfeoffed him as the Marquis of Chien-ling 建陵.[137]

[448] During the first month of the second year of the Later Reign (23 February to 24 March 142 B.C.), the earth quaked three times in one day. General Chih 郅 attacked the Hsiung-nu.[138]

---

[131]*Chung Tai-fu* 中大夫; Bielenstein (p. 212) has Palace Grandee.

[132]*Wei-wei* 衛尉.

[133]*Yu shu-chang* 右庶長.

[134]Earlier, under Ch'in law, officials and common people were not allowed to gather and drink together, but when a *p'u* 酺 (bacchanal) was declared, they could (cf. *Grand Scribe's Records,* 1:134, n. 118 and n. 68 to our translation of *Shih chi* Chapter 10 above). Bacchanals were often allowed at times of crisis. Presumably this bacchanal was imperially sanctioned, but its cause remains unknown.

The *Han shu* (5.150) dates this simply "in the summer."

[135]The region around the southwest part of Chu-shan 竹山 County in modern Hopei about seventy miles southeast of modern An-k'ang 安康 City (Wang Li-ch'i, 11.279n.). This is the only earthquake of Emperor Ching's reign that is recorded in *Chung-kuo li-shih ti-chen t'u-chi, Yüan-ku chih Yüan shih ch'i* 中國歷使地震圖集，遠古至元時期 (Atlas of the Historical Earthquakes in China, The Period from Remote Antiquity to the Yüan Dynasty; Peking: Chung-kuo Ti-t'u Ch'u-pan-she, 1990], p. 27).

[136]As Liang Yü-sheng (7.275) points out the date designation *jen-ch'en* did not occur during the eighth month. Liang is troubled to admit that the same date for Wei Wang's appointment to Chancellor is given on *Shih chi*, 22.1132; an account of his promotion on *Han shu,* 19B.766, dates it simply within 143 B.C.

[137]Wei Wang served as Chancellor until just after Emperor Wu took the throne (140 B.C., *Shih chi,* 22.1133). Aside from the dating of this appointment, the enfeoffment of Wei here is also an error; he was made Marquis of Chien-ling eight years earlier in 151 B.C. (see *Shih chi,* 11.443 and 19.1014).

[138]Chih Tu 郅都 held several positions during the tenure of Emperor Ching, the highest that of Capital Commandant (*Chung-wei* 中尉). Due to his harsh treatment in a particular legal case, Empress Dowager Tou managed to have charges brought against him. He retired from his post in the capital, but was appointed by the Emperor as the Governor of Yen-men 鴈門 on the northern border. When he arrived to take up his post, the

There was a five-day bacchanal. [The Emperor] ordered the Scribes of the Capital and the commanderies not to feed grain to horses, [otherwise] they [the horses] would have to be presented to the local officials.[139] He ordered the convict-laborers to be clothed in seven-hemp cloth[140] and the cessation of using horses to pound grain.[141] Because the harvest did not measure up, he prohibited all in the world from eating beyond what they would harvest in a season. He reduced the number of ranking marquises [in the capital] and sent them to [their] states.[142]

In the third month (23 April to 23 May 142 B.C.), the Hsiung-nu entered Yen-men 鴈門.[143]

In the tenth month (26 Nov. to 25 Dec. 142 B.C.),[144] the fields of Ch'ang-ling 長陵 were rented out.[145] There was a great drought.[146] In the kingdom of Heng-shan 衡山, and in Ho-tung 河

Hsiung-nu withdrew their troops and kept them away until Chih died. They even made an archery target that looked like Chih Tu, but none of the archers could hit it. Chih was eventually executed because of further charges brought by the Empress Dowager (see his biography on *Shih chi*, 122.3132-4).

Liang Yü-sheng (7.275) notes that there is no mention of Chih Tu's attack in the parallel passage of the *Han shu* (5.151). While Chih Tu is not referred to, however, the *Han shu* records this Hsiung-nu incursion into Yen-men in its account of this month, claiming that the governor was Feng Ching 馮敬 and that he died in the fighting.

[139]None of the usual sources (Lu Zongli, Bielenstein, *Ch'in Han shih*) have a gloss for *Nei-shih chün* 內史郡; we follow the parsing suggested by Wang Li-ch'i (11.279): 令內史，郡不得食馬粟，沒入縣官.

Pan Ku appears to have tried to clarify the term by omitting *shih* 史 (Scribes) in the *Han shu* (5.151) parallel. The reason given there for this action was that there had not been a good harvest in the previous year. Yen Shih-ku (*ibid.*) believes that it was horses that were presented to government officials. We follow this reading. *Han chi* and *Tzu-chih t'ung-chien* also follow the *Han shu* account (see Wang Shu-min, 5.422).

[140]According to Hsu Cho-yun, this was a coarse cloth of the poorest quality and probably worth the least amount of money. Convict-laborers typically wore such cloth. "*Tsung*" ‰÷ (of "seventh grade" *ch'i-tsung* 七‰÷) was the unit of measure of the density of the filling thread in the cloth. This cloth was likely as coarse as fine medical gauze (see Hsu Cho-yun, *Han Agriculture: The Formation of Early Chinese Agrarian Economy [206 B.C.–A.D. 220]*, ed. Jack L. Dull [Seattle and London: University of Washington Press, 1980], p. 131).

[141]Chavannes (2:508, n. 1) suggests this was probably because men could grind grain with less waste.

[142]Following the policy set by his father, Emperor Wen, in 178 B.C. (cf. *Shih chi*, 10.422).

[143]A commandery located on the border of modern Shantung and Inner Mongolia, near the region south of Huang-ch'i Hai 黃旗海 and Tai Hai 岱海. Yen-men Pass was located in the southern part of this commandery, near the Great Wall, and was a key north-south travel junction (Wang Li-ch'i, 11.279n.).

[144]Liang Yü-sheng (7.276) points out that the tenth month (the first of the year) should not follow the third month. He suggests that the text here should read "the seventh month" (relying on the similarity of the Han-dynasty graphs for "ten" and "seven").

[145]This was the site of Han Kao-tsu's tomb. Located in the northeast part of Hsien-yang in modern Shensi (Wang Li-ch'i, 11.279n.).

[146]Among the various events dated by these annals in the tenth month, *Han shu* (5.152) mentions only

東[147] and Yün-chung 雲中[148] commanderies, the people suffered epidemics.

In the tenth month of the third year of the Later Reign (16 November-14 December 141 B.C.), the sun and the moon were both red for five days.[149]

On the last day of the twelfth month (11 February 141 B.C.), it thundered.[150] The sun appeared purple. Five planets moved in retrograde and guarded the constellation of T'ai-wei 太微 (Grand Tenuity).[151] The moon passed through the center of the constellation T'ien-t'ing 天廷 (Heaven's Court).

On the *chia-yin* 甲寅 day of the first month (28 February 141 B.C.), the August Heir was capped.[152]

On the *chia-tzu* 甲子 day (9 March 141 B.C.), the Hsiao Ching Huang-ti 孝景皇帝 (The Filial and Lumious August Emperor) passed away.[153] In his testamentary edict he bestowed an increase of one rank to the noble kings and on down to heirs of fathers among the common people,[154] and one hundred cash to all households in the world.[155] The palace women were sent out to return to their homes, with no [service] to be required again.[156] The Heir ascended the

this drought and says it took place in autumn.

[147]South of Shih-lou 石樓 county and west of Ch'in-shui 沁水 county in modern Shansi (Wang Li-ch'i, 11.279n.).

[148]South of Ssu-tzu-wang-ch'i 四子王旗 and north of Ch'ien-fang-tzu 前房子 in Modern Inner Mongolia (Wang Li-ch'i, 11.279n.).

[149]The Chung-hua editors have removed the word *shih* 食 (eclipse) which appears before *ch'ih* 赤 (red) in the Chung-ling edition and various other earlier texts (such as the *Po-na* edition, 11.6b) based on Chang Wen-hu's comments (1.109).

[150]According to Chavannes, thunder in February was regarded as a sign. He cites no source for this explanation, so it is possible that this information was gleaned from the Chinese scholar with whom Chavannes read the *Shih chi* in the early 1890s in Peking (Chavannes, 2:508, n. 4), although Chiao Hung 焦竑 (1541-1620; cited in Takigawa, 11.15-6) suggests the same thing.

[151]*T'ai-wei* is one of the five celestial courts. For a description of its place in Han astronomy, see Sun Xiaochun and Jacob Kistemaker, *The Chinese Sky during the Han: Constellating Stars and Society* (Leiden: E. J. Brill, 1997), pp. 124-8. See also n. 21 above.

[152]A ceremony performed when a young noble reaches twenty, symbolizing his coming of age (Wang Li-ch'i, 11.279n.).

[153]The *Han shu* (5.153) account says he died in the Wei-yang Palace; he was forty-eight *sui*.

[154]According to the *Han shu* (5.153) account, this occurs immediately following the capping of the Heir.

[155]According to the testamentary edict described on *Han shu*, 5.153, kings, marquises and higher-ranking officials received substantially more.

[156]Emperor Ching here repeats the practice of his father, Emperor Wen (see our translation of the testamentary edict he left as recorded on *Shih chi*, 10.434 above). Wang Ming-sheng 王鳴盛 (1722–1798; cited on Takigawa, 11.16) notes that later Han emperors beginning with Emperor Wu ordered their palace women to

throne; he became Hsiao Wu Huang-ti 孝武皇帝 (The Filial and Martial August Emperor).

In the third month (11 April-10 May 141 B.C.), he enfeoffed the younger half-brothers of the Huang T'ai-hou 皇太后 (August Empress Dowager), [T'ien 田] Fen 蚡,[157] as Marquis of Wu-an 武安,[158] and [T'ien] Sheng 勝,[159] as Marquis of Chou-yang 周陽.[160] [Ching-ti] was interred at Yang-ling.[161]

[449] His Honor the Grand Scribe says, "When the Han arose, Hsiao Wen[-ti] spread great virtue and the world cherished peace [that resulted]. By the time of Hsiao Ching[-ti], there was no further worry about [those lords] of different *cognomens*.[162] Yet Ch'ao Ts'o 晁錯 pared and stripped away the [fiefs of the] feudal lords, finally causing the Seven Kingdoms to all rise up, join in alliance, and move toward the western regions together.[163] This was because the feudal lords were too vigorous, and because Ts'o in dealing with them was not [sufficiently] deliberate. When Chu-fu Yen 主父偃 (d. 127 B.C.) [later] spoke on this,[164] the feudal lords were weakened, and finally pacified. Does not the key to peace or crisis lies in planning?

*   *   *   *   *

The noble lords were arrogant and dissipated; [the kingdom of] Wu was the head in making rebellion. When the capital armies carried out punishments, and the Seven Kingdoms admitted their guilt, the world was brought into line and a great peace led to abundant wealth.

---

remain after their deaths to maintain sacrifices at their (the emperors') tombs. It was not until Wang Mang 王莽 (45 B.C.–A.D. 23) released Emperor P'ing's 平 (r. A.D. 1–6) palace women upon his death that the practiced was again repeated.

[157]T'ien Fen (d. 131 B.C.), after Emperor Wu ascended the throne, was enfeoffed as the Marquis of Wu-an 武安. He also served as Grand Commandant and Chancellor (Wang Li-ch'i, 11.279n.).

[158]Wu-an was a county that corresponds to modern Wu-an county in Hopei (Wang Li-ch'i, 11.279n.).

[159]T'ien Sheng was T'ien Fen's younger brother (Wang Li-ch'i, 11.279n.).

[160]Situated northwest of Wen-hsi 聞喜 county in modern Shansi (Wang Li-ch'i, 11.279n.).

[161]*Han shu* 5.153 dates this to the *kuei-yu* 癸酉 day of the second month (18 March 141 B.C.).

[162]Referring to the kings such as Han Hsin appointed by Kao-tsu who later rebelled.

[163]On Ch'ao Ts'o's policies and summaries of his memorials see his biography in *Shih chi* Chapter 101. Many of his dealings with Ching-ti were carried out in private audiences.

[164]Chu-fu Yen was a palace attendant, and later a Regular Grand Master during the reign of Wu-ti who submitted a famous memorial and remonstrated several times on the subject of the marquises gaining too much power. He advocated the idea of allowing marquises to enfeoff their own sons within their existing marquisates, which would cause a gradual decrease in their size and power. Emperor Wu adopted this policy, which was instrumental in the strengthening of the Han central government. See *Shih chi* Chapter 112 for details.

[Thus] I wrote "The Basic Annals of the Filial and Luminous [Emperor], Number 11."[165]

---

[165]This is the account given by Ssu-ma Ch'ien in his postface, *Shih chi*, 130.3303.

TRANSLATOR'S NOTE

To any reader who is familiar with Ssu-ma Ch'ien's prose style in the *Shih chi*, this chapter must seem an obvious departure from the conventions and tone he has set forth in most of the first ten chapters. The detailed anecdotes and reconstructed dialogues so common in the earlier basic annals, as well as in the later memoirs and hereditary houses, are curiously absent from this chapter. Burton Watson considers the chapter 'exasperatingly dull,' with its simple contents of adminstrative acts, personnel changes and records of natural phenomena.[166] Following Chavannes' earlier comments, Watson notes that several commentators throughout history have considered this chapter not to be the work of Ssu-ma Ch'ien. Watson claims that there is no evidence for this view. We also believe that this chapter was written by the Grand Scribe, but the speculations of past and present commentators about the chapter's authenticity are not completely unwarranted.

The issue of the authenticity of ths chapter and nine others allegedly missing from the *Shih chi*, has been the subject of many studies. The problem is first raised in Ssu-ma Ch'ien's *Han shu* biography, where there is a section that reads, ". . . ten fascicles [of the *T'ai-shih-kung shu*] are missing, there are titles but no text."[167] Chang Yen comments on this passage of text:

> After Ssu-ma Ch'ien's death, the "[Basic] Annals of [Emperor] Ching 景紀,"[168] the "[Basic] Annals of [Emperor] Wu 武紀,"[169] the "Treatise on the Rites 禮書,"[170] the "Treatise on Music 樂書,"[171] the "Treatise on the Military 兵書," the Chronological Table of Generals and Ministers Since the Rise of the Han 漢興以來蔣相年表,"[172] the "Memoir of the Calendar Makers 日者列傳,"[173] the "Hereditary House of the Three Sovereigns" 三王世家,[174] the "Memoir of the Tortoise and Milfoil [Diviners] 龜茅列傳,"[175] and the "Memoir

---

[166]See Watson, *Han*, 1.311, n. 1.

[167]See *Han shu*, 62.2724.

[168]*Shih chi*, 11.439.

[169]*Shih chi*, 12.451.

[170]*Shih chi*, 23.1157.

[171]*Shih chi*, 24.1175.

[172]*Shih chi*, 22.1119.

[173]*Shih chi*, 127.3215.

[174]*Shih chi*, 60.2105.

[175]*Shih chi*, 128.3223.

of Fu, Chin, [and the Marquis of K'uai-ch'eng] 傅靳[蒯成]列傳"[176] were lost. During the reigns of Emperor Yüan 元 (r. 48-32 B.C.) and Emperor Ch'eng 成 (r. 32-6 B.C.) Master Ch'u [Ch'u Shao-sun 褚少孫 (ca. 104-ca. 30 B.C.)][177] repaired the omissions, composing the "Annals of Emperor Wu," the "Hereditary House of the Three Sovereigns," and the memoirs of the "Tortoise and Milfoil [Diviners]" and "Calendar Makers." His words and phrases were rustic and vulgar, and not [Ssu-ma] Ch'ien's original meaning.

This, along with a citation in the *Han shu* "Bibliographic Monograph" that lists a *T'ai shih kung* 太史公 in 130 fascicles, with ten having titles but no text,[178] are some of the earliest mentions of such omissions. Other sources suggest that Emperor Wu had read the "Basic Annals of Emperor Ching," and, angered by Ssu-ma Ch'ien's critical comments on his father, excised the chapter.[179]

This note is not the place to review all the scholarship discussing the authenticity of this chapter, as well as the other alleged missing chapters. Having reviewed such scholarship ourselves, however, we are in agreement with Liang Yü-sheng's conclusions about the "Basic Annals of Emperor Ching the Filial." After thoroughly evaluating the various arguments of authorship, he agrees with the Sung scholar Chen Te-hsiu 真德秀 (1178-1235) in concluding that Ssu-ma Ch'ien was indeed the writer of this chapter, noting, among other things, that it contains information that is not in the *Han shu* account.[180] Liang Yü-sheng, from our observations, tends to be a most skeptical critic. His consideration of this chapter as authentic is noteworthy.

Hopefully, understanding the importance of this chapter in the textual history of the *Shih chi* will make the prosaic nature of the text somewhat more bearable.

[176]*Shih chi*, 98.2707.

[177]There is little biographical information about Ch'u Shao-sun. Most of what we know comes from his mention in the biography of Wang Shih 王式 on *Han shu*, 88.3610. For a thorough study of his life, which incorporates all remnants of biographical information, see Timoteus Pokora, "Ch'u Shao-sun–the Narrator of Stories in the *Shih-chi*," *Estratto di Annali dell' Instituto Orientale di Napoli*, 41 (1981): 403-430.

[178]See *Han shu*, 30.1714.

[179]See *Hsi-ching tsa-chi* 西京雜記, *SPTK*, 6.3b-4a. Wei Hung 衛宏 is also quoted in the "Chi-chieh" as having written a similar account in his *Han chiu yi chu* 漢舊儀注 (Liang Yü-sheng, 7.278).

[180]Liang quotes Chen's *Ching chi lun* 景記論.

BIBLIOGRAPHY

I. Translations

Chavannes, 2:496–510.
Watson, *Han*, 1:311–7.
Yoshida, 2:674-87.
Viatkin, 2:247-53, notes 467-75.

II. Studies

Bielenstein, Hans. "An Interpretation of the Portents in the Ts'ien Han-shu," *BMFEA* 22 (1950): 127–43.

Ch'in Chung-hsing 秦中行. "Han Yang-ling fu-chin ch'ien-t'u mu te fa-hsien," 漢陽陵附近鉗徒墓的發現, *Wen-wu* 文物 2 (1972): 51–3.

Eberhard, Wolfram. "The Political Function of Astronomy and Astronomers in Han China," in *Chinese Thought and Institutions*, ed. John K. Fairbank. Chicago: University of Chicago Press, 1957,pp. 33-70.

Loewe, "Liu Qi 劉啟," *Dictionary,* pp. 338-44.

Nanba Toshisada 那波利貞. "Kyôshôhon *Shiki* 'Kôkei hongi,' Dai jûichi kaisetsu" 舊抄本史記孝景本紀第十一解説, in *Shinagaku* 支那學 8.3: 125–53 and 8.4 (1936): 121–66. An excellent collation and study of a Japanese manuscript edition of this chapter.

Shan-hsi Sheng K'ao-ku Yen-chiu-so Han ling K'ao-ku-tui 陝西省考古研究所漢陵考古隊. "Han Ching-ti Yang-ling nan-ch'ü ts'ung tsang k'eng fa chüeh ti-erh hao chien-pao" 漢景帝陽陵南區從葬坑發掘第二號簡報, *Wen wu* 6 (1994): 4-23.

Shan-hsi Sheng K'ao-ku Yen-chiu-so Han ling K'ao-ku-tui 陝西省考古研究所漢陵考古隊. "Han Ching-ti Yang-ling nan-ch'ü ts'ung tsang k'eng fa chüeh ti-yi hao chien-pao" 漢景帝陽陵南區從葬坑發掘第一號簡報, *Wen wu* 4 (1992): 1-13.

The Filial and Martial [Emperor], Basic Annals 12

[**12.451**] Hsiao Wu Huang-ti 孝武皇帝 (The Filial and Martial August Emperor, 156-86 B.C., r. 140–87 B.C.) was a middle son[1] of Hsiao Ching[-ti] 孝景 [帝] (The Filial and Luminous [Emperor]).[2] His mother was called Wang T'ai-hou 王太后 (Empress Dowager Wang)[3] In the fourth year of [Emperor] Hsiao Ching (153 B.C.), as an imperial son he became King of Chiao-tung 膠東.[4] In the seventh year of Hsiao Ching[-ti] (150 B.C.), the Heir, Li 栗,[5] was deposed to become King of Lin-chiang 臨江,[6] and the King of Chiao-tung was made Heir. Hsiao Ching[-ti] passed away in his sixteenth year (141 B.C.)[7] and the Heir ascended the throne as the Hsiao Wu Huang-ti.

---

[1]His *praenomen* was Ch'e 徹. Ssu-ma Chen (in his "So-yin") concludes that Emperor Wu was the ninth son of Ching-ti based on the listing of Wu-ti's elder brothers in the "Ching Shih-san wang chuan" 景十三王傳 (Memoir of the Thirteen Kings of the [Emperor] Ching), *Han shu*, 53.2409). Modern scholars (e.g., Loewe, *Dictionary*, p. 274) have not found Ssu-ma Chen's reasoning convincing and simply list Liu Ch'e as a middle son of Ching-ti.

On the non-official accounts of Emperor Wu's life and reign, see the massive study by Thomas Eric Smith, "Ritual and the Shaping of Narrative: The Legend of the Han Emperor Wu," Unpublished Ph.D. dissertation, 2v., The University of Michigan, 1992.

[2]See *Shih chi*, Chapter 11.

[3]There is a brief account of Empress Dowager Wang on *Shih chi*, 49.1975-6.

[4]See also *Shih chi*, 11.442 and our translation above.

Chiao-tung was a small kingdom in the center of the Shantung peninsula with its capital at Chi-mo 即墨 about forty-five miles north-northwest of modern Tsingtao (T'an Ch'i-hsiang, 2:20).

[5]The Heir, Li 栗, was Emperor Ching's eldest son, Liu Jung 劉榮. Li was the *cognomen* of his mother and Liu Jung was known by this title because he was deposed as a result of his mother's loss of favor (*Shih chi*, 49.1976). This deposition happened in winter, see *Shih chi*, 11.443. Liu Jung was subsequently charged with a crime and forced to commit suicide in 148 B.C. (see *Shih chi*, 59.2094-5 and 17.847-8; according to the "Ta-shih chi" 大事記, *Shih chi*, 22.1132, he died in 146 B.C.).

[6]Lin-chiang was first founded by Hsiang Yü and ruled by Kung Ao 共敖 (*Shih chi*, 7.316; *The Grand Scribe's Records*, 1:196, n. 161). It then approximated the Ch'in commandery of Nan-chün 南郡 and covered most of what is today central and western Hupei along with a small part of eastern Szechwan (T'an Ch'i-hsiang, 2:11-2). With the accession of the Han, it became Nan-chün Commandery again. In 155 B.C. Emperor Ching reestablished the kingdom of Lin-chiang and made his son, Liu O-yü 關于, king (*Shih chi*, 59.2094). When Liu O-yü died in 154 B.C., the kingdom was again abolished. It was revived in 150 B.C. in order to find a place—apparently a rather impotent and insignificant place—for Liu Jung to rule. After his death it reverted to the status of a commandery (see Wang Hui, p. 516 and Loewe, *Dictionary*, pp. 785 and 796).

[7]Another account of his death is given in *Shih chi*, 11.448, but this passage also mentions the posthumous

When Hsiao Wu Huang-ti first ascended the throne, he was particularly respectful of sacrifices to ghosts and spirits.[8]

[452] In his first year (140 B.C.), it was already more than sixty years since the Han arose and the world was orderly and at peace; the civil officials all looked to the Son of Heaven to conduct the *Feng* 封 and *Shan* 禪 sacrifices and to change the primes and the standards.[9] The Sovereign inclined toward the Confucian art of politics and summoned the Worthy and the Good, so that Chao Wan 趙綰 (d. 139 B.C.), Wang Tsang 王臧 (d. 139 B.C.)[10] and others became honorable officials and ministers by virtue of their letters and learning. [The Emperor] wished them to deliberate about how in ancient times a Ming T'ang 明堂 (Hall of Light)[11] was erected south of the city wall in which to hold audiences with the feudal lords. They drafted plans to conduct tours of inspection, to hold the *Feng* and *Shan* sacrifices,[12] and to change the calendar and the colors of court vestments and vehicles,[13] [but] the plans were not completed. It happened that the Empress Dowager Tou 竇,[14] who was studying the Huang-Lao 黃老 teachings and did not like the political arts of the Confucians, sent men to secretly[15] gather information on

title Hsiao Wu-ti 孝武帝 (The Filial Martial Emperor) and therefore seems to be interpolated. Emperor Wu was sixteen the year his father died.

[8]On *Shih chi*, 28.1384 this sentence begins *chin T'ien-tzu* 今天子 , "The present Son of Heaven . . . . " The rest of this chapter is then nearly identical with the last part of Chapter 28. On the textual problems posed by this chapter, see the Translator's Note.

[9]For the *Feng* Sacrifice, the emperor ascended Mount T'ai 泰 and offered sacrifices to Heaven. For the *Shan* Sacrifice, the emperor offered sacrifices to earth on Mount Liang-fu 梁父 (see *Grand Scribe's Records*, 1:138, n. 158 and n. 270 to our translation of *Shih chi* Chapter 10 above).

The translation of *cheng tu* 正度 here follows Wu and Lu (12.392n.) who argue that *cheng* 正 refers to the "prime" or "first month" of the year as well as the first day of each month, while *tu* 度 refers to the system which designated the colors of court vestments and most other aspects of imperial life in association with the Five Elements or Five Phases (*Wu hsing* 五行).

[10]Chao Wan was a native of Tai 代 (see *Grand Scribe's Records,* 7:137, n. 74). Wang Tsang was from Lan-ling 蘭陵 (several miles south and east of modern Tsao-chuang 棗庄 in Shantung [T'an Ch'i-hsiang, 2:20]). Both men were scholars of the *Shih ching*. See also *Shih chi*, 121.3121–2 and n. 16 below.

[11]The Ming T'ang was a universe in miniature with a square base (reflecting earth) and a round-roofed central hall (in concert with heaven); see the thorough description and references given in Knechtges, *Wen xuan*, 1:114-16, n. 140.

[12]The *Feng* Sacrifice was directed to Heaven, the *Shan* Sacrifice to Earth; see *The Grand Scribe's Records,* 1:138, n. 158 and n. 270 to Chapter 10 above.

[13]*Fu* 服 were not restricted only to vestments, but included as well items related to vehicles, rites and sacrifices (see *The Grand Scribe's Records*, 1:45 n. 63).

[14]This was Emperor Wu's paternal grandmother, called Tou Chi 竇姬 (Beauty Tou). Her biography is on *Shih chi* 49.1972-5.

[15]Takigawa (12.3) notes that this same passage in two other *Shih chi* editions as well as the parallel passage on *Shih chi*, 28.1384 all include the character *ssu* 伺 (to spy on) after *wei* 微 "secretly." Mizusawa (12.328) adds four other editions that read the same (including the Palace Edition 12.2a); the parallel passage

embezzlement by Chao Wan and the rest.[16] Chao Wan and Wang Tsang were summoned and investigated. Chao Wan and Wang Tsang committed suicide, and all the initiatives they undertook were abandoned.

Six years later (135 B.C.), Empress Dowager Tou passed away. The following year (134 B.C.), the Sovereign summoned to court Kung-sun Hung 公孫弘 (*ca.* 200-121 B.C.) and other scholars of letters and learning.

The next year (133 B.C.), the Sovereign for the first time traveled to Yung 雍[17] to conduct the *Chiao* 郊 (Suburban) Sacrifice at the Wu Chih 五畤 (Five Altars);[18] after this the *Chiao* Sacrifice was regularly performed every three years.[19] Around this time the Sovereign also sought out the Shen Chün 神君 (The Spirit Mistress) and lodged her in the T'i-shih Kuan 蹏氏觀 (Ms. T'i's Tower) in the middle of the Shang-lin 上林 (Sovereign's Forest) Preserve.[20] The Shen Chün was a woman of Ch'ang-ling 長陵[21] who [died of] anguish and grief over her

on *Han shu,* 25A.1215 also reads *wei ssu.*

[16]According to the *Han shu* (6.157) account in the second year of Emperor Wu the Filial, Chao Wan, Grand Master of the Imperial Scribes, knowing that the Empress Dowager disdained Confucian teachings and favored Huang-Lao, asked to be allowed not to submit memorials to her. This angered her and resulted in Chao Wan's imprisonment and suicide as well as the suicide of Wang Tsang, Prefect of the Palace Attendants. See also Dubs, 2:30 and n. 10 above.

Another version of Chao Wan and Wang Tsang's attempt to bring Confucian ideas to Emperor Wu's court can be found in the biography of their master, Shen P'ei 申陪 (*Shih chi,* 121.3118). On *Shih chi,* 103.2765, Wang Tsang's downfall is attributed to his advocating *wen hsüeh* 文學,"letters and learning," which ties to the passage just below relating how Emperor Wu summoned *wen-hsüeh chih shih* 文學之士 after Empress Dowager Tou's death.

[17]Yung was located just south of modern Feng-hsiang 鳳翔 in Shensi (T'an Ch'i-hsiang, 2:15).

[18]On the significance of the Chiao Suburban Sacrifice and its first performance in Ch'in, see *Grand Scribe's Records,* 1:121, n. 433. Here "Cheng-yi" gives the names of the Five Altars as the Fu Altar 鄜畤, the Mi Altar 密畤, the Wu-yang Altar(s) 吳陽畤, and the Pei Altar 北畤 and attributes the first sacrifice to the White Emperor 白帝 at the Fu Altar to Duke Wen 文 of Ch'in (r. 765-716 B.C.); to the Azure Emperor 青帝 at the Mi Altar to Duke Hsüan 宣 of Ch'in (r. 675-664 B.C.); to the Red Emperor 赤帝 and Yellow Emperor 黃帝 at the Upper and Lower Wu-yang Altars to Duke Ling of Ch'in 秦靈 (r. 424-415 B.C.); and to the Black Emperor 黑帝 at the Pei Altar to Emperor Kao-tsu of Han (r. 206-195 B.C.); cf. *Grand Scribe's Records,* 1:91, n. 40.

[19]In Chapter 28, "So-yin" cites the *Han chiu yi* 漢舊儀 (Old Regulations of the Han Dynasty) according to which, "in the first year sacrifice is made to Heaven, in the second year to Earth, and in the third year [to the Five Emperors] at the five sacred altars. The series of sacrifices takes three years, and the Emperor makes the journey in person" (*Shih chi,* 28.1384). See also Marianne Bujard, "Le 'Traité des Sacrifices' du *Hanshu* et la mise en place de la religion d'État des Han," *Bulletin de l'École Française d'Extrême-Orient* 84 (1997): 111-27.

[20]Shang-lin was the name of the imperial hunting preserve first established during the Ch'in dynasty and later expanded by Emperor Wu. It ran along the south bank of the Wei River from modern Hu 戶 County west for some thirty miles (T'an Ch'i-hsiang, 2:5).

[21]Ch'ang-ling was located some fifteen miles north of modern Sian, in Shensi (T'an Ch'i-hsiang, 2:15).

[infant] son's death[22]; for this reason, she appeared in spirit form to her sister-in-law, Yüan-jo 宛若. Yüan-jo sacrificed to the spirit in her home and large numbers of people came to take part. [*453*] P'ing-yüan Chün 平原君 (Mistress P'ing-yüan)[23] also went there to sacrifice [to the spirit]; after this her descendants thereby became honored and distinguished. When Wu-ti[24] ascended the throne he treated the Shen Chün to sumptuous rites and relocated her shrine within the imperial hunting preserve. The spirit's words could be heard, but her form could not be seen.

At this time Li Shao-chün 李少君 also had an audience with the Sovereign; by means of [his skills in] sacrificing to the Tz'u Tsao 祠竈 (God of the Furnace),[25] dietary practices,[26] and methods for retarding old age, the Sovereign accorded him great respect. Li Shao-chün had formerly been a houseman of the Marquis of Shen-tse 深澤[27] who recommended him [to the Emperor] as a magician.[28] He kept his age and birthplace a secret, always claiming to be seventy [years old], capable of manipulating spirits, and retarding old age. He traveled among the courts of the feudal lords by virtue of his [magical] methods. He had no wife or children. On hearing [*454*] he was able to manipulate spirits and achieve immortality, people lavished even more gifts on him, so that he was always more than amply provided with money, silk clothing, and food. People all thought that he managed no productive enterprises and yet was abundantly supplied with everything, and not knowing where he was from, people's faith in him increased all the more, and they competed to serve him. Shao-chün derived his livelihood from his proficiency in [magical] methods, and he was especially skillful in making artful statements

[22]Chapter 28 (*Shih chi*, 28.1384) has *yi tzu ssu* 以子死 for *yi tzu ssu pei-ai* 以子死悲哀 here, which has led to a somewhat forced interpretation of *yi tzu ssu* as "died in childbirth"; cf. Watson, 2:25 and Chavannes, 3:463. The latter cites the *Han shu* version, *yi ju ssu* 以乳死, and Meng K'ang's gloss, *ch'an ju erh ssu yeh* 產乳而死也, "died giving birth," in support.

[23]Emperor Wu's maternal grandmother Tsang Erh 臧兒. A brief biography may be found on *Shih chi*, 49.1975-7.

[24]This is the only instance where the Emperor's posthumous title Wu-ti is used in this chapter; in the parallel passage in Chapter 28 (28.1384) the text reads *chin shang* 今上. Other references to the sovereign in this paragraph and elsewhere typically use *chin shang* or simply *shang*.

[25]"So-yin" cites *Shuo-wen* 説文 and *Chou-li* 周禮 which identify the God of the Furnace (also called the Kitchen God) as Chu Jung 祝融. He notes further that *Huai-nan Tzu* 淮南子 says Yen Ti 炎帝, the Flaming Emperor, was the official in charge of fire who became the God of the Furnace after death.

[26]The expression used is *ku tao* 穀道, literally "Way of grain," the meaning of which is obscure. Contradictory glosses refer to both the consumption of and abstinence from food grains.

[27]Surnamed Chao 趙; his enfeoffment was terminated by Emperor Ching (see "Chi-chieh"). He is variously referred to as Chao Chiang-yeh 趙將夜 (*Shih chi*, 18.933-4) and Chao Chiang-hsi 趙將夕 (*Han shu*, 16.585). According to *Shih chi*, 22.1126, he was made a general in 177 B.C. For details surrounding his enfeoffment and its termination see *Shih chi*, 18.933, and *Han shu*, 16.585.) Shen-tse was located northeast of Chin 晉 County in modern Hopei (T'an Ch'i-hsiang, 2:26).

[28]The *fang* 方 here refers to *fang yao* 方藥, an ancient kind of pharmacist whose prescriptions could create various 'magical' effects (according to Wu and Lu, 12.393n.).

that later proved uncannily accurate. He once accompanied the Marquis of Wu-an drinking,[29] among the company there was an old man of over ninety. Shao-chün then spoke about a place where he had wandered and practiced archery with the old man's grandfather. The old man had traveled with his grandfather as a boy and recognized the place; the whole company was completely amazed. [Another time] Shao-chün appeared before the Sovereign and the Sovereign asked him about an ancient bronze vessel the Sovereign possessed. Shao-chün said: "Duke Huan 桓 of Ch'i (r. 685-643 B.C.) displayed this vessel in the Po-ch'in [T'ai] 柏寢[臺] (Cypress Chamber [Terrace]) in his tenth year (676 B.C.)."[30] Shortly after, when the inscription was examined, the bronze indeed proved to be Duke Huan of Ch'i's. The whole palace was astonished and took Shao-chün to be a spirit, someone who had lived hundreds of years.

[455] Li Shao-chün told the Sovereign: "If you sacrifice to the Furnace,[31] you will summon the spirits; once you summon the spirits, cinnabar grains can be transformed into yellow gold; the yellow gold once made, if you fashion drinking and eating utensils from it, you can prolong your life; with prolonged life you can visit the immortals who live on the [Isles of] P'eng-lai 蓬萊[32] in the middle of the sea; on seeing them, by means of performing the *Feng* and *Shan* sacrifices you will never die. This is what the Huang-ti 黃帝 (The Yellow Emperor) did. Your servant once wandered across the sea and saw Master An-ch'i 安期[33] who fed me jujubes as big as melons.[34] The immortal Master An-ch'i made it to [the Isles of] P'eng-lai. When

---

[29]This was T'ien Fen 田蚡 (d. 131 B.C.), uncle of Emperor Wu and younger brother of the Empress Dowager Tou by the same mother. He was enfeoffed by Emperor Wu in 141 B.C. and also served as Grand Commandant and Chancellor (Wang Li-ch'i, 12.279n.).

Wu-an was located in Wei Commandery 魏郡 (T'an Ch'i-hsiang, 2:26).

[30]Takigawa (12.5) cites Shen Ch'in-han 沈欽韓 (1775-1832) who claims it was built later, based on a passage in *Yen Tzu ch'un-ch'iu* (*Yen Tzu ch'un-ch'iu chi-shih* 晏子春秋集釋, Wu Tse-yü 吳則虞, ed. [Peking: Chung-hua, 1962], 6.379); there it says the Cypress Chamber Terrace was newly built in the reign of Duke Ching 景 of Ch'i (r. 547–490 B.C.). Fu Ch'ien (see "Chi-chieh") says Po-ch'in was a placename and *K'uo-ti chih* 括地志 (cited in "Cheng-yi") locates it in Ch'ien-sheng 千乘, about ten miles north and west of modern Po-hsing 博興 in Shantung (T'an Ch'i-hsiang, 1:39).

[31]It is clear from what follows that *tsao*   "furnace" here does not refer to the domestic hearth or its resident spirit as some commentators suggest, but to the alchemical furnace. On this point see Chavannes, 2:465, n. 1.

[32]On these isles see also *Shih chi*, 6.247; *Grand Scribe's Records*, 1:142.

[33]For the legend of Master An-ch'i, "So-yin" quotes *Lieh-hsien chuan* 列仙傳: "Master An-ch'i was a native of Lang-ya 琅邪 who sold medicinal herbs by the side of the Eastern Sea. His contemporaries all said he was one thousand years old." "Cheng-yi" also cites *Lieh-hsien chuan*: "Master An-ch'i was a native of Fu-hsiang T'ing 阜鄉亭 in Lang-ya. He sold medicinal herbs by the sea. The First Emperor of Ch'in engaged him in conversation for three nights running and rewarded him with many thousands in cash. Master An-ch'i went out, and leaving everything at Fu-hsiang T'ing, he departed, leaving behind a testament, using a one-ounce crimson jade shoe as recompense; it said: 'In a thousand years look for me at the foot of Mount P'eng-lai.'"

[34]*Shih chi*, 28.1385 and the Po-na (12.3b) edition both have *chü* 巨 "giant" for *ch'en* 臣 "your servant,"

it suits him, he reveals himself, otherwise he stays hidden." At this, the Son of Heaven began to sacrifice in person to the God of the Furnace. He also sent practitioners of [magical] methods to sea to search for P'eng-lai, Master An-ch'i, and the rest, and had attempts made to transform cinnabar grains and medicinal concoctions into yellow gold.[35]

After some time, Li Shao-chün fell ill and died.[36] The Son of Heaven believed that he had transformed himself [into an immortal] and did not die, so he had the Scribe from Huang 黃 and Ch'ui 錘,[37] K'uan-shu 寬舒, carry on Li's [magical] methods.[38] In the search for P'eng-lai and Master An-ch'i, they were unable to find anything, but on the seacoast of Yen 燕 and Ch'i 齊 many strange and outlandish imitators[39] imitated [Li], one after another expounding on spiritual matters.

[456] A man from Po 亳[40] by the name of Miu Chi 謬忌[41] submitted a memorial on the methods of sacrifice to the T'ai-yi 泰一 (Grand Unity), saying: "The Grand Unity is the highest heavenly spirit,[42] and the Grand Unity's assistants are called the Wu Ti 五帝 (Five Emperors).[43]

which could be taken to mean Master An-ch'i was the one doing the eating. *Han shu* (25A.1217) has "your servant."

[35]See Chavannes, 2:465, n. 1, on the importance of this passage for the history of alchemy.

[36]The "Cheng-yi" cites a legendary account of his death from the *Han shu ch'i-chü* 漢書起居.

[37]Huang and Ch'ui counties were located near modern Huang 黃 and Wen-teng 文登 counties in Shantung (Wang Li-ch'i, 12.285n.; T'an Ch'i-hsiang, 2:20).

[38]The translation here is based on Wu and Lu (12.394n.); see also the passage on *Shih chi,* 6.244 concerning the First Emperor of Ch'in's visit to Huang and Ch'ui 腄.

[39]*Shih chi,* 28.1386, and *Han shu,* 25A.1217, both omit *hsiang-hsiao* 相效.

[40]Po (also written 薄) was a county located several miles south and east of modern Ts'ao 曹 County in Shantung (T'an Ch'i-hsiang, 2:19).

[41]Following "So-yin" which takes *po* 薄 as an interpolation arising from subsequent use of 薄 for 亳 when referring to Miu Chi as Po Chi 薄忌. *Yu* 誘, on the other hand, is said to be an error for *miu* 謬; *Shih chi,* 28.1386 and *Han shu,* 25A.1218), both read *Miu* 謬 (cf. Wang Li-ch'i, 12.285n.).

[42]"So-yin" here notes that T'ai-yi "Grand Unity" refers to the star T'ien-yi 天一 "Heavenly Unity" within the asterism Tzu-wei Yüan 紫微垣 (Purple Tenuity Enclosure) near the Pole. He cites Sung Chün who held that both T'ien-yi and T'ai-yi were alternative names for the North Pole; see also n. 141 below. In fact, T'ien-yi and T'ai-yi were two stars in Draconis very close to the Pole; for their locations see Sun and Kistemaker, *The Chinese Sky During the Han* (Leiden: E. J. Brill, 1997), pp. 96 and 166-7. For another interpretation of this term, see Li Ling, "An Archaeological Study of Taiyi (Grand One) Worship," *Early Medieval China,* 2 (1995-6): 1-39, and the numerous studies cited by Li Chien-min 李建民 in n. 7 on p. 54 of his "T'ai-yi hsin-cheng—yi Kuo-tien Ch'u chieh wei hsien-so" 太一新證—以郭店楚簡為線索, *Chûgoku shutsudo shiryô kenkyû* 中國出土資料研究, 3(1999): 46-62 (thanks to Mark Csikszentmihalyi for this reference).

[43]"Cheng-yi" lists the various appellations of the Five Heavenly Emperors as follows: "*Kuo-yü* 國語 says: 'The Ch'ing-ti 青帝 (Azure Emperor) [was] Ling Wei Yang 靈威仰; the Ch'ih-ti 赤帝 (Red Emperor), Ch'ih Piao Nu 赤熛怒; the Pai-ti 白帝 (White Emperor), Pai Chao Chü 白招矩; the Hei-ti 黑帝 (Black Emperor), Yeh Kuang Chi 葉光紀; the Huang-ti 黃帝 (Yellow Emperor), Han Shu Niu 含樞紐.' *Shang-shu ti-ming yen* 尚書帝

In ancient times the Son of Heaven sacrificed to the Grand Unity every spring and autumn in the southeastern suburbs, employing the *T'ai-lao* 太牢[44] for seven[45] days. An altar was constructed that was open to the ghost roads of the eight directions." At this, the Son of Heaven ordered the Grand Supplicator[46] to establish such shrines in the southeastern suburbs of Ch'ang-an, where sacrifices were regularly offered according to the methods of [Miu] Chi. Thereafter, someone [else] submitted a memorial to the throne saying: "In ancient times, once every three years the Son of Heaven would employ a complete set of *T'ai-lao* 太牢 Sacrifices to sacrifice to the spirits of the San-yi 三一 (Three Unities): the T'ien-yi 天一 (Heavenly Unity), the Ti-yi 地一 (Earthly Unity), and the T'ai-yi 泰一 (Grand Unity)." The Son of Heaven consented to this and ordered the Grand Supplicator to lead the sacrifices to them on [Miu] Chi's altar to the Grand Unity according to this method. Afterward, someone again submitted a memorial to the throne saying: "In ancient times the Son of Heaven regularly conducted Exorcistic Sacrifices in spring and autumn; in sacrificing to the Huang-ti he employed an owl and a "broken mirror"[47]; to Ming Yang 冥羊 (Dark Ram) he employed a sheep; in sacrificing to Ma Hsing 馬行 (Horse Traveler) he employed a black stallion; to the Grand Unity, the Kao-shan Shan-chün 皋山山君 (The Mountain Lord of Mount Kao),[48] and Ti Chang 地長 (Earth Elder) he employed an ox; to Wu-yi Chün 武夷 君 (The Lord of Wu-yi)[49] he employed dried fish; and to the Yin Yang Shih-che 陰陽使者 (The Envoys of Yin and Yang) he employed an ox." The officials in charge of sacrifices were ordered to lead [rites] according to these methods, sacrificing alongside [Miu] Chi's altar to the Grand Unity.

命驗 says: 'The Azure Emperor's name is Ling Wei Yang; the Red Emperor's name is Wen Tsu 文祖, the Yellow Emperor's name is Shen Tou 神斗; the White Emperor's name is Hsien Chi 顯紀; the Black Emperor's name is Hsüan Chü 玄矩.'" The near identity between the Yellow Emperor's names (e.g., "Containing the Pivot," "Spirit Dipper") and terminology associated with circumpolar stars points to the connection between the Huang-ti and the celestial pole.

[44]According to Wang Li-ch'i (12.285n.), *T'ai-lao* literally means "Great Vessel" and is used metonymically to refer to the cooked meat which is sacrificed. This usually contains beef, lamb, and pork, although in this chapter there are examples of a sacrifice with only beef (or more accurately veal—see the translation of *Shih chi,* 12.461 and n. 80 below). See also *Grand Scribe's Records,* 7:283, n. 14.

[45]"Chi chieh" quotes Hsü Kuang's comment that the sacrifices lasted ten days, not seven.

[46]*T'ai-chu* 太祝.

[47]*P'o ching* 破鏡 "broken mirror" is somewhat implausibly identified as a creature resembling a wildcat that was notorious for devouring its father. The owl was thought malevolent because it was believed to devour its mother. Both were dispatched as surrogates to exorcise all such impious influences. Meng K'ang 孟康 (cited in "Chi-chieh") says that according to one view "broken mirror" means just what it says. No details are known about the other spirits mentioned in what follows.

[48]*Shih chi,* 28.1386 has *Tse* 澤 for *Kao* 皋 (and does not duplicate the graph *shan* 山). Neither location is found in T'an Ch'i-hsiang, though there was a Kao-lan 皋蘭 Mountain located just southwest of modern Lan-chou 蘭州 City (T'an Ch'i-hsiang, 2:34).

[49]Wu-yi Mountain was located south of Ch'ung-an 崇安 County in modern Fukien Province (Wang

[457] After this there were white deer in the Son of Heaven's [game] preserve. He had their hides made into a kind of currency[50] to make known this auspicious portent and initiated the minting of a white metal coinage.[51]

The following year (123 B.C.),[52] during the *Chiao* Sacrifice at Yung, a one-horned animal was captured which looked like a *Piao* 麃 deer.[53] The authorities concerned said: "Your Majesty solemnly and reverently carried out the *Chiao* Sacrifice and the Supreme Deity has repaid your offerings by bestowing this one-horned animal; [*458*] probably this is a unicorn." At this, the Emperor offered it up at the Five Altars, and added a burnt offering of an ox at each. He bestowed on each of the feudal lords white-metal [coins] to allude to this auspicious sign in harmony with Heaven and Earth.[54]

At this time, the King of Chi-pei 濟北,[55] thinking the Son of Heaven was about to perform the *Feng* 封 and *Shan* 禪 sacrifices, thus submitted a memorial presenting Mount T'ai 泰山 to the throne together with nearby towns. The Son of Heaven accepted them and compensated the King with other counties in exchange. When the King of Ch'ang-shan 常山[56] committed an offense and was banished, the Son of Heaven enfeoffed the king's younger brother at Chen-ting 真定[57] to continue the sacrifices to the former kings [of Ch'ang-shan], and then he made Ch'ang-

Li-ch'i, 12.286n.).

[50]The *Han shu*, "Shih-huo chih" 食貨志 (*Han shu*, 24B.1163) states that the hide currency was one *ch'ih* square and worth 400,000 cash. No mention of this event is made in the parallel *Han shu* version of this passage (25A.1215ff.); cf. Dubs, 2:64.

[51]Chavannes (2:468, n. 1) notes that this passage anticipates events of 120 B.C. which are reported in the "P'ing-chün shu" 平準書 (*Shih chi* 30.1427ff.). The coins were minted in three denominations from a silver and tin alloy. The largest, called *pai-hsüan* 白選, was round, weighed eight ounces, was worth three thousand cash (*chin*), and was inscribed with dragons. The next, called *chung ch'a hsiao* 重差小, was square, worth five hundred cash, and inscribed with horses. The last, called *fu hsiao* 復小, was oval, worth three hundred cash, and was decorated with turtles. The three animals were said to represent Heaven, Earth, and man. See the informative comments in Dubs, 2:64, n. 15.

[52]*Han shu*, Chapter 25A.1219, makes it two years later; cf. Dubs, 2:57. See also Wang Shu-min (12.434).

[53]For details on this animal, see Dubs, 2:85, n. 24.

[54]The *Shih chi* (28.1387) and *Han shu* (25A.1219) versions have *yeh* 也 for *ti* 地 here. The Po-na version (12.5b) has *ti*.

[55]In modern Shantung, southeast of T'ai-an 泰安 County (see Ch'ien Mu, *Ti-ming-k'ao*, p. 281; Wang Li-ch'i, 7.175n., and T'an Ch'i-hsiang, 2:8).

[56]This was Liu Po 劉勃, grandson of Emperor Ching, who had been unfilial in violating mourning prohibitions. This occurred in 107 B.C., according to Hsü Kuang ("Chi-chieh").

Ch'ang-shan was located in the central part of modern Hopei and the central and eastern parts of modern Shansi (Wang Li-ch'i, 7.175n.; T'an Ch'i-hsiang, 2:26).

[57]South of Cheng-ting 正定 County in modern Hopei, the fief was established as Chen-ting Kuo by Emperor Wu (Wang Li-ch'i, 12.286n; T'an Ch'i-hsiang, 2:26).

shan into a commandery.[58] Thereafter, all the Wu Yüeh 五嶽 (Five Sacred Peaks)[59] were situated in commanderies [under the direct control] of the Son of Heaven.

The following year (122 B.C.), a native of Ch'i 齊, Shao Weng 少翁 (The Youthful Gaffer), through his [magical] methods with ghosts and spirits, gained an audience with the Sovereign. The Sovereign had a favorite, Lady Wang 王夫人,[60] who had expired. It was said that Shao Weng used his [magical] methods and techniques to summon her spectral apparition and that of the Ghost of the Furnace at night, while the Son of Heaven watched them at a distance from among the curtains. At this, the Emperor appointed Shao Weng as General of Accomplished Letters[61] and lavishly rewarded him, treating him with the courtesy due an imperial guest. [The General of] Accomplished Letters said: "Inasmuch as Your Majesty desires to communicate with the spirits, if the furnishings of the palace and apartments as well as your own vestments are not patterned after the spirits, they will not come." Then [the Emperor] had [five] carriages made decorated with cloud-emanation [patterns], each driven on the day its power was in the ascendancy,[62] to ward off malevolent ghosts. He also built a terraced chamber in the center of the Kan-ch'üan Kung 甘泉宮 (Sweet Springs Palace),[63] which was decorated with images of Heaven, Earth, the Grand Unity, and all the other spirits, and there he placed the sacrificial [offering] vessels to attract the spirits of Heaven. After more than a year, his [magical] methods grew weaker and the spirits failed to come, so he wrote something on silk and fed it to an ox. Then, feigning ignorance, he said there was something extraordinary in the ox's belly. The ox was slaughtered, examined, and the document retrieved. The document's wording was utterly bizarre

[58]This happened in 107 B.C.

The Northern Sacred Peak 北嶽, Mount Heng 恆, was located northwest of Ch'ü-yang 曲陽 County in modern Hopei. The name was changed to Ch'ang Shan to avoid the taboo on Emperor Wen, Liu Heng's, *praenomen* (Wang Li-ch'i, 12.286n.).

[59]The Five Sacred Peaks were Mount Heng in the north (see n. 58 just above), Mount T'ai 泰 in the east (just over twenty miles south of modern Tsinan in Shantung [T'an Ch'i-hsiang, 2:20]), Mount Hua 華 in the west (just over ten miles southwest of the confluence of the Wei and Yellow rivers in modern Shensi [T'an Ch'i-hsiang, 2:15]), Mount T'ien-chu 天柱 (Heavenly Pillar) in the south (about eighty-five miles southwest of modern Hofei in Anhwei [T'an Ch'i-hsiang, 2:24]), and T'ai-shih 太室 (The Great House) in the center (about twenty-five miles southeast of modern Lo-yang near the modern town of Teng-feng 登封 in Honan [T'an Ch'i-hsiang, 2:19]); cf. Wu and Lu, 12.394n.).

[60]*Han shu*, 25A.1219, gives her *cognomen* as Li 李.

[61]*Wen-ch'eng Chiang-chün* 文成將軍.

[62]The implication is that the color and decoration of each carriage symbolized one of the Five Phases—Wood, Metal, Water, Fire, Earth—each of which was associated in divination with two of the ten Heavenly Stems: Wood with *chia-yi* 甲乙; Fire with *ping-ting* 丙丁; Earth with *wu-chi* 戊己; Metal with *keng-hsin* 庚辛; Water with *jen-kuei* 壬癸.

[63]Kan-ch'üan Palace was located on Kan-ch'üan Mountain, fifteen miles northwest of modern Ch'un-hua 淳化 County in Shensi (T'an Ch'i-hsiang, 2:15).

and the Son of Heaven became suspicious about it. Someone[64] recognized the calligraphy. Having questioned the man, it was indeed [determined to be] a forged document.[65] At this, the General of Accomplished Letters was executed and the affair was hushed up.

[459] After this buildings like the Po-liang [T'ai] (Cypress Beams [Terrace]) were also built with bronze pillars and statues of immortals in whose upraised palms dew was collected.[66]

The year after [the General of] Accomplished Letters died (118 B.C.), the Son of Heaven fell gravely ill at Ting Hu 鼎湖 (Tripod Lake);[67] he caused all the shamanesses and physicians to come, [but] he did not improve. [Earlier,] Fa Ken 發根 of Yu-shui 游水[68] had said: "In Shang-chün 上郡 [Commandery][69] there is a shamaness who fell ill and ghosts descended upon her."[70] The Sovereign summoned her and sacrificed to her in the Kan-ch'üan Palace. When he became ill [himself], he sent someone to ask the Spirit Mistress [through the shamaness], who responded: "The Son of Heaven must not worry about this illness; when the illness has improved slightly, he should make an effort to join me in Kan-ch'üan [Palace]." At this the Emperor's illness improved slightly; he then favored[71] Kan-ch'üan with his presence, and his sickness really was completely cured. He granted a general amnesty throughout the world and established the Shou Kung 壽宮 (Palace of Longevity)[72] for the Spirit Mistress. Among those most honored by the Spirit Mistress was the T'ai-yi 太一 (Grand Unity),[73] whose assistants were called Ta Chin 大禁

---

[64]Elsewhere both *Han shu* (25A.1219: 天子識其手) and *Shih chi* (28.1388: 天子識其手書) explicitly say the Emperor recognized the calligraphy, but here we have only *yu shih* 有識, "there was a recognition."

[65]The Chung-hua editors have emended the text here: *wei* 為 has been changed to *wei* 偽. This was done in spite of Chang Wen-hu's (1.111) rejection of this change (although he notes that *wei* 為 here *means wei* 偽). Chang Wen-hu also observes that all but one edition he has examined read *wei* 為. The Po-na edition (12.6b), which Chang Wen-hu was not able to consult, also reads *wei* 為. The Chung-hua editors explain their decision on Chang Wen-hu, 1.111: "for the convenience of the reader, we have changed *wei* 為 to *wei* 偽": 以便利讀者，改「為」為「偽」.

[66]According to sources cited in "So-yin," this imposing edifice, with pillars thirty *chang* in height, was in the Chien-chang Kung 建章宮 (Palace of Established Emblems). The collected dew was mixed with jade powder and drunk to promote longevity.

[67]The name of a palace whose ruins are located on the border of Lan-t'ien 藍田 County near Yi-ch'un 宜春 in modern Shensi Province (Wang Li-ch'i, 12.287n.; T'an Ch'i-hsiang, 2:15).

[68]Yu-shui was located in eastern Tung-hai 東海 Commandery near the east coast in what is now Kiangsu Province (T'an Ch'i-hsiang, 2:20).

[69]Shang Commandery was located west and northwest of Yen-an 延安 in modern Shensi Province (Wang Li-ch'i, 12.287n.; T'an Ch'i-hsiang, 2:17).

[70]*Han shu* (25A.1220), and *Shih chi* (28.1388) do not take this as a direct quote.

[71]*Han shu* (25A.1220), and *Shih chi* (28.1388) both have *ch'i* 起 "arose" before "favored."

[72]Wu and Lu (12.396) noted that the ruins of the Shou Kung are located a few miles northwest of modern Sian in Shensi. The palace was a part of the Northern Palace (see just below in this paragraph and *San-fu huang-t'u,* p. 172).

[73]The original Chin-ling text reads Tai-fu 大夫 here instead of T'ai-yi; it has been emended by the

(Grand Prohibiter), Ssu Ming 司命 (Arbiter of Fate), and the like,[74] and who all accompanied her. They could not be seen, but their voices could be heard; they sounded like human speech. Sometimes they departed and sometimes they came, and when they came it was like the soughing of the wind. Dwelling among the curtains of the chamber, they sometimes spoke in the daytime, but usually by night. The Son of Heaven would first perform the purgation rites and only thereafter enter [her chamber]; relying on the shamaness to act as host; [*460*] they would partake of the food and drink, whatever they wanted to say[75] being relayed [through the shamaness]. The Emperor further established the Shou Kung and the Pei-kung 北宮 (North Palace) and had feathered banners unfurled and ritual paraphernalia set out to perform rites for the Spirit Mistress. Whatever the Spirit Mistress said the Sovereign would have someone write down, and [these writings] he named *Hua fa* 畫法[76] (Record of Mantic Arts). What the spirit spoke about was just common knowledge and nothing out of the ordinary, and only the Son of Heaven was pleased with it. This business was kept secret, however, and no one knew about it at the time.

Three years later (114 B.C.), the authorities concerned said that in originating [reign periods] it would be appropriate to name them after auspicious signs from Heaven, and it was not appropriate to enumerate "first," "second," [etc.]. The first origination 元 (140 B.C.) should be called Chien-yüan 建元 (Establishing the Originations); the second origination (134 B.C.), named for the comet,[77] should be called Yüan-kuang 元光 (The Origination in Resplendence);

Chung-hua editors based on Chang Wen-hu's (1.111) observation that parallel passages in both *Shih chi* (28.1388) and *Han shu* (25A.1220) read "T'ai-yi." Wang Shu-min (12.437) cites arguments by late-Ch'ing scholars on the merits of the two expressions in this context, and concludes that T'ai-yi is the preferred reading.

[74]Nothing is known about the Grand Prohibiter. The Arbiter of Fate was the deity in charge of the realm of the dead and the name given to an asterism in Aquarius north of lunar mansion Hsü 虛. The earliest mention of this spirit is in Ch'ü Yüan's 屈原 "Li-sao" 離騷 (Encountering Sorrow). For the location of Ssu-ming in the sky see Sun and Kistemaker, *The Chinese Sky During the Han*, p. 169.

[75]The text appears corrupt at this point. *Shih chi*, 28.1388 has *so yi yen* 所以言, and *Han shu*, 25A.1220 reads *so yü yen* 所欲言, both of which make better sense than the text here: *so yü che yen* 所欲者言.

[76]The Po-na and Palace versions (12.7b and 12.7a, respectively) have *shu* 書 for *hua* 畫. Wang Shu-min (12.428) notes that in general most older editions of *Shih chi* read *shu*. The "Cheng-yi" in some versions (such as the Palace edition) reads *shu yin hua* 書音畫. This would seem to support *shu* as the correct reading. However, *hua* has two pronunciations (音獲，音畫) whereas *shu* has only one (cf. *Chung-wen ta tz'u-tien*, 6.679 and 4.1449, respectively). Thus, it seems that editors of many early *Shih chi* editions perpetuated the error of *shu* for *hua* and subsequently changed the wording of the "Cheng-yi" as well (as Wang Shu-min suggests). The parallels in *Han shu* (25A.1220) and in *Han Wu-ti ku-shih* 漢武故事 (*Ku hsiao-shuo kou-ch'en* 古小說鉤 沈, Lu Hsün 魯迅, ed. [Peking: Jen-min Wen-hsüeh, 1953], p. 295) both read *hua*.

[77]Literally *ch'ang hsing* 長星 "elongated star" which appeared in July-August of the sixth year of the Chien-yüan reign period (135 B.C.). For an account of the comet, see Dubs, 2:34. This comet was identified by diviners as "Ch'ih Yu's Banner," an omen of war that evoked the cosmic battle between the legendary miscreant Ch'ih Yu and the Huang-ti; cf. Bodde, *Festivals in Classical China*, p. 121. For an illustration of the second century B.C. Ma-wang-tui cometary atlas, Ch'ih Yu's banner, see *Chung-kuo ku-tai t'ien-wen wen-wu t'u-chi* 中 國古代天文文物圖集 (Peking: Wen-wu Ch'u-pan she, 1980), p. 23, PL 21. For a detailed discussion of the

[*461*] the third origination (122 B.C.), because during the *Chiao* Sacrifice a one-horned animal was captured, should be called Yüan-shou 元狩 (The Origination of the Hunt).

In the winter of the following year (113 B.C.), having performed the *Chiao* Sacrifice at Yung, the Son of Heaven had [his officials] deliberate about it: "Now We have personally performed the *Chiao* Sacrifice to the Supreme Deity, but have not made an offering to the Hou-t'u 后土 (Mother Earth)[78] and, according to the rites, this is inappropriate." The authorities concerned deliberated with the Prefect of the Grand Scribes,[79] the official in charge of sacrifices, K'uan-shu, and others: "For Heaven and Earth the sacrificial oxen has horns the size of a silkworm cocoon or a chestnut. Now if Your Majesty sacrifices in person to Mother Earth, it would be appropriate to build Five Altars on a round hillock in the middle of a marshy place and on each altar there should be a set of yellow-calf *T'ai-lao* sacrifices.[80] When the sacrifices are over, the victims should be completely buried. The vestments of those in attendance at the sacrifice should exalt the color yellow." At this the Son of Heaven proceeded to the east[81] where he first established sacrifices to Mother Earth on a mound at Fen-yin 汾陰 (South Bank of the Fen),[82] according to the deliberations of K'uan-shu and the others. The Sovereign personally performed

Ma-wang-tui cometary atlas, Ch'ih Yu's Banner, and the various other terms applied to comets in Han sources, see Michael Loewe, "The Han View of Comets," in *Divination,* pp. 61-84.

[78]Loewe, *Chinese Ideas,* p. 17, notes that the Hou-t'u, along with the T'ai-yi, were the two major deities in state worship of this period. Yüan K'o, *Shen-hua,* pp. 164-5 observes that Hou-t'u (according to the *Li chi*) was an assistant to the Huang-ti.

Although Hou-t'u is sometimes translated as "Lord of the Earth" (in this chapter Ti-chu 地主 is so translated), Loewe normally refers to the Hou-t'u as "The Earth Queen" (see *Crisis and Conflict,* p. 28, or *Ways to Paradise,* p. 57, for example). In discussing the term Ao 媼, "So-yin" (*Shih chi,* 8.342) cites various texts claiming that the God of the Earth (*Ti-shen* 地神) and Hou-t'u were both referred to by the term Ao 媼 which usually denotes an elderly woman. *Hou* 后 can mean "the principle wife" and in the usage Hou-t'u seems to be antithetically balanced to the male Huang T'ien 皇天. Thus our rendering, "Mother Earth." For a general survey of the controversy concerning the sex of the Hou-t'u see Anne Birrell, *Chinese Mythology, An Introduction* (Baltimore: The Johns Hopkins University Press, 1993), pp. 161-2.

[79]Only *Han shu* (25A.1221) identifies Ssu-ma T'an by name here.

[80]Although Michael Loewe (*Crisis and Conflict,* p. 168) believes this sacrifice contained the normal bull, sheep and pig in addition to calves, it seems rather that this is an example of a *T'ai-lao* sacrifice that involves only veal. Such is the understanding of the two modern Chinese translations normally consulted (Wu and Lu, 12.414; Wang Li-ch'i, 12.302n.) and apparently also that of Pan Ku—the parallel passage on *Han shu,* 25A.1222 reads: 黃犢牛具.

[81]This was in 113 B.C.

[82]Fen-yin County was located southwest of Wan-jung 萬榮 County in modern Shansi (Wang Li-ch'i, 12.287n.; T'an Ch'i-hsiang, 2:16). The mound was four to five *li* by about two *li,* and ten *chang* high (see "Chi-chieh").

the prostrations at the *Wang* 望 (Sacrifice from Afar),[83] as in the rites for the Supreme Deity. After the rites were concluded the Son of Heaven returned by way of Hsing-yang 滎陽.[84] On the way he passed by Lo-yang 雒陽[85] where he issued a decree stating: "The [line of the] Three Dynasties has long been severed, their remoteness has made its continuation difficult. Let an area of thirty *li* [on a side] be taken to enfief the descendant of Chou as the Lord of the Chou Viscounts and Barons 周子南君,[86] so that he might perform the sacrifices to the former kings [his ancestors] there."[87] In this year, the Son of Heaven for the first time traveled on a tour of inspection through commanderies and counties, proceeding by degrees toward Mount T'ai 泰山.

[462] In this [same] spring, the Marquis of Lo-ch'eng 樂成[88] submitted a memorial to the throne which spoke of Luan Ta 欒大. Luan Ta was a Man of the Palace [in the service of the King] of Chiao-tung 膠東[89] who had formerly had the same teacher as the General of Accomplished Letters. Shortly thereafter, he became Master of Medical Methods[90] to King [K'ang] 康 of Chiao-tung. The older sister of the Marquis of Lo-ch'eng had become King K'ang's queen, but was childless. When King K'ang died, the son of another consort was enthroned as King. But King

---

[83]An ancient sacrifice to important nature spirits, e.g., mountains and watercourses, earliest recorded in the "Shun tien" 舜典 Chapter of *Shang shu*. See *Grand Scribe's Records*, 1:9, n. 103, and *Chung-wen ta tz'u-tien*, 4.14697.

[84]Located northeast of Hsing-yang 滎陽 County in modern Honan (Wang Li-ch'i, 11.287n.; T'an Ch'i-hsiang, 2:16).

[85]Located northeast of modern Loyang 洛陽 City in Honan, at the time this was the capital of Ho-nan Commandery (Wang Li-ch'i, 12.288n.).

[86]Although Yen Shih-ku (*Han shu*, 6.184) argues Tzu-nan was the designation of his fief (and the *Grand Scribe's Records*, 1.84 followed this interpretation), Wang Shu-min (12.439–40) cites various texts to demonstrate that Tzu-nan was a composite of titles: *Tzu* 子 (Viscount) and *Nan* 南 (also written *nan* 男; Baron). *Han shu*, 6.183 refers to him as Chia 嘉, the son of a concubine, and Yen Shih-ku (*Han shu*, 6.184n.) reveals that he had the Chou *cognomen* Chi 姬. His name is confirmed by Ssu-ma Ch'ien's comments on *Shih chi*, 4.171 (*Grand Scribe's Records*, 1:83–4), which also maintain that his position was comparable to a high-ranking lord. Loewe (*Dictionary*, p. 182) notes he died in 107 B.C. and provides other information on his ancestry. See also Dubs, 2:75, who translates his title as "Baronet Baron Descendant of Chou." "Cheng-yi" (on *Shih chi*, 4.171) cites evidence that the fief encompassed three thousand households with an area of thirty *li* on a side.

[87]*Han shu*, 6.183-4 contains a fuller text of this decree.

[88]According to Hsü Kuang (cited in "Chi-chieh"), his *cognomen* was Ting 丁, his *praenomen* Yi 義, and he was later executed at the same time as Luan Ta.

Lo-ch'eng, located several miles south and west of modern Chiao 郊 County in Honan (see T'an Ch'i-hsiang, 2:22), was first enfeoffed at the beginning of the Han, but was terminated as a fief in Ting Yi's tenure as marquis (see *Shih chi*, 18.925–6).

[89]This was Emperor's Ching's son, Liu Chi 劉寄, who was posthumously titled King K'ang 康王 of Chiao-tung (r. 148-120 B.C.; see also Loewe, *Dictionary*, p. 314, and his biography in *Shih chi* Chapter 59).

[90]*Shang-fang* 尚方, an official responsible for preparing medical prescriptions (see Wang Li-ch'i, 12.288n.; Bielenstein, p. 67, renders this title "Master of Techniques").

K'ang's queen had acted licentiously and could not get along with the king, each threatening the other with legal action. King K'ang's queen, on hearing that [the General of] Accomplished Letters [Shao Weng] had already died, and wishing to ingratiate herself with the Sovereign, dispatched Luan Ta through the good offices of the Marquis of Lo-ch'eng [her brother] to seek an audience to expound on his [magical] methods. After having executed [the General of] Accomplished Letters, the Son of Heaven felt remorse over his premature death and regretted that his methods had not been exhaustively tried; when Luan Ta obtained an audience the Emperor was delighted. [Luan] Ta was a man who was tall and handsome, capable of speaking about innumerable [magical] methods and strategems, who ventured to speak expansively, and handled [everything] without hesitation. [Luan] Ta expansively said: "Your servant once ventured into the middle of the sea and saw An-ch'i 安期, Hsien-men [Kao] 羨門 [高] and the other [immortals]. But they considered me a humble commoner and would not take your servant into their confidence. Moreover, because they considered King K'ang to be no more than a feudal lord, he was unworthy to receive their [magical] methods. Your servant spoke of this often to King K'ang, but he still did not make use of me. Your servant's master said: 'Yellow gold can be made; the breaches in the Ho dikes can be plugged; the drug of immortality can be obtained, and immortals may be summoned.' [But] your servant feared he would meet the same fate as Shao Weng, so we practitioners of [magical] methods all kept our peace. How dare I speak of my methods!" The Sovereign replied, "[The General of] Accomplished Letters [Shao Weng] merely died from eating horse's liver.[91] If you are truly able to carry on his [magical] methods, what could I possibly begrudge you?" [Luan] Ta said: "Your servant's masters seek nothing of men, it is men who seek of them. If Your Majesty is determined to invite them here, then ennoble your envoys, make them imperial relatives, treat them with the courtesy due guests, and do not humble them. Let your envoys each hang their seals of office from their girdles, and then you can send them to converse with spirtual beings. Whether the spiritual beings will accede or not is still uncertain, but if you bestow high honors on your envoys, then they may be induced to come." At this the Sovereign first had [Luan Ta] make chess pieces fight to verify his minor [magical] methods; the chess pieces threw themselves against each other of their own accord.

[463] At this time the Sovereign was distressed about the breaches in the Ho dikes and the failure to make yellow gold. So he appointed [Luan] Ta the rank of General of the Five Benefits.[92] In just over one month, Luan Ta acquired four bronze seals: he wore on his girdle those of General of Heavenly Practitioners,[93] General of Earthly Practitioners,[94] General Grand Communicator,[95] and General of the Heavenly Way.[96] The Emperor issued an edict to the [Grand

---

[91] Wang Shu-min (12.441–2) cites several texts which show that horse liver was thought to be poisonous.

[92] *Wu-li Chiang-chün* 五利將軍.

[93] *T'ien-shih Chiang-chün* 天士將軍.

[94] *Ti-shih Chiang-chün* 地士將軍.

[95] *Ta-t'ung Chiang-chün* 大通將軍.

[96] *T'ien-tao Chiang-chün* 天道將軍. Some editions and parallel accounts do not contain this title. Takigawa (12.18) and Wang Shu-min (12.443) believe it an interpolation, a belief strengthened by the title's reintroduction in the text below.

Master of the] Imperial Scribes[97]: "Long ago, Yü 禹 dredged the Nine Chiang 九江[98] and determined the courses of the Four Streams 四瀆.[99] Recently, the Ho has overflowed its banks onto the plain and the corvée laborers at the dikes have not rested. Having ruled the world for twenty-eight years; it seems Heaven has sent Us this practitioner, [Luan] Ta, who is able to comprehend it. Hexagram Ch'ien 乾 "The Creative" speaks of a 'flying dragon' and there is 'the wild goose draws near the slope,'[100] whose import would seem to correspond to this situation. Let the General of Earthly Practitioners, [Luan] Ta, be enfeoffed with two thousand households as Marquis of Lo-t'ung 樂通."[101] The Emperor bestowed on him an official residence of a full marquis[102] and a thousand servant-boys, let him ride in an equipage from among the emperor's unwanted carriages and horses, and [bestowed] hangings, draperies, utensils, and implements with which to fill his household. Moreover, [the Emperor] gave him in marriage [his daughter] the Elder Princess Wey 衛,[103] granted him [a dowry of] ten thousand chin of gold, and changed the name of her manor [so that] she was called Princess of Tang-li 當利公主 (The Princess Who Was Matched to [Five] Benefits)."[104] The Son of Heaven went in person to the General of the Five Benefit's residence, and the envoys sent to present greetings and inquire after his needs formed an unbroken stream on the roads. From the Grand Princess[105] to generals and ministers on down, all feted him [Luan Ta] in their homes and presented him gifts. At this, the Son of Heaven further had a jade seal engraved with the inscription "General of the Heavenly Way" 天道將軍. He sent an envoy wearing feather clothes, who at night stood on white rushes while the General of the Five Benefits, also wearing feather clothes and standing on white rushes, received the seal to show that he [Luan Ta] was not considered a subject [of the Emperor]. [Luan Ta] was to hang [the seal of] the T'ien-tao 天道 (Heavenly Way) on his girdle and moveover provide the way to the heavenly spirits for the Son of Heaven. At this point, [the General of] the Five Benefits regularly sacrificed at his home during the night, intending to cause the spirits to descend. The spirits

[97] Yü-shih [tai-fu] 御史大夫, Bielenstein's "Grandee Secretary," p. 230.

[98] See Grand Scribe's Records, 1:26, n. 65.

[99] See Shih chi, 3.97; Grand Scribe's Records, 1:45.

[100] This second quotation is not from the first hexagram but from hexagram number fifty-three, Chien 漸 "Gradual Progress," line text for six in the second place; see Edward L. Shaughnessy, I Ching: The Classic of Changes (New York: Ballantine Books, 1996), p. 157. Hexagram Chien employs the image of the wild goose at various stages of life and like hexagram Ch'ien evokes gradual progress toward soaring flight.

[101] Lo-t'ung was located southeast of Ssu-hung 泗洪 County in modern Kiangsu (Wang Li-ch'i, 11.289n.).

[102] The rank of Lieh-hou 列侯 (Full Marquis) bestowed on Luan Ta was the highest of the twenty ranks of nobility in Ch'in and Han times (see Wang Li-ch'i, 12.289n.).

[103] The eldest daughter of the Empress Wei 衛 (see "Chi-chieh").

[104] Tang-li was the name of a County whose seat was southwest of Yeh 掖 County in modern Shantung (Wang Li-ch'i, 1.289n; T'an Ch'i-hsiang, 2:20).

[105] T'ai-chu 大主, an abbreviated form of T'ai-ch'ang kung-chu 大長公主 (Grand Elder Princess); see Wang Shu-min, 12.444; not in Bielenstein. Hsü Kuang (cited in "Chi-chieh") says she was Wu-ti's aunt, whom Wei Chao (also cited in "Chi-chieh") argues was the daughter of Empress Dowager Tou 竇.

did not arrive, but hundreds of ghosts gathered; yet [Luan Ta] was quite capable of manipulating them. After this, he packed for a journey, and was said to have put to sea off the eastern coast in search of his master. A few months after his [first] audience with the Emperor, [Luan] Ta had hung **[*464*]** six seals of office from his girdle and his preeminence astounded the world. Along the seacoast between Yen 燕 and Ch'i 齊 there was none who did not seize his wrist in his fist[106] and declare himself in possession of secret [magical] methods capable of attracting spirits and immortals.

In the middle of the sixth month of this summer (113 B.C.),[107] when the shamaness Chin 錦 from Fen-yin was performing a sacrifice to Mother Earth on behalf of the common people at the mound in Wei 魏,[108] she looked and saw [a place where] the earth was shaped like a hook. When she dug and looked, she found a tripod. It was large and quite unlike most others, with inscribed décor, but lacking a dedicatory inscription. Marvelling at it, she told the [local] officials. The officials informed Sheng 勝, the Grand Administrator[109] of Ho-tung 河東,[110] who informed [the court]. The Son of Heaven sent an envoy to verify [the matter] and ask the shamaness Chin about finding the tripod to establish that **[*465*]** there was no trickery or deception involved. Then he sacrificed in accordance with the rites. Going forth to receive the tripod he arrived at Kan-ch'üan, and taking it with him, the Sovereign offered it [to Heaven]. On reaching Chung-shan 中山 (Middle Mountain)[111] the weather cleared, it warmed up, and there was a yellow cloud covering it [the mountain]. There was a deer that passed by and the Sovereign shot it himself, taking advantage of this to use it in the sacrifice. On arriving in Ch'ang-an, the honorable officials, ministers and grandees all deliberated [among themselves] and requested that the precious tripod be treated with utmost respect. The Son of Heaven said: "Recently the Ho has overflowed and several harvests have not measured up; for this reason We traveled on a tour of inspection to sacrifice to Mother Earth to pray for the increase of grain on behalf of the people. This year there has been no response by way of an abundant harvest. Why has this tripod appeared?" The authorities concerned all said: "We have heard that long ago when the Ta-ti 大帝 (The Great Emperor)[112] arose he made one sacred tripod, the number one symbolizing unified rule—Heaven, Earth, and the myriad things being completely brought together. The Huang-ti made three precious tripods to symbolize Heaven, Earth, and Man. Yü collected bronze

---

[106]A gesture of agitation and determination (see Wang Li-ch'i, 12.289n.).

[107]For the date of this entry and further description of the event, see Dubs, 2:71, 75.

[108]This is the same altar to the Hou-t'u mentioned above, here identified by reference to the former state within whose territory it lay.

[109]*T'ai-shou* 太守.

[110]A commandery in the southwest area of Shensi, its seat was northwest of the present day Hsia 夏 County (Wang Li-ch'i, 12.289n.).

[111]A mountain southeast of Ch'un-hua 淳化 County in modern Shensi (Wang Li-ch'i, 12.289n.; T'an Ch'i-hsiang, 2:15).

[112]Probably a reference to the mythical ruler Fu-hsi 伏犧 (see "So-yin").

from the Nine Provinces and cast nine tripods.[113] All of them used the sacred tripods to cook sacrificial offerings to the Supreme Deity, the spirits, and ghosts [of the ancestors]. On encountering a sage ruler the tripods arose; they were removed to Hsia and Shang. When the virtue of Chou declined and the altar to the Earth in Sung was gone, the tripods sank under water, lay hidden, and finally vanished. The Laudes says: 'From the hall they go to the gate-house base, from the sheep they go to the oxen; there are big tripods and small . . . they are not noisy, not clamorous; that secures the tranquillity of those of a great old age.'[114] Now when the tripod reached Kan-ch'üan, it shone profusely, its dragon patterns scintillating; the beneficence received is boundless. In accordance with this [shooting of the deer] on Middle Mountain, when the yellow-white cloud descended to cover Middle Mountain, it served as an auspicious sign, just as the wild animals had. Brought down by your great bow and suite of four arrows, [the deer] was gathered at the foot of the altar mound where the grand reward sacrifice [of thanksgiving to the ancestors] was held. Only one who received the Mandate and ruled as Emperor could know its [Heaven's] intentions and accord his virtue with [Heaven]. It is fitting that the tripod be displayed before the ancestral tablets and preserved in the Emperor's Court,[115] to accord with these bright omens." The imperial decree said: "So be it."

[467] Those who had gone to sea in search of P'eng-lai said that the isles were not distant, and that their inability to reach P'eng-lai was likely due to their not perceiving the emanations from it. Then the Sovereign dispatched a specialist in watching for the emanations to attend to its [P'eng-lai's] emanations.

That autumn (113 B.C.), the Sovereign favored Yung with a visit and was about to perform the *Chiao* Sacrifice. Some said, "The Five Emperors are but the assistants of the Grand Unity. It would be appropriate to establish sacrifices to the Grand Unity and for the Sovereign personally to perform the *Chiao* Sacrifice to it." The Sovereign harbored doubts about the matter and remained undecided. A man of Ch'i 齊, Kung-sun Ch'ing 公孫卿, said, "This year the precious tripod was obtained, and this winter the solstice falls on the *hsin-ssu* 辛巳 day of the new moon at dawn (24 December 113 B.C.), just as in the time of the Huang-ti." Ch'ing possessed a document written on wooden tablets which said, "The Huang-ti obtained a precious tripod at Yüan-ch'ü 宛朐[116] and asked Kuei Yü-ch'ü 鬼臾區[117] about it. [Kuei Yü-]ch'ü replied: 'Your Majesty[118] has obtained the precious tripod and sacred counting sticks; this very year the

---

[113]See *Grand Scribe's Records*, 1:62, n. 81.

[114]This passage has been extracted from the "Ssu yi" 絲衣, Mao #292, in the "Chou Sung" 周頌 section of the *Shih ching* (tr. Bernhard Karlgren, *The Book of Odes* [Stockholm: Museum of Far Eastern Antiquities, 1950], p. 252).

[115]Probably a reference to the temple dedicated to the Supreme Deity at Kan-ch'üan and referred to below as the Shen-t'ing 神庭 (Spirit Court; see Wang Li-ch'i, 12.290n.).

[116]A county whose seat was southwest of Ho-tse 荷澤 County in modern Shantung (Wang Li-ch'i, 12.291n.; T'an Ch'i-hsiang, 2:7).

[117]According to tradition, the name of one of the Yellow Emperor's ministers (see Wang Li-ch'i, 12.291n.).

[118]The Chung-hua editors have deleted the graph *huang* 黃 (the original read Huang-ti 黃帝) here;

winter solstice falls on the *chi-yu* 己酉 day of the new moon at dawn, thus according with the cycles of Heaven which will now end and begin again.' At that, the Huang-ti, by manipulating the counting sticks, made a calendar[119] and generally every twenty years the winter solstice once again coincided with the new moon at dawn. Projecting the calculation ahead twenty times, for a total of three hundred eighty years, was when the Huang-ti will become an immortal and ascend to Heaven." [Kung-sun] Ch'ing wishing to memorialize the Emperor went through So Chung 所 忠;[120] So Chung, seeing the document was heterodox, suspected it to be a fabrication and declined, saying: "The affair of the precious tripod has already been decided. What is the point of pursuing the matter?" [Kung-sun] Ch'ing went through one of the Emperor's favorites to memorialize him. The Sovereign was greatly pleased and summoned [Kung-sun] Ch'ing for questioning. The latter replied, "I received this document from Shen-kung 申功[121] who has since died." The Sovereign asked, "What kind of a man was Shen Kung?" [Kung-sun] Ch'ing answered: "Shen Kung was a man of Ch'i who, to communicate with Master An-ch'i, received the words of the Huang-ti. He left no writings; there is only this document about the tripods. It says, 'The rise of Han ought once again to correspond to the time of the Huang-ti. The sage ruler of the Han is among the grandsons or great-grandsons of Kao-tsu 高祖 (The Exalted Ancestor). The precious tripod will appear and then he will communicate with the spirits and perform the *Feng* and *Shan* sacrifices. Of the seventy-two kings who performed the *Feng* and *Shan* sacrifices, only the Huang-ti was able to climb Mount T'ai 泰山[122]to perform the *Feng* Sacrifice.' Shen Kung said: 'The ruler of Han also ought to go up and offer the *Feng* Sacrifice; if the Sovereign performs the *Feng* Sacrifice, he will be able to ascend into Heaven as an immortal. In the time of the Huang-ti, there were ten thousand feudal lords, and the sacred spirits receiving *Feng* Sacrifices [*468*] amounted to seven thousand. There were eight famous mountains in the world, three among the Man 蠻 and Yi 夷 [tribes] and five in the Central States. In the Central States, Mount Hua 華 山,[123] Mount Shou 首山,[124] [Mount] T'ai-shih 太室 (Great Chamber),[125] Mount T'ai, and Mount

although the text may be easier to read without the *huang*, parallel passages on *Shih chi*, 28.1393, and *Han shu*, 25.1228 both read Huang-ti, suggesting that the deletion may have been ill-advised.

[119]See the parallel passage on *Shih chi* 1.6 (*Grand Scribe's Records*, 1:3).

[120]So Chung was a favorite (or several favorites—see Loewe, *Dictionary*, p. 500) of Emperor Wu. As Remonstrant Grand Master (*Chien Tai-fu* 諫大夫; see "Cheng-yi" on *Shih chi*, 117.3063), he was one of Wu-ti's closest ministers and was known for attempting, rather unsuccessfully, to collect Ssu-ma Hsiang-ju's writings for the throne (see *Shih chi*, 117.3063-72).

[121]In parallel passages (*Shih chi*, 28.1393, and *Han shu*, 25A.1228) he was called Shen Kung 申公 (Master Shen); although "Cheng-yi" believes *kung* 功 is in error, Wang Shu-min (12.448–9) points out that the two graphs were interchangeable. See also Loewe, *Dictionary*, p. 469.

[122]T'ai shan is located about forty miles south-southeast of modern Tsinan in Shantung (T'an Ch'i-hsiang, 2:19).

[123]The Western Sacred Peak, in eastern Shensi a few miles southeast of the confluence of the Yellow and Wei rivers (T'an Ch'i-hsiang, 2:15).

[124]South of Yung-chi 永濟 County in modern Shansi (Wu and Lu, 12.401n.).

[125]I.e., Mount Sung 嵩山, the Central Sacred Peak, southeast of Loyang and north of Teng-feng 登封

Tung-lai 東萊,[126] these five mountains, were regularly visited by the Huang-ti to commune with the spirits. On the one hand, the Huang-ti devoted himself to military campaigns; on the other, [he devoted himself] to studying the immortals. He was worried that the families of the hundred *cognomens* criticized his ways, and so he brought to judgment and beheaded those who denied the ghosts and spirits. After over a hundred years had passed he was able to communicate with the spirits. The Huang-ti performed the *Chiao* Sacrifice to the Supreme Deity at Yung, and lodged there for three months. [Kuei Yü-]ch'ü's designation was Ta-hung 大鴻 (Great Crane), and when he died he was buried at Yung; this is the old Hung-chung 鴻冢 (Crane Tumulus). Afterward, the Huang-ti received ten thousand spirit-beings in the Ming T'ing 明廷 (Court of Light);[127] this Court of Light was [none other than] Kan-ch'uan. The so-called Han-men 寒門 (Cold Gate) is just Ku-k'ou 谷口 (The Mouth of the Valley).[128] The Huang-ti had copper extracted from Mount Shou and had a tripod cast at the foot of Mount Ching 荊山.[129] When the tripod was finished, a dragon with whiskers dangling from its chin came down to meet him. The Huang-ti mounted and rode it; over seventy of his ministers and palace women followed him and mounted the dragon, after which the dragon took off. Those remaining lower-ranking subordinates were not able to get on, but all clung to the dragon's whiskers. The dragon's whiskers pulled out, causing the Huang-ti's bow to fall to the ground. When the people looked up and saw that the Huang-ti had ascended to Heaven, they hugged his bow and the dragon's whiskers and wailed. For these reasons later generations called the place Ting Hu 鼎湖 (Tripod Lake), and his bow Wu Hao 烏號 (Crow Call).'" At this the Son of Heaven said: "Ah! If We could truly be like the Huang-ti, leaving Our wives and children would be like doffing a slipper!" Then he appointed [Kung-sun] Ch'ing Attendant and sent him east to attend to the spirits at [Mount] T'ai-shih 太室 (Great Chamber).

[469] The Sovereign then performed the *Chiao* Sacrifice at Yung; he reached Lung-hsi 隴西,[130] went west to ascend Mount K'ung-t'ung 空桐,[131] and then favored Kan-ch'üan with a visit. He ordered the official in charge of offerings, K'uan-shu, and the others to prepare the altar for sacrifices to the Grand Unity. The altar was modeled after [Miu] Chi of Po's altar to the Grand Unity, with three levels. The altars to the Five Emperors were located below it on all sides, each in its given direction, the Huang-ti's to the southwest, and eight ghost roads were cleared through [to the main altar]. Those [offerings] used for the Grand Unity were like those at each

County in Honan (Wu and Lu, p. 401n.).

[126]There are two mountains by this name, one north of Lai-yang 萊陽 County and one southeast of Huang 黃 County in Shantung (Wang Li-ch'i, 12.291n.).

[127]Wang Li-ch'i (12.291n.) equates the Ming T'ing with the Ming T'ang 明堂 (Hall of Light).

[128]This was a valley at the foot of Mount Chung 中 (see Wu and Lu, 12.401n.).

[129]Located on the border of Ling-pao 靈寶 County in Honan (Wang Li-ch'i, 12.291n.).

[130]A commandery in the southeast part of modern Kansu Province, its seat was at Ti-tao 狄道, modern Lin-t'ao 臨洮 County (Wang Li-ch'i, 12.291n.; T'an Ch'i-hsiang, 2:34).

[131]That is, K'ung-t'ung 崆峒 Mountain, west of P'ing-liang 平涼 County in Kansu Province (Wang Li-ch'i, 12.291n.).

altar at Yung, with the addition of sweet wine, jujubes, dried meat, and the like. A single, long-haired ox was killed to make up the grand set of sacrificial animals, with accompanying sacrificial vessels and stands. For the Five Emperors, only the [sacrificial offerings] in vessels and stands and sweet wine were presented. Below this on the ground in the four directions the hosts of spirit followers together with the Northern Dipper were offered libations and food in succession. After sacrificing, the remaining sacrifical meat was all immolated. The color of this ox was white, the deer was placed inside it, and the hog inside the deer, water being added to stew them. An ox was used to sacrifice to the sun; to the moon a sheep or a hog were sacrificed. The Grand Supplicator and Master of Ceremonies[132] for the Grand Unity wore purple robes decorated with embroidery. Each of the Five Emperors was accorded his color; for the sun it was red, for the moon, white.

[470] On the *hsin-ssu* 辛巳 day of the new moon in the eleventh month (24 December 113 B.C.), at winter solstice, in the dawn light, the Son of Heaven first performed the *Chiao* Sacrifice and a prostration to the Grand Unity. At dawn he performed the *Chao* 朝 (Morning) Sacrifice to the [rising] sun, and in the evening the *Hsi* 夕 (Evening) Sacrifice to the moon, and then bowed. In presenting himself to the Grand Unity he followed the rites of the *Chiao* Sacrifice at Yung.[133] The invocation accompanying the sacrifice said, "Heaven has for the first time bestowed upon the August Emperor the precious tripod and sacred counting stalks, the new moon has once again become the new moon, ending [the cycle] and beginning again.[134] The August Emperor respectfully prostrates himself to [Heaven]." The vestments [used in the rites] exalted yellow, and the fires of the sacrifice filled the altar, alongside which were arrayed the ritual vessels for cooking the sacrifices. The authorities concerned declared, "Above the sacrifice there appeared a light."[135] The honorable officials and ministers said: "When the August Emperor for the first time presented himself to the Grand Unity during the *Chiao* Sacrifice at Yün-yang 雲陽,[136] the authorities concerned held jade discs and excellent sacrificial victims were presented for the sacrifice. That night there was a beautiful gleam of light, and at daylight a yellow emanation rose up to Heaven." The Grand Scribe, the Official in Charge of Offerings, K'uan-shu, and others said: "The sacred spirits in their beneficence bestow auspicious tokens of assistance and prosperity. It is fitting that because of this there be established in this place of brilliant portents an altar platform to the Grand Unity to make manifest the [auspicious] response. Let the Grand Supplicator lead sacrifices from the autumn[137] through the La 臘 Festival.[138] The Son

---

[132]*Tsai* 宰; Bielenstein (p. 224) renders *tsai* as "Butcher."

[133]Cf. Dubs, 2:77.

[134]That is, the cycle begun in the time of the Huang-ti has now come full circle.

[135]For further accounts of the mysterious lights, see Dubs, 2:78.

[136]Where the Kan-ch'üan Palace was located (T'an Ch'i-hsiang, 2:15).

[137]The original Chin-ling edition text read *ssu* 祀 here; the Chung-hua editors, presumably basing themselves on Chang Wen-hu (1.114), changed the text to *ch'iu* 秋 (reading: 令太祝領，秋及臘閒祠。), making it agree with the parallel passages on *Shih chi*, 28.1395, and *Han shu*, 25A.1231. The Palace (12.15a) and the Po-na (12.15b) editions both read *ssu.* An alternate parsing and translation, maintaining the *ssu,* might read: 令太祝領祀，及臘閒祠。; "Let the Grand Supplicator lead sacrifices; when it is the La Festival period, he should offer

of Heaven should appear at the *Chiao* Sacrifice once every three years."

[471] That autumn (112 B.C.), in preparation for a punitive expedition against Nan Yüeh 南越,[139] the attack was announced in prayers to the Grand Unity. A banner decorated with images of the sun, moon, Northern Dipper, and rampant dragons was mounted on a shaft made from the wood of the thorn tree, to symbolize the T'ien-yi 天一 (Heavenly Unity)[140] and its three stars,[141] vanguard of the Grand Unity. [The banner] was called Ling-ch'i 靈旗 (The Efficacious Flag). When one prayed for military success, the Grand Scribe would hold it aloft and point in the direction of the country to be attacked.[142] At the same time, the General of the Five Benefits [Luan Ta], who had been sent as an envoy, did not venture to put to sea, and [instead] went to Mount T'ai to sacrifice. The Sovereign sent men to follow him surreptitiously and verify [any results]; in fact there was nothing for them to see. [The General of] the Five Benefits falsely said he had seen his master [beyond the sea], but his [magical] methods were exhausted, for the most part having elicited no response. The Sovereign then executed [the General of the] Five Benefits.[143]

[472] That winter (111 B.C.),[144] Kung-sun Ch'ing was waiting on the spirits in Ho-nan 河南,[145] when atop the city wall of Kou-shih 緱氏[146] he saw the tracks of an immortal. There was a creature like a pheasant walking back and forth on top of the wall. The Son of Heaven in person favored the Kou-shih city wall with a visit to view the tracks; he asked [Kung-sun]

sacrifices."

[138]Celebrated during the last month of the year. For a detailed study of the La Festival, see Bodde, *Festivals*, pp. 49ff.

[139]At the time Nan Yüeh referred to the area of modern Kwangtung, Kwangsi, and the northern part of Vietnam.

[140]"Chi-chieh" says T'ien-yi is a combination of three stars.

[141]"Heavenly Unity" (7 Dra) is probably used interchangeably with "Grand Unity" (8 Dra) here. The mention of the Dipper has led to confusion among some commentators about exactly which stars are referred to in what follows. The opening section of the "T'ien-kuan shu," *Shih chi*, 27.1289, leaves little room for doubt that the asterism identified with the Supreme Unity is not the Big Dipper itself, but rather is located close to the Pole within the Purple Palace 紫宮 or Purple Tenuity Enclosure 紫微垣. According to Ssu-ma Ch'ien, the brightest star in the array is Grand Unity 太一 (8 Dra) and beside it are three others called the Three Eminences (San kung 三公); see Sun and Kistemaker, *The Chinese Sky During the Han*, pp. 96, 154, 166-7, 173. Cf. also the commentary at *Han shu*, 25A.1232, and *Chung-wen ta tz'u-tien*, 2.1592b. On the Grand Unity's vanguard see Li Ling, "An Archaeological Study of Taiyi (Grand One) Worship," pp. 18ff.

[142]"The Grand Scribe" presumably refers to Ssu-ma Ch'ien's father, Ssu-ma T'an 司馬談 (d. 110 B.C.).

[143]Cf. Dubs, 2:81.

[144]Wang Shu-min (12.454) points out that both *Han shu* and *Han chi* date this event to the winter of 110 B.C.

[145]Here the name of a commandery with its seat at Lo-yang 洛陽 to the northeast of modern Lo-yang in Honan (T'an Ch'i-hsiang, 2:16).

[146]K'ou-shih County was located within the territory of the ancient state of Hua 華 about five miles southeast of modern Yen-shih 偃師 in Honan (T'an Ch'i-hsiang, 2:16). Cf. Dubs, 2:85.

Ch'ing, "You wouldn't be imitating Accomplished Letters [Shao Weng] and Five Benefits [Luan Ta], would you?" [Kung-sun] Ch'ing replied: "The immortals are not those who seek out the ruler of men; it is the ruler of men who seeks them. If his way is not accommodating and patient, the spirits will not come. When I speak of spirit matters they seem unnatural and exaggerated, but if one persists for a number of years the spirits can be induced to come." After this, in anticipation of an imperial visit, each and every commandery and kingdom cleared the roads and refurbished or built palaces and towers, as well as famous mountain shrines dedicated to the spirits.

That year (111 B.C.), after the destruction of Nan Yüeh, the Sovereign had a favorite subject, Li Yen-nien 李延年,[147] who gained audience because of skills in music. The Sovereign considered him excellent and ordered the honorable officials and ministers to deliberate: "In the sacrifices among the common people there is still the music of instruments and dancing. Now when the *Chiao* Sacrifice is performed there is no music. How can this be appropriate?" The honorable officials and ministers replied, "In ancient times, when sacrificing to Heaven and Earth there was always music, and their spirits could be invoked and accorded the proper rites." Someone said, "The T'ai-ti 泰帝 (Great Emperor)[148] had the Su Nü 素女 (White Maiden) play the fifty-string zither, but it was too melancholy. The Emperor could not bear it; for this reason he broke her zither [in half] to make a twenty-five string zither." Therefore, during the thanksgiving offering [for the victory over] Nan Yüeh, when prayers and sacrifices were offered to the Grand Unity and Mother Earth, music and dancing were used for the first time. In addition, choirs of boys were summoned, and from this time on the twenty-five string zither and Hou's harp-zither[149] began to be made.

In the winter of the next year (110 B.C.), the Sovereign deliberated and said, "In ancient times, the weapons were first stored and the soldiers discharged, and thereafter the *Feng* and *Shan* sacrifices were performed." Thereupon he made a tour of inspection to the north to Shuo-fang 朔方[150] and drilled over one hundred thousand soldiers.[151] On returning [*473*] he

---

[147]Li Yen-nien (d. 87 B.C.) from Chung-shan 中山 (Ting 定 County in modern Hopei) was a famous musician. He began his career as a maker of musical instruments and attained the rank of Chief Commandant of Harmony (*Hsieh-lü tu-wei* 協律都尉; see also Wang Li-ch'i, 12.292n.).

[148]According to the "So-yin" and "Cheng-yi," this was Fu-hsi. But Wang Shu-min (12.455) cites a number of sources in support of his argument that the T'ai-ti was the Huang-ti.

[149]According to the "Chi-chieh," this instrument was an invention of a musician named Hou T'iao 侯調. Parallel passages on *Shih chi*, 28.1396, and *Han shu*, 25A.1232 read *k'ung hou* 空侯. Wang Hsien-ch'ien (*Han shu pu-chu*, 25A.34b-35a) observes that several *Han shu* editions, as well as a quotation of *Han shu* in a commentary to Ts'ao Chih's 曹植 (192-232) "K'ung Hou yin" 箜篌引, read *k'an hou* 坎侯; Wang believes that *k'an* was an attempt to represent the sound of the instrument and Hou the *cognomen* of its inventor. The treatise on music in the *Sui shu* (15.378) claims it was imported from the Western Regions. Little else was known about it until the recent discovery of intact examples in excavated Han tombs. See also the illustration (originally T'ang dynasty) in *Han-yü ta tz'u-tien*, 8.1206.

[150]The name of a commandery in the Ho-t'ao 河套 region of modern southwestern Inner Mongolia (Wang Li-ch'i, 12.292n.; T'an Ch'i-hsiang, 2:17).

sacrificed at the tumulus of the Huang-ti at Mount Ch'iao 橋山,[152] and then discharged the soldiers at Hsü-ju 須如.[153] The Sovereign said, "We have heard that the Huang-ti did not die; now there is this tumulus. Why is that?" Someone responded, "After the Huang-ti became an immortal and ascended to Heaven, his ministers buried his clothes and hats [there]." After reaching Kan-ch'üan, as he was about to conduct the affairs [for the *Feng* and *Shan* sacrifices] on Mount T'ai, a *Lei* 類[154] sacrifice was first performed to the Grand Unity.

From the time the precious tripod was obtained, the Sovereign together with the honorable officials, ministers and various scholars deliberated about [instituting] the *Feng* and *Shan* sacrifices. The *Feng* and *Shan* sacrifices had been rarely performed, and had been cut off for a long time; no one knew their ceremonies and rituals. The assembled Confucian scholars culled material selected from the *Shang shu* 尚書 (The Documents of High Antiquity),[155] the *Chou kuan* 周官 (Offices of Chou),[156] and the "Wang Chih" 王制 (Kingly Regulations)[157] pertaining to the *Wang* 望 (From Afar) Sacrifice and the [royal officiant's] shooting of the [sacrificial] ox.[158] A man of Ch'i, Master Ting 丁公, who was over ninety years old, said: "The *Feng* [Sacrifice] is in accord with an immortal name. The [First] Emperor of Ch'in was unable to ascend [the mountain] and perform the *Feng* Sacrifice.[159] If Your Majesty insists on ascending [the mountain], go up a little and if there is no wind or rain, then make the ascent and perform the *Feng* Sacrifice." At this, the Sovereign ordered the assembled Confucian scholars to practice shooting the [sacrificial] oxen and to draft the ceremonies for the *Feng* and *Shan* sacrifices. After several years, the time had come to carry out [these sacrifices]. The Son of Heaven had already paid heed to the words of Kung-sun Ch'ing and the practitioners of [magical] methods about how the Huang-ti and earlier [rulers] had conducted the *Feng* and *Shan* [sacrifices]; they all had been able to summon strange creatures and commune with the spirits. The Emperor desired to imitate

---

[151]*Han shu* (25A.1223) adds the detail that these were "mounted troops" 騎. Chavannes (2:496, n. 2) notes that this was actually an elaborate maneuver staged to impress the Hsiung-nu; cf. also Dubs, 2:84.

[152]Also called Mount Tzu-wu 子午, in Huang-ling 黃陵 County in modern Shensi Province. According to tradition the Yellow Emperor's grave mound is located on the mountain (Wang Li-ch'i, 12.292n.; T'an Ch'i-hsiang, 2:17).

[153]*Han shu* (25A.1233) has *liang* 涼 instead of *hsü*; its location is unknown.

[154]According to *Chou li* 周禮 ("Ch'un-kung, Hsiao-tsung-po" 春宮・小宗伯; *Chou li cheng-yi* 周禮正義, Sun Yi-jang 孫詒讓 (1848-1908), comm. [Peking: Chung-hua, 1987], 36.1428), *Lei* 類 was the name of either a regular seasonal sacrifice to the heavenly spirits, sun, moon, and constellations similar to the *Wang,* or an occasional sacrifice offered in connection with natural disasters, in advance of military campaigns, etc. See *Chung-wen ta tz'u-tien,* 10.44590.

[155]Also known as the *Shu ching* 書經 (Book of Documents).

[156]From the end of the Former Han period it became known as the *Chou-li* 周禮 (Rites of Chou).

[157]The "Kingly Regulations" is a chapter in the *Li chi* 禮記; see also Chavannes, 2:458, n. 4.

[158]According to "So-yin," the Son of Heaven shoots the ox himself to emphasize that it is his personal sacrifice (cf. the passage in *Kuo-yü,* 18.564-5).

[159]In fact, *Shih chi* records that he did; see *Grand Scribe's Records,* 1:138.

the Huang-ti's having been able to contact the spirits, immortals, and gentlemen of P'eng-lai, to transcend the [mundane] world and compare in virtue to the Chiu-huang 九皇 (Nine August Ones).[160] Moreover, he selected from the methods of the Confucians to embellish them [the sacrifices]. The assembled Confucian scholars, having been unable to discuss and clarify the affairs of the *Feng* and *Shan* rites, and furthermore constrained by rigid adherence to ancient documents like the *Shih* 詩 (The Odes) and the *Shu* 書 (The Documents), dared not improvise. The Sovereign had ritual vessels for the *Feng* Sacrifice manufactured and showed them to the assembled Confucian scholars; one of the assembled Confucian scholars said, "These are not the same as in ancient times." Hsü Yen 徐偃 further added, "The performance of the rites by the various scholars under the Grand Master of Ceremonies[161] is not as good as that of [the state of] Lu." Chou Pa 周霸 gathered together [the Confucian scholars] to plan the *Feng* [and *Shan*] affairs. At this, the Sovereign demoted [Hsü] Yen and [Chou] Pa, dismissed the assembled Confucian scholars, and did not employ them.

[474] In the third month (31 March to 28 April 110 B.C.),[162] the Emperor proceeded eastward and favored Kou-shih with a visit, and as prescribed by the rites he ascended the T'ai-shih 太室 (Great Chamber) of the Chung-yüeh 中嶽 (Central Sacred Peak).[163] While at the foot of the mountain[164] the officials in his entourage heard what sounded like the words, "Ten thousand year's longevity!" They asked those [who had been] above on the mountain about it, and they had not spoken the words; they asked those [who had remained] below, and they had not said them. At this, the Emperor founded a shrine to the T'ai-shih supported by three hundred households [from around the foot of the mountain] and named the town Sung-kao 崇高 (Revering the Heights).[165] [The Emperor] went eastward and ascended Mount T'ai. On the mountain the grass and leaves of the trees had not yet sprouted, so he ordered men to carry a stone stele up the mountain and erect it at the summit of Mount T'ai.

Subsequently, the Sovereign went on a tour of inspection to the eastern seaboard and

---

[160]One interpretation argues that the Nine August Ones may refer to the Chiu-chu 九主 (Nine Rulers), nine kings of antiquity (see *Grand Scribe's Records,* 1:43, text and n. 32). Wu and Lu (12.404n.) give alternate lists of these nine rulers.

[161]*T'ai-ch'ang* 太常.

[162]This took place in the first month according to the *Han shu* (6.190) and *Han chi* (14.2b, *SPTK*).

[163]The Central Sacred Peak actually referred to two nearby peaks surmounted by stone chambers, the one on the east was called the Great Chamber and the one on the west the Shao-shih 少室 (Lesser Chamber). Together the whole was called Mount Sung-kao 嵩高 (Wang Li-ch'i, 12.293n.; T'an Ch'i-hsiang, 2:16).

[164]*Han shu,* 25A.1234 places the officials "on the mountain."

[165]On Sung-kao see also n. 162 above.
The expanded *Han shu* (25A.1234) account incorporates significantly more of the text of the imperial edict commemorating the occasion and the founding of the town: "Let the officials in charge of the sacrifices add to the sacrificial offerings at the Great Chamber and let the cutting of plants and trees on the mountain be prohibited. Let three hundred households from around the foot of the mountain be the fief of Sung-kao, their sole occupation being to provide for the sacrifices; they should be exempted from providing anything else"; cf. Dubs, 2:86.

conducted the rites of offering to the Pa-shen 八神 (Eight Spirits).[166] People from Ch'i who submitted memorials to the throne expounding on spirits, strange creatures, curiosities and [magical] methods numbered in the tens of thousands, but nothing could be verified. Then more boats were sent out with orders that the several thousands of individuals who had spoken about the sacred mountains in the middle of the sea should seek out the spirit beings of P'eng-lai. Kung-sun Ch'ing usually went ahead carrying a caduceus to await events on each famous mountain.[167] When he reached [Mount] Tung-lai, he said that during the night he saw a man several *chang* 丈 in height who disappeared at his approach; he saw that his footprints were extremely large, like those of a wild beast. Among the assembled ministers some said they had seen an old man leading a dog; he said, "I wish to see the Chü Kung 巨公 (Colossal Master),"[168] [*475*] whereupon he suddenly disappeared. Having seen the footprints, the Sovereign did not yet believe in it, but when some of his ministers mentioned the old man, he became utterly convinced it was an immortal. He lingered awhile on the seacoast, placing post carriages at the disposal of the practitioners of [magical] methods, and secretly sent men in the thousands to search for immortals.

In the fourth month (30 April-29 May 110 B.C.) the Sovereign reached Feng-kao 奉高 on his return journey.[169] He reflected on [the fact that] the words of the assembled Confucian scholars and practitioners of [magical] methods in discussing the *Feng* and the *Shan* [sacrifices] differed from one man to the other, were inconsistent, and difficult to put into effect. The Son of Heaven arrived in Liang-fu 梁父[170] where in accordance with the rites he sacrificed to the Ti Chu 地主 (Lord of the Earth). On the *yi-mao* 乙卯 day (17 May 110 B.C.), he ordered those Confucians among the Palace Attendants[171] to don their leather caps and padded sashes, shoot the sacrificial ox, and perform the sacrifice. The *Feng* Sacrifice was conducted at the foot of Mount T'ai to the east, the ritual being like that for the *Chiao* Sacrifice to the Grand Unity. The sacrificial mound was one *chang* and two *ch'ih* 尺 on a side and nine *ch'ih* high. Below it there were documents written on jade tablets whose contents were kept secret. After the ceremony was completed, the

---

[166]The identity of the Eight Spirits is somewhat obscure. "So-yin" quotes Wei Chao's gloss that the eight refer to Heaven, Earth, Yin, Yang, Sun, Moon, the Lords of the Constellations (*Hsing-ch'en Chu* 星辰主), and the Lords of the Seasons (*Ssu-shih Chu* 四時主). In support, Ssu-ma Chen cites a passage from *Han shu* (25A.1202), which on the whole agrees with Wei Chao, with the exception of "Lords of the Constellations," for which that text substitutes the "Lords of the Military" (*Ping Chu* 兵主)."

[167]He is carrying a caduceus to symbolize that his authority comes directly from the emperor. This would also have allowed him privileges and benefits befitting an imperial envoy.

[168]The "So-yin" quotes the *Han shu yin-yi* 漢書音義 to the effect that the "Colossal Master" indicated Emperor Wu himself.

[169]Feng-kao was located a little over five miles northeast of the present T'ai-an 泰安 County in Shantung (Wang Li-ch'i, 12.294n.; T'an Ch'i-hsiang, 2:19).

[170]The name given to the foothills of Mount T'ai in the southeastern part of T'ai-an County in modern Shantung (Wang Li-ch'i, 12.294n.; T'an Ch'i-hsiang, 2:19).

[171]*Shih chung* 侍中.

Son of Heaven, accompanied solely by the Palace Attendant and [Chief Commandant] of Imperial Equipages,[172] [Huo] Tzu-hou [霍]子侯,[173] ascended Mount T'ai where the *Feng* Sacrifice was performed anew, this time in strictest secrecy. The next day, the Emperor descended via the path on the north slope. On the *ping-ch'en* 丙辰 day (18 May 110 B.C.), he performed the *Shan* Sacrifice on Mount Su-jan 肅然 (Solemn Appearing)[174] below Mount T'ai on the northeast, the ritual used resembling the sacrifice to the Mother Earth. For each [ceremony] the Son of Heaven dressed in vestments that exalted yellow and in all he prostrated himself, and music was exhaustively employed. Rushes with three-lobed stalks[175] from between the Chiang and Huai [rivers] were used to make the sacred mats, and more earth in each of the five colors was matched and added to the altar mound. Rare animals, flying birds, and white pheasants and various other animals from distant quarters of the world were all released and used to augment the sacrificial offerings. Animals like rhinoceroses and elephants were not offered up. They arrived at Mount T'ai and afterward they left. During the *Feng* and *Shan* sacrifices the night seemed to be lit up by a gleam of light, and during daylight white clouds rose from the middle of the altar mound.

[476] On returning from the *Feng* and *Shan* sacrifices, the Son of Heaven seated himself in the Ming T'ang,[176] and the assembled ministers in turn offered their salutations. At this, the Emperor issued an edict to the [Grand Master of the] Imperial Scribes: "With an insignificant body, We have inherited the most exalted status; [We] tremble with fear at it lest [We] not be up to the task. For [Our] virtue is scant and meager, and [We] have no understanding of the rites and music. When [We] performed the sacrifice to the Grand Unity, it seemed there was a phenomenon of an auspicious gleam of light, which suddenly could be seen.[177] [We] were deeply shaken by these unnatural happenings and wished to stop, but [We] dared not, finally ascending Mount T'ai and offering the *Feng* Sacrifice; then [We] went to Liang-fu, and afterward performed the *Shan* Sacrifice at Mount Su-jan. Having renewed [ourself] thereby, [We] felicitate all officers and grandees by granting them a new beginning. To every one hundred households among the people let there be given one ox and ten *shih* of wine; to the elderly eighty years and over,[178]

---

[172]*Feng-chü* [*tu-wei*] 奉車[都尉].

[173]This was the *agnomen* of Huo Shan 霍嬗 (d. 110 B.C.), son of the famous general Huo Ch'ü-ping 霍去病 (Wang Li-ch'i, 12.294n.). As Loewe (*Dictionary,* p. 175) points out, he was the only person who accompanied Wu-ti in his ascent of Mount T'ai and then died very suddenly on the mountain (see *Shih chi,* 20.1038 and the text below, 12.476). "So-yin" (*Shih chi,* 28.1399) records two explanations of his death: he was either killed by Wu-ti or attained immortal status through transformation on the mountain. Both explanations share the view that this sudden illness was a euphemism.

[174]Located in the northwest of Yeh-wu 葉蕪 County in modern Shantung (Wang Li-ch'i, 12.294n.).

[175]See Chavannes, 2:426, n. 4.

[176]Or more precisely, in the location where the Ming T'ang 明堂 was thought to have once stood and where it would soon be rebuilt (see "Chi-chieh" and Dubs, 2:87, n. 25.2).

[177]The *Han shu* (6.191) version of this edict reads: 屑然如有聞, "faint sounds were heard."

[178]*Han shu,* 6.191 reads "over seventy."

orphans, and widows, add two bolts of hemp and silk cloth. Po 博,[179] Feng-kao 奉高, Yi-ch'iu 蛇丘,[180] and Li-ch'eng 歷城,[181] shall be exempted from this year's land tax and [capitation] taxes. Let there be a general amnesty throughout the world, like the amnesty order in the year *yi-mao* 乙卯 (120 B.C.). Where this tour [of inspection] has passed, none shall be sentenced to light penal servitude[182] and those crimes that occurred prior to two years ago shall be exempted from prosecution." The Emperor further issued an edict that said: "In ancient times, when the Son of Heaven conducted a tour of inspection every five years and held [sacrificial] events on Mount T'ai, the feudal lords all had a place to lodge when they came to pay him homage. Let the feudal lords be ordered each to construct lodgings at the foot of Mount T'ai!"

After having completed the *Feng* and *Shan* sacrifices on Mount T'ai without a calamity involving wind or rain,[183] the practitioners of [magical] methods one after another spoke about P'eng-lai and the sacred mountains, as if they were now nearly within reach. At this, the Sovereign was pleased at the prospect of encountering them and again went east to the seacoast to gaze into the distance, in hopes of encountering P'eng-lai there. His [Chief Commandant] of Imperial Equipages, [Huo] Tzu-hou, became violently ill and died within a day.[184] The Emperor then departed, heading northward along the coast until he reached [Mount] Chieh-shih 碣石,[185] where he made an inspection tour starting at Liao-hsi 遼西 Commandery that traversed the northern borderlands and reached Chiu-yüan 九原.[186] In the fifth month, the Emperor reached Kan-ch'üan

[179]Po was the name of a county which had its seat in the northeast part of T'ai-an County in modern Shantung, (Wang Li-ch'i, 12.294n.; T'an Ch'i-hsiang, 2:19).

[180]Yi-ch'iu was the name of a county which had its seat in the southwest part of T'ai-an County in modern Shantung (Wang Li-ch'i, 12.294n.; T'an Ch'i-hsiang, 2:19).

[181]Li-ch'eng was the name of a county which had its seat in modern Tsinan City in modern Shantung, (Wang Li-ch'i, 12.294n.; T'an Ch'i-hsiang, 2:19).

[182]*Fu-tso* 復作: A form of lighter punishment under Han penal law in which the convicted were obliged to perform labor service in lieu of wearing fetters or criminal dress. According to one opinion, this punishment was reserved for women, the term of service ranging from three months to one year (Wang Li-ch'i, 12.294n. and 296n.). Hulsewé, *Han law,* pp. 240ff. argues that *fu tso* meant "still had to work" and was applied to criminals sentenced to hard labor who even after an amnesty were required to "fulfill the years, months and days of their original punishment" (p. 240). Following Hulsewé, this sentence would read: "Where this tour [of inspection] has passed, there shall be no [sentence of] continuing to work [after an amnesty]." See also the commentary to the term on *Han shu,* 8.236.

[183]Here recalling Master Ting's admonition cited above in the text (*Shih chi,* 12.473): "If Your Majesty insists on ascending [the mountain], go up a little and if there is no wind or rain, then make the ascent and perform the Feng Sacrifice."

[184]Chavannes notes (2:504, n. 1) that as the sole witness to the secret rites atop Mount T'ai, Huo Tzu-hou was probably poisoned (see also n. 173 above).

[185]Located northwest of modern Ch'ang-li 昌黎 County in Hopei (Wu and Lu, 12.406n.).

[186]Liao-shi Commandery was located in the central and western part of modern Liaoning Province and the Ch'eng-te 承德 region of Hopei. Its seat was at Ch'ieh-lü 且慮, which lay east of Lu-lung 盧龍 County in

on the return journey. The authorities concerned proposed that, since the appearance of the precious tripod was commemorated by inaugurating the Yüan-ting 元鼎 (Tripod Origination) reign period, the present year should be the inaugural year of the Yüan-feng 元封 (*Feng* Sacrifice Origination) reign period.

[477] That autumn (110 B.C.), there was a *pei* 茀[187] star in [the constellation] Tung ching 東井 (Eastern Well).[188] Just over ten days later, there was a *pei* star in [the constellation] San T'ai 三能.[189] The Observer of Emanations,[190] Wang Shuo 王朔, said: "While I was watching, only I saw the star appear like a gourd,[191] and in the time it takes to eat a meal it was gone again."[192] The authorities concerned said: "Your Majesty inaugurated the *Feng* and *Shan* sacrifices for the House of Han; Heaven is no doubt responding with a *Te hsing* 德星 (Star of Virtue)!"[193]

In the winter of the next year [109 B.C.], the Emperor conducted the *Chiao* Sacrifice to the Five Emperors at Yung. On his return, he performed prostrations, prayers, and sacrifices to the Grand Unity. The liturgy of praise accompanying the sacrifice said: "The Star of Virtue, expansive in its brilliance, is auspicious. The Shou hsing 壽星 (Star of Longevity)[194] appeared

modern Hopei (Wang Li-ch'i, 12.295n.; T'an Ch'i-hsiang, 2:27-28).

Chiu-yüan was the name of a county which had its seat west of modern Pao-t'ou City in Inner Mongolia (T'an Ch'i-hsiang, 2:17). According to the "Chi-chieh," the round-trip journey covered some eighteen thousand *li*, or about six thousand miles.

[187]The term *pei* or *fu* 茀 is more commonly written *po* 孛 when referring to a kind of comet: "When a comet comes into line with the earth and the sun, its tail is no longer visible and its light may appear nebulous. The Chinese had a special term for a comet in opposition, *po hsing* 孛星, clearly distinguishing it, at least theoretically, from a nova" (see Joseph Needham *et al., Science and Civilisation in China,* Vol. 3, *Mathematics and the Sciences of the Heavens and the Earth* [Cambridge: Cambridge University Press, 1959], p. 431; see also Loewe, "The Han View of Comets," p. 71).

[188]Lunar Mansion #22, corresponding to Gemini and the astrological space associated with the state of Ch'in.

[189]Otherwise known as San-t'ai 三台, an asterism created by linking three close pairs of stars in Ursa Major, just south of the bowl of the Big Dipper and some forty degrees east of Gemini. See Sun and Kistemaker, *The Chinese Sky During the Han,* p. 153.

[190]*Wang ch'i* 望氣.

[191]*Shih chi,* 28.1399, and *Han shu,* 25A.1236 both read *T'ien hsing* 填星 for *ch'i hsing* 其星 here. Wu and Lu (12.1245n.) equate *T'ien hsing* with a comet and say the passage is intended to indicate Heaven's critical reaction to Wu-ti's dependence on *fang shih* 方士 practitioners. See also the following note.

[192]Judging from Wang Shuo's testimony about the brevity of the apparition, the "star" may have been a bolide, or exceptionally bright meteor.

[193]The context suggests that "Star of Virtue" here refers to the comet. However, the term also commonly inidicated the planet Jupiter, which would have been visible in Gemini throughout most of the night in mid-January, 109 B.C.

[194]Canopus, or Alpha Carinae, otherwise known as the "Old Man of the Southern Pole," Nan-chi lao-jen 南極老人, was just visible low on the southern horizon late at night in mid-January, 109 B.C.; see Sun and

with it, its gleam shining far and wide. The Hsin hsing 信星 (Saturn)[195] appeared brightly, and the August Emperor respectfully prostrated himself in response to the Grand Supplicator's sacrifices."

That spring, Kung-sun Ch'ing 公孫卿 said he had seen a spirit man on Mount Tung-lai who is supposed to have said, "[I want to] see the Son of Heaven."[196] At this the Son of Heaven favored Kou-shih City with a visit and appointed [Kung-sun] Ch'ing as Regular Grand Master.[197] He then went to [Mount] Tung-lai and, having sojourned for several days,[198] did not see anything except the footprints of a great man. The Emperor again dispatched practitioners of [magical] methods in the thousands to seek out spirits and anomalies and collect medicinal fungi.[199] There was a drought this year. Therefore, there being no formal reason stated for his having gone out, the Son of Heaven prayed [for rain] at Wan-li-sha 萬里沙[200] and, on passing Mount T'ai, offered sacrifices there. On his return he reached Hu-tzu 瓠子,[201] where he personally oversaw the blocking of the breaches in the Ho dikes.[202] He stayed for two days, sank offerings[203] [in the Ho] [*478*], and left. He dispatched two excellencies[204] to command the troops blocking breaches

Kistemaker, *The Chinese Sky During the Han*, p. 156.

[195]Late in the evening in mid-January, 109 B.C., Saturn would have been observable in Virgo at the same time Jupiter and Canopus were visible.

[196]Both *Shih chi*, 28.1399, and *Han shu*, 25A.1236 read *yü chien* 欲見, "desired to see," for the *chien* 見, "see," here.

[197]*Chung Tai-fu* 中大夫.

[198]The Chung-hua editors punctuate after "for several days": 遂至東萊，宿留之數日，毋所見，見大人跡. Wu and Lu (12.406) and Wang Li-ch'i (12.295) also follow this reading. But Ku and Hsü (12.14 [232]) end the sentence after Tung-lai 東萊. Watson (2:45) follows this parsing. Chavannes (3:506) believes the break should come after *su liu chih* 宿留之, beginning the next sentence with *Shu jih* 數日.

[199]This is no doubt Spirit Fungus, *Ling-chih* 靈芝, which, in addition to being a symbol of longevity, has medicinal applications.

[200]Ten-thousand-*li* Sands, a waste some one hundred miles across located between Chao-yüan 招遠 and Yeh 掖 counties in modern Shantung, where a shrine was located (Wang Li-ch'i, 12.295n.; T'an Ch'i-hsiang, 2:20).

[201]Southwest of P'u-yang 濮陽 County in modern Honan Province (Wang Li-ch'i, 12.195n.; T'an Ch'i-hsiang, 2:19).

[202]The break at Hu-tzu-k'ou 瓠子口, where the Yellow River dike failed in 132 B.C., caused disastrous flooding for the next twenty-three years, in part due to an earlier failed repair effort and subsequent reluctance to contravene the will of Heaven in causing the flood. Finally, in 109 B.C., Emperor Wu sent tens of thousands of troops to repair the breaks in the dikes, and on his return from Wan-li-sha, personally oversaw the work. At this time, everyone in the Emperor's entourage from the rank of general on down was ordered to carry brush for the repairs, and Emperor Wu himself composed a "Song of Hu-tzu" ("Hu-tzu ko" 瓠子歌) commemorating the effort; see "Ho-chü shu" 河渠書, *Shih chi*, 29.1409-13.

[203]The offerings to the Lord of the River consisted of a white horse and jade *pi* discs.

[204]The two were Chi Jen 汲仁 and Kuo Ch'ang 郭昌 (see Loewe, *Dictionary*, pp. 142 and 138, respectively).

in the Ho dikes and lead the flood waters off into two channels, so as to restore the Ho at that place to its former course from the time of Yü.

At this time, after having annihilated Nan Yüeh, a man of Yüeh, Yung Chih 勇之, said: "It is customary among the people of Yüeh to believe in ghosts and at their sacrifices they always saw ghosts; of this there are numerous proofs. Formerly, the King of Tung-ou 東甌[205] was reverential toward the ghosts, and lived to be 160 years old. But subsequent generations became negligent and indifferent, and so they declined and died." Thus the Emperor ordered a shamaness from Yüeh to establish prayers and sacrifices in the Yüeh [style], installing a platform without altar; she also sacrificed to the Spirit of Heaven, the Supreme Deity, and the hundred ghosts, divining by means of chickens. Because the Sovereign placed his faith in these [methods of divination], the Yüeh sacrifices and chicken divination thenceforth began to be employed.[206]

Kung-sun Ch'ing said, "The immortals can be seen; Your Majesty always goes forth in such haste, and for this reason doesn't see them. Now, if Your Majesty can build a tower like that of Kou-shih City wall, and there set out dried meat and jujubes, immortals could probably be induced to come. Moreover, the immortals are fond of dwelling in towers." At this, the Sovereign ordered the Fei Lien 蜚廉[207] and the Kuei Kuan 桂觀 (The Cassia Towers) to be built at Ch'ang-an, and the Yi and Yen-shou Kuan 益延壽觀 (Towers of Increase and the Prolonged Longevity)[208] to be built at Kan-ch'üan, and dispatched [Kung-sun] Ch'ing [*479*] with an [imperial] caduceus to install the [sacrificial] parephenalia and to watch for spiritual beings. Then [the Emperor] built the T'ung-t'ien T'ai 通天台 (Terrace for Comunicating with Heaven),[209] and installed the sacrificial implements at its base, in anticipation of summoning the spirits, immortals and their like. At this, the palace at Kan-ch'üan was expanded by adding a Front Hall, and all the palace rooms were enlarged for the first time.

In the summer, a [Spirit] Fungus grew inside a room of the Hall. The Son of Heaven having blocked the Ho [dikes] and raised the Terrace for Communicating with Heaven,[210] a brilliant light was said to have appeared, and the Emperor issued an edict saying, "As a nine-

---

Chi Jen's elder brother, Chi An 汲黯, was sent on a similar mission in 132 B.C.

[205]I.e., Tsou Yao 騶搖, the King of Tung-hai (became king in 192 B.C. because of his service to Kao-tsu under Wu Jui). He was designated 'King of Tung-ou' because his capital was located there. See *Shih chi,* 114.2979, and Loewe, *Dictionary,* p. 753 (under the entry for Tsou Wu-chu 騶無諸).

[206]According to the "Cheng-yi," divination with chickens involved first obtaining a chicken and a dog and presenting an invocatory prayer; then the animals were killed and boiled together; finally the chicken's eyes were removed and the cracks in the eyesockets were 'read.' If they appeared in the form of a human, this was a good omen; otherwise the omen was inauspicious.

[207]"Chi-chieh" says this was a supernatural bird that could cause winds to blow; on *Shih chi,* 117.3034, "Chi-chieh" notes that the Fei Lien was the god of wind.

[208]Wang Shu-min (12.464) notes that there are two theories about this name; the first (which we follow) argues that the Yi Kuan and the Yen-shou Kuan are separate buildings; the second, that *yi* 益 is an interpolation.

[209]*Han shu,* 6.192 says it was part of the Kan-ch'üan Palace.

[210]Built in the interior of the Palace, the Terrace was thirty *chang* high and from it the city of Ch'ang-an was visible, some sixty miles distant ("So-yin").

stemmed [Spirit] Fungus has grown in a room in Kan-ch'üan Palace, let there be a general amnesty and no light penal servitude."[211]

The following year [108 B.C.], there was a punitive attack on Ch'ao-hsien 朝鮮 (Korea);[212] in summer, there was a drought. Kung-sun Ch'ing said: "In the Huang-ti's time, when the *Feng* Sacrifice was performed there was a drought that dried the earthen altar mound [*feng*] for three years." The Sovereign then issued an edict saying: "Does Heaven intend with this drought to dry the earthen altar mound? Let all the world be ordered reverently to sacrifice to the Ling-hsing 靈星 (Efficacious Star)"[213]

[480] The following year [107 B.C.], the Sovereign performed the *Chiao* Sacrifice at Yung, opened the Hui-chung 回中 Road,[214] and made a tour of inspection on it. In the spring, he reached Ming-tse 鳴澤[215] then returned via Hsi-ho 西河 [Commandery].[216]

In the winter of the next year [106 B.C.], the Sovereign conducted a tour of inspection of Nan 南 Commandery; reaching Chiang-ling 江陵,[217] he turned eastward. He ascended Mount T'ien-chu 天柱 (Heaven's Pillar)[218] in Ch'ien 潛 [County] and performed rites there, designating it Nan Yüeh 南嶽 (Southern Sacred Peak). He embarked at Hsün-yang 尋陽[219] and boated down

---

[211]On *fu tso* see also n. 182 above.

Another version of this edict is recorded on *Han shu,* 6.193.

[212]At the time, Ch'ao-hsien referred to portions of modern Liaoning and Chilin provinces and the northern part of the Korean peninsula. The Han 漢 dynasty exercised sovereignty over this area together with the three Han 韓 kingdoms in the southern part of the peninsula (Wang Li-ch'i, 12.296n.).

[213]"Cheng-yi" identifies Ling-hsing here as Lung-hsing 龍星 (Dragon Star); i.e., the vast Cerulean Dragon constellation in the Eastern Palace of the heavens which extended from Virgo to Scorpio (see also n. 248 below).

During Kao-tsu's time (*Shih chi,* 28.1380), there was an edict that ordered each commandery and state to establish annual sacrifices to the Lung-hsing; the Lung-hsing was thought to govern agricultural matters and is associated with rain making, thus Wu-ti is probably sacrificing to it because of the drought.

[214]Hui-chung was located northwest of Lung 隴 County in modern Shensi (Wang Li-ch'i, 12.296n.; T'an Ch'i-hsiang, 2:15). Yen Shih-ku (*Han shu,* 6.195) argues that Wu-ti built this road to connect to the Hsiao 蕭 Pass.

[215]Ming-tse was the name of a marsh northwest of Chuo-chou 涿州 City in modern Hopei; one commentator identifies the Ming-tse with the Ming-tse 鳴澤 at Mount Tu-lu 獨鹿 (都盧), now called T'an-cheng hsia 彈箏峽, located west of P'ing-liang 平涼 County in modern Kansu (Wang Li-ch'i, 12.296n.).

[216]Hsi-ho Commandery was established by Wu-ti in 125 B.C. It incorporated portions of Inner Mongolia, Shansi, and Shensi. The commandery seat was at P'ing-ting 平定, within the boundaries of Sheng 勝 County in the modern Inner Mongolia Autonomous Region (Wang Li-ch'i, 12.296n.; T'an Ch'i-hsiang, 2:18).

[217]Nan Commandery, with its seat at Chiang-ling (modern Chiang-ling County), incorporated the southwestern part of modern Hupei (Wang Li-ch'i, 12.296n.; T'an Ch'i-hsiang, 2:22).

[218]Mount T'ien-chu, also known as Mount Wan 皖 and Mount Ch'ien 潛, in Ch'ien County, is located in the southwestern part of Huo-shan 霍山 County in modern Anhwei (Wang Li-ch'i, 12.296n,; T'an Ch'i-hsiang, 2:24).

[219]Hsün-yang County was located southwest of Huang-mei 黃梅 County in modern Hupei (Wang Li-ch'i,

the Chiang 江 [Yangtse River] as far as Tsung-yang 樅陽,[220] [along the way] passing by P'eng-li 彭蠡[221] where he sacrificed to the famous streams and mountains of the region. Turning north he reached Lang-ya 琅邪,[222] then travelled via the seacoast. In the middle of the fourth month, he reached Feng-kao where he performed the *Feng* Sacrifice.

Earlier, the Son of Heaven performed the *Feng* Sacrifice at Mount T'ai; at the foot of Mount T'ai on the northeast was the location of the Ming T'ang in ancient times, a location confined and almost inaccessible. The Sovereign wished to build a Ming T'ang next to Feng-kao, but did not know its standard [dimensions]. A man from Chi-nan 濟南,[223] Kung-su Tai 公玉帶,[224] submitted a sketch of the Ming T'ang from the time of the Huang-ti. The sketch had a hall in the center that lacked walls on all four sides. Its roof was thatched with rushes, and water flowed through it. The ramparts surrounding the palace had been made into a covered walkway, atop which were multistoried towers. That which entered from the southwest was named the K'un-lun 昆侖 [Path],[225] where the Son of Heaven entered to perform prostrations and sacrifices dedicated to the Supreme Deity. At this, the Sovereign ordered a Ming T'ang like that in [Kung-su] Tai's plan to be constructed on the banks of the Wen 汶 River[226] at Feng-kao. When the *Feng* Sacrifice was performed in the fifth year [of the Chien-yüan era [106 B.C.], he sacrificed to the Grand Unity and the Five Emperors, [placing them] in the highest positions in the Ming T'ang, and ordered the sacrificial seat of Kao Huang-ti 高皇帝 (August Emperor Kao) to be placed opposite them. He sacrificed to Mother Earth in the Lower Chamber, using twenty *T'ai-lao*

12.296n.; T'an Ch'i-hsiang, 2:24).

[220]Tsung-yang County was located near modern Tsung-yang County in Anhwei Province (Wang Li-ch'i, 12.296n.; T'an Ch'i-hsiang, 2:24), so that Emperor Wu traveled roughly ninety miles down the Yangtse River.

[221]P'eng-li was the name of a marsh located between Hsün-yang and Tsung-yang, later it turned into the lake now known as P'o-yang 鄱陽 Lake (Wang Li-ch'i, 12.296n; T'an Ch'i-hsiang, 2:24).

[222]Lang-ya was a seaside town on the southeast coast of Shantung in the commandery by the same name. The commandery seat was at Tung-wu 東武, modern Chu-ch'eng 諸城 County (Wang Li-ch'i, 12.296n.; T'an Ch'i-hsiang, 2:20).

[223]Chi-nan Commandery incorporated the counties of Li-ch'eng, Chi-nan, and Chang-ch'iu 章丘, in modern Shantung Province (Wang Li-ch'i, 12.296n.; T'an Ch'i-hsiang, 2:20).

[224]The Chung-hua edition (1982 reprint) which has served as the base text for this translation reads Kung-wang 公王 for Kung-su 公玉. But the earliest printing (1959 hardcover) of the Chung-hua text reads Kung-su. The original Chin-ling edition (12.18b) also has Kung-su. Wu and Lu (12.408) follow this reading. The *Shih chi jen-ming so-yin* 史記人名索引 (Peking: Chung-hua, 1982, p. 244), edited by the *Shih chi* specialist Wu Shu-p'ing 吳樹平, reads this name as Kung-yü Tai 公玉帶, presumably following *Han shu* accounts (25B.1401 and 1403; see also Yen Shih-ku's comments on a pre-Ch'in usage of Kung-yü as a *cognomen*, 25B.1401).

[225]K'un-lun is the mythical axis mundi and abode of immortals located in the far northwest which was supposed to be encircled by five ramparts with a dozen multistoried towers. This path is called K'un-lun because of the associations the name has with immortality.

[226]The River Wen flowed by Mount T'ai on the northeast, passing by Feng-kao County on the southwest and emptying into the Ch'ü-yeh 巨野 Marsh (Wang Li-ch'i, 12.296n.; T'an Ch'i-hsiang, 2:19-20).

complete sets of animals. The Son of Heaven entered through the K'un-lun Path, first performing prostrations to the Ming T'ang as in rites for the *Chiao* Sacrifice. When the rites were finished, the offerings were immolated at the base of the Hall, whereupon the Sovereign ascended [*481*] Mount T'ai on whose summit secret rites were conducted. At the base of Mount T'ai sacrifices were performed to the Five Emperors, each in his proper quarter, the Huang-ti being worshipped together with the Ch'ih-ti 赤帝 (Red Emperor);[227] the authorities concerned waited upon the sacrificial ceremonies there. On the summit of Mount T'ai, a bonfire was lit, and below all responded [with bonfires].

Two years later (105 B.C.), at dawn on the *chia-tzu* 甲子 day [25 December] in the eleventh month, new moon and winter solstice coincided. Those responsible for computing the calendar took this day as the point of origin [for the new calendar]. The Son of Heaven in person reached Mount T'ai and at dawn on the day *chia-tzu* in the eleventh month, the day of the new moon and winter solstice, he sacrificed to the Supreme Deity, but did not[228] perform the *Feng* and *Shan* sacrifices. The sacrificial liturgy said: "Heaven has once again bestowed on the August Emperor the sacred counting sticks of the Supreme Origin; the cycles have come round and begin again. The August Emperor reverently prostrates himself before the Grand Unity." The Emperor went east, reached the seacoast, and examined the practitioners of [magical] methods and those who had put to sea in search of spirit beings, but none had achieved any results; nevertheless, he dispatched more and more of them and hoped to encounter them [spirit beings].

In the eleventh month, on the *yi-yu* 乙酉 day [15 January 104 B.C.], there was a conflagration in the Po-liang [Terrace]. In the twelfth month, on the new moon *chia-wu* 甲午 day [24 January], the Sovereign personally performed the *Shan* Sacrifice on Mount Kao-li 高里[229] and sacrificed to Mother Earth. He went to the Po-hai 渤海[230] and was about to sacrifice to P'eng-lai and the like using the *Wang* Sacrifice, hoping thus to reach those otherworldly courts.

[482] The Sovereign returned [to the capital] and, because the Po-liang Palace had burned down, held audience and received the annual accounting at Kan-ch'üan. Kung-sun Ch'ing said, "Twelve days after the Huang-ti completed the Ch'ing-ling T'ai 青靈臺 (Black Efficacious Tower) it burned down, so the Huang-ti built the Ming-t'ing 明庭 (Court of Light). This Court of Light was Kan-ch'üan." Many of the practitioners of magical arts said that ancient rulers had made Kan-ch'üan their capital. After that, the Son of Heaven held audience with the feudal lords at Kan-ch'üan, who then built residences there. Yung Chih [of Yüeh] then said, "The custom in Yüeh is that whenever there is a fire and the house is rebuilt, it must be made larger, in this way subduing [the evil] and causing it to submit." At this, the Emperor built the Chien-chang [Kung] 建章[宮] (Established Emblems [Palace]),[231] with dimensions on such a scale that it had

---

[227]There being five emperors and only four cardinal directions (the Huang-ti ruling over the Center) honoring two emperors in the southern quarter was a necessary expedient.

[228]*Shih chi*, 28.1401, and *Han shu*, 25A.1244, both have *wu* 毋 for *mei* 每 which is certainly correct.

[229]Kao-li was the name of the southern foothills of Mount T'ai southwest of modern T'ai-an City in Shantung (Wang Li-ch'i, 12.297n.).

[230]The modern Gulf of Po-hai enclosed by the Shantung and Liaotung peninsulas (T'an Ch'i-hsiang, 2:4).

[231]Located to the west of the Wei-yang Palace (see following note); see also Wu and Lu, 12.409n. and

a thousand gates and ten thousand inner doorways and with a Front Hall taller than the Wei-yang 未央[宮] (Eternal) [Palace].[232] On the east the Feng-ch'üeh 鳳闕 (Phoenix Gate-tower) was over twenty *chang* high. On the west, was T'ang-chung 唐中 [Pond][233] along with Hu-chüan 虎圈 (Tiger Enclosure) measuring several tens of *li* [in circumference]. On the north was built a great pond called the T'ai-yeh Ch'ih 泰液池 (Ultimate Liquid Pond) with its Chien T'ai 漸臺 (Water-immersed Terrace)[234] over twenty *chang* in height. In its center there were a P'eng-lai, a Fang-chang 方丈, a Ying-chou 瀛洲, and a Hu-liang 壺梁,[235] made to resemble the magical mountains in the middle of the sea, with their turtles, fish, and so on. In the south there was the Yü-t'ang 玉堂 (Jade Hall), Pi-men 璧門 (Jade Annulus Gate), Ta-niao 大鳥 (Great Bird), and the like. Then [the Sovereign] erected the Shen-ming T'ai 神明臺 (Spirit Brilliance Terrace), the Ching-han lou 井幹樓 (Well-railing Tower), each measuring over fifty *chang* [in height], with carriage roads connecting them all to one another.

[483] In summer, the Han [dynasty] changed the calendar, taking the first month as the beginning of the year.[236] Among the colors yellow was exalted, and the officials' seals of office were all changed to [consist of] five characters.[237] Accordingly, this became the origination year of the T'ai-ch'u 太初 (Grand Inception [104-101 B.C.]) reign period. That year (104 B.C.), in the west a punitive attack was launched against Ta-yüan 大宛 (Ferghana).[238] Locusts swarmed in vast numbers. Ting Fu-jen 丁夫人, Yü Ch'u 虞初 of Lo-yang, and others employed their magical methods to make offerings and to curse the Hsiung-nu and Ta-yüan.

[484] The next year [103 B.C.], the authorities concerned said that the Five Altars at Yung had no sets of cooked sacrificial animals so the fragrance of the offerings was deficient. The Emperor ordered the officials in charge of the sacrifices to provide the altars with sets of calves as sacrificial animals, with each of the five colors to consume the one it had overcome,[239]

San-fu huang-t'u, p. 167.

[232]Wei-yang was the name of a palace complex of vast proportions built by Han Kao-tsu. It was located northwest of modern Sian, in Shensi. See also n. 500 in the translation of *Shih chi* Chapter 8 above.

[233]T'ang-chung was located northwest of modern Ch'ang-an County in Shensi (Wu and Lu, 12.409n.).

[234]Chien t'ai was the name of the Office of Standards responsible for maintaining uniformity in measurement of length, weight, musical tones, and time. The constellation by the same name in Lyra (γ Lyr) was said to preside over music, sundials, and the water-clock (clepsydra). The hour circle passing through it coinciding with the position of the sun at mid-winter when the standards were recalibrated; see Sun and Kistemaker, *The Chinese Sky during the Han,* p. 172.

[235]Fang-chang, Ying-chou, and Hu-liang are all names of mythical island abodes of immortals.

[236]Until this time the Han had retained the Chou calendar which started the year in the tenth month.

[237]This was done because of the Five Phases association of the Han with earth and the number five ("Chi-chieh").

[238]A state which can be located in what is now Russia (T'an Ch'i-hsiang, 2:37); see also the memoir on Ta-yüan, *Shih chi,* Chapter 123.

[239]For example, sacrifices to the Red Emperor would privilege the color white, signifying the overcoming of the power of metal (white) by fire (red).

except that wooden models of horses would be substituted for colts in the sacrifices.[240] In the case of those sacrifices to the famous mountains and watercourses that used colts, all were to substitute wooden models of horses. Only when the Emperor passed by and performed the sacrifices in person were colts to be used. In other respects the rites were to be performed as in the past.

The following year (102 B.C.), the Emperor made a tour of inspection to the eastern seaboard to look into [reports of] spirit beings, immortals, and the like, but there was no confirmation. Among the practitioners of [magical] methods there were some who said, "In the Huang-ti's day he built five ramparts with twelve towers at Chih-ch'i 執期[241] in order to watch for spirit men, calling the place Ying Nien 迎年 (Welcome Harvest)." The Sovereign let such a place be built as prescribed, and called it Ming Nien 明年 (Bright Harvest). The Sovereign personally sacrificed to the Supreme Deity according to the rites, his vestments exalting the color yellow.

Kung-su Tai said: "In the time of the Huang-ti, although he performed the *Feng* Sacrifice at Mount T'ai, [his counsellors] Feng Hou 風后, Feng Chü 封鉅,[242] and Ch'i Po 岐伯[243] advised the Huang-ti that, on performing the *Feng* Sacrifice at East Mount T'ai[244] and the *Shan* Sacrifice at Mount Fan 凡山,[245] if the signs matched, he would achieve immortality." After ordering the sacrificial sets of offerings to be put in place, the Son of Heaven proceeded to East Mount T'ai, but finding it small and inconsequential and not measuring up to its reputation, he ordered the officials in charge of the sacrifices to perform the rites and did not conduct the *Feng* and *Shan* sacrifices there. Subsequently, he ordered [Kung-su] Tai to conduct the sacrifices and watch for spirit beings. In the summer, he returned to Mount T'ai to perform the fifth year ceremonies as

---

[240]This change of policy testifies to the desperate lack of good horses during the Han, especially when, as now, they were needed for the campaigns against the Hsiung-nu and the Ta-yüan. The two clauses that follow at this point, 獨五帝用駒，行親郊用駒 "only the Five Emperors use colts, when [the Emperor] travels in person to perform the Suburban Sacrifice, use colts" appear corrupt. The *Shih chi* version (28.1402) has 獨五月嘗駒，行親郊用駒 "only in the fifth month Ch'ang Sacrifice [use] colts, and when [the Emperor] travels in person to perform the Suburban Sacrifice, use colts," which is no less awkward and contains an obvious non sequitur. The version in *Han shu* (25B.1244) lacks the two problematic clauses, but follows with 及諸名山川用駒者，悉以木偶馬代。獨行過親祠，乃用駒 closely paralleling what follows in the *Shih chi* Chapter 12 version, while also clarifying the last sentence 行過，乃用駒 of that version. The *Han shu* version thus seems preferable and has been adopted here. Cf. also the remarks by Wang Li-ch'i (12.298n) and Liang Yü-sheng (16.818-9).

[241]A place known only in legend.

[242]According to Ying Shao (cited in "Chi-chieh"), this was the Huang-ti's tutor.

[243]According to the "Cheng-yi," this was the imperial physician to the Huang-ti.

[244]A mountain located between Yi-yüan 沂源 and Yi-shui 沂水 Counties in modern Shantung (Wang Li-ch'i, 12.298n.; T'an Ch'i-hsiang, 2:20).

[245]A mountain located in southwest Ch'ang-le 昌樂 County in modern Shantung (Wang Li-ch'i, 12.298n.; T'an Ch'i-hsiang, 2:20).

before, with the addition of a *Shan* Sacrifice at Mount Shih-lü 石閭 (The Stone Gateway).[246] This Mount Shih-lü was located in the southern foothills of Mount T'ai, and most of the practitioners of [magical] methods claimed this was the immortals' communal gateway, so the Sovereign personally performed the *Shan* Sacrifice there.

[485] Five years later (97 B.C.), the Emperor once again went to Mount T'ai to perform the *Feng* Sacrifice. On his return he passed by and performed a sacrifice to Mount Ch'ang 常山.[247]

Those sacrifices that the present Son of Heaven instituted were the Grand Unity, the Mother Earth, and the *Chiao* Sacrifice which he personally performed every three years. On behalf of the House of Han he established the *Feng* and *Shan* sacrifices which are performed every five years. [Miu] Chi of Po's [sacrifice] for the Grand Unity, the Three Unities, the Dark Ram, the Horse Traveler, and the Ch'ih Hsing 赤星 (Red Star) makes five,[248] K'uan-shu's officials in charge of the sacrifices celebrated them annually at the appropriate season. At all six sacrifices[249] the Grand Supplicator was in charge. As for the other famous sacrifices like those for the Pa Shen 八神 (Eight Spirits) and various deities, for Bright Harvest, and for Mount Fan, when the Emperor passed by on a tour of inspection they were performed, on his departure they were discontinued. Sacrifices initiated by practitioners of [magical] methods were each their individual charge; when the individual died they were discontinued. State officials responsible for sacrifices did not have charge of them. All other sacrifices continued as in the past. The present Sovereign performed the *Feng* and *Shan* sacrifices, and after twelve years (98 B.C.) he had traveled the circuit of all Five Sacred Peaks and Four Watercourses and returned to the capital. Yet the practitioners of [magical] methods who sacrificed to and watched for spirit beings, and who put to sea in search of P'eng-lai, in the end could not verify [any spirits]. And the spirits for which Kung-sun Ch'ing watched, though he offered the footprints of a giant by way of justification, [they] also came to nothing. The Son of Heaven grew increasingly weary and disdainful of the strange and outlandish talk of the practitioners of [magical] methods, but to the end he remained bound to and did not break with them, continuing in hopes of finding a real one. From this time on the practitioners of [magical] methods who promoted sacrifices to the spirits grew ever more numerous, but the results are there for all to see.

[486] His Honor the Grand Scribe says: "I accompanied [the Emperor] on his tours of inspection when he sacrificed to Heaven and Earth and to all the spirits, to the famous mountains

[246] A mountain located in southern T'ai-an County in modern Shantung (Wang Li-ch'i, 12.298n.).

[247] That is, Mount Heng 恆山, the Northern Sacred Peak, located about thirty miles north of modern Ch'ü-yang 曲陽 in Hopei (T'an Ch'i-hsiang, 2:26).

[248] According to Ssu-ma Chen ("So-yin"), this is a reference to sacrifices to the 'Efficacious Star' 靈星 already mentioned above, which Ssu-ma Chen identifies as Arcturus (Alpha Boo), the star marking the left horn of the Cerulean Dragon; cf. Sun and Kistemaker, *The Chinese Sky During the Han*, p. 147.

[249] That is, the five enumerated plus the regular sacrifice to the Supreme Unity conjoined with that to the Hou-t'u.

and rivers, and when he performed the *Feng* and *Shan* sacrifices. I entered the Shou Kung (Palace of Longevity) and assisted in the language of the sacrifices by the Spirit [Mistress]. I studied in depth and observed the words[250] of the practitioners of [magical] methods and officials in charge of sacrifices, and at this point withdrew to discuss and put in chronological order all the practices connected with worship of spirits and ghosts from the ancient past down to the present, to completely disclose both the external and internal aspects of these affairs. When later there are gentlemen [with an interest], they will be able to peruse them here. As for the particulars of the ritual utensils, jade implements, silks, and the rites of presentation and recompense, those records are preserved by the authorities concerned.

*   *   *   *   *

The fifth [imperial] generation after the Han arose, it [reached] prominence in the Chien-yüan [reign]; in foreign affairs [Wu-ti] drove out the Yi and the Ti, internally he refined laws and regulations, performed the *Feng* and *Shan* [sacrifices], revised the first month of the year, changed the color of [court] clothing. [Thus] I made "The Basic Annals of the Present Sovereign, Number Twelve."[251]

---

[250]*Shih chi,* 28.1404 has *yi* 意 "ideas, beliefs," for *yen* 言, "words," here, which seems a better fit.

[251]Comments from Ssu-ma Ch'ien's postface, *Shih chi,* 130.3303.

Translator's Note

The problems posed by Chapter 12 have more to do with the vicissitudes of transmission than with the language of the text. The annalistic account of Emperor Wu's reign along the lines of Chapter 5 in *Han shu* that one expects to find under the rubric "Basic Annals of Emperor Wu the Filial" is nowhere in evidence. Instead, we have an account of the re-creation of state ritual and Wu-ti's perennial preoccupation with the occult reproduced verbatim from Chapter 28, the "Treatise on the *Feng* and *Shan* Sacrifices." Even the present title of the chapter is an interpolation, substituting for the original "Chin shang pen chi" 今上本紀 (Basic Annals of the Present Sovereign) advertised in Ssu-ma Ch'ien's "Postface" (Chapter 130).[252] The original account of Emperor Wu's reign is one of the seven chapters[253] dealing with the first century of Han rule that have been missing since the *Shih chi* surfaced in the Later Han dynasty, and numerous conjectures have been put forward over time to account for their loss. One of the more speculative theories has it that this chapter, together with the preceding one dealing with the reign of Wu's father Ching-ti, was suppressed by Emperor Wu, who was outraged by the historian's unflattering account. It is hardly likely that Emperor Wu ever saw any version of Ssu-ma Ch'ien's history, and in any case other chapters that preserve trenchant criticisms have survived intact.[254] This and other theories have been systematically debunked by Liang Yü-sheng[255] and need not detain us. We can only deplore the loss of Ssu-ma Ch'ien's eyewitness account of the political events of his own time, which would certainly have made for fascinating reading, and translate what we now find in its place.

Two main themes stand out in this chronological account of ritual and mantic preoccupations during Emperor Wu's reign. The first is the restoration and regular performance of the recreated state sacrificial rituals, in particular the *Feng* and *Shan* sacrifices so intimately connected with dynastic prestige and legitimacy, and the second is Wu-ti's personal preoccupation with the occult, especially his tireless efforts to communicate with spirits and immortals in hopes of achieving immortality. Re-creating the state ritual as it was supposed to have been performed in the time of the Yellow Emperor entailed first and foremost the staging on a regular schedule of the quasi-legendary *Feng* and *Shan* sacrifices at cosmologically symbolic locations

---

[252]The text translated here also contains the occasional corruption and one or two suggestive interpolations, such as the anachronistic reference to the sovereign as "Emperor Wu" (*Shih chi*, 12.453) seen above. The few minor variations among the versions of the text preserved in *Shih chi*, Chapter 28, and in *Han shu*, Chapter 25 are not adequate to establish filiation, but are sometimes helpful in deciphering obscure or garbled passages and are duly noted.

[253]Not ten, see Liang Yü-sheng, 6.280. Cf. also Michael Loewe, ed., *Early Chinese Texts: A Bibliographical Guide*, p. 406.

[254]Grant Hardy, *Worlds*, p. 190.

[255]Liang Yü-sheng, 6.277-80.

throughout the world, especially Mount T'ai and the other Sacred Peaks. The strenuous round of royal progresses accomplished between 110 and 98 B.C. required the Emperor and his entourage to travel tens of thousands of *li* in their circumambulation of the world. In order to perform the sacrifices, not only did the ritual specialists have to reconstruct the requisite liturgy and music, but numerous altars, shrines, and most crucially, the sacred precincts of the Ming T'ang at the foot of Mount T'ai. The difficulties this undertaking posed for bookish court erudits is reflected in the Emperor's frustration with their inability to achieve a consensus about the form and content of the ancient rituals. This created an opening for charlatans who were only too eager to gain the emperor's favor and win fame and fortune with claims of intimate knowledge of ancient traditions, including those from the time of the Yellow Emperor himself.

In contrast to this effort to raise the imperial sacrifices to a level of dignity and splendor commensurate with the prestige of the dynasty, Chapter 12 is also replete with accounts of Emperor Wu's penchant for indulging practitioners of [magical] methods and gentleman purveyors of occult skills *fang-shih* 方士. The meteoric rise to high rank and vast wealth of the most successful of these specialists in the mantic arts became legendary, and one gains a clear impression of the impact their careers must have had on courtiers, as well as on other ambitious self-promoters from the eastern seaboard who "swarmed in droves" as a result. In addition to stoking Emperor Wu's burning ambition to contact the immortals of P'eng-lai and achieve immortality, others of these ritual specialists were instrumental in promoting the elevation of esoteric religious devotions, such as worship of the *T'ai-yi* 太一 (The Grand Unity), to the level of a state cult. However, the overall impression created by this account of occult developments, unlike that of the restoration of imperial sacrifices, is a portrayal of Emperor Wu as the hapless victim of numerous scams and deceptions. The denouements of particularly embarrassing episodes of imperial gullibility, such as the downfall of the notorious Luan Ta, are said to have been "hushed up," and on several occasions, Ssu-ma Ch'ien barely conceals his disdain for this defect in the imperial personality. The parallel with the historian's portrayal of Ch'in Shih-huang (*Shih chi* Chapter 6) in this regard seems unmistakable.

Bibliography

Translations

Chavannes, 3:324-405.
Yoshida, 2:688-750.
Viatkin, 2:254-86; notes 475-83.
Watson, *Han,* 1.319 (partial).

Studies

Chang Sheng-fu 張勝發. "'Chin-shang pen-chi' k'ung-pai shuo kuan-chien" 今上本紀空白説管見, *Wei-nan Shih-chuan hsüeh-pao* 渭南師專學報 1988.3. Not seen.
Chin Hui 金惠. "Chieh-k'ai *Shih chi* Chin-shang pen-chi ('Wu-ti pen-chi') ch'üeh-shih chih mi" 揭開史記今上本紀（武帝本紀）闕失之謎, *Tung-fang tsa-chih* 13.5 (1979): 48-52.
Inada Takashi 稲田孝. "Kan u *Shiki* 'Butei honki'" 関于史記武帝本紀, *Tôkyô Gakugei Daigaku kiyô (Jimbun Kagaku)* 東京学芸大学記要（人文科学）, 29 (1978): 266-73.
Juan Chih-sheng 阮芝生. "San Ssu-ma yü Han Wu-ti feng shan" 三司馬與漢武帝封禪, *T'ai-ta li-shih hsüeh-pao* 臺大歷史學報, 20 (1996): 307-40.
Lo Fang-sung 羅芳松. "Han Wu-ti ho *Shih chi* ch'eng-shu de kuan-hsi" 漢武帝和史記成書的關系, *Ch'eng-tu Ta-hsüeh hsüeh-pao* 1985.1. Not seen.
Shih Ting 施丁. "Ssu-ma Ch'ien hsieh 'Chin-shang (Han Wu-ti)'" 司馬遷寫'今上（漢武帝.' In Shih Ting, *Ssu-ma Ch'ien yen-chiu hsin-lun* 司馬遷研究新論. Chengchow: Ho-nan Jen-min, 1982, pp. 137-63.
Yü Kuei-fu 玉貴福. "Ts'ung *Shih chi* k'an Ssu-ma Ch'ien tui Han Wu-ti de t'ai-tu" 從史記看司馬遷對漢武帝的態度, *Kuang-hsi Min-tsu Hsüeh-yüan hsüeh-pao* 廣西民族學院學報 1983.3. Not seen.

Frequently Mentioned Commentators

Chang Shou-chieh 張守節 (fl. 725)

Ch'ien Ta-chao 錢大昭 (1744-1813)

Ch'ien Ta-hsin 錢大昕 (1728-1804)

Chin Cho 晉灼 (fl. 275)

Fu Ch'ien 服虔 (fl. 188)

Ho Cho 何焯 (1661-1722)

Hsü Kuang 徐廣 (352-425)

Ju Ch'un 如淳 (fl. 230)

Kao Yu 高誘 (fl. 205-212)

Ku Yen-wu 顧炎武 (1613-1682)

Liang Yü-sheng 梁玉繩 (1745-1819)

Meng K'ang 孟康 (ca. 180-260)

Ssu-ma Chen 司馬貞 (fl. 745)

Wang Hsien-ch'ien 王先謙 (1842-1918)

Wang Nien-sun 王念孫 (1744-1832)

Wei Chao 韋昭 (204-273)

Yen Shih-ku 顏師古 (583-645)

Ying Shao 應劭 (ca. 140-203/204)

Biographical Sketches of *Shih chi* Commentators

Hsü Kuang 徐廣 (*tzu* Yeh-min 野民, 352–425).[1] One of the first major *Shih chi* commentaries, the *Shih chi yin-i* 史記音義 (Sounds and Meanings of the *Shih chi*) was written by Hsü Kuang, who hailed from Ku-mu 姑幕 in Tung-wan 東莞 Commandery.[2] His father, Hsü Tsao 徐藻, was the commissioner of waterways and his older brother, Hsü Miao 徐邈 (344-397), was the leader of the heir apparent's front guard. Hsü Kuang's family had always loved learning, and he was no exception. Of the hundred schools and all the various arts, there was none which he did not master. His family was poor but they had allegedly never had ambitions for material goods or careers.

Hsü's marriage apparently did not prosper as much as his scholarship. His wife, the daughter of Liu Mi 劉謐, did not share his lack of concern for worldly affairs and material goods. She was angry about his passion for learning and often criticized him, but Hsü remained resolute in his disciplined dedication to scholarship. The friction between Mr. and Mrs. Hsü continued for over ten years; the state of the family finances worsening day by day, until Mrs. Hsü finally left Mr. Hsü. Had she had more faith in her husband, her pecuniary passions would have been realized, as Emperor Wu the Filial 武 (of the Chin, r. 373–97) saw value in Hsü Kuang's broad learning and appointed him as an assistant in the Palace Library (*pi-shu lang* 秘書郎), where he worked collating the books of the imperial archives. During the Lung-an 隆安 reign period (402) the director of the Imperial Secretariat (*shang-shu ling* 尚書令) Wang Hsün 王珣 recommended him to be a gentleman attendant in the Ministry of Sacrifices (*tz'u-pu lang* 祠部郎).

Hsü Kuang's career spanned the courts of two dynasties. He continued to serve at

[1]The following biographical information is based on Hsü Kuang's biographies found in three of the standard histories. The accounts can be found in: Fang Hsüan-ling 房玄齡 (578–648) *et al.*, *Chin shu* 晉書 (History of the Chin) (Peking: Chung-hua shu-chü, 1974), 82.2158–59; Li Yen-shou 李延壽 (ca. 629), *Nan shih* 南史 (History of the South) (Peking: Chung-hua shu-chü, 1975), 33.858–59; and Shen Yüeh 沈約 (441–513), *Sung shu* 宋書 [History of the (Liu) Sung] (Peking: Chung-hua shu-chü, 1974), 55.1547–1549. The *Nan shih* and *Sung shu* versions of Hsü's biography also contain two or three "Discussions" (*yi* 議) which Hsü had submitted to the throne. Further evidence of the stature of Hsü Kuang's work is the number of times he is cited in the *Wen-hsüan chu*. Four of his different works, the *Chü fu chih* 車服志, his *Shih chi* annotations, "Fu Hsieh Chü-ch'i tsang huan shih" 赴謝車騎葬還詩, and *Chin chi* 晉紀 are cited a total of twenty-seven times. The dates of birth and death listed for Hsü Kuang are corroborated by Hsü's biographies in the *Chin shu* and *Sung shu*. It is noteworthy, however, that in *Nan shih*, 33.859 it states that Hsü lived over eighty years.

[2]According to T'an Ch'i-hsiang, 3:51–2, Ku-mu was actually in Ch'eng-yang 城陽 Commandery, approximately fifteen miles east of the eastern border of Tung-wan Commandery. This location is approximately sixty miles west of modern Tsingtao city in Shantung province.

court under the reign of Emperor Wu 武 of the Liu Sung 劉宋. At the beginning of the
I-hsi 義熙 reign period (405–419), Emperor Wu ordered him to write *Chü fu i chu* 車服儀
注 (Carriages, Clothing and Ceremonies, Annotated) appointing him as an administrative
adviser to a defense command (*chen-chün tzu-i ts'an-chün* 鎮軍諮議參軍) overseeing the
record keepers (*chi-shih* 記室), and enfeoffing him as a fifth-rank marquis of Le-ch'eng 樂
成 district.[3] He was quickly promoted to be a supernumerary senior recorder (*san chi
ch'ang shih* 散騎常侍), overseeing the editorial directors (*chu-tso lang* 著作郎). In the
following year (406), Hsü Kuang began a history of the Chin 晉, which he completed in
416. In the sixth year (410), he was promoted to be the general of the Imperial Guard.
Around this time Hsü Kuang admonished Emperor Wu about a calamitous hailstorm that
had occurred in the empire. Emperor Wu must have approved of Hsü Kuang's admonition,
as he was promoted again, this time to chamberlain for the National Treasury (*ta ssu-nung
大司農*)[4] and overseer of the editorial directors (*ling chu-tso lang* 領著作郎).[5] Hsü Kuang
was shortly promoted again to be director of the Palace Library (*pi-shu chien* 秘書監).[6]

Historical hindsight illustrates Hsü's success in the Liu Sung imperial bureaucracy.
Hsü himself was not privy to such an objective viewpoint at the fall of the Chin. When
Emperor Wu received the throne, Hsü Kuang was filled with grief, with tears flowing.
Hsieh Hui 謝晦, a Liu Sung official, saw him and said, "Master Hsü has done nothing
wrong." Hsü Kuang stopped sobbing and replied, "I am different from you, sir. You assist
the mandate of Heaven to make a king rise, meeting a thousand years of good luck. I have
for my whole life received the favor of Chin, thinking fondly back to the former sovereign."
Thereupon he resumed his sobbing and sniveling.[7] Little did he know he would continue

---

[3]Located on the coast of modern Chekiang, approximately thirty miles north of
Wenchow (T'an Ch'i-hsiang, 4:25–6).

[4]This was an extremely high position. According to Charles O. Hucker, it was "one of
the Nine Chamberlains in the central government; had very broad responsibilities for the
registration of agricultural lands, the collection of land taxes, the storage of state grain supplies,
management of the state monopolies of such commodities as salt and iron, management of the
state's price stabilization schemes. . ." (see Hucker, p. 473).

[5]There were most likely two editorial directors, who had concurrent positions in the
Secretariat or the Palace Library (see Hucker, p. 184).

[6]At this time it appears that the Director was responsible "to oversee archival materials
in the halls (*ke* 閣) in the outer palace grounds; it was traditionally considered that this (reign
of Emperor Hui of the Chin, r. 290–306) marked the beginning of a governmental rather than a
personal imperial institution. The Director soon was in charge of a substantial agency called
Court of the Palace Library, normally having a Vice Director and four specially esteemed Assistants,
each in charge of a Hall or Bureau with a subordinate staff of Clerks and Proofreaders. Although
from time to time both the names and functions of the Palace Library and the Secretariat seem to
have been interchangeable, the Palace Library was increasingly devoted to archival-editorial
work" (see Hucker, p. 377).

[7]This account appears in each of the three biographies mentioned above.

to climb the ladder of imperial bureaucracy to a height he had not reached under the Chin.

In the first year of the Yung-ch'u 永初 reign period (420–23), Hsü was appointed as the grand master of palace leisure (*chung-san tai-fu* 中散大夫), but he asked to be excused from service, as he was aging and wished to return to the land of his ancestral tomb. His wish was granted. It is noted that he passed away in the second year of the Yüan-chia 元嘉 reign period (425) at the age of seventy-four. Prior to his death, his biographies indicate that he completed a history of the Chin entitled *Chin chi* 晉紀 (The Annals of Chin) and another work entitled *Ta li wen* 答禮問 (Answers to Ritual Questions). Interestingly, there is no mention in any of his biographies of the *Shih-chi yin-i*, a work which Hsü's many positions in and around the Imperial Library uniquely qualified him to write.

Ying Shao 應紹 (*praenomen*, Chung-yüan 仲瑗;[8] active 165-ca. 204) was one of the most often cited scholars in the "Commentaries of the Three Scholars." These citations came from his commentaries on *Han shu* and a number of other works concerning Han social customs, official ceremonies, bureaucratic establishments, and legal institutions.[9] A native of Ju-nan 汝南 commandery,[10] Ying Shao was born into a noble family,[11] which for generations had been closely associated with the leading family of the region, the Yüans 袁.[12] His father Ying Feng 應奉 was a scholar-official and his position reached as high as Colonel Director of the Retainers (*ssu-li hsiao-wei* 司隸校尉) during the Yen-hsi 延熹 period of Emperor Huan 桓 (158-166). Ying Shao's interest in Han historiography may have been influenced by his father, who edited materials from the *Shih chi*, *Han shu*,

[8]His *agnomen* was also given as Chung-yüan 仲援, Chung-yüan 中遠, or Chung-yüan 仲遠 (see *Hou Han shu*, 48.1609 and 35.1211). 仲瑗 may be the correct one, since the meaning of 瑗 "a round flat piece of jade" is related to his *praenomen* 劭 "beautiful, magnificent." Moreover, his younger brother's *agnomen* Hsün 珣 also carries a jade radical. Wu Shu-p'ing 吳樹平 also finds several additional pieces of evidence which support Chung-yüan as his *agnomen*. See Wu Shu-p'ing, "*Feng-su t'ung-i* tsa k'ao" 風俗通義雜考, *Wen shih* 7 (1979): 54.

[9]Ying Shao's biography can be found in *Hou Han shu*, 48.1609-15. For an annotated translation of this biography, see Michael Nylan, "Ying Shao's *Feng Su Tung Yi*: An Exploration of Problems in Han Dynasty Political, Philosophical and Social Unity," Unpublished Ph.D. Dissertation: Princeton University, 1982, pp. 321-38.

[10]Ju-nan is a commandery with its seat in P'ing-yü 平與 (about twenty miles northeast of modern Ju-nan, Honan; T'an Ch'i-hsiang, 2:45).

[11]According to *Hou Han shu*, 48.1615, members of the Ying family served as government officials under Han for seven consecutive generations.

[12]One of the eminent figure of that clan was Yüan Shao 袁紹 (d. 202), who rose to be a powerful general after the Han collapsed and Ying Shao joined his staff in his later years. For a discussion of the relationship of these two families, see Michael Nylan, "Ying Shao," pp. 30-4.

and *Han chi* and compiled the *Han shih* 漢事 (The Affairs of Han), in seventeen *chüan*.[13] Shao's nephew Ying Yang 應瑒 was famous for his literary talent and was one of the "Seven Masters of the Chien-an 建安 Period."

During the reign of Emperor Ling 靈 (r. 168-189), Ying Shao was recommended as Filially Pious and Incorrupt (*hsiao-lien* 孝廉).[14] Later he was appointed as an aide to Ho Miao 何苗 (d. 189), General of Chariots and Cavalry (*Chü-ch'i chiang-chün* 車騎將軍).[15] In 189, he became the Grand Administrator of T'ai-shan 泰山 Commandery.[16] In the same year, the death of Emperor Ling and the subsequent strife between the eunuchs and great ministers led to the turmoil of the empire. Tung Cho 董卓 (d. 192) advanced to the capital with his troops and he soon became military dictator, deposing the child emperor and enthroning Emperor Hsien 獻 (r. 189-220). Yüan Shao fled the capital and together with Ts'ao Ts'ao 曹操 (155-220) and other military leaders formed an alliance against Tung Cho. During this period, Ying Shao showed his continuous allegiance to the throne and supported the anti-Tung Cho alliance.[17] In 191, Ying Shao successfully defeated a group of Yellow Turban rebels and forced them to withdraw from his commandery. Two years later, when Ts'ao Ts'ao's father and other family members passed the T'ai-shan commandery, they were attacked and killed by T'ao Ch'ien 陶謙, the Shepherd of Hsü 徐 Province.[18] Ying Shao feared Ts'ao Ts'ao would punish him for being unable to protect his father , so he fled the commandery and sought refuge with Yüan Shao, then the Shepherd of Chi 冀 Province.[19] In the next year, he was appointed as Colonel of Military Strategy (*chün-mou hsiao-wei* 軍謀校尉) under Yüan Shao. Thereafter he spent the rest of his life in Yüan's camp. While Ying Shao placed much hope on Yüan and wished him to become a "hegemon" who would be committed to the protection of the Han state,[20] Yüan's disastrous defeat by Ts'ao Ts'ao in 200 ruined all his hopes. Ying probably died in 203 or 204,[21] before Ts'ao Ts'ao took control of all of northern China.

[13]*Hou Han shu*, 48.1608.

[14]Wu Shu-p'ing, "Tsa-k'ao" (pp. 54-5) claims this event took place between 168-173.

[15]Wu Shu-p'ing, "Tsa-k'ao" (p. 55) dates this event to 187 or 188.

[16]The seat of T'ai-shan commandery was at Feng-kao 奉高 (about fifteen miles east of modern T'ai-an 泰安, Shantung; T'an Ch'i-hsiang, 2:44). Wu Shu-p'ing, "Tsa-k'ao" (pp. 54-5), based on several other sources, claims Ying Shao had held a number of minor posts such as Gentleman and county prefect before he became the Grand Administrator.

[17]See Michael Nylan, "Ying Shao," pp. 50-1.

[18]Hsü Province covers modern Kiangsu, southern Shantung, and parts of Anhwei (T'an Ch'i-hsiang, 2:44).

[19]Chi Province covers southern Hopei, and parts of Shantung, Honan, and Shansi (T'an Ch'i-hsiang, 2:46).

[20]See Michael Nylan, "Ying Shao," p. 20.

[21]His biography in *Hou Han shu* did not specify the date of death. In *San kuo chih*, 1.11, it is said that Ying Shao had already died at the time when Ts'ao Ts'ao pacified Chi Province. Since we know Ts'ao pacified the Chi province in 204, Ying Shao should have died in

Ying Shao was a prolific writer. According to *Hou Han shu* (48.1614), he left 136 works, in addition to his "Collected commentaries" (*chi-chieh* 集解) on *Han shu*. According to *Sui shu* (33.953), the book was called *Han shu chi-chieh yin yi* 漢書集解音義 (Collected Commentaries on the Meaning and Pronunciation of the *Han shu*), in twenty-four *chüan*. The book is now lost but parts of it are preserved in the current "Commentaries of Three Scholars" to the *Shih chi*. He was also said to have annotated Hsün Yüeh's 荀悦 (148-209) *Han chi* 漢紀 (Record of the Han [dynasty]).[22] His other major work is *Feng-su t'ung yi* 風俗通義 (The Comprehensive Discussion of Customs). This text was intended to rectify social customs and to restore traditional moral principles at a time when the political unity and the orthodox Confucian values were disintegrating. His other works[23] include: 1) *Han yi* 漢儀 (Han Institutions), submitted to the throne in 196, was basically a record and discussion of the precedent legal code and law cases so as to assist the contemporary ruler to "decide doubtful cases and elucidate right and wrong"[24]; 2) *Han kuan yi* 漢官儀 (Han Bureaucratic Institutions), written in 197, a first-hand account of the court institutions and regulations of officialdom of Han times.

that year or a year earlier. See Wu Shu-p'ing, "Tsa-k'ao," p. 56.

[22]See *Erh-shih-wu shih pu pien* 二十五史補編 (Peking: Chung-hua Shu-chü, 1956), 2:2351-2.

[23]For a list of the known titles of Ying Shao's works, see Michael Nylan, "Ying Shao," pp. 237-38, n. 75.

[24]*Hou Han shu*, 48.1612. See also Michael Nylan, "Ying Shao," pp. 52-3.

Glossary

Our base glossary, of which this is a selection, is still growing and evolving. Most of the terms here were used in the renditions of the basic annals (*pen-chi* 本紀) of *The Grand Scribe's Records* (i.e., volumes 1 and 2), but some are general to the entire translation project. We have attempted to use the same word in English to translate a Chinese term whenever possible. This list is not intended to be complete, but rather a sampling of some of the most often used and/or troublesome terms and phrases which should give the reader an idea of one of the sources of our admittedly sometimes awkward, but literal translations. Examples of usage are given as needed below. Most of the abbreviations should be self-evident, but Pn. stands for 'Proper noun,' vp. for 'verb phrase,' and m. for 'measure word.'

A

ai 哀 **v./adj./n.** "to mourn, grieve, lament, pity; mournful, grieving, pitiful; pity"; *Shih chi*, 4.147: 聞其夜啼，哀而收之; *Grand Scribe's Records*, 1:74: "They heard it cry during the night and, out of pity, they adopted it"; *Shih chi*, 5.194: 秦人哀之，為作歌黃鳥之詩; *Grand Scribe's Records*, 1:102: "The Ch'in people mourned for them and wrote the poem 'Yellow Birds' to sing their praises."

an 安 **n.** "peace of mind"; *Shih chi*, 9.408. 大臣得安; *Grand Scribe's Records*, 2:130: "The great ministers will gain peace of mind."

ao 媼 **n.** "Mother" (term of address preceded by surname)

C

cha 詐 **n.** "deception"; see also *mou* 謀.

chan tao 棧道 **n.** "plank roadways or roads" (roads built along mountain sides out of planks of wood that were supported against the steep slopes by wooden piles; our translation follows the gloss given in "So-yin" (*Shih chi*, 8.367); *Shih chi*, 8.367: 去輒燒絕棧道以備諸侯盜兵襲之，亦示項羽無東意; *Grand Scribe's Records*, 2:44: "Once the King of Han left [a place], he quickly burned the plank roadways at once as a precaution against bandit troops from the feudal lords launching a surprise attack on him and also to show Hsiang Yü that he had no thoughts of the East."

chao 招 **vt.** "to summon" (8.352)

chao 詔 **n.** "decree, edict"; *feng-chao* 奉詔 "to receive an edict"

che 折 **v.** "to break"; *Shih chi*, 8.343: 折券棄責; *Grand Scribe's Records*, 2:9: "broke the markers and cancelled his debt."

269

chen 鎮 **v.** "to guard, keep in order"; *Shih chi*, 5.202: 獻公即位，鎮撫邊境，徙治櫟陽，且欲東伐，復繆公之故地，脩繆公之政令; *Grand Scribe's Records*, 1:109: "After Duke Hsien acceded to the position, he guarded and calmed the borders, moved the capital to Yüeh-yang, and prepared to launch an expedition east in order to recover Duke Mu's former territory and to implement Duke Mu's orders"; *Shih chi*, 8.381: 鎮國家，撫百姓，給餽饟，不絕糧道，吾不如蕭何; *Grand Scribe's Records*, 2:68: "As for guarding a country, calming its people, providing provisions and field rations, and not allowing supply lines to be cut, I am not as good as Hsiao Ho."

ch'en 臣 **n.** "vassal (in pre-Ch'in times), minister, official, subject; your servant (in direct address)."

cheng 爭 **v.** "to dispute, argue over"

cheng tu 正度 **n.** "primes and standards"

ch'eng 誠 **n./adj./adv.** "sincerity, sincere, sincerely, really"; *Shih chi*, 1.11: 絜誠以祭祀; *Grand Scribe's Records*, 1:5: "With purity and sincerity he offered sacrifices"; *Shih chi*, 2.80: 德誠施皆清矣; *Grand Scribe's Records*, 1:34: "If a lord's kindness is applied with sincerity, they will all become peaceful"; *Shih chi*, 5.186: 臣誠私利祿爵; *Grand Scribe's Records*, 1:95: "I really coveted the salary and position."

ch'eng 稱 **v.** "to call"

   ch'eng chih 稱制 **v.o.** "to cause [orders] to be called decrees"; *Shih chi*, 9.400: 太后稱制，議欲立諸呂為王，問右丞相王陵。王陵曰：「高帝刑白馬盟曰『非劉氏而王，天下共擊之』」; *Grand Scribe's Records*, 2:115: "The T'ai-hou caused [her orders] to be called decrees. . . ."

chi/yi 姬 **n.** "lady, Beauty, Belle, consort" (Ju Ch'un, *Shih chi*, 9.395, says that this graph should be pronounced *yi* 怡 when referring to the title); *Shih chi*, 5.186: 晉驪姬作亂; *Grand Scribe's Records*, 1:95: "Chin's Consort from the Li caused a revolt"; *Shih chi*, 7.311: 范增説項羽曰：「沛公居山東時，貪於財貨，好美姬」; *Grand Scribe's Records*, 1:190: "Fan Tseng advised Hsiang Yü: 'When the Magistrate of P'ei was living east of the Mount, he was greedy for wealth and fond of beautiful women [or "beauties"]"; *Shih chi*, 9.395: 及高祖為漢王，得定陶戚姬，愛幸; *Grand Scribe's Records*, 2:105: "When the Exalted Ancestor was King of Han, he obtained a Beauty Ch'i from Ting-t'ao and loved and favored her"; *Shih chi*, 85.2508. 子楚遂立姬為夫人; *Grand Scribe's Records*, 7:313: "Tzu Ch'u then installed the lady as his principle wife."

chi 計 **v.** "consider, lay plans, plan"; **n.** "plan"; see also *mou* 謀.

chi shou 稽首 **v.o.** "to touch one's head to the ground"; (*Shih chi*, 71.2312: 樂羊再拜稽首曰; *Grand Scribe's Records*, 7:149: "Yüeh Yang knelt down, touched his forehead twice to the ground twice, and said . . . "; see also *kuei* 跪, *pai* 拜, *tun-shou* 頓首.

chi wei 即位 **v.o.** "to ascend the throne"

chiao 矯 **vt.** "falsify an order"

   chiao chih 矯制 **v.o.** "to forge decrees", *Shih chi*, 9.407: . . . 矯制以令天下; *Grand Scribe's Records*, 2:129: ". . . forged decrees so as to issue orders to the world."

chiao 驕 **adj.** "arrogant, extravagant";

   chiao-tz'u 驕恣 **adj.** "extravagant and dissipated"

chieh 節 **n.** "caduceus (the staff of a herald; *chieh* is a bamboo staff decorated with oxtails carried by an envoy or herald)"

chieh 劫 **v.** "to coerce, force, plunder, kidnap"; *Shih chi*, 6.274: 追劫樂母置高舍; *Grand Scribe's Records*, 1:161: "Having kidnapped Yen Le's mother and placed her in his [own] house,"; *Shih chi*, 7.329: 彭越疆劫外黃; *Grand Scribe's Records*, 1:203: "P'eng Yüeh coerced the people of Wai-huang [into rebelling]"; *Shih chi*, 8.349: 因劫眾，眾不敢不聽; *Grand Scribe's Records*, 2:19: ". . .taking advantage of this opportunity, coerce the populace so they will have to listen to you."

ch'ieh 竊 **adv.** "in secret, secretly, in private, privately"; *Shih chi* 3.106: 西伯昌聞之，竊嘆; *Grand Scribe's Records*, 1:50: "The Lord of the West, Ch'ang, on hearing this sighed in secret"; *Shih chi*, 6.231: 十二年，文信侯不韋死，竊葬; *Grand Scribe's Records*, 1:131: "In the twelfth year (235 B.C.), Lü Pu-wei, Marquis Wen-hsin, died. He was buried in secret."

  ch'ieh-wen **adv.v.** 竊聞 "to hear privately"; *Shih chi*, 9.397: 竊聞太后怨戚夫人，欲召趙王并誅之; *Grand Scribe's Records*, 2:110: "I have privately heard that the T'ai-hou harbors resentment for Lady Ch'i and wants to summon the King of Chao and execute them together"; *Shih chi*, 85.2506: 呂不韋曰：「秦王老矣，安國君得為太子。竊聞安國君愛幸華陽夫人; *Grand Scribe's Records*, 7:311: "Lü Pu-wei said, 'Now that the King of Ch'in is old, the Lord of An-kuo has become Heir. I have privately heard that the Lord of An-kuo loves and favors the Lady of Hua-yang . . . .'"

chien 漸 **n.** "point of departure, first step in the process"

chien 諫 **v./n.** "to admonish, remonstrate; admonishment"; see also *ch'üan* 勸.

ch'ien 遷 **n./v.** "banishment"; "to move, banish"

ch'ien 塹 **n.** "moat"

chih 卮 **n.** "scyphus [two-handled goblet], cup, goblet"

chih 執 **v.** "to seize" (8.382)

chih 制 **v./n.** "to restrain, control; to regulate;" "regulations, orders"

  chiao chih 矯制 "to forge decrees"; *Shih chi*, 9.407: 矯制以令天下; *Grand Scribe's Records*, 2:129: ". . . forged decrees so as to issue orders to the world."

chih 治 **vt.** "to regulate"

  chih-shih 治事 **v.o.** "to regulate affairs, administer"

chih 置 **vt.** "to set up, put, place; to establish (political region—commandery, county, etc.)"; *Shih chi*, 1.6: 置左右大監，監于萬國; *Grand Scribe's Records*, 1:3: "He set up the Left and Right Grand Superintendents to superintend the myriad states"; *Shih chi*, 3.105: 多取野獸蜚鳥置其中; *Grand Scribe's Records*, 1:50: "And gathered many wild beasts and birds to put in them"; *Shih chi*, 5.207: 又攻楚漢中，取地六百里，置漢中郡; *Grand Scribe's Records*, 1:113: "He also attacked Han-chung in Ch'u and took six-hundred *li* [on a side] of land, where Ch'in established the Han-chung Commandery; *Shih chi*, 65.2167: 魏置相，相田文; *Grand Scribe's Records*, 7:44: "When Wei established the position of Prime Minsiter, he appointed T'ien Wen"; *Shih chi*, 68.2231: 已乃立三丈之木於國都市南門，募民有能徙置北門者予十金; *Grand Scribe's Records*, 7:90: "He erected a three-*chang* pole at the south gate of the capital's market and advertised for men able to move [the pole] and set it up at the north gate. He offered ten *chin*."

chih 智 **adj.** "intelligent, wise, clever, witty"; *Shih chi,* 2.77: 知人則智，能官人：*Grand Scribe's Records,* 1:33: If he were able to know people, then he would be intelligent and [therefore] capable of appointing people to official positions"; *Shih chi,* 6.245: 聖智仁義，顯白道理; *Grand Scribe's Records,* 1:140: "Being sagacious, intelligent, benevolent, and righteous, he manisfested the Way and reason"; *Shih chi,* 7.308. 且天之亡秦，無愚智皆知之; *Grand Scribe's Records,* 1:188. "Moreover, Heaven itself is destroying Ch'in; all men, both wise and foolish, now know this"; *Shih chi,* 67.2198. 智者不疑也; *Grand Scribe's Records,* 7:62: "A wise man would not hesitate"; **n.** "intelligence, wisdom, wits"; *Shih chi,* 7.328. 漢王笑謝曰：「吾寧鬥智，不能鬥力。」; *Grand Scribe's Records,* 1:202: "The King of Han laughed and declined, 'I would rather fight with my wits than with my strength'"; *Shih chi,* 8.392: 陳平智有餘，然難以獨任; *Grand Scribe's Records,* 2:86: "Ch'en P'ing has more than enough intelligence, but can hardly be relied on by himself."

ch'ih 馳 **vi.** "hasten, gallop, speed"

  Ch'ih-tao 馳道 **n.** "Speedway"; *Shih chi,* 6.241: 是歲，賜爵一級。治馳道; *Grand Scribe's Records,* 1:138. "In this year, he granted everyone an increase of one rank. He built the Speedway."

ch'in 寢 **v.** "to sleep, lie"; *Shih chi,* 64.2157: 君寢不安席; *Grand Scribe's Records,* 7:34: "Our lord takes no comfort from lying on his sleeping mat"; less frequently as a **n.** "chamber"; *Shih chi,* 6.286: 康公享國十二年。居雍高寢; *Grand Scribe's Records,* 1:171: "Duke K'ang enjoyed a reign of twelve yeras over the state, dwelling in the Exalted Chamber in Yung."

ch'in 琴 **n.** "[twenty-five stringed] zither"; see also *chu* 筑 and *se* 瑟.

ch'in-pao 侵暴 **v.o.** "impose violence, bring savageness upon"; sometimes also used as *pao-ch'in*

ch'ing 青 **adj.** "dark, green, blue"; see also *ts'ang* 蒼.

ch'ing 請 **v.** "to request, to ask"

  ku-ch'ing 固請 **v.** "to insist, implore"; *Shih chi,* 8.389-90: 十餘日，高祖欲去，沛父兄固請留高祖; *Grand Scribe's Records,* 2:83: "After more than ten days, Kao-tsu wanted to leave, but the elders of P'ei insisted that Kao-tsu stay longer";

chiu 九 **n./adj.** "nine; many"; *San-kung chiu-ch'ing* 三公九卿 **adj. n. adj. n.** "The Three Honorable Officials and the Nine Ministers."

chiu 就 **v.** "move towards, head for"; see also *wang* 往.

chu 祝 **v.** "to supplicate"; see also *tz'u* 祠 and *ssu* 祀.

chu 屬 **vt.** "to entrust (troops) to, put (troops) under the command of, put (troops, generals) under someone"; see also *fu* 附.

chu 筑 **n.** "dulcimer"; *Shih chi,* 8.389: 高祖擊筑，自為歌詩曰; *Grand Scribe's Records,* 2:82: "Kao-tsu struck the dulcimer, and sang a song he had composed himself"; see also *se* 瑟 "zither" and ch'in 琴 "[twenty-five stringed] zither."

chu 諸 **adj.** "all, various"

  chu-hou 諸侯 **adj.–n.** "the various lords; the feudal lords"; *Shih chi,* 7.321: 春，漢王部五諸侯兵，凡五十六萬人，東伐楚; *Grand Scribe's Records,* 1:198: "In the spring, the King of Han forced the troops of five feudal lords, 560,000 in all, to march east to attack Ch'u."

chu-hou wang 諸侯王 **n.** "noble kings," an early Han-dynasty term to designate the subordinate nature of the royally-born "kings" as opposed to those who earned their throne through merit fighting with Kao-tsu or the patronage of Empress Lü; *Shih chi,* 9.406: 辛巳，高后崩，遺詔賜諸侯王各千金，將相列侯郎吏皆以秩賜金; *Grand Scribe's Records,* 2:127: On the *hsin-ssu* day, Kao-hou passed away, leaving an edict granting the noble kings each one-thousand *chin*."

ch'u 除 **vt.** "to abolish, eliminate, clear (of objects), clean up, remove; put an end to"; *Shih chi,* 3.106: 以請除炮格之刑; *Grand Scribe's Records,* 1:50: "[The Lord of the West] requested the punishment of roasting on a rack be abolished"; with a state (as in *kuo ch'u* 國除), "to abolish"

> ***ch'u-ch'ü*** 除去 **vt.** "to eliminate"; *Shih chi,* 6.268: 以除去上生平所不可者; *Grand Scribe's Records,* 1:157: "To eliminate those whom you have not approved of your whole life."

ch'u 初 **adv.** "earlier"

ch'u 處 **v.** "to live, stay"; **n.** "place, location, whereabouts; place to turn to" (or "place of refuge"); *Shih chi,* 3.102: 更無定處; *Grand Scribe's Records,* 1:47: "without fixing its location"; *Shih chi,* 5.193: 戎王處辟匿，未聞中國之聲; *Grand Scribe's Records,* 1:101: "The King of the Tung lives in obscurity and has never heard the tones of the Central States"; *Shih chi,* 6.257: 行所幸，有言其處者，罪死; *Grand Scribe's Records,* 1:149: "Wherever he went, those who spoke of his whereabouts were sentenced to death"; *Shih chi,* 8.346: 及高祖貴，遂不知老父處; *Grand Scribe's Records,* 2:13: But when Kao-tsu became honored, he could not even learn the whereabouts of the elderly father"; see also *chü* 居.

> ***ch'u shih*** 處士 **n.** "untried" or "unemployed scholar"; *Shih chi,* 3.94: 或曰，伊尹處士，*Grand Scribe's Records,* 1:43: "Some sources say that Yi Yin was an untried scholar."

chü 居 **v.** "to live, reside, dwell"; *Shih chi,* 1.10: 黃帝居軒轅之丘，; *Grand Scribe's Records,* 1:4: "The Huang-ti lived at the hill of Hsüan-yüan"; *Shih chi,* 1.10: 青陽降居江水; *Grand Scribe's Records,* 1:4: "Ch'ing-yang was ordered to live down by The Chiang River";

chü 踞 **v.** "sitting with legs apart/spread, legs akimbo"

> ***chü-ch'uang*** **v.o.** 踞床 "sitting with legs apart on his sleeping-couch, legs spread or akimbo."

chuan 傳 **n.** "pass, permit"; a wooden pass (often with the reason and name of the person) which permits the holder to go through a pass or into a restricted area (see Li Chün-ming 李均明, "Han chieh so-chien ch'u-ju fu, chuan yü ch'u-ju ming-chi" 漢簡所見出入符，傳與出入名籍, *Wen shih* 19 [1983]: 27-35).

> ***chuan-she*** 傳舍 **n.** "post house, road house"; see also Ma Hung-lu 馬洪路, *Hsing-lu nan* 行路難 (Hong Kong: Chung-hua, 1990), pp. 134-5.

ch'üan 勸 **v.** "to exhort"; see also *chien* 諫

chuang 壯 **v.** "to reach manhood"

ch'uang 床 **n.** "sleeping-couch, bed"

chün-hsiang 軍餉 **adj. n.** "field or garrison rations"

F

fa 法 **n.** "model"

  fa chia 法駕 **adj. n.** "model equipage"

fa sang 發喪 **v.o.** "to announce (the) mourning" or "to set out in a funeral march, start the funeral cortege/procession"; *Shih chi*, 5.193-4: 為發喪，哭之三日; *Grand Scribe's Records*, 1:101: "[Duke Mu] . . held funeral marches for them, and mourned for three days"; *Shih chi*, 6.264: 恐諸公子及天下有變，乃祕之，不發喪; *Grand Scribe's Records*, 1:154: "[Li Ssu] because he was afraid lest the noble scions and the world rise up, thus he kept the matter secret and did not start the funeral"; *Shih chi*, 6.265: 行從直道至咸陽，發喪; *Grand Scribe's Records*, 1:155: "They took the Straight Road back to Hsien-yang and started the funeral."

fan 反 **v./n.** "betray, revolt, turn the back on; rebellion"; see also *luan* 亂 and *p'an* 叛

  mou-fan 謀反 **v.o.** "plotting rebellion/revolt";

fang 方 **adj.** "square, **n.** "region, direction"

fei 廢 **v.** "to dismiss, forsake, remove, neglect, abolish, demote, to depose" (a king or an heir)"; *Shih chi*, 3.17: 商容賢者，百姓愛之，紂廢之; *Grand Scribe's Records*, 1:51: "Shang Jung was a worthy man and the families of the hundred cognomens loved him, but Chow dismissed him"; *Shih chi*, 4.126: 殷之末孫季紂，殄廢先王明德，侮蔑神祇不祀 . . . ; *Grand Scribe's Records*, 1:62: "Chow, the last descendant of the Yin, forsook his ancestor's bright virtue, defied the deities, . . . "; *Shih chi*, 7.320: 韓王成無軍功，項王不使之國，與俱至彭城，廢以為侯，已又殺之。臧荼之國，因逐韓廣之遼東，廣弗聽，荼擊殺廣無終; *Grand Scribe's Records*, 1:197: "Since Ch'eng, the King of Han, had not earned any merit in battle, King Hsiang did not let him go to his fief, but took him to P'eng-ch'eng, where he demoted him to a marquis and afterwards killed him."

feng-su 風俗 **n.** "customs and practices"

fu 符 **n.** "tally"; *Shih chi*, 6.237: 符、法冠皆六寸; *Grand Scribe's Records*, 1:136: "The length of tallies and the height of judicial caps were all six *ts'un*"; tallies were slips of wood six *ts'un* in length (14 cm) which were numbered (as opposed to *chuan*) and had serrated edges so they could be matched up; they afforded the bearer access to a restricted area (see Li Chün-ming 李均明, "Han chieh so-chien ch'u-ju fu, chuan yü ch'u-ju ming-chi" 漢簡所見出入符，傳與出入名籍, *Wen shih*, 19 [1983]: 27-35).

  fu-chieh 符節 **n.** "tallies and caducei"; *Shih chi*, 8.362: 秦王子嬰素車白馬，係頸以組，封皇帝璽符節; *Grand Scribe's Records*, 2:38: "The Ch'in king, Tzu-ying, came riding in a white chariot harnessed with white horses, a cord tied around his neck, and holding the seals, tallies and caducei of the august emperor."

fu 祓 **v.** "to purify oneself and perform an exorcism, perform the purgation rites"; *Shih chi*, 4.1321: 周公乃祓齋; *Grand Scribe's Records*, 1:64: "The Duke of Chou purified himself to perform an exorcism"; *Shih chi*, 9.405: 三月中，呂后祓; *Grand Scribe's Records*, 2:125: "In the middle of the third month, Empress Lü performed the purgation rites."

fu 附 **v.** "to come in support, adhere, to support, to attach oneself to someone, to ally oneself to, bind oneself to, give loyalty to"

fu-hsiung 父兄 **n.** "elders"

H

hao 豪 **adj.** "leading, stalwart, valiant, gallant, exceptional"

hao-li 豪吏 **n.** "stalwart officers"

ho-ch'in 和親 **n.** "marital alliance"

hou chiu yüeh 後九月 **adv.** "(in) the month after the ninth" (i.e., an intercalary month)

hou t'u 后土 **v.o.** "to be in charge of the land"; *Shih chi*, 1.35: 至於堯，堯未能舉。舜舉八愷，使主后土，以揆百事，莫不時序; *Grand Scribe's Records*, 1:13: "When it came to Yao's time, he was not yet able to select Shun. He picked the Eight Joyous Ones and let them be in charge of the land, thereby [allowing them] to manage all kinds of affairs, all of which were organized in a timely manner."

Hou t'u 后土 **n.** "Mother Earth"; *Shih chi*, 12.0461: 其明年冬，天子郊雍，議曰：「今上帝朕親郊，而后土毋祀，則禮不答也。」; *Grand Scribe's Records*, 2:230: "In the winter of the following year (113 B.C.), having performed the *Chiao* Sacrifice at Yung, the Son of Heaven had [his officials] deliberate about it: "Now We have personally performed the *Chiao* Sacrifice to the Supreme Deity, but have not made an offering to the Hou-t'u (Mother Earth)."

hsi 喜 **sv./adj.** "to be happy, pleased"; *Shih chi*, 4.142: 厲王喜; *Grand Scribe's Records*, 1:71: "King Li was pleased"; *Shih chi*, 8.347: 後人告高祖，高祖乃心獨喜，自負; *Grand Scribe's Records*, 2:17: "Kao-tsu was secretly pleased and thought highly of himself"; **v.** "to be fond of"; *Shih chi*, 8.342: 高祖為人. . . 仁而愛人，喜施，意豁如也; *Grand Scribe's Records*, 2:5: "Kao-tsu was a man who. . . loved people, was fond of largesse, and openhearted."

hsi 襲 **v.** "to inherit"

　　hsi-hao 襲號 (為) **v.o.** "to inherit the title (as . . .)" usually in connection with becoming emperor; *Shih chi*, 6.267: 皇帝曰：「金石刻盡始皇帝所為也。今襲號而金石刻辭不稱. . .*Grand Scribe's Records*, 1:156: "The [Second] Emperor said: "The inscriptions on the monuments were all done by the First Emperor. Now I have inherited his title and the monument inscriptions failed to use [his posthumous title]."

hsia 下 **v.** "to subdue"; *Shih chi*, 8.370: 下河內，虜殷王，置河內郡; *Grand Scribe's Records*, 2:48: "They subdued Ho-nei, captured the King of Yin, and set up Ho-nei Commandery."

hsia-wu 狎侮 **v.** "to slight, disparage, treat with disrespect, be rude to"; *Shih chi*, 8.344: 高祖因狎侮諸客，遂坐上坐，無所詘; *Grand Scribe's Records*, 2:11: "Taking advantage [of Master Lü's high opinion of him], Kao-tsu, to slight the other guests, proceeded to take the place of honor without a second thought."

hsiang 饗 **v.** "to feast"; *Shih chi*, 8.362: 秦人大喜，爭持牛羊酒食獻饗軍士; *Grand Scribe's Records*, 2:39: "The people of Ch'in were greatly pleased and strove to bring oxen, sheep, wine and food to feast the officers in his army."

hsien 險 **n.** "defile, redoubt"; see also *ku* 固 and *tsu* 阻

hsin 信 **n.** "trust, belief, sincerity"; *Shih chi*, 8.387: 上曰：「豨嘗為吾使，甚有信; *Grand Scribe's Records*, 2:78. "The sovereign said, "Hsi was once an envoy for me, he really had my trust""; **adj.** "trustworthy, true, truthful"; *Shih chi*, 4.120: 「齊栗，信哉！予無知; *Grand Scribe's Records*, 1:59: "Be reverent and true to yourselves. I am ignorant"; *Shih chi*, 7.298. 居縣中，素信謹; *Grand Scribe's Records*, 1:181: "He lived at the county seat, was always truthful and careful"; **v.**

"to trust, verify"; *Shih chi,* 4.138.   五辭簡信; *Grand Scribe's Records,* 1:69: "When the Five Testimonies are examined and verified"; *Shih chi,* 65.2167: 大夫之上，士卒未附，百姓不信; *Grand Scribe's Records,* 7:44: "When the great vassals have not given their loyalty, or the families of the hundred cognomens their trust . . . ."

hsing 幸 **v.** "to favor, visit, favor with a visit"

hua-tsei 猾賊 **adj.** "cunning, crafty, deceiptful"

hui 會 **v.** "to gather, call to a meeting, assize"

huan 患 **n./v.** "worry, worries, dismay, distress"

huang 皇 **adj.** "imperial"

   huang-tzu 皇子 **n.** "imperial scion" (see *kung-tzu* 公子 "noble scion")

hung 薨 **vi.** "to pass on" (of nobles); *Shih chi,* 5.213: 四十二年，安國君為太子。十月，宣太后薨; *Grand Scribe's Records,* 1:119: "In the forty-second year, Lord An-kuo became Heir. In the tenth month, the Queen Dowager Hsüan passed away . . . "; see also *peng* 崩 "to pass away" (of kings); *tsu* 卒 "to expire" (also of nobility), *ssu* "to die" 死 (of common people and those kings/nobles Ssu-ma Ch'ien despises).

huo-lu 貨賂 **n.** "goods and wealth"

J

jao 擾 **n./v.** (1) "confusion; to confuse"; see also *luan* 亂

   jao luan 擾亂 **v.o.** "to throw into confusion"

   jao lung 擾龍 **v.o.** "to tame dragons"

   ta-jao 大擾 **n.** "chaos"

jen 人 **n.** "person, people (especially of a place); a native of; someone"; *Shih chi,* 1.30: 堯曰：「終不以天下之病而利一人」; *Grand Scribe's Records* 1:11: "Yao said, 'In the final analysis I will not displease the people and benefit a single person"; *Shih chi,* 1.31: 自從窮蟬以至帝舜，皆微為庶人; *Grand Scribe's Records* 1:11: "From Ch'iung-ch'an down to the Emperor Shun, they were all obscure and were common people"; *Shih chi,* 1.32: 舜，冀州之人也; *Grand Scribe's Records* 1:11: "Shun was a native of Chi-chou (The Land of Chi)"; *Shih chi,* 1.37: 於是四門辟，言毋凶人也; *Grand Scribe's Records* 1:13: "Thereupon the four gates [of the city] were opened up, showing that he had barred those evil people"; *Shih chi,* 2.77: 知人則智，能官人；能安民則惠，黎民懷之; *Grand Scribe's Records,* 1:33: "If he wre able to know people, then he would be intelligent and therefore capable of appointing people to official positions. If he could bring peace to people, then he would be gracious and therefore the common people would embrace him"; *Shih chi,* 2.88: 桀謂人曰; *Grand Scribe's Records,* 1:38: "He [Chieh] said to someone"; **m.** *Shih chi,* 1.35: 昔高陽氏有才子八人; *Grand Scribe's Records,* 1:13: "In the past the Kao-yang Clan had eight sons of good disposition"; see also *jen min, min, pai hsing, shu min,* and *wan min*

jen min 人民 **n.** "populace, people"; *Shih chi,* 8.359-60: 宛，大郡之都也，連城數十，人民眾，積蓄多，吏人自以為降必死，故皆堅守乘城;   *Grand Scribe's Records,* 2:35: [Yüan] is the capital of a great commandery. It joins several dozen walled cities together, its populace is large, its provisions plentiful, its officers themselves believe that to surrender would mean certain death; *Shih chi,* 10.419:

天下人民未有嗛志; *Grand Scribe's Records* 2:157: "The people of the world have not fulfilled their desire"; see also *jen, min, pai hsing, shu min,* and *wan min*

K

kang-yi 剛毅 **adj.** "obstinate and resolute; steadfast and resolute"; *Shih chi,* 6.237: 剛毅戾深。 *Grand Scribe's Records,* 1:136: "His (First Emperor's) government was obstinate and resolute, perverse and unfathomable."

ke 割 **vt.** "to cut, hack; cede (territory)"

k'ou 寇 **n.** "raiders, plunderers, marauders"

ku 固 **adj./n.** "originally, decidedly; stronghold"; see also *hsien* 險 and *tsu* 阻
 ku-ch'ing **v.** 固請 "to implore"

k'uan-jung **adj.** 寬容 "lenient"

k'uan-hou **adj.** 寬厚 "generous and kind, tolerant and kind"

kuei 跪 **v.** "to kneel"

kuei 鬼 **n.** "ghost, spirit, demon"; *Shih chi,* 6.257: 人主時為微行以辟惡鬼，惡鬼辟，真人至; *Grand Scribe's Records,* 1:149: "If a ruler of men from time to time disguises himself as a commoner and walks around to exorcise evil demons, then the evil demons will be expelled and the Perfected will arrive"; see also *shen* 神.

kuei shen 鬼神 **n.** "spirits, ghosts and spirits"; *Shih chi,* 1.11: 依鬼神以制義; *Grand Scribe's Records,* 1:5: "By complying with ghosts and spirits, he prescribed right conduct."

k'uei 饋 **v.** "to offer food, send food to"; *Shih chi,* 5.189: 更舍上舍，而饋之七牢; *Grand Scribe's Records,* 1:98: "Duke Mu moved him to the finest lodge and offered him the food for seven *lao* sacrifices."

kung 公 **n.** "duke, Your Honor, an honorable person"; for Ch'u region "magistrate"; **adj.** "honorable"
 kung-ch'ing 公卿 **n.** "the honorable [officials] and ministers" (previously rendered as "dukes and ministers, high officials"); we read *kung* as an honorific; thus *San-kung chiu-ch'ing* 三公九卿 becomes "The Three Honorable [Officials] and the Nine Ministers."

kung 共 **adv.** "together, in common, in concert, collectively, working together"

L

lan 蘭 **n.** "orchid"

lau 勞 **v.** "to thank for services rendered"

lei 壘 **n.** "earthworks, embankments (military earthen walls)"

li 吏 **n** "officer, functionary"

lin 臨 **v.** "to hold memorial services for"

ling 令 **n./v.** "command, order; to command, order" (most often as a verb); *Shih chi,* 1.30: 二十年而老，令舜攝行天子之政; *Grand Scribe's Records,* 1:10: "After twenty years he [Yao] stepped back from his duties because of age and ordered Shun to take charge of the administration of a Son of Heaven, recommending him to Heaven"; *Shih chi,* 1.51: 令益予眾庶稻，可種卑溼; *Grand Scribe's Records,* 1:22: "He [Yü] ordered Yi to give the common masses rice to enable them to plant the low, wet lands"; see also *ming* 命.

lou 樓 **n.** "tower, multistoried building"

luan 亂 **n./vt.** "disorder, chaos, rebellion, strife; to create, cause disorder"; see also *fan* 反, *p'an* 叛, and *pien-shih* 變事

  wei-luan 為亂 **v.o.** "to rebel, make rebellion"

lüeh 略 **vt.** "overrun"

  lüeh-ti 略地 **v.o.** "to overrun territory"

lun 論 **v.** "to arbitrate, decide; to sentence"; *Shih chi*, 87.2562: 二世二年七月，具斯五刑，論腰斬咸陽市; *Grand Scribe's Records*, 7:355: "In the seventh month of the second year of the Second Emperor [208 B.C.] it was proclaimed that [Li] Ssu should be sentenced to the five punishments and cut in half at the waist in the market place of Hsien-yang."

M

meng 盟 **n./v.** "oath, convenant; to make an oath, swear a covenant"; see also *Grand Scribe's Records*, 7:102, n. 37, and *sha-hsüeh* 啑血

miao 廟 **n.** "temple, shrine"

mien 免 **vt.** "to dismiss, remove [from a position]"; *Shih chi*, 5.210: 十年 . . . 薛文以金受免。*Grand Scribe's Records*, 1:116: "In the tenth year (297 B.C.), . . . Hsüeh Wen was dismissed because he accepted money"; *Shih chi*, 70.2284: 其後二年，使與齊、楚之相會齧桑。東還而免相，相魏以為秦; *Grand Scribe's Records*, 7:126-7: "In the second year after this (323 B.C.), [Ch'in] sent him to meet the Primer Ministers of Ch'i and Ch'u at Nieh-sang. He then turned his carriage east and was removed as [Ch'in's] prime minister, serving Wei as prime minister on behalf of Ch'in."

min 民 **n.** "people, common people (those ruled)"; *Shih chi*, 8.371: 平原民殺之; *Shih chi*, 8.384: 子肥為齊王，王七十餘城，民能齊言者皆屬齊; *Grand Scribe's Records* 2:71: "Those people who are able to speak the Ch'i language are all to belong to Ch'i"; *Shih chi*, 9.403: 上有歡心以安百姓，百姓欣然以事其上; *Grand Scribe's Records* 2:122: "The sovereign must have a cheerful heart to bring contentment to the people, before the people can joyously serve their sovereign"; see also *jen, jen min, pai hsing, shu min,* and *wan min.*

ming 命 **n./v.** "to order; "to order, command" (most often as a noun); *Shih chi*, 1.3: 蚩尤作亂，不用帝命; *Grand Scribe's Records*, 1:3: "Ch'ih-yu raised troops to rebel and did not implement the emperor's orders"; *Shih chi*, 3.95: 不用命，乃入吾網; *Grand Scribe's Records*, 1:43: "If you don't listen to this order, you will fall into my net!"; *Shih chi*, 3.95: 今夏多罪，天命殛之; "Now The Hsia has committed many crimes and Heaven has ordered me to condemn him"; see also *ling* 令.

mou 謀 **v.** "to conspire, to plot, to consult"; *Shih chi*, 5.195: 晉人患隨會在秦為亂，乃使魏讎餘詳反，合謀會，詐而得會，會遂歸晉; *Grand Scribe's Records*, 1:102: "The Chin people, troubled by Sui Hui's fomenting rebellion from Ch'in, had Wei Ch'ou-yü pretend to defect to Ch'in. They conspired against Hui, and got hold of him through decption. Hui then returned to Chin"; *Shih chi*, 5.196: 二十四年，晉厲公初立，與秦桓公夾河而盟。歸而秦倍盟，與翟合謀擊晉; *Grand Scribe's Records*, 1:103: "In the twenty-fourth year (580 B.C.), when Duke Li of Chin was newly invested, he made a covenant with Duke Huan of

Ch'in from opposite sides of the Ho. When he returned, Ch'in ignored the covenant and plotted with the Ti to assault Chin"; *n.* "plan, plot"; *Shih chi,* 6.232: 韓非使秦，秦用李斯謀，留非，非死雲陽; *Grand Scribe's Records,* 1:132: "Han Fei was sent as an envoy to Ch'in. Ch'in adopted Li Ssu's plan and detained [Han] Fei. [Han] Fei died in Yün-yang"; see also *chi* 計

mu 募 **vt.** "to solicit, enlist, recruit"

   mu-hsi 募徙 **v.phr.** "to enlist and move [people]"; *Shih chi,* 5.212: 二十一年，錯攻 魏河內。魏獻安邑，秦出其人，募徙河東賜爵，赦罪人遷之; *Grand Scribe's Records,* 1:117: "In the twenty-first year (286 B.C.), [Ssu-ma] Ts'o atttacked Ho-nei in Wei. Wei presented An-yi. Ch'in expelled [Ho-nei's] people, enlisted people [of Ch'in] to settle there with awards of rank, or pardoned convicts and sent them there."

   mu-min 募民 **v.o.** "to advertise for men/people; to solicit people"

N

nai 乃 **conj.** "then"

nei 內 **adj./n.** "interior, within; palace"

nüeh 虐 **v./adj.** "to tyrannize; tyrannical"

P

pa 拔 **vt.** "to seize", see also *ch'ü* 取 "to take"

pa 罷 **vt.** "to dismiss (troops)"

pai 拜 **vt.** "to appoint, to kneel and bow the head"

pai hsing 百姓 **n.** "the familes of the hundred cognomens (pre-Han–see *Grand Scribe's Records,* 1:2, n. 16), people (Han)"; *Shih chi,* 5.187: 丕鄭子丕豹奔秦，説繆公 曰：「晉君無道，百姓不親，可伐也」; *Grand Scribe's Records* 1:96: "P'i Cheng's son, P'i Pao, fled to Ch'in and spoke [or "gave advice"] to Duke Mu, "The Lord of Chin is unreasonable and the families of the hundred cognomens are no longer close to him"; *Shih chi,* 8.381: 鎮國家，撫百姓，給餽饟，不絕糧道， 吾不如蕭何; *Grand Scribe's Records* 2:67: "As for guarding a country, calming its people, providing provisions and field rations, and not allowing supply lines to be cut, I am not as good as Hsiao Ho"; see also *jen, jen min, min, shu min, wan min*

p'an 版 **vt.** "to desert, turn against, rebel"; see also *fan* 反, *luan* 亂

pao 暴 **adj.** "violent, brutal"

   pao-feng 暴風 **n.** "squall, tempest"; *Shih chi,* 1.22: 堯使舜入山林川澤，暴風雷雨， 舜行不迷; *Grand Scribe's Records,* 1:9: "Yao had Shun go to the mountains, the forest, the rivers, and the swamps; through squalls and thunderstorms, Shun went on without losing his way."

   pao-n'i 暴逆 **adj.** "brutal (or "violent") and treacherous"

pei 悲 **"sorrowful" adj.** (see also *ai* 哀 "to mourn, grieve; mournful, grieving)

peng 崩 **vi.** "to pass away" (of rulers); see also *hung* 薨 "to pass on" (of nobles); *ssu* "to die" 死 (of common people and those kings/nobles Ssu-ma Ch'ien despises), *tsu* 卒 "to expire" (also of nobility).

pi 壁 **n.** "barricade, fortification(s)"

   chien-pi 堅壁 **v.o.** "to secure fortifications"

p'i 琵 **n.** "lute"

pieh 別 **adj.** "adjutant, deputy" as in *pieh-chiang* 別將 "deputy general"

pien 便 **adj.** "skilled or good at" (8.379); **n.** "advantage"

pien 變 **n./v.** "changing situation, emergency, exigency, crisis; to change"

   pien shih 變事 **adj. n.** "seditious affairs"

p'ing 平 **vt.** "to pacify, suppress; to make peace"; see also *ting* 定 "to stabilize"

pu 卜 **v.** "to divine by shells and bones"; see also *shih* 筮 "to divine by stalks of plants"

S

san 三 **n./adj.** "three, a few"; *San-kung chiu-ch'ing* 三公九卿 "The Three Honorable Officials and the Nine Ministers"

   san tsu 三族 **v. phr.** "to exterminate one's three kindred"; although n. 46 on p. 91 of volume one of *The Grand Scribe's Records* notes that "the families of the father, mother and wife of an individual guilty of a capital crime" were those put to death, there are various theories about this punishment (see also "Extermination of Relatives," in A. F. P. Hulsewé, *Remnants of Han Law*, v. 1 [Leiden: E. J. Brill, 1955], pp. 112-4 ff.); *Shih chi*, 5.179: 二十年，法初有三族之罪; *Grand Scribe's Records*, 1:91: "In the twentieth year (746 B.C.), the punishment of three kindred was first written into law"; *Shih chi*, 5.182: 三年，誅三父等而夷三族，以其殺出子也; *Grand Scribe's Records*, 1:92: "In the third year (695 B.C.), he executed the Three Elders and the others and exterminated their three kindred because they had killed Ch'u Tzu"; *Shih chi*, 8.386: 九年，趙相貫高等事發覺，夷三族; *Grand Scribe's Records*, 2:75-6: "In the ninth year (198 B.C.), the affairs of the Prime Minister of Chao, Kuan Kao, and the others came to light. He and his three kindred were exterminated."

se 色 **n.** "color, look(s), sight; (female) beauty" (the visual aspect of an object)

se 瑟 **n.** "[fifty-string] zither"; *Shih chi*, 69.2248. 秦成，則高臺榭，美宮室，聽竽瑟之音; *Grand Scribe's Records*, 7.101: "If Ch'in succeeds, they will raise high terraces and pavilions, make beautiful houses and buildings, and listen to the music of pipes and zither."

sha hsüeh 啑血 **v.o.** "to sip/drink blood, smear blood on the lips" (usually as part of the *meng* 盟 oath/convenant; the blood used was that of various animals–see also *Grand Scribe's Records* 7:102, n. 37).

shan 擅 **v.** "to act without authority"; *Shih chi*, 8.376: 項羽已救趙，當還報，而擅劫諸侯兵入關，罪三; *Grand Scribe's Records*, 2:60: "After Hsiang Yü had rescued Chao, he should have returned and reported [to King Huai], but without authority he forced the troops of the feudal lords to enter the Pass."

shao 少 **n.** "young, youth"

   shao-nien 少年 **adj. n.** "young bloods"

she 社 **n.** "altar (of soil/earth), local communal altar" (see Mu-chou Poo, *In Search of Personal Welfare, A View of Ancient Chinese Religion* [Albany: State University of New York Press, 1998], p. 149); *she* was often mentioned together with *chi* 稷 , the worship of grain, in official cult practices. During the Chou, people of varied status may have had their own *she.* In Han times the lowest level of officially established *she* was the county. According to one source, twenty-five families could establish one communal *she*-altar, and there were cases where five or ten families established a still smaller "private" *she* for the blessing of the fields. The "Lord of the *She*" (*She kung* 社公) during the Han dynasty developed into what eventually became *T'u-ti kung* 土地公 or "Lords of the Earth."

she 射 **v.** "to shoot"; *Shih chi,* 3.104: 為革囊，盛血，卬而射之，命曰「射天」; *Grand Scribe's Records,* 1:49: "[Emperor Wu-yi] made a leather pouch, filled it with blood, and shot at it, declaring he was 'Shooting at Heaven.'"

she 赦 **v.** "to grant or issue an amnesty, to pardon"; *Shih chi,* 7.329: 項王然其言，乃赦外黃當阬者; *Grand Scribe's Records,* 1:203: "Seeing the truth of his words, King Hsiang pardoned all the men of Wai-huang who were to have been massacred"; *Shih chi,* 8.369: 大赦罪人; *Grand Scribe's Records,* 2:48: "He broadly pardoned those who had committed offenses"; *Shih chi,* 8.381: 六月，大赦天下; *Grand Scribe's Records,* 2:68: "In the sixth month (24 June-23 July 202 B.C.), he granted a general amnesty throughout the world."

she yi 攝衣 **v.o.** "to straighten, tidy one's clothes"

shen 甚 **adv.** "extreme(ly), exceeding(ly), very, quite, awfully; surely (followed by a negative)"

shen jen 神 **n.** "spirits (or deities)"; see also *kuei* 鬼

shen jen 神人 **n.** "spirits (or deities) and human beings (people), spiritual beings"; *Shih chi,* 1.39: 八音能諧，毋相奪倫，神人以和。」; *Grand Scribe's Records,* 1:15: "Make the eight sounds capable of being in harmony and do not let them lose the relationship to each other. The spirits and the human beings will be harmonized by means of music"; *Shih chi,* 12.462: 使各佩其信印，乃可使通言於神人; *Grand Scribe's Records,* 2:232: "Let your envoys each hang their seals of office from their girdles, and then you can send them to converse with spirtual beings."

shih 食 **v.** "to provide with provisions, take sustenance from, hold a fief"; *Shih chi,* 9.398: 今王有七十餘城，而公主酒食數城; *Grand Scribe's Records,* 2:112-3: "Now Your Majesty has more than seventy walled cities and the princess has [only] several walled cities to provide her with provisions."

shih 筮 **v.** "to divine by stalks of plants"

shih 弒 **vt.** "to kill a superior, to fell"

shih 筮 **v.** "to divine by stalks of plants"

shih 事 **n.** "incident, affair"

pien shih 變事 **adj./n.** "seditious affairs"

ssu-shih 死事 **vp.** "died in a military affair"

shih 恃 **v.** "to rely upon"; *Shih chi,* 9.407:固恃大臣諸侯; *Grand Scribe's Records,* 2:129: "He certainly needs to rely upon the great ministers and marquises"; *Shih chi,* 68.2235: 書曰：『恃德者昌，恃力者亡。』; *Grand Scribe's Records,* 7:94: "The *Documents* says, 'One who relies on virtue prospers, One who relies on force perishes.'"; *Shih chi,* 76.2367: 毛遂按劍而前曰：「王之所以叱遂者，以楚國之眾也。今十步之內，王不得恃楚國之眾也，王之命縣於遂手; *Grand Scribe's Records,* 7:205: "Mao Sui put his hand on his sword and stepped foward. 'Your Majesty shouts at me because you have the forces of Ch'u behind you. But within ten paces you cannot rely on the forces of Ch'u. Your life hangs in my hands.'"

shih 勢 **n.** "physical features, topography, aspect, geographical location, circumstances, conditions, power, influence; set-up, position, tendency" (see also comments by Karel van der Leeuw's review of F. Jullien's *Le propension des choses, China Review International,* 4.2 [Fall 1997]: 326-7, and Roger T. Ames, *The Art of Rulership* [Honolulu: University of Hawaii Press, 1983], pp. 65 ff.); *Shih chi,* 5.193: 問其地形與其兵勢盡察;   *Grand Scribe's Records,* 1:101: "The Duke asked about the physical features of the land and the military strength of the Jung"; *Shih chi,* 6.252: 地勢既定; *Grand Scribe's Records,* 1:145: "After the topography was regulated, . . . "; *Shih chi,* 6.255: 如此弗禁，則主勢降乎上，黨與成乎下; *Grand Scribe's Records,* 1:147: "If things like this are not banned, then the ruler's power will be diminished above, and factions will form below"; *Shih chi,* 6.300: 今陳勝首事，不立楚後而自立，其勢不長; *Grand Scribe's Records,* 1:183: "Now when Ch'en Sheng initiated this affair, he failed to enthrone a descendant of Ch'u, but enthroned himself instead; thus his power did not grow."

shih-yi 食邑 **n.** "fief manor"

shih shih 是時 **adv.** "at this time"

shou 授 **v.** "to give (superior to inferior), bestow, grant"

shou 守 **v.** "to guard, to take charge of"

   shou-fan 守藩 **v.o.** "to guard the frontier"; *Shih chi,* 6.280: 乃使蒙恬北築長城而守藩; *Grand Scribe's Records,* 1:145: "Then he had Meng T'ien build the Great Wall in the north and guard the frontier."

shu 屬 **vt.** "to entrust (troops) to, put (troops) under the command of, put (troops, generals) under someone"; see also *fu* 附.

shu 術 **n.** "path, political arts, technique, method"; *Shih chi,* 12.452: 會竇太后治黃老言，不好儒術; *Grand Scribe's Records,* 2:220: "It happened that the Empress Dowager Tou, who was studying the Huang-Lao teachings and did not like the political arts of the Confucians."

shu min 庶民 **n.** "common people, multitude"; *Shih chi,* 4.135: 商王帝辛大惡于民，庶民不忍，訴載武王，以致戎于商牧; *Grand Scribe's Records* 1:67: "When the Shang King Ti-hsin [pi.e., Chow] brought great evil to the people, the common people couldn't endure him and were happy to support King Wu by raising troops at Mu in Shang"; see also *jen, jen min, min, pai hsing* and *wan min.*

ssu 祀 **n.** "sacrifice"; *Shih chi,* 12.451: 孝武皇帝初即位，尤敬鬼神之祀; *Grand Scribe's Records,* 2:220: "When Hsiao Wu Huang-ti first ascended the throne, he was particularly respectful of sacrifices to ghosts and spirits"; see also *chu* 祝 and *tz'u* 祠.

ssu 死 **v.** "to die" 死 (of common people and those kings/nobles Ssu-ma Ch'ien despises); see also *hung* 薨 "to pass on" (of nobles); *peng* 崩 "to pass away" (of rulers); *ssu* "to die" 死 (of common people and those kings/nobles Ssu-ma Ch'ien despises), *tsu* 卒 "to expire" (also of nobility).

ssu-ma 司馬 **o.t.** "marshal" *(passim)*

ssu-shih 死事 **vp.** "died in a military affair"

sui 遂 **adv.** "finally, consequently, then"

sui 祟 **n.** "evil influence"; *Shih chi*, 6.273: 卜曰：「涇水為祟。」; *Grand Scribe's Records*, 1:161: "The oracle was: 'The Ching River is casting its evil influence'"; *Shih chi*, 9.405: 卜之，云趙王如意為祟; *Grand Scribe's Records*, 2:121: "When they divined by shells and bones about it, the result read: 'Ju-yi the King of Chao is casting his evil influence.'"

T

ta-ni wu-tao 大逆無道 **adj.** "treasonous and unprincipled"; *Shih chi*, 8.370: 今項羽放殺義帝於江南，大逆無道; *Grand Scribe's Records*, 2:49: "Now Hsiang Yü has exiled and killed Yi-ti South of the Chiang; this is treasonous and unprincipled"; *Shih chi*, 8.376: 夫為人臣而弒其主，殺已降，為政不平，主約不信，天下所不容，大逆無道，罪十也; *Grand Scribe's Records*, 2:61: "To be a man who was a vassal and yet felled his ruler, who killed those who already surrendered, who in administering was not fair, who though in charge of an agreement was not trustworthy, is something the world cannot forgive, it is treasonous and unprincipled. This is his tenth offense."

ta-p'u 大酺 **n.** "grand bacchanal"

tai fu 大夫 **n.** "honorable guests, grandees"; *Shih chi*, 8.344: 蕭何為主吏，主進，令諸大夫曰 . . . ; *Grand Scribe's Records*, 2:11: "Hsiao Ho (d. 195) was the chief of personnel in charge of the presentation, so he issued an order to all the honorable guests saying . . ."; *Shih chi*, 12.465: 至長安，公卿大夫皆議請尊寶鼎; *Grand Scribe's Records*, 2:234: "On arriving in Ch'ang-an, the honorable [officials], ministers and grandees all deliberated [among themselves] and requested that the precious tripod be treated with utmost respect."

tan 憚 **v.** "to dread"

t'an 袒 **vt.** (also 襢) "to bare the upper arm" (sometimes just to remove an upper garment); baring the left arm is a sign of respect or loyalty (formal rite, bearing the right a sign of guilt or readiness to accept punishment (see also Hsü Chia-lu 許嘉璐, p. 235); *Shih chi*, 10.414: 一呼士皆左袒，為劉氏，叛諸呂; *Grand Scribe's Records*, 2:147: "And with a single call, all the officers bared their left arms. They acted for the Liu Clan and turned against the Lüs."

tang tz'u shih 當此時 **adv.** "meanwhile"

t'ang-mu yi 湯沐邑 **n.** "bath-town"

tao 盜 **n** "bandits"; see also *tsei* 賊

te 德 **n.** "power, psychic power" (in giver as felt by receiver); prestige (especially in a military context); rewards, favors; potency"

t'e 特 **adv./v.** "vainly; to single out"

ti hsing **n.** 地形 "topography"

ti-tzu 適子 **n.** "legitimate son"; *Shih chi*, 5.177: 我復與大駱妻，生適子成; *Grand Scribe's Records*, 1:89: "I, too, gave [my daughter] to be Ta Lo's wife, and she gave birth to his legitimate heir, Ch'eng."

t'ien 填 **v.** "to fill in, fill [a vacancy]; to subdue"; *Shih chi*, 6.238-39: 丞相綰等言：「諸侯初破，燕、齊、荊地遠，不為置王，毋以填之。」; *Grand Scribe's Records*, 1:137: "[Wang] Wan, the Chancellor, and the others said: "The feudal lords have just been destroyed, and the territories of Yen, Ch'i, and Ching are distant; if we do not establish kings there, there is no way we can subdue them."

t'ien-hsia 天下 **n.** "the world"

ting 定 **vt.** "to stablize"

ting 鼎 **n.** "tripod"; *Shih chi,* 1.6: 獲寶鼎，迎日推筴; *Grand Scribe's Records,* 1:3: "He acquired a precious tripod and, by manipulating the counting sticks, made a calendar"; *Shih chi,* 10.430: 因說上設立渭陽五廟。欲出周鼎; *Grand Scribe's Records,* 2:175: "He took the opportunity to advise the sovereign to establish a temple to the Five [Emperors] in Wei-yang, intending to make the Tripods of Chou come out."

to 奪 **v.** "to take away, seize"

ts'ang 蒼 **adj.** "blue, green, laucous"; see also *ch'ing* 青 (N.B., *lü* 綠, *ts'ui* 翠, and *pi* 碧, other synonyms for green, are not commonly found in the *Shih chi; ts'ang* is the most common word for green/blue); *Shih chi,* 9.404: 自決中野兮蒼天舉直！; *Grand Scribe's Records,* 2:123: "If I put an end to myself midst the fields, would blue heaven do what is just?"

   ts'ang-t'ou 蒼頭 **adj./n.** "blue caps"; *Shih chi,* 7.298. 異軍蒼頭特起; *Grand Scribe's Records,* 1:181: "Distinguishing themselves from other forces by wearing blue caps."

tsei 賊 **n.** "thieves"; see also *tao* 盜

tso 左 **adj.** "left" (*passim*)

   tso t'an 左袒 **v.** "to bare the left arm" (a gesture which in the early Chinese social code indicated a sign of respect or loyalty, see Hsü Chia-lu, p. 235); see also *yu t'an* 右袒 "bearing the right arm" (to accept punishment)

tsu 族 **vt.** "to wipe out a clan"; see also *san-tsu* 三族

tsu 阻 **n.** "obstacle, defile"; *Shih chi,* 6.252: 夷去險阻; *Grand Scribe's Records,* 1:145: "Removing defiles and obstacles"; *Shih chi,* 7.330: 項王至，漢軍畏楚，盡走險阻; *Grand Scribe's Records,* 1:203: "When King Hsiang arrived, the Han army, fearful of Ch'u, all fled into the defiles and the mountains"; **v.** "to use as a buffer"; *Shih chi,* 6.224: 阻其山以保魏之河內; *Grand Scribe's Records,* 1:128: "Using the mountains there as a buffer, he defended Ho-nei in Wei"; see also *hsien* 險 and *ku* 固.

tsu 卒 **v.** "to expire" (of nobility); see also *hung* 薨 "to pass on" (also of nobles); *peng* 崩 "to pass away" (of rulers); and *ssu* "to die" 死 (of common people and those kings/nobles Ssu-ma Ch'ien despises).

ts'un-wen 存問 **v.** "inquire about conditions (often from elders of an area), express sympathy and solicitude" (often to people in an area suffering from disaster or warfare)

tsung miao 宗廟 **adj. n.** "ancestral temple, temple of the royal house"; *Shih chi,* 6.236: 賴宗廟之靈，六王咸伏其辜，天下大定; *Grand Scribe's Records,* 1:135: "With the help of the divine spirits from our ancestral temple, all these six kings have been brought to account for their crimes and the world is generally pacified."

ts'ung 從 **vt.** "to accompany, to pursue (an enemy), to follow (some other leader), to submit or subordinate oneself to"

   ts'ung-chi 從騎 **adj. n.** "personal horse"

   ts'ung kuan 從官 **n.** "accompanying officials, suite of officials"; *Shih chi,* 6.264: 會暑，上輼車臭，乃詔從官令車載一石鮑魚以亂其臭; *Grand Scribe's Records,* 1:155: "It happened to be hot and His Highness' insulated carriage smelled. Thus there was an edict for the accompanying officials to order one tan of salted fish loaded on a carriage so as to disguise the smell"; *Shih chi*, 9.404: 王后從官皆諸呂; *Grand Scribe's Records*, 2:124: "The queen's suite of officials were all from the Lüs."

t'u 屠 **vt.** "to put to the sword (city or place), slaughter (people or animals)"

tun-shou 頓首 **v.o.** "to knock/strike/touch the forehead on/against the ground"; see also *chi shou* 稽首, *pai* 拜, and *kuei* 跪.

t'un 屯 **v.** "to set up camp"

t'ung 僮 **n.** "servant-boys"; *Shih chi*, 12.463: 賜列侯甲第，僮千人; *Grand Scribe's Records*, 2:233: "The Emperor bestowed on him an official residence of a full marquis and a thousand servant-boys."

tzu 資 **n.** "resources, status"

tzu-sha 自殺 **v.** "commit suicide"

tzu-tzu 自恣 **v.** "to act/do as one pleases, please oneself (with a bad connotation)"; *Shih chi*, 9.404-5: 趙王不得自恣; *Grand Scribe's Records*, 2:124: "The King of Chao was not able to do as he pleased"; *Shih chi*, 63.2144: 其言洸洋自恣以適己，故自王公大人不能器之; *Grand Scribe's Records*, 7:24: "His words billowed and swirled without restraint, to please himself, and so from kings and dukes down, the great men could not utilize him."

tz'u 慈 **adj.** "compassionate, merciful"

  tz'u-jen **adj.** 慈仁 "merciful and humane, compassionate and humane"

tz'u 賜 **v.** "bestow, grant"; see also *yü* 予 and *shou* 授

tz'u 祠 **v./n.** "to offer sacrifices, sacrifice; worship (the ancestors)"; *Shih chi*, 12.452: 宛若祠之其室，民多往祠; *Grand Scribe's Records*, 2:222: "Yüan-jo sacrificed to the spirit in her home and large numbers of people came to take part"; *Shih chi*, 12.456: 於是天子令太祝立其祠長安東南郊，常奉祠如忌方; *Grand Scribe's Records*, 2:225: "At this, the Son of Heaven ordered the Grand Supplicator to establish such shrines in the southeastern suburbs of Ch'ang-an, where sacrifices were regularly offered according to the methods of [Miu] Chi"; see also *chu* 祝 and *ssu* 祀.

W

wan min 萬民 **n.** "myriad people"; *Shih chi*, 9.402: 凡有天下治為萬民命者; *Grand Scribe's Records*, 2:122: "He who has the mandate to possess the world and manage the myriad people . . . "; see also *jen, jen min, min, pai hsing* and *shu min*.

wang 往 **v.** "to go"; *Shih chi*, 1.38: 舜曰：「然，往矣。」; *Grand Scribe's Records*, 1:14: "Shun said, 'So be it! Go!'"

wei jen 為人 **vp.** "[X] is a man who";

  wei pien 為變 **v.o.** "to cause trouble"

wei 微 **adj.** "in obscurity, in hiding, secretly"

  wei shih 微時 **adj./n.** "when X was [still] unknown"—an epithet for Kao-tsu; *Shih chi*, 9.395: 高祖微時妃也; *Grand Scribe's Records*, 2:105: ". . . a consort from the time when Kao-tsu was [still] unknown."

  wei ssu 微伺 **vt.** "to spy on from hiding, secretly observe"; *Shih chi*, 9.404: 王后從官皆諸呂，擅權，微伺趙王; *Grand Scribe's Records*, 2:124: "The queen's suite of officials were all from the Lüs and they acted on their own authority, spying from hiding on the King of Chao . . .”; *Shih chi*, 66.2179: 且嚭使人微伺之; *Grand Scribe's Records*, 7:57: “Moreover, I have had a man secretly observing him.”

wei 慰 v. “to console”

   wei-hsin 慰心 v.o. “to console (someone's) heart”

wu 物 n. “being, thing”; *Shih chi*, 6.257: 盧生說始皇曰：「臣等求芝奇藥仙者常弗遇，類物有害之者; *Grand Scribe's Records*, 1:149: “Scholar Lu advised the First Emperor [to conceal his whereabouts]: ‘This vassal and others who looked for magic muschrooms and elixirs of long life and immortals regularly failed to find them. It seems there were beings impeding the effort’”; *Shih chi*, 9.405: 三月中，呂后祓，還過軹道，見物如蒼犬; *Grand Scribe's Records*, 2:125: “In the middle of the third month (24 March–22 April 180 B.C.), Empress Lü performed the purgation rites; on her return, as she passed the Chih Road, she saw a being which looked like a blue-green dog . . .”; *Shih chi*, 75.2362: 馮驩曰：「夫物有必至，事有固然。」; *Grand Scribe's Records*, 7:200: “Feng Huan said, ‘. . . Some things are sure to arrive, and some matters are necessarily so.’”

wu-hsing 五行 n. “five phases, five elements”

Wu Tai-fu 五大夫 pn. “Full Grand Man” (Ch'in title)

wu-tao 無道 adj. “unprincipled, devoid of (moral) principle”; see also *ta-ni wu-tao* 大逆無道

Y

ya 雅 adv. “always, never (w/negatives)”

yen 言 n. “words; report”

yen 嚴 adj./n. “severe; severity”

   yen-wei 嚴威 v.o. “lend severity to one's majesty”; *Shih chi*, 9.407: 而諸呂又擅自尊官，聚兵嚴威 . . .; *Grand Scribe's Records*, 2:129: “Yet the Lüs have further acted on their own to exalt their positions, raised troops to lend severity to their majesty . . . ”; *Shih chi*, 87.2563: 太史公曰：李斯以閭閻歷諸侯，入事秦 . . . 持爵祿之重，阿順苟合，嚴威酷刑; *Grand Scribe's Records*, 7.387: “His Honor the Grand Scribe says, ‘Beginning in a simple hamlet, Li Ssu traveled among the feudal lords, then came to serve Ch'in . . . Holding the highest title and salary, he was slavish in his conformity and unscrupulous in his agreement, lent severity to [the emperor's] majesty and harshness to his punishments.”

yen yin 燕飲 vp. “to drink and feast together casually (especially when there should be more formality, as in the case of a king and his subject)”; *Shih chi*, 9.398: 十月，孝惠與齊王燕飲太后前，孝惠以為齊王兄，置上坐，如家人之禮;*Grand Scribe's Records*, 2:112: “In the tenth month, Hsiao Hui-[ti] and the King of Ch'i feasted and drank together in front of the T'ai-hou; Hsiao Hui-[ti] considering that the King of Ch'i was his elder brother, placed him in the honored seat, as was the custom among family members.”

yi 異 n./adj./v. “; difference; rare, different; to make different, distinguish (from)”; *Shih chi*, 1.43: 致異物; *Grand Scribe's Records*, 1:16: “he acquired rare animals . . . ”; *Shih chi*, 4.114: 何異; *Grand Scribe's Records*, 1:56: “What is the difference?”; *Shih chi*, 7.298: 異軍蒼頭特起; *Grand Scribe's Records*, 1:181: “distinguishing themselves from the other forces by wearing blue caps."

yi 邑 **n.** "trade town, small walled town, township; manor"

yi 議 **vt.** "to deliberate, to ask for discussion of, cause the question to be deliberated"; *Shih chi*, 6.236: 其議帝號; *Grand Scribe's Records*, 1:135: "You shall deliberate on the imperial designation"; *Shih chi*, 9.400: 太后稱制，議欲立諸呂為王，問右丞相王陵; *Grand Scribe's Records*, 2:115-6: "The T'ai-hou caused [her orders] to be called decrees, and caused the question of whether to enthrone the Lüs to be deliberated, questioning the Chancellor of the Right, Wang Ling."

yin 因 **adv./v.** "accordingly, then; take advantage of"

yu 囿 **n.** "grounds"; *Shih chi*, 8.369: 諸故秦苑囿園池，皆令人得田之; *Grand Scribe's Records*, 2:48: "As for all the former Ch'in [imperial] reserves, grounds, gardens, and ponds, he ordered that the people be able to farm them"; see also *yüan* 園, *yüan* 苑.

yu ssu 有司 **n.** "authorities, authorities concerned, government officials; petty officials, functionaries"; *Shih chi*, 4.152: 管仲辭曰：「臣賤有司也」; *Grand Scribe's Records*, 1:76: "Kuan Chung declined saying, 'Your vassal is a lowly functionary'"; *Shih chi*, 9.411: 夜，有司分部誅滅梁、淮陽、常山王及少帝於邸; *Grand Scribe's Records*, 2:137: "By nightfall the authorities divided up to execute the kings of Liang, Huai-yang and Ch'ang-shan, along with Emperor Shao in their [respective] residences."

yu-yü 猶豫 **v.** "to hesitate"; see also *tso t'an* 左袒 "to bare the left arm" (a gesture of respect or loyalty)

yu t'an 右袒 **v.** "bearing the right arm" (to accept punishment); see also

yü 予 **vt.** "to give, confer" (see also *tz'u* 賜, *kei* 給); "permit; praise"

yü 語 **n.** "account"; *Shih chi*, 5.203: 其事在商君語中; *Grand Scribe's Records*, 1:109: "These matters can be found in the account of the Lord of Shang."

yü tz'u 於此 **adv.** "at this, at this point"

yü 獄 **adj.** "criminal"; *Shih chi*, 6.264: 趙高故嘗教胡亥書及獄律令法事，胡亥私幸之; *Grand Scribe's Records*, 1:154: "Chao Kao had once taught Hu-hai calligraphy and criminal laws and ordinances. Hu-hai was partial to him"; **n.** "prison"; *Shih chi*, 10.427: 五月，齊太倉令淳于公有罪當刑，詔獄逮徙繫長安; *Grand Scribe's Records*, 2:170: "In the fifth month, the Prefect of the Grand Granary of Ch'i, Master Ch'un-yü, committed an offense and deserved to be punished. The Officer of the Imperial Prison arrested him and moved him to Ch'ang-an for imprisonment."

yü-li 獄吏 **n.** "a law officer who presides in criminal courts, an officer of the court, a warden"; *Shih chi* 6.253: 三十四年，適治獄吏不直者，築長城及南越地; *Grand Scribe's Records*, 1:146: "In the thirty-fourth year Ch'in exiled those law officers who presided in criminal courts but did not uphold justifice and had them build the great wall or sent them to the territory of Nan Yüeh."

yü-yüan 獄掾 **n.** "warden"

yüan 怨 **v.** "resent, harbor resent for"

yüan 原 **adj.** "original"; **n.** "plain, highland, source" (often in Pn.); *Shih chi*, 2.65: 原隰底績，至于都野; *Grand Scribe's Records*, 1:28: "In both the highland and lowlands, [Yü achieved success all the way to the desolate areas"; *Shih chi*, 2.65: 過九江，至于敷淺原; *Grand Scribe's Records*, 1:30: "Crossing the Nine Chiang, to the Plain of Fu-ch'ien"; *Shih chi,* 4.146: . . . 原必塞；原塞，國必亡; *Grand Scribe's Records,* 1:73: " . . . when the source of the rivers is blocked, the state will surely perish."

Yüan-miao 原廟 **Pn.** "Origin Shrine"; see also *T'ai-miao* 太廟

yüan 苑 **n.** "garden, reserve"; *Shih chi,* 8.369: 諸故秦苑囿園池，皆令人得田之; *Grand Scribe's Records,* 2:48: "As for all the former Ch'in [imperial] reserves, grounds, gardens, and ponds, he ordered that the people be able to farm them"; see also *yu* 囿, *yüan* 園.

yüan 園 **n.** "garden"; *Shih chi,* 8.369: 諸故秦苑囿園池，皆令人得田之; *Grand Scribe's Records,* 2:48: "As for all the former Ch'in [imperial] reserves, grounds, gardens, and ponds, he ordered that the people be able to farm them"; see also *yu* 囿, *yüan* 苑.

yüan 垣 **n.** "ramparts, embankment"

yüeh 約 **n.** "agreement, to come to an agreement"

yüeh 説 **adj.** "to be pleased"

yung 用 **v.** "to use, employ, hold"

yung-shih 用事 **v.o.** "to exercise power, have charge of affairs"; *Shih chi,* 1.38: 堯老，使舜攝行天子政，巡狩。舜得舉用事二十年，而堯使攝政; *Grand Scribe's Records,* 1:13: "When Yao stepped back, he had Shun take charge of the administration of the Son of Heaven and inspect local governments. After Shun had been promoted, he had charge of affairs for twenty years, and then Yao put him in charge of administration."

yung-hsiang 永巷 **n.** "the Long Lane, i.e., the harem" (it also became a place of imprisonment for palace women); *Shih chi,* 9.397: 呂后最怨戚夫人及其子趙王，迺令永巷囚戚夫人，而召趙王; *Grand Scribe's Records,* 2:109: "Empress Lü, harboring the greatest resentment for Lady Ch'i and her son the King of Chao, ordered the Long Lane [officials] to confine Lady Ch'i and summoned the King of Chao."

yung-hui 擁簪 **v.o.** "to hold/clasp a broom (often a sign of respect used to greet an honored guest)"

Shih chi Chi-chieh (Collected Explanations of the Grand Scribe's Records) Preface

[1] Pan Ku 班固 (32–92) has an account which reads[1]: "Ssu-ma Ch'ien relied on *Tso shih* 左氏 (Mr. Tso) and the *Kuo yü* 國語 (Conversations from the States), he took from the *Shih pen* 世本 (Genealogical Origins) and the *Chan-kuo ts'e* 戰國策 (Intrigues of the Warring States), he followed the *Ch'u Han ch'un-ch'iu* 楚漢春秋 (Annals of Ch'u and Han), joining them to [a narration of] later events until he reached the T'ien-han 天漢 era (100–97 B.C.).[2] In his account of Ch'in and Han he is detailed. When it comes to taking from the classics, selecting from the commentaries, and separating the affairs recorded in the various schools,[3] very often he leaves things out and sometimes there are contradictions. Surely these [sources] in which he waded and hunted were broad and extensive. Threading together classics and commentaries, galloping madly through the period of several thousand years from ancient to modern, former to later, in this he already showed diligence. Yet again, in his judging of right and wrong, he goes somewhat against the Sages; in discussing the Great Way, he gives precedence to Huang-Lao 黃老 and slights the Six Classics; in recounting the wandering knights-errant he rejects gentlemen awaiting an apt position to promote heroic scoundrels[4]; in telling of 'those who amass wealth,' he reveres those who have potential and profit and disparages those in poverty or humble station.[5] These are the points where his vision was obscured.

[1]Aside from Watson's translation of this section in *Ssu-ma Ch'ien,* pp. 68-69, Chang Lieh's 張烈 rendition in his *Han shu chu-yi* 漢書注譯 (Haikow: Hai-nan Kuo-chi Hsin-wen, 1997), 3.2751-52 and 2761 has also proved a useful reference.

[2]These sources are listed in an approximate chronological progression. The *Tso chuan* 左傳 was known to Pan Ku as *Tso shih* 左氏 (cf. *Han shu,* 30.1713). On the textual history of the *Kuo yü* 國語 (Conversations of the States) see the notice by Chang I-jen, William G. Boltz and Michael Loewe in *Early Chinese Texts, A Bibliographic Guide,* Michael Loewe, ed. (Berkeley: The Society of the Study of Early China and the Institute of East Asian Studies, University of California, 1993), pp. 264-5. For the *Chan-kuo ts'e* 戰國策 (Intrigues of the Warring States) see the entry by Tsuen-hsuin Tsien in Loewe, *Early Chinese Texts,* pp. 1-11. The *Shih pen* 世本 (Genealogical Origins) was apparently based on genealogies of the pre-Ch'in era and probably edited in the version that exists today by Liu Hsiang 劉向 (77-6 B.C.); lost in the Sung dynasty, it was reconstructed by Ch'ing scholars and is most easily available in the modern compendium *Shih-pen pa-chung* 世本八種 (Shanghai: Shang-wu, 1957) which contains a preface further tracing its textual history. On the *Ch'u Han ch'un-ch'iu* 楚漢春秋 see Chin Te-chien's 金德建 entry "Ch'u-Han ch'un-ch'iu te chi-shih fan-wei he hsing-chih" 楚漢春秋的記事範圍和性質 in Chin's *Ssu-ma Ch'ien so-chien shu-k'ao* 司馬遷所見書考 (Shanghai: Shang-hai Jen-min, 1963), pp. 320-7.

[3]We read *shu chia* 數家 as "various schools," i.e., the *Chu-tzu pai-chia* 諸子百家 (One Hundred Schools); cf. also Pan Piao's 班彪 biography on *Han shu,* 40.1325 and Watson's translation in his *Ssu-ma Ch'ien,* p. 68.

[4]The account of the knights-errant can be found in *Shih chi* Chapter 124.

[5]Referring to the "Huo-chih lieh-chuan" 貨殖列傳, *Shih chi* Chapter 129.

However, even Liu Hsiang and Yang Hsiung who were extensively read in many books both claimed [Ssu-ma] Ch'ien had the 'talent of an excellent historian'[6] and admired his skill in recounting events and their causes, his eloquence without flowery language, his substantiveness without becoming vulgar; his writing is direct, his narrative complete. He does not falsely lend praise to people nor hide their faults. For this reason people call his work a 'true record.'"[7]

I think that which [Pan] Ku said is acclaimed as correct by the present age. Although at times there are flaws [in the *Shih chi*], Ssu-ma Ch'ien was actually able to control [his materials] to form his own school,[8] to put it in general terms, he was indeed a capacious talent famous in his age.

[3] When one examines and compares [various editions of] this book, [one finds] the literary phrasing is not the same, there are some accounts which are longer, some shorter, so there is no way to discern their reliability; among those contemporaries who are deluded [by this] some decide on "this reading," others follow "that reading, so that correct and incorrect are exchanged, false and true are mixed together. [*4*] Formerly, the Palace Attendant Grandee Hsü Kuang 徐廣 of Tung-wan 東莞 investigated the accuracy of many editions,[9] for these [reasons] he wrote the *Yin-yi* 音義 (Pronunciations and Meanings [of the *Grand Scribe's Records*]), completely arraying variants and recording explanations; there were some things that he clarified, but it is greatly regretted that he omitted [so much].

I have used my humble opinions to increase and extend Mr. Hsü['s work]. I took from the Classics, the commentaries, and the Hundred Schools, together with the sayings of the Former Confucians, and anything of benefit I copied them all. I removed the unfounded language and took their essential truths. Where the meaning sometimes resides in what was suspect, I laid out [texts] of several scholars. As for the one who the *Han shu yin-i* 漢書音義 (Pronunciations and Meanings in the History of the Han) calls "Your subject, Tsan 瓚," no one knows his name. Now I directly say: "Tsan says."[10] Further, for all those who have no name [recorded],[11] I have only said *"Han shu yin-i."* From time to time I present my own insignificant ideas and there are [some things in them] which can

---

[6]This expression is not found in their extant writings; *Hsi-ching tsa-chi*, 4.3a, suggests he was generally known under this epithet, but this may reflect no more than a reflection on this passage by the compilor of the *Hsi-ching tsa-chi*.

[7]Original can be found on *Han shu*, 62:2737-38.

[8]*Ch'eng yi-chia yen* 成一家言 has been widely debated and is also understood as "to complete [a book] of a single family" among other readings. On this controversy see Chang Ta-k'o 張大可, *Ssu-ma Ch'ien yi-chia yen* 司馬遷一家言. In *Ssu-ma Ch'ien yü Hua Hsian ts'ung-shu* 司馬遷與華夏叢書. Sian: Shan-hsi Jen-min Chiao-yü Ch'u-pan-she, 1995.

[9]On Hsü Kuang and his work see the entry by Scott W. Galer in the "Biographical Sketches of *Shih chi* Commentators" section appended to this volume.

[10]There are a number of books by this title recorded in the various bibliographies of the dynastic histories (see *Sui shu*, 33.953 and *Chiu T'ang shu*, 46.1988). None of these works is by anyone named "Ts'an," however. "So-yin" (*Shih chi*, "Chieh-chieh hsü," p. 5) identifies him as Fu Tsan 傅瓚.

[11]"Cheng-yi" notes that the name Meng K'ang 孟康, to whom the *Han shu yin-yi* is attributed in the bibliographies of the T'ang official histories (cf. *Chiu T'ang shu*, 46.1988, and *Hsin T'ang shu*, 58.1454), has been added by later scholars.

augment and supplement [the comments of previous scholars]. Like [the light of] those small stars connects with the morning sun,[12] or the flying dust collects on Sacred Mount Hua 華,[13] I take Hsü as my base text and call [my comments] the *Chi-chieh* 集解 (Collected Explanations). Places where there is no detailed information [in other works] I left blank, not daring to offer my personal theory. Since the minds of people are not identical, what they hear and see they perceive as different words. What Mr. Pan [Ku] called "neglecting and omitting . . . [and] . . . having contradictions," I shall not argue in detail which to accept and which to reject. I am ashamed not to have the 'great learning of Hsü Ch'en' 胥臣 or the 'broad familiarity with things' of Tzu Ch'an 子產.[14] Since I am reckless in speech and have insignificant learning, I defile old history. How can it be sufficient to involve [in my commentary] those who have virtue? I hope this will be more worthy than those who do not use their minds at all.

translated by William H. Nienhauser, Jr.

[12]Alluding to Mao #21, "Hsiao hsing" 小星.

[13]Suggesting that his work is cumulative and although only "flying dust" will eventually make a Sacred Mount Hua.

[14]Hsü Ch'en (see Fang Hsüan-ch'en, p. 390), was a minister of the state of Chin. Hsü was his *nomen* and Ch'en his *praenomen*. He was also called Chiu Chi 臼季,(Chiu was his fief and Chi his *agnomen*). "The great learning of Hsü Ch'en" is a quotation from the fourth of the "Chin yü" 晉語 sections of the *Kuo yü* (Shanghai: Shang-hai Ku-chi, 1988, 10.382).

Tzu Ch'an was the grandson of Duke Mu 穆 of Cheng (r. 627-606 B.C.). According to *Tso chuan* (Yang, *Tso chuan,* p. 1221, Chao 1), the Lord of Chin once called Tzu-ch'an "a gentleman with a broad familiarity of things" because he expounded so eloquently on the origins of the lord's illness.

Ssu-k'u ch'üan-shu Resumes on Shih chi and Shih chi Chi-chieh

Introduction

The compilation of the *Ssu-k'u ch'üan shu* 四庫全書, as well as its *Annotated Catalog* (*Ssu-k'u ch'üan-shu tsung-mu t'i-yao* 四庫全書總目題要) has been the topic of many scholarly inquiries throughout the twentieth century, both in China and the West. The foci of these studies vary, but nearly all discuss the immensity of the task of compilation, the inevitable resulting errors, and the power struggles among the editors. These issues are important to all scholars who have need to utilize the vast collection of "the Emperor's Four Treasuries," from social scientist to literary critic. A knowledge of the strengths, weaknesses, and miscellaneous idiosyncracies of China's largest *ts'ung shu* is helpful in assesing the value of the individual texts contained therein. Careful readings of the bibliographic summaries in the *Annotated Catalog* can provide such information, if used with caution.

The purpose of this appendix is not a general analysis on the composition and reliablility of the *Annotated Catalog*, but rather an annotated translation of the *t'i yao* entries on the *Shih chi*, and its three primary commentaries, namely the *Chi-chieh*, *So-yin*, and *Cheng-i*.[1] (For excellent studies of the *Annotated Catalog* as a whole, please refer to the selected bibliography, compiled by Bruce Knickerbocker, following the translations.) A close reading of the accompanying notes will illustrate that the editors of the *Annotated Catalog* were careless in more than one instance, with errors ranging from incorrect citations to complete misrepresentation. It is our hope that the annotated translations of these bibliographic summaries will provide accurate and updated information regarding the textual history of the *Shih chi* as it appeared in the *Ssu-k'u ch'üan shu*, and to also point out some of the weaknesses of the *Annotated Catalog*, in order to remind sinologists from all fields to utilize its summaries with care.

---

[1]The *Chi-chien, So-yin, and Cheng-yi* are here referrred to as the separate titles they once were. After the Sung dynasty, however, they were incorporated into the standard San-chia chu 三家注 (Three Scholar's Commentary) and became parts of the received text of the *Shih chi.* We therefore generally refer to these titles in the notes as "Chi-chieh," "So-yin," and "Cheng-yi."

N.B. Abbreviations in these notes refer to Bruce Knickerbocker's Bibliography appended to this section.

Ssu-k'u ch'üan-shu Resume for the *Grand Scribe's Records*[2]
The Grand Scribe's Records in 130 *chüan.* The Palace Treasury Edition[3]

Compiled by Ssu-ma Ch'ien 司馬遷 (145-86? B.C.) of the Han 漢, supplemented by Ch'u Shao-sun 褚少孫 (*ca.* 104-*ca.* 30 B.C.).[4] The traces of the events of Ch'ien's life are all in his own memoir in the *Han shu* 漢書 (History of the Han Dynasty).[5] Shao-sun, relying on Chang Shou-chieh's 張守節 (fl. 725-735) *Cheng yi* 正義 (Rectified Interpretations) citing the theories of Chang Yen 張晏 (fl. 250),[6] is considered to be a native of Ying-ch'uan 穎川 who was an *Po-shih* 博士 (Erudite) during the reigns of Emperor Yüan 元 (r. 48-32 B.C.) and Emperor Ch'eng 成 (r. 32-6 B.C.).[8] [Chang Shou-chieh] also cites the *Ch'u Yi*

[2]My thanks to J. Michael Farmer and Bruce Knickerbocker, who contributed to portions of the draft translation of this section, and to the current (Fall 2000) Saturday *Shih chi* Seminar, who offered a number of suggestions for emendation of the translation and the notes. I assume responsibility for all errors and infelicities. The base text used for this translation is *Ch'in-ting Ssu-k'u ch'üan-shu tsung-mu* 欽定四庫全書總目 (rpt. Taipei: Shang-wu Yin-shu-kuan, 1983), 45.4a-6b.

[3]The "nei-fu k'an-pen" 內府刊本 referred to here is that prepared by the Wu-ying Tien 武英殿 as a part of the twenty-four dynastic histories published in 1739; generally known as the "Tien pen" 殿本, it was in turn based on the Pei-chien 北監 (Northern Academy) edition of 1598 prepared by Liu Ying-ch'iu 劉應秋 *et al.* See also Ho Tz'u-chün, pp. 207-11.

[4]There is little biographical information about Ch'u Shao-sun. Most of what we know comes from his mention in the biography of Wang Shih 王式 on *Han shu,* 88.3610. For a thorough study of his life, which incorporates all remnants of biographical information, see Timoteus Pokora, "Ch'u Shao-sun—the Narrator of Stories in the *Shih-chi,*" *Estratto di Annali dell'Instituto Orientale di Napoli,* 41 (1981): 403-30.

[5]See *Han shu,* 62.2707-39.

[6]Chang Yen 張晏 was from Chung-shan 中山 during the Three Kingdoms period. He authored the *Hsi Han shu yin shih* 西漢書音釋 (Sounds and Explanations on the History of the Western Han). See Kuo Yün-k'ai 郭雲楷, *Tseng-kuang Shang yu lu t'ung pien* 增廣尚友錄統編 (Shanghai: Chin Chang T'u-shu-chü Yin-hang 錦章圖書局印行, 1927), 7.3b. See also Yves Hervouet, *Le Chapitre 117 du Che-ki (Biographie de Ssu-ma Siang-jou)* (Paris: Presses Universitaires de France, 1972), p. 232.

[7]The Ying-ch'uan region was located in the Western part of modern Honan province, near Hsü-ch'ang City 許昌市 (T'an Ch'i-hsiang, 3:7-8).

[8]This information is not found in any remaining notes from Chang Shou-chieh's *Cheng-yi.* It is conceivable that it was once included in the *Cheng-yi,* yet since it is still intact in the *So-yin,* an earlier work, this seems to be a mistake. See Ssu-ma Chen's 司馬貞 (fl. 720)

chia chuan 褚顗家傳 (Family Memoir of Ch'u Yi)[9] which considers Shao-sun to be the grandson of the younger brother of Ch'u Ta 褚大,[10] the Prime Minister of Liang 梁. [Shao-sun] was an Erudite during the reign of Emperor Hsüan 宣 (r. 73-48 B.C.)[11] and lived in P'ei 沛.[12] He served the great Confucian scholar Wang Shih 王式 and for this reason was called Master.[13] The two theories of [Chang Yen] and the [*Ch'u Yi chia-chuan*] are different. But the time between the end of the reign of Emperor Hsüan and the beginning of the reign of Emperor Ch'eng is not more than seventeen or eighteen years, and the gap from one to the other is indeed not far.

In examining [Ssu-ma] Ch'ien's postface, in all there are 12 basic annals, 10 chronological tables, 8 treatises, 30 hereditary houses, and 70 memoirs for a total of 130 chapters.[14] Ssu-ma Ch'ien's memoir in the *Han shu* claims that [the *Shih chi*] is missing 10 chapters, with [titles] recorded but no text.[15] Chang Yen's commentary considers that

"So-yin" note preceding *Shih chi,* 12.451.

[9]This text, according to Pokora, was "mentioned evidently" by Wei Ling 韋稜 (sixth century) in the *Han shu hsü-hsün* 漢書續訓 (Continued Instructions of the *History of the Han Dynasty*; cited in "So-yin," *Shih chi,* 12.451). He notes that *Ch'u Yi chia chuan* is recorded in the *Sui shu* 隋書 "Bibliographic Monograph" as *Ch'u-shih chia chuan* 褚氏家傳 by Ch'u Yi 褚顗 and others, in one *chüan*. He also notes that both of the T'ang histories, in their respective bibliographic monographs, present slightly different information: *Ch'u-shih chia chuan* by Ch'u Chieh 褚結, annotated by Ch'u T'ao 褚陶, also in one *chüan*. See Pokora, "Ch'u Shao-sun," p. 405. See also *Harvard-Yenching Institute Sinological Index Series,* No. 10, "Combined Indices to Twenty Historical Bibliographies" (rpt. Taipei: Chinese Materials and Research Aids Service Center, Inc., 1966), 5:09832.

[10]Ch'u Ta is listed as a disciple of Tung Chung-shu 董仲舒. He also served as chancellor to the state of Liang. See *Shih chi,* 121.3129.

[11]The *Ssu-k'u* editors perpetuate their error here and in the following two sentences by continuing to quote Chang Shou-chieh. The error is taken a step further with this quotation, as it should be attributed to Wei Ling 韋稜, as quoting *Ch'u-shih chia chuan*. See note preceding chapter in *Shih chi,* 12.451. Wei Ling lived in the sixth century and was a scholar and high dignitary. See Pokora, "Ch'u Shao-sun," p. 405; Yao Ssu-lien 姚思廉 (d. 637), *Liang shu* 梁書 (Peking: Chung Hua Shu-chü, 1973), 12.225-26; Li Yen-shou 里延壽 (ca. 629), *Nan shih* 南史 (Peking: Chung Hua Shu-chü, 1975), 58.1437.

[12]P'ei 沛 district corresponds to P'ei County in modern Kiangsu province (T'an Ch'i-hsiang, 2:19-20).

[13]Wang Shih 王式 had earlier served as a tutor to the King of Ch'ang-yi 昌邑 (See *Han shu,* 88.3610; Pokora, "Ch'u Shao-sun," pp. 403-7.) The designation *Hsien-sheng* 先生 was a step below the *Po-shih* 博士 in the Han-dynasty bureaucracy. See Pokora, "Ch'u Shao-sun," pp. 420-1.

[14]See *Shih chi,* 130.3319.

[15]See *Han shu,* 62.2724.

after Ssu-ma Ch'ien's death, the "Basic Annals of Emperor Ching," 景帝[16] the "Basic Annals of Emperor Wu," 武帝[17] the "Li shu" 禮書 (Treatise on the Rites), [18] the "Yüeh shu" 樂書 (Treatise on Music), [19] the "Ping shu" 兵書 (Treatise on the Military),[20] the "Han hsing yi-lai chiang-hsiang nien-piao" 漢興以來將相年表 (Chronological Tables of Generals and Ministers Since the Rise of the Han),[21] the "Jih-che lieh-chuan" 日者列傳 (Memoir of the Diviners),[22] the "San-wang shih-chia" 三王世家 (Hereditary Houses of the Three Kings),[23] the "Kuei ts'e lieh-chuan" 龜筴列傳 (Memoir of the Tortoise and Milfoil Diviners),"[24] and the "Fu, Chin lieh-chuan" 傅靳列傳 (Memoirs of Fu, Chin [and the Marquis of K'uai-ch'eng])[25] were lost. Liu Chih-chi's 劉知幾 (661-721) *Shih t'ung* 史通 (Mastery of History), on the other hand, considers that the 10 chapters were not completed, having titles only, and criticized Chang Yen's opinion as incorrect.[26] Today, when we examine the memoirs of the Diviners and the Tortoise and Milfoil Diviners, they have [sections headed by] by "His Honor the Grand Scribe says" as well as "Master Ch'u says."[27] This is clear evidence of the addition of a fragmented text. We should consider Liu Chih-chi as correct. However, the "Ch'un-ch'iu Chia" 春秋家 (School of Annals) [section] of the *Han shu* "Yi-wen chih" 藝文志 (Treatise on Literature) records the *Shih chi* in 130 chapters, and does not speak of deficencies.[28] Probably the official edition of that time

[16]*Shih chi,* 11.439.

[17]*Shih chi,* 12.451.

[18]*Shih chi,* 23.1157.

[19]*Shih chi,* 24.1175.

[20]As quoted in the "Chi-chieh," Chang Yen does not mention the "Ping shu" 兵書, but the "Lü shu" 律書; see *Shih chi,* 130.3321. When Chang Yen is quoted with regard to this matter in the *Han shu* (see *Han shu,* 62.2724-5, n. 13), *ping* is in place of *lü*. Since the "Chi-chieh" is the earliest of the three commentaries, and Chang Yen is cited in each of the three, it is plausible that a copying error resulted in this mistake. Yen Shih-ku's 顏師古 (581-645) comments in n. 13, on *Han shu,* 62.2724, say that Chang Yen was wrong, thus leading us to believe that he must not have been looking at the "Chi-chieh" commentary. However, Takigawa (25.2) and Wang Li-ch'i (25.897) argue that *"P'ing shu"* and *"Lü shu"* were alternate titles for the same chapter.

[21]*Shih chi,* 22.1119.

[22]*Shih chi,* 127.3215.

[23]*Shih chi,* 60.2105.

[24]*Shih chi,* 128.3223.

[25]*Shih chi,* 98.2707.

[26]See Liu Chih-chi 劉知幾 (661–721), *Shih-t'ung t'ung-shih* 史通通釋 (*Pai-pu ts'ung-shu*), 12.6b. 至宣帝時遷外孫楊惲祖述其書遂宣布焉而十篇未成有錄而已。 "At the time of Emperor Hsüan (r. 73–48 B.C.), [Ssu-ma Ch'ien's] grandson Yang Yün transmitted from his ancestor his book and made it [known to the] public. But there were ten chapters which were not complete, having titles only."

[27]See *Shih chi,* 127.3221 and 128.3223-5.

[28]Again, contrary to the editors of the *Ssu-k'u t'i-yao,* the *Han shu* "Treatise on

already had [Ch'u] Shao-sun's amendments combined into one volume. Looking at its two memoirs of the "Diviners" and the "Tortoise Shell and Milfoil Diviners," both have [sections] that say, "When your subject was a Palace Attendant." This book must have been presented [to the imperial court]." For this reason there is this designation ["your subject"]. The words "Master Ch'u said" were probably interpolated by people of later times, so as to mark them separately. Chou Mi's 周密 (1232-1298) *Ch'i-tung yeh-yü* 齊東 野語 (Rustic Words from the East of Ch'i) draws words from the comment on Ssu-ma Hsiang-ju's 司馬相如 memoir as saying "Yang Hsiung 揚雄 (53 B.C.–A.D. 18) believes that ornate rhapsodies encourage [indulgence] a hundred times while indirectly criticizing once."[29] [*Ch'i-tung yeh-yü*] also draws from Kung-sun Hung's 公孫宏 memoir as saying, "During the Yüan-shih 元始 reign period of Emperor P'ing 平 (r. 1–6), an edict bestowed Hung's descendants with noble rank."[29] Chiao Hung's 焦竑 (1540-1620) *Pi-sheng* 筆乘 cites [the line] from Chia Yi's 賈誼 (200–168 B.C.) memoir that "Chia Chia 賈嘉 was most fond of learning; by the time of Emperor Shao the Filial 孝昭 (r. 86–73 B.C.), he was ranked as one of the Nine Ministers 九卿."[30] None of these things could have been seen by [Ssu-ma] Ch'ien.[31]

Wang Mao-hung's 王懋竑 (1668-1741) *Pai-t'ien tsa-chu* 白田雜著 also says that the *Shih chi* only records years and does not have the year names.[32] Today, at the top of the "Shih-erh chu-hou nien-piao" 十二諸侯年表 (Chronological Table of the Twelve Feudal Lords), there is a line [which reads] "*keng-shen* 庚申, *chia-tzu* 甲子, etc."[33] This was added by people of later times. It is not only that some [things] were scattered and lost, but at the same time that some things were altered. These years are distant, and now [these lost or altered things] cannot be examined. However, although the words and phrases were disordered, perhaps [this situation] was inevitable.

As for the book as a whole, it is still Ch'ien's original version. Chiao Hung's *Pi-sheng*, based on Ju Ch'un's 如淳 note on the "Comment" on Chang T'ang's 張湯 memoir, considers Feng Shang 馮商 and Meng Liu 孟柳 to be among those who

---

Literature" does indeed speak of deficiencies. It records, "*His Honor the Grand Scribe* in 130 *p'ien*; [titles for] ten *p'ien* are recorded but have no text" 太史公百三十篇。十篇有錄無書。See *Han shu*, 30.1714. For an important discussion of the early transmission of the *Shih chi*, see Ch'en Chih 陳直, "Han Chin jen tui *Shih chi* te ch'uan-po chi ch'i p'ing-chia" 漢晉人對史記的 傳播及其評價 in *Chung-kuo shih-hsüeh lun-chi* 中國史學論集, Wu Tse 吳澤 ed. (Shanghai: Shanghai Jen-min, 1980), pp. 234–58.

[29]See Chou Mi (1232–1298), *Ch'i-tung yeh-yü* (*Pai-pu ts'ung-shu*), 10.2b. This passage is also recorded in Chiao Hung 焦竑, *Chiao-shih Pi sheng* 焦氏筆乘, *Yüeh-ya T'ang ts'ung-shu* 粵雅堂叢書 (*Pai-pu ts'ung-shu*), 2.10b.

[30]See Chiao Hung, *Chiao-shih Pi sheng*, 2.10b.

[31]Each of these three situations appears to be anachronistic, suggesting that they were added to the text sometime after Ssu-ma Ch'ien completed it.

[32]See Wang Mao-hung, *Pai-t'ien tsa-chu* (*SKCS*), 8.13b-14a.

[33]See *Shih chi*, 14.512, 515, etc.

supplemented it.[34] [Chiao Hung] also considers, based on Yang Ching's 楊經 memoir in the *Hou Han shu* 後漢書 (History of the Later Han), that [they] had cut Ch'ien's book to something over 100,000 words, pointing out that the current *Shih chi* is not the original book.[35] This is not true. Since the Chin 晉 and the T'ang 唐, his manuscript has been transmitted without any major differences. Only when in the twenty-third year of the K'ai-yüan 開元 reign period of the T'ang dynasty (735 A.D.), a decree exalted the "Lao Tzu lieh-chuan" 老子列傳 (Memoir of Lao Tzu) above the "Po Yi lieh-chuan" 伯夷列傳 (Memoir of Po Yi).[36]

Ch'ien Tseng's 錢曾[37] *Tu-shu min-ch'iu chi* 讀書敏求記[38] says that there is still

[34]Here the Ssu-k'u editors must be referring to the *Han shu*, as there is no comment by Ju Ch'un about Feng Shang and Meng Liu in any notes in Chang T'ang's biography in the *Shih chi*. See *Shih chi*, 122.3137-44 and 3154-5. The *Han shu*, however, does contain this reference. In *chüan* fifty-nine, "The Biography of Chang T'ang," Ju Ch'un says: "Pan Ku's *Catalog* (*Mu lu* 目錄) [says] Feng Shang was a person of Ch'ang-an. During the time of Emperor Ch'eng, because he knew how to compose books he waited for a summons at the Golden Horse Gate (*Chin-ma Men* 金馬門). He received a summons to append more than ten *chüan* of the *T'ai-shih kung shu*." Another note by Yen Shih-ku says: "Yen Shih-ku said: 'Liu Hsin's 劉歆 *Seven Epitomes* (*Ch'i lüeh* 七略) said that Feng Shang was a person of Yang-ling 陽陵. He studied the [Book of] *Changes* and served Wu-lu Ch'ung-tsung 五鹿充宗. He knew how to compose books, was broadly versed and had an excellent memory. He waited together with Meng Liu for a summons. He narrated several biographies, but before he was finished, he met with an illness and died.'" See *Han shu*, 59.2657.

[35]The Ssu-k'u editors err on Yang's name: it should be Yang Chung 楊終, not Yang Ching (經). See *Hou Han shu*, 48.1599.

[36]"Exalted . . . above" in the sense of "giving primacy to" by causing it to be placed at the head of the memoir section. See Ch'ien Tseng 錢曾 (1629-after 1699), *Tu-shu min-ch'iu chi* 讀書敏求記, *Hai-shan Hsien-kuan ts'ung-shu* 海山仙館叢書 (*PPTSCC*), 2.1a.

[37]Ch'ien Tseng 錢曾 (1629-after 1699) was a bibliophile and twenty-fifth generation descendant of Ch'ien Liu 錢鏐 (852-932), founder of the state of Wu-Yüeh, one of the "Ten Kingdoms" which arose during the transitional period between the T'ang and Sung dynasties. His father and grandfather were also bibliophiles, thus his collection was primarily inherited from his grandfather Ch'ien Ch'ien-yi 錢謙益 (1582-1664). See Hummel, p. 157.

[38]The *Tu-shu min-ch'iu chi* was compiled by Ch'ien Tseng between 1669 and 1684. The work, in 4 *chüan*, lists 601 Sung and Yüan works and manuscripts with detailed comparative annotations concerning editions. It was first printed in 1726 by Chao Meng-sheng 趙孟升 and passed through at least three subsequent printed editions during the Ch'ing period. The catalog was highly prized by scholars and apparently even circulated in manuscript form. An annotated and collated edition by Chang Yü 章鈺 appeared in 1926 under the title *Ch'ien Tsun-wang tu-shu min-ch'iu chi chiao-cheng* 錢遵王讀書敏求記校證. Ch'ien also compiled other catalogues. For more information, see Hummel, p. 157.

a Sung woodblock print.[39] Today we have not seen it. During the Southern Sung Chang Ts'ai 張材 of Kuang-han 廣漢 also excised Ch'u Shao-sun's amendment. Chao Shan-fu 趙山甫 also regarded its incompleteness as a defect. He took Shao-sun's writings and published them separately as an appendix.[40] Today we have likewise not seen his edition. The edition which is circulating widely in this generation is this one [i.e, the Ssu-k'u edition]. As for the forged Sun Shih 孫奭 subcommentary of *Meng Tzu*, which quotes the episode from the *Shih chi* about Hsi Tzu 西子 and the gold and money,[41] our current edition does not have that [section]. Probably someone in the Sung falsely attributed it to an ancient book. It is not an omission from our current edition. Additionally, the *Hsüeh-hai lei-pien* 學海類編[42] records a *Shih chi chen-pen fan-li* 史記真本凡例 (Guidelines to the True Edition of the *Grand Scribe's Records*) by Hung Tsun 洪遵 (1120-1174)[43] in one *chüan*. Regarding the original text, [Hung Tsun] freely cut and revised it, claiming that it was the original manuscript that Ssu-ma Ch'ien hid in the famous mountain. That instance was similar to that of the Liang dynasty King of P'o-yang's 梁鄱陽王 true copy of the *Han shu*.[44] These stories are even more absurd and unreliable. Of those who have

[39]Ch'ien Tseng, *Tu-shu min-ch'iu chi*, 2.1a.

[40]Hu Yü-chin 胡玉縉 (1859–1940) notes that Lu Hsin-yüan's 陸心源 (1834–1894) *Ts'ang-shu chih* 藏書志 listed a fragmented edition (*ts'an pen* 殘本) by Keng Ping 耿秉 (*fl. ca.* 1174), which recorded a preface by Chang Yü 張杅 (not Chang Ts'ai, as in the text above). Keng's preface noted that during the *ping-shen* 丙申 year (of the Ch'un-hsi 淳熙 reign period; i.e., 1176), Chang Chieh-chung 張介仲 engraved the *T'ai-shih kung shu* 太史公書, but omitted whatever had been amended by Ch'u Shao-sun. Two years later Chao Shan-fu 趙山甫 took the parts which had been omitted and published them as a separate portfolio. See Hu Yü-chin, *Ssu-k'u ch'üan-shu tsung-mu t'i-yao pu-cheng* 四庫全書總目提要補正 in Yang Chia-lo 楊家駱, ed., *Ssu-k'u ta tz'u-tien* 四庫大辭典 (Taipei: Chung-kuo Tz'u-tien-kuan Fu-kuan Ch'ou-pei-ch'u Yin-hang 中國辭典館復館籌備處印行, 1967), p. 322.

[41]Sun Shih 孫奭 (962-1033) was the author of the *Meng Tzu yin-yi* 孟子音義. For biographical information see T'o T'o 脱脱, *et al.* (1313–1355), *Sung shih* 宋史 (Peking: Chung-hua, 1977), 431.13801-08. See also Herbert Franke, ed., *Sung Biographies* (Wiesbaden: Franz Steiner, 1976), pp. 977-79. There is no mention of the "Hsi Tzu chin ch'ien shih" (西子金錢事) in the *Meng Tzu yin-yi*. Hu Yü-chin notes that the "*Shih chi*" referred to is not the one written by Ssu-ma Ch'ien. See Hu Yü-chin, p. 323.

[42]The *Hsüeh-hai lei-pien* 學海類編 (Classified Anthology from the Ocean of Learning) is a group of titles compiled by Ts'ao Jung 曹溶 (1613-1685). The titles were selected from his personal library. The *ts'ung-shu* was enlarged by a pupil, Tao Yüeh 陶越, and comprises 440 monographs in its present form. It was first printed in 1831, and reprinted by Commercial Press in 1920. It is contained in the *PPTSCC*. See Hummel, p. 740.

[43]See Hung Tsun, *Ting-cheng* Shih chi *chen-pen fan-li* 訂正史記真本凡例, *Hsüeh-hai lei-pien*, 1b. Hung Tsun was the older brother of Hung Mai 洪邁 (1123-1202). See *Sung shih*, 373.11565-69, and also Herbert Franke, *Sung Biographies*, pp. 481-3.

[44]See Chiao Hung, 2.11a/b. See also Yao Ssu-lien 姚思廉 (d. 637), *Liang shu* 梁書

commented on this text, there are now only the three commentaries of P'ei Yin 裴駰 (fl. 438), Ssu-ma Chen 司馬貞 (fl. 745) and Chang Shou-chieh still extant. In earlier times, each [commentary] was in a separate volume. Beginning in the Northern Sung they were published together. In the edition published by the Ming *Kuo-tzu chien* 國子監 (Academy of the Sons of the State) there are considerable revisions and omissions.[45] The Nan-chien 南監 (Southern Academy) edition went so far as to put "San-huang pen-chi" 三皇本紀 (The Basic Annals of the Three August Emperors) which Ssu-ma Chen added before "Wu-ti pen-chi" 五帝本紀 (The Basic Annals of the Five Emperors), causing the old appearance [of the *Shih chi*] to be lost. So [we, the editors] have collected all the discourses, investigations, and comparisons, and therefore now record them in a collected volume; in order to observe and peruse, we again separately record the writings of the three [commentators] in order to preserve the complete edition herein.

(Peking: Chung-hua, 1973), 40.573.

[45] Although there are three editions published by the Kuo-tzu Chien in Nanking during the Ming dynasty, this seems to refer to the most recent, that prepared by Feng Meng-chen 馮夢禎 (1546-1605) *et al.* in 1599 (see Ho Tz'u-chün, pp. 170-3).

Ssu-k'u ch'üan shu Resume for the "Chi-chieh" 集解 (Collected Explanations)
on *The Grand Scribe's Records* in 130 *chüan*[46]

Edition collected and presented by the Governor of Chiang-su 江蘇.
Compiled by P'ei Yin 裴駰 (*fl.* 438) of the Sung 宋 (420-479) dynasty. [Pei] Yin's *agnomen* was Lung-chü 龍駒. He was a native of Wen-hsi 聞喜 in Ho-tung 河東.[47] His official rank reached as high as the Adjutant to South Commandant. The traces of the events of his life were attached to the biography of P'ei Sung-chih 裴松之 (372-451) in the *Sung shu*.[48] P'ei Yin thought Hsü Kuang's 徐廣 (353-425) *Shih chi yin-yi* 史記音義 roughly had some insights, yet he disliked extremely the abridged parts. Then he collected materials from the Nine Classics, the various histories, the *Han shu yin-yi* 漢書音義 and various other works and compiled this work separately. He often cited old ideas of former Confucian scholars. Chang Shou-chieh's 張守節 (*fl.* 725–735) *Cheng-i* 正義 had a detailed list of the works [P'ei] cited. Yet, Chang didn't write in his list that he often cited Yü Fan's 虞翻 (164-232) comment on *Kuo yü*, Liu Hsi's 劉熙 commentary of *Meng Tzu*, Mr. Hsüeh's 薛 (fl. 200) commentary of *Han-shih wai-chuan* 韓詩外傳. It is understood that at that time he cited so many works that Chang couldn't count all of them. The original edition was in eighty *chüan*. The records in the "Bibliographic Monograph" of the *Sui* [*shu* 隋書 ([History of the] Sui) and in the T'ang histories were all the same.[49] This edition was produced by Mao Chin's 毛晉 (1599-1659) Chi-ku ko 汲古閣.[50] It was divided into 130 *chüan*. Thus, the original organization cannot be reconstructed. Yet the notes and text still follow that of the old edition. The Ming dynasty Academy 監 Edition, which attached the *So-yin* 索隱 and the *Cheng-yi* 正義 behind it and freely deleted and revised the text, resulted in many errors. For example, in the "Basic Annals of the Five Emperors," below the sentence "in the past the Kao-yang clan had eight talented sons" and the sentence "the Kao-hsin clan had eight talented sons," the four words "names seen [in]

[46]My thanks to Cao Weiguo, who contributed a draft translation of nearly half of this section. I alone am responsible, however, for any errors remaining in the text.

[47]The seat of Ho-tung Commandery was on the Yellow River, 120 miles west of modern Loyang in Shansi province (T'an Ch'i-hsiang, 4:46–7).

[48]See *Sung shu,* 64.1701. His biography is only a single line. It reads: "His son, Yin, was the Adjutant to South Commandant. The writings and essays that [P'ei] Sung-chih wrote and the *Chin chi* (Chin Annals), together with the *Shih chi* by Ssu-ma Ch'ien commented on by Yin, circulate among the present generation."

[49]See *Chiu T'ang-shu* 舊唐書, 46.1987 and *Hsin T'ang-shu* 新唐書, 58.1453 (Chung-hua Shu-chü editions).

[50]This was the edition included in the "Seventeen Histories." For more information on this edition, see Yang Yen-ch'i 楊燕起, *Shih chi yen-chiu tzu-liao so-yin ho lun-wen, chuan-chu t'i-yao* 史記研究資料索引和論文專著提要 (Lanchow: Lan-chou Ta-hsüeh, 1988), p. 12.

Tso chuan" are omitted.[51] In the "Basic Annals of the First Emperor of Ch'in," below the sentence "[The people along the Ho] left for the east in light carts with double horses to go for food,[52] the eight words "Hsü Kuang says: 'One [edition] without the word "double" is omitted. In "The Basic Annals of Hsiang Yü," below the sentence "In the ninth month the Governor (守) of K'uai-chi . . . ,"[53] the nine words "Hsü Kuang says: 'At that time he was not yet referred to as "governor (太守)" are omitted. In the "Basic Annals of Emperor Wu," below the sentence, "sacrificed to the lord on high in the Ming T'ang 明堂"[54] the eighteen words, "Hsü Kuang says: 'performed once every five years, but now just the second year, hence only *szu* 祀 'sacrifice' in the Ming T'ang'" are omitted. [In the same chapter], below the sentence "but its results are there for all to see,"[55] the seven words "also several editions all without word 'can'" are omitted. In the "Treatise on the Rivers and Canals," below the sentence [beginning] "Banks prone to collapse. . .,"[56] the six words "Ju Ch'un says: 'river [water] banks'" are omitted.

In the "Memoir of Ssu-ma Hsiang-ju," below the sentence "sailing far away on the seas," this edition cited Kuo P'u 郭璞: "Ch'ing-ch'iu is the name of a mountain. On its top there are fields; there is also a country which produces nine-tailed foxes. It is located overseas."[57] In Ssu-ma Ch'ien's postface to the *Shih chi*, below the sentence [beginning] "'The Great Commentary' of the *Book of Changes*," this [edition (i.e., the *Ssu-k'u* edition] cites Chang Yen as saying, "[this] refers to the "Appended Words" (*hsi tz'u* 繫辭) of *Yi ching* 易經 (The Book of Changes).[58] The Academy Edition mistook all [of these] for *Cheng-yi*.

As for variances of words and sentences, many examples can be found throughout. For example, in the "Basic Annals of Hsia," below the sentence "Nine Chiang presented large turtles," K'ung An-kuo 孔安國 (fl. 126-117 B.C.) said, "they came from the waters of the Nine Chiang."[59] The Academy Edition made it "from the mountain." In "The Basic Annals of Emperor Wen the Filial," below the sentence "[Sung] Ch'ang 宋昌 arrived at the Wei Bridge," [this edition] cites Su Lin 蘇林 (*fl.* latter half of third century) as saying, "Three *li* north of Ch'ang-an." The Academy Edition adds the two characters "Wei

---

[51]This example is noted in notes one and three in *Shih chi,* 1.36. For all following examples, I will simply cite the *chüan* and page number of the example sentence in the *Shih chi.*

[52]See *Shih chi,* 6.225-26; *The Grand Scribe's Records,* 1:129.

[53]See *Shih chi,* 7.297; *The Grand Scribe's Records,* 1:180. Charles Hucker notes that from the Ch'in to the Sui, the title *t'ai-shou* 太守 was the "governor" of a *chün* 郡, responsible for military and civil affairs and often also called by the title general (*chiang-chün* 將軍). He also notes that *shou* 守 was often used as an abbreviation for *t'ai-shou* (Hucker, pp. 431 and 482).

[54]See *Shih chi,* 12.481.

[55]See *Shih chi,* 12.485-86.

[56]See *Shih chi,* 29.1412.

[57]See *Shih chi,* 117.3015.

[58]See *Shih chi,* 130.3288-9.

[59]See *Shih chi,* 2.61.

Bridge."[60] [In the same chapter] below the sentence ". . . the Marquis of Ch'i 祁, Ho 賀 as General . . . " it cites Hsü Kuang as saying, "*cognomen* Tseng 繒." The Academy Edition adds one *ho* 賀 character.[61] [In the same chapter] below the sentence "There should appear a jade quintessence," [it] cites the *Jui ying t'u* 瑞應圖 as saying, "[As for] the jade quintessence, the Five Emperors each refined it, then [it] appeared." The Academy Edition says "five principles."[62] Note: The wording "Five Emperors each refined it" cannot be explained. It seems that we should take the Academy Edition as correct. [In the same chapter] below the sentence "Han 悍, the Director of Dependent States [was] made General of Military Encampments," [it] cites Hsü Kuang as saying, "*cognomen* Hsü." The Academy Edition adds one Han character.[63] In "The Basic Annals of Emperor Ching the Filial," below the sentence ". . . enfeoffed P'ing 平, the grandson of Chou K'o 周苛, the former Grand Master of the Imperial Scribes, as Marquis of Sheng 繩," [it] cites Hsü Kuang as saying, "one [edition] says *ying* 應."[64] The Academy Edition adds one *p'ing* character.[65] In "The Basic Annals of Emperor Wu the Filial," below the sentence "From the Princess Supreme. . . ," [it] cites Hsü Kuang as saying, "Emperor Wu's paternal aunt." The Academy Edition adds the two characters *t'ai chu* 太主 (princess supreme).[66] In "The Memoir of the Diviners of Tortoise and Milfoil," below the sentence "The hedgehog is humiliated by the magpie . . . ," it cites Kuo P'u as saying, "The hedgehog despises its intentions [and] in its heart considers it despicable." The Academy Edition says "and in his heart considers it despicable."[67]

All of these types [of errors] probably occured because anciently the exegesis was simple and elemental. People of later times relied on their own understanding to augment the text, losing the old text.

As for the transmission of the commercial editions,[68] errors and omissions are especially extensive. For example, in "The Basic Annals of Hsia," below the sentence ". . . the Feng Waters 灃水 joined them. . . ," [the "Chi-chieh"] cites K'ung An-kuo as saying, ". . . the Feng Waters joined—joined in the Wei [River]."[69] The commercial editions lack

---

[60]See *Shih chi*, 10.415-6.

[61]See *Shih chi*, 10.425-6.

[62]Reading *ch'ang* 常 instead of *ti* 帝. See *Shih chi*, 10.430.

[63]See *Shih chi*, 10.434-5.

[64]The *ying* 應 was in place of *p'ing* 平, according to the positioning of note two (in the second set of notes) on *Shih chi*, 11.444.

[65]See *Shih chi*, 11.444.

[66]See *Shih chi*, 12.463-4. The *Shih chi* has the character *ta* 大 instead of *t'ai* 太.

[67]The Academy Edition adds the character *erh* 而. See *Shih chi*, 128.3237. The note in the *Shih chi*, containing the aforementioned statement, cites the *Huai-nan Tzu* 准南子 as its source. Kuo P'u is quoted as saying something entirely different.

[68]Ma Tailoi believes that there were several commercial editions of the *Shih chi* circulating at this time. Ascertaining which specific edition the *Ssu-k'u* editors are referring to is next to impossible (personal communication with Ma Tailoi, Fall 1997).

[69]On this reading cf. Wu and Lu, 2.43-4, n. 4-5.

one "joined."[70] In "The Basic Annals of Hsiang Yü," below the sentence "Hsiang Po 項伯 was enfeoffed as the Marquis of She-yang 射陽," [the commercial editions] omit the nine words "Hsü Kuang says: 'Hsiang Po's *praenomen* [is] Ch'an 纏, his *agnomen* [is] Po 伯.'"[71] These [commercial editions] are even poorer than the Academy Edition. Only in the "Memoir of Goods and Wealth," below the sentence "one thousand *t'ai* of fermented yeast and salted soya-bean," the Academy Edition cites Sun Shu-ao's 孫叔敖 (*fl.* 600 B.C.)[72] words, "*T'ai* is a tile container, it has the capacity of six *sheng* 升, the pronunciation is *t'ai*."[73] This must be an error for Sun Shu-jan 孫叔然.[74] This edition also repeats it the same. From this we see one can never avoid negligence in collation. In the end it is better than the Academy Edition of the Ming.

translated by Scott W. Galer

[70]See *Shih chi*, 2.65-6; *The Grand Scribe's Records*, 1:28.

[71]See *Shih chi*, 7.338; *The Grand Scribe's Records*, 1:208.

[72]On Sun Shu-ao, see William H. Nienhauser, Jr., "A Reexamination of 'The Biographies of the Reasonable Officials' in the Records of the Grand Historian," *EC* 16 (1991): 209–33.

[73]See *Shih chi* 69.3276.

[74]Other than this citation, Sun Shu-jan is only mentioned three times in the twenty-five dynastic histories. Only one instance gives any biographical information. In Wang Lang's 王朗 biography in the *San-kuo chih* 三國志, it notes that Sun was a student of Cheng Hsüan 鄭玄 (127–200; *San kuo chih*, 13.419).

Bibliography

I. Editions and Concordances

Chi Yün 紀昀 (1724-1805), *et al.,* comps. *Ch'in-ting Ssu-k`u ch'üan-shu tsung-mu* 欽定四庫全書總目. Canton: Kuang-tung Shu-chü, 1868; Shanghai: Ta-tung Shu-chü, 1926; Taipei: Yi-wen Yin-shu-kuan, 1964.

Hung, William, ed. *Ssu-k'u ch'üan-shu tsung-mu chi wei-shou shu-mu yin-te* 四庫全書總目及未收術目引得. Harvard-Yenching Institute Sinological Series no. 7. Peking: Yen-ching Ta-hsüeh T'u-shu-kuan, 1932 (Rpt. Taipei: Ch'eng-wen, 1966).

Yang Chia-lo 楊家駱. *Ssu-k'u ta tz'u-tien* 四庫大辭典. Nanking: Tz'u-tien Kuan, 1935 (Rpt. 2v. Peking: Chung-kuo Shu-tien, 1987).

Ying-yin Wen-yüan-ko Ssu-k'u ch'üan-shu 影印文淵閣四庫全書. 1500v. Taipei: T'ai-wan Shang-wu Yin-shu-kuan, 1983-1986.

II. Studies and Supplements

Chang, Peter, *et al. The Wen-yüan Pavilion Ssu-k'u ch'üan-shu Photolithographic Facsimile Edition Subscription Registration Procedures.* Taipei: The Commercial Press, 1982 [?].

Ch'en Yüan 陳垣 (1880–1981). *Ch'en Yüan hsüeh-shu lun-wen chi* 陳垣學術論文集, v. 2. Peking: Chung-hua, 1982.

Cheng Heng-hsiung 鄭恆雄. *Chung-wen tsan-k'ao tzu-liao* 中文參考資料. Taipei: Hsüeh-sheng Shu-chü, 1982, pp. 61–6.

Chung-kuo Ti-yi Li-shih Tang-an Kuan 中國弟一歷史檔案館. *Tsuan-hsiu Ssu-k'u ch'üan-shu tang-an* 纂修四庫全書檔案. 2v. Shanghai: Shang-hai Ku-chi Ch'u-pan-she, 1997.

Goodrich, Luther Carrington. *The Literary Inquisition of Ch'ien-lung. Baltimore,* Waverly Press, 1935 (Rpt. New York, 1966).

Guy, R. Kent. *The Emperor's Four Treasuries: Scholars and the State in the Late Ch'ien-lung Era.* Cambridge, Mass.: Council on East Asian Studies, Harvard University, 1987.

Hu Yü-chin 胡玉縉 (1858-1940) and Wang Hsin-fu 王欣夫. *Ssu-k'u ch'üan-shu tsung-mu t'i-yao pu-cheng* 四庫全書總目提要補正. 2v. Peking: Chung-hua Shu-chü, 1964 (Rpt. Shanghai: Shang-hai Shu-tien Ch'u-pan-she, 1998).

Hummel, Arthur W. *Eminent Chinese of the Ch'ing Period (1644–1912)*. 1943–44. Rpt. Taipei: Ch'eng-wen, 1967, s.v. "Chi Yün" and "Chu Yün."

Hung, William, "Preface to an Index to *Ssu-ku ch'üan-shu tsung-mu* and *Wei-shou shu-mu*," *HJAS* 4 (1939): 47–58.

Kuo Po-kung 郭伯恭. *Ssu-k'u ch'üan-shu tsuan-hsiu k`ao* 四庫全書纂修考. Shanghai: Shang-wu Yin-shu-kuan, 1937 (Rpt. Shanghai : Shang-hai Shu-tien, 1992).

Ma, Y.W. "Chi Yün" 紀昀, in William H. Nienhauser, Jr., ed. *The Indiana Companion to Traditional Chinese Literature,* pp. 247–49.

Shao Yi-ch`en 邵壹辰 (1810-1861), comp. *Tseng-ting Ssu-k'u chien-ming mu-lu piao-chu* 增訂四庫簡明目錄標注. Edited and annotated by Shao Chang 邵章. Revised edition by Shao Yu-ch'eng 邵友誠. Peking: Chung-hua, 1959.

Teng Ssu-yü and Knight Biggerstaff, comps. *An Annotated Bibliography of Selected Chinese Reference Works.* 1950. Third ed. Cambridge, Mass.: Harvard University Press, 1971, pp. 18–22.

Wang Shu-min 王樹民. "*Ssu-k'u ch'üan-shu* ho yu-kuan chu-tso" 四庫全書和有關著作, in *Shih-pu yao-chi chieh-t'i* 史部要藉解題. Taipei: Mu-to Ch'u-pan-she, 1983, pp. 302–7.

Wang T`ai-yüeh, 王太岳, *et al. Ssu-k'u ch'üan-shu k'ao-cheng.* 10v. Taipei: T'ai-wan Shang-wu Yin-shu-kuan, 1967.

Wang Yün-wu 王雲五, ed. *Hsü-hsiu Ssu-k'u ch'üan-shu t'i-yao* 續修四庫全書提要. 13v. Taipei: T'ai-wan Shang-wu Yin-shu-kuan, 1972.

Wu Che-fu 吳哲夫. *Ssu-k'u ch'üan-shu tsuan-hsiu chih yen-chiu* 四庫全書纂修之研究. Taipei: Kuo-li Ku-kung Po-wu-yüan, 1990.

Yü Chia-hsi 余嘉錫 (1883–1955). *Ssu-k'u ch'üan-shu t'i-yao pien-cheng* 四庫全書提要辨證. 4v. Peking, 1937 (Rpt. Peking: Chung-hua, 1980; Taipei: Yi-wen Yin-shu-kuan, 1959; and others).

Wu Wei-tsu 吳慰祖. *Ssu-k'u ts'ai-chin shu-mu* 四庫採進書目. Peking: Shang-wu Yin-shu-kuan, 1960.

Selected Recent Studies of the *Shih chi* and Related Works

This selected bibliography contains primarily works related to the Han annals along with other relevant studies published since 1993 or not listed in the bibliographies in volumes 1 and 7 of *The Grand Scribe's Records.*

Arminio, Joseph Anthony. "The Grand Strategy of the Han Empire in the Second Century B.C." Unpublished Ph. D. dissertation, Massachusetts Institute of Technology, 1989.

Bissell, Jeff. "Literary Studies of Historical Texts: Early Narrative Accounts of Chong'er, Duke Wen of Jin." Unpublished Ph D. dissertation, University of Wisconsin, 1996.

Bujard, Marianne. *Le sacrifice au Ciel dans la Chine ancienne, théorie et pratique sous les Han occidentaux.* Paris: École française d'Extrême-Orient, 2000.

___. "The 'Traité des sacrifices' du *Hanshu* et la mise en place de la religion d'État des Han," *BEFEO* 84 (1997): 111-27.

Cha, Joseph Hyosup. "The Historical Significance of the Reigns of Emperors Wen and Ching of the Former Han Dynasty, 180–141 B. C." Unpublished Ph. D. dissertation, University of Chicago, 1973.

Chang Chia-ying 張家英. *Shih chi shih-erh pen-chi yi-ku* 史記十二本紀疑詁. Harbin: Hei-lung-chiang Chiao-yü, 1997.

Chang Ch'un-shu 張春樹. "Qin-Han China in Review: The Field, New Frontiers, and the Next Assignment," *Chûgoku Shigaku* 4 (1994): 47–59.

___. "Military Aspects of Han Wu-ti's Northern and Northwestern Campaigns," *HJAS* 26 (1966): 148–73.

Chang Hsin-k'o 張新科 and Wang Kang 王剛. "20 shih-chi *Shih chi* hsüeh te fa-chan tao-lu" 20 世紀史記學的發展道路, *Huai-yang Shih-fan Hsüeh-yüan hsüeh-pao* 22.1 (2000): 40-6.

___. *Shih chi yü Chung-kuo wen-hsüeh* 史記與中國文學. Sian: Shan-hsi Jen-min Chiao-yü, 1995. Ssu-ma Ch'ien yü hua-hsia wen-hua ts'ung-shu.

___ and Yü Chang-hua 俞樟華. *Shih chi yen-chiu shih-lüeh* 史記研究史略. Sian: San-Ch'in Ch'u-pan-she, 1990.

Chang Lieh 張烈, ed. *Han shu chu yi* 漢書注譯. 4v. Haikow: Hai-nan Kuo-chi Hsin-wen Ch'u-pan Chung-hsin Ch'u-pan Fa-hsing, 1997.

Chang Ta-k'o 張大可. *Ssu-ma Ch'ien yi-chia yen* 司馬遷一家言. Sian: Shan-hsi Jen-min Chiao-yü, 1995.

Chang K'o 張克, *et al. Shih chi jen-wu tz'u-tien* 史記人物辭典. Nanning: Kuang-hsi Jen-min, 1991.

Chang Wei-hua 張維華. *Lun Han Wu-ti* 論漢武帝. Shanghai: Shang-hai Jen-min, 1957.

Chang Wei-yüeh 張維嶽. *Ssu-ma Ch'ien yü Shih chi hsin-t'an* 司馬遷與史記新探. Taipei: Sung-kao Shu-she, 1985.

Chang Yüan-chi 張元濟. *Po-na pen Erh-shih-ssu shih chiao-k'an chi—Shih chi chiao-k'an chi* 百衲本二十四史校勘濟—史記校勘記. Shanghai: Shang-wu, 1998.

Ch'e Hsing-chien 車行健. "Ts'ung Ssu-ma Ch'ien *Shih chi* 'T'ai-shih-kung tzu-hsü' kan Han-tai shu-hsü te t'i-chih" 從司馬遷史記太史公自序看漢代書序的體制, *Chung-kuo wen-che yen-chiu chi-kan* 17 (September 2000): 263-88.

Ch'en, Ch'i 陳琪. "'Yao tien' yü 'Wu-ti pen-chi' tzu-chü chih pi-chiao yen-chiu" 堯典與五帝本紀字句之比較研究 *Shu-mu chi-k'an* 17.3 (December 1983): 50-72.

Ch'en Chih 陳直. *Han shu hsin-cheng* 漢書新證. Second printing; Tientsin: T'ien-chin Jen-min, 1979 (1959).

Ch'en Meng-chia 陳夢家. "Han-ch'u chi ch'i ch'ien te chi-nien ts'ai-liao" 漢初及其前的紀年材料, in Ch'en's *Liu-kuo chi-nien* 六國紀年. Shanghai: Hsüeh-hsi Sheng-huo, 1955.

Ch'en Ts'ang-chieh 陳蒼杰. "Liu Pang nien-piao" 劉邦年表, in *Liu Pang chuan* 劉邦傳. Peking: Yi-ch'ün, 1985.

Ch'en T'ung-sheng 陳桐生. *Chung-kuo shih-kuan wen-hua yü Shih chi* 中國史官文化與史記. Shantou: Shan-t'ou Ta-hsüeh, 1993. Explores various aspects of Ssu-ma Ch'ien's historiography; useful bibliography.

___. *Shih chi yü chin-ku-wen ching-hsüeh* 史記與今古文經學. Sian: Shan-hsi Jen-min Chiao-yü, 1995. *Ssu-ma Ch'ien yü hua-hsia wen-hua ts'ung-shu.*

Cheng Chih-hung 鄭之洪. *Shih chi wen-hsien yen-chiu* 史記文獻研究. Chengtu: Pa Shu Shu-she, 1997.

Ch'eng Chin-tsao 程金造, ed. *Shih chi "So-yin" yin-shu k'ao-shih* 史記索隱引書考實. Peking: Chung-hua, 1994.

___. *Ssu-ma Ch'ien p'ing-chuan* 司馬遷評傳. Nanking: Nan-ching Ta-hsüeh, 1994.

Chi Ch'ao 嵇超, *et al. Shih chi ti-ming so-yin* 史記地名索引. Peking: Chung-hua, 1990.

Chi-lin Shih-fan Ta-hsüeh 吉林師范大學, ed. *Lü T'ai-hou* 呂太后. Kirin: Ch'i-lin Jen-min, 1977.

Chou Ching 周經. *Ssu-ma Ch'ien Shih chi yü tang-an* 司馬遷史記與檔案. Peking: Tang-an Ch'u-pan-she, 1986.

Chou Hsiao-t'ien 周嘯天 and Yu Ch'i 尤其, eds. *Shih chi ch'üan-pen tao-tu tz'u-tien* 史記全本導讀辭典. 2v. Chengtu: Ssu-ch'uan Tz'u-shu, 1997. Despite the title, this is merely a *pai-hua* rendition of the text.

Chou Hsien-min 周先民. "Kung Kao-che wei—*Shih chi* chung kuan-yü chün-ch'en kuan-hsi te chu-t'i" 功高者危一史記中關於君臣關系的主題, *Nagoya Daigaku Chûgoku gogaku bungaku ronshû* 7 (1994): 1–18.

___. *Ssu-ma Ch'ien te shih-chuan wen-hsüeh shih-chieh* 司馬遷的史傳文學世界. Taipei: Wen-chin, 1995.

Dawson, Raymond. *Historical Records.* Oxford, New York and Toronto: Oxford University Press, 1994. Renditions of all or parts of *Shih chi* chapters 6, 7, 28, 29, 48, and 85-88.

Drège, Jean-Pierre. *Les bibliothèques en Chine au temps des manuscrits (jusqu'au xe siècle).* Paris: École Française d'Extrême-Orient, 1991.

Durrant, Stephen. *The Cloudy Mirror: Tension and Conflict in the Writings of Sima Qian*. Albany: State University of New York Press, 1995.

___. "Redeeming Sima Qian," *Chinese Review International* 4.2 (Fall 1997): 307-13.

___. "Self as the Intersection of Traditions: The Autobiographical Writings of Ssu-ma Ch'ien," *JAOS* 106 (1986): 33-40.

___. "Ssu-ma Ch'ien's Conception of *Tso chuan*," *JAOS* 112 (1992): 295-301.

___. "Takigawa Kametaro's Commentary on Chapter 47 of *Shih-chi*," In *Proceedings of the Second Annual International Conference on Chinese Language Works Outside of China*. Taipei: Lien-ching, 1989, pp. 995-1007.

Emmerich, Reinhard. "Bemerkungen zu Huang und Lao in der Frühen Han Zeit, Erkenntnisse aus *Shiji* und *Hanshu*," *MS* 43 (1995): 53-140.

Fan Fu-yüan 范福元. *Han Wu-ti* 漢武帝. Peking: Chung-hua, 1960.

Fields, Lanny B. "Hsia Wu-chu: Physician to the First Ch'in Emperor" *JA* 28.2 (1994): 97-107. A discussion of Hsia Wu-ch'u (fl. 227) as a possible source for the account of the Ch'in dynasty in the *Shih chi*.

Fujikawa Masakazu 藤川正數. "Kandai ni okeru daijin dappuku no sei ni tsuite" 漢代における大臣奪服の製について. *Nippon Chûgoku gakkai hô* 16 (1964): 75–89.

Fujita Katsuhisa 藤田勝久. "Baôtai hakusho *Sengoku jûôka sho* no kôsei to seikaku" 馬王堆帛書戦国縦横家書の構成と性格, *Ehime Daigaku Kyôyôbu kiyô* 19 (1986).

___. Sun Wen-ko 孫文閣, trans. "Chin-nien lai Jih-pen te *Shih chi* yen-chiu" 近年來日本的史記研究, *Ku-chi cheng-li yen-chiu hsüeh-k'an* 57 (1995): 45-8.

___. "Meiji ikô no *Shiki* kenkyû" 明治以降の史記研究, *Ehime Daigaku Hôbungakubu ronshû* 愛媛大学法文学部論集 11 (2001): 15-41.

——. "Nihon ni okeru Sengokushi kenkyû no dôkô" 日本における戦国史研究の動向, *Chûgoku shigaku* 4 (1994): 167–86.

___. "Nihon *Shiki* kenkyû bunken mokuroku" 日本史記研究文獻目録. Unpublished working draft in manuscript.

___. *Shiba Sen to sono jidai* 司馬遷とその時代. Tokyo: University of Tokyo Press, 2001.

——. "*Shiki* Ro Kô ni mieru hongi Shiba sen no rekishi shisô" 史記呂后にみえる本紀司馬遷の歴史思想, *Tôhôgaku* 86 (1993.7): 21–35.

——. *Shiki Sengoku shiryô no kenkyû* 史記戦国史料の研究. Tokyo: Tokyo University, 1997. An thoughtful study of Ssu-ma Ch'ien's use of sources.

___. "*Shiki* sengoku shikun retsuden no shiryôteki seikaku" 史記戦国四君列伝の史料的性格, *Kodai bunka* 43.1 (1991): 1–15.

——. "*Shiki* 'Gi seka' no shiryôteki kôsatsu" 史記魏世家の史料的考察, *Ehime Daigaku Kyôyôbu kiyô* 27.1 (1994): 83–106.

——, Kudô Motô 工藤元男 and Sanae Yoshio 早苗良雄, annot. and trans. *Sengoku jûôka sho, Baôtai hakusho* 戦国縦横家書－馬王堆帛書. Kyoto: Hôyû Shoten, 1994.

Fukushima Masashi 福島正. "*Shiki* 'Shin hongi' enshi" 史記秦本紀冤詞, *Ôsaka Kyôiku Daigaku Kiyô–Jinbun kagaku* 40.1 (1991): 13–27.

Han Chao-ch'i 韓兆琦, ed. *Shih chi hsüan-chu chi-p'ing* 史記選注集評. Kweilin: Kuang-hsi Shih-fan Ta-hsüeh, 1995.

___ and Lü Po-t'ao 呂伯濤. "Ssu-ma Ch'ien yü *Shih chi*" 司馬遷與史記, in Han and Lü, *Han-tai san-wen shih-kao* 漢代散文史稿. Taiyuan: Shan-hsi Jen-min Ch'u-pan-she, 1986, pp. 95-167.

Hardy, Grant Ricardo. "Can An Ancient Chinese Historian Contribute to Modern Western Theory? The Multiple Narrations of Ssu-ma Ch'ien," *History and Theory* 33.1 (1994): 20-38.

___. *Worlds of Bronze and Bamboo, Sima Qian's Conquest of History*. New York: Columbia University Press, 1999.

Hayashi Minao 林巳奈夫. *Kandai no bunbutsu* 漢代の文物. Kyoto: Kyôto Daigaku Jimbun Kagaku Kenkyûjo, 1976.

Hirase Takao 平勢隆郎. *Shinpen Shiki tôshû nenpyô—Chûgoku kodai nenki no kenkyû joshô* 新編史記東周年表—中国古代紀年の研究序章, Tokyo: Tôkyô Daigaku Shuppankai, 1995.

Ho Tz'u-chun 賀次君. *Shih chi shu-lu* 史記書錄. Shanghai: Shang-wu Yin-shu-kuan, 1958.

Hsiang Li-ling 項立岭 and Lo Yi-chün 羅義俊. *Liu Pang* 劉邦. Peking: Jen-min, 1976.

___. "Liu Pang nien-piao" 劉邦年表, in *Liu Pang*. Peking: Jen-min, 1976.

Hsü Hsing-hai 徐興海, ed. *Ssu-ma Ch'ien yü Shih chi lun-chi* 司馬遷與史記論集. Sian: Shan-hsi Jen-min Chiao-yü, 1995.

___, ed. *Ssu-ma Ch'ien yü Shih chi yen-chiu lun-chu chuan-t'i so-yin* 司馬遷與史記研究論著專題索引. Sian: Shan-hsi Jen-min Chiao-yü, 1995.

Hsü Shuo-fang 徐朔方. *Shih Han lun-kao* 史漢論稿. Nanking: Chiang-shu Ku-chi, 1984.

Hsü Te-lin 徐德鄰. "Lun Ssu-ma Ch'ien pi-hsia te Liu Pang hsing-hsiang" 論司馬遷筆下的劉邦形象, *Pei-fang lun-ts'ung* (May 1988): 53-7.

Hu Che-fu 胡哲敷. *Han Wu-ti* 漢武帝. Peking: Chung-hua, 1935.

Huang Hsin-yeh 黃新業. *Ssu-ma Ch'ien p'ing-chuan* 司馬遷評傳. Peking: Kuang-ming Jih-pao Ch'u-pan-she, 1991.

Huang Lin 黃霖. *Yeh-hsin chia Lü Hou* 野心家呂后. Shanghai: Jen-min, 1977.

Ikeda Hideo 池田英雄. *Shikigaku 50 nen—Ni-Chû Shiki kenkyû no dôkô (1945-1995 nen)* 史記学５０年－日中史記研究の動向 (1945-1995 年). Tokyo: Meitoku, 1996.

Ikeda Shirôjirô 池田四郎次郎. *Shiki hochû* 史記補注. 2v. Tokyo: Benseisha 勉誠社, 1976.

Ikeda Shirôjirô 池田四郎次郎 and Ikeda Eiyû 池田英雄. *Shiki kenkyû shomuku kaidai (kôhon)* 史記研究書目解提, 稿本. Tokyo: Meitoku Shuppansha, 1978.

Ishikawa Misao 石川三佐男. "*Shiki* no 'Kutsu Gen den' ni tsuite" 史記の屈原伝について, *Shibun* 97 (1989): 68-101.

___. "*Shiki* no 'Kutsu Gen den' to *Shoku ô hongi* 'Penrei den' ni tsuite–So no densetsuteki jinbutsu to 'oni'" 史記の屈原伝と蜀王本紀鼈列伝について–楚の伝説的人物と鬼, *Akita Daigaku Kyôiku Gakubu Denkyû Kiyô–Jinbun Kagaku Shakai kagaku* 43 (1992): 15–36.

Itô Tokuo 伊藤徳男. *Shiki jippyô ni miru Shiba Sen no rekishikan* 史記十表に見る司馬遷の歴史観. Tokyo: Hirakawa Shuppansha, 1994.

Juan Chih-sheng 阮芝生. "Hua-chi yü liu yi–*Shih chi* 'Hua-chi lieh-chuan' hsi-lun" 滑稽與六藝—史記滑稽列傳析論, *T'ai-ta li-shih hsüeh-pao* 29 (November 1996): 341-78.

___. "San Ssu-ma yü Han Wu-ti Feng Shan" 三司馬與漢武帝封禪, *T'ai-ta li-shih hsüeh pao* 29 (November 1996): 307-39.

Kamata Shigeo 鎌田重雄. "Kandai no *Shôsho* kan: Ryô *Shôsho* ji to roku *Shôsho* ji to o chûshin toshite" 漢代の尚書観（領尚書事と録尚書事とを中心として）, *Tôyôshi kenkyû* 26.4 (1968): 113–37.

Kanda Kiichirô 神田喜一郎. Review of Ho Tz'u-chün's 賀次君 *Shih chi shu-lu* 史記書錄 in *Chûgoku bungaku hô* 中国文学報 10 (April 1959): 146-51.

Kao Chen-to 高振鐸. "Li-tai tui *Shih chi* t'i-ch'u te yi-nan wen-t'i pien-hsi" 歷代對史記提出的疑難問題辨析, *Ku-chi cheng-li yen-chiu hsüeh-k'an* 古籍整理研究學刊 (1986.4).

Katô Shigehi 加藤繁. "Sen Kan" 前漢, in *Tô Sô jidai ni okeru kingin no kenkyû* 唐宋時代に於ける金銀の研究. Rpt. Tokyo: Tôyô Bunko 東洋文庫, 1965 [1927], pp. 633-48.

Kawakubo Hiroe 川久保広衛. "*Shiki* 'Shin So shi saigetsu hyô' ni tsuite" 史記秦楚之際月表ついて, *Nishôgakusha Daigaku Tôyôgaku Kenkyûjo Shûkan kiyô* 21 (1991): 21–53.

Kobayashi Haruki 小林春樹. "Shiba Sen ni okeru *Shiki* chojutsu no dôki ni tsuite-*Shiki* kenkyû josetsu" 司馬遷における『史記』著述の動機について-『史記』研究序説. *Shikan* 127 (1992).

Kolb, Raimund. *Die Infanterie im Alten China*. Main am Rhein: Phillipp von Zabern, 1991.

Ku Kuo-shun 古國順. *Shih chi shu Shang shu yen-chiu* 史記述尚書研究. Taipei: Wen-shih-che Ch'u-pan-she, 1985.

Kudô Motô 工藤元男. "Baôtai shutsudo *Sengoku jûôka sho* to *Shiki*" 馬王堆出土戦国縦横家書と史記, in *Chûgoku seishi no kisoteki kenkyû* 中国正史の基礎的研究. Tokyo: Waseda Daigaku Shuppanbu, 1984, pp. 1–26.

Kuo Yi 郭逸 and Kuo Man 郭曼, comm. *Shih chi* 史記. 2v. Shanghai: Shang-hai Ku-chi, 1997.

Kurosu Shigehiko 黒須重彦, trans. *Shiki* 史記. Tokyo: Gakushû Kenkyûsha, 1984.

Lewis, Mark Edward. "Sima Qian and Universal History," in Lewis, *Writing and Authority in Early China* (Albany: State University of New York Press, 1999), pp. 308-17.

Li Chen-yü 李真瑜. "*Shih chi* yü *Ch'u Han ch'un-chiu*" 史記與楚漢春秋, *Jen-wen tsa-chi*, 1986.6: 29-36.

Li Chieh-min 李解民. "*Shih chi* 'Kao-tsu kung-ch'en hou-che nien-piao' piao-tien shang-ch'üeh" 史記高祖功臣侯者年表標點商榷. *Wen-shih* 35 (1992): 126–137.

Li Mien 李勉, ed. *Shih chi ch'i-shih p'ien lieh-chuan p'ing-chu* 史記七十篇列傳評注. Taipei: Kuo-li Pien-yi Kuan, 1996.

Li T'ang 李唐 *Han Wu-ti* 漢武帝. Taipei: Ho-Luo T'u-shu 河洛圖書, 1978.

___. *Han Kao-tsu* 漢高祖. Taipei: Ho-Luo T'u-shu 河洛圖書, 1978.

Li Te-yüan 李德元. "T'ang-tai tien-ting *Shih chi* yen-chiu te chien-shih chi-ch'u" 唐代奠定史記研究的堅實基礎 *T'ung-hua Shih-yüan hsüeh-pao* 通化師院學報 (1991.1).

Li, Wai-yee. "The Idea of Authority in the *Shih chi* (Records of the Historian)," *HJAS* 54 (1994): 345-405.

Li Yung-hsien 李永先. "Ssu-ma Ch'ien shih 'chieh-lu' 'pien-t'a' ho "p'i-p'an' Lü Hou ma?" 司馬遷是揭露鞭撻和批判呂后嗎？ *Liao-ning Shih-yüan hsüeh-pao* (1980.3).

Lin Lü-chih 林旅芝. *Han Wu-ti chuan* 漢武帝傳. Hong Kong: Hsiang-kang San-sheng T'u-shu Wen-chü Kung-ssu 香港三省圖書文具公司, 1958.

Ling Chih-lung 淩稚隆 (fl. 1576-1587), ed. *Shih chi p'ing-lin* 史記評林. Changsha: Wei-shih Yang-ho Shu-wu, 1874. Rpt. Tokyo: Kyûko Shoin, 1989; Tientsin: T'ien-chin Ku-chi, 1997.

Liu Hua-ch'ing 李華清 *et al. Han shu ch'üan yi* 漢書全譯. 5v. Kweichow: Kuei-chou Jen-min, 1995.

Liu Nai-ho 劉乃和, ed. *Ssu-ma Ch'ien ho Shih chi* 司馬遷和史記. Peking: Pei-ching Ch'u-pan-she, 1987.

Liu Ts'ao-nan 劉操南. *Shih chi Ch'un-ch'iu Shih-erh Chu-hou shih shi chi-cheng* 史記春秋十二諸侯史事輯證. Tientsin: T'ien-chin Ku-chi, 1992; 1995.

Loewe, Michael. *A Biographical Dictionary of the Qin, Former Han and Xin Periods (221 BC-AD 24).* Brill: Leiden, 2000. As indispensable as it is expensive.

___. "Changes in Qin and Han China: The Religious and Intellectual Background," *Chûgoku Shigaku* 4 (1994): 7–45.

Lu Wen-ch'ao 盧文弨 (1717–1795) and Wu Shu-p'ing 吳樹平, *et al.*, comms. *Shih chi 'Hui Ching chien hou-che nien-piao' chiao-pu* 史記惠景間侯者年表較補. Peking: Chung-hua, 1982.

Lu Yao-tung 廖耀東. "*Shih chi* lieh-chuan chi ch'i yü pen-chi te kuan-hsi" 史記列傳及其與本紀的關係, *T'ai-ta li-shih hsüeh pao* 29 (November 1996): 379-405.

Lu, Zongli. "Problems Concerning the Authenticity of *Shih chi* 123 Reconsidered," *CLEAR* 15 (1993): 51-68.

Miyazaki Ichisada 宮崎市定. *Shiki to kataru* 史記と語る. Tokyo: Iwanami, 1996. Essays on how to read the *Shih chi,* its various genres, and a brief piece on women who appear in it; originally published in the early 1990s as part of Miyazaki's collected works.

Mizusawa Toshitada 水澤利忠. *Shiki 'Seigi' no kenkyû* 史記正義の研究. Tokyo: Kyûko Shoyin, 1993.

Murayama Makoto 村山孚. *Shiba Sen Shiki rekishi kikô* 司馬遷史記歴史紀行. Tokyo: Shôbunsha, 1995.

Nienhauser, William H. Jr., ed. Cheng Tsai-fa, Lu Zongli, William H. Nienhauser, Jr. and Robert Reynolds, trans. *The Grand Scribe's Records. Volume 1, The Basic Annals of Pre-Han China. Volume 7, The Memoirs of Pre-Han China.* Bloomington and Indianapolis: Indiana University Press, 1994.

Nienhauser, William H., Jr. "A Century (1895-1995) of *Shih chi* 史記 Studies in the West," *Asian Culture Quarterly* 24.1 (Spring 1996): 1-51.

___. "The Study of the *Shih chi* 史記 (The Grand Scribe's Records) in the People's Republic of China," in *Das andere China.* Wiesbaden: Harrassowitz, 1995, pp. 381-403.

___. "Historians of China," *CLEAR* 1 (1995): 207-17.

___. "The Implied Reader and Translation: The *Shih chi* as Example," in *Translating Chinese Literature.* Eugene Eoyang and Lin Yao-fu, eds. Bloomington: Indiana University Press, 1995, pp. 15-40.

___. "Travels with Edouard—V. M. Alekseev's Account of the Chavannes' Mission of 1907 as a Biographical Source," *Asian Culture Quarterly* 22.4 (Winter 1994): 81-95.

Nylan, Michael. "The Ku Wen Documents in Han Times," *TP* 81 (1995): 25-50.

___. "Ssu-ma Ch'ien: A True Historian?"*EC* 23-24 (1998-99): 203-46.

Ozaki Yasushi' 尾崎康. *Seishi Sô Gen ban no kenkyû* 正史宋元版の研究. Tokyo: Kyûko Shoin, 1989, pp. 161-231. Discussion of Sung editions of the *Shih chi.*

Page, John. *Los adversarios: Dos biografías de Las memorias históricas de Sima Qian.* Mexico City: El Colegio de México, 1979. Lightly annotated translations of Chapters 7 and 8.

Pankenier, David W. "The Mandate of Heaven," *Archaeology* 51.2 (1998): 26-35.

___. "'The Scholar's Frustration' Reconsidered" *JAOS* 110 (1990): 434-59.

Park Jae-Woo 朴宰雨. "Han-kuo *Shih chi* wen-hsüeh yen-chiu te hui-ku yü ch'ien-chan" 韓國史記文學研究的回顧與前瞻, *Wen-hsüeh yi-ch'an* (1998.1): 20-8.

___. *Shih chi, Han shu pi-chiao yen-chiu* 史記漢書比較研究. Peking: Chung-kuo Wen-hsüeh, 1994.

Pei-ching Ch'i-ch'e Chih-tsao Ch'ang Kung-jen Li-lun Yen-chiu So 北京汽車制造廠工人理論研究所, ed. *Lü Hou ch'i-jen—Lü Hou chi chu Lü p'an-kuo ts'uan-ch'üan tzu-liao hsüan-yi* 呂后其人一呂后及諸呂叛國篡權資料選譯. Peking: Chung-hua, 1977.

Peterson, Willard J. "Ssu-ma Ch'ien as Cultural Historian," In *The Power of Culture, Studies in Chinese Cultural History.* Hong Kong: Chinese University of Hong Kong Press, 1994, pp. 70-9.

Psarras, Sophia-Karin. "Exploring the North: Non-Chinese Cultures of the Late Warring States and Han," *MS* 42 (1994): 1-125.

Puett, Michael. "The Ambivalence of Creation: The Rise of Empire in Early China (Vols. One and Two)." Unpublished Ph. D. dissertation, University of Chicago, 1994.

Satô Taketoshi 佐藤武敏. *Shiba Sen no kenkyû* 司馬遷の研究. Tokyo: Kyûko, 1997.

Shih Chih-mien 施之勉. "Shih *Shih chi* 'Han-hsing yi-lai chiang-hsiang ming-ch'en nien-piao' tao-shu li" 釋史記漢興以來將相名臣年表倒書例, *Ta-lu tsa-chih* 52.2 (June 1976): 47.

Shih Ting 施丁, ed. *Han shu hsin chu* 漢書新注. 4v. Sian: San Ch'in, 1994.

Suiyama Hiroyuki 杉山寬行. "'Kô U honki' o yomu" 項羽本紀を読む, *Nagoya Daigaku Bungakubu kenkyû ronshû –Bungaku* 42 (1996): 289-99.

Sung Yün-pin 宋雲彬. "Liu Pang nien-piao" 劉邦年表, in *Liu Pang* 劉邦. Peking: Chung-hua, 1964.

T'ai-ta li-shih hsüeh-pao 臺大歷史學報. 23 (June 1999). A special issue titled "*Shih chi* hsin t'an-so" 史記新探索 featuring articles by Jan Chih-sheng 阮芝生 (who also edits the journal), Yi P'ing 易平, and Yen Hung-chung 閻鴻中.

Takahashi Minoru 高橋稔. "*Shiki* to rekishikatari ni tsuite" 史記と歷史語りについて, *Higashi Ajia bunka ronsô* (1991): 33-48.

Terakado Hideo 寺門日出南男. "*Shiki* hyô no ito" 史記表の意図, *Chûgoku kenkyû shûkan* 5 (January 1988): 12–28.

Ts'ang Hsiu-liang 倉修良, ed. *Shih chi tz'u-tien* 史記辭典. Tsinan: Shan-tung Chiao-yü, 1991.

Ts'en Chung-mien 岑仲勉. "*Shih chi* 'Liu-kuo piao' ho tui chin-jen k'ao-ting chih shang-ch'üeh" 史記六國表和對近人考訂之商榷, *Chung-shan Ta-hsüeh hsüeh-pao* 3 (June 1956): 74–99.

Tsukamoto Terukazu 塚本照和. "*Shiki* 'Ro Taigô hongi' o yomu" 史記呂大后本紀を読む, *Tenru Daigaku Gakuhô bessatsu* 4 (1992): 83–109.

Tu Ch'eng-hsiang 杜呈祥. "*Shih chi* 'Liu-kuo piao' ting-wu" 史記六國表訂誤, *T'ien-chin yi-shih-pao tu-shu chou-k'an* 12 (August 1935).

Tuan Shu-an 段書安. *Shih chi San-chia chu yin-shu so-yin* 史記三家注引書索引. Peking: Chung-hua, 1982.

Twitchett, Denis and Michael Loewe, eds. *The Cambridge History of China, Volume I: The Ch'in and Han Empiers, 221 B.C.-A.D. 220.* Cambridge: Cambridge University Press, 1986.

van Ess, Hans. "The Apocryphal Texts of the Han Dynasty and the Old Text/New Text Controversy," *TP* 85 (1998): 29-64.

___. "Die geheime Worte des Ssu-ma Ch'ien," *OE* 36.1 (1993): 5-27.

___. "The Meaning of Huang-Lao in *Shiji* and *Hanshu*," *Études chinoises* 12.2 (Autumn 1993): 161-177.

Viatkin, Rudolf V. *Istoricheskie zapiski ("Shi tszi").* 7v. Moscow: Nauka, 1972-.

Wang Hsi-p'eng 汪錫鵬. "*Shih chi* 'Feng Shan shu' fa-wei" 史記封禪書發微, *Chiang-hsi Shih-fan Ta-hsüeh hsüeh-pao (Che-hsüeh She-hui k'o-hsüeh)* 60 (October 1990): 64–7.

Wang Hui 王恢. "Tu *Shih chi* 'Kao-tsu kung-ch'en hou-che nien-piao'" 讀史記高祖功臣侯者年表, *Shu-mu chi-k'an* 14.3 (December 1980): 17–28.

___. *Shih chi pen-chi ti-li t'u-k'ao* 史記本紀地理圖考. Taipei: Kuo-li Pien-yi-kuan, 1990.

Wang Shu-min 王叔岷. "Lun Ssu-ma Ch'ien so liao-chieh te Lao Tzu" 論司馬遷所了解的老子, *BIHP* 70.1 (March 1999): 303-8.

Watson, Burton. "The *Shih chi* and I," *CLEAR* 17 (1995): 199-206. Watson's reminiscences on his study of the *Shih chi*.

___. *Records of the Grand Historian: Han Dynasty I and II* (Revised Edition). 2v. Hong Kong and New York: Renditions-Columbia University Press, 1993.

___. *Records of the Grand Historian: Qin Dynasty. V. 3.* Rev. ed. Hong Kong and New York: The Research Centre for Translation, The Chinese University of Hong Kong and Columbia University Press, 1993.

Wu Hsün 吳恂 (1890-1973). *Han shu chu-shang* 漢書注商. Shen Pei-tsung 沈北宗, ed. Shanghai: Shang-hai Ku-chi, 1983.

Wu Kuo-t'ai 吳國泰. *Shih chi chieh-ku* 史記解詁. Tientsin: T'ien-chin She-hui K'o-hsüeh Yüan Ch'u-pan-she, 1993.

Wu Shu-p'ing 吳樹平, Lu Zongli 呂宗力, Liu Ch'i-yü 劉起釪, *et al. Ch'üan-chu ch'üan-yi Shih chi* 全注全譯史記. 3v. Tientsin: T'ien-chin Ku-chi, 1996. These huge tomes provide a useful commentary.

Yang Chung-hsien 楊鐘賢 and Hao Chih-ta 郝志達. *Wen-pai tui-chao ch'üan-yi Shih chi* 文白對照全譯史記. 5v. Peking: Kuo-chi Wen-hua, 1992.

Yang Hsü-min 楊緒敏. "*Shih-t'ung* tsun Pan yi Ma pien" 史通尊班抑馬辨, *Hsü-chou Shih-yüan hsüeh-pao* 徐州師院學報 (1983.3).

Yang Shu-ta 楊樹達 (1885-1956). *Han shu k'uei-kuan* 漢書窺管. Shanghai: Shang-hai Ku-chi, 1984.

Yang Yen-ch'i 楊燕起. "*Shih chi* te piao" 史記的表, *She-hui k'o-hsüeh (Lan-chou)* 34 (December 1985): 96–103.

____. *Shih chi te hsüeh-shu ch'eng-chiu* 史記的學術成就. Peking: Pei-ching Shih-fan Ta-hsüeh, 1996.

Yoshida Kenkô 吉田賢抗 and Mizusawa Toshitada 水澤利忠. *Shiki* 史記. 10v. Tokyo: Meiji Shoin, 1973–1996.

Yoshihara Hideo 吉原英夫. *Shiki ni kansuru bunken mokuroku* 史記に関する文献目録. Hokkaido: Hokkaidô Kyoiku Daigaku, 1997. A fifty-page bibliography of editions (since 1911) and studies.

____. "*Shiki* ni mieru 'chôja' ni tsuite" 『史記』に見える「長者」について, *Kanbungaku ronshû* (1991).

Yoshimoto Michimasa 吉本道雅. *Shiki o saguru: sono naritachi to Chûgoku shigaku no kakuritsu* 史記を探る－その成り立ちと中国史学の確立. Tokyo: Tôhô Shoten, 1996.

Zufferey, Nicolas. "Érudits et Lettrés au debut de la dynastie Han," *Asiatische Studien/Études asiatiques* 52.3 (1998): 915-65.

INDEX

Place names and titles that occur too frequently (e.g., *Han shu* and the state of Ch'i) are not included in this index. In some cases we have followed Pinyin romanization for scholars whose names normally appear that way in English publications (e.g., Wu Shuping). The index is keyed to the translations, translators' notes, introduction, and the acknowledgements only.

K

Z

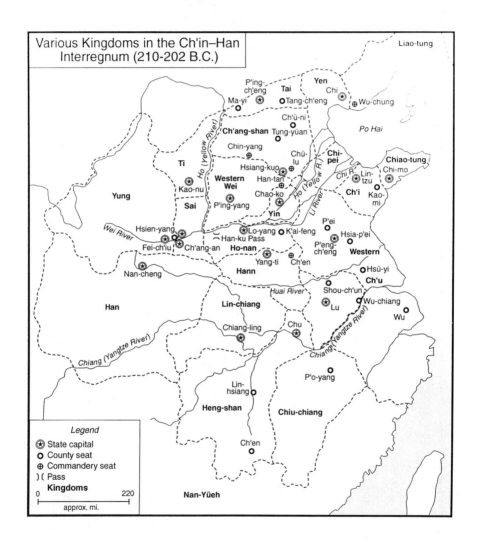

Various Kingdoms in the Ch'in–Han Interregnum (210-202 B.C.)

Liao-tung

P'ing-ch'eng
Tai
Yen
Chi
Wu-chung
Ma-yi
Tang-ch'eng
Po Hai
Ch'ü-ni
Ch'ang-shan
Tung-yüan
Chin-yang
Chü-lu
Chi-pei
Chiao-tung
Ti
Chi R.
Chi-mo
Hsiang-kuo
Western
Wei
Han-tan
Lin-tzu
Yung
Kao-nu
Ch'i
Kao-mi
Sai
P'ing-yang
Chao-ko
Yin
Wei River
Hsien-yang
Lo-yang
K'ai-feng
P'ei
Fei-ch'iu
Ch'ang-an
Ho-nan
P'eng-ch'eng
Hsia-p'ei
Yang-ti
Ch'en
Western
Nan-cheng
Hann
Hsü-yi
Han
Lin-chiang
Huai River
Shou-ch'un
Ch'u
Lu
Wu-chiang
Wu
Chiang-ling
Chu
Chiang (Yangtze River)
Chiang (Yangtze River)
P'o-yang
Lin-hsiang
Heng-shan
Chiu-chiang
Ch'en
Nan-Yüeh

Ho (Yellow River)
Ho (Yellow River)
Li River

Han-ku Pass

Legend
⊛ State capital
○ County seat
⊕ Commandery seat
)(Pass
Kingdoms
0   220
approx. mi.

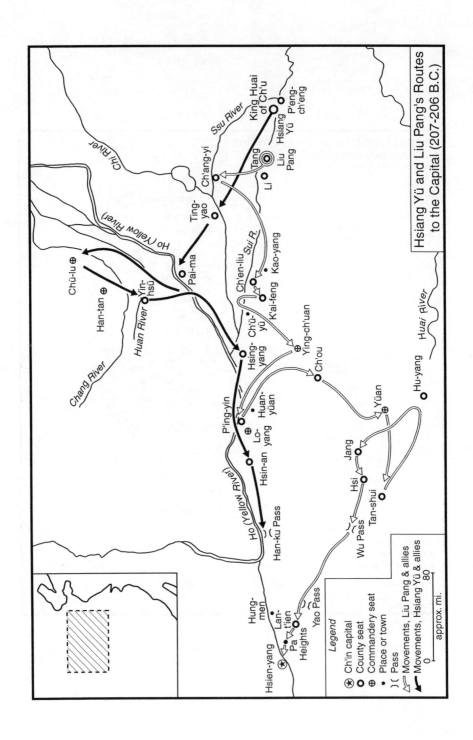

Hsiang Yü and Liu Pang's Routes
to the Capital (207-206 B.C.)

Ssu River
Ch'i River
Ho (Yellow River)
Chang River
Huan River
Sui R.
Huai River
Ho (Yellow River)

King Huai
of Ch'u
Liu Hsiang Yü P'eng-
Pang ch'eng
Ch'ang-yi
Tang
Li
Ting-yao
Pai-ma
Ch'en-liu
K'ai-feng Kao-yang
Chü-lu
Yin-hsü
Han-tan
Hsing-yang
Chü-yü
Ying-ch'uan
Ch'ou
P'ing-yin
Huan-yüan
Lo-yang
Hsin-an
Hu-yang
Yüan
Jang
Hsi
Han-ku Pass
Tan-shui
Wu Pass
Hung-men
Lan-t'ien
Pa Heights
Yao Pass
Hsien-yang

Legend
⊛ Ch'in capital
○ County seat
⊕ Commandery seat
• Place or town
)(Pass
➡ Movements, Liu Pang & allies
⇨ Movements, Hsiang Yü & allies

0   80
approx. mi.

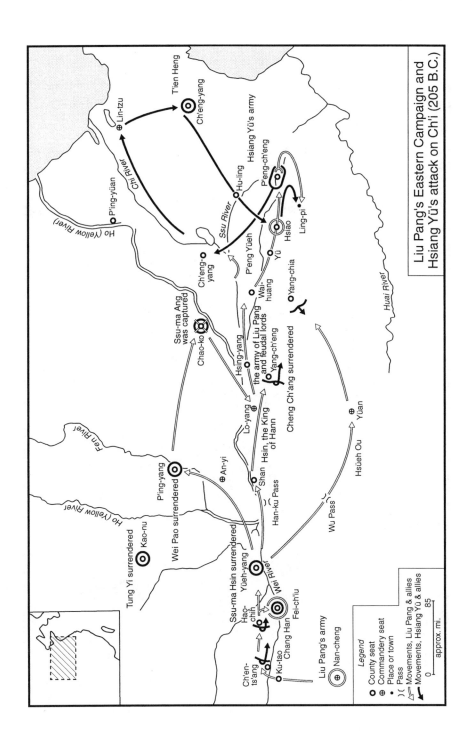

Liu Pang's Eastern Campaign and
Hsiang Yü's attack on Ch'i (205 B.C.)

Legend
◎ County seat
⊕ Commandery seat
• Place or town
)(Pass
→ Movements, Liu Pang & allies
⇨ Movements, Hsiang Yü & allies

0   85
approx. mi.

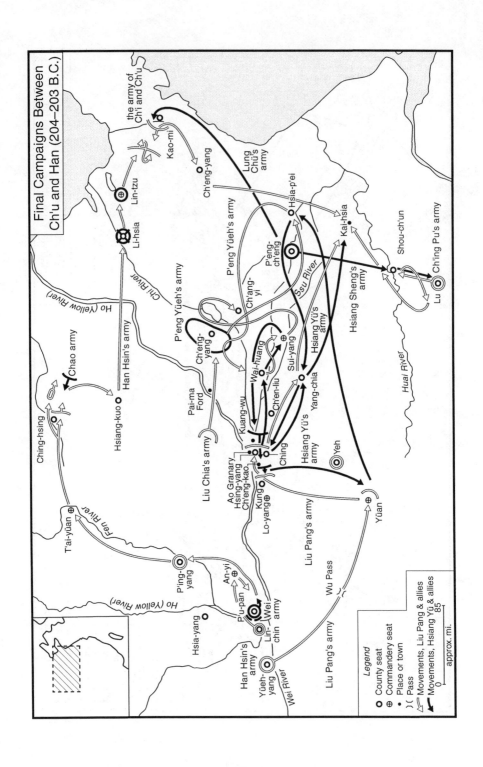

Final Campaigns Between
Ch'u and Han (204–203 B.C.)

the army of Ch'i and Ch'u

Kao-mi

Ch'eng-yang

Lin-tzu

Li-hsia

Lung Chü's army

Hsia-p'ei

P'eng-ch'eng

Kai-hsia

Ho (Yellow River)

Chi River

Han Hsin's army

P'eng Yüeh's army

P'eng Yüeh's army

Ch'ang-yi

Shou-ch'un

Lu

Ch'ing Pu's army

Hsia-yang

Hsiang-kuo

Chao army

Ch'ing-hsing

Ch'eng-yang

Ssu River

Hsiang Sheng's army

Huai River

Pai-ma Ford

Liu Chia's army

Kuang-wu

Wai-huang

Sui-yang

Chen-liu

Hsiang Yü's army

Yang-chia

T'ai-yüan

Fen River

Ao Granary
Hsing-yang
Cheng-kao

Kung

Ching

Yeh

Hsiang Yü's army

Yüan

Ho (Yellow River)

Ping-yang

An-yi

Lo-yang

Liu Pang's army

Wu Pass

Pu-pan

Lin-chin army

Wei

Liu Pang's army

Hsia-yang

Han Hsin's army

Yüeh-yang

Wei River

Legend

◎ County seat
⊕ Commandery seat
• Place or town
)(Pass
⇨ Movements, Liu Pang & allies
➜ Movements, Hsiang Yü & allies

0   85
approx. mi.

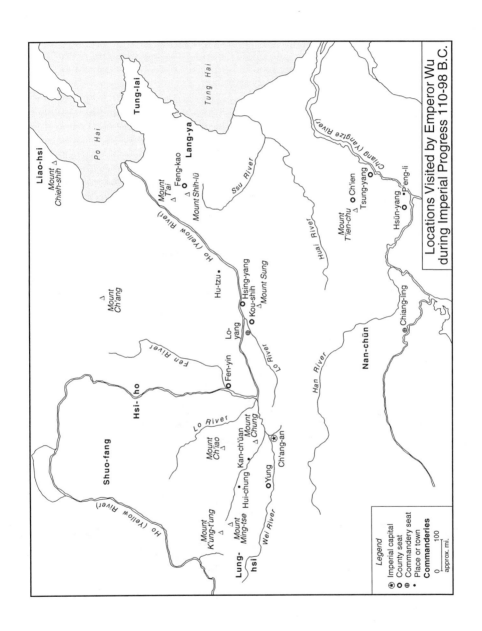

Locations Visited by Emperor Wu
during Imperial Progress 110-98 B.C.

Legend

- ⊛ Imperial capital
- ⊙ County seat
- ⊕ Commandery seat
- • Place or town
- **Commanderies**

0   100
|————————|
approx. mi.